GIZA

THE TRUTH

GIZA

THE TRUTH

The People, Politics, and History Behind the
World's Most Famous Archaeological Site

Ian Lawton & Chris Ogilvie-Herald

INVISIBLE CITIES PRESS
MONTPELIER, VERMONT

Invisible Cities Press
50 State Street
Montpelier, VT 05602
www.invisiblecitiespress.com

Cataloging-in-Publication Data is available from the Library of Congress

ISBN: 1-931229-13-9

Manufactured in Canada

CONTENTS

PART II: MODERN METHODS

CONTENTS

LIST OF PLATES

LIST OF FIGURES

FOREWORD

The credit for the original idea of writing this book goes to Chris. As someone who had been involved in the 'Egypt arena' for a number of years, he felt there was a gap in the market. And so we embarked on a project which, over an intense six-month period, oscillated between heady excitement and downright hard work. If we had to choose between illicit exploration of the Plateau and sitting in our respective offices at all hours of the day and night, desks strewn with books and correspondence, the decision would not take long!

Undoubtedly our first task must be to make a sincere apology to the Egyptian authorities, since during our research trip in the autumn of 1998 we entered at least two restricted areas on the Giza Plateau without permission. This was an extremely difficult decision to make, since Dr. Zahi Hawass, the director of the site, is generous in granting permission to bona fide researchers to visit such areas. However, our intention was to obtain irrefutable photographic evidence which would prove, one way or another, whether clandestine activities were taking place. And we knew that, as two relative unknowns, this permission would almost certainly be denied us. All we can say is that we have the utmost respect for the monuments, and they were never at risk from our careful intrusions.

We would like to take this opportunity of expressing our sincere gratitude to the many people who have helped with this work by answering our requests for information and sharing with us their experiences and insights, all of which gave us a better understanding not only of events but also of the people involved. In no particular order they are: Nigel Appleby and Adam Child for information on Operation Hermes. Andrew Collins for providing us with a copy of Joseph Jochman's *The Hall of Records* and other research material, and for his efforts to bring our work to the attention of the public. Lambert Dolphin for forwarding a copy of his report 'Applications of Modern Sensing Techniques to Egyptology', for permission to reproduce diagrams, and also for his answers to our myriad questions and queries. Christopher Dunn for forwarding a copy of his *Giza Power Plant*, and his constructive approach to corresponding with us. Ralph Ellis for his unreserved sharing of material which helped us to comprehend a political minefield. Rand Flem-Ath for his efforts in recommending our work to others. Rudolf Gantenbrink for responding to our multiple queries, which resulted in a truer understanding of his work, and for permission to reproduce still shots from Upuaut's camera. Amargi Hillier for his painstaking and timely updates on events at Giza. Joseph Jahoda for his advice, experience and enlightening communications, and above all his gentlemanly conduct in the face of adversity. Ahmed Osman for Arabic translations, advice and constant encouragement. Clive Prince for his translation of Dormion and Goiden's *Les Nouveaux Mysteres de la Grande Pyramide*, and for sharing research material. John Reid and Harry Brownlee for the photograph of the Petrie drill-core 'No. 7' and for sharing their papers on ancient machining and acoustic technology. David Rohl for his considerable support and encouragement. Colin Reader for sharing his research into the age of the Sphinx, and for his constructive feedback. Gabor Scott for his conference video-tapes. Nigel Skinner-Simpson for his friendship and excellent research skills. Greg Taylor for publicising our work on his Daily Grail web site. John Anthony West for providing a copy of Robert Schoch's paper 'How Old Is the Sphinx?' And the staff at the British Library, the Egypt Exploration Society, and the Petrie Museum, for their assistance with our research.

Thanks must also go to the following people and organizations who have responded to our requests for information or have given other assistance: Alan Alford, The Association for Research and Enlightenment, Filip Coppens, Simon Cox, Thomas Danley, Dr. Farouk El Baz, Adrian Gilbert, Dr. Zahi Hawass, Jim Hurtak, Dr. Ed Krupp, Dr. Mark Lehner, Master Travel, Peter Renton and Paul Ellson, Boris Said, Dr. Joseph Schor, SRI International, Linda Tucker, and Waseda University.

If we have omitted anyone who has helped us from the above list, we humbly apologise for our oversight.

In addition Chris would in particular like to give unreserved thanks to the following people: Barbara Keller for her sharing of material and insights, and her timely communications; Tej Lavani who unselfishly stepped in and lent his laptop when his own computer failed; his mother, Elizabeth, whose unwavering encouragement, assistance and personal belief in her son was a persistent driving force for him to succeed; and, above all, he would like to express his undying gratitude and love to his wife, Malathi, for always being there, for her love, encouragement, support and belief in both this project and her husband.

Finally, in an article in the UK *Independent* of February 10, 1998 titled 'The Real Mystery of the Sphinx: Why Do Falsehoods Drive Out Truth?', journalist Boyd Tonkin takes publishers to task in their willingness to promote the 'chaotic, waffling works' of crackpot authors, knowing they will sell well to an excitable public, while at the same time marginalising the amount of money and the number of publishing slots they provide to properly researched and argued work. He suggests that 'they have sold whatever authority their imprints might once have claimed for a cargo of flyblown nonsense'. Above all, therefore, we would like to thank our agents, Simon Trewin in the UK and Elizabeth Joyce in the United States, all the staff at Virgin in the UK – especially Kerry Sharpe, Anna Cherrett, Susan Atkinson, Rod Green and Humphrey Price – and at Invisible Cities Press in the United States – especially Joel Bernstein and Rowan Jacobsen – for at least giving us a chance to improve on the quality of these works, and to set the record straight about Giza in particular.

Ian Lawton
Hamble
and
Chris Ogilvie-Herald
London
August 2001

Some Notes on Style

As co-authors we have primarily used the term 'we' throughout this book for simplicity, even though some of the experiences or actions may have only related to one of us. In the vast majority of cases the opinions expressed are jointly held, unless we state otherwise.

Where extracts from other authors' work have been quoted, any comments inserted by us for clarification have been placed in square brackets. Similarly, italics in these quotes are used for our own emphasis unless otherwise stated.

Internet information and addresses are correct at the time of writing; we cannot accept any responsibility for changes or updates made thereafter.

We have included brief chronological summaries of the major events in the exploration, theory development and politics of the Plateau respectively in Appendix V to assist those of you who are unfamiliar with these events.

References to the work of other authors in the endnotes are abbreviated, with full details provided in the Bibliography at the end.

INTRODUCTION

The Great Pyramid looms large before us in the darkness, seeming even more vast than usual. We thread our way through the never-ending back streets of the village of Nazlet el-Samman. The locals sleep mainly in the day, but they have seen us around here many times in the last week. We have made sure of that. We wave to them nonchalantly, greet them quietly with 'salam alekuum', and no one bothers us.

We reach the edge of the Plateau. It is a quick climb up the rocky escarpment, but steep, and at the top we stop to catch our breath. We are lucky. The night is relatively murky. We stop to slip on the local galabayas, which we hope will blend in with the meditation group we intend to tag on to. Underneath we have waistcoats whose pockets bulge with torches, cameras, notebooks and other essential equipment. We trust that in the darkness we will just look as if we have feasted on too much shish kebab.

It is now 2 a.m. We are nervous but calm. If the gods are on our side, all will be well. And if we believe in our hearts that what we are doing is for the general good, not just for our own selfish ends, then the gods will be on our side. We hope.

Right on cue, the group arrive from their sumptuous hotel in their air-conditioned coach. How the other half live! But we have no time to ponder the inequalities of life and the apparent benefits money can bring. We have work to do.

Again luck is on our side. No guards yet. We run quickly towards the rear of the coach, then slow our pace. Our timing is perfect. We join the back of the line of white-robed innocents, and blend in perfectly. No one suspects. Now we need our next piece of luck. As we climb the steps up to the entrance, we pray that there will not be a head count. The guards welcome us nonchalantly, for we are just another group who bring in money, but not much to them. We are in!

Slowly we climb the Ascending Passage, bent double under the low ceiling. Our hearts beat faster as we wait to see if the final piece of luck is on our side. We emerge into the Grand Gallery, and crane our necks to the top. Yes! The ladder up to the Relieving Chambers is there, and in place against the wall! Someone is definitely looking after us.

At the top, we all creep down the passage into the King's Chamber. The guide chats for a few minutes about what will happen. Then the guard leaves. In a few minutes we are plunged into darkness. All is quiet, except for the welcome noise of the fan in the wall. It is quieter than the old one, but it is enough. We wait. Gradually the group enters its state of karma. We are at the back, by the passage. Quietly and slowly we creep out. Back down the passage. Back to the base of the ladder.

The guard has retired to the entrance. We are alone in the Grand Gallery. All systems are go. We remove our galabayas, because we know from experience that they do not make ideal garments for exploration. Quietly and slowly we climb up, one rung at a time. At the top we stop briefly to don our head torches. We are high above the floor, nearly 30 feet up. Thankfully the ladder is tied to the wall, for it is steeply inclined. In perhaps the scariest part of the operation we lever ourselves off the ladder and into the passage, and begin the crawl towards our goal. The loose stones on the floor scrape at our exposed knees, but we hardly notice.

At the end of the passage, we come out into a small chamber in which we can stand. We see that a succession of short ladders lead up to the higher chambers, but we must ignore these for the moment. Our target lies ahead. We have to lie on our sides to squeeze through the narrow slit that gives access to the first chamber, Davison's. And as we pick ourselves up, our torches reveal a long, low room matching the size of the King's Chamber beneath it. There is some rubble in the far corner, and the unevenness of the floor blocks is in stark contrast to the smoothness of the monolithic ceiling blocks. But, as our heads turn to the corner nearest us, our torches reveal what we have come to explore. A passage leading off to the side.

We know this passage was begun by Captain Caviglia in the nineteenth century. But rumours have been abounding for several years that it has been extended to look for a secret chamber. We have been told on the grapevine that supposedly eminent researchers have been sharing video footage of this secret excavation, all under strict nondisclosure agreements. Many people have suggested this is the real reason why the pyramid has been closed to the public for some time now. We must discover the truth.

We hurry towards it, excitement mounting. Crawling inside, we can see that after about 10 feet it turns sharp right to follow the south wall of the chamber, heading west. Faster now . . . we must get to the corner to see where it leads. Scrambling around it, we see the passage extends for a further 15 feet. By the time we are halfway along, we can already see what lies ahead. We have waited for so long for this moment. Now we know the truth . . .

The passage ends in a blank wall!

This is just one of the many experiences we have shared in writing this book. It is not untypical. Time and again we have been regaled by local Egyptians, fellow researchers and a variety of other sources, all claiming in hushed conspiratorial tones to have information on clandestine operations at the Giza Plateau. These usually involve the discovery and exploration of secret passages and chambers in and around the Great Pyramid and Sphinx, and, often as not, the fabled Hall of Records is introduced into the mix. As open-minded individuals who believe in the *possibility* that an advanced civilisation could have existed millennia ago on Earth,* and could have stored some form of records to enlighten or warn future civilisations, we were initially flushed with excitement at these apparent revelations – a feeling many of you will have shared when reading about or discussing such awesome possibilities.

---

* For his part, Chris has an entirely open mind on the issue of 'lost civilis- ations'. However, he emphatically does not subscribe to the High Civilisation/ Atlantis/Catastrophe model proposed by the American psychic Edgar Cayce, and many modern alternative researchers.

However, coupled with official and other denials, these stories became so conflicting that we could stand the confusion no longer. We *had* to research these rumours first-hand, on location, if only to clear our heads! It would be arrogant and foolish of us to suggest that, in two busy weeks at the Plateau in the Autumn of 1998, we were able to investigate all these rumours in full – and can now present a complete picture in this book with no questions left unanswered. Of course we can't. But what we can do is shed considerably more light on the picture than has been cast before. And we do see a clear trend, which emerged almost as soon as exploration commenced at the Plateau, and which has become exacerbated in recent years – at least in part due to a combination of millennium fever and the ability of new Internet technology to spread rumours like wildfire, so that to many they become reality. What we have undoubtedly uncovered, and will prove in this book, is that much of the rumour mill surrounding the Plateau is at best misleading, and at worst complete garbage.

It would be churlish of us to suggest that all researchers of the Plateau are charlatans who deliberately mislead the public merely to enhance their status and their bank accounts. Many do fervently believe what they are saying, but appear to be motivated by one common factor – a desire to stamp their name on history by finding the elusive answers to the enigmas of the Plateau. In this quest they seem to become taken over by a kind of 'Plateau Fever' – perhaps a special strain of 'Millennium Fever' – which inhibits their ability to look independently and objectively at the evidence.

Does this mean that everything that orthodox science and archaeology tell us about the Plateau is correct? Undoubtedly no! There is a balance to be struck between orthodoxy and open-mindedness, which in our view is rarely achieved by protagonists on either side.

What this book therefore hopes to accomplish is to provide you, the reader, with a balanced picture of the four main aspects of the Plateau: its *exploration* from ancient times to the present day; the *theories* surrounding its edifices – who built them, when, how and why (and note that we have no 'pet' theories of our own to promote at the expense of others); the *Hall of*

4

Records – whether it exists, and if so where, and what it contains; and the *politics* that have come to dominate the Plateau in recent years.

This type of book has been attempted in part before, most notably in a seminal work by Peter Tompkins entitled *Secrets of the Great Pyramid*, first published in 1971, and recently republished. However, even this highly regarded work suffers from some major defects. As its title suggests, it takes little account of the other edifices on the Plateau apart from the Great Pyramid itself, which is in our view a fundamentally flawed approach which has been copied by most 'alternative' (i.e., nonorthodox) researchers both before and since; for, as we will see, *context is king* in understanding the enigmas of Ancient Egypt. It concentrates heavily on the mathematical properties supposedly inherent in the structure of the Great Pyramid – and since Tompkins is clearly an advocate of these theories it can hardly be regarded as an entirely independent and objective study. The Hall of Records, which was not as commonly discussed then as now, is not mentioned. And of course much of the political excitement and intrigue surrounding the Plateau has occurred only since Tompkins's book was published.

One might also suggest that various studies by orthodox Egyptologists have already fulfilled our objective. Most notably Dr Eiddon Edwards's *The Pyramids of Egypt* – a standard reference text which has been updated repeatedly since its first publication in 1947 – and Dr Mark Lehner's *The Complete Pyramids* – the most current treatise, which was published as late as 1997 – are superb reference works. However, they are relatively 'dry' textbooks, and again they tell only some of the story: because their authors refuse to accept any alternative theories, these are not discussed at all. The Hall of Records is a no-go area for them – even though in his early days, prior to his conversion to the orthodox cause, Lehner wrote an entire book devoted to the subject. And of course they cannot, by their nature, delve into the politics and personalities that make the subject come alive, as well as being essential to a proper understanding.

In order to cover all these aspects and more, this book is

split into three parts: Part I, Prologue, provides the essential background information required to place recent explorations and political wranglings into context. It examines the history of exploration of the Plateau from classical times to the middle of this century, ensuring that *all* edifices on the Plateau are considered and not just the Great Pyramid. It summarises the various theories that have been put forward about when, why and how the pyramids were built, ensuring that due attention is paid to all the Third and Fourth Dynasty pyramids – not just those on the Plateau – and as a result allowing both orthodox and alternative views to be considered. And it looks at the various legends of the Hall of Records throughout history, ensuring that some of the less well-known esoteric material on this subject is presented.

If we have succeeded in our objectives, this will be the first time you will have encountered such a balanced treatment of these topics. We believe that determining the truth about the Plateau and its incredible structures requires that due deference be paid to the centuries of scholarship of orthodox Egyptologists. However, at the same time our minds must be a little more open to unorthodox *possibilities* than this body allows – for example of the existence of advanced ancient civilisations, and of the potential value of material that has supposedly been 'channelled' from other dimensions. While covering all viewpoints, we will not, however, remain entirely astride the fence. Where we consider any theory – of whatever persuasion – to be flawed or even downright crackpot, we will comment accordingly; similarly if we regard a theory as being particularly persuasive when all the evidence is considered, we will say as much. In this way we hope to provide you with the best perspective you can possibly obtain, and have not hitherto been able to in distilled and condensed form.

In Part II, Modern Methods, we will document the true story of the explorations of the Plateau in the last 30 years, most of which involved searches for secret chambers in the Great Pyramid and others, and an underground network of tunnels and chambers under the Plateau – and especially under or near the Sphinx. The details of much of this work have never before been made readily available to the public in their entirety, and we will rectify that omission. We will examine the much-publicised and ground-breaking research that led to the questioning of the age of the Sphinx, and the discovery of a 'door' in one of the shafts in the Great Pyramid by a small remote-controlled robot. We will also consider the equally well known theories that suggest that the pyramids align with certain star constellations. Are these theories and discoveries really as 'orthodoxy-shattering' as they are made out to be? We will find out . . .

In Part III we bring the picture right up to date with a review of the various explorations, discoveries and associated controversies that have rocked the Plateau in the 1990s. We will get behind the multiple rumours that have proliferated via the emerging power of the Internet, many of them dealing with secret tunnelling and excavation, and the various pieces of 'evidence' that purport to back them up. We will reveal new details about the most highly publicised recent search for the Hall of Records. We will look at the various supposedly newly discovered shafts that have been excavated recently on the Plateau. And we will reveal that intertwined in all these projects are a number of 'key players' whose relationships have ebbed and flowed – sometimes dramatically hostile, sometimes cordial and respectful – with huge implications for the projects themselves and the way they have been presented to, or in some cases hidden from, the public.

It is hardly surprising that politics has come to dominate all exploration and discussion of the Plateau over the last decade. Consider the rewards on offer for major new discoveries that could challenge the whole basis of mankind's understanding of his past and his future. At the very least they could lead to considerable riches and worldwide recognition – even immortalisation in mankind's 'Hall of Fame'. In a more sinister light, the keys to Ancient Wisdom could unlock untold power – perhaps even the power to change mankind for ever. As a result, 'Plateau Fever' is kicking in with a vengeance, and some egos are vibrating at a new, higher frequency! Where such egos appear to take themselves a little too seriously – some even appearing to proclaim themselves as new 'messiahs' – we will take sharp aim and let the arrows fly!

In an ideal world a work such as this would not have to dirty its hands with political machinations. Indeed both the authors attempted to shrug off the coils of the commercial world precisely because we wanted to escape these often negative aspects of our lives. But, mankind being what it is, this is an idealistic viewpoint, and, unless you want to bury your head in the sand and cut off from the rest of society completely, it is impossible to avoid the inevitable interaction with these forces. It is all very well suggesting that a new dawn of spiritual understanding is overtaking the old materialism, but even many of those who espouse this view are continually proving by their own hypocritical actions that this is an extremely slow process. Idealism is often caught up with a kind of blind hope, which unfortunately requires naivety to underpin it – exactly the conditions that allow the unscrupulous to exploit the innocent.

When the stakes are this high, some people become ruthless. There are even suggestions that major governmental organisations are involved. We will examine whether or not this is likely; and, if they are, have they decided that paternalism is called for – to protect mankind from its own ignorance? Who really is involved in the exploration of the Plateau, and what are their motives? We will delve into the recesses of apparent cover-ups and conspiracies, claims and counterclaims, in an attempt to deliver the truth to the public at what many see as a pivotal point in our history – the new millennium.

And let us never forget: according to many, the time for the discovery of the Hall of Records is at hand . . .

Part I
PROLOGUE

ONE

EARLY EXPLORATIONS

Of all the monuments of the Ancient World, none are more enigmatic than those found at the Giza Plateau – a rocky outcrop situated at the edge of the Libyan desert on the west bank of the Nile, just across from modern Cairo. Its three best-known structures – the Great, Second and Third Pyramids – dominate the landscape for miles around, guarded by the majestic Sphinx. Their construction has been attributed by Egyptologists to the Old Kingdom rulers Khufu (Greek Cheops), Khafre (Chephren) and Menkaure (Mycerinus) respectively, in the Fourth Dynasty *c.* 2575–2465 BC.

No photographs or video images, and certainly no words, can hope to capture the incredible majesty of these structures. If they look imposing now, we can only imagine how they would have looked in antiquity, when they were entirely covered in a polished, gleaming, white limestone casing which would have reflected the powerful sun for miles around, perhaps surmounted – at least in the case of the largest or 'Great Pyramid' – by a golden capstone.

The Great Pyramid alone covers an area of 13 acres, and was laid out with incredible precision to align with the points of the compass. It contains more than 2 million blocks of limestone and granite weighing between 2 and 70 tonnes each, representing more masonry than that required to construct *all* the cathedrals, churches and chapels built in England in the last 2,000 years. It rises through 201 courses of masonry to an original height of 481 feet, which represents approximately four-fifths of the height of the Telecom Tower in London. Meanwhile, the method of its construction, with such huge yet accurately worked blocks and with a steep face angle of nearly 52 degrees, baffles many modern engineers and architects.

However, it should not be overlooked that the Second

Pyramid rises to an original height of 471 feet, which is only 10 feet less – and, because it is built on slightly higher ground, it usually appears taller. It has a steeper slope of some 53 degrees, which renders the base area about 6 per cent less. This no less incredible edifice (at least from its external dimensions) has managed to retain some of its limestone casing blocks, which remain visible on the upper quarter – although now robbed of their gleam by the patina of age. Meanwhile the spectacle is completed by the smaller Third Pyramid: although it rises to less than half the height of its brethren at 213 feet, reducing its base area by a similar proportion, it too was clearly constructed with great skill.

The pyramids' influence and power is such that hundreds of books have been written over the centuries which attempt to answer the perennial questions: Who built them, when, how and why? We should not be deceived by the modern textbooks that insist that *all* these questions have been answered definitively. There is plenty of evidence to suggest that some enigmas remain – although perhaps not as many as the more excitable alternative researchers would have us believe. At the dawn of a new millennium – with an ever more prevalent view that orthodox science and religion are missing the point when they suggest they know all the answers – the focus is back on the Giza Plateau. Yet while we should still marvel at its edifices, and the skill and mind-set of its builders, perhaps a degree of caution – indeed a 'reality check' amid a seemingly never ending sea of ill-informed speculation – is appropriate.

Our first task is to review the early explorations of the Plateau by what we might call the 'Founding Fathers'. This mixture of academics, researchers, scientists, archaeologists, explorers, fortune seekers and sometimes downright eccentrics have all shared one common purpose – to unlock the secrets of the Giza Plateau. We owe them a great deal.

This chapter sets out to achieve a number of objectives that will make up for the shortfalls in most other popular works on the subject. It describes the explorations of the *entire* Plateau, not just the Great Pyramid. It is based on both the most up-to-date information and the original work of the pioneers themselves, each where appropriate. We trust that this means nothing is overlooked in our quest to ensure that the information is as reliable and historically accurate as possible, in order that there is no propagation of the misconceptions that have already received too much exposure – partly due to poor investigation and lack of simple scholarship. To achieve this a variety of sources have been used and, in many cases, cross-checked.

The list has been narrowed down to three primary sources, each of which has its strengths and weaknesses. Peter Tompkins's *Secrets of the Great Pyramid* was completed in 1971 as a culmination of twenty years of research, and although it was primarily written as a treatise on the mathematical and geometric properties of the Great Pyramid, it also contains a relatively thorough account of the explorations up to 1970. However, not only does it concentrate primarily on the Great Pyramid to the exclusion of the others, it is also clear that some of Tompkins's details are incorrect, especially in relation to older sources. In these cases we have turned to the work of Colonel Richard Howard Vyse: not only did he personally contribute a great deal to the exploration of the Plateau, which he documented in his *Operations Carried Out on the Pyramids of Gizeh . . .*, published in three volumes in 1840, but in this work he also collated probably the most comprehensive set of accounts of explorations over the centuries ever produced, from classical times on. Finally, the most up-to-date views of orthodox Egyptology are provided by Dr Mark Lehner's detailed and comprehensive *The Complete Pyramids*, published in 1997. Where other sources have been used to fill in any gaps these are duly noted, while we have also added our own observations, comments and interpretations where appropriate.

Most of the measurements of the internal dimensions of the three Giza Pyramids are taken from the detailed surveys performed by Vyse.[1] Some readers may find it confusing that the measurements in the early chapters are provided in feet and inches, but this is to allow due deference to the early explorers, most of whom worked in these units of measure. A simple conversion is that a foot is approximately a third (0.3048) of a metre. Meanwhile readers who are unfamiliar with the layout of the Giza Plateau are advised to refer regularly to Figure 1 for clarification.

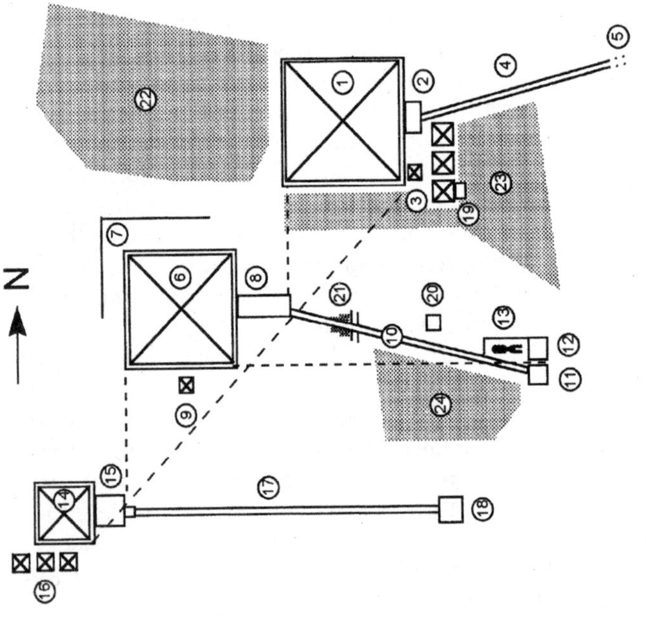

1 Great Pyramid (GP)
2 GP Mortuary Temple
3 GP Satellite Pyramids
4 GP Causeway
5 to GP Valley Temple...
6 Second Pyramid (2P)
7 2P Enclosure Walls
8 2P Mortuary Temple
9 2P Satellite Pyramid
10 2P Causeway
11 2P Valley Temple
12 Sphinx Temple

13 Sphinx
14 Third Pyramid (3P)
15 3P Mortuary Temple
16 3P Satellite Pyramids
17 3P Causeway
18 3P Valley Temple
19 Temple of Isis
20 Campbell's Tomb
21 Water Shaft
22 Western *Mastaba* Field
23 Eastern *Mastaba* Field
24 Central *Mastaba* Field

- - - - - Significant Alignments

FIGURE 1: MAP OF THE GIZA PLATEAU

The Caliph's Capers

As befits a megalomaniac with an unquenchable thirst for power and control, in the latter part of the fourth century BC, Alexander (inappropriately named 'the Great') destroyed much of the evidence of Ancient Wisdom that many enlightened commentators are now convinced existed in the temples and libraries of cities dotted all over the Ancient World. He was tutored by Aristotle himself, was hailed as a supposedly erudite man, and showed signs of being a good political ruler once he had made his conquests. Nevertheless, this image does not fit well with the initial destruction he wrought, most notably of the seats of learning at Persepolis and especially Heliopolis. The latter housed the astronomical and mathematical records of the Egyptian priestly elite – the descendants of the same elite that had perhaps guarded ancient scientific knowledge for several millennia – and there is increasing evidence that this knowledge was highly advanced, even by modern standards.

Such attempts at gaining power by the suppression of knowledge were continued by various religious zealots and power-crazed political leaders over the ensuing centuries. The great library of Alexandria, founded in Alexander's own city by Ptolemy I after his death, was in turn destroyed by the Roman Emperor Theodosius in AD 389. However, the conquest of Alexandria by Mohammed in AD 640 led to an Arab renaissance, and the first recorded attempts to recover this lost wisdom. The still extant ancient texts from around the world were eagerly sought and translated – partly so they could learn as much as possible about practical geography and navigation, which in turn required an understanding of mathematics and astronomy. In the ensuing centuries successive Caliphs of Baghdad effectively developed the new seat of learning of the world in what were otherwise the 'Dark Ages'.

Nearly two centuries later, the Caliph Abdullah al Mamun came to power. An intellectual and avid seeker of the truth, he translated Ptolemy's astronomical treatise *Almagest* in his youth, and attempted to check Ptolemy's work and extrapolate the circumference of the globe by measuring one degree of latitude using astronomical observation. This was in an era when the religious 'scholars' of the West were insisting that the

Earth was flat, and would continue to promote this dogma for many centuries.

It would appear that the Arabs of this era suffered from the same human shortcomings that we do to this day. Theirs was clearly a highly intellectual society, and yet a significant proportion of the Arab writings that have come down to us from this era and the ensuing centuries is riddled with myths, rumours and distortions, yet presented as fact and truth. The pyramids of the Giza Plateau were one of the focuses for these exaggerations, and the following extract from the Arab writer Abd al Hokm, although written after Mamun's time, is indicative of the sort of rumours with which he would have been bombarded. He tells how the pyramids were built by King Saurid Ibn Salhouk 300 years before the Great Flood, after he had a dream which foretold that great catastrophe and it was confirmed by his astronomer priests:[2]

> . . . and he commanded in the meantime to build the Pyramids, and that a vault (or cisterne) should be made, into which the river Nile should enter, from whence it should run into the countries of the West, and into the land Al-Said; and he filled them with talismen, and with strange things, and with riches, and treasures, and the like. He engraved in them all things that were told him by wise men, as also all profound sciences . . . The science of Astrology, and of Arithmetic, and of Geometry, and of Physics. All this may be interpreted by him that knows their characters, and language . . . Then he built in the Western [Second?] Pyramid thirty treasuries, filled with store of riches, and utensils, and with signatures made of precious stones, and with instruments of iron, and vessels of earth, and with arms which rust not, and with glass which might be bended, and yet not broken . . . He made also in the East [Great?] Pyramid, diverse celestial spheres, and stars, and what they severally operate, in their aspects: and the perfumes which are to be used to them and the books which treat of these matters. He put also in the coloured [Third?] Pyramid, the commentaries of the Priests, in chests of black marble, and with every priest a book, in which were the wonders of his profession, and of his actions, and of his nature, and what was done in his time, and what is, and what shall be, from the beginning of time, to the end of it . . . The Coptites write in their books that there is an inscription on them . . . 'I King Saurid built

the Pyramids in such and such a time, and finished them in six years. He that comes after me, and says that he is equal to me, let him destroy them in six hundred years . . .'

This account is almost identical except in a few details to that of Masoudi, written c. AD 950, which was compiled and translated by one of the foremost experts in the field, Dr Sprenger.[3] The one major difference is in the apparent length of time that Saurid took to build the pyramids, which in Masoudi appears to be sixty years as opposed to Hokm's six years. Nevertheless, Dr Sprenger suggests, 'Arabian authors have given the same account of the Pyramids, with little or no variation, for above a thousand years; and they appear to have repeated the traditions of the ancient Egyptians, mixed up with fabulous stories and incidents, certainly not of Mahometan invention.' He goes on to say, 'Every writer, indeed, seems to have enumerated as many marvellous things as his imagination could suggest.'

As to the issue of retrieving these supposed treasures from the pyramids, a number of Arab accounts from this time and later suggest that in AD 820 Mamun set his heart on breaking into the Great Pyramid to release them. For example, Hokm reports that the entrance in the Pyramid was opened for him 'with fire, and vinegar. Two smiths prepared, and sharpened the iron, and engines, which they forced in, and there was a great expense in the opening of it . . .'[4]

This view is supported by, for example, Makrizi, writing in the fifteenth century,[5] by the infamous *Thousand and One Tales of the Arabian Nights*, and by other Arab sources, as will be seen later. As a result it has now become almost universally accepted, at least by the alternative school, that Mamun was the first person to breach the upper reaches of the edifice, even though most enlightened researchers would accept that the lower reaches had already been explored. In fact there are arguments to suggest that this was not the case, and that the entire edifice had already been explored in remote antiquity. Since this issue is a critical one, we will return to it later. Meanwhile the following account is the traditional one from Tompkins *et al.* – which, with the possible exception of the

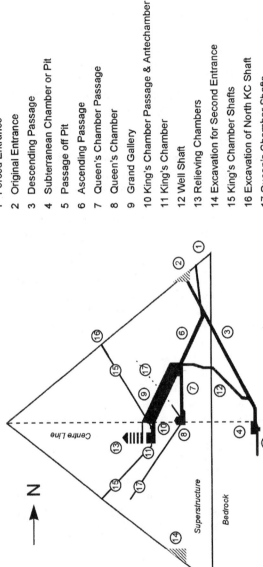

1 Forced Entrance
2 Original Entrance
3 Descending Passage
4 Subterranean Chamber or Pit
5 Passage off Pit
6 Ascending Passage
7 Queen's Chamber Passage
8 Queen's Chamber
9 Grand Gallery
10 King's Chamber Passage & Antechamber
11 King's Chamber
12 Well Shaft
13 Relieving Chambers
14 Excavation for Second Entrance
15 King's Chamber Shafts
16 Excavation of North KC Shaft
17 Queen's Chamber Shafts

FIGURE 2: THE GREAT PYRAMID IN PROFILE, LOOKING WEST

circumstances of the initial tunnelling, can probably be regarded as reasonably authentic.

Mamun assembled a vast team of architects, stonemasons and engineers and supposedly attempted to locate the entrance hidden under the casing blocks of the north face, to no avail. Undaunted, he then decided to force an entrance in the hope of linking up with an internal passageway. He chose a point at the centre of the north face, seven courses up (see Plate 1). In order to remove the hard limestone casing blocks, his men lit fires around them and then cooled them rapidly with vinegar to induce fractures. Once past these they could more easily chisel their way through the softer limestone of the core blocks.

They tunnelled for approximately 100 feet, and still found nothing. Then perhaps the greatest 'coincidence' in the history of the Great Pyramid occurred. One of the workmen heard the muffled thud of something heavy falling within the body of the pyramid, not too far away to their left. Redoubling their efforts, they altered course and broke through into what is now known as the 'Descending Passage', where a large limestone ceiling block had been dislodged and lay on the floor. Crawling back up the passage, which was about 4 feet high, 3 feet 6 inches wide, and sloped at an angle of 26 degrees, they discovered the original entrance – which turned out to be not only 55 feet above the base on the seventeenth course, but also 24 feet *east* of the centre line.

Retracing their steps, Mamun's men passed their tunnel and continued on down the Descending Passage, which for the most part was cut into the bedrock of the Plateau. Finally, after some 320 feet, the passage levelled out for 27 feet before opening into the northeast corner of what is now referred to as the 'Subterranean Chamber'. This measured 46 feet east–west, 27 feet north–south, and a maximum of approximately 11 feet high, had a relatively smooth roof but extremely uneven floor, and lay some 580 feet under the apex, although to the south thereof. At the base of the far wall opposite the entrance was a further horizontal passage, about 2 feet 6 inches square and rough-hewn, which progressed snakelike for some 53 feet before ending in solid masonry.

Thus the first of the Great Pyramid's enigmas surfaced:

although the model of a descending passage leading to a subterranean chamber is repeated throughout Egyptian pyramids, why was there only dust and debris therein? Why did it appear so unfinished? And, since it is commonly assumed from the quality of the excavation of the passage in the south wall that it is an original feature, why dig a further passage which went nowhere? From torch marks on the ceiling Mamun concluded that this chamber had already been explored (presumably by people who still knew where the original entrance was, unless 'his' entrance had been forced much earlier) – but had they found anything and looted it, or had it always been empty?

Mamun now turned his attention to the stone that had been dislodged into the Descending Passage near his own tunnel. It had been concealing a large granite plug in the entrance to what appeared to be a further passage leading *up* towards the centre of the pyramid, a passage not mentioned in classical accounts. Was this the key to finding the secret chambers?

Attempting to chisel out the hard granite block was impossible, so the workmen dug into the adjacent limestone blocks to the west. After tunnelling alongside three huge granite 'sealing' plugs, they finally broke into the 'Ascending Passage'. This was just as narrow, low and slippery as its descending counterpart, with the same 26-degree angle. The team crawled upward for some 124 feet until the passage levelled off and grew tall enough for them to stand.

Confronted this time by a low horizontal passage, they crawled along it for 127 feet to find that it ended in a step which dropped the floor by 2 feet before opening into the northeast corner of another chamber, approximately 17 feet north–south by 19 feet east–west, beautifully formed from limestone blocks. The walls were perfectly worked (although they were reported by subsequent explorers to have been coated with a layer of salt sometimes as much as half an inch thick); the floor rough-hewn – again giving the appearance of being unfinished; and the gabled roof, over 20 feet high at the apex, consisted of huge polished monoliths. Christened the 'Queen's Chamber' because under Arab tradition women were buried in tombs with gabled roofs, it lay directly under the apex of the pyramid. But, yet again, according to most reports they were frustrated: it was empty. However, in the east wall a corbelled niche had been carved to a depth of 3 feet 6 inches and a height of 15 feet, with four courses ranging from just over 5 feet at the base to 20 inches at the top.

Recognising that this was the next great enigma of the Great Pyramid, they chiselled back into the recesses of the niche for some 40 feet in the hope of finding a hidden entrance to another chamber, but to no avail. (According to Tompkins they tunnelled back for only a further 3 feet, but we know from accounts of explorations in the seventeenth century that the tunnel was 40 feet deep by this time. Given the relative lack of intrusive tunnelling in the intervening period since Mamun's explorations, it is most likely that this tunnel was dug by his men or at least around this time.) Had the niche once contained a statue of some sort which had been looted? Or were Mamun and his men the first to enter the chamber since it had been sealed in antiquity? And, if it had contained nothing, what was it for?

Exiting the Queen's Chamber, the team returned to the Ascending Passage, and, when they held their torches up over a vertical step above the Queen's Chamber passage, they realised they were at the base of a huge gallery. It sloped up at the consistent 26-degree angle, was 28 feet high and 156 feet long, and had corbelled sides again formed by perfectly worked Turah limestone blocks – which would have originally shone brilliant white – in seven courses which narrowed from just under 7 feet at the base to 3 feet 6 inches at the top. Dubbed the 'Grand Gallery' and marvelled at for its architectural mastery, it was clearly the next great enigma – its purpose rendered more mysterious by the nature of its flooring: a 3-foot-6-inch-wide channel in the centre was flanked along its length by ramps on both sides, each 20 inches wide and 2 feet high – with small recesses or notches, about a foot long and 6 inches wide, cut into the tops next to the walls at regular intervals. Why was this stunning gallery built, and did the notches present a clue?

At the top of the Gallery lay a huge block raised 3 feet off the floor, the top of which provided a square platform. At the far edge of this 'Great Step', and in the base of the far wall of the Gallery, lay the entrance to another horizontal passage, this time extending for only a few feet before opening out into a

21

small antechamber whose walls were formed by polished, red-granite blocks, not the usual limestone. The side walls of this antechamber contained four sets of slots via which portcullis-style doors would have been lowered. The passage continued in the far wall, but again they had to crawl for only a few feet before it opened into the northeast corner of the apparent focal point of the pyramid – the flat-roofed 'King's Chamber', which, at approximately 34 feet east–west, 17 feet north–south and 19 feet high, was considerably larger than the others. Not only that, but its walls, floor and ceiling were all of beautifully worked and polished red granite. And at last they had found *something* – near the west wall lay a lidless coffer carved from a single block of red granite; although its interior was polished to a smooth finish, its exterior was rough and unpolished. Its external dimensions were approximately 3 feet 3 inches wide, 7 feet 6 inches long and 3 feet 5 inches deep (without the lid).

The general consensus has it that, disappointed at his lack of apparent success in finding anything of significance, Mamun had his men dig a small excavation under the coffer itself, and a larger borehole into the floor on the north wall, near the coffer – none of which revealed any new passages or chambers. Meanwhile, some Arab accounts tell a somewhat different story about what Mamun found. For example, Hokm relates:[6]

> ... there was an ewer of green emerald, in it were a thousand dinars very weighty, every dinar was an ounce of our ounces: they wondered at it, but knew not the meaning of it. Then Al Mamun said, cast up the account, how much hath been spent in making the entrance: they cast it up, and lo it was the same sum which they found, it neither exceeded, nor was defective.

This is clearly the basis or a distortion of another account by Tompkins which suggests that Mamun deliberately secreted the exact money owed to his men inside the pyramid to pacify them and make up for the lack of treasure therein, putting this fortune down to the will of Allah. Hokm continues as follows:

> They found towards the top of the Pyramid a chamber in which there was an hollow stone: in it was a statue of stone like a man,

22

and within it a man, upon whom was a breast-plate of gold set with jewels, upon his breast was a sword of unvaluable price, and at his head a Carbuncle, of the bigness of an egg, shining like the light of the day, and upon him were characters written with a pen, no man knows what they signify.

However, we have seen that certain elements of Hokm's account are highly exaggerated, and accordingly little weight should probably be placed on his assertions. These types of exaggeration have been peddled by local Egyptians and other more fanciful or deceitful types through the ages and continue to this day – although perhaps now more in relation to secret chambers that have yet to be discovered. Perhaps for the locals who live in relative poverty, their endless quest to generate intrigue and, more particularly, baksheesh can be understood. Nevertheless it is infuriating for the newcomer to Egypt, who is excited at the possibility of making new discoveries, to find that they must wise up in pretty short order. And of course some people, even those who should know better, never learn.

If Mamun was responsible for the first discovery of the upper chambers since they were sealed, and these accounts are broadly correct, we future generations are much in his debt. After all, if he hadn't been motivated by his desire to uncover Ancient Wisdom, and if fortune had not smiled on him, we might still be trying to persuade the Egyptian authorities to authorise drillings in the Great Pyramid to locate the chambers he discovered more than a thousand years ago. In truth, whoever opened them up, whether in Mamun's epoch or before, it must be accepted that – improved technology notwithstanding – we have discovered very little extra by comparison in the intervening period.

Arabian Accounts

For some 700 years between the ninth and sixteenth centuries, we have only the accounts of Arab writers to shed any further light on Giza. There has been a tendency to dismiss almost all of this plethora of Arabian histories with disdain. Although we have been somewhat scathing about the reports of those such as Hokm, we nevertheless believe that this blanket dismissal is a mistake. There are a few accounts that are less fanciful and arguably therefore more reliable, which shed important light on the subject. One in particular, which has been almost forgotten in modern literature, is Edrisi's *History of the Pyramids*, written *c.* 1245.

Among other things he recounts a visit into the interior of the Great Pyramid, which appears to be a first-hand account. It is extremely difficult to follow, owing to the vagueness of the language used. Nevertheless, once the various features he records have been identified, they do match what we now know of the interior pretty well, with little apparent exaggeration or embellishment. He even records the recesses cut into the platforms at the side of the Grand Gallery.[7]

More importantly, Edrisi adds three new pieces of information that do not commonly emerge from accounts of Mamun's explorations. First, 'To the right of him, who ascends, is a well situated between the two alleys [the Ascending Passage and the Grand Gallery] and the just-mentioned door [the horizontal passage to the Queen's Chamber], but below the second alley.' This is surely sufficient evidence to indicate a feature that is commonly thought to have been rediscovered only early in the seventeenth century, and is now known as the 'Well Shaft'. We will return to this feature later.

Second, he reports something that, if we have interpreted his account correctly, we have not seen mentioned in *any* other account, ancient or modern: 'By this door, or opening, a square room is entered with an empty vessel in it.' It is clear that the 'room' to which he refers is the *Queen's* Chamber and at first sight one might dismiss this as being a description of the niche therein, until one gets to the description of the King's Chamber, about which he says, 'An empty vessel is seen here similar to the former.' He is clearly suggesting that the Queen's Chamber also contained a coffer, similar to the one in the King's Chamber. Since this account appears to be reliable, we must take this seriously, and it raises a number of important questions: If such an additional coffer did exist, how does this affect the symbolic interpretations of the Great Pyramid? And, since it is quite clear that this artefact was not *in situ* by the time detailed accounts came to be written about the interior in the sixteenth and seventeenth centuries, who removed it in the intervening period?

As if this account hadn't provided us with enough rare information, we have a third *tour de force*. Still referring to the Queen's Chamber, Edrisi says, 'On the roof of the room are writings in the most ancient characters of the heathen priests.' It is sensible, given the absence of any other original votive inscriptions in the interior of this or any other of the three Giza Pyramids, to assume this was graffiti of some sort. But we must also assume that it was not written in Arabic or Latin, otherwise Edrisi would have recognised it. This must mean that the symbols were hieroglyphs, and must have been placed there in pre-Classical antiquity. We have already seen that Mamun supposedly noted torch marks on the ceiling of the Subterranean Chamber. But, if this new analysis is correct, then it surely adds fuel to the argument that the *upper reaches* of the edifice had also been violated previously, and probably in *remote* antiquity.

Of course it is possible that our interpretations are not correct, or that Edrisi himself recorded false information. But, when his account is compared to those of many others, both Arabian and European, coming both before and after him, it appears to stack up extremely well in terms of detail, credibility and lack of exaggeration. It should not therefore be dismissed lightly.

Another Arab historian from this period is far more frequently quoted. Writing about his visit to Giza *c.* 1220, Abd al Latif reports the following about the interior of the Great Pyramid:[8]

> The opening into the interior leads to narrow passages, to deep wells, and to pits and precipices, as I am assured by those, who have had the courage to explore them in search of treasures. No way through the building has been discovered; the most frequented passage ascends to a square chamber in the higher part of the Pyramid, containing a stone sarcophagus. The opening, by which the Pyramid is now entered, is not the original entrance, but a forced passage made, it is said, by the Caliph Mamoon. Many of my companions entered this opening, and went up into the chamber constructed in the top of the Pyramid. Upon their

return, they related the wonderful things they had seen, and told us that the passage was nearly stopped up with bats and dirt; that the bats were as large as pigeons, and that in the upper part were openings and windows, which appeared to have been made to admit air and light. When I again visited the Pyramids, I entered this passage with several people, but having penetrated about two-thirds into the interior, and having through fear completely lost my senses, I returned half dead.

There are a number of observations to be made from this account. First, Latif's account of the interior is not a first-hand one. Second, he reasserts the common view that Mamun was responsible for the forced entrance. Third, his companions report that the passages were nearly 'stopped up with bats and dirt' – this is not something mentioned by Mamun, nor even by Edrisi, who entered the interior only a few decades after Latif's companions. Nevertheless it is a feature commonly reported by explorers of the sixteenth century onwards, and it is important for the following reason: bats could inhabit and proliferate inside the pyramid only once it had been opened, and remained open. Their presence or absence at particular times therefore forms an important part of the jigsaw in determining when and how the edifice may have been breached – and is again a subject to which we will return. Fourth, his companions also report that 'in the upper part were openings and windows, which appeared to have been made to admit air and light.' While from our current knowledge of the interior the idea of 'windows' is clearly entirely fanciful, we will see later that there are two narrow shafts which lead from the King's Chamber to the outside of the edifice which may have been completely unblocked at this time. Is this what his companions were describing, and, if so, can we reliably conclude that they were open to admit air and light at this time?

Latif is also one of the first historians to describe the Sphinx from first-hand observation. Although it would have been buried up to its neck in sand when he saw it, he reports that its face was 'covered with a reddish tint, and a red varnish as bright as if freshly painted'.[9] (In fact even in the first century AD, the Roman historian Pliny had asserted that 'the face of the

26

monster is coloured red',[10] although it is by no means certain that he viewed it personally.) Latif also specifically mentions its fine nose, although this was subsequently broken off as part of a deliberate religious desecration sometime in the late-13th or 14th century – not by Napoleon's men, as is often suggested. It is interesting that in his time it had already attained its more modern Arabic name of Abu Hol or 'Father of Terror' – but its original Egyptian name had been Horemakhet or 'Horus in the Horizon'. The name Sphinx, which has stuck in the Western world, is a Greek creation, the etymology of which is riddled with misleading connotations.

Desecration and Disaster

Part of Latif's account, which is that element most commonly reported, is his apparent personal observation that the Great Pyramid's limestone casing was intact and covered in hieroglyphs. In fact he reports the same of the Second Pyramid:[11]

> The stones were inscribed with ancient characters, now unintelligible. I never met with a person in all Egypt, who had even heard of any one who understood them. The inscriptions are so numerous, that copies of those alone, which may be seen upon the surface of the two Pyramids, would occupy above ten thousand pages.

From the previous context it is clear that he is referring to the two largest pyramids at Giza. However, around the turn of the fourteenth century a series of earthquakes rocked northern Egypt and demolished many of the buildings in its cities. As a result, over the course of the next few generations, the locals stripped off all of the casing stones on the Great Pyramid (22 acres of up to 8 feet in thickness), using them in the reconstruction of the new capital city of El Kaherah on the site of modern-day Cairo. The debris from this destruction rose to such a height that Mamun's entrance was covered up. The only consolation was that the original entrance to the Descending Passage was revealed, surmounted by two huge gables (see Plate 1).

While we cannot be certain, it would appear that the Great

Pyramid was the first of the Giza group to be defaced in this way. And, although such desecration would probably have taken place over an extended period of time, there are reports even as late as the seventeenth century which, as we will see, tend to suggest that the bulk of the casing stones on the Second and Third Pyramids were still intact at this relatively late date.

In fact these finely worked and gleaming casing stones covered all the major pyramids, as well as many of the smaller satellite pyramids and mastabas. And it is not just the Giza group that have suffered this desecration – all these edifices have been stripped of their casing at some time or another. In fact the only pyramid that survives with much of its casing intact to this day is the Bent Pyramid at Dashur, supposedly built by Khufu's father, Sneferu. To us, walking around this magnificent structure – which is about 80 per cent of the size of the Great Pyramid – reveals just how imposing a pyramid looks when its casing remains in place. Close up, the impression of *vastness* is significantly heightened, and the faces seem to expand upward and sideways for ever (see Plate 21). The mind truly boggles at the thought of how the Giza Plateau would have looked in its prime.

Meanwhile, the fact that the Great and Second Pyramids have been defaced also means that any writing that may have existed on their surfaces – and which may have provided some answers to the perennial questions – has been lost to us. In the first instance this observation of Latif's is dismissed as fantasy by almost all modern authors of whatever persuasion. However, our investigations have revealed that his was by no means an uncorroborated account (see Appendix I).

The Dawn of Decoding

After the relative lack of scholarship encountered in the work of all the explorers and writers we have so far encountered, which as we have seen causes so many problems in the interpretation of their accounts, it is refreshing to move on to the first explorer of modern times who applied emerging scientific and scholarly procedures both in his explorations and in the way he documented them. In 1638 an Englishman called John Greaves, who was Professor of Astronomy at Oxford University, visited the Plateau. Like other brave mavericks before him, he recognised that Ptolemy, Pythagoras and other scholars of the Classical Period had all admitted, with greater or lesser degrees of honesty, that their work was based on earlier knowledge derived from Egypt and Mesopotamia.

According to Tompkins, Greaves was fascinated by ancient systems of measurement and he fervently wanted to establish the ancient datum used to derive the dimensions of the Earth. This latter point is somewhat overplayed by Tompkins. In his own work, *Pyramidographia*, published in 1646, Greaves does not mention the determination of the circumference of the Earth. He does concede that the ancient Egyptians may have encapsulated their units of measure in the dimensions of the King's Chamber and its coffer, to fix and record them for posterity, since they had already lasted several thousand years and would likely last several thousand more.[12]

However, he also makes it clear that, while he firmly believed the ancient Egyptians were advanced in mathematics and astronomy, they did *not* reflect this knowledge in the *external* measurements of the Great Pyramid. Indeed he scoffs that to suggest they built pyramid shapes to 'express the first and most simple of mathematical bodies', or 'to represent the mysteries of pyramidal numbers', is 'to play with truth, and indulge too much in fancy'.[13] It is possible that he may not have been too happy with the way his views have been misrepresented by Tompkins.

On entering the Great Pyramid he was confronted by the ubiquitous storm of huge bats as mentioned by Latif's companions. Unable to reach the bottom of the Descending Passage, which was still blocked by the debris of Mamun's excavations, he worked his way around and up into the Ascending Passage and attained the Queen's Chamber, where he noticed the niche and tunnel behind it, but was quickly repelled by the stench of vermin. Retracing his steps, he ascended to the King's Chamber. Here he marvelled at the quality of the workmanship in the chamber and the coffer, and set about measuring and recording their dimensions.

He established that the coffer rang like a bell when struck, and noted the excavation in the floor near it. He also particularly noted the existence of two small square openings cut opposite each other into the north and south walls of the chamber, about 3 feet from the floor, which disappeared horizontally into the recesses of the masonry for some 6 feet or more – the southern one of which showed evidence of blackness and soot, leading him to assume they were receptacles for lamps; however it appears he did not question why they went back so far if this was their only purpose. Finally it is clear from the following observation that plenty of visitors had been in the chamber before him, although whether before or only after Mamun is unclear:[14]

> . . . if they [the walls of the King's Chamber] were not veiled, and
> obscured by the steam of tapers, they would appear glittering
> and shining.

On returning down the Grand Gallery, he noticed that at its base a stone block had been removed from the raised ramp on the west side, and realised this was the opening into the 'Well Shaft', which, as we have already seen, was specifically referred to at least by Edrisi some 400 years previously, and perhaps even by Pliny way before that when he reported: 'In the interior of the largest Pyramid there is a well, eighty-six cubits deep, which communicates with the river [Nile], it is thought'.[15]

Indeed, just to prove that even Greaves himself did not believe he was the first person to discover this shaft – as some would now have us believe – he says, 'At the end of it [the Ascending Passage], on the right hand, is the well mentioned by Pliny: the which is circular, and not square, as the Arabian writers describe'.[16] However, he does provide us with the first detailed account of its layout. He squeezed through the opening, which was only about 2 feet 6 inches in diameter, into a small pit, and then into a vertical shaft which led off it, kinking gently one way then another until opening out into a small 'grotto' about 60 feet down. This grotto was cut into the domed outcrop of Plateau bedrock, which rises at the centre to a height of about 22 feet above the exterior base, and on which the pyramid is anchored. Greaves dropped a lighted torch to establish that the shaft continued down for some distance, but decided to return since the intrusive presence of the bats and their stench was once again overpowering him.

Sir Isaac Newton was at the time also attempting to decode the units of measure used by the ancients. He took Greaves's measurements of the King's Chamber and derived his 'profane' or 'Memphis' cubit of approximately 20.6 British inches, which produced chamber dimensions of 20 × 10 cubits. He also believed there was an alternative measure, the 'sacred' cubit of just over 25 British inches. According to Tompkins he further suspected, unlike Greaves, that the external dimensions of the Great Pyramid measured in these latter units would provide the accurate measure of the circumference of the Earth, which he needed to complete his Theory of Gravitation.

Greaves had attempted to measure the outside of the edifice, but his results were rendered inaccurate by the mountain of rubble that had built up when the casing stones were removed – a problem that would continue to hinder accurate measurement for some time to come – and Newton could not make them fit. Over the next few decades various scientists began to compute the length of one degree of circumference of the Earth by stellar observation and measurement, and therefore derived a figure for the circumference close enough to allow Newton to ratify his Gravitational Theory *without* the use of the pyramid's dimensions (although this fact is often misrepresented).

Greaves also pointed out the Second Pyramid's external appearance: ' . . . the sides . . . are smooth, and equal, the whole fabric (except where it is opposed to the south) seeming very entire, free from any deformed ruptures, or breaches'. Furthermore, perusal of his drawings of the three edifices reveals that, while he renders the Great Pyramid with clearly stepped sides throughout, by contrast he clearly draws both the Second and Third Pyramids with smooth sides. Although his observations were wrong in some areas, it would seem that the balance of probability favours the casing stones being substantially intact on both the Second and Third Pyramids at this time.

Davison Delves

Although no major exploration or discovery was reported for another 130 years, the general advance of scientific procedures meant that a number of early attempts were made to map the Plateau during this period. Benoit de Maillet, Claude Sicard, Richard Pococke and Friderik Norden all contributed to a greater or lesser degree – the last of them especially being the first to map some of the mortuary temples and causeways on the Plateau in his *Travels*, published in 1755.

In 1765 Nathaniel Davison – who would later become British Consul General in Algeria – entered the Great Pyramid while holidaying there. Unlike his predecessors he left us no clear record of his motives, but he did make several discoveries. Despite the continued problem of the bats, he had himself lowered down the Well Shaft by assistants, and continued past the grotto for another hundred or so feet before apparently reaching the bottom, finding it blocked by sand and rubbish.

Disappointed, he turned his attention to looking for other unexplored features. The popular story as told by Tompkins has it that at the top of the Grand Gallery he noticed that his voice echoed from above, and using candles on poles he ascertained that there was a small rectangular opening about 2 feet wide at the end of the east wall, just below the ceiling blocks. Using a rickety series of ladders he inched his way up above the yawning chasm of the Gallery, and peering into the hole was confronted by over a foot of bat dung. He forced his way through it and into the narrow passage, through which he crawled for some 25 feet with only his handkerchief to prevent him from retching. His reward was to come out into the north-east corner of a chamber too low in which to stand, with its uneven floor giving a height that varied between 2 and 4 feet, but otherwise of similar proportions to the King's Chamber beneath it – except about 4 feet longer at roughly 38 feet.

Through the dung he was able to determine that the floor consisted of nine huge rough-worked granite slabs, now estimated to weigh between 25 and 45 tonnes each, and realised that he was sitting on the top of the King's Chamber ceiling blocks. Even more intriguing, he noticed that, as well as the north and south walls being lined with granite blocks, the low ceiling in this 'Relieving Chamber' consisted of eight even larger granite monoliths, now thought to weigh as much as 70 tonnes each – but, not unreasonably given the conditions, he left the chamber without exploring further.

However, more clarity can be achieved when one establishes from Lehner that two other explorers were already trying to find this chamber, and describing it as directly above the King's Chamber and of lower height. They were the German orientalist Karsten Niebuhr and a French merchant called Meynard. This would suggest that rumours were circulating based on the fact that someone else had already been in there unrecorded, although we cannot tell when. And once again it shows how reports of explorations can be distorted and simplified. Nevertheless, it is clear that Davison was the one who braved the ladders and dung to carve his initials in the chamber that would thereafter bear his name.

There is one other aspect of this chamber that we should consider. Although the passage leading to it is better carved than, for example, the Well Shaft, it is clear that it was cut through after the blocks had been put in place. Who had dug it, when and why? These are questions to which we will return.

Jomard Juggles

Little else occurred of relevance in the latter part of the eighteenth century, except that Napoleon conquered Egypt after a fierce battle against the ruling Mamelukes adjacent to the Plateau in 1798. As a corollary to his military activities he assembled a huge team of savants brought together from all professional disciplines, who were tasked with documenting the ancient monuments of the whole of Egypt, as part of a French revival of this ancient seat of learning. Although French domination was soon halted by the English, during the three years before their expulsion the savants remained and formed the Institut d'Egypte.

As far as the Great Pyramid was concerned, although they measured and recorded its internal dimensions carefully, they found nothing new of note apart from a further increase in the profusion of bats and their excreta. Nevertheless, one of the savants in particular, Edme-Francois Jomard, was aware of the theory that had excited Newton that the circumference of the Earth was encoded into the Great Pyramid's structure, and set about measuring the external dimensions as accurately as possible.

Aware that he could not measure the base without clearing some of the debris and sand that still lay piled up, he enlisted an army of Turks to set about the task. This led to an important breakthrough: parts of the pavement or esplanade on which the edifice had been erected were uncovered, along with two of the sockets where the cornerstones had been laid on the northern side, although of the cornerstones themselves there was no trace. Each of these sockets measured 10 feet by 12 feet, had been hollowed some 20 inches into the bedrock, and were perfectly level, both in themselves and with each other. However, the piles of debris along the side ensured that measurement of the base was still a laborious and essentially inaccurate process.

Consequently, Jomard's measurements were still insufficiently accurate for him to prove his 'geodesic dimension' hypothesis. His work was incorporated into the monumental multivolume work prepared by the savants, on Napoleon's instructions, following their return from Egypt – in fact their *Description de l'Egypte* took a total of 25 years to produce. However, Jomard's contribution to Egyptology was ridiculed by contemporary scholars, especially of course by those who could not conceive that their beloved Greeks had *not* been the originators of all knowledge.

The end of the eighteenth century also marked a turning point for the study of Egyptology, when the French discovered the trilingual Rosetta Stone in the Nile Delta. It was handed over to the British as part of the capitulation and deposited in the British Museum, but several decades elapsed before a young French scholar considered by many to be the 'Founder of Egyptology', Jean François Champollion, managed to establish the first translation of Egyptian hieroglyphs and basic grammar from the remaining combination of Greek and demotic Egyptian on the tablet. In allowing the secrets of ancient texts to be unlocked for the first time in at least two millennia, this was to prove a major breakthrough in the understanding of the high culture of Ancient Egypt.

The Circus Strongman

Early in the nineteenth century, two Italians made their mark on the history of the Plateau. The first was Giovanni Battista Belzoni, a huge, former London circus strongman who – as unlikely as it may seem – found his vocation in the exploration of the Plateau after a hydraulic machine he had invented did not sell well. In 1818 he became the first explorer of the modern era to gain access into the Second Pyramid, and the following is based directly on his own *Narrative of the Operations and Recent Discoveries within the Pyramids, Temples, Tombs and Excavations in Egypt and Nubia,* published in 1822. Belzoni started tunnelling at a point central in the north face, which he fancied to be the spot where the original entrance should be. It is clear that by this time the bulk of the casing stones on the Second Pyramid had been removed, and that, as with the Great Pyramid, this had led to a significant build-up of rubble around the base, above the level at which he wanted to work. His workmen toiled for sixteen days, primarily shifting rubble, until they encountered a more or less horizontal tunnel – which itself was strewn with loose debris and sand, which had to be removed before further progress could be made. After a further four days they reached an aperture above them, which rose vertically to the outside face, and it became quite clear to Belzoni that – far from having found the original entrance as planned – they were following a rough-hewn intrusive tunnel which had been excavated after the monument was built.

However, keen to see where it led, they continued to clear the debris for a further two days before breaking into a cleared tunnel, which headed almost horizontally for over 100 feet towards the centre of the edifice. It was dangerous in that parts of the exposed ceiling blocks were hanging precariously askew and loose. At the end there had been a complete cave-in of the roof and – given the danger of complete collapse in other parts – they decided to leave well alone. A further tunnel about halfway along led down and in towards the centre for some 40 feet before terminating in an apparent dead end, but again it was in a similarly perilous state. The entrance to this intrusive passage remains visible to the right of the original upper

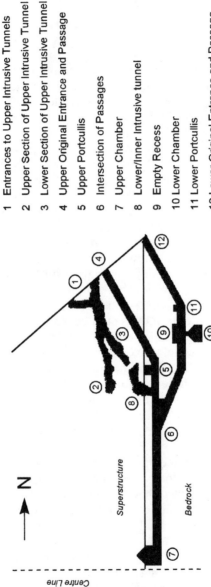

1 Entrances to Upper Intrusive Tunnels
2 Upper Section of Upper Intrusive Tunnel
3 Lower Section of Upper Intrusive Tunnel
4 Upper Original Entrance and Passage
5 Upper Portcullis
6 Intersection of Passages
7 Upper Chamber
8 Lower/Inner Intrusive tunnel
9 Empty Recess
10 Lower Chamber
11 Lower Portcullis
12 Lower Original Entrance and Passage

FIGURE 3: THE SECOND PYRAMID IN PROFILE, LOOKING WEST

entrance, with the entrance to the accompanying vertical shaft above it.

After a day of reflection, Belzoni's resolve to breach the pyramid was strengthened. He took the time to peruse the entrance of the Great Pyramid again, and was reminded of its offset to the east. Was this the answer to his present problem? Returning to the Second Pyramid he set his team to work again, this time about 40 feet to the east of the centre line. After three days they encountered three huge red-granite slabs which bordered the original upper entrance, all inclined into the plane of the pyramid's side. Clearing the remaining rubble, they revealed a granite-lined passage, which descended at an angle of 26 degrees for some 105 feet.

Belzoni reports that this upper passage was filled with debris, which took a further two days to extract. It would appear that if this passage had been sealed with limestone plugs, as that in the Great Pyramid probably had, this exercise should have taken longer. We can only conclude that either these plugs had been broken up in antiquity, or the passage was never plugged and the debris Belzoni encountered was only fragments of casing stones and other rubbish which had fallen into the passage. However, the latter would be somewhat anomalous because, as we will see later, the lower passage in this pyramid was later found with its plugs intact by Vyse.

Once the passage was cleared, at the bottom they encountered what at first appeared to be a dead end, but on closer inspection was revealed to be a huge granite portcullis slab, 6 feet high, 5 feet wide, and 15 inches deep. It was fitted into cut grooves in the walls and ceiling, and was in fact stuck some 8 inches off the floor. After much difficult work with levers in the confined space, Belzoni's men raised it high enough for him to squeeze underneath. The passage continued horizontally for some 18 feet, now with its ceiling level with the base of the superstructure, until its floor dropped off vertically for some 15 feet to meet a lower passage, which was at this point climbing up at a 26 degree angle. Seeing that this latter passage headed back to the outside, Belzoni let himself down by rope and then climbed back up the gradual ascent of the new floor – which rose to a point somewhat lower than the previous passage before heading into a new horizontal passage, approximately 128 feet in length.

Knowing that he was nearing his goal, he scrambled along it and entered into the northeast corner of a pent-roofed rectangular chamber measuring approximately 46 feet east–west by 16 feet north–south, and 22 feet high at the centre. Its walls were entirely carved out of the bedrock, with only the sloping limestone roof slabs protruding into the superstructure. In the poor candlelight he could make out little more than the blocks of stone that were strewn about the floor having been prised from it – evidently by previous intruders searching for treasure.

These blocks initially obscured his view, but on closer inspection Belzoni saw what he had expected: at the western end, just as in the Great Pyramid, lay a finely carved black-granite coffer some 8 feet 6 inches long, 3 feet 6 inches wide and 3 feet deep – although this time with the added security of being partly let into the floor and retained by a surround of cut-granite slabs (see Plate 4). It had no markings; its lid was intact (not broken in two as often reported – it is still there in one piece today) but pushed to one side, and it was filled with earth and stones which, it was discovered a few days later, masked some bones which were subsequently found to be those of a bull. The fact that he was not the first person to enter the sanctuary since the edifice had been closed up was confirmed beyond doubt when Belzoni found multiple charcoal inscriptions on the walls, one of which was clear enough to be transcribed and translated from the Arabic as follows:[17]

> The Master Mohammed Ahmed, lapicide, has opened them; and the Master Othman attended this; and the King Alij Mohammed at first to the closing up.

Also in the upper chamber, he noticed two square horizontal openings in the north and south walls, comparing them to those in the Great Pyramid's King's Chamber. Although, for example, Dr Edwards has more recently supported such a comparison,[18] it is clear on inspection with adequate lighting, that these do not go back into the bedrock for anything more than a few inches, and are therefore not comparable to those in either the

King's or Queen's Chamber (see Plate 9). It is also clear that small-diameter channels could not have been excavated through solid bedrock.

Returning down the horizontal passage, Belzoni now wished to explore the lower passage he had observed on his way in. He found that the entrance was partially blocked by rubble, which was peculiar this far inside the edifice, given that this lower passage was also an original feature rather than a forced entrance. However, on his way in he had noticed the beginnings of an intrusive tunnel disappearing upward from the roof at the junction of the two passages – and he subsequently established that it proceeded towards the lower arm of the upper intrusive tunnel. Belzoni was unable to investigate this fully, but Vyse subsequently established that these two tunnels had originally joined up, and would have allowed access into the interior, but had been blocked by a cave-in of the masonry. Although Belzoni himself does not question this point, it would appear therefore that the rubble had been left by the excavators of the intrusive tunnel.

Clearing the rubble sufficiently to squeeze through, he found that the lower passage descended at the same 26-degree angle as its upper counterpart for a length of some 48 feet before levelling out for about 50 feet, still heading north to the outside of the edifice. Halfway along this horizontal section he found an empty recess on the east side, 11 feet long by 6 feet deep, while opposite it on the west side was a short passage of some 22 feet, descending at the consistent angle of 26 degrees, leading to the centre of the east side of a rectangular lower chamber, this time measuring 34 feet east–west by 10 feet north–south. Again, this had a pent roof and was about 9 feet high at the centre, though at this lower elevation the chamber, including its roof, was entirely cut from the bedrock and unlined. The walls were as smooth and straight as those in the upper chamber, and also exhibited a few examples of similar graffiti. Apart from a number of small blocks of stone lying around, this lower chamber was completely empty.

Returning to the lower horizontal passage, he continued north to the end, where he discovered the grooves for another granite portcullis, although this one had been broken into fragments, which lay around the floor. Finally, the passage rose back out towards the exterior, again at 26 degrees, for some 50 feet before he found it blocked by a large stone, and had to return the way he had entered. He did not attempt to clear the top end of this lower passage, but did subsequently calculate correctly that it emerged right at the base of the north face, and was about 100 feet in length. The entirety of the lower passage was unlined, cut simply but accurately into the bedrock.

Since Belzoni clearly noted that the horizontal element of the upper intrusive tunnel ended in a cave-in, it is instructive to ask how much further it might go. Or does the cave-in signify the end of the intrusion? We know that Vyse did not explore it further, nor have we seen it mentioned elsewhere. It would seem that whoever dug this element was attempting to locate chambers in the superstructure rather than to break into the lower recesses, which would tend to suggest that the upper chambers in the Great Pyramid had probably been found when it was dug, effectively acting as a spur to find similar chambers in this edifice (an influence that has continued to spur other more recent explorers, as we will see). As for the question as to *when* the Second Pyramid was first broken into, we will return to this issue later (see also Appendix II).

The Genoese Merchant

The second Italian adventurer was Giovanni Battista Caviglia, a Genoese sea captain who became so entranced by the Giza Plateau that he gave up the sea and set up home there in 1817, staying for the next twenty years. Although he did not write up his exploits in a formal work, they were recorded sufficiently for Vyse to incorporate them into his own, and the accounts that follow are primarily taken therefrom. Like many of his predecessors, he was convinced that other chambers existed in the Great Pyramid that awaited discovery.

He first explored the Well Shaft, and having ascertained that it was blocked at the bottom, as Davison had discovered, he persuaded his workmen to lift buckets of sand and debris up from its depths in the hope of exploring it further. However, conditions were so appalling that he allowed them to stop, and turned his attention to the Descending Passage, which he decided to clear of the debris that had blocked it for centuries. With this refuse partially cleared, he was able to crawl down the remainder of the passage and into the Subterranean Chamber – the first person to enter it perhaps since Mamun. However, it was itself choked almost to the ceiling with debris, rubbish and sand. As he apparently coughed up blood from the stifling heat and fetid air, his efforts appeared to be rewarded when he crawled back out and came upon a low doorway on the west side of the passage, just after it started to slope back up. Ordering the workmen to dig upward into the hole behind it, he noticed a strong smell of sulphur – which they had been using to try to clear the air in the bottom of the Well Shaft.

It was not long before they had dislodged sufficient earth and rock that a pile of debris fell on top of them, a gust of cool air hit their lungs, and the Well Shaft and Descending Passage had been reunited. Another major enigma had surfaced: who had dug this shaft, and why take so much trouble to dig *another* tunnel through the bedrock for several hundred feet, when all it did was join up the two main ones?

Caviglia completed the clearing of the Subterranean Chamber, and in his search for additional chambers it would appear that he excavated a vertical shaft in its floor, although he does not appear to have progressed to any great depth (in fact it is unclear whether he continued an excavation that already existed – commenced perhaps by Mamun or someone else of that epoch – or started from scratch[19]). While we have seen that Mamun apparently noted torch marks on the ceiling of this chamber, Caviglia additionally noted some Latin characters inscribed on it in charcoal, which he transcribed.[20]

Although he seems to have paid little attention to the Queen's Chamber, he did explore the tunnel behind the niche (which we assume to have been dug by Mamun or a contemporary). His disappointment in finding that it progressed back for some 40 feet before coming to an abrupt halt was probably heightened when all he found at the end were the inscribed names of two previous European travellers, 'Paisley' and 'Munro'.[21]

Most particularly Caviglia seems to have become intrigued by the two small openings in the walls of the King's Chamber, which Greaves had assumed to be receptacles for lighting.

Although the proper excavation of these openings is always assumed to be the work of Vyse, in fact it is clear that Caviglia had already ascertained before Vyse arrived several years later that these were shafts that, after their initial horizontal run of some 6 feet, bent upward into the masonry behind the walls. And they were original features – the blocks had been deliberately carved out, rather than cut through after they were laid. Not only that, but it would appear that attempts had been made to establish their course long before – for example, Greaves had noted soot deposits within one of them nearly 200 years previously, which, rather than being lighting-related, may have represented attempts to hold a lighted torch in them to see what happened to the smoke.

It is highly likely that Caviglia did the same, and that he and possibly unknown predecessors had also attempted to insert rods into them to see how far up, and in what direction, they travelled. Caviglia also opened up the mouth of the southern shaft, although for what purpose remains unclear. However, the most conclusive proof that they had been examined before would be uncovered later by Vyse, as we will see.

Caviglia clearly decided that these shafts might communicate with an undiscovered chamber, and excavated a series of tunnels in their vicinity. This can best be illustrated by an extract from Vyse's diaries relating the circumstances in which the two men met:[22]

> I returned to Alexandria; and on the 23rd [of February 1836] I had the pleasure of being introduced to Mr. Caviglia, with whom I had a long conversation. He informed me that he had made the excavation in the Subterraneous Chamber; that to the south of Davison's Chamber, and the one also along the Northern Air Channel; and that he had attempted to force the mouth of the Southern Air Channel in the King's Chamber. He stated his belief that these channels led to other apartments, which, by excavating in their direction, might be easily discovered. He also mentioned the vertical direction he supposed the Southern Air Channel to take.

We should be clear about the two primary tunnels which

Caviglia dug at this time, because they will be important later. (Refer to Figure 4 for their layout.) The first started at the southeast corner of Davison's Chamber, and after about 10 feet – enough to get behind the hard granite blocks that lined the southern wall – it turned sharp right and ran through the limestone blocks behind the southern wall for a little less than half its length, or something like 15 feet – a sufficient distance to meet the southern shaft if it had risen vertically. We now know that it does not, but rises at an angle, so Caviglia encountered neither the shaft nor any other chamber with which it communicated. This is of course the tunnel we explored personally, as mentioned in the Introduction. Turning his attention to the northern shaft, he dug upward from the west side of the short passage leading from the Grand Gallery into the King's Antechamber, where his tunnel met and followed along underneath the shaft for about 15 feet, but again he encountered nothing except solid masonry.

Another of Caviglia's most important excavations on the Plateau was at the Sphinx. Its human head, carved from a natural outcrop of the bedrock, was all that had been visible for some time. Its leonine body is carved out of the slope of the Plateau, forming an enclosure with steep high walls to the south and west, and a decreasing wall to the north sloping down to a flat surface to the east, or front, of the monument. This enclosure rapidly fills with sand swept in from the desert unless it is regularly cleared. From historic records we know that the enclosure was cleared at various times between the New Kingdom and Graeco–Roman eras. These clearances revealed the true majesty of the monument – it is 240 feet long and 66 feet high. Nevertheless, for most of its life, and probably since Roman times, the Sphinx had lain buried up to its neck.

In 1818, at the request of the then British Consul General Henry Salt, and with great difficulty because of the shifting sand, Caviglia and his workmen excavated in front of the Sphinx.[23] As they dug down they began to unearth fragments of stone, which were later confirmed to be the long pointed 'beard' – which is always displayed in pictorial representations of sphinxes, and had broken off – and a fragment of a serpent's head, which they assumed must have once formed part of the Sphinx's headdress.

At the base they unearthed a small open-air chapel, 10 feet long and 5 feet wide, directly underneath the Sphinx's chin and nestling between its paws. Constructed in the New Kingdom era *c*. 1550–1070 BC, this included a large granite stela at the back which became known as the Dream Stela of Thutmose IV. It was badly worn at the base when first uncovered, and is almost indecipherable today. Meanwhile, there were two smaller limestone stelae honouring Ramesses II, one on either side – the left-hand one in place, the right-hand one having fallen over. Both of these smaller stelae were subsequently sent back to Britain by Vyse, and are now in the Louvre in Paris. A small lion statue had been placed in the entrance, and various other rudely carved lions and sphinxes were scattered around. They also noted that all the foregoing, including the stelae, had been painted red – which ties in with both Pliny's and Latif's observations, and suggests that the entire monument had been decorated in this fashion. Just in front of the outer walls to this chapel, between the front of the Sphinx's paws, was a small square altar which still showed the signs of burnt offerings that had been made upon it.

They also found a number of Greek inscriptions on the paws, one of which stated that the Sphinx was 'the guardian of the tomb of [the Egyptian god] Osiris'.[24] This appeared to confirm the perception of Egyptologists at the time, including Samuel Birch of the British Museum, who suggested that the pedestals on which the sphinxes in the two stelae reside 'have the form of a doorway', and further:[25]

The form of these pedestals has been supposed to allude to a communication through the Sphinx to the Second Pyramid, or to a temple within the body of the image.

These two factors seem to have been linked by both Salt and Birch at the time, who suggested that the 'doorway' would lead to the tomb of Osiris, which would be in one or other of the stated locations. In fact rumours had previously surrounded the work of Napoleon's engineers, who had dug down to a point where they had probably just uncovered the top of the main stela before they had to break off their excavation. Local onlookers at the time had interpreted this as the 'secret door' about which so much folklore had already existed for centuries. Such rumours about secret passages and chambers in and around the body of the Sphinx clearly stem from these Greek sources, and they continue to this day, perhaps now even stronger. As we have already seen they are often linked to the other rumours concerning secret chambers in the Great Pyramid and underground communications between it, the Second Pyramid, and the Sphinx – rumours that themselves probably have their origins in the accounts of the classical historian Herodotus, as will be seen in the next chapter. It is perhaps more surprising that in due course we will see that the specific desire to locate the tomb of Osiris continues even among the Egyptian authorities to this day.

Meanwhile, Caviglia continued his excavations in front of the Sphinx, and cleared the area further east. Here he uncovered a wide flight of 30 steps leading up to a large raised platform measuring about 40 feet by 30 feet, upon which were several small altars. Finally a further 13 steps ascended on the far side of this to an extended walkway about 135 feet long. At the time this was believed to be how the front of the Sphinx had always looked, and it would be another 100 years before further excavation proved that these constructions were of Roman origin, which as we will see masked a much more interesting monument underneath.

Victorian Vandal?

Colonel Richard Howard Vyse himself is the next major player in the history of the Plateau. We have already mentioned him on numerous occasions, not least because he is such a good source for information on older accounts. Of aristocratic English stock, he has been much derided in the modern era for a variety of reasons. Descriptions of him as 'humourless, artless and somewhat of a trial to his family', and as someone who, in 1835, came to the Plateau as a 'fashionable amusement seeker', are still regularly trotted out. And yet these suggestions that he was a frivolous young man seem to be glaringly at odds with the facts.

He became entranced by the Pyramids after his first visit, and also by Caviglia's work, and they soon collaborated – in fact initially Caviglia became his superintendent of works. Vyse's money allowed him to hire whole armies of workmen, plus the services of two civil engineers, John Perring and James Mash, to whom he allocated the task of surveying the entire Plateau. After travelling to Syria for a number of months after his first visits, Vyse returned and set up what appears to have been a highly professional operation, basing it in one of the tombs in the eastern cliff. He directed his operations tirelessly for nearly a year from the end of 1836, apparently fuelled by his strong Christian belief that this was his Master's bidding.

He has also been lambasted by modern archaeologists for his tendency to resort to blasting with gunpowder at the slightest obstacle, and there is clearly some justification for this criticism since the monuments still bear the scars of this work. But what alternatives did he have if he wanted to find out more, in a limited time, without an inexhaustible supply of money, and without modern, less intrusive technology? Should he have waited, sure in the knowledge that the archaeologists of today would do the job much better in another 150 years' time? And what of his many predecessors who hacked at beautiful granite floors and walls, not to discover more about the monuments but in the avaricious search for treasure? They do not seem to be given such a hard time.

Anyone who cares to question Vyse's motives and indeed scholarship has evidently not read *Operations*. The diary format does make it difficult to follow particular threads of his work, since most of them take place over a period of weeks or months, and multiple operations tend to be all jumbled in together. However, it reveals much about the character and integrity of the man, albeit that some of his observations, for example on the ethics and habits of many of the locals he hired as workmen, are far from couched in modern politically correct language. But he was a proud man of aristocratic English stock who went to great lengths to get things done, often in the face of severe obstacles, and often with great diplomacy.

Some of the survey results, plates and inscriptions in *Operations* remain the prime source of historical and archaeological record for a host of artefacts, measurements and other details – not only of the operations conducted under Vyse's supervision, but also of previous historical accounts, of Caviglia's previous work under Salt, and of Perring's surveys of the Plateau and other Egyptian pyramid sites conducted after Vyse's departure. We feel strongly that it is time for the lampooning of this man to cease, and that he should be given the credit he richly deserves. Meanwhile, the following accounts are taken directly from his own records.

Operations inside the Great Pyramid

Starting with his operations inside the Great Pyramid, Vyse's contribution is probably second only to that of Mamun (or whoever really opened up the edifice). Like Caviglia, he too believed there were chambers yet to be discovered, and most of his work was dedicated to locating them. Starting with the Queen's Chamber, and working on the basis of a close examination of the joints between blocks, his workmen commenced by removing the floor block in front of the niche, but found nothing and replaced it. They then removed the blocks under the step in the passage near the entrance to the chamber, but again found nothing. However, in both cases they came across cavities of some 3 or 4 feet in depth, apparently formed by gaps between the core blocks, filled with sand and 'black particles'. As will be seen later, the latter were found in abundance by Vyse, and he interprets them as being remnants of 'decayed stone'.

They also bored small holes down into the floor blocks of the Queen's Chamber passage for some 10 feet, finding nothing unusual, and dug back into the top of the wall in the northwest corner of the chamber to establish that the sloped ceiling blocks overlapped the wall blocks by several feet – this design isolating the finely worked wall linings from the great weight of masonry above them. (In fact Vyse discovered by similar excavation that the ceiling blocks in the Second Pyramid's upper chamber overlapped in the same way, although this time in an apparent attempt to buttress the roof on to the bedrock and against the weight above it.)

Vyse appears to have done relatively little in the other two main chambers. In the King's Chamber, he merely had his men further excavate the hole in the floor near the coffer, originally made, supposedly, by Mamun. Over time four of the floor blocks have been removed, only two of which remain nearby in the chamber. The excavation underneath, although irregular in shape, extends down under the chamber for some 30 feet.[26] Meanwhile, intrigued by Herodotus's tales of chambers far underground beneath the Great Pyramid, which we will examine later, Vyse ordered the extension of Caviglia's excavation in the floor of the Subterranean Chamber, which it was to a depth of 38 feet through the solid bedrock.[27] Neither of these operations revealed any new chambers.

Turning his attention to Davison's Chamber, despite the fact that he clearly disagreed with Caviglia's view that the southern shaft rose vertically, Vyse in fact continued Caviglia's tunnel behind the south wall. It is not entirely clear from his descriptions, but it would appear from our own observations that this continuation probably consisted of digging cavities a few feet up, down, and left at the end of the tunnel, and then a few feet forward. Nothing new was revealed, and the operation was discontinued.[28] Meanwhile he found that he could push a thin rod up through a crack in the ceiling blocks of Davison's Chamber for several feet, and concluded that a larger chamber might exist above.

Since chiselling through the tough granite slabs lining the ceiling and north and south walls would clearly not work, Vyse resorted to gunpowder to blast his way through the limestone blocks behind the wall at the northeast corner – upward from the end of the access passage. When the dust settled, he crawled his way up into another chamber which, to his chagrin, was virtually identical, only between 2 and 4 feet high due to the rough floor, with granite-lined walls and another series of eight granite monoliths forming the low ceiling, these latter estimated to weigh as much as 70 tonnes each. It was empty, save for a covering of black dust on the floor, which he again put down to disintegrated rock. Samples of this dust were subsequently examined by some French scientists and declared ligneous, while the British Museum suggested it was formed from the crushed remains of insects.

Over a three-month period, repetition of these operations revealed a total of four new chambers, all the same with mainly granite linings (although the use of granite for the wall linings decreased with each successively higher chamber, with all lime-stone walls in the uppermost). They had rough-hewn floors and smoothed, flat ceilings formed of massive granite monoliths – except for the uppermost, which had a gabled roof made up of huge, sloping limestone blocks.[29] (Refer to Figure 4 for the layout of the chambers, and see Plates 5 to 8.) Vyse named them in turn Wellington's, Nelson's, Lady Arbuthnot's (after the wife of a lieutenant general who visited the site during the operations), and Campbell's (after Colonel Campbell, the British Consul in Cairo at the time). He, and many others after him, concluded that, since the roof of the King's Chamber underneath was flat and not pent or corbelled, the chambers were designed to relieve the stresses of the huge weight of masonry above it, especially in the event of earthquakes, to which the area had at times been prone. While this theory is probably correct, the many writers who heap praise on this innovative design may be somewhat mistaken, as we will see later.

Perhaps the most interesting of all his finds was not the chambers per se, but a series of red-painted hieroglyphs on the walls of the Relieving Chambers. These walls are now almost entirely covered in the graffiti of subsequent visitors, but the original hieroglyphs are concentrated on the limestone (*not* granite) blocks comprising the north, south and west walls of Lady Arbuthnot's and Campbell's Chambers, and the west walls of Nelson's and Wellington's. Some are upside down, and all are roughly painted, indicating they are quarry marks and not decorative inscriptions. When Vyse had them copied and sent to Birch at the British Museum, he established that at least one of the ovals, signifying the cartouche of a king, contained the name of Suphis, Shofo, or as we know him Khufu (the most complete cartouches have been reproduced in Figure 5).[30] It is this mark which more than any other piece of evidence has

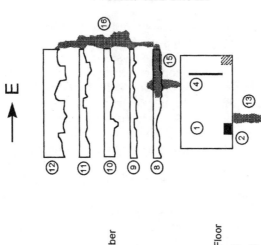

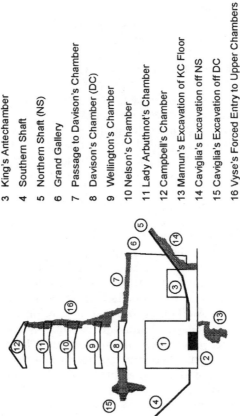

1 King's Chamber (KC)
2 Coffer
3 King's Antechamber
4 Southern Shaft
5 Northern Shaft (NS)
6 Grand Gallery
7 Passage to Davison's Chamber
8 Davison's Chamber (DC)
9 Wellington's Chamber
10 Nelson's Chamber
11 Lady Arbuthnot's Chamber
12 Campbell's Chamber
13 Mamun's Excavation of KC Floor
14 Caviglia's Excavation off NS
15 Caviglia's Excavation off DC
16 Vyse's Forced Entry to Upper Chambers

FIGURE 4: CROSS-SECTIONS OF KING'S AND RELIEVING CHAMBERS

**THE "KHUFU" CARTOUCHE ON THE SOUTHERN
ROOF BLOCKS OF CAMPBELL'S CHAMBER**

**THE "KHNUM-KHUF" CARTOUCHE ON THE
SOUTH WALL OF LADY ARBUTHNOT'S CHAMBER**

FIGURE 5: TWO OF THE CARTOUCHES IN THE RELIEVING
CHAMBERS[31]

been used by Egyptologists to date the construction of the Great
Pyramid to the reign of this Fourth Dynasty Pharaoh, *c.* 2550
BC. Furthermore, it appeared to corroborate what various
Classical historians had recorded, as we will see later: that the
pyramid had been built in the reign of Cheops, who was one
and the same.

This analysis has been challenged recently from a variety of
sources, but one thing should be remembered: it is beyond
question that these chambers had never been entered between
the time of their construction and Vyse's forced entry. They
were sealed off, never intended to be seen, and no one could
have gained access to them without leaving some trace of their
own forced entry. Therefore, unless it can be conclusively
proved either that Vyse faked the cartouches himself (as some
have suggested) or that their translation is faulty, the evidence
must be considered sound. While we will return to this
important topic later, we should also point out that no other

original inscriptions of any kind have ever been found inside the Great Pyramid.

Operations outside the Great Pyramid

Turning their attention to the outside of the Great Pyramid, Vyse and his team used gunpowder on the south side in an abortive and admittedly ill-judged attempt to find a second entrance in the same relative location as that on the north side – about 24 feet to the *west* of centre.[32] He reasoned, as many have since, that the relative size of the edifice as against the small volume of chambers found therein might mean that there were more to be discovered;[33] and further that there may be an equivalent passage from the south which led to other chambers *between* the King's, Queen's and Subterranean Chambers. Having blasted with great difficulty into core blocks, which were well cemented and overlapped, he ordered his men to clear the blocks vertically from above. In the end this work left a huge and ugly scar, about 30 feet high, which is still clearly visible today. Having found nothing even at a depth of 30 feet in, they gave up the scheme.

Meanwhile, as he surveyed the north face of the Pyramid, Perring came across the outlet for the northern shaft from the King's Chamber about halfway up at the 102nd course. His task was made easier because someone (not Caviglia, as is sometimes reported) had *already* attempted to explore it by enlarging the opening to a diameter of about 3 feet. The shaft was full of rubbish, and another of Vyse's assistants, an Englishman by the name of JR Hill, was given the task of clearing it using boring rods. After several weeks, it was established that the intrusive enlargement had been carried on to a depth of approximately 37 feet before the shaft returned to its normal 8-inch-square section. When the internal end – which was also choked with rubbish – was finally cleared, they poured water down the shaft from the outside: it came right through to the King's Chamber, proving that there was no connection with another chamber.[34]

Although it is usually reported that the southern shaft was cleared first, this is not the case. *After* his success with the northern shaft, Hill was asked to locate the outlet for the southern shaft, which he found without great difficulty in the equivalent position on the south face. It too was blocked, and he was forced to blast away some core blocks in order to have space to erect a scaffold to support the boring rods. After several days of blasting he came across a most unexpected and unusual find: a substantial fragment of an iron plate, about 12 inches by 4 inches and $\frac{1}{8}$ inch thick. As two modern-day researchers, Graham Hancock and Robert Bauval, have pointed out in their book *Keeper of Genesis*,[35] this find was sufficiently important – given that the plate had been found embedded in a monument dating conservatively to some 2,000 years before the supposed Iron Age in Egypt – for Hill to write a certification for it before it was dispatched to the British Museum.[36]

> This is to certify that the piece of iron found by me near the mouth of the air-passage [shaft], in the southern side of the Great Pyramid at Gizeh, on Friday, May 26th, was taken out by me from an inner joint, after having removed by blasting the two outer tiers of the stones of the present surface of the Pyramid; and that no joint or opening of any sort was connected with the above mentioned joint, by which the iron could have been placed in it after the original building of the Pyramid. I also shewed the exact spot to Mr. Perring, on Saturday, June 24th.

While this discovery did not call the age of the pyramid into question, it certainly added another enigma – indeed a dilemma for the orthodox scholars. The builders of the pyramids were not supposed to have the technology to mould an iron plate! In fact Hancock and Bauval quote the report of an independent scientific test on the plate, carried out on a fragment in 1989, which contained the following findings: first, that the plate had a negligible nickel content, and could not therefore have been fashioned from a meteorite; second, that it had been smelted at between 1,000 and 1,100 degrees Celsius; and, third, that it contained traces of gold on one face, which suggest it may have been gold-plated.[37] They also revel, in this case reasonably enough, in the discomfort of the British Museum personnel who attempted to dismiss this analysis and Hill's certification (suggesting the plate had been deliberately inserted there in

Vyse's time), without any firm counterarguments. Needless to say, this element of the story is, perhaps selectively, omitted by Lehner.

Hill's continued clearance of the southern shaft was complicated by the fact that a piece of rock was lodged about 7 feet in and had to be removed with great care in case it fell further and blocked the shaft lower down. Nevertheless, this final obstruction was cleared, and he noted that beneath the blockage the shaft was 'blackened with fires made from time to time in the lower part to discover its direction.'[38]

Furthermore, Perring, who was in the King's Chamber at the time, felt a sudden rush of cool air as the full ventilation from both shafts being open was effected. Since their clearance, the temperature in the chamber has supposedly remained at a constant 68 degrees Fahrenheit, irrespective of the season. This led Vyse and many subsequent researchers to assume they were ventilation shafts, a form of early air conditioning. Jomard had theorised that the King's Chamber could be some form of repository for weights and measures, which require an even temperature and constant barometric pressure to remain accurate – for example, the Paris Observatory had been built 85 feet below ground to achieve these conditions – and this discovery appeared to ratify his theory. However, there are a number of factors that contradict this analysis, as we will shortly see. So another great enigma had emerged: if these shafts were not built for ventilation, what was their purpose? And what role was played by the iron plate?

After all this blasting, tunnelling and clearing, neither Caviglia nor Vyse had found the type of 'secret' chamber in the Great Pyramid which they had been convinced existed. Vyse at least was forced to conclude that the Great Pyramid was nothing more than a funerary edifice for Khufu's burial. Meanwhile, it seems the relationship between the two became soured almost as soon as it began when, with Vyse absent on a trip up the Nile, Caviglia disobeyed his instructions and concentrated all his and the team's efforts on excavating shaft tombs in the central mastaba field – particularly one that was labelled Campbell's Tomb in similar fashion to the Relieving Chamber. This continued for some time after Vyse's return, until, after a huge disagreement, Caviglia retired to Paris, where he remained to the end of his days.

Vyse reluctantly goes into great length about their disagreement in the Appendix to *Operations*, and, although his observations are written in the more polite and restrained manner of the time, this was clearly a fine prototype for some of the political wranglings that have so dogged the Plateau in recent years. It has all the elements: Caviglia accused Vyse of stealing his secrets, claiming somewhat without justification that he was on the point of discovering the additional Relieving Chambers himself when he was fired. He further claimed Vyse was monopolising excavation rights, after he attempted to obtain Vyse's permission to return to the Plateau, but was again quite reasonably denied, given his outrageous statements. And all this was conducted in a highly publicised letter-writing campaign in the press – as we will see, some things never change! Meanwhile, after Caviglia's departure, Perring took over as Vyse's superintendent.

Turning to the base of the Great Pyramid, we note that the debris and sand had increased again, and even the corner sockets uncovered by the French forty years earlier were once again obscured. Vyse ordered his workmen to clear the debris from the centre of the northern face, and yet another vital discovery was made: two of the original limestone casing blocks were still intact and in place on the lowest course. They were highly polished, finely worked, the largest measuring approximately 8 feet wide by 8 feet deep by 5 feet high, and weighing about 15 tonnes (see Plate 2). This discovery achieved a major breakthrough: it allowed the angle of the pyramid's slope to be determined accurately at 51 degrees 51 minutes – ostensibly allowing a more accurate figure for the height to be determined by trigonometry. However, this still depended on the accuracy of the base measurement, which at this time remained problematic.

Furthermore, this clearing operation on the north side uncovered a large section of the original platform or 'pavement' which surrounded the pyramid, and has since been determined to extend over 30 feet on the north side, and a few feet on the three other sides (the surrounds of the other two pyramids at Giza were similarly paved). The blocks forming this pavement were once again finely honed to a high degree of accuracy on both their upper and lower sides, as was the underlying bedrock, in order to form a level foundation on which to base the edifice. In fact more recent surveys show that the maximum deviation of the pavement from dead level is less than 1 inch across the entire area, and even then some of this variation could have been caused by subsidence. The pavement was also found to extend underneath the lowest course of core masonry for an indeterminate length.

Operations at the Second Pyramid

At the Second Pyramid, Vyse discovered the entrance to the lower passage which Belzoni had seen only from the blocked interior, and blasted through the obstructions to clear it. He noted that it was deliberately sealed up with a number of 'jointed and cemented' limestone plugs, the first 10 feet long, the remainder 6 or 7 feet.[39] This is the only descending entrance passage in one of the three Giza Pyramids to be found with intact sealing blocks in modern times, and it has led to speculation that they were all sealed in this way. Uniquely, it is also the only passage that slopes at an angle of 22 degrees, whereas all the others slope at 26 degrees or thereabouts. Perring also lifted the floor blocks of the upper chamber in the hope that they concealed a lower chamber underneath but, finding nothing, he replaced them. They also excavated the many grottos and shafts in the enclosure walls, which had been cut from the sloping bedrock to the north and west of the Second Pyramid as part of the levelling operation for the foundations; however, these were primarily found to be later tombs.

Operations at the Third Pyramid

At the Third Pyramid Vyse had one of his greatest successes. Since he knew of no modern record of anyone having breached its interior, he determined to carry on from where both Belzoni and Caviglia – both of whom had attempted to find a way in – had left off.[40] This pyramid had been badly disfigured by Saladin's son, Malek Abd al Aziz Othman ben Youssef, who attempted to dismantle it in 1196 so he could reuse the stone. In fact after eight months he was able to create only a relatively small 'dent' in the north face – a tribute to the quality of the core masonry, and to the general building techniques of the Ancient Egyptians.

Given the relatively small size of this structure, the difficulties in clearing the sand and rubble from the lower courses and his mistaken belief that Youssef had been attempting to explore the pyramid from this excavation rather than dismantle it, Vyse decided to bore straight into it via the earlier intrusion – something that Caviglia had begun some time before with little success. His tunnel progressed horizontally for some 60 feet to near the centre line, at which point he angled it straight downward. After a short horizontal section he again sent it straight down, reaching the bedrock after the shafts had descended for a total of about 80 feet. Since all this was achieved only with some difficulty, and they still found nothing after several months of effort, he was forced to turn his attention to the outside and attempt to locate the original entrance.

With the tendency for illogical reasoning that he occasionally displayed, Vyse employed his workmen for some days in clearing the pavement on the north side some distance from the base, under which he felt the entrance would lie despite the fact that there was little or no precedent for this. Finally he realised that he must clear the base of the north face, where, in a short time, his men revealed unstripped casing stones on the lower courses. Not only were they unusually made of granite, but their faces displayed a more rounded nature than those on the other pyramids – indeed, they are still in place on these lower courses today, and resemble sandbags stacked up against the base. (It is now clear that this granite casing was employed up to the sixteenth course before the builders reverted to the traditional limestone; and that the first two courses of the Second Pyramid were the same.) Although the bulk of the casing blocks gave this appearance of remaining unfinished, Vyse noticed that in the centre they had been smoothed flat for about 20 feet, which suggested an entrance point (in fact the same smoothing occurs at the centre of all four sides, but he may not have known this at the time, and in any case the north side would always be the first point of exploration). He ordered his men to remove the debris from the centre of this flattened

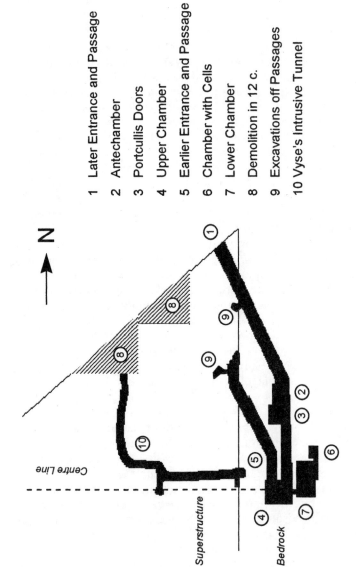

1 Later Entrance and Passage
2 Antechamber
3 Portcullis Doors
4 Upper Chamber
5 Earlier Entrance and Passage
6 Chamber with Cells
7 Lower Chamber
8 Demolition in 12 c.
9 Excavations off Passages
10 Vyse's Intrusive Tunnel

FIGURE 6: THE THIRD PYRAMID IN PROFILE, LOOKING WEST

section, revealing an entrance into a descending passage at a height of 13 feet above the base, and – unusually – placed centrally.

Although Vyse was able to establish that the passage sloped at the consistent angle of 26 degrees, and was granite-lined for some 29 feet before reaching the bedrock, he initially found it blocked at its lower extremes with stone fragments and sand. He also noticed that an excavation had been forced upward for about 5 feet behind the lowest granite ceiling block – both of which clearly indicated that the passage had been entered before. He further surmised that it had been originally sealed with plug stones – just as he had found the lower passage in the Second Pyramid to be – the removal of which at some point had been effected with some force and clumsiness, judging by the rough and damaged state of the walls and ceiling, especially nearer the entrance.

After several days, the passage, which turned out to be 104 feet long, had been cleared sufficiently to reveal an antechamber at its base, although sand and other debris still filled this horizontal section to within 2 feet of its roof. Once cleared further, the antechamber was revealed to have plastered walls decorated with simple reliefs of long, thin, rectangular panels reaching nearly from floor to ceiling all round – nothing too elaborate, but the first decoration of any kind to have been found in one of the Giza Pyramids. Several large blocks in their original position on the floor indicated that this antechamber had originally been sealed up so that it was inaccessible.

Beyond this was a further chamber, which contained the grooves for three vertical portcullises, although these had been broken up by previous intruders. Beyond this, a horizontal passage led due south for some 41 feet before giving on to the northeast corner of a large ('upper') chamber, measuring some 46 feet east–west, 13 feet north–south and 16 feet in height. It was entirely carved from the bedrock, and was unlined (see Plate 10). There were a number of unusual features surrounding this chamber. First, an original passage immediately above the one by which Vyse had entered led back to the north. Again horizontal for the first 17 feet, it then rose at an angle of 27 degrees for some 64 feet before stopping level with the base of the superstructure. A number of subsequently forced tunnels off the end of this had evidently been dug in antiquity in attempts to locate other passages or chambers in the superstructure. From a close inspection of the chisel marks in the two main descending passages, Vyse and Perring concluded that this upper one had been constructed first, from the *outside* (that is, *before* the superstructure had been built), while the lower one had been constructed subsequently from the *inside*. Even more intriguing, it was clear, from the remnants of plugging blocks therein and plaster on the walls, that this upper passage had been blocked off as well.

Second, the western part of this upper chamber narrowed in height and width, as well as containing an empty recess for a sarcophagus in the floor, while a passage in the western wall led down to an empty, low-ceilinged side chamber with a roughly finished granite floor. It was evident that this had originally been blocked off and coated with plaster, but had been broken into by earlier intruders – and, from the degree to which its floor blocks were worn and glazed, Vyse concluded that it had been visited by many people before him.

Third, the northern and southern walls of this upper chamber contained a number of small but shallow recesses, similar to but more numerous than those in the Second Pyramid's upper chamber (see Plate 11). These may have been used for lighting, as we have previously suggested. However, in this case, since they are more rounded than square, Vyse himself conjectures that they may have retained wooden beams which were necessary to assist the further construction which we will shortly review (the chamber in Sneferu's pyramid at Meidum has similar holes, which still contain the wooden supports that might have been used to manoeuvre a coffer).

And, fourth, the chamber contained Arabic graffiti similar to that found by Belzoni in the Second Pyramid, indicating it had been broken into at a similar time.

When first found, this upper chamber contained a large quantity of rubbish, which had to be cleared and sorted. This operation revealed another sloping passage, about 32 feet long, leading westward down into the bedrock from the centre of the floor, which Vyse concluded had also been sealed up with plugs.

After the debris had been cleared, a 10-foot-long horizontal passage with two more chambers leading off it was revealed. The first, attained after descending a short flight of steps on the right of the passage, was a small rectangular room unusually oriented north–south, measuring 18 feet long by 6 feet wide by 7 feet high. It had four 'cells', 8 feet deep by 3 feet wide, in the east wall, and two in the north. It was again unlined, and was essentially empty apart from rubbish. The second, the 'lower' chamber, lay at the end of the passage (see Plate 12). Entered via its southeast corner, it was again oriented north–south, measuring approximately 22 feet long by 9 feet wide. Vyse assumed it must be the main burial chamber, since it was entirely lined with polished granite blocks and had a sloped but rounded roof, 11 feet high at the centre. It was also clear that the rough granite floor of the side chamber at the west end of the upper chamber constituted the top side of the roof blocks of this lower chamber – and that its primary purpose must have been to assist the construction of the latter.

In this lower chamber he found one of his most prized discoveries – a black basalt coffer decorated in typical Old Kingdom 'palace façade' style, with rectangular reliefs similar to those in the antechamber but somewhat more complex (see Figure 7). Again this was the only authentic coffer discovered in one of the three Giza Pyramids that was decorated, although once again it was empty. The following is Vyse's description of the coffer, along with some associated finds which were made shortly afterwards:[41]

The sarcophagus did not bear any inscription or hieroglyphics. The lid had been fixed by two pins in the usual manner, and also by a dovetail, which was rounded; and a plate of metal seemed to have been applied so carefully underneath it, that in order to insert a lever for its removal, it had been found necessary to cut a groove across the rim of the sarcophagus. The lid was not found in the sepulchral [lower] chamber, but pieces of it were afterwards discovered. When the large apartment [the upper chamber] was finally cleared out, the greater part of the lid of the sarcophagus was found near the entrance of the passage descending to the sepulchral chamber; and close to it fragments of the top of a mummy-case (inscribed with hieroglyphics, and

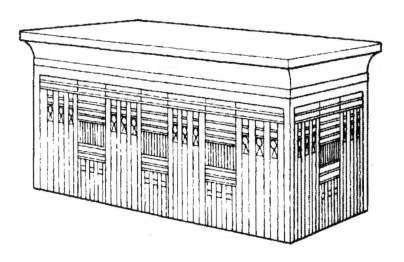

FIGURE 7: DRAWING OF THE BASALT COFFER FOUND IN
THE THIRD PYRAMID[42]

amongst them, with the cartouche of Menkaure) were discovered
upon a block of stone, together with part of a skeleton consisting
of ribs and vertebrae, and the bones of the legs and feet enveloped
in coarse woollen cloth of a yellow substance to which gum was
attached. More of the board and cloth were afterwards taken out
of the rubbish.

Vyse removed the basalt coffer from the Third Pyramid, and
arranged to have it transported back to England. However, in
a cruel twist of fate, the ship sank in deep water off the coast
of Spain, robbing him of one of his finest trophies. Meanwhile,
the human bones, linen wrappings and fragments of wooden
coffin, which he describes above as found among the debris in
the upper chamber, were pieced together and sent to the British
Museum, where they still reside. Unfortunately, they have subsequently been carbon-dated and found to belong to the much
later Saite Period (or 26th Dynasty, c. 664–525 BC), while the
design of the wooden coffin (see Figure 8) corroborates this
dating. Meanwhile, after his return, Vyse was to uncover infor-

FIGURE 8: PERRING'S DRAWING OF THE WOODEN COFFIN
FOUND IN THE THIRD PYRAMID[43]

mation from the account of Edrisi that would add more
confusion to the possible original contents of the Third Pyramid,
as will be seen later.

Other operations at Giza

Vyse and Perring performed many more excavations on the
Plateau. Presumably having heard some of the rumours that
already existed concerning the Sphinx, Vyse was convinced
there might be a secret chamber within its body. He used boring
rods to drill a hole in the top, behind the head (although he
refers to it as the 'shoulder'), which progressed to a depth of
some 27 feet before the rods became stuck and embedded. Since
they had encountered no cavities, at this point the project was
abandoned. They excavated the two sets of three satellite pyramids to the south of the Third and to the east of the Great
Pyramid, finding they had all been broken into at some point
in the past. Most of them were found to contain sarcophagi
located within the standard 'subterranean-chamber-reached-via-
descending-passage' layout, and plenty more quarry marks were
recorded, including one that incorporated the name Menkaure.

They unearthed the bridged entrance on the south perimeter
of the Plateau now known as the 'Wall of Crows', the top of
which they found to be composed of two huge limestone monoliths over 20 feet in length. Finally, they continued the
excavation of several shafts in the central mastaba field which,
as we have seen, had been begun by Caviglia but initially
afforded undue priority. The first was Campbell's Tomb, in
which they uncovered a beautifully decorated sarcophagus

which Vyse presented to the British Museum, and established to be a 26th Dynasty construction. The others, referred to as 'Shaft No. 1, 2' etc, lay between the Sphinx and the Second Pyramid. These have some similarities to a shaft that has been excavated more recently, which will be referred to later.

Having contributed a great deal to the study and understanding of the Giza Plateau during his stay, despite the destruction his gunpowder wrought in places, Vyse returned to England towards the end of 1837. He left Perring to continue their exploration, surveying and measurement work both on the Plateau and increasingly at the other pyramid complexes at Dashur, Abusir, Saqqara, Abu Roash, Meidum and elsewhere (a map of these major sites is included in Appendix VI). Once home, he set about writing *Operations*, the first two volumes of which were published three years later; while a third volume, an invaluable appendix containing a condensed version of Perring's continued work at the other sites, was added in 1842.

The French Founders

Over the next few decades, two Frenchmen would make their mark on the study of Egyptology. The first, Karl Richard Lepsius, studied Egyptology before embarking on a massive survey of Egyptian antiquities in the period from 1842 to 45. His most famous contributions were his excavations away from the Plateau: of the Step Pyramid at Saqqara – where he uncovered a door frame in the substructure which bore King Djoser's name; and of the so-called 'Labyrinth' at Hawara – which Herodotus had described as an even greater wonder than the Giza Pyramids, but was in fact the largest of all known mortuary temples, that of Amenemhet III of the Twelfth Dynasty. His many finds were to form the basis of the Berlin Museum collection, and his work was written up in his massive twelve-volume *Denkmaler*.

The second was Auguste Mariette, who again studied Egyptology from an early age and in 1850 was sent to Egypt by the Louvre and placed in charge of the newly created Egyptian Antiquities Service, a position that would be held by the French for the next 100 years. His excavations made several major contributions: he discovered the 'Serapeum', a huge catacomb at Saqqara which contained the massive sarcophagi of the sacred Apis bulls. More important for our purposes, he was the first modern excavator of the Valley Temple, connected to the Second Pyramid by its causeway, both attributed by Egyptologists to Khafre. This temple lies close to the front of the Sphinx but to the south (while for clarity the separate temple later excavated immediately in front of the Sphinx is known as the Sphinx Temple); and, since the whole of this lower or eastern part of the Plateau had been covered in by sand and debris for many centuries or even millennia, all that had been visible of the Valley Temple was a few blocks of stone and some hollows.

What Mariette uncovered between 1853 and 1858 remains the best-preserved outlying building on the Plateau (see Plates 13 to 16). The Valley Temple was revealed to comprise a T-shaped pillared hall accessed via a rectangular entrance hall, with various ancillary corridors and chambers. It appears to have been on two levels, the ground floor being predominantly roofed over while the first floor may have consisted, at least in part, of an open terrace. The fascination of this building lies in the quality of the red-granite ashlars that line its interior, and of the pillars and ceiling lintels of the same material. Most of these are still in place, and the quality of their workmanship is magnificent. Originally they would have been polished to a high sheen, as would the alabaster floor, which is now in a poorer state of repair.

Unfortunately, only some of the ceiling lintels are still in place – the remainder were found on the floor when Mariette excavated, which he sadly decided to blast to pieces to effect their removal. Meanwhile, the core of the outer walls is composed of huge limestone monoliths, some of which are reported to weigh as much as 100, and in some reports 200 tonnes, and have clearly been quarried from the Sphinx enclosure (because this fact is central to the arguments surrounding the possible redating of the Sphinx, we will return to it later). Although these now show severe signs of weathering, some argue that the building was originally cased with red granite on the outside as well.

Within a pit in the floor of the entrance hall – where it had presumably been placed to hide it from robbers – Mariette discovered the celebrated life-size statue of Khafre, exquisitely carved from a solid block of black diorite, which now resides in the Cairo Museum. Not only did this statue add weight to the view that the Second Pyramid had been built by Khafre, it also remains one of the finest examples of Ancient Egyptian sculpture of any dynasty.

Mariette made one other notable find on the Plateau: while excavating what is known as the 'Temple of Isis', built on the east side of the southernmost of the three subsidiary pyramids to the east of the Great Pyramid, he discovered a small stela, which is now known as the Inventory Stela – since it supposedly records repair work performed by Khufu on the Plateau, including on the Sphinx. Much has been made of this stela by alternative researchers anxious to question the orthodox dating of the Sphinx, which maintains that it was carved by Khafre as an ancillary to his Valley Temple complex. However, as will be seen later, there are good reasons for concluding that the account on this stela is a highly edited and fictitious one prepared by Saite Period 'restorers'.

The Astronomer Royal

While these various excavations were underway, John Taylor, a former editor of the *London Observer*, was becoming the next standard-bearer of the proposition that the Great Pyramid's dimensions incorporated mathematical and geodesic knowledge. Although he never visited the Plateau personally, he presented his theories in *The Great Pyramid: Why Was It Built, and Who Built It?* in 1859. While we will examine these in more detail in a later chapter, suffice to say his work intrigued the man who would later become the Scottish Astronomer Royal – Charles Piazzi Smyth. The two men struck up a spirited but brief correspondence shortly before Taylor's death, which led the underfunded Smyth to travel to Giza in order to make his own measurements of the edifice. Over a three-month period at the beginning of 1865, he used the most advanced instruments so far employed to furnish himself with the most detailed set of interior and exterior measurements possible.

However, the key to the theories about encoded knowledge still lay in obtaining an accurate measurement of the perimeter;

once again this was foiled by the huge quantities of debris that still lay around the base. Significant differences existed between Smyth's figures and those of Perring and Jomard before him, and, despite Smyth juggling them with what must be considered arbitrary assumptions (effectively taking the mean of each pair of figures and seeing which result best suited his theories), in no way did he obtain definitive proof. Much reluctance existed among Smyth's scientific contemporaries to accept anything other than classical theories of knowledge evolution. This, coupled with his devout religious beliefs, which led him to theorise that such knowledge must have been granted to certain Ancient Egyptians by 'the Author of all Wisdom', resulted in his being vociferously ridiculed to an even greater extent than Taylor had been before him.

Smyth's position was not strengthened by his later association with another religious zealot, Robert Menzies, who was one of the first to suggest that the layout and dimensions of the interior passages in the Great Pyramid were deliberately designed to incorporate a 'timeline' of biblical prophecy of all the major events in mankind's history – including the 'second coming'. This theory may have had some roots in the Arab legends. For example, Hokm and Masoudi talk of the 'books' stored in the Third Pyramid: 'with every priest a book, in which were the wonders of his profession, and of his actions, and of his nature, and what was done in his time, and what is, and what shall be, from the beginning of time, to the end of it'. It was expounded in subsequent decades by David Davidson, Morton Edgar and others – perhaps the best contenders for the title 'Pyramidiots'. Although it became increasingly ridiculed over the decades, apart from other factors because many of the prophecies failed to come to fruition, as we will see there are still those who cling to this belief now.

Meanwhile, it is interesting to note that Smyth's most celebrated work, *Our Inheritance in the Great Pyramid* – in which he set out his theories – was first published in 1864: the year *before* he conducted his surveys at Giza (although it was subsequently updated).

Masonic Meddling?

In 1872 two brothers, Waynman and John Dixon, travelled to the Plateau to explore the Great Pyramid. The former, an engineer, was intrigued by the King's Chamber shafts, and considered that there may be similar features in the Queen's Chamber. One of his companions, a Dr Grant, noticed a crack in the south wall of the latter in roughly the right place, albeit somewhat higher off the floor at a little over 5 feet, and slightly more to the east. Dixon inserted a piece of wire through the crack and, finding it went in a considerable distance, he set his general factotum Bill Grundy to work with a hammer and chisel. After only a short time the chisel dropped through the masonry into a cavity. This was soon revealed to be a shaft, again about 8 inches square, and again travelling vertically for about 6 feet before disappearing upward into the body of the pyramid at an angle of about 30 degrees. The same procedure revealed a similar shaft in the north wall.

The Dixons attempted to test the shafts with jointed iron rods similar to those of a chimney sweep – one of which got stuck in the northern shaft some distance up and remains there to this day. They also lit fires in the openings to see what happened. Smyth's contemporary account of the Dixons' work, published in an updated edition of *Inheritance* in 1880, indicates that the smoke in the southern shaft did not billow back into the chamber, nor could it be seen on the outside of the edifice. Try as they might they could not locate an exit point for either shaft on the north and south faces. Undoubtedly the Dixons began to suspect that the shafts were unlikely to exit fully because they had been deliberately sealed off with about 5 inches of regular masonry at their internal ends, masonry that formed part of the large surrounding blocks and was not readily removable. Of course we now know that they do not extend through to the outside, as will be seen later. They were therefore unlikely to be ventilation shafts – and, given their similarities, this cast doubt on the function of the shafts in the King's Chamber. The enigma of the shafts had been reinforced.

However, their exploration of the northern shaft led on to another discovery of some importance. This is best reviewed by quoting from Smyth:[44]

Something else, however, was discovered inside the channels, viz, a little bronze grapple hook; a portion of cedar-like wood, which might have been its handle; and a grey-granite, or green-stone ball, which, from its weight, 8,325 grains [1 pound 3 ounces], as weighed by me in November, 1872, must evidently have been one of the profane Egyptian *mina* weight balls, long since valued by Sir Gardiner Wilkinson at 8,304 grains.

Once again Bauval deserves credit as the first researcher for over a century to bring the existence of these relics to light, and his initial account provided in *The Orion Mystery* (co-written with Adrian Gilbert in 1994) furnishes us with more details taken from Smyth's private diaries and correspondence with the Dixons.[45] The ball may have been used as a plumbline, while the two-pronged hook might have been an astronomical sighting device, or even possibly a *pesh-en-kef* tool used in the 'opening-of-the-mouth' ceremony performed by priests on the dead king, supposedly to allow his soul to escape. The portion of wood, of which only diagrams now exist, was reported to be about a third of an inch square in section and just under 5 inches long. It was broken off at one end; and had (if our interpretation of Smyth's writing is correct) 'many holes and gouges [or squares?], and with two little teeth like small stones set in it'. The Dixons noted that the northern shaft at least was as 'clean and white as the day it was made', and, since they had clearly been sealed since construction, the artefacts could have been placed or left inside them only when the edifice was built. Apart from the granite coffer, they therefore represent the only original artefacts ever found inside the Great Pyramid in modern times.

Bauval was anxious to trace the relics. They had effectively 'gone missing' for nearly a century. Apart from Smyth's account, they were not mentioned in the work of the foremost Egyptologists at the time or afterwards, nor in Edwards's *The Pyramids of Egypt*. In fact, Edwards, who was in close contact with Bauval at the time, claimed he had never heard of them. Bauval decided to force the issue by going to the newspapers in the hope of jogging someone's memory, and was rewarded shortly afterwards when Dr Vivian Davies of the British Museum admitted that the relics had been donated to it by the Dixon family in 1972, and had now been located. Bauval's original investigation and reporting of this incident appear to be fairminded and a fine example of investigative journalism. However, by the time he had started his association with Hancock and came to write up the account several years later in *Keeper of Genesis*, it had turned into a trail of conspiracy which cast Smyth, the Dixons, the Egyptian Exploration Society and the whole foundation of Egyptology into its net – the possible linking factor being Freemasonry.[46]

While even Bauval admits that some of his initial theories in this area may have been a little overimaginative, a far worse slant was placed on the role of Professor Edwards in this new version. Whereas in *The Orion Mystery* the words are warm and friendly, and a photograph of the two together is even incorporated, in *Keeper of Genesis* it is suddenly 'revealed' that the written receipt provided when the Dixon relics were handed in to the British Museum was in the hand of none other than Edwards himself – the then Keeper of Egyptian Antiquities. We find it strange that this record of events is only to be found in Bauval's second book, even though the actual events took place before *The Orion Mystery* was published.

The fact that a new journalistic style was creeping into Bauval's work is emphasised by the great play he makes in the later work of the fact that the piece of cedar wood – the only artefact of the three that could have been carbon-dated to provide a construction date for the Great Pyramid – had gone missing. He makes a clear implication that this was also part of the conspiracy. However, we found his point somewhat diluted when, in a lecture delivered by him in October 1998 in London, he showed a video clip in which he is inspecting the relics at the British Museum shortly after they resurfaced. The cigar box in which they had always been kept was clearly shown, with its original label mentioning only the hook and the ball, *not* the cedar wood. It would appear that the wood went missing very early on – a long time before carbon dating had been conceptualised. Consequently, there appears to be little possibility of conspiracy, and certainly not one involving the modern authorities. Of course without the carbon-datable wood, the relics remain interesting, but their omission from the accounts of modern Egyptologists is more understandable. For his part, Lehner accords them only the briefest of mentions in his recent work.[47]

We have emphasised the role played by Robert Bauval in this saga for two reasons: first, on a positive note, because he deserves praise for bringing the iron plate and the Dixon relics to the public's attention; and second, not so positive, because his conversion to conspiracy theorist appears to us in many cases to be based on a perverse interpretation of the evidence and arguments that do not bear close scrutiny. Since he plays an increasingly influential role in the political aspects that will unfold later in this work, we feel we should bring these issues out as they arise. Furthermore, there is another twist to this story: Bauval claims that a similar piece of wood and metal hook have been found recently in the northern shaft. These claims will be examined in more detail later.

The Father of Egyptian Archaeology

Fascinated by the encoding theories of Taylor and Smyth, the next man to enter the fray was the celebrated Egyptologist William Flinders Petrie. In 1880, as a young surveyor of 26, he set off for Egypt armed with even more sophisticated equipment than that at Smyth's disposal. Using triangulation, he recorded the layout and dimensions of the Plateau's edifices so meticulously that he would spend a whole day taking and retaking readings from a single station. He was amazed at the accuracy of their layout, and particularly of the Great Pyramid's alignment to the cardinal points.

Petrie's instruments allowed him to measure to between one-hundredth and one-thousandth of an inch, depending on the degree of accuracy required, and these were used in both the interior and exterior of the monuments. As far as the exterior of the Great Pyramid was concerned, he uncovered further casing stones under the rubble and was amazed at their accuracy, estimating their mean variation from a straight line and from square to be no more than 1 in 7,500. Despite their size and weight, he also established that their joints were so accurate that the film of mortar between them was on average no thicker than 0.02 of an inch – and yet was still so strong that when attempts were made to separate the blocks they shattered before the bond gave way. He also determined that the mean deviation of the walls of the Descending Passage – which once again had to be cleared of debris – was an incredible 0.25 of an inch over the entire 350-foot length.

Petrie's approach apparently incorporated delightful British eccentricity: while measuring the interior of the Great Pyramid, he would discourage inquisitive tourists from interrupting his work by walking around its outside, clad in pink underwear alone – apparently an effective method, especially with Victorian ladies! Notwithstanding this, it was his painstaking and scientific approach that earned him the deserved nickname 'the Father of Egyptian Archaeology'. However, his new measurements for the base of the Great Pyramid were some 70 inches less than Smyth's, and as a result he was forced to refute the latter's theories about encoding. Once he published *The Pyramids and Temples of Gizeh* in 1883, he effectively quashed further discussion of this subject for several decades.

Petrie was also the first person to examine in detail the question of how the Ancient Egyptians were able to machine and work such hard materials as granite, basalt and diorite at all, let alone so accurately. He estimated that the coffer in the King's Chamber had been fashioned using jewel-tipped saws and drills, and performed similar analyses on many artefacts found on the Plateau and elsewhere (for example in the pre- and Early Dynastic mastaba tombs at Abydos). These included concave bowls which were hollowed out with such precision and symmetry that they balanced perfectly – in one case even on a base which came to a point. From this he concluded: 'Truth to tell, modern drill cores cannot hold a candle to the Egyptians . . . their fine work shows the marks of such tools as we have only now reinvented.' In fact he was understating his own case, because he believed firmly that in his time no one had invented the technology to copy all the craftsmanship he uncovered. This view has been resurrected in modern times with equal determination, and will be examined later.

Twentieth-century Greats

After Mariette's death in 1881, his relatively tight rein over excavations as the Director of Antiquities was relaxed somewhat by his successor, Gaston Maspero. Maspero contributed a great deal to Egyptology, for example by immediately excavating the Fifth Dynasty pyramids at Saqqara, including that of Unas, the main burial chamber walls of which were covered in hieroglyphic texts. These were the oldest and finest examples of what became known as the *Pyramid Texts*, which would again shed more light on Ancient Egyptian culture. Meanwhile, Egyptologists from around the world were queuing up to mount expeditions backed by various institutions.

The next half-century up to the outbreak of World War Two saw a huge expansion of major explorations all over Egypt – Lehner lists nearly sixty, an average of more than one a year.[48] Petrie was joined by such greats as the German Ludwig Borchardt and the American George Reisner. Borchardt performed most of his work away from Giza, although he did assist with a detailed survey of the Great Pyramid undertaken by JH Cole in 1925. Reisner directed excavations at the mastaba fields to the east, west and south of the Great Pyramid over several decades, and unearthed the mortuary temple and other structures in the vicinity of the Third Pyramid from 1906–10. He also excavated the Third Pyramid's Valley Temple, found to have been finished in a hurry with only the foundations made of stone, while the rest was crude brickwork and may not even have been finished; its causeway was similarly crude compared with its counterparts, and rapidly completed.

Meanwhile, another German, Uvo Holscher, excavated the mortuary temple to the east of the Second Pyramid at about the same time. Both of these mortuary temples are highly significant structures, which, although found to be in very poor repair, were – like the Valley Temple – constructed from huge limestone monoliths weighing as much as 200 tonnes each, although now massively eroded (see Plates 17 and 18).

In 1925 a Frenchman, Emile Baraize, began once again to clear the enclosure surrounding the Sphinx, and in particular the area to the east where he uncovered the Sphinx Temple. The latter had lain under the sand for millennia, at least since the Roman platforms and stairways excavated by Caviglia had been built, and more likely well before that. This edifice was similar in size to the Valley Temple lying next to it to the south, and its walls displayed the same monolithic limestone core blocks that had also been quarried from the Sphinx enclosure. It too had been lined with granite, probably both on the inside and outside, but its state of repair was again considerably worse than its counterpart. Baraize also cleared and investigated a tunnel in the rump of the Sphinx, which is entered from low down right at the base. It appears that he found nothing of interest therein – although we cannot be sure because, despite working on the Sphinx and its surroundings for a period of eleven years, he published no reports of his activities. We will be returning to 'Baraize's Tunnel' later. At the base on each side he excavated other small temples thought to date to the New Kingdom era. He also performed extensive repairs to the Sphinx using cement, which not only made it harder for modern archaeologists to trace the progression of repairs in earlier times (a key element in the argument over its age, as will be seen later), but also caused damage itself over the intervening years due to the acidity of the mixture.

In the 1920s a home-grown talent finally started directing operations of an equivalent scale to those of his foreign counterparts: a combination of his nationality and the thoroughness of his work led to Selim Hassan becoming a hero in his native Egypt – a position he retains to this day, long after his death. He cleared the central mastaba field, which lies between the Sphinx and the Second Pyramid, and in doing so revealed a deep vertical shaft running off a tunnel under the middle causeway, which was filled with water at its lower level, although he reported that he could see a 'colonnaded hall' under the water. No matter how much he attempted to pump the water out in the hope of investigating further, the level remained the same. This shaft was what we now refer to as the 'Water Shaft', which has been the focus of much attention on the Plateau in recent years, and to which we will return later. Hassan also followed up on Baraize's work on the Sphinx and Sphinx Temple, excavating there from 1936 to 38. His work was written up in meticulous detail in the multivolume *Exca-*

vations at Giza, and *The Sphinx: Its History in the Light of Recent Excavations*, published in 1946 and 1949 respectively.

One of the most dedicated of the twentieth-century Egyptologists was Jean-Philippe Lauer, who arrived at Saqqara in 1926 and spent the next seventy years primarily piecing together the complex surrounding Djoser's Step Pyramid. However, in 1946 he excavated and mapped the remains of the last significant structure on the Plateau, which we have yet to mention: the Great Pyramid's mortuary temple. Although only the beautifully finished black basalt floor remains, this was clearly an impressive structure which mixed basalt and granite for the first time. To complete the picture, we know that a huge causeway led from this structure to the east – the foundations of which rose as high as 130 feet to surmount the steep drop off the northeastern edge of the Plateau, and were still visible at the turn of the twentieth century. Little was known about any possible valley temple until in the late 1980s a consortium called AMBREC, engaged in sewerage installation for the Cairo suburbs to the east of the Plateau, came across another basalt pavement on the valley floor. Dr Zahi Hawass, the Director of the Giza Plateau and a man we will encounter regularly in this work, was responsible for the archaeology on this project, and declared it likely that this was the only surviving element of what must again have been an impressive but unreconstructable structure.[49]

The number and complexity of excavations started to wane in the 1930s, especially those involving foreigners, as a result of the build up of Egyptian nationalism. This justifiable desire on the part of the Egyptians to take full responsibility for unearthing and maintaining the treasures of their own cultural heritage – albeit ensuring they were accessible to the world at large – was undoubtedly fuelled by the tensions over the ownership of the Tutankhamun treasures unearthed by Howard Carter in the Valley of the Kings in the 1920s. However, the onset of World War Two more or less brought all work to a halt.

After the cessation of hostilities, Abdelsalam Hussein of the Antiquities Service commenced the 'Pyramids Study Project', the aim of which was to systematically survey, clear, document and conserve all the major pyramid sites. This was continued after his death by Ahmed Fakhry, although the huge project was never completed. Between 1963 and 1975 two Italians, Vito Maragioglio and Celeste Rinaldi, undertook a comprehensive survey of all the Old through to Middle Kingdom pyramids, including those at Giza, publishing their results meticulously in eight volumes entitled *L'Architettura delle Piramidi Menfite*.

Apart from these efforts, little exploration of note occurred at Giza until a revival commenced in the mid-1960s. We will move on to this 'modern' period in Part II.

TWO

WHEN WERE THE PYRAMIDS BUILT?

The next three chapters will examine three perennial questions in turn: when were the pyramids erected, and by whom? What was their purpose? And how were they constructed? These questions have intrigued humankind for millennia, and the profusion of books written on the subject renders the task of summarising the theories a daunting one – especially if a balanced critique of all theories across the orthodox and alternative spectra is to be provided without undue bias. These questions have an additional significance in this work, inasmuch as many of the major players involved in the political machinations (to be covered later) at least purport to hold strong views on these questions, views which have a major influence on their motivation and actions.

The first question that must be tackled is when they were built, and by whom. If we can gain a clear picture in this area, it will create a far better framework in which to consider the other questions. If it becomes clear that the balance of evidence lies in favour of the orthodox view that the Giza Pyramids were built some 4,500 years ago by known kings of Egypt, then the arguments of those alternative researchers who suggest they were constructed millennia before this – perhaps as early as 10,000 BC or even before – and that they are the legacy of a lost civilisation, or even of visitors from other planets, become somewhat discredited. As it is often these same researchers who suggest that they were built as guidance beacons for incoming spacecraft, or as repositories for the Ancient Wisdom of prior civilisations, then our ability to narrow down their function is similarly enhanced by examining the questions in the right order.

Most alternative researchers deliberately focus on the 'why' (and to a lesser extent the 'how') question first, sometimes using great ingenuity to concoct their theories. To many people, these are attractive and eye-catching, and of course the books, documentaries, conferences and tours in which such ideas are expounded can be extremely lucrative. Aware that they cannot leave the 'when and who' question completely to one side, some *selectively* pick as many holes in the orthodox view as they can and hope for the best. This approach may generate money and sometimes fame, but it lacks scholarship, truth and integrity, is disingenuous and misleading, and not only does not assist but positively hinders the general public's appreciation of the true mysteries that nevertheless remain.

Context is King

First, the Giza Pyramids should be placed *in context*. *Context is king* in dating these edifices, and this context is rarely given a fair hearing by alternative researchers. To obtain a balanced view, a clear understanding of the other major pyramids built by the Ancient Egyptians away from Giza is needed – which ones had been built before and which after, and what, if anything, any of them has been found to contain. One should also be as informed about the Second and Third Pyramids at Giza as the Great Pyramid. We will begin by reviewing the orthodox Egyptologists' view of the progression of the Egyptian dynasties and of pyramid building therein. This information has been primarily sourced from the works of Dr Lehner and Professor Edwards, and also from the archaeologist Paul Jordan's *Riddle of the Sphinx*, published in 1998.

After a massive exertion of scholarly effort over the last century in particular, Egyptologists have now arrived at a position where they have a framework for Ancient Egyptian history that groups around 330 kings into 30 dynasties.[50] These dynasties are grouped into periods or eras, on the basis that not all dynastic changes brought about significant political or cultural change. The prime source of information for this chronological framework is the 'King List' prepared by the Egyptian priest Manetho in his *Aegyptiaca*, written in the third century BC. Unfortunately, the original text no longer survives, and only edited versions of it from the first to third centuries AD are available for scrutiny. Other lists exist that add to the picture, including the Turin Canon, a New Kingdom papyrus prepared in the time of Ramesses II, the king lists found in tombs at Abydos, Saqqara and Karnak, and the Palermo stone.

A number of complications arise from the use of these sources. For example, Manetho wrote in Greek and used the kings' secular names, whereas some of the other sources were written in Egyptian and used their religious names. Apart from this problem of matching the different languages and naming conventions, the lists of names in the various sources invariably differ at times. Also, the lengths given for each reign vary. These differences would have arisen from a variety of factors: inadequate information to begin with; fallible copying; even deliberately distortive editing carried out by the various scribes down the centuries for religious and political reasons. All these problems have caused great difficulties for a succession of scholars who have attempted to piece the various elements of the jigsaw together, but their efforts have been rewarded by the more or less universal acceptance of the *progression* of the framework, and of the major kings who make it up. There are some lesser-known kings whose position may still be in doubt, but for our purposes the bulk of the framework is sound.

Attaching an *absolute* chronology to the framework is the most contentious problem that remains. At the time these sources were being prepared, a universally accepted absolute dating mechanism such as we have today did not exist. Even now the Western world's convention of dating events to the supposed birth of Christ, or its increasingly common secular alternative 'before the common era' (BCE), remains at odds with the various dating mechanisms used in the East. The Ancient Egyptians did not use absolute dates, instead they prepared king lists with the length of each reign, recording important events by the number of years into a particular king's reign in which they occurred. On top of this problem, and the variation in reign lengths from list to list, the 'intermediate' periods tended to be ones of disunity and disorder, meaning that reigns could overlap.

Despite these problems, an important breakthrough in the attempt to establish an absolute chronology for the framework came when three separate references in the ancient texts were found which recorded the heliacal rising of Sirius. These allowed scholars to retrospectively correlate the Sothic calendar with our present-day system, providing a small but vital set of absolute dates for particular years in the reigns of the three kings concerned. Since this breakthrough, the chronology has been continually updated and refined, and cross-referenced with new and old archaeological finds.

More recently carbon dating technology has been applied to the pyramids. This is something of an inexact method, best suited to resolving problems of prehistory to an accuracy of at best a few hundred years, rather than those of detailed history down to an accuracy of a few years. Moreover, its results must be carefully interpreted. As a rule with carbon dating, a result can be predicted with around 70 per cent certainty if a span of 100 years is quoted, and can be raised to around 95 per cent certainty if a span of 200 years is quoted; moreover any year within the range has an equal probability of being right. Nevertheless, attempts have been made to verify the general chronology.

According to Jordan,[51] the only real discrepancies came with some datings of material derived from the Giza Pyramids and others of the Third and Fourth Dynasties, producing results that suggested that these edifices were between 200 and 300 years older than the orthodox chronology. However, he says that other results from this same era more or less corroborate the orthodox dating, and because the discrepancies were in wood samples there are arguments surrounding the possible use of already ancient trees or the reuse of wood, making solid judgements impossible.

While Jordan may be simplifying the results of carbon dating somewhat, and we will therefore return to it later, at this point we can say that even if all the Early Dynastic and Old Kingdom dates are several centuries out, for our purposes these differences are immaterial to the arguments. What is important is that the carbon dating surveys have provided invaluable support to the *relative* chronology of the edifices built in this era. This is the first piece in the jigsaw that suggests that the Giza Pyramids, and the Great Pyramid in particular, cannot be taken out of this context of progression.

The result of all this scholarly effort is that, while a number of different chronologies are used by Egyptologists today, they do not vary greatly. Figure 9 lays out the various periods, the dynasties within them, and the dates for each dynasty taken from the chronological system developed by Professor John Baines and Dr Jaromir Malek in their *Atlas of Ancient Egypt*. It also shows the average and maximum size of the *major* pyramids erected in each dynasty, excluding the multiple smaller satellites.

Pyramid Progression

The funerary edifices of the First and Second Dynasties were relatively simple buildings called mastabas – oblong structures formed from mud bricks with sloping, sometimes stepped, sides, and flat tops. These were erected over a deep pit, and were concentrated primarily in Saqqara, just south of Giza. Much further to the south, at Abydos, tombs with little or no apparent superstructure have been found that also date to these dynasties, causing some confusion. The consensus now appears to be that the royal tombs were primarily those at Abydos, while those at Saqqara were for nobles and officials.

Pyramid building did not commence until the Third Dynasty, and a brief perusal of the statistics in Figure 9 reveals that the height of the pyramid age occurred at its commencement in the Third and Fourth Dynasties. After this the number and size of pyramids drops off rapidly. Figure 10 provides the orthodox view of the most significant structures built during the Third and Fourth Dynasties in chronological order, showing the kings believed to be responsible for building them.

If this information is right, once one appreciates that all the pyramids in the table that have less than 10 years available appear to be unfinished, the average time available for each edifice to be built is about 20 years. The only exception to this, according to the orthodox chronology, is Sneferu, who supposedly built three pyramids in the space of 24 years. In order to make the latter's accomplishments appear more realistic, attempts have been made to attribute the pyramid at Meidum to a king called Huni, who reigned at the end of the Third Dynasty from 2599–2575 BC. It is true that Huni has no

FIGURE 9: PYRAMID BUILDING ACROSS THE EGYPTIAN DYNASTIES[52]

Period	Dynasties	Dates (BC)	Length (Yrs)	No. Major Pyramids	Ave. Size ('000 cu. m)	Max. Size ('000 cu. m)
Early Dynastic	1st–2nd	2920–2649	271	0	–	–
	3rd	2649–2575	74	3	137	330
Old Kingdom	4th	2575–2465	110	10	1,110	2,583
	5th	2465–2323	142	7	118	257
	6th	2323–2150	173	4	108	108
	7th–8th	2150–2134	16	1	7	7
1st Intermediate	9th–11th	2134–2040	94	1	?	?
Middle Kingdom	11th–14th	2040–1640	400	9–13	172	288
2nd Intermediate	15th–17th	1640–1550	90	0	–	–
New Kingdom	18th–20th	1550–1070	480	1	?	?
3rd Intermediate	21st–25th	1070–712	358	0	–	–
Late	25th–30th	712–343	369	0	–	–

FIGURE 10: PYRAMID BUILDING IN THE THIRD AND FOURTH DYNASTIES[53]

Pharaoh	Name	Location	Dates (BC)	Time (Yrs)	Height (m)	Volume ('000 cu. m)	Vol. per Yr ('000 cu. m)
3RD DYNASTY							
Djoser	Step Pyramid	Saqqara	2630–2611	19	60	330	17
Sekhemkhet	–	Saqqara	2611–2603	8	7*	34	4
Khaba (?)	Layer Pyramid	Zawiyet el-Aryan	2603–2599	4	20*	47	12
4TH DYNASTY							
Sneferu	–	Meidum	2575–2551	8 (ave.)	92	639	149 (ave.)
Sneferu	Bent Pyramid	Dashur	2575–2551	8 (ave.)	105	1,237	149 (ave.)
Sneferu	Red Pyramid	Dashur	2575–2551	8 (ave.)	105	1,694	149 (ave.)
Khufu	Great Pyramid	Giza	2551–2528	23	147	2,583	112
Djedefre	–	Abu Roash	2528–2520	8	?*	131	16
Khafre	2nd Pyramid	Giza	2520–2494	26	144	2,211	85
Menkaure	3rd Pyramid	Giza	2490–2472	18	65	235	13

* Unfinished

major pyramid attributed to him as yet – although a small, mud-brick stepped pyramid at Abu Roash has been credited to him by some, even though reversion to this material would be somewhat out of context. However, the ancient name of Meidum is Djed Sneferu ('Sneferu Endures'), and his name – not Huni's – has been found in texts at the site. This argument cannot therefore be considered sound. Since the total volume of Sneferu's three pyramids is just over 3.5 million cubic metres, compared with the 2.5 million of Khufu's Great Pyramid, one is left to suggest that he must have used half as many people again as his son in order to achieve his prolific work rate.

Some have calculated the number of blocks per day that would need to be laid for this chronology to be correct, and have suggested that the results are impossible. Although we will return to this subject later, in our view this approach is misleading, and involves too much manipulation of statistics. It is incredible to think that a monument of the size of the Great Pyramid could have been erected in as little as 20 years, but the more interesting investigation is to establish what methods were used to achieve this feat. There is too much evidence that the orthodox chronology is more or less correct for logistics alone to be used as an argument against it.

Perhaps more significant is that it is clear that the Giza Pyramids were not the first to be erected, nor should their predecessors be regarded as unduly inferior. The earliest major pyramid in Egypt in which stone was used was erected at Saqqara in the reign of Djoser in the Third Dynasty. This 'stepped' pyramid is still standing and mostly complete to this day, and is a testament to the quality of the building techniques used (see Plate 19). It was surrounded by the largest complex of any of the pyramids, with fine temples, courtyards, causeways and enclosures – many with exquisitely carved columns and walls. Its designer was reputed to be Imhotep, who is often revered as the world's first known 'genius'.

Meanwhile, between seven and ten smaller stepped pyramids, which are often overlooked, have been discovered in a variety of locations, ranging from Elephantine in the far south to Abu Roash in the north. These are known as the 'provincial' stepped pyramids and are more crudely made of mud brick, leading some Egyptologists to suggest that they predate Djoser's stone edifice, built as practice runs either by him or by his predecessor. Since their ruins are relatively unexplored we await further discoveries that may shed more light on their attribution.

The construction of major stepped pyramids continued with two that were probably never finished, and of which little of the superstructures remains – the first built by Sekhemkhet at Saqqara, the second possibly by Khaba at Zawiyet el-Aryan. These were followed by Sneferu's first attempt at Meidum, which started out with a step design but was completed as the first smooth-faced pyramid (the last additions to the outer superstructure have either been removed or collapsed, leaving what looks like a simplified stepped pyramid underneath). Although the single chamber within this was built in the superstructure at ground level for the first time, introducing the ingenious method of corbelling the roof to absorb the stresses of the masonry above it, it is clearly rough and unfinished.

Sneferu went on to build the two greatest pyramids outside the Giza Plateau, that reveal much about the progression of pyramid building. Both are at Dashur, the first referred to as the 'Bent' Pyramid because of the way its face angle reduces significantly from 55 to 43 degrees about halfway up (see Plate 20); the second known variously as the 'Northern' or 'Red' Pyramid. The construction quality of both is proved by the extent to which their superstructures remain intact, while the former retains much of its original casing. Both of them start to approach the size of the Giza Pyramids, and each has three superbly constructed internal chambers, which rival those in the Great Pyramid, with perfectly worked and sometimes massive granite lining blocks, and beautifully finished corbelled roofs (see Plates 22 and 23). The roofs were still utilised to absorb stresses, and, since they are higher although much shorter than the roof of the Grand Gallery, they must surely be regarded as the prototypes for it. Fortunately, the Northern Pyramid has recently been reopened to the public after many years of inaccessibility on military land, and of all the pyramids we have inspected we found that its interior especially has an awe-inspiring feel. (For a more detailed examination of the enigmas of Sneferu's multiple pyramids, see Appendix II.)

Despite experiments with certain elements of the internal and external design, all the major Third and Fourth Dynasty pyramids were built to a common model (see Appendix IV for details). They were all oriented to the cardinal points with increasing accuracy. They were all finished with a smooth casing. They all had an entrance on the north face which gave on to a descending passage. They all contained at least one chamber below or just at ground level, and many of them contained two or even three chambers. They all, at least if completed, would have had a surrounding complex which included in varying degrees enclosure walls, satellite pyramids, mortuary temples, causeways and valley temples.

Furthermore there was a gradual increase in the size of the edifices (see Figure 11), and in the size and quality of the blocks used. This was coupled with a switch from the earlier style of inclining the core and casing blocks downward into the structure to prevent collapse, to the later one – introduced first in the Red Pyramid – of laying them horizontally. This proved easier in terms of erection, although the quality of general design – and especially of the intersection of the outermost blocks with their neighbours – had to be far superior for it to be successful.

It should therefore be evident that those who argue that the Giza Pyramids suddenly sprang from nowhere in the orthodox chronology, with no precedents, are talking nonsense. In particular it is clear that the Great Pyramid forms an integral part of the developmental context that we have described, and cannot be isolated from it. The only attributes of the Great Pyramid that really stand out, with no known precedent or antecedent, are the two chambers that lie high up in the superstructure, and the shafts that lead off them. These are anomalies to which we will return, particularly because they have been the cause of so much speculation. But the other so-called anomalies of the Great Pyramid can be traced back to earlier precedents – for example the corbelling of the Grand Gallery, the multiple lined chambers and passages, the portcullis arrangements, the fine external casing, and the alignment. One is tempted to ask why myriad books have not been written about the Bent Pyramid, which, apart from being bent, has *two* entrances – one in the north face and one in the west face, leading to a separate set of chambers. This is also a unique anomaly, but perhaps one that cannot sell so many books.

Moving on past the Giza Pyramids and the Fourth Dynasty, even by the Fifth and Sixth Dynasties the pyramids were far smaller (see Figures 9 and 11). Their inner cores were constructed from stone infill rather than blocks – so that with a high-quality casing the same external effect was achieved but with far less expense and effort. Once this casing had been stripped off, most of these structures collapsed into the mounds of rubble which we see today. By contrast the pyramid temples continued to become larger and more complex.

In the First Intermediate Period, political upheaval and rivallry ensured that pyramid building virtually ceased. It was revived in the Middle Kingdom, but still with relatively modest monuments which became decreasingly standardised – entrances were no longer on the north face, and passages and chambers were laid out in a far more circuitous design. By the time of the New Kingdom, pyramid building was abandoned completely, with kings buried in tombs cut into the rock face of the southern mountain region at Thebes known as the 'Valley of the Kings'.

Many critics of the orthodox view have suggested that the decline in the quantity and quality of pyramid building after the Fourth Dynasty does not make sense. Indeed it does seem strange that the acme of the genre should have been reached relatively quickly, and then dropped off with similar rapidity. But this is what the facts suggest, and what is the alternative? We have seen that there is a progression leading up to the Giza Pyramids, which indicates that they did not spring from nowhere – so attempting to place them far earlier in the chronology does not make any sense. But, given the rapidity of the decline, nor would it make sense to reposition them at a later point.

As much as this argument is derided by alternative researchers who do not have a valid alternative that fits the known facts, we are left to surmise that it was a combination of religious and economic factors that led to the demise of pyramid building. This *may* have been allied to the relatively swift loss of the skills and technology developed in the early stages of pyramid

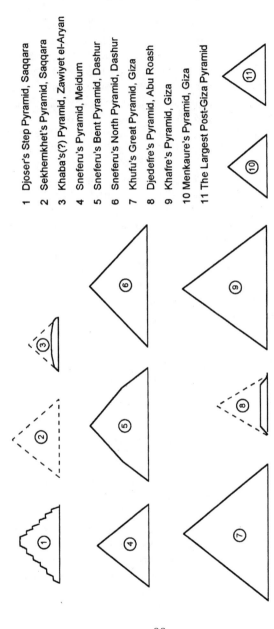

1 Djoser's Step Pyramid, Saqqara
2 Sekhemkhet's Pyramid, Saqqara
3 Khaba's(?) Pyramid, Zawiyet el-Aryan
4 Sneferu's Pyramid, Meidum
5 Sneferu's Bent Pyramid, Dashur
6 Sneferu's North Pyramid, Dashur
7 Khufu's Great Pyramid, Giza
8 Djedefre's Pyramid, Abu Roash
9 Khafre's Pyramid, Giza
10 Menkaure's Pyramid, Giza
11 The Largest Post-Giza Pyramid

FIGURE 11: SCALE DIAGRAMS OF MAJOR THIRD- AND FOURTH-DYNASTY PYRAMIDS[54]

evolution. As a corollary, many would agree that there has been a considerable decline in the quality of architectural design and planning in Britain, especially in the last half-century. Does this mean that St Paul's Cathedral is an anomaly, which must therefore have been built by another civilisation? No – it means that over several centuries our culture has changed, albeit not for the better.

The Foundations of Attribution

We have seen that there is a general progression in the building of pyramids during the Third and Fourth Dynasties, and that the *order* in which Egyptologists place them appears to be confirmed by carbon dating. But what evidence has allowed Egyptologists to attribute these edifices to the specific kings listed above?

The attributions of the pre-Giza pyramids will be examined first. The Step Pyramid at Saqqara is perhaps the easiest of them all: multiple reliefs, inscriptions and statues of Djoser have been found both inside it and in the outlying buildings. Around Sekhemkhet's Pyramid, also at Saqqara, the king's name has been found on many clay jar stoppers. As for the Layer Pyramid at Zawiyet el-Aryan, Khaba's name has been found on a number of stone vessels in mastabas to the north, although this is not currently regarded as definitive proof of its attribution – an example of the high standards that Egyptologists set *for themselves*. The alternative camp seem to overlook the fact that competition and rigorous debate *between* professional Egyptologists over the decades is an in-built control over their standards of scholarship. Moving on to Sneferu, and the start of the Fourth Dynasty, his name is found both around the first of his pyramids at Meidum and in the translation of its old place name. As for his other two pyramids at Dashur, his cartouche has been found in quarry marks on the back of casing stones from both, as well as on statues found nearby.

Turning to Giza, the first evidence we have is not archaeological but provided by the Classical historians. The most important of these is Herodotus, who in *c*. 440 BC made the following observations:[55]

[124] The priests said that up to the reign of King Rhampsinitus Egyptian society was stable and the country was very prosperous, but that under their next king, Cheops, it was reduced to a completely awful condition. He closed down all the sanctuaries, stopped people performing sacrifices, and also commanded all the Egyptians to work for him. Some had the job of hauling blocks of stone from the quarries in the Arabian mountain range as far as the Nile, where they were *transported across the river in boats* and then passed on to others, whom he assigned to haul them from there to the Libyan mountains. *They worked in gangs of 100,000 men for three months at a time.* They said that it took ten years of hard labour for the people to construct the causeway along which they hauled the blocks of stone, which I would think involved not much less work than building the pyramid, since the road is five stades long, ten fathoms wide, and eight fathoms high at its highest point, and is made of polished stone, *with figures carved on it.* So they spent ten years over this road and *the underground rooms which Cheops had constructed as his sepulchral chambers in the hill on which the pyramids stand, which he turned into an island by bringing water from the Nile there along a canal. The actual pyramid took twenty years to build.* Each of its sides, which form a square, is eight plethra long and the pyramid is eight plethra high as well. It is made of polished blocks of stone, fitted together perfectly; none of the blocks is less than thirty feet long.

. . .

[127] *The Egyptians said that after a reign of fifty years Cheops died and the kingdom passed to his brother Chephren.* He carried on in the same manner as his brother, and not least in the sense that he too built a pyramid, although it did not reach the size of his brother's. I know because in fact I measured them both myself. *There are no underground chambers in Chephren's pyramid, nor does a channel come flowing into it from the Nile, as in the case of the other one, where a conduit was built so that the Nile would encircle an island on which, they say, Cheops himself is buried.* The bottom layer of Chephren's pyramid was made out of patterned Ethiopian stone and the whole thing is the same size as the other pyramid, but forty feet less tall. Both of them stand on the same hill, which is about a hundred feet high. *They said that Chephren's reign lasted fifty-six years.*

[128] So by their own reckoning, this terrible period in Egypt

lasted 106 years, and the sanctuaries, locked for all these years, were never opened. *The Egyptians loathe Chephren and Cheops so much that they really do not like to mention their names.* Instead, they say the pyramids belonged to a shepherd called Philitis, who at this time used to graze his flocks on the same land.

. . .

[134] He [Mycerinus] too left a pyramid as a memorial. His pyramid is much smaller than his father's, each side of the square base being twenty feet short of three plethra, and the bottom half of it is made out of Ethiopian stone . . .

We have reproduced these paragraphs from Herodotus's work in full, with our own italics for emphasis, because they contain suggestions related to other subjects to which we will return on many occasions. Many commentators have suggested that Herodotus's reports are highly unreliable: for example, his description of the contempt in which Khufu and Khafre were held, because of the way they supposedly enslaved the population in the building of the pyramids, has enraged Egyptologists and Egyptians themselves. To them suggestions of such a servile and dominated populace are misleading and insulting, particularly since recent excavation work has proved that the building population were well housed and fed, and did not appear to work under penance.

Although the blame for these misconceptions can initially be laid at Herodotus's door, it is nonetheless wrong to suggest that everything he records is unreliable. Although he clearly admits that in most cases he was merely recording what the Egyptian priests at the time told him – and it is evident that at this time they were highly contemptuous of both Khufu and Khafre, although not of Menkaure – he explicitly asks his readers to make of the reports what they will. It is clear that he did visit the Plateau himself, and in certain circumstances he is quite ruthless in his judgements where he thinks that the stories he is being told are nonsensical or far-fetched, particularly if he is able in some way to argue against them through personal observation or logic.[56] On the other hand, we cannot ignore the fact that his measurement of the blocks (none 'less than thirty feet long') is clearly incorrect unless badly translated, so his reliability is mixed.

Specifically in relation to the attribution of the Pyramids, despite Herodotus's use of their Greek names we can see that the Egyptian priests who briefed him clearly attributed the Great, Second and Third Pyramids to Khufu, Khafre and Menkaure respectively. The prime difference is that he suggests the reigns of the first two were in the region of fifty years each, compared with the modern chronology, which more or less halves this figure. The Roman historian Diodorus Siculus, writing in the first century AD, provides an account that is entirely in accord with Herodotus's except that he attempts to render Khufu's name in Egyptian, not Greek, and ends up with Chemis.[57] For their part, Strabo (a Greek historian also of the first century AD) and Pliny do not mention the builders at all, while Manetho himself, in preparing his King List, specifically recorded that the Great Pyramid was built in the reign of Suphis, that is Khufu.

What about the archaeological evidence of the attributions of the Giza Pyramids? Taking the Great Pyramid first, we have already discussed the quarry marks found in the sealed Relieving Chambers by Vyse. It has been incorrectly suggested that these are fakes perpetrated by Vyse, and so much has been made of this assertion that it will be considered in depth shortly. But do we have anything else? The answer is yes. Vyse records that similar quarry marks were found on core blocks in the first five courses of the edifice.[58] Did Vyse have the time and opportunity to fake these too? We think not.

Furthermore, we know that the funerary accoutrements of Queen Hetepheres, undoubtedly one of Sneferu's queens, were buried in a deep shaft next to the Great Pyramid's northernmost satellite – possibly after her original tomb was plundered. Although we cannot be sure that she was Khufu's mother, Sneferu was certainly his father, and the association of such a close relative with what is clearly a contemporary structure should be regarded as added contextual evidence. In our view those who attempt to suggest that other parts of the Plateau complexes – such as temples and satellite pyramids – were erected either long before or after the pyramids themselves are on scholastically weak ground. Suggestions of *adoption* at a later stage are theoretically more sound, but still do not fit the facts. This is quite apart from the huge quantity of inscriptions bearing Khufu's name that have been found in the mastaba tombs of officials, dignitaries and relatives surrounding the edifice and also on the remains of the decorated blocks of his causeway.[59] It is, however, interesting to note that only one statue of Khufu has ever been found, and this is only a tiny figurine standing a mere 2 inches high.

One of the main pieces of archaeological evidence linking the Second Pyramid to Khafre is the beautiful life-size statue found by Mariette in a pit in the Valley Temple floor. Alternative-camp suggestions that the statue could have been placed in the temple later on by an adoptive king taking over a predecessor's monuments, and that there is little other evidence, appear to have some validity. However, Selim Hassan reveals that during his excavations of the Plateau he recovered the 'smashed remains of between three and four hundred statues of Khafre, all executed in fine stone, such as diorite, granite and alabaster'.[60] Furthermore, a stela set up near the Sphinx by the New Kingdom ruler Amenhotep II acknowledges not only Khafre but *also* Khufu.[61]

As for the Third Pyramid, we have already seen that Vyse found an intrusive 'burial' dating to the Saite Period in the upper chamber, with Menkaure's cartouche inscribed on the lid of the wooden coffer – indicating that the priests of the time attributed this edifice to him. To back this evidence up, he also found a similar red-painted cartouche on the ceiling of a chamber in the central satellite pyramid. Again it has been suggested that Vyse faked these pieces of evidence, but this claim will be disproved along with the others shortly.

Zahi Hawass has also reported that during the excavation of the 'workers' city' at the south edge of the Plateau, multiple tombs – many in the shape of small mud brick pyramids – were found, showing that the workforce was not composed of slave labour. More important for the current discussion, multiple pieces of Old Kingdom pottery litter this site, and indeed the whole Plateau.[62] This is highly important contextual evidence.

It is true that much of this evidence can be attacked on a piecemeal basis – although many of the attacks are entirely lacking in scholarship. Nevertheless, when the entirety of the contextual, historic, archaeological, carbon dating and circumstantial evidence is weighed in the balance, the scales tip in favour of the orthodox dating and attribution. The entirety of the alternative arguments remain so fundamentally flawed that they scarcely tip the scales at all.

Alternative Attacks

Alternative theories are not new, and have been put forward down the centuries. However, recent years have seen a proliferation in the number of authors who pass themselves off as bona fide 'alternative Egyptologists', and present their arguments in what sometimes appear to be highly scientific and scholarly terms. As well as attracting those interested in ancient history, their theories have gained widespread credence with those searching for spiritual enlightenment in the run-up to the new millennium. We are therefore keen that the true picture be presented so that people can concentrate their search for meaning and enlightenment in the right areas. Bearing this in mind, many of the misconceptions which are continually perpetrated must be revealed in their true light.

There are four main areas of attack. In decreasing order of importance, they are: first, that quarry marks found inside the Great and Third Pyramids were faked by their discoverer, Vyse; second, that the Inventory Stela is genuine; third, that the Giza Pyramids are unique in containing no original inscriptions; and fourth – an argument that represents more of a compromise between the orthodox and alternative positions – that they are built on the site of earlier structures. We will deal with each of these in turn. However, we should remind ourselves that these attacks are usually linked with, indeed necessitated by, the desire to attribute functions other than funerary ones to the edifices – albeit that the full discussion of the 'why' question will be left to the next chapter. Furthermore, one of the most celebrated of the alternative attacks with respect to the age question is that relating to the possible redating of the Sphinx to a much earlier epoch; this issue too must be left for a later chapter.

Vyse is Victimised

Sitchin attacks

The 'alternative-dating' argument that has gained by far the most exposure in recent years is that Vyse and his accomplices faked the Khufu cartouches in the Relieving Chambers. The first person to perpetrate this accusation in any detail was the New York-based writer Zecharia Sitchin. For those readers unfamiliar with this author, he has written a series of books under the blanket title *The Earth Chronicles*, commencing with *The Twelfth Planet* in 1976. In this first volume he developed a reinterpretation of Ancient Mesopotamian texts to support his contention that humankind was genetically created by a race of visitors from outer space, called the Anunnaki (the biblical Nefilim), who came from an undiscovered planet in our solar system called Nibiru. Although to some this may sound a highly fanciful notion, we have had reason as part of a separate study to investigate these claims in detail, and we can confirm that these ancient texts do indeed make highly interesting reading.

What has all this to do with the dating of the Great Pyramid? you may ask. The answer is that the nature of Sitchin's apparent scholarship, so trumpeted by his many devotees around the world, is highly suspect. And, since it is his attack that so many subsequent writers have reproduced apparently without question, it is apposite to take a brief look at the nature of his work.

Sitchin is perhaps one of the best examples we have yet encountered of a writer whose work appears highly scholarly if one is not an expert in the subject under discussion. Admittedly, his appalling lack of references for his source material rings alarm bells with any serious researcher, but to the unsuspecting his breadth of knowledge appears unrivalled. However, to condense a long investigation into a few sentences, we found that, for example, he negligently mistranslates and misquotes Mesopotamian source texts to suit his purposes. We say this because, once the original texts have been traced (not always easy given the lack of references), it becomes clear that not only does he omit preceding and following lines from his extracts – lines that can destroy his fanciful interpretations once the full context is understood – but on occasion he even omits *intervening* lines that would have the same effect.

This cannot be the action of a man who is misguided or mistaken, as other detractors have often suggested; rather, in our view, it clearly demonstrates gross negligence with the result that his readers are misled. Since we believe that there remain highly revealing passages in the Mesopotamian texts *as translated by proper scholars* that deserve a great deal of public attention, such distortion – which tends, when revealed, to ensure that 'the baby is thrown out with the bathwater' – is to be condemned in the strongest possible terms. This is the background to the man who first 'exposed' Vyse as a liar and a cheat!

Sitchin's 'investigation' into Vyse did not emerge until his second book, *The Stairway to Heaven*, was published in 1980;[63] this book represented his first foray into Egypt and its enigmas. One might suggest that this work is not deserving of detailed scrutiny, but he devotes a whole chapter to this issue and if one did not know better, his arguments appear persuasive. They have certainly fooled a host of supposedly eminent researchers in the intervening years, some of whom have based their entire 'alternative scenarios' around them. We must therefore summarise, and expose the weaknesses in, the salient points.

As a general observation, it is abundantly clear from the many extracts that Sitchin quotes from Vyse's *Operations* that he has read this work. Since we have done the same, and formed exactly the opposite view of the character and integrity of both Vyse and his colleagues, we must wonder whether Sitchin actually believes the distorted web that he weaves from Vyse's accounts – or is this just another attempt to disfigure the truth? Whichever is the case, the main elements of his argument follow, split for convenience between 'practical' and 'linguistic and interpretation' issues, with each point accompanied by our refutation in italics.

Practical issues
- Caviglia initially turned down Vyse's offer of financial assistance, and Vyse was 'in shock' and 'disgusted' to find that the

firman granting him permission to excavate was also in the name of Campbell and another associate, Mr Sloane.
COMMENT: *This is a false version of events, and is not recounted in the writings of Vyse.*

- Vyse deliberately got rid of Caviglia so that he could not blow the whistle on his forgery plans.
COMMENT: *This is untrue. First, Caviglia was sacked six weeks before the first entry (into Wellington's Chamber) was forced. At this time Vyse had nothing more than suspicions about what might lie above Davison's Chamber. Second, the real causes of the disagreement between the two are described in great depth in* Operations, *and they primarily involve Caviglia's desire to use money and manpower conducting operations at various tombs, while Vyse wanted the focus switched to the interior of the Great Pyramid. They also involve a multitude of other matters too numerous to reproduce here.*

- Vyse had the motivation to forge the marks because he was desperate to make a name for himself.
COMMENT: *First, the discovery of the Relieving Chambers in their own right was highly significant. Second, Vyse was the first explorer to enter the Third Pyramid in modern times. Third, he unearthed the basalt coffer therein. Fourth, he and his team made a whole catalogue of other discoveries which we have already documented. Consequently his achievements hardly required artificial inflation.*

- Vyse developed the idea of forging quarry marks only because Caviglia had uncovered some in Campbell's Tomb, which were causing a great stir.
COMMENT: *This is untrue, although to be fair Sitchin makes less of this point than many of his successors who imitated his work. Quarry marks had already been discovered in abundance at Egyptian sites by this time, and Vyse and his team were responsible for uncovering many more. They were not in themselves any great novelty. Furthermore Vyse had taken over responsibility for the excavation of Campbell's Tomb as soon as Caviglia left the Plateau, and could easily have claimed credit for the previous as well as new finds therein had he wanted to so do. However, perusal*

of his diaries reveals that – even though they were written up for publication after their disagreement – Vyse was always scrupulously fair in attributing credit to Caviglia where it was due.

• When the tunnel was wide enough for Vyse and Hill to first inspect Wellington's Chamber, his 'thorough inspection' revealed nothing but the black powder that covered the floor and the fine workmanship of the ceiling blocks. When he returned that night with Hill, Perring and another associate, James Mash, the first set of quarry marks had 'suddenly appeared'.

COMMENT: Vyse did not make a 'thorough inspection' when he first went into the chamber. Furthermore, the marks in this chamber are only on the limestone blocks of the west wall (just as in Nelson's Chamber above it), that furthest from the entrance tunnel, and it is even conceivable that there was a film of black dust on the wall, which meant they were not immediately apparent. Meanwhile, Vyse's diaries clearly state that in the intervening period the workmen carried on enlarging the hole. Finally, although Vyse did not reproduce the marks in this chamber in his book, we know that only one of the quarry marks in Wellington's Chamber, and none of those in Nelson's Chamber, is a cartouche. For someone so desperate to effect a forgery, who did not know whether he would locate additional chambers, Vyse seems to have been remarkably prepared to mess about daubing many (as far as he knew) meaningless marks in these first two. If all he wanted to do was forge the king's name, why bother at all with the multiple other inscriptions that occur in all the chambers? We now know that the other marks primarily recorded the names of the various work gangs responsible for the blocks – such as '(The crew) The White Crown of Khnum-khufu is powerful! (Craftsman division)' – and, since this aspect of the quarry marks was not understood even by hieroglyphics experts at the time, no one would have thought it important to fake them.

• Davison's Chamber, discovered before Vyse's time, contains no quarry marks.

COMMENT: This is one of the few points that are difficult to counter. However, first, it is entirely circumstantial evidence, which actually proves nothing. Second, in common with the two chambers above it, Davison's north and south walls comprise granite blocks that were never inscribed with quarry marks (it is also interesting to note that Perring theorised that the marks appeared only on stone quarried away from the Plateau). Also, none but the highest of the chambers has inscriptions on the east wall, so we would expect marks only on the west wall of this chamber. Why are there none even on this? If any ever did exist, there are two possibilities: either they were chemically eroded by the excreta of the bats that inhabited this inaccessible and low-ceilinged chamber at least from the time of Mamun; or, since we believe that the tunnel leading to Davison's Chamber was dug by the priests shortly after the edifice was completed (we will examine this theory in more detail in the next chapter), it is not inconceivable that out of pride and respect they would have washed any marks off the walls, given that this chamber would now be 'open for inspection'.

- The quarry marks are upside down or sideways, indicating that whoever painted them was having to crouch or lie down. COMMENT: *However constricted the space in which one was working, in what way would it be easier to paint something upside down? Sideways perhaps, but not upside down. Surely it is far more plausible that they are not upright precisely because they are quarry marks, which serve merely to identify a batch of blocks for a particular part of the pyramid – in contrast to the separate and accurately oriented lines and arrows, which can also be seen in the chambers, and which were drawn by the masons to assist final assembly and alignment.*

- The quarry marks are not 'precise, delicate and in proportion', as are all other Egyptian hieroglyphic inscriptions. COMMENT: *These are not inscriptions that were intended to be seen – they are rough-daubed quarry marks.*

- There are no inscriptions on the east walls, except in Campbell's Chamber, because 'whoever daubed them preferred to write on the intact walls to the north, south and west, rather than on the damaged [by Vyse's tunnelling] east walls'.

COMMENT: *Anyone who has actually been inside these chambers, or who studies the diagrams published by Vyse and Perring, will know that Vyse's tunnel hardly touches the east walls at all. It ran up the northeast corner primarily behind the granite blocks of the north walls. We fancy that this line of argument reveals not Vyse's desperation but Sitchin's – and it certainly makes us wonder whether the man who started all this nonsense has conducted a proper physical examination of the chambers himself.*

- Although some of the cartouches appear to be part hidden by floor blocks, which overlap inside the walls, paint specks have subsequently been found on the adjacent floor blocks, which confirm that the brush used to daub the marks touched the floor blocks while they were *in situ*.

  COMMENT: *There is no reference or attribution for this assertion – we are only told that the revelation supposedly came about 100 years after Vyse's discoveries. Either this information is false in origin or interpretation, or these specks may have rubbed off from the marks over the years and become ingrained in the floor. In any case, as we will see shortly, new evidence has emerged that some of the marks carry on round the corners and into the crevices between the blocks, or on down behind the sides of the floor blocks, which strongly contradicts this argument. Perhaps most important of all, at one point an original 'levelling' line, drawn horizontally across several adjacent blocks on the south wall of Lady Arbuthnot's Chamber once they were* in situ, *is clearly superimposed on the quarry mark underneath.*[64]

- The forgeries were actually perpetrated by Hill, not Vyse himself, 'probably alone, certainly at night when all others were gone'.

  COMMENT: *Quite why Hill gets the blame is unclear, except for the unpleasant innuendo that 'having been a copper mill employee when he first met Vyse, he ended up owning the Cairo Hotel when Vyse left Egypt'. This is a gross distortion of information, which Sitchin could only have obtained from* Operations: *in fact, first, Vyse states that Hill was the superintendent of the copper mill, not just a worker. Second, as a foreigner he was not allowed to own the hotel, he merely rented it. Third, Vyse indicates it was merely 'a hotel in Cairo' (which was known originally as the 'English Hotel'); it was not the Sitchin-devised and far grander sounding 'Cairo Hotel'. As to the possibility of Hill's being alone at night, Sitchin himself admits that from an early stage Vyse put the tunnelling team working on the Relieving Chambers on to round-the-clock shifts to speed up the process: even if they were all bribed, the regular dismissal of so many different labourers to allow Hill time to work alone would hardly have remained a secret for long.*

Linguistic and interpretation issues
Turning to the linguistic as opposed to practical issues, these have been thoroughly refuted by a British researcher, Martin Stower, on his Internet web site. While we will only summarise the arguments – because they can become lengthy and involved – any reader who wishes to immerse themselves should refer to Stower's original rebuttals.[65]

• The quarry marks contain two different kings' names, and this came about as follows. Given that the decipherment of hieroglyphics was still in its infancy at the time, Hill and Vyse initially used the main reference work available, Sir John Gardner Wilkinson's *Materia Hieroglyphica*, to fake the cartouches in Wellington's and Lady Arbuthnot's Chambers. At this time the work showed only a cartouche that is commonly translated 'Khnum-Khuf' (see cartouche in Figure 5). However, by the time they opened Campbell's Chamber they had obtained a copy of Wilkinson's new work, *Manners and Customs of the Ancient Egyptians*, which had been published only earlier in that year of 1837. This contained the 'standard' Khufu cartouche with which we are all now more familiar, the one found only in Campbell's Chamber (see cartouche in Figure 5).
COMMENT: *This is pure speculation. First, scholars now accept that Egyptian kings had as many as five different*

names for different purposes, all written differently; therefore both the cartouches in the chambers are accepted versions of Khufu's names. Second, Sitchin has ignored the presence of yet another version of the king's name in Lady Arbuthnot's Chamber, which was unknown at the time of the discoveries because as a 'Horus-name' – in Khufu's case 'Horus-Medjedu' or 'Medjeru', as confirmed by other inscriptions found elsewhere – it was not even enclosed within the normal identifying cartouche. Third, the cartouches often appear in a different orientation from that in the source books of the time; not only are they sometimes upright instead of horizontal, but the order of the symbols is sometimes reversed. Only an expert would have known that the order in which the symbols are read depends on the orientation of the animal figures – with the correct order starting with the opposite side from that in which they are facing. These factors, and the presence of the various work-gang names of which the cartouches form part, prove that they could not have been forged from existing reference works.

- Vyse found a partial cartouche inscribed on a fragment of brown stone outside the pyramid on 2 June. In the diary entry for that day he says it was part of the 'standard' Khufu cartouche, but he had 'discovered' this in Campbell's Chamber on 27 May and had not yet had confirmation from the British Museum that the cartouche was Khufu's. The only way he could have known at this time was because he already had Wilkinson's new book, which he had used to copy the inscription in the uppermost chamber.

  COMMENT: *Again, pure distortion. Vyse wrote up his diaries retrospectively, and time and again, in order to better explain a discovery or other point, he inserts information at the entry for a particular date which he only came upon later – normally making this 'retrospective edit' clear. Sitchin would have been quite familiar with this style of Vyse's, and yet he distorts the argument all the same.*

- Birch stated that the writing was semi-hieratic or linear-hieroglyphic, which appeared long after the Fourth Dynasty (hieratic is a simplified form of hieroglyphic writing which requires less knowledge and effort, while linear means painted rather than sculpted or inscribed). He further stated that some of the marks included forms of grammar never encountered before or since.

COMMENT: *It is now accepted by all experts in hiero-glyphics, that these forms of writing did indeed exist in the Fourth Dynasty. Given that some of the more modern reference works which Sitchin himself quotes make this quite clear – for example, Reisner's* Mycerinus *and Grinsell's* Egyptian Pyramids *– he must have been aware of it even as he was putting forward his spurious arguments.*

• In respect of the 'solar disc' element of the cartouches, we now know that this would normally be transcribed as a solid disc or as an empty circle when inscribed using proper hieroglyphics, whereas in linear script it is represented as a circle with a dot in the centre. Wilkinson's first work failed to correctly distinguish between the two, sometimes showing the former, sometimes the latter. *It is unclear why Sitchin makes this point initially. However, he later goes on . . .* All the reference works at the time confused the symbol for the 'solar disc' with the symbol for the letters 'Kh', which is a circle with multiple diagonal lines inside, and according to Birch pictorially represents a sieve (*although this pictographic interpretation as a sieve has now been challenged*). Vyse and Hill copied this mistake, incorporating the sun disc instead of the sieve symbol into all their cartouches, thereby spelling out 'Ra-ufu' and 'Khnem-ra-uf'. This is an elementary mistake of spelling and grammar which ancient scribes would never have committed.

COMMENT: *Again, pure distortion, although this is compounded by the existence of so many copies of the transcriptions of the marks, which are often too small to clearly distinguish the contents of the disc (as were the copies from* Operations *from which our reproductions are derived). Stower has inspected the same British Museum originals that Sitchin supposedly did, and has clearly proved that the discs in these do contain the 'multiple lines' for the 'Kh' symbol rather than any representation of the solar disc.*[66] *This is important because, although current close-up photographs of the actual marks in the Relieving Chambers bear this out and ought to constitute the definitive proof, there have been suggestions that they have been recently doctored to incorporate the multiple lines.*

So we are not accused of being selective ourselves, we should note that Sitchin makes a number of other less substantial claims. He bemoans the lack of proper archaeological supervision of the discoveries. He suggests the diaries are generally vague about the inscriptions, and further that Vyse refused to send copies of them to the British Consul as soon as they were requested. He states that both Mariette and the British Egyptologist Sir Alan Gardiner refused to acknowledge the inscriptions, and finally he quotes Perring, who happened to comment in his own book that the state of preservation of ancient red paint marks in the quarries was so good that they could not be told apart from modern ones – implying that he was dropping a hint of the forgery. Each of these claims can be dismissed as the others were, but we would be here for ever and have more pressing business.

We trust that, with Stower's invaluable assistance on the linguistic issues, our comments have firmly placed Sitchin's 'Khufu Fraud' theory where it belongs. Before we move on to his next allegation, there is another piece of relevant evidence that is rarely disclosed. Referring to his team's search for an additional entrance to the Great Pyramid, Vyse states that 'red quarry marks were continually found upon the stones that were removed at the southern front', although it is clear from his reproductions that none of these contained cartouches.[67] On his web site Stower provides additional evidence of similar marks taken from LV Grinsell's *Egyptian Pyramids*, published in 1947:

> On some of the backing stones of the first 5 or 6 courses, on the south, east and west sides, there are builder's inscriptions and marks mostly in red but occasionally in black. Two of them contain the name Khnmw-khuf [sic], and two others the name Medjedu, both of which are names belonging to Kheops [sic].

Although Grinsell's drawings appear never to have been published, it is clear that he did spend many hours personally inspecting both these marks and those on other pyramids. Did Vyse and his team fake these too? It has been suggested that the Great Pyramid was renovated (although the suggestion is in fact that this occurred before Khufu's time), but even if the edifice were already quite old at this time it would almost certainly have remained reasonably intact. Consequently, any external renovation would have at most involved the remortaring and refacing of the casing blocks – it would not have involved the extensive quarrying of new core blocks. These additional quarry marks therefore provide a conclusive 'double whammy'.

Sitchin then goes on to attempt to cast even more doubt on the integrity of Vyse, Hill and Perring by suggesting that they fraudulently introduced the remains of the wooden coffer bearing Menkaure's cartouche into the Third Pyramid – specifically that they must have found the remains elsewhere and then secretly introduced them into the rubbish in the upper chamber. His main support for this is that the coffer and mummy fragments come from different periods – although when he quotes Edwards as saying the former are Saite Period, the latter 'early Christian', he is clearly not aware that Coptic Arabs were already in existence by this time, and that neither Edwards nor Lehner deliberately implies that the remains are from two separate intrusive burials. But even if they were this would hardly represent definitive proof of a forgery by Vyse, since it appears that the pyramids were entered on multiple occasions in antiquity, and anything could have been introduced and or removed on each of these occasions.

Indeed, far from attempting to trumpet this great new evidence for the attribution of the Third Pyramid, Vyse's account shows an almost careless disregard for the wooden coffer and mummy fragments – he was far more interested in the basalt coffer, which bore *no* inscriptions. Meanwhile, Vyse also uncovered an inscription containing Menkaure's name on the ceiling of a chamber in one of his satellite pyramids, a fact that Sitchin overlooks. Is he supposed to have faked this as well? And, if not, why is this acceptable and his other discovery not?

Sitchin ends with one more stab – implying that Perring's

discovery of a quarry mark bearing Djoser's cartouche at the Step Pyramid was probably more than mere coincidence. The fact that Perring was a highly conscientious and able man who meticulously recorded remains at many more sites than just the few examples he quotes seems to have escaped Sitchin's attention. For example, *Operations* contains details of a multitude of red quarry marks and other inscriptions discovered by Perring at Abusir, Saqqara, Dashur and the Turah quarries after Vyse had returned to England, all of which Birch translates and comments on in some depth in Volume III.[68] In any case, we have seen that Sitchin suggests that Perring 'dropped hints' about the forgeries – was this supposed to be some form of personal atonement? Even his thought processes are inconsistent.

Finally, there is an intriguing footnote to Sitchin's part in this saga. In his third book, *The Wars of Gods and Men*, published in 1985, he reveals a new piece of 'evidence':[69]

At the end of 1983, a reader of that book [*The Stairway to Heaven*] came forward to provide us with family records showing that his great-grandfather, a master mason named Humphries Brewer, who was engaged by Vyse to help use gunpowder to blast his way inside the pyramid, was an *eyewitness to the forgery* [Sitchin's italics] and, having objected to the deed, was expelled from the site and forced to leave Egypt altogether!

There is nothing to back up this potential bombshell. Again, Stower has dug further and established more details from three separate articles written by, or based on interviews with Sitchin. The first provides the following additional information:[70]

In April, 1983, Walter M. Allen of Pittsburgh, Pennsylvania, prompted by an article he read which summarized Sitchin's forgery conclusions, wrote to Sitchin and told him that the forgery was actually witnessed by Allen's great-grandfather, Humphries Brewer. Mr. Brewer was born in Box, Wiltshire, England on February 28, 1817. He studied at the University of Berlin and became a leading quarry master and tunnel builder. In 1837, Humphries Brewer was recruited by the British Medical Service to go to Egypt to assist in the construction of an eye hospital. The project was abandoned, and Brewer joined the team of Col.

Vyse, who was then excavating, measuring and stone-blasting at the Giza Pyramids. While working for Vyse, Brewer had a dispute with Vyse's assistants, Raven and Hill, about the painted marks inside the Great Pyramid. He said that faint marks had been repainted, and that some were new. He had words with Hill and Vyse and he was barred from the site. In 1842, Humphries Brewer was invited by the University of Berlin to return to Egypt on a project, but Col. Vyse would not permit him to do so.

Humphries Brewer reported all of these facts in letters to his father, who was disturbed by them. The Brewer letters were kept in the family and in 1954 the information was given to Walter M. Allen's mother, who told it to Walter. He then recorded the information in his ham-radio logbook in which he was preparing a history of the family.

One of the other articles also reveals that:

> Although the original letters could not be traced for me, a comparison of dates, names and other data included in the records leaves no doubt that Humphries Brewer was indeed an eyewitness to the forgery within the Great Pyramid.

So the only 'family records' that apparently still exist are those in Allen's logbook. The real contemporary evidence, the letters supposedly written by Brewer to his father, have never been produced, either *to* Sitchin or *by* him. Sitchin asserts that dates, names and other data corroborate these claims. Yet we know that Vyse was scrupulous in recording the names and activities of his senior staff, and also meticulous about giving credit for important discoveries to those involved, even if, as in the case of Caviglia, he had already fallen out with them. Since Brewer was apparently 'the *very* stonemason from England whom Col. Vyse engaged to use gunpowder inside the pyramid' (Sitchin's words), it is surely appropriate to ask why his name is entirely absent from the three volumes of Vyse's *Operations*. And unless Sitchin can come up with better evidence than this – at the very least the contents of the logbook, verified by an independent witness and preferably scientifically tested to authenticate its date – it is inadmissible.

Sitchin's motivation in all these matters is inextricably tied into two further lines of argument. First, if all the evidence of attribution *inside* the Giza Pyramids was faked, then the last barrier to the authenticity of the Inventory Stela is removed. This stela can be interpreted as suggesting that the Sphinx existed before Khufu's time, but as we will see, Sitchin manages to distort its interpretation sufficiently to suggest that the Great Pyramid existed before his time as well. He suggests that the Pyramids and Sphinx predated all the other monuments on the Plateau, which were later additions of the Fourth Dynasty. In this he is clearly ignorant of a fact that even most alternative researchers have grudgingly accepted – that the carving of the Sphinx was contemporaneous with the building of the Sphinx Temple. His theory is therefore ill-thought-out, and entirely ignorant of the main body of Egyptian scholarly knowledge. In any case, as we will shortly prove, this stela is probably a late forgery.

Second, he argues that the Giza Pyramids were built long before all the others by the Anunnaki, to serve as guidance beacons at the entrance to a triangulated approach corridor for their spacecraft, leading to a landing platform at Baalbek in the Lebanon (the right-hand marker for the entrance to the corridor is supposed to be Mount St Katherine in southern Sinai, this and Giza being supposedly equidistant from Baalbek). The problem of why they all have complex internal features that would not assist this function is not one that Sitchin addresses in this book – although he does make an attempt in a subsequent volume, as will be seen later. It should be clear from this that his work slips effortlessly between *apparent* scholarship and entirely fanciful whimsy.

Copycats

Despite the ease with which they can be countered, Sitchin's arguments have been reproduced ad nauseam in recent years by researchers who do not seem to have tried to validate them for themselves. Some of them are authors who have earned widespread acclaim, making their irresponsibility all the more perplexing.

Perhaps the best known are the two we have already encountered, Graham Hancock and Robert Bauval. In *Keeper of*

Genesis they use Sitchin's main points,[71] adding that Egyptologists are guilty of 'intellectual chicanery', and that 'attributing the Great Pyramid to Khufu on the basis of a few lines of graffiti is a bit like handing over the keys to the Empire State Building to a man named "Kilroy" just because his name was found spray-painted on the walls of the lift'. Their attitude in this matter was always a perplexing one. Anyone who reads this book, which remains their primary work on Egypt at the time of writing, can become extremely confused about their views on the dating of the Pyramids. As will be seen later, Hancock and Bauval believe they were *laid out* to reflect the stars of Orion's belt as they would have appeared *c.* 10,500 BC, even though they are forced by other astronomical alignments to accept the orthodox view that they weren't actually *built* until 8,000 years later. In reality they disagree with the orthodox chronology only in respect of the Sphinx and its associated temples, but their work has to be read several times over to establish this owing to the lack of clarity with which it is written.

Apart from their attack on Egyptologists for not accepting Sitchin's claims when they agree with their chronology anyway, their lack of clarity serves to obfuscate these issues. This is nowhere better demonstrated than in their inconsistency towards Vyse and Hill. We have already seen that they make great play of the iron plate discovered by Hill in the mouth of the southern King's Chamber shaft, and of the validity of the certification he provided for it. And yet they push forward with Sitchin's allegations that both Vyse and Hill were complete charlatans in respect of the quarry marks, bent on deceiving the world of Egyptology on a grand scale. This is laughable, especially since – in suggesting that Egyptologists have got the importance of the two discoveries the wrong way round – they discuss them both in the same section of the book under the entirely appropriate heading 'Double Standard'!

As the evidence against Sitchin's claims has mounted and become more widely publicised, Hancock at least has now seen sense and withdrawn his support for them in a laudable statement published on our own *EgyptNews* Internet mailing list in

July 1998. The relevant part of his 'admission of guilt' runs as follows:[72]

> I have rightly been taken to task for uncritically supporting Zecharia Sitchin's forgery theory. I reported this theory in Fingerprints (published 1995) and in Keeper/Message (published 1996). As an author and researcher I hope that my work will always be 'in progress' and never finished or set in stone. When I come across new evidence that casts doubt on theories that I previously endorsed I am ready to change my views and admit to past mistakes. As John West kindly reported in his open letter to Stower I have changed my views on the validity of the forgery theory. The relieving chambers are strictly off limits to the public and are extremely difficult to gain access to. I had been unable to obtain permission to visit them prior to the publication of Keeper/Message in 1996. However, in December 1997, Dr. Zahi Hawass allowed me to spend an entire day exploring these chambers. There were no restrictions on where I looked and I had ample time to examine the hieroglyphs closely, under powerful lights. *Cracks in some of the joints reveal hieroglyphs set far back into the masonry.* No 'forger' could possibly have reached in there after the blocks had been set in place – blocks, I should add, that weigh tens of tons each and that are immovably interlinked with one another. The only reasonable conclusion is the one which orthodox Egyptologists have already long held – namely that the hieroglyphs are genuine Old Kingdom graffiti and that they were daubed on the blocks before construction began.

The purpose of including this extract is to note that Hancock has spent time inspecting the quarry marks in detail, something that we were unable to do during our own visit in the autumn of 1998 (we were short on time, and our main priority was to investigate Caviglia's tunnel). Hancock's statement confirms that some of the marks go round the corners and down the crevices *between* the blocks, proving their authenticity – although of course photographic evidence of this would be useful.

Two more books published in 1996 by well-respected authors reveal that they fell into exactly the same trap of accepting Sitchin's work without question. Colin Wilson's *From Atlantis to the Sphinx* repeats Sitchin's allegations, and describes him as 'obsessively scholarly', with an 'extremely acute mind' and whose 'erudition is enormous'.[73] Enough said. Meanwhile, in Andrew Collins's *From the Ashes of Angels* the allegations are, more appropriately, demoted to a footnote.[74]

The writer who has championed Sitchin's cause more vociferously than anyone, and at the time of writing is about the only serious member of the alternative camp who still refuses to back down on certain points, is the British researcher Alan Alford. Since Sitchin himself has added nothing to the debate for many years, Alford's position as the main defender of his work requires examination. His first book, *Gods of the New Millennium*, again published in 1996, was intended to be an objective reappraisal of Sitchin's theories about the genetic creation of man. To be fair, there was some new and interesting work in some areas. However, he also relied heavily on Sitchin's literal and often distorted interpretations of Mesopotamian texts, to such an extent that, if the detailed story and prehistoric chronology put forward by Sitchin was fabulous, Alford's revised and expanded version was positively fantastic. As part of this approach, Alford again regurgitated Sitchin's arguments regarding the supposed 'Khufu Fraud', and like Hancock and Bauval, added nothing new.[75]

Alford has since conducted a genuine reappraisal of these theories, and has realised that much of this work was misguided. His latest book, *The Phoenix Solution*, first published in 1998, concentrates on Egypt, and is a more useful work as a result. It is refreshingly argued, and attempts to take a detailed and indeed revolutionary look at the *context* of the Third and Fourth Dynasty pyramids and of their progression. This makes a far better contribution to the 'why' question and the 'pyramids-as-tombs' debate than his previous attempt. However, part of his new hypothesis is a revised chronology in which the Great and Second Pyramids predate *all* the others. His full hypothesis will be examined later, but the 'Khufu Fraud' theory is *essential* to his arguments.

Although in this latest work Alford primarily follows Sitchin's original arguments with respect to the quarry marks, he has made some concessions and alterations, which will be considered briefly.[76] First, however, we should point out that, wherever he quotes Vyse, his source appears to be Leonard Cottrell's *The Mountains of Pharaoh*, published in 1956; and in fact he makes no secret of the fact that, despite championing the anti-Vyse cause and engaging in a sometimes fierce and very public ongoing debate with Stower on the Internet, he has never actually read Vyse's *Operations* for himself! He defends this omission by suggesting that in order to retain his independent stance as 'Devil's Advocate', he does not want to be indoctrinated by Vyse's propaganda. We can only comment that this is an unusual departure from the standard approach to scholarly research, which considers all the evidence available.

In any case, he starts by reiterating Sitchin's points about the absence of marks in Davison's Chamber, and also on the eastern walls bar Campbell's. Given our previous comments on this, we wonder whether he too has conducted a proper physical examination of Vyse's tunnel or the Relieving Chambers himself.

He repeats the date-manipulation criticism again, and then turns 'more seriously' to the Third Pyramid frauds – even though in a footnote he accepts the strongest argument against Sitchin's view, that is, the widespread evidence for multiple intrusive burials. He then adds a new twist, suggesting that, based on Vyse's promotions – he retired from active service in 1825 on half-pay, but was elevated to full colonel in January 1837, and then to major general in November 1846 – 'one cannot help but wonder whether Howard Vyse was being utilised by the British secret services, and, if so, what interest such authorities might have had in seeing the Great Pyramid firmly attributed to the Egyptian king Khufu'. This is great conspiracy theory, but hardly persuasive evidence.

Having been forced to acknowledge Stower's contribution in ensuring that the original linguistic-forgery arguments are now entirely discredited, Alford comes up with another ingenious amendment: Vyse must have copied the marks from existing inscriptions *outside* the pyramid, not from the contemporary books which, we have seen, did not contain the range of inscriptions found in the chambers. The problem with this argument is that no one, not even the foremost Egyptologists of the day, knew enough about these extended inscriptions to realise they were worth copying. If Vyse had wanted to forge the king's name, it is most likely that he *would* have kept it simple and stuck to the cartouches that were well known. Alford nevertheless goes on to suggest that the incompleteness of many of the inscriptions indicates that they were copied from worn originals. If he is happy with this as an explanation for worn inscriptions outside the edifice, why not those inside it as well?

After discussing the upsides and downsides for Vyse of perpetrating a forgery, he then suggests that he daubed the unimportant inscriptions first so that he could insert the cartouches later without attracting suspicion – once his own ongoing explorations had revealed that no proper chamber would be discovered that did contain proper inscriptions! Again ingenious, but all too contrived. With a last throw of the dice, Alford turns to the 'context' of the inscriptions, suggesting that he is 'uncomfortable' with terms like 'Khufu inspires love' being chosen by workers as a name for their king (although in a footnote he accepts that it can be translated 'Khufu's friends'), and similarly with 'Craftsmen's Crew' for heavy lifters.

Valiant though Alford's attempts are, his desperation becomes ever more evident, the reason for which is that in his view the Relieving Chamber inscriptions are the 'one single piece of evidence' that prevent Egyptologists from being able to break free from their restricted paradigm. The reality is that they are the one piece of evidence that *conclusively* undermines his amended chronology – although there are many other pieces of more *circumstantial* evidence, which are also lined up against him. Hopefully at some point he will realise that he is committing the very error that he accuses Egyptologists and others of committing – that of 'arguing from a position of preconception or prejudice'. He is so keen to replace the orthodox chronology with his revised version that he fails to objectively assess the now huge weight of evidence against the 'Khufu Fraud' argument.

In the case of the quarry marks, there is one very important thing to remember: some of the more esoteric and hypothetical arguments can be extended, refined and used in counterattack ad infinitum – a process that is no better displayed than in some of the correspondence between Stower and Alford on the

Internet. Even if one does have to delve into the detail, it is important to stand back and look at the bigger picture. On whose side does the balance of probability lie? We hope we have done more than enough to prove that it rests with Vyse and his team, and not with Sitchin and Alford.

The Invented Inventory

Another of the prime pieces of 'evidence' used by alternative theorists to attack the orthodox chronology is the Inventory Stela discovered by Mariette in the 'Temple of Isis', next to one of the Great Pyramid's satellites. Although most alternative theorists confine their use of this stela to support the redating of the Sphinx, both Sitchin and, less stridently, Alford insist on using it to support a redating of the Great Pyramid as well. A translation of the opening lines of the stela is provided by Jordan, as follows.[77]

> Long live . . . the King of Upper and Lower Egypt, Khufu, given life . . . He found the House of Isis, Mistress of the Pyramid, by the side of the hollow of Hwran (the Sphinx) . . . and he *built his pyramid* beside the temple of this goddess and he built a pyramid for the King's Daughter Henutsen beside this temple. The place of Hwran Horemakhet is on the south side of the House of Isis, Mistress of the Pyramid . . . He restored the statue, all covered in painting, of the Guardian of the Atmosphere, who guides the winds with his gaze. He replaced the back part of the nemes head-dress which was missing with gilded stone . . . The figure of this god, cut in stone, is solid and will last to eternity, keeping its face looking always to the east . . .

If this were a genuine inscription made in Khufu's time then the evidence for the Sphinx predating him would be relatively strong, given the details mentioned such as the repair to the back of the head – which it is believed *was* carried out in ancient times after lightning damaged the monument. However, it is also clear that, even if the inscription were genuine, the evidence for the Great Pyramid already being in existence is much flimsier. According to Sitchin, it relies on assuming that Isis would be referred to as the 'Mistress of the Pyramid' only if it already existed,[78] and yet the stela clearly refers to him 'building his pyramid'. But is the stela genuine anyway?

Although even Egyptologists were initially excited by it, it soon became clear to most of them that there were severe problems with its authenticity. As Lehner points out:[79]

> The 26th Dynasty saw an attempt to resurrect the glory of the Old Kingdom. At Giza there was an active priesthood of the Sphinx as *Horemakhet* and there were also people calling themselves priests of Khufu, Khafre and Menkaure. Ironically, the worship of the powerful kings who built the largest structures in Egypt was now carried out in the tiny Temple of Isis, built against the southernmost of the pyramids of Khufu's queens (Gl-*c*) in the 21st dynasty. A small stela there related another story about Khufu, namely that having found the Isis Temple in ruins he restored the images of the gods, and repaired the headdress of the Sphinx. The style of the text and the deities mentioned all point to its having been written in the 26th dynasty; the story was no doubt told to give greater antiquity and authenticity to the fledgling cult. But its erroneous implication that the Sphinx and Isis Temple predate Khufu shows just how far the perceived history of the site was slipping from fact.

For his part, Jordan likens the Saite Period priests' resurrection of the cult of the Fourth Dynasty kings to the Victorian Gothic revival, describing the stela as 'a pious fraud in which a latter-day king borrows the name of Khufu to cloak his own operations at Giza in glory, and to promote the antiquity of the cult of Isis at Giza'. He goes on to establish a number of points regarding its age. First, the stela is poorly executed. Second, the Cult of Isis itself was little known in the Fourth Dynasty. Third, there exist a variety of anachronistic titles for gods whose statues are listed in other parts of the stela. Fourth, 'Hwran' and 'Horemakhet' were not used as names for the Sphinx before the Eighteenth Dynasty. And, fifth, the 'Temple of Isis' in which the stela was found has clearly been built into, and partly out of, an older temple which was attached to the satellite pyramid – which in turn was 'attached' to the already existing Great Pyramid. So it is clearly a later work that contains considerable distortions.

Although Alford accepts its late date, and does not place the same naive (or perhaps cynical) reliance on it as Sitchin, he suggests that the important feature of the stela is not what it contains but what it omits.[80] He asks if the Saite priests were praising Khufu and his achievements, why would they mention that he built a small pyramid for Henutsen but fail to mention that he built the Great Pyramid – unless he did *not* build it? This argument is countered both by the phrase 'he built his pyramid . . .' and by Jordan's view that they were not commemorating Khufu's achievements but their own.

Sign your name!

It is often asked why such apparent egotists as those who built the Giza Pyramids did not plaster their names more freely on their edifices. Previous mastabas, temples and even the earliest pyramids – most notably that of Djoser – had been copiously decorated with reliefs, friezes and statues. Hieroglyphic writing had been invented at least 500 years beforehand, and an inscribed stela found in the Early Dynastic tomb of Merka at Saqqara proves that it was used in tomb adornment from the earliest times.[81] Furthermore, the pyramids of later dynasties contained statues and inscriptions. Clearly the Fourth Dynasty pyramids do stand out somewhat in their lack of decoration – the only concrete evidence of this is the simple reliefs discovered on the antechamber walls of the Third Pyramid, and on the coffer that Vyse removed from its lower chamber.

However, there are variations in style from dynasty to dynasty – just as there are from decade to decade in modern architectural trends – and in our view this is clearly one of them. Moreover, Herodotus observed that the Great Pyramid's causeway was richly decorated, and this has been borne out by fragments discovered in recent times. It is also possible that at least the Great Pyramid did originally have some hieroglyphic inscriptions on its casing (see Appendix I). Meanwhile, we have already seen that the mortuary and valley temples on the Plateau at least contained multiple statues, although most have never been found; and we know from fragmented remains that the walls of the Great Pyramid's mortuary temple were covered with delicately carved reliefs.[82] Therefore, this assertion that the

Fourth Dynasty kings' edifices were completely unadorned and anonymous is not as simple as it might appear, and cannot be regarded as sufficient evidence to lift the Fourth Dynasty pyramids *en masse* out of their place in the orthodox chronology.

Another associated objection is often heard: Egyptian kings often put up their own inscriptions on earlier monuments with little regard for maintaining an accurate record of their origin, making dating based on inscriptions hazardous. There is some truth in this: for example the Inventory Stela is clearly a somewhat distorted version of the process. However, there are also cases when, for example, Saite Period restorers clearly tried to restore the correct names to monuments from which they had been previously removed: the inscribed wooden coffer in the Third Pyramid is in a way an example of this. As will be seen shortly, Alford subscribes heavily to this 'adoption theory', but the arguments are mixed and each case must be taken on its merits. A blanket objection such as this cannot in our view seriously damage the mass of scholarly effort put in by Egyptologists over many decades – especially since they are as much on the lookout for authenticity and the possibility of false 'adoptive claims' as anyone.

Earlier Structures?

There have been suggestions that the three Giza Pyramids were built on top of earlier structures. The arguments for this fall into three main categories: that the lower courses of the pyramids contain larger blocks which could reveal an earlier construction; that the edifices show significant signs of replanning, possibly over a long period; and that they were only renovated and adopted in the Early Dynastic or Old Kingdom eras, having been constructed much earlier.

Larger first courses

It is argued that the core blocks of the first few courses, particularly those of the Second Pyramid, are far larger than those higher up. This is true – external observation of all three edifices reveals this to be the case, while we know from Vyse that when his intrusive tunnel in the Third Pyramid was nearing the base he encountered blocks 'of enormous size, particularly near the foundation'. However, it surely makes sense to use larger blocks near the base, where they do not have to be lifted up so high. Furthermore, we have already seen that some of the core blocks of the lower courses of the Great Pyramid were daubed with quarry marks similar to those in the Relieving Chambers.

The situation can be confused in relation to the unevenness of the Plateau underneath the edifices. Vyse reports that a number of large blocks were used at both the Second and Third Pyramids as a foundation to raise up the surrounding platform to the required level.[83] Conversely, Lehner notes that the north-east corner of the Great Pyramid, and the northwest corner of the Second, were constructed out of the bedrock which stood proud of the pavement level for the first few courses – this bedrock being fashioned into steps to merge with the core blocks on either side.[84] Therefore, the arguments for earlier structures *above ground* are not persuasive.

Replanning

The second, and not mutually exclusive, argument is that the descending passages and under- or near-ground chambers may have been constructed long before. In order to understand this we need to review the evidence for replanning of the structures.

The Third Pyramid provides clear evidence that redesign of the sub- and superstructures went hand in hand. The original descending passage, which now ends underneath the edifice, would have led to the upper chamber only, and the floor of the latter would have been higher. Meanwhile, the original planned superstructure would have been about half the size in base and height, since even the redesigned chambers remained under the apex. We must assume that at some point it was decided to increase the size of the edifice, which necessitated lowering the floor of the upper chamber so that a new descending passage would still emerge on the outside near the base (refer back to Figure 6).

Given that the Second Pyramid also has two descending passages, in this case with two entirely separate chambers, it is possible – indeed likely – that it too was replanned. The older lower chamber lies only about one-sixth of the way into the superstructure, indicating that either the whole edifice was shifted a long way to the south so that the new upper chamber would still be underneath the apex, or – more likely – the whole size of the edifice was considerably increased but with its northern perimeter remaining in the same place.

There have been suggestions that both these 'replans' arose from the need to establish certain alignments between the edifices on the Plateau, and this will be looked at more closely later. However, our initial observation is that if these alignments were so important they would have been the primary consideration from the outset.

Turning to the Great Pyramid, the arguments become far more complex. Although there is only one descending passage, uniquely there are also chambers high up in the superstructure. Although it is often suggested that the Subterranean Chamber was deliberately built as a foil for grave robbers, there are a number of pieces of evidence to support the view that at some point it was decided to abandon the entire subterranean operation and to place the main chamber (or chambers) up in the superstructure.

First, the Subterranean Chamber is unfinished. Second, the small tunnel in the far wall may have signalled the intention to place a new chamber further to the south, an idea that was also abandoned – this would have created a 'dual-chamber' system, as found in the superstructure. Third, there is a niche measuring some 6 feet long by 6 feet wide by 4 feet high in the west wall of the horizontal passage leading to the chamber; this was almost certainly planned as an antechamber, which would have incorporated a portcullis system, but was again abandoned. Fourth, at the beginning of the twentieth century Ludwig Borchardt examined the walls of the Ascending Passage and noticed that the blocks at the lower end were laid parallel to the ground, whereas higher up they were laid parallel to the slope of the passage. He concluded from this that the point of transition marked the height to which the superstructure had risen when the plan to build the main chamber in the superstructure, rather than underground, was put in place. Consequently this lower part of the passage was rough-hewn out of the already laid blocks, while thereafter the walls – being deliberately formed – are much smoother. These arguments are certainly persuasive.

119

Although it is not directly relevant to the discussion of earlier structures, we should finish off the remaining arguments concerning the replanning of the Great Pyramid – those relating to the possible replanning of the upper reaches themselves. Many Egyptologists have suggested that, given the unfinished nature of the Queen's Chamber floor, and the fact that there is a drop in the floor of the last part of the passage leading to it, it too was abandoned in favour of the King's Chamber. The proponents of this theory claim that further support for the abandonment principle is found in the fact that the Queen's Chamber shafts stop somewhere inside the masonry, and do not exit to the outside as do their King's Chamber counterparts. However, we have already seen that these shafts were deliberately sealed off with masonry at their inner ends as part of the original design, rather than hastily plugged as an afterthought. More compelling still, we will later see that recent discoveries have proved that the southern shaft continues for some 200 feet up into the masonry. This evidence tends to militate against the Queen's Chamber abandonment theory.

Unlike many of his colleagues, Lehner does not subscribe to the replanning view, at least not in respect of the Great Pyramid. He argues instead that most Old Kingdom pyramids had three chambers, and that each chamber in the Great Pyramid had a specific purpose in 'catering for different aspects of the king's spiritual welfare'. In particular he points to the fact that the Queen's Chamber was sealed off like a *serdab* ('statue house'), and that the niche would have contained a *ka* statue representing the king's spiritual double.[85] For our part we have to admit that we remain open-minded about the arguments in relation to the *upper* reaches of the Great Pyramid, but would still contend that the weight of evidence supports the theory of the replanning of the *substructure* in this pyramid, and of the sub- and superstructures in the other two.

To sum all this up in relation to earlier structures, of course, it is still *possible* that the 'first-plan' substructures were constructed considerably earlier. However, this is unlikely, since the model of sloping-descending-passage-and-subterranean-chamber is one found only in conjunction with pyramid super-structures – the early mastabas tending to have vertical shafts sometimes combined with sloping trenches which were largely open-roofed. Consequently, even if earlier pyramid structures had been placed above the substructures on the Plateau and were subsequently demolished or rebuilt, context would argue that they could be no older than the commencement of the Pyramid Age. In any case, replanning is evident in most of the Third and Fourth Dynasty pyramids, which tends to suggest it was all contemporary.

Adoption and renovation

Alford's revised chronology is the reason he is so determined to continue to champion the 'Khufu Fraud' theory. The 'Adoption' hypothesis he puts forward will now be looked at because it is interesting even if flawed. His arguments in relation to chronology are sometimes complex, and he develops them over several chapters so that they are not always easy to follow.[86] Nevertheless, they can be summarised as follows:

- The Great Pyramid is so superior in design and execution to *all* the other pyramid structures that it must have been built long before them – probably by a 'lost race' of nonsedentary intellectuals who had no need for writing, and left no trace of their culture when they moved on from Egypt when their task was accomplished. This established Giza as a sacred site from the earliest pre-dynastic times. Alford is at pains to point out that he does not believe this race were alien visitors, although this was the theory put forward in his first book.
- The poorer-constructed, simpler-designed but nevertheless similarly sized Second Pyramid was erected in late pre-dynastic times by early Egyptians wishing to emulate the Great Pyramid. They had discovered some of the technology and skills – perhaps within the Great Pyramid itself – without having the same mind-set or experience to put them to full use. Since he suggests that the Sphinx, and the various megalithic temples attached to it and the two large pyramids, were built at the same time, we can assume that he would accept that by this time the *complexes* were taking on a funerary significance (although he does not make this clear).
- The entire site was renovated *c*. 3000 BC, particularly the Great Pyramid. In this way he attempts to keep his theories in line with the carbon dating evidence, as the mortar tested from the Great Pyramid came only from the outer layers. This argument is backed

up with the claim that the outer core of the edifice which we see now is inferior to the interior construction.

- In the Fourth Dynasty, first Khufu then Khafre *adopted* the Great and Second Pyramids respectively, probably building only the causeways. Meanwhile, they used the associated temples for religious rituals, and decorated them with their statues and inscriptions. Having nothing left to adopt, Menkaure built a much smaller pyramid and (presumably, although Alford doesn't say) its associated temples and causeway.

This is an intriguing set of ideas which at first sight have some appeal, but, apart from the all-important fact that the Khufu inscriptions in the Relieving Chambers are genuine, it has further inconsistencies. First, it effectively dismisses the 'Older Sphinx' theory, since in this scenario its date is put back only between 500 and 1,000 years. Second, although his renovation idea fits in with the carbon dating evidence, it had to have occurred some 500 years later to allow the Khufu inscriptions on the outer-core blocks to be explained, plus renovation would have been more likely to involve refitting original blocks rather than quarrying new ones. Third, the renovation idea is not supported by the findings of Vyse's team – they encountered cavities of up to 3 or 4 feet in diameter when they dug underneath the passage leading to the Queen's Chamber – these were filled with sand and rubble, and were almost certainly wide gaps between core blocks which had been filled. The inner (in Alford's terms, original) core construction may therefore have been as imperfect as the outer. We do not share his view about the general superiority of construction of the Great Pyramid, and, while we accept that some elements of its *interior* design do stand out, we do not feel the same need to shift its place in the chronology.

Fourth, he discusses the full implications of the carbon dating surveys – that the dates for *all* the Third and Fourth Dynasty pyramids should be revised, and that the *relative* chronology of the existing orthodoxy is fine. Despite this, he insists on shifting only the Great and Second Pyramids backward in his chronology.

Fifth, he suggests that the megalithic temples were extensively refurbished, whereas we believe that their construction was entirely single-phase, as will be seen later.

Finally, under his scenario presumably the Third Pyramid's mortuary and valley temples were built at the same time as the pyramid to which they were attached – in the Fourth Dynasty. Why then does at least the mortuary temple display exactly the same megalithic structure as, for example, the Sphinx and Valley Temples – which under his chronology were supposedly built far earlier and are not Fourth Dynasty designs?

One final piece of Alford's analysis should be mentioned. He suggests that the 'alignments' of the two Giza 'Great Pyramids' with the two Dashur pyramids indicate that the former predate the latter.[87] Although he maintains that 'it does not take a genius to see which pair of pyramids had been oriented to the other', we clearly failed this particular test and are forced to admit that his logic in making this assertion escapes us.

Carbon Dating Revisited

Jordan does not indicate the source of the carbon dating results that we described above, but we do know that in 1984 a 'Pyramids Carbon Dating Project' was conducted. 64 samples of organic material extracted from the pyramids and associated structures were carbon dated. After calibration, the dates averaged 374 years earlier than one of the major accepted chronologies.[88]

In an article dating back to 1986, Lehner, who was personally involved, reports the following about fifteen samples of mortar taken from the Great Pyramid:[89]

The dates run from 3809 to 2869 BC. So generally the dates are . . . significantly earlier than the best Egyptological date for Khufu . . . In short, the radiocarbon dates, depending on which sample you note, suggest that the Egyptological chronology is anything from 200 to 1200 years off. You can look at this almost like a bell curve, and when you cut it down the middle you can summarise the results by saying our dates are 400 to 450 years too early for the Old Kingdom Pyramids, especially those of the Fourth Dynasty . . . Now this is really radical . . . I mean it'll make a big stink. The Giza pyramid is 400 years older than Egyptologists believe.

Meanwhile, the official report of the project includes detailed results which can be summarised as follows in relation to the Giza edifices:[90]

Edifice	No. Samples	Earliest Date (BC)	Latest Date (BC)	Average Date (BC)
Great Pyramid	15	3101*	2869	2985
Second Pyramid	7	3196	2723	2960
Third Pyramid	6	3076	2067	2572
Sphinx Temple	2	2746	2085	2416

* This excludes the *one* sample out of 15 that showed serious deviation from all the others: it came from the southwest corner of the 198th course and gave 3809 BC (+/– 160 years), although another sample from the same spot gave only 3101 BC (+/– 414 years).

From this it is clear that the results are far less extreme if the one seriously anomalous sample from the Great Pyramid is excluded. Furthermore, the general *order* of the orthodox chronology can be seen to be supported. We should also note that the discrepancies between the various orthodox chronologies are not immaterial when viewed in the light of these results. For example, writing in 1990, the Egyptologist JP Lepre preferred a chronology some 240 years earlier for the Old Kingdom than that of Baines and Malik quoted at the beginning of this chapter.[91]

What is to be made of these results? Clearly it was reasonable for Lehner to suggest that a discrepancy of 400 years would make 'a big stink'. To Egyptologists anxious to protect the details of their chronology, this would be a major blow. But even if carbon dating were a reliable method for detailed historical verification, which we have already indicated it is not, are differences of 400 or even 1,000 years really that radical to non-Egyptologists? What are the implications? It certainly does not mean that the whole of orthodox Egyptology goes out of the window – although it might mean that there is much work to do in re-evaluating the reign lengths accorded to each king, and perhaps in searching for kings currently omitted from the list. It *may* have an impact on the 'why' question, which we will consider shortly. But it is not the sort of evidence that can support those who suggest that the pyramids were built *several* thousands of years before by other civilisations.

Members of the alternative camp, Hancock and Bauval in particular,[92] once again take delight in slamming the scholarly community for their apparent desire to sweep such results under the carpet, without allowing for the fact that this reticence is more likely caused by the inherent fallibility of the method used. As usual we must ask what their real point is, since we have already seen that they support the conventional dating. There is plenty of innuendo, but all it does is confuse the reader as to where they actually stand.

Alford goes into some detail about carbon dating, and he stresses its unreliability, despite then making extensive (but in our view *selective*) use of its results. He indicates that contamination and other factors can significantly distort the results.[93] He also provides three examples of the highly anomalous individual results that can derive from the process.[94] First, one sample of mortar from the Sphinx Temple dated as late as 2085 BC. Second, and by contrast, a sample of wood from one of 'Khufu's Boats', found in a pit near the Great Pyramid, dated far too early at 3400 BC. Third, according to Lehner, a female skeleton found underneath Djoser's Step Pyramid has been dated to 'generations before Djoser's time'. There are *possible* explanations for all of these: the first perhaps arose due to later repairs; the second possibly because the wood had been reused from a much earlier piece, or was already old when used; the third perhaps because the site had been used for burials long before the pyramid was erected. However, in our view they indicate that we must be extremely careful about using carbon dating evidence to refine a detailed chronology, unless *consistently material anomalies* are encountered.

Lehner mentions another survey conducted in 1995 when more than 300 samples were collected from monuments ranging from the First-Dynasty tombs at Saqqara to Djoser's pyramid, the Giza pyramids, and a selection of Fifth- and Sixth-Dynasty and Middle Kingdom pyramids.[95]

It would appear that the results of this survey had not been published at the time Lehner's book came out in 1997, and as far as we are aware at the time of writing this remains the case. However, elsewhere he has emphasised that the results of the earlier survey do, at the very least, confirm that the orthodox *sequence* of early pyramid building is correct.[96]

As for other carbon-datable relics, particularly related to the Great Pyramid, we have already seen that – although Hancock and Bauval made a great fuss about it – the piece of cedar wood found in the northern Queen's Chamber shaft has been missing for many years. But Bauval has not stopped there. Not only has he suggested since 1994 that there is another similar piece of wood still in the northern shaft – and recently resurrected his campaign to have it removed – but he has also revealed of late that he is in possession of a finger thought to have been found trapped in a crevice in the floor of the upper chamber in the Second Pyramid. These sagas will be scrutinised closely in a later chapter, but suffice to say at this stage, we do not believe either is an original 'relic' that can shed light on the age of the edifices.

Conclusion

A great deal of rubbish has been written about the age of the pyramids, passing itself off as scholarly research, and much of the blame for this can be attached to one original instigator who has done so much to unfairly blacken Vyse's reputation. Fortunately, many members of the alternative camp are beginning to see the truth – that there is every reason to believe that the chronology developed by orthodox Egyptologists over many decades is, to all intents and purposes, accurate. Above all, the Great Pyramid itself cannot be removed from its rightful place in this chronology, which places considerable restrictions on the range of purposes for which it might have been constructed, as we will now find out . . .

THREE

WHY WERE THE PYRAMIDS BUILT?

The orthodox line that has been established in textbooks for many decades is that all Egyptian pyramids are funerary edifices. This line of argument is mercilessly ridiculed by the alternative camp, apparently for lack of evidence. It is therefore important to start by examining the arguments on each side.

Attention will then be turned to the suggestion that mathematical, geometric and other knowledge has been encoded into the design of the pyramids. This also has its roots buried in legends dating back many centuries. Although it is possible that it is in itself the origin of the Hall of Records concept, these two notions tend to be regarded as separate. Again, many alternative researchers present this argument as if it were a foregone conclusion; but is their case as concrete as they suggest? And even if such knowledge were proven to exist, does it necessarily mean that the edifices are something other than tombs? Although the two theories are usually presented as mutually exclusive as part of the polarisation of the two camps, conceptually there is no reason why they should not sit comfortably together.

This is not the case with the third set of theories, those suggesting that the Great Pyramid was built as an astronomical observatory. Nor indeed with the last set to be considered – those suggesting that the Great Pyramid was built by highly advanced ancient civilisations for a bewildering array of purposes. These theories include the suggestions that it acted as a guidance beacon for incoming spacecraft, or as a massive energy generator.

Above all it should be remembered that all these latter theories tend to concentrate on the Great Pyramid with little regard for its counterparts. This would be fine if this pyramid could be lifted out of the orthodox chronology, but this is a contrived solution which flies in the face of the evidence.

Funerary Edifices?

The positions adopted by the most radical players in the modern alternative camp are as follows:

> The common – and indeed authoritative – assumption that the Pyramid was just another tomb built to memorialise some vainglorious Pharaoh is proved to be false. (Peter Tompkins, *Secrets of the Great Pyramid*, 1971)[97]

> ... Nor have historians, succeeded in producing any convincing theory as to why such an enormous undertaking, combined with such incredible accuracy, should have been deemed necessary for the construction of a mere tomb and funerary monument to a dead king who in any case apparently never occupied it. (Peter Lemesurier, *The Great Pyramid Decoded*, 1977)[98]

> If lack of evidence constitutes the criterion for judging the crankiness of any given theory, then there is one theory crankier than all the fantasising of the pyramidologists and the UFO freaks. This is the theory that the great pyramids were built as tombs, and as tombs only. In support of this theory there is no direct or indirect evidence whatsoever. While the numerous small pyramids of Middle and Late Kingdom Egypt were clearly and obviously designed as tombs, and have disclosed a wealth of mummies and coffins, the eight 'great' pyramids assigned to the Third and Fourth Dynasties of the Old Kingdom have revealed no sign of either coffin or mummy. (John Anthony West, *Serpent in the Sky*, 1979)[99]

> The Old Kingdom pyramids never held a Pharaoh's body because they were never meant to hold a king's body. (Zecharia Sitchin, *The Stairway to Heaven*, 1980)[100]

> To the surprise of many who have taken the tomb theory at face value, no body, no mummy, nothing at all connected in any remote way with a burial or a tomb, has ever been found inside the Great Pyramid ... [There is not] one shred of evidence that any pyramid was ever intended to be a tomb. (Alan Alford, *Gods of the New Millennium*, 1996)[101]

> The bottom line on the pyramids-as-tombs theory is that there is as yet no positive evidence whatsoever for original pyramid burials prior to the Sixth Dynasty. (Alan Alford, *The Phoenix Solution*, 1998)[102]

It is now becoming widely recognised by people who research the pyramid issue that of all the pyramids excavated in Egypt, there was not one that contained an original burial. Considering that more than eighty pyramids have been discovered in Egypt, this fact alone practically negates the tomb theory. (Chris Dunn, *The Giza Power Plant*, 1998)[103]

It is clear from these extracts that most of their authors reject the tomb theory absolutely. A number of factors are used by the alternative camp to support this view, including:

- The apparent lack of looting evidence and of mummies.
- The fact that sarcophagi have been supposedly missing, lidless, oversize for the passages, or sealed but empty.
- The fact that on occasion multiple sarcophagi have been found in one pyramid, or multiple chambers, or even that one king built multiple pyramids.

On the face of it these are all valid observations which support alternative theories, but in our view they can all be proved to be either incorrect or explainable. Each of these points will be examined in detail in Appendix II.

The tombs theory – significant support
The body of orthodox opinion has a somewhat superior provenance, and is supported by many of the 'founding fathers' – the first men to enter the edifices in the modern era. Although this does not in itself prove the superiority of such opinions, these explorers did see at first hand the condition of the chambers when they reopened them, and this must count for something. By contrast, apart from some of the more far-fetched Arab accounts, the only 'major player' from the past who may be considered a member of the alternative camp is Smyth, and as we have seen he supported arguably one of the most far-fetched theories, that of the 'biblical' timeline. The development of the less far-fetched and apparently scholarly body of alternative thinking is a relatively recent phenomenon.

Some of its more vociferous detractors would have us believe that the 'pyramids-as-tombs' theory has been dreamt up by unimaginative Egyptologists in the last few centuries, and that they dare not let it go for fear of the unknown despite the mountain of contrary evidence that confronts them. However, it is clear that this theory has persisted for millennia. The Classical historians Herodotus, Strabo and Diodorus all believed the Giza Pyramids were constructed as sepulchres, although Pliny makes no comment on their purpose. The Arab historian Latif not only supports this view, but adds weight to the theory that the pyramids had all been ransacked repeatedly in antiquity in search of treasure.[104]

> It is also stated, that when the Persians conquered Egypt, they forced open the tombs in search of treasure, and took away great riches from the Pyramids, which were the sepulchres of the kings: and that the Greeks afterwards did the same.

What of the explorers? After his investigation of the Second Pyramid, Belzoni formed the following opinion:[105]

> The circumstance of having chambers and a sarcophagus (which undoubtedly contained the remains of some great personage), so uniform with those in the other pyramid, I think leaves very little question, but that they were erected as sepulchres; and I really wonder, that any doubt has ever existed, considering what could be learned from the first pyramid, which has been so long open. This contains a spacious chamber with a sarcophagus; the passages are of such dimensions as to admit nothing larger than the sarcophagus; they had been closely shut up by large blocks of granite from within, evidently to prevent the removal of that relic. Ancient authors are pretty well agreed in asserting, that these monuments were erected to contain the remains of two brothers, Cheops and Cephren, kings of Egypt. They are surrounded by other smaller pyramids intermixed with mausoleums on burial-grounds. Many mummy-pits have been continually found there; yet with all these proofs, it has been asserted, that they were erected for many other purposes than the true one, and nearly as absurd as that they served for granaries.

As for Vyse, we have already seen that after his unsuccessful attempts to locate secret chambers in the Great Pyramid he was forced to conclude that ' . . . the King's Chamber is the principal apartment, and the security of the sarcophagus within it the great object for which the pyramid was erected.'[106]

By the time Perring had completed his investigations of all the major Third and Fourth Dynasty pyramid sites, and had repeatedly encountered mountains of rubbish, floors that had been dug up, and fragmented sealing blocks and portcullises – indeed the type of vandalism they had witnessed together in the Third Pyramid – Vyse was forced to go further: '. . . in some instances, the [Ancient] Egyptians themselves broke open and destroyed these ancient tombs.'[107]

Vyse was clearly convinced that all the edifices had been broken into shortly after they were completed. The perpetrators had either been part of the construction crew themselves, or had obtained accurate information on the concealed entrances and internal layout from others who were.[108] This is a theory supported by a number of modern Egyptologists, and with good cause. For a start, there is a consistent lack of the sort of ancillary damage that one would expect if the robberies had been carried out by those unfamiliar with the layout of the pyramids. There is little evidence of repeated hacking at the surrounds of external entrances, or of the walls of passages and chambers in which doorways were blocked off and concealed.

One of the best examples is the entrance into the third or upper chamber in the Red Pyramid, which is 25 feet up in the south wall of the second chamber. It is highly likely that this was originally sealed off, and we can assume that it would have been cleverly concealed with a block that gave no hint of what lay behind it. Yet it was found and removed with no evidence of any false starts with other blocks. By contrast, the state of the floor in the third chamber suggests it was dug up by later robbers who were unaware that nothing lay beneath it, and were simply operating by guesswork alone. It is also possible that the short passage that connects the two sets of chambers in the Bent Pyramid, which is clearly not part of the original design, was also tunnelled by robbers who knew the layout, although it is also possible that this was part of an escape route for the builders responsible for lowering the portcullis, and was dug during the construction.

Vyse also felt that there was sufficient evidence to suggest that all the descending passages had been sealed with limestone blocks for some distance from the entrance. This meant that the effort required to break in was substantial. Why did the robbers go to so much trouble? Clearly, if they were party to accurate information about the layout, they probably knew what was inside. Their supreme and determined efforts can be explained only by the suggestion that the Old Kingdom rulers were indeed buried along with substantial treasure. Once these initial marauders had opened up the edifices and removed the best booty, there is every reason to suppose that successive intruders over many centuries would have picked the chambers clean of all souvenirs.

Perhaps the most conclusive evidence that contemporary tomb robbing was rife comes from Jean Vercoutter's *The Search for Ancient Egypt*, published in 1992.[109] He describes in detail the trial of the robbers of the tomb of the Thirteenth Dynasty King Sebekemsaf, and reports that 'trials of this kind take up yards and yards of papyrus . . . they demonstrate how widespread such robbery was, and give an idea of the lavish contents of the royal tombs'. He even suggests that in later Arab times there were 'manuals offering tips on how to do it' – the best known of which is called the *Book of Buried Pearls*.

The Great Pyramid Puzzle

High-level chambers

In addition to the general argument, the particular circumstances of the Great Pyramid cause significant complications for the pyramids-as-tombs theory. Although we have seen that many of the features that some of the alternative camp would have us believe are unique – the Grand Gallery, portcullis arrangement, alignment to the cardinal points and so on – are not, the reason for this complication is its primary and *genuinely* unique feature: that it has chambers *high up* in its superstructure. Although the Meidum and Dashur Pyramids, and the Second Pyramid have chambers that either butt into or are entirely enclosed by the superstructure, they are all at or near ground level. By contrast, the Queen's and King's Chambers lie at about one-fifth and two-fifths of the height of the Great

Pyramid respectively, and are accessed by a separate Ascending Passage, which branches off from the normal Descending Passage.

Before looking at the implications of this for the pyramids-as-tombs theory, a few general issues surrounding this layout should be considered. The question that is always raised by the alternative camp is, why did the builders go to so much trouble to implement such a difficult design? In answer, we know that contemporary tomb robbing was a major problem for the Old Kingdom kings, and at the start of his reign Khufu would have seen that many of his predecessors' tombs had already been ransacked – including perhaps those of his father and mother. Having his architects design ingenious methods of concealed burial was therefore a major priority for a king who, above all else, needed to ensure that his body remained intact so his spirit could live on in peace in the afterlife.

The leading architects and masons would by this time have become some of the most influential men in ancient Egyptian society, and would have been vying for the key posts in Khufu's entourage by coming up with ever more ingenious designs for his great monument. While some of them would have been the experienced men who worked on the various evolutions of Sneferu's pyramids, others would have been young and bursting with new ideas.

All this sounds pretty reasonable. However, Alford and others raise another serious objection: Why did this process not continue in the subsequent generations? This is a hard one to answer, and as with so many of these issues it primarily requires speculation, as unsatisfactory as that may be. The main piece of pertinent evidence that should be considered is an analysis of the Great Pyramid by the French engineer Jean Kerisel. He made a detailed survey of the edifice in the early 1990s, and argues that the construction method was fatally flawed because the builders were attempting to use two types of stone with substantially differing levels of compressibility.

Kerisel believes that fine fractures initially emerged as a result of the contraction of the nummulitic limestone masonry that surrounded the granite linings in the King's and Relieving Chambers. These then enlarged and deepened until they crossed some of the beams. The architects would have been worried by the cracks, and ordered a halt to the work to dig the tunnel that allowed access to the lowest chamber. Two different kinds of plaster show that repair work to the fissures took place twice. The Relieving Chambers were clearly heavily overloaded and warped. This is backed up by the fact that recent gravimeter measurements show the upper part of the pyramid has a lesser density – Khufu clearly ordered a lighter construction. It would appear that Khufu's successors took advantage of this lesson, since none of them ever again ventured to insert chambers of this type in the middle of their pyramids.[110]

This analysis contradicts Petrie's theory (which still has widespread credibility among Egyptologists) that the cement repairs were performed by the priests responsible for the maintenance of the edifice *after* the pyramid was constructed, as a result of earthquakes; furthermore he suggests this is why the Well Shaft was dug from the bottom up. In our view this latter suggestion is entirely at odds with the known facts (see Appendix III). As a result, Kerisel's analysis seems more compelling – even though both alternatives provide an answer as to when the passage to Davison's Chamber was built, and why.

It is further supported if a similar analysis of the Queen's Chamber is conducted. Of course this had a pent rather than a flat roof, and one might argue that the major stresses were taken by the King's Chamber above it anyway. But according to Kerisel's theories one of the major reasons why this chamber shows minimal signs of cracks would be that its lining is made from the same material as the surrounding core blocks – limestone. The question that immediately springs to mind is, why didn't the subsequent generations of builders learn from this and continue to build chambers in the superstructure, but composed entirely of limestone? The answer is that they did not have the benefit of this analysis. The effort involved in lifting the 50-to-70-tonne granite monoliths that formed the roofs of the King's and Relieving Chambers was of an entirely different order of magnitude from that of lifting the smaller and lighter limestone blocks. This had never been tried before. And, if Kerisel is right, Khufu and his architects caused so much grief for his builders that none of his successors wanted to repeat the performance.

After this step too far, the overwhelming urge to push forward the design barriers probably came to a dramatic halt.

There are important additional implications if this theory is correct. First, those who search ardently for additional chambers in the superstructure of other pyramids are likely to be disappointed. Second, those who search for additional chambers in the superstructure of the Great Pyramid itself are also likely to be disappointed, albeit that the logic for this is less secure.

There is every indication that for a while *size* remained important for Khufu's successors. Khafre built a monument almost equal in size to that of Khufu, although he made sure that only the roof of his upper chamber poked into the superstructure. And Nebka, who Lehner suggests came next in line before Menkaure, seems to have planned a similarly huge edifice at Zawiyet el-Aryan, although this was substantially incomplete due to his short reign. Quite what it was that persuaded Menkaure and all subsequent kings to build considerably smaller pyramids remains a mystery. We can speculate that it was either due to economic factors, changes in religious emphasis, or a combination of the two. Does admitted uncertainty on this point invalidate the pyramids-as-tombs theory? Given the mass of other contextual evidence, we think not.

Security and sealing

A number of features built into the Great Pyramid can be argued to represent security-related mechanisms, including the Subterranean Chamber acting as a 'dummy', plugging blocks being used to seal the Descending as well as the Ascending Passage, and the portcullis system in the King's Antechamber. Furthermore, there is incontrovertible evidence that the Well Shaft is an original feature which was dug from the top down and acted as an escape route for the workers responsible for lowering the granite sealing plugs down from the Grand Gallery. All these issues have been the subject of considerable debate, and the evidence is lengthy and the arguments complex. They are therefore discussed in detail in Appendix III.

When were the lower reaches first breached?

Classical historians provide plenty of circumstantial evidence that the lower reaches of the Great Pyramid had been entered at least by their time, which was long before Mamun. Even if it was not particularly accessible in their day, Herodotus mentions underground chambers, Pliny the 'well', and Strabo – although he appears not to have visited Giza personally – mentions a 'doorway' in the entrance, an issue we consider in detail in Appendix III: 'At a moderate height in one of the sides is a stone, which may be taken out; when that is removed, there is an oblique passage leading to the tomb.'[111]

Only Diodorus's account gives no clue that the interior might have been entered before – strangely mentioning the entrance to the Second but not that to the Great Pyramid, even though he may have actually visited the Plateau.[112]

Although it is possible that these historians were only relating information that had been passed down from the time of the builders, this is unlikely. Also, there is hard evidence that the edifice had been entered before Mamun came to the Plateau, all of which has already been mentioned in passing. First, Mamun reported torch marks on the ceiling of the Subterranean Chamber. Second, Caviglia reported finding Latin characters on the same ceiling. We cannot be sure when these were daubed, but we know the Descending Passage had been blocked for some centuries before he cleared it, so these could well date to Classical times. Third, Mamun reported being able to crawl back up the Descending Passage to the original entrance without undue effort, and, since we have postulated that it too would have been plugged for some distance with sealing blocks, these must have been removed previously.

Although this evidence strongly suggests that the lower reaches of the edifice had been entered in antiquity, possibly shortly after it was constructed and repeatedly thereafter, it does not prove that the upper reaches were breached before Mamun's time. It is only this that could overwhelmingly prove that the main burial chamber was robbed – which would be why Mamun found it empty – thereby providing support for the pyramids-as-tombs theory even in relation to the Great Pyramid. Therefore, this issue will now be considered.

When were the upper reaches first breached?

This is by far the most difficult element of the whole jigsaw of the Plateau to piece together. It requires the analysis of a multitude of different pieces of evidence, several of which conflict. Many researchers from both camps tend to skip over the details, especially those that do not fit their preferred explanation; in truth we were tempted to join them due to the complexity of the analysis that must be undertaken. Nevertheless our aim is to present all the evidence without being selective, even if this makes the arguments more complex and leads to a less definitive conclusion.

The reasons for the complexity are primarily twofold: first, the uniqueness of the layout; second, the lack of verifiable detail in accounts of Mamun's exploits. It is highly likely that Mamun *was* responsible for digging the intrusive tunnel that provided a second entrance into the Pyramid (see Appendix III). However, it is far more complex to judge whether he was also responsible for the tunnel that by-passes the granite plugs at the base of the Ascending Passage. There is another crucial factor that affects our judgement: could the Well Shaft have been used to enter the upper reaches in early antiquity?

Taking these issues in reverse order, the Well Shaft will be examined first. In *The Great Pyramid* (1927), David Davidson (a supporter of the 'encoded-timeline' theories promoted by Menzies, Smyth and Edgar) included a sketch that suggested that the block that had originally sealed the upper entrance to the shaft had been pushed out from below. Others have since relied on this analysis, but they are now in the minority. Apart from the physical improbability of attempting to dislodge a well-cemented and sizeable block from below in a cramped space, a close examination of the chisel marks on the *topside* of the blocks that surround the upper entrance to the shaft reveals that it was *chiselled out from above*.[113] This is a piece of evidence we would love to omit, because it would make this discussion a great deal easier. Many Egyptologists have suggested that the Upper Chambers were plundered in antiquity by robbers who knew about the Well Shaft and used it to gain access into the upper reaches. This is a nice, simple theory which would make perfect sense if it were not for this piece of evidence. However, if the block sealing the Well Shaft was removed from above there can be only two explanations:

- The shaft was originally built in secret as an escape route for the workers, without official sanction. The entrance would have been sealed off, but when the plugging blocks had been released down the Ascending Passage they would have chiselled out the block sealing the shaft and escaped. However, there is no general precedent for the Ancient Egyptian kings deliberately entombing their workers alive along with them. Consequently, we must reluctantly turn to the alternative . . .
- The shaft was discovered only *after* the tunnel that by-passes the granite plugs in the Ascending Passage had been dug. Consequently, whoever dug this tunnel was indeed the first person to enter the upper reaches of the edifice.

We cannot be sure of the accuracy of the accounts of Mamun's exploration. It is therefore *possible* that he did find a body in the King's Chamber, and a lid on the sarcophagus, and various other funerary ancillaries – as suggested by Hokm's account. However, if the pyramids-as-tombs theory is to remain vindicated in the Great Pyramid, we must examine the possibility that Mamun was *not* responsible for digging the by-pass tunnel. There are a number of possibilities that may point to this being the case:

- First, the older accounts of Mamun's explorations are unreliable. Because of this, both his omissions and statements can be used to argue for and against any given point, with little solid justification. However, it is worth postulating that, while most of the accounts talk about his using fire and vinegar to tunnel the intrusive entrance, few of them mention the circumstances of the tunnelling to by-pass the plugs. Is it reasonable to suggest that the circumstances of the 'miraculous' dislodging of the limestone block that concealed the granite plugs – without which piece of fortune Mamun could never have discovered the Ascending Passage *unless it was already by-passed* – were embellishments to make a better story, and have consequently grown to become part of pyramid folklore?
- Second, in Edrisi's first-hand account of entering the pyramid he records having seen what could only be hieroglyphs on the Queen's Chamber ceiling, and Edrisi's accounts are accurate and detailed in

most respects. This is not definitive proof that the chamber had been entered in antiquity, but it certainly adds to the picture.

- Third, a large portion of the corner of the coffer in the King's Chamber has been broken off. It is probable that this occurred as a result of someone trying to prise off the lid – the original existence of which is proved by some rarely mentioned evidence of fittings (see Appendix II) – rather than through the petty efforts of vandals or souvenir hunters. The implication of this is that either Mamun *did* find a lid on the coffer, and almost certainly prised it off himself, or someone else had been in there before him. Again, not definitive proof, but the arguments are building up.

- Fourth, there is rarely mentioned evidence that a 'bridge slab' originally spanned the gap in the floor between the Ascending Passage and the Grand Gallery (this gap occasioned by the horizontal passage leading off to the Queen's Chamber), and also that the portcullises in the King's Antechamber were originally in place (see Appendix III). None of the accounts of Mamun's exploration record his having to demolish these obstacles. Is this simple omission, or had they already been removed?

These points might start to swing the balance in favour of a pre-Mamun by-passing of the plugs. But another, complicating issue exists: what happened to the debris resulting from the digging of the by-pass tunnel? The standard accounts suggest that Mamun explored the Subterranean Chamber first, then turned his attention to by-passing the Ascending Passage, and the rubble from this operation was allowed to fall down the Descending Passage, thereby blocking it until Caviglia cleared it. Reports from Vyse and other contemporaries of Caviglia's work are likely to be more reliable than much of the other evidence currently being considered, so we can assume that the Descending Passage was blocked when he found it. But by what? It is possible that this was primarily the debris from the post-Mamun stripping of the casing stones, combined with the sand that would have blown in and accumulated once the edifice was opened up by him. This in turn allows for the possibility that the debris from the by-pass tunnel was entirely separate, and – although if intruders dug the tunnel they almost certainly *would* have let the debris fall down the Descending Passage – it could have been cleared long before by restorers.

This in turn would have allowed the Subterranean Chamber to be visited by travellers in Classical times.

Before attempting to draw any preliminary conclusions from all this, there is one further piece of evidence that must be reviewed, although once again it raises more questions than it answers.

The Denys of Telmahre affair

Lehner, along with many others, quotes the observations of one Denys of Telmahre, described as a 'Jacobite Patriarch of Antioch'. Denys supposedly accompanied Mamun's party to Giza and, furthermore, recorded that the Great Pyramid was already open.[114] Lehner and co. therefore suggest that Mamun did not dig the intrusive tunnels, he only rediscovered and possibly enlarged them. If this were true and as simple as it sounds, all our worries would be over. Unfortunately these are gross oversimplifications.

Perusal of Vyse's *Operations* reveals what Denys actually recorded. The first is a translation provided by Latif, as follows:[115]

> I have looked through an opening, fifty cubits *deep*, made in *one of those buildings* [the Giza Pyramids], and I found that it was *constructed of wrought stones, disposed in regular layers.*

This extract is backed up by a reproduction by Vyse of Denys's own account.[116] Both clearly indicate that what Denys did was look into *one* of the pyramids on the Plateau, but he doesn't say which one. Furthermore, from his use of the word 'deep' it would appear that he was looking into a passage that went *down*, not *in* horizontally. Finally, his description of 'wrought stones, disposed in regular layers' seems to confirm that he was looking into one of the original descending passages, not into the horizontal and forced entrance in the Great Pyramid. As we maintain our view that the latter was forced by Mamun or a contemporary, logic dictates that the original Descending Passage in the Great Pyramid was concealed at this time. So Denys must have been looking into one of the descending passages in either the Second or the Third Pyramid.

Unless we have picked up entirely the wrong element of Denys's account, this tells us nothing whatsoever about the state of the Great Pyramid at the time of Denys's visit, and – even if it is true that he accompanied Mamun – of the latter's explorations.[117]

Lehner mentions another account, that of Abu Szalt of Spain, which he suggests is sober and trustworthy. In Lehner's words, 'He tells of Mamun's men uncovering an ascending passage. At its end was a quadrangular chamber containing a sarcophagus.' This in itself does not tell us much, but Lehner then adds what appears to be a direct quote: 'The lid was forced open, but nothing was discovered excepting some bones completely decayed by time.'[118]

At the time of writing we have been unable to check this intriguing account further. In any case, while it may add support to the pyramids-as-tombs theory, as with all other reports of this age it cannot be regarded as definitive proof.

Buried elsewhere?

For those who still believe that Mamun was the first to reach the King's Chamber and found an empty coffer, we present one final alternative, proposed by Noel F Wheeler and others.[119] Their theory is that, for fear of defilers, Khufu was not buried in the Great Pyramid at all, but elsewhere in secret. Provided one accepts the context that it was always *intended* as a funerary edifice, this explanation would still demand that he complete his pyramid, and conduct a false burial therein. This would include the lowering of the portcullises and granite plugs, and the incorporation of the Well Shaft to allow the last workmen to escape. Clearly he was expected to erect a magnificent pyramid, as were all kings at the time, but the best way to preserve the anonymity of his resting place, and ensure his body remained intact to allow his spirit to continue in the afterlife, would be to be buried in an unmarked and deep-shaft tomb.

If he did execute this plan, it would have two likely preconditions. First, it would have to be kept secret – only one or two of his most trusted advisers would have been informed. Second, given the unparalleled complexity of the interior of his pyramid, he would almost certainly have chosen this path only once the

Great Pyramid's construction was either well under way or even nearing completion.

What could have led Khufu to this drastic course of action? It is possible that the original tomb of Hetepheres – his father's wife if not his mother – had been ransacked, possibly at Dashur (for more on Hetepheres' reburial, see Appendix II). If this were the case, he would almost certainly have ordered her reburial in a deep unmarked shaft next to his pyramid. Was this what forced him to change his mind, if indeed he did?

Wheeler goes further with his analysis, arguing that a number of factors point to the entire edifice being completed with a minimum of detail, and with some elements left incomplete. He singles out:[120]

- The unfinished state of the Queen's Chamber and of the passage leading to it – both of which are valid observations but could be explained by replanning.
- The rough and apparently unfinished state of the exterior of the King's Chamber coffer, which ought to be the focal point of the edifice. This is probably the most valid of his observations.
- Only three sealing plugs were used instead of the full complement of 25. Again, a valid but not conclusive argument.
- The supposed evidence that the three main portcullises were never installed. On this point, he is almost certainly mistaken (see Appendix III).

While we have some sympathy with Wheeler's extended argument, it clearly has some flaws, and we can disagree with this extension without its affecting the validity of his basic 'buried-elsewhere' proposition. There is, however, another piece of evidence that backs up his basic theory. Diodorus makes the following observation:[121]

Although the kings [Chemis/Khufu and Cephres/Khafre] designed these two for their sepulchres, yet it happened that neither of them were there buried. For the people, being incensed at them by the reason of the toil and labour they were put to, and the cruelty and oppression of their kings, threatened to drag their carcasses out of their graves, and pull them by piece-meal, and cast them to the dogs; and therefore both of them upon their beds commanded their servants to bury them in some obscure place.

Diodorus's account is not the best by any means, but this observation is a unique one although it does link in with Herodotus's general comments regarding the unpopularity of both Khufu and Khafre. Could it have some basis in truth? Many Egyptologists also suspect that, for example, Djoser was buried in his 'Southern Tomb' and not underneath his pyramid.

It is possible that these early kings decided to be buried elsewhere. JP Lepre in particular presents a compelling argument that all early kings had two burial edifices, one in the north and one in the south, to represent the duality of their reign over both Upper and Lower Egypt. On this basis he suggests that the reason that so many coffers have been found empty, even when sealed, is that the pyramids in which they were found may have been merely cenotaphs connected with ritual practices. As a corollary he even suggests that, since most of these edifices are in the north, their real tombs may be found much further to the south. He suggests that the old 'twin cities' of Abydos and nearby Thinis (the latter being the ancient capital of Upper Egypt before the unification of the two lands by Menes) may hold a cache of hidden rock tombs or shaft graves of Old Kingdom kings similar to the New Kingdom ones found more or less by accident in the Valley of the Kings as late as the 1920s.[122]

Preliminary conclusion

The 'burial-elsewhere' theory is a perfectly valid alternative regarding the Great Pyramid, and possibly others. However, it requires just as much speculation as the previous interpretations of when the upper reaches of the Great Pyramid were first breached. Both have their merits and neither deserves to be singled out. This is not woolly-minded, merely an acceptance that on a few issues more than one theory has equal validity.

Above all, it is important to detach oneself from the detail, and remember the *context*. We have all the ancillary evidence from the other pyramids; we have the fact that all the pyramids, including the Great Pyramid, were clearly the focal point of *funerary complexes*; we have the fact that the Great Pyramid cannot be removed from the chronology, and, in Appendices II and III we prove that it *was* sealed with plugs and portcullises just like all the others, that its coffer *was* designed to take a lid, and that the Grand Gallery and its slots and grooves, and the Well Shaft, all had specific functions in a funerary edifice. Therefore – even if it is almost impossible to state with any certainty whether or not Mamun was the first person to breach the upper reaches of the edifice – we stand by the theory that the Great Pyramid was primarily designed as a tomb for King Khufu.

The only other aspect of the Great Pyramid that has not been revisited in this analysis is the enigmatic 'air' shafts in the King's and Queen's Chambers. We believe that these almost certainly do have a symbolic rather than a practical function, and will now turn to issues of symbolism, which are not mutually exclusive to the tombs theory. A more detailed examination of the shafts will be undertaken in a later chapter.

Symbolism, Ritual and Initiation

Even if the pyramids were built primarily as tombs, an almost unique phenomenon occurs when we move on to our next topic. Not only most members of the alternative camp but also those of the orthodox persuasion tend to express the opinion that these incredible edifices must have served a higher purpose than the mere *incarceration* of a dead king; and that this higher purpose is related to ritual and symbolism. Although to many in the alternative camp this view is a replacement for the tombs theory, to the orthodox it is a corollary. It is also interesting that in recent years some of the less fanciful members of the alternative community have broadened their horizons to the point where they too accept that these two elements may go hand in hand. For example, Andrew Collins suggests:[123]

> No-one really knows for sure why the Great Pyramid – or its two neighbouring pyramids . . . – was actually built . . . Although it might well have acted as a tomb for its founder, it also probably played a major role as a place of funerary rites and rituals associated with the journey of the soul of the Pharaoh in the afterlife.

This is not so very different from Lehner's suggestion in relation to the King's Chamber shafts that they 'allowed the king's spirit to ascend to the stars',[124] which ties in with his other assertion that the Queen's Chamber niche contained a *ka* statue that acted as the king's spiritual double. Although Hancock and Bauval claim that the three Giza pyramids were never designed to serve primarily as burial places, they do continue to say:[125]

> We do not rule out the possibility that the pharaohs Khufu, Khafre and Menkaure may at one time have been buried within them – although there is no evidence for this – but we are now satisfied that the transcendent effort and skill that went into the construction of these awe-inspiring monuments was motivated by a higher purpose.

The major factor that motivates this type of speculation is the variety of ancient Egyptian texts that have been found inscribed on tomb walls, on stelae and on papyri. These include the *Book of the Dead*, the *Book of What is in the Duat*, the *Book of Gates*, the *Pyramid Texts* and the *Coffin Texts*. Most of these have been found in multiple but clearly related forms, and although they usually date to later dynasties they are clearly versions of older texts. We do not have the space or time in this work to examine these in any detail, but commentaries and discourses thereon can be found in the work of many other authors.[126] However, they all indicate the great importance of symbolism, ritual and initiation in the process of obtaining everlasting life.

Indeed it is suggested that these texts are deliberately incomprehensible to those who are not initiated into their true meaning, and as a result the translations and interpretations that are generally available can make parts of them seem absurd to most of us, while only those with true understanding can appreciate the profound significance of the originals. This view is backed up by the fact that, for example, there are 37 different hieroglyphs all of which are translated as 'Heaven', but which must have at least subtle if not significant differences in meaning were they to be unleashed from the straitjacket of modern religious and cultural beliefs.

Tompkins suggests that this view is corroborated by the secret knowledge perhaps still retained by a few select members of sects such as the Freemasons, Knights Templar and Rosicrucians, many of whom support the general principle of the pyramids being used for initiation into knowledge so powerful that it was, and still is, withheld from the masses. Of course such bodies – shrouded in secrecy as they are despite a number of recent attempts to record their origins and practices – attract much derision, and even those who believe their origins to be genuine often suggest that what was once pure and profound has been degraded over the millennia. But who are we to judge? Meanwhile, the work of theosophers such as Helena Blavatsky at the turn of the twentieth century and other more recent 'channellers' seems to support the concept of the pyramids being used for initiation.[127]

It appears that this initiation process would have worked along the following lines. The initiate, having been brought through many stages of evolution and suffered many trials in order to reach their stage of readiness, would be placed in some kind of trance – perhaps while lying in a coffer – in which it appears they might stay for several days. This trance might have been induced by some form of hypnosis by priests or other adepts, or by the triggering of harmonic properties. In the case of the Great Pyramid and possibly at least the Red Pyramid also, new and as yet unpublished theories about the acoustic properties of their layouts may prove highly persuasive – this subject will be revisited later.

What would have been achieved by this initiation? Perhaps the answer lies in the fact that the Ancient Egyptians believed that their deeds on Earth would determine their fate in the afterlife, indeed would be 'weighed' by the gods immediately after death to determine their fate. Perhaps therefore the 'astral journey' triggered by these mechanisms was in some sense a practice run in which they at least felt they could obtain a preliminary judgement. There may have been much more again to these initiations, which opened up the mind of the subject to the entire nature and reality of the cosmos, maybe including the type of concepts at which our greatest minds of modern times have attempted to chip away, such as the true nature of space and time, and of alternative dimensional realities. Tompkins quotes from the work of William Kingsland on the *Book of the Dead* as follows:[128]

> The ultimate goal of initiation, says Kingsland, was 'the full realization of the essential divine nature of man, the recovery by the individual of the full knowledge and powers of his divine spiritual nature, of that which was his source and origin, but to the consciousness of which he is now dead through the "Fall of Man" into matter and physical life.'

Hancock has more recently coined an interesting expression when he suggests that the pyramids may be compared to 'flight simulators' used by the pharaohs during their lives to practise their journey to the *duat*, and prepare for immortality after death. Although we do not agree with many of the theories expounded by Tompkins, Kingsland, and indeed Hancock, nevertheless we find these observations intriguing.

What is to be made of all this? It is our aim to be open-minded, and if a set of ideas works for us, we will acknowledge this fact. But bringing this discussion back to the practical realities, we have seen that the 'air' shafts remain an enigma for which a symbolic or ritual purpose is probably more persuasive than a practical one. We have also seen that the housing of a *ka* statue is as good an explanation for the Queen's Chamber niche as any other, although it is somewhat watered down if the 'abandonment' theory is correct. However, there are some restrictions that must be placed on this analysis.

To recap, not only were the edifices built primarily as tombs, but they were also clearly subject to considerable security using portcullises and plugs – even in the case of the Great Pyramid. To support his rejection of the pyramids-as-tombs theory, Alford uses the fact that cathedrals and churches were not built primarily as burial sites. This is true, but nor were they originally designed and built with massive blocks of stone sealing their naves and aisles. The presence of such mechanisms would suggest that they were not designed to allow rituals to be conducted on an ongoing basis after the king's death.

All the coffers found in the pyramids were designed to have lids, which may be considered to reaffirm their use for burial and not ritual purposes. Perhaps most telling of all, we know from their unfinished state that in a number of cases the king died *before* his edifice was complete, which would also suggest that they were not designed to be used for rituals and initiations during his life. This is a big problem, particularly for the initiation theories. Of course if the Great Pyramid could be taken out of context, one could argue – as many of the supporters of these theories do – that it was originally designed for ritual, symbolic and initiation purposes, and then reused as a funerary edifice. However, we have seen that it cannot. While the mortuary and other temples that formed part of the funerary complex were undoubtedly the focal points for elaborate rituals both at the time of the king's death and on a daily basis thereafter,[129] the only possibility for the *pyramids themselves* – and perhaps the Great Pyramid in particular – is that they may have come to be used for rituals and initiations long *after* the king's death, for example by restoration priests of later dynasties.

To sum up, despite reservations about initiations and ongoing rituals, we feel that as well as having a burial function the pyramids clearly did have a far deeper symbolic function specifically connected with the king's journey to the afterlife. In this context it is worth mentioning that the original Egyptian word for the Greek name 'pyramid' is *mer*, which *may* be derived from components that translate as 'the Place of Ascension'.[130]

Repositories of Knowledge?

This section will consider a variety of the alternative theories that have been developed over more than a century. All these theories are in some way or another connected to the concept of the pyramids – and the Great Pyramid in particular – being 'repositories' for knowledge. They range from the relatively practical knowledge of geometry to the possibility that the Great Pyramid is the *Book of Revelation* embodied in stone. The next section will look at the possibility of advanced knowledge of astronomy, while the broader concept of buried or hidden records revealing 'Ancient Wisdom' will be covered in a later chapter dealing with the Hall of Records.

Encoded geometric knowledge

We have already indicated that the main objective of Tompkins's *Secrets of the Great Pyramid* is to prove that advanced mathematic and geometric relationships are encoded into the structure and dimensions of the Great Pyramid. These arguments have won almost universal acceptance, even in some parts of the orthodox community, but we will examine whether they stand up to close scrutiny. Similar logic will also be applied to the other pyramids on the Plateau to see how they fare, as *context* must be brought to bear on this issue.

The first assertion is that the relative dimensions of the edifice incorporate the geometric constant *pi*, which defines the relationship of a circle's radius to its circumference and area. Even though most academics through the ages have led us to believe that this constant was discovered by the Greeks, it is now known that the Egyptian *Rhind Papyrus*, dated to *c.* 1700 BC, is the earliest *written* proof that the Egyptians knew about *pi* – and derived an approximate value to two decimal places of 3.16. The suggestion that they may even have known about it long before originated in the work of John Taylor, who as we have already seen wrote *The Great Pyramid: Why Was It Built, and Who Built It?* in 1859. Although the theory was developed by the more infamous Smyth shortly afterwards, it was Taylor who first took Jomard's and Vyse's measurements and concluded that the *pi* relationship could be established in the Great Pyramid's dimensions. In order to understand this the following definitions should be established: 'height' is the vertical height through the centre of the pyramid; 'base' is the length of the base of one side of the pyramid; 'perimeter' is the length around the entire base perimeter of the pyramid, i.e. four times the base; and 'apothem' is the distance down the face from the apex to the centre of the base of one side. The form of this relationship in the pyramid is:

$$pi = \frac{2 \times \text{base}}{\text{height}}$$

The relationship can be, and often is, expressed in a number of forms, all of which give the same result. For example, another alternative is:

$$pi = \frac{\text{perimeter}}{2 \times \text{height}}$$

This analysis has subsequently been extended to suggest that a second important relationship is embodied in the dimensions involving the constant *phi* – often referred to as the 'Golden Section' or 'Golden Mean'.[131] This constant is derived from the following principle: take a line AC and divide it at a point B whereby the length of the whole line (AC) is greater than that of the longer section (AB) in the same proportion as the length of the longer section (AB) is greater than that of the shorter section (BC).

The resulting proportion of each pair of lines is 1.61803 or *phi*. Furthermore, *phi* lies at the heart of the Fibonacci series, in which each new number (n) is the sum of the previous two, as follows: 1, 2, 3, 5, 8, 13, 21, 34, 55, 89 . . ., etc. As the series progresses, the relationship $n \div (n - 1)$ defines *phi* ever more accurately. Tompkins suggests that this proportion formed the basis for the hermetic knowledge underlying many great masterpieces composed during the Renaissance and thereafter – being used especially, for example, by Leonardo da Vinci. Furthermore, it has links with the study of harmonics, and it is often argued that it is the natural proportion that underlies the basic structure of life itself.

With respect to the Great Pyramid, Tompkins and others suggest that Herodotus wrote that he had been informed by the

Egyptian priests that the area of each of its faces was equal to the square of its height. However, what he actually says in the translation we have consulted is, 'Each of its sides, which form a square, is eight plethra long and the pyramid is eight plethra high as well'.[132] This is clearly different. By mathematical reduction (using the unique properties whereby $phi + 1 = phi^2$, and $1 + 1/phi = phi$), this principle can be more simply expressed by the formula:

$$phi = \frac{2 \times \text{apothem}}{\text{base}}$$

The link between these two relationships is no accident. *Any* structure that has the angle of 51 degrees 51 minutes defining the relationship between its height and base obeys *both* of these formulae, and furthermore *only* such an angle produces either result.[133] Consequently, it is something of a distortion to suggest that not only does the Great Pyramid exhibit the *pi* proportion but *also* the *phi* proportion, since the mathematics render this automatic.

We have conducted an investigation of the accuracy of the relationships based on the latest and most up-to-date measurements for the Meidum, Dashur and Giza Pyramids from Lehner.[134] The results can be seen in Figure 12. There are a number of points that should be made in relation to this data:

- The height of the edifices is always somewhat in doubt, due to the missing capstones and upper courses. As a result, two sets of calculations have been made, one using the *quoted* height and the other using the height as *derived* by trigonometry (i.e deriving it from the other more reliable measurements of slope and base).
- The results have been evaluated by calculating the absolute and percentage errors between the derived values of *pi* and *phi* and the actual values to 5 decimal places, i.e. 3.14159 and 1.61803.
- The values for the apothems have again been *derived* by trigonometry.

It is clear from this that the *pi* results for the Great Pyramid are reasonably impressive, the calculations producing 3.143 and

FIGURE 12: CALCULATED VALUES FOR THE *PI* AND *PHI* RELATIONSHIPS IN THE PYRAMIDS

Pyramid	Slope in degrees	Base	Height (Quot'd)	Height (Der'd)	Apothem (Der'd)	*pi* (b/o Quot'd Height)	*pi* (b/o Der'd Height)	*phi* (b/o Der'd Apothem)
Meidum	51.843	144.000	92.000	91.637	116.539	3.130	3.143	1.619
Error (%)						1.378	0.040	0.035
Bent	n/a	188.000	105.000	n/a	n/a	3.581	n/a	n/a
Error (%)						14.038	n/a	n/a
Red	43.367	220.000	105.000	103.902	151.313	4.190	4.235	1.376
Error (%)						33.449	34.797	−14.985
Great	51.867	230.330	146.590	146.701	186.505	3.143	3.140	1.619
Error (%)						0.029	−0.047	0.088
Second	53.167	215.000	143.500	143.526	179.320	2.997	2.996	1.668
Error (%)						−4.618	−4.635	3.094
Third	51.337	103.400	65.000	64.618	82.755	3.182	3.200	1.601
Error (%)						1.272	1.871	−1.073

3.140 based on the quoted and derived heights respectively. The same is true of the *phi* result at 1.619. All of these results produce an error of less than 0.1 of a per cent from the actual values. Although it is a point rarely mentioned, it is also clear that both the *pi* and *phi* results for the pyramid at Meidum are similarly impressive. However, although the Third Pyramid gets within 2 per cent, the results are hopelessly out when applied to the other edifices. Since we maintain that none of the pyramids should be taken out of context, it must be asked why these relationships would be deliberately incorporated into two or three only, and not their counterparts.

Alford has also performed new work on this issue, and has attempted to apply 'Pyramid Geometry' to the two pyramids at Dashur.[135] In brief, he uses another form of the *pi* relationship which incorporates a new constant 'N', as follows:

$$\text{height} = \frac{\text{N} \times \text{base}}{2 \times pi}$$

The results in Figure 12 show that the normal attempts at deriving *pi* and *phi* are hopelessly out for both of the Dashur Pyramids (although since the Bent Pyramid has two slopes we have only calculated a simple *pi* value for this using the base and the quoted height). While Alford only *rearranges* the formula we used previously, he argues that, whereas the value of the new constant N for the Great Pyramid is exactly 4, its value for the upper section of the Bent Pyramid and for the Red Pyramid is in both cases 3, while the overall value for the Bent Pyramid is 3.5. He then makes great play of the 'significance' of the numbers 3 and 4. All his calculations are quite correct using the data supplied above. However, he does not mention that this revised approach does not work out well for the other two Giza Pyramids, since values of 4.19 and 3.95 were established for N for the Second and Third Pyramids respectively.

Furthermore it must be appreciated how he has achieved these 'amazing results'. Yet another constant has been inserted into an equation that already has two – the value '2' and *pi*. Under normal circumstances in mathematics, one tries to eliminate all unnecessary constants and work with as simple a formula as possible. If his formula is rearranged by merging the constants N and '2', his values for N are effectively halved, deriving the constants 2, 1.75 and 1.5 for the three edifices in question. These are still interesting, as with so much of Alford's analysis, but his arguments do seem somewhat contrived.

This view is reinforced when, although Alford does not admit to the lack of significant values for N produced by the other Giza Pyramids, he points out that the sine and cosine values produced by the angle of the Second Pyramid are exactly 0.8 and 0.6 respectively, again 'highly significant' numbers, as is their total 1.4, etc, etc. If all the numbers regarded as 'significant' by Tompkins, Alford et al. were listed, we would probably have every integer between 0 and 9, and a whole array of other non-whole numbers in between. We are aware that the interplay between and symbolism of, for example, harmonics and geometry is something that has exercised a profound influence on great minds in all civilisations ancient and modern, but this hand is repeatedly and monotonously overplayed. As a result, one ends up feeling that you can produce any result you want provided you play with the numbers for long enough. Even more examples of this will be seen shortly.

In summary, the issue of encoded geometry must be one on which we remain open-minded. But, even if one considers that these relationships are incorporated into the dimensions of the Great Pyramid and one or two others, this factor must be viewed in light of the fact that the remainder do not incorporate them, and that the primary function of all the monuments was a funerary one – albeit interwoven with much symbolism and ritual. While the two propositions are by no means mutually exclusive in our view, undue concentration on the issue of encoded geometry alone, and in respect of the Great Pyramid alone, tends to be misleading. By the same token, even if we were to disagree with the encoded-geometry theory, it would not automatically imply that we reject the possibility that the Ancient Egyptians, Mesopotamians and others may still have had advanced geometric knowledge.

Encoded geodesic knowledge

It is difficult to be as open-minded about some of the other theories presented by Tompkins, the prime one of which suggests that the Great Pyramid's dimensions also incorporate knowledge of the circumference of the Earth ('geodesy' is the study of the Earth's dimensions). Whereas with encoded geometry we were dealing entirely with *relationships* that stand irrespective of the units of measure used by the Ancient Egyptians, and of absolute measurements for the edifice, this theory is entirely dependent on making assumptions about both. This renders the analysis far more open to debate.

The theory rests on two principles. First, modern units of measure (feet, metres, etc.) must be accurately converted into archaic units such as the cubit and longer stadia – of which a variety existed in Ancient and Classical times – with sufficient corroborative proof from texts and ancient buildings that the conversion ratios have not been 'doctored' to fit the proposition. Second, using these conversion ratios it is necessary to accurately measure the Pyramid's dimensions – base, height and apothem – and prove that predominantly whole numbers were used both in the layout of the edifice and when extrapolating these dimensions into geodesic measurements. Linking these principles are various suggestions from Classical historians, for example that a stadium represented 1/600 of a geographical degree.

Tompkins incorrectly attributes the origins of this theory to Greaves – who was in fact interested only in establishing the ancient units of measure themselves. It was Jomard who started the ball rolling, but again Taylor and Smyth and various others picked up on the theory and attempted to verify it. Early on it was suggested that a modern British inch increased by a one-thousandth part produced a figure for the polar axis of the Earth of five hundred million such inches; Newton's sacred cubit of 25 of these inches would then give a polar axis of 20 million cubits, and a polar radius of 10 million cubits. The theory went somewhat off track when Taylor supposedly found these units in the dimensions of the Great Pyramid in multiples of approximately 366, theorising that the edifice also incorporated accurate knowledge of the real length of the year. Smyth tried to bring it back into line but was still juggling with inaccurate measurements, and when Petrie established a base length for the edifice that was some 70 inches shorter than Smyth's, the theory was forced into hibernation.

Undaunted, Tompkins suggests that the issue was resolved by JH Cole's accurate survey figures of 1925.[136] He switches to using metres and Jomard's 'Geographical' cubits of 0.462 of a metre (or 18.2 British inches), and concentrates on the latter's discovery that Classical sources had suggested the Great Pyramid had a base of 500 cubits and an apothem of 400 cubits. However, even these figures do not tie up correctly: they give a base of 498.6 cubits, an error of 0.3 per cent, and an apothem of 403.75 cubits, an error of 0.9 per cent. On the basis of these units he then suggests that the base represents $\frac{1}{8}$ of a minute of longitude – giving a circumference of the Earth of 39,790 kilometres – and the apothem $\frac{1}{10}$ of a minute of longitude – giving a circumference of the Earth of 40,274 kilometres. Comparison of these with modern estimates of 40,000 kilometres reveals errors of 0.5 and 0.7 per cent respectively. Despite the fact that these are arguably significant percentage errors, it is clear that – because of the huge multiples used in these calculations – a deliberate manipulation of the second or third decimal place in the base units can effectively be used to produce the desired result.

Smyth and others have also suggested that the positioning of the Great Pyramid very close to the 30th parallel (the line of latitude) is deliberate, and that it acted as a geodesic landmark. This added support to the theory that the Ancient Egyptians had an advanced knowledge of geodesy. Although its true latitude is 29 degrees 58 minutes, 51 seconds, about one mile to the south, it is argued that this difference is either down to errors in observation arising from atmospheric refraction, or the mere practicality of the fact that the area immediately to the north of the Plateau is extremely sandy and unsuitable for the erection of such a huge edifice. That the Great Pyramid is in this location is clearly not in dispute. But the suggestion that this positioning is deliberate once again ignores the *context* of the other pyramids, and really holds water only if the Great Pyramid is taken out of the orthodox chronology. As will be

seen later, there are a great ͏
of the Giza Plateau, and inde͏

Smyth also tried to prove that t͏
incorporate the imputed orbital rad͏
sun.[137] He took the edifice's height in i͏
– and, based on the supposed fact that it͏
10:9, he multiplied this figure by 10⁹. This ͏
produced a figure of 91.84 million miles – whi͏
mates vary between 91 and 92 million. To show how ͏
the figures used by Smyth and his contemporaries w͏
current measurement of the height in inches is 5,770, whi͏
slope has a ratio of 1.27:1 as opposed to his 1.11:1 (i.e. 10͏
9). This is a fine example of the sort of rubbish that can be
generated when a highly imaginative mind juggles with endless
permutations of figures (which may be inaccurate anyway) until
they appear to produce an astounding result.

Other madcap theories have accompanied these better-known
ones. It has been suggested that the King's Chamber coffer not
only acted as a record of ancient Egyptian units of measure, but
that its dimensions reflect incredible astronomical knowledge of
the relative masses and orbits of the planets in the solar system.

These often wildly inaccurate manipulations of data can only
denigrate the study of the pyramids. Plus, these theories clearly
do not apply to any of the other pyramids, so that *context* is
once again completely ignored.

Prophecies and predictions
We have already seen that, prompted by the work of Robert
Menzies and then Smyth himself, a variety of 'pyramidiots',
including David Davidson and Morton Edgar, have attempted
to interpret the interior layout of the Great Pyramid's passageways and chambers as a timeline for biblical prophecies and
predictions.[138]

Although this theory was discredited for many years, it has
been resurrected by Peter Lemesurier in his *The Great Pyramid
Decoded*, first published in 1977. His work is incredibly
detailed, but sadly the imagination is far better than the actual
theory.

WERE THE PYRAMIDS BUILT?

a that the Great
observatory is the
ices to the cardinal
nly 5 minutes 30
it), and the average
r cent). There is no
servation of circum-
precision, and that a
hrough. However, the
ificant to the Ancient
ation that *all* the other
iat the accuracy clearly
Given the similarity of
0 degrees (see Appendix
nding passages in all the
sighting channels which
nitial above-ground sight-

many other theories about the layout
of other pyramid sites.
the Great Pyramid's dimensions
ches of the Earth around the
ches – supposedly 5819
slope has the ratio
piece of juggling
current esti-
inaccurate
our
the

pyramids wo
either increased the pro
ings or ensured that the passages themselves retained their
incredible straightness, or both.

To illustrate this point, taking the Great Pyramid as our
example, the angle of 26 degrees 31 minutes of the Descending
Passage would point directly at a circumpolar star at 3 degrees
29 minutes from the pole at the 30th parallel. In attempting to
ascertain the likelihood that Alpha Draconis was the polar star
used (due to the effects of the precession of the equinoxes
different stars orbit the celestial pole in different epochs), the
great archaeo-astronomer Sir John Herschel, a contemporary
of Vyse, illustrated that, at 63 feet down, the size of the passage
would mean that the entrance allowed an arc covering a total
of 7 degrees 7 minutes to be visible – or 3 degrees 33 minutes
either side of the centre point.[139] Although his data for the date
of the edifice was inaccurate, we now know that this arc would
include the position of Alpha Draconis in the pyramid-building
epoch.

This analysis means that it is now universally accepted that
the Ancient Egyptians had a relatively advanced level of astronomical knowledge; at the very least, they clearly knew that the
Earth was round and rotated on its axis. That this knowledge

was widespread in the Ancient World is indicated by the similarity of the passages and often corbelled roofs of the multiple burial mounds found all over Europe – for example at Newgrange in Ireland and Maes-Howe in the Orkneys – although most of these appear to be aligned to the sun at the solstices. Additional study by the growing body of archaeoastronomers of, for example, the multitude of Mayan and other temples in South America, of Mesopotamian ziggurats in the Near East, and of temples and pyramids dotted all over Indo-China, has added widespread evidence of this global knowledge.

1894 saw the publication of a book entitled *The Dawn of Astronomy* by Sir Norman Lockyer. At the time, Lockyer's work was vilified, but it is now regarded as being years ahead of its time. He argued that many Egyptian temples – for example those at Luxor, Edfu and Karnak – were aligned with the sun at the solstices or equinoxes to produce highly accurate calendars. These were more favourable than star calendars because precession had less effect, making them accurate over a longer period. Where temple edifices had been oriented towards stars, he suggested that there was ample evidence that they had been continually updated with newly aligned buildings and corridors which maintained their orientation by allowing for the effects of precession. In recent decades this work has been rediscovered and expanded upon by great minds like those of Rene Schwaller de Lubicz and Giorgio de Santillana.[140]

But what does all this mean for the pyramids themselves? Moses B Cotsworth, sadly supported by Lockyer, suggested that the development of the Third- and Fourth-Dynasty pyramids can be explained as refinements to a sundial system which was fully refined by the size of the Great Pyramid. They attributed similar purposes to British structures such as Silbury Hill, on which they argued a maypole would be raised for accurate measurement of shadows. This may be true for the latter, but the intricate interiors of the former render this highly unlikely.

Alternatively, could the Grand Gallery have been designed as a stellar observatory? This theory was put forward in 1883 by the British astronomer Richard Proctor in *The Great Pyramid, Observatory, Tomb, and Temple* – based on ideas he came across in the writings of the Roman neo-Platonic philosopher

Proclus in his commentary on Plato's *Timaeus*.[141] Proctor suggested that at least the upper end of the gallery (the south wall), could have been left open to the skies. He claimed that the roofing slabs of the gallery do not bear directly on each other, so that they could have been removed to reveal more of the sky, and that the regularly spaced niches in the side ramps were there to support observation benches. He then goes on to speculate that the core masonry changes at the 35th course (about the level of the roof of the Queen's Chamber) indicate that the Grand Gallery was originally left standing proud on a flat platform – making it similar to other ancient structures that are undoubtedly observatories found in, for example, India.[142] He continues by saying that, once the true transits of meridian stars had been established as a reference point, additional observers on the flat platform would have been able to map the movement of all the other stars visible in the northern hemisphere, while the combination of gallery and platform would have allowed the sun and planets to be mapped as well. Finally he suggests that the accuracy of the measurements would have allowed the Ancient Egyptians to deduce the rate of precession without extremely long observational timeframes. As to why the pyramid was then completed as a true pyramid, supporters of this theory argue that it was reused as a burial edifice long after it had served its original purpose. All we can say is, great set of ideas – shame about the lack of understanding of context and chronology.

There are in addition a number of more modern theories regarding the layout of the Giza Pyramids which suggest their astronomical alignment, most notably with the three belt stars of Orion. However, these will be considered in a later chapter.

Millennium Madness?

Partly for completeness, and partly for sheer entertainment, what follows is a brief review of the other more far-fetched theories regarding the purpose of the Great Pyramid that have tended to proliferate in the approach to the millennium. Many of these are clearly ludicrous when placed in the context of the other pyramids, since – apart from any other flaws – they rely entirely on taking the Great Pyramid out of the accepted chronology and dating it much earlier.

Spaceman
Although writing some twenty years before the millennium, Zecharia Sitchin set the tone in stunning fashion when, in *The Stairway to Heaven*, he suggested that not only the Great Pyramid but possibly also its two Giza counterparts were built by the Anunnaki as guidance beacons for their visiting space-craft.[143] To be fair to Sitchin this amazing piece of analysis is followed up by a reasonably in-depth review of the various Old Kingdom pyramids, which shows that he had made an effort to research the context of the subject a little. However, since this is all distorted in order to take the Giza pyramids out of their context, it counts for little.

Nevertheless, his imagination made a dramatic return to form five years later when, in *The Wars of Gods and Men*, Sitchin turned his attention to the interior of the edifice.[144] He describes one of the Anunnaki gods inspecting its contents, and finding the various crystals and other energy-emitting devices located in the Queen's Chamber niche, the Grand Gallery recesses, and – of course – the central 'guidance unit' residing in the King's Chamber coffer. This is all reported in the context of 'pyramid wars', which supposedly took place some time in the ninth millennium BC and resulted in these objects being smashed or carried off. All this dramatic information was derived by 'following and correctly interpreting' the ancient Mesopotamian text *Lugal-e*. There is more, but for all our sakes it is best that we stop here.

Energy generator (1)
We have already seen that in his first book, *Gods of the New Millennium*, Alan Alford tended to use Sitchin's basic work and then elaborate on it. In respect of the purpose of the Great Pyramid he did this in some style, suggesting that it was not only a guidance beacon but also a giant 'water fuel cell'.[145] His ingenuity in matching the various features of the edifice to the various components that would be required is, as always, impeccable. It is, however, sadly flawed. Fortunately, Alford has

now seen the error of his ways, at least in respect of this issue, and, while he still refuses to accept the orthodox chronology or the tombs theory, his views on the function of the Great Pyramid are now more securely grounded in reality.

Energy generator (2)

Another researcher whose initial work we admired is the British engineer Chris Dunn. Over the last few years he has done a great deal to fuel the important debate about the techniques used to machine some of the amazing artefacts found at predynastic and Old Kingdom sites, and also some of the advanced engineering aspects of the Great Pyramid. These topics will be returned to later. However, we are sad to report that even he appears to have fallen prey to 'millennium fever', since his recently published book *The Giza Power Plant* follows similar lines of thought. Dunn argues that the unique acoustic properties of the edifice indicate it was designed as a form of 'Tesla-style' energy-generation device, which used harmonics to harness the Earth's natural vibrational energies and convert them into microwave radiation. This is an ingenious piece of research, but his insistence that such properties were used for energy generation is, as ever, fundamentally flawed by its failure to consider *context*.

This is just a selection of the theories put forward recently by some of the better-known names in the field of 'alternative Egyptology'. There are many, many more, but they all suffer from the same fundamental problems. We will therefore leave them to rest in peace, and move on.

Conclusion

To sum up, we firmly believe that *all* the Egyptian pyramids were built *primarily* as funerary edifices. That is not to denigrate their extraordinary beauty and incredible execution, nowhere better illustrated than in the Great Pyramid itself. But despite its unique interior, despite the fact that Khufu may not have been buried therein, despite its enigmatic 'air shafts' – which almost certainly have a symbolic rather than functional purpose – and despite the fact that it does appear to incorporate geometric relationships into its proportions, even this amazing edifice cannot escape from its roots in the orthodox chronology of pyramid progression, placing it firmly in the same category and context.

FOUR

How Were the Pyramids Built?

How often have we heard the cry, 'Modern technology has remained completely unable to explain the methods by which the pyramids were constructed!'? This clamour comes particularly from those who have spent minimal time examining the real evidence and reasoning put forward by the orthodox camp. Although all Egyptologists have their various pet theories – especially about the methods by which such a huge quantity of masonry was erected – in many respects their archaeological approach has yielded sound and perfectly feasible theories. Once again, using the work of Lehner, Edwards and this time to a lesser extent Lepre, the evidence as to how the stone was quarried, transported, worked, raised and finished will be reviewed.[146]

The orthodox view of the construction of the pyramids will be looked at under four headings: preparation, erection, completion and logistics. To simplify the general analysis the special considerations of the huge granite monoliths that have been raised to a considerable height in the interior of the Great Pyramid will be left aside during this initial discussion, and examined in a separate section. Finally, the main elements of the alternative theories that may be required to bolster the orthodoxy will be reviewed.

Preparation

Quarrying

The limestone that forms the bulk of the stone in all the Third- and Fourth-Dynasty pyramids was quarried in three main locations. At Giza there was a plentiful supply of nummulitic limestone, which contains small fossilised shells (nummulites) from which its name derives. It is of relatively poor quality, but is perfectly suited for the inner-core blocks which form the bulk of the edifices, and which do not require accurate or attractive finishing. It was quarried from the natural cliff that ran along an approximate northeast to southwest diagonal on the eastern edge of the Plateau, and evidence suggests that the quarrying was begun by Khufu's men directly to the south of the Great Pyramid – in fact to the south of and about halfway along what is now the causeway to the Second Pyramid. Subsequent development by Khafre and Menkaure extended these quarries, although a substantial amount of core material for the Second Pyramid came from the levelling of its own enclosure to the north and south.

Additional core material, particularly for the other pyramid sites, came from the Mokattam Hills about twenty miles to the east of Giza, across the Nile. That the Giza Plateau had its own source for the bulk of the material made the erection of the edifices there a far simpler task, as transportation effort was considerably reduced. The casing stones, however, needed to be of higher quality to achieve durability and an attractive finish, and the pure white limestone for this task came from quarries at Turah and Maura, which lay to the south of the Mokattam Hills opposite Memphis.

The opencast quarries at Giza allowed the workers to excavate the sides of the blocks using copper chisels, examples of which can be examined in, for example, the Cairo Museum and the Petrie Museum in London. Edwards even suggests, in our view sensibly, that they may have used copper axes or picks to facilitate their task – although he admits that no examples have yet been found. Since limestone is relatively soft, the proposed use of copper tools presents no particular problems. Meanwhile, in the quarries at, for example, Turah, where the high-quality strata lay underground, the quarrymen were faced with the additional difficulty of excavating an initial tunnel across the top of the blocks.

To dislodge the blocks from the ground, it is normally proposed that they chiselled out recesses around the base into which wooden wedges could be hammered which, when soaked with water, would expand to crack the block along its base so it could be prised away from the underlying material. Lehner disagrees with this analysis, suggesting that the width of the channels found to have existed in the quarries at Giza shows that the blocks were prised up with wooden levers. Neither of these methods would have presented too many problems, and both could have been used at different times or in different places.

The core blocks, which didn't require much finishing, would probably have been squared off to the required degree at the quarry, again primarily using copper chisels. The casing blocks could have been part-finished at the quarry, but undoubtedly received final finishing – especially of the front face – *in situ*. The wood and stone tools required for squaring were essentially the same as are used today – the set square, the horizontal plumb line, and the vertical plumb line – and examples of all of these have been found.[147] The more complex shaping work was performed using copper drills and saws.

Transportation

Stone that had to be transported from across the Nile almost certainly came by barge. Although it has been suggested that the Ancient Egyptians were sufficiently skilled architects and engineers to have built a bridge, this could have been useful only when the Nile was *not* in full flood. Since it was only during the three-month period when it *was* in full flood that the bulk of the agricultural workforce was available to assist with the nonskilled transportation work, this is an unlikely solution. That *limestone* blocks that averaged something like 2.5 tonnes in weight should have been transported by barge is not an unreasonable assumption.

When the annual Nile floods occurred the waters came quite close to the Plateau and to other pyramid sites. From the knowledge that a huge and possibly artificially created lake exists near Dashur, Lehner has postulated that a similar lake with an extended canal system may have been developed at Giza, which would fit in with the positioning of at least the Second and Third Pyramids' valley temples, which are relatively close to the main edifices. Such efforts would have reduced the extent to which stone had to be transported overground.

Be that as it may, how was the stone moved overground on

the quarry side where necessary, and especially at the pyramid site itself? There is ample archaeological evidence that this was achieved by roping the blocks to a sledge. Roadways were constructed into which reinforcing wooden planks were inserted. With this stable base, and the assistance of water or other lubricating fluids being consistently applied to the front of the sledge's runners, experiments have proved that a relatively small number of men are required to haul heavy loads. Most estimates suggest that a third of a tonne per man is a reasonable hauling average using this method – at least on the flat – which translates into seven or eight men for a 2.5 tonne block.

This analysis is substantially reinforced by a relief from the Twelfth-Dynasty tomb of a nobleman called Djehutihotep at el-Bersheh, which depicts 172 men in 4 ranks dragging a colossal statue estimated from its scale to weigh something like 60 tonnes (see Figure 13). It also clearly shows a man on the statue clapping his hands to keep the rhythm, while another pours

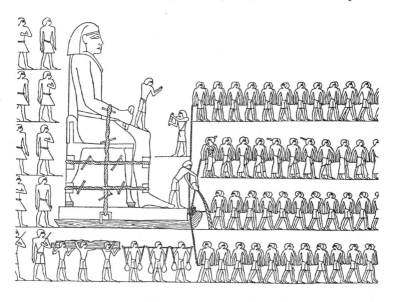

FIGURE 13: TWELFTH DYNASTY RELIEF SHOWING A STATUE
BEING TRANSPORTED ON A SLEDGE[148]

lubricating fluid under the front of the sledge.[149] In addition, Lepre reveals that a number of hieroglyphs indicate that the sledge was the method used,[150] while Lehner notes that the remains of a transport road have been excavated at Lisht, which was up to 36 feet across and consisted of a 'fill of limestone chips and mortar with wooden beams inserted'.

It has been suggested that oxen may have been used to assist the hauling process. However, there are no depictions of this, and, since Ancient Egypt was not overendowed with cattle, those that were kept were more likely used for agricultural purposes. Some alternative theorists have suggested that it is ridiculous to suppose that a culture that was sufficiently advanced in astronomy and construction to build and align the Great Pyramid with such incredible accuracy should not have already invented the wheel. This may be a fair suggestion, but no evidence to support it has been found, and it is also clear from reliefs and hieroglyphs that, even if they did have the wheel, this was not the preferred method of transporting heavy loads.

Another orthodox theory put forward is that wooden circle quadrants were attached to four sides of the blocks to effectively turn them into 'wheels' which could be rolled (see Figure 14). This view is often castigated on the basis that the quadrants found have not contained holes to attach them to the blocks. However, a recent study performed by an engineer, Dr Dick Parry of Cambridge University, has revealed that at least one of these quadrants dating to the New Kingdom was not solid but composed of two flat quadrants joined by a series of wooden bars, around which ropes could have been coiled to secure the quadrants to the block and also assist hauling. Furthermore the bars would act as an ideal support against which chocks could be wedged while the hauliers were resting especially on inclined slopes.

On this basis Parry conducted a small-scale experiment to examine the reduced-friction efficiency of this method when compared with a lubricated sledge, and his results were then confirmed in a full-scale experiment conducted by the Obayashi Corporation in Japan: they established that a 2.5-tonne weight could be pushed along on the flat by two or three men at a 'fast

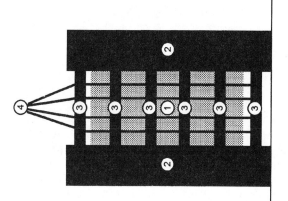

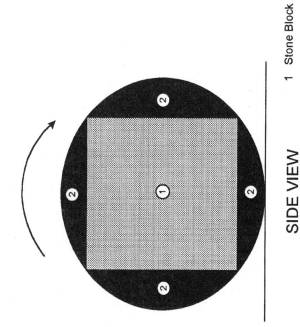

FRONT VIEW

SIDE VIEW

1 Stone Block
2 Wooden Quadrants
3 Wooden Bars
4 Binding & Hauling Ropes

FIGURE 14: A SCHEMATIC DIAGRAM OF THE USE OF WOODEN QUADRANTS TO HAUL BLOCKS

walking pace'.[151] This is an impressive result, and it is possible that this method was used on occasion. However, the lack of uniformity in the dimensions of the core blocks, let alone the more awkwardly shaped casing blocks, would in our view render the use of such cradles unlikely for widespread application. Furthermore, the reliefs and hieroglyphic evidence suggest that the sledge was the preferred method.

As far as Giza is concerned, the bulk of the transportation effort would have involved hauling the core blocks over the relatively short distance between the quarries and the pyramids themselves. Stones brought in from elsewhere were probably pulled up the foundations of the causeways from the 'harbour' – these causeways only subsequently being completed for the funeral procession. However, since the likely route of any blocks once near the pyramid itself relies entirely on our assumptions about how they were raised into place, further discussion of the detailed route will be left until later.

Surveying[152]

The alternative camp make a great fuss about the accurate alignment of the Great Pyramid to the cardinal points, but this presents no real problems in terms of technology – at least not in a theoretical sense.

It is known that the Ancient Egyptians possessed a variety of instruments for observing the stars. These included the 'astrolabe' – a triangular block with a rotating bar which is the precursor of the sextant, the 'bay' – a wooden stick with a small 'v' cut out at the top, and the *merkhet* – a type of plumb line. First they would have provided themselves with a 'false horizon'. This would probably have consisted of a temporary wall, built on a levelled platform at the heart of the intended site, just high enough to obscure any natural or man-made features. It would have been accurately levelled by plumb line, and oriented roughly east–west by simple observation of a pole star. They would then have set up an observation point at a reasonable distance from the wall, used their instruments to accurately mark off the rising (i.e. east) and setting (i.e. west) points of a pole star on the wall, dropped the lines down accurately to the base, and drawn a line bisecting the angle between the observation point and the two sighting marks. As long as the observation point was at a reasonable distance, this would have provided a true north–south line, which could be accurately extrapolated and used as the initial datum.

That the practice of carrying such observations through into the construction of the edifice was no mean feat is demonstrated by the lesser accuracy of the alignment of some of the other edifices. For example, while the Great Pyramid's sides have an average deviation of only 3 minutes 06 seconds, the figures for the others are as follows: Second Pyramid – 5 minutes 26 seconds; Bent Pyramid – 9 minutes 12 seconds; Third Pyramid – 14 minutes 3 seconds; and Meidum Pyramid – 24 minutes 25 seconds. Nevertheless, even this worst figure represents an error of only 0.1 per cent.

Levelling

All the platforms for the pyramids were levelled with great accuracy, again nowhere more than at the Great Pyramid, which has less than 1 inch of variation from dead level over its entire base – an error of less than 0.01 per cent. It is commonly suggested that this was achieved by digging a network of shallow trenches and filling them with water. However, the presence of the considerable mound of bedrock that was left protruding in the centre of this edifice precludes this solution. A single continuous trench around the perimeter of the edifice would overcome this objection, a solution backed up by Lepre's assertion that such a trench has been found on the north side of the Second Pyramid.

Lengths of flax-fibre or palm-fibre cord, in conjunction with more hardy and accurate measuring rods, would then have been used for levelling right across the site, and further up as the edifice progressed. Nevertheless, even the largest deviation in the sides of the Great Pyramid is only 7.9 inches, or 0.09 per cent, – a great credit to the surveyors, particularly because the diagonals could not be checked properly because of the central mound.

Erection

Although in general the blocks tend to be smaller in the pre-Giza pyramids, to a large extent the same construction methods must have been used, with variations and refinements, in all the early pyramids. For example, they all have larger blocks on the lower courses. However, this does not mean that the methods used to *raise* the blocks into place were always the same – indeed a different approach would almost certainly have been employed in the stepped pyramids, which had ready-made platforms. A variety of methods have been put forward, and can be simplified into the following categories: simple levers, leverage machines, straight ramps and spiral ramps. These will be looked at in turn, but first we will take time out to review the most recently conducted experiment in recreating a pyramid.

The NOVA Experiment[153]

In the mid-1990s, Lehner teamed up with stonemason Mark Hopkins and, with the help of a team of Egyptian quarrymen, masons and labourers, attempted to build a small-scale replica pyramid on the Plateau. Owing to tight deadlines imposed by the sponsors of the project – the NOVA television company – they were allowed three weeks to perform the quarrying, and a further three weeks to construct the replica. They used a total of 44 men, and quarried and laid 186 blocks ranging from about 1 tonne to 2.5 tonnes in weight, producing a pyramid 20 feet high and with a base of 30 feet per side.

They proved that it was possible to quarry and manoeuvre stones of the average size of the blocks used in the pyramids using techniques that would have been available to the Ancient Egyptians. For example, they built a short inclined roadway-cum-ramp of the type described above, and found that, while the use of wooden rollers proved a time-consuming and inefficient method of sliding the blocks, the use of a lubricated wooden sled did allow a team of ten men to haul a 2-tonne block up the gentle slope with relative ease.[154]

Simple levers were predominantly used in conjunction with the ramp to raise the stones. This was found to be a dangerous and precarious exercise, with limited space proving a real problem even as low as at the second course on such a small-scale model. Not only did levers need to be applied to both sides of the blocks, but they found that they needed to carve slots in the bases of the blocks to receive them and avoid side slip; such slots are not regularly found on the core blocks of the pyramids. As the blocks were chocked higher and higher, even with planed support planks, the whole ensemble became highly unstable. They therefore concluded that ramps must have been used all the way up on the originals.

As soon as this programme was aired the alternative camp had a field day. Rumours were soon flying that the team had cheated and used iron tools, and worse still that they had employed a dumper truck to transport and position many of the blocks. This criticism seemed to validate all their arguments about Egyptologists manipulating the facts to suit their purposes, and we have to admit that we too got caught up in the initial scepticism. However, in Lehner's own account of the project in *The Complete Pyramids*, he readily admits to this 'cheating'. Both aspects of assistance were clearly employed to save time in the tight schedule – the iron tools being quicker but not in any way invalidating the use of copper tools on limestone, while, in addition to transporting some of the blocks, the dumper could be used to assist their erection and positioning only on the lower courses, which are not the major problem area anyway. The NOVA team can perhaps be criticised for not making this assistance clear in the television programme itself.

Simple levers
Although the use of simple levers would require no infrastructural investment, it is clear from the experience of the NOVA Experiment that this could not have been the sole method employed in raising the pyramid blocks. However, levers may have been used for final positioning, as will be seen below.

Leverage machines
The method that requires the next least infrastructural investment is the use of leverage 'machines'. This is exactly the method that Herodotus describes as being reported to him by the Egyptian priests:[155]

[125] The pyramid was built up like a flight of stairs (others use the image of staggered battlements or altar steps). When that first stage of the construction process was over, they used appliances made out of short pieces of wood to lift the remaining blocks of stone up the sides. First they would raise a block of stone from the ground on to the first tier, and when the stone had been raised up to that point, it was put on to a different device which was positioned on the first level, and from there it was hauled up to the second level on another device. Either there were the same number of devices as there were tiers, or alternatively, if the device was a single manageable unit, they transferred the same one from level to level once they had removed the stone from it. I have mentioned two alternative methods, because that is exactly how the information was given to me. Anyway, they finished off the topmost parts of the pyramid first, then the ones just under it, and ended with the ground levels and the lowest ones.

Initially, this appears reasonable, although arguably only the multiple arrangement – one machine on each course on each face – would provide any semblance of speed and efficiency.

Lepre favours this method, especially for the higher courses, and has designed a model of a 'double-fulcrum counterweight' system. This utilises the leverage from smaller counterweights placed further from the main fulcrum than the block to be raised, and also a complex double-counterweight to lower the arms back into place after the block has been removed.[156] It would require minimal manual effort, and could be fabricated from wood, rope and stone alone. Although the scale to which his model was designed is unclear, it would appear that it could be too large to fit on the casing ledges alone, especially as they became narrower with the smaller courses higher up. Consequently, a number of core blocks behind the casing gap would also have to be omitted in order to make the requisite space. It is feasible that all the casing could be left off to allow these machines to operate, but this would be a less efficient method overall. It is therefore possible that perhaps one 'staircase' or 'gap' would be left on each side, on which the machines would be arranged on each course. At the end, the gaps would be filled in from the top down.

Lepre's machine would appear to work were it not for one

important fact: it is clearly designed to sit on the upper level, and to lift the blocks upward and inward from the level below. This would make it impossible for the final core and casing blocks to be laid from the top down in the space already occupied by the machine. That is not to say that a redesign might not overcome this problem. Indeed another researcher, Jason Baldridge, having criticised the physics of Lepre's design, has devised a far simpler solution which relies on wooden poles and stone fulcrum blocks to *swivel* the blocks upward and inward (see Figure 15).[157] On the face of it there is no reason why his solution – which relies on the simple addition of weight into a basket at the longer end of the pole until it balances the weight of the block – should not overcome this problem, while at the same time representing a far simpler solution. Like Lepre he suggests that the heavier and larger blocks in the first five or six courses would have been raised by a ramp, after which a 20-foot-wide gap would be left in the side (in fact he suggests that a one-block-wide row would extend outwards to create the required platform, which would then presumably be pared down to form the casing).

Such machines might well have been used on both the stepped and true pyramids, especially on the higher courses. However, there are potential problems with this method regarding the heavier blocks of the Great Pyramid, as will be seen later.

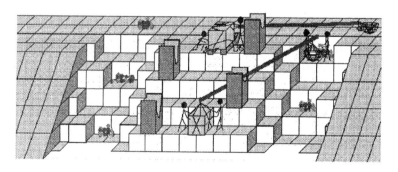

FIGURE 15: SIMPLE LEVERAGE MACHINE DESIGN FOR
LIFTING PYRAMID BLOCKS[158]

Ramps in general

The next alternative involves the use of ramps. There is no question that this would require a great deal of manpower and material, both to build them and to dismantle them afterwards. However, it is equally clear from archaeological remains that ramps *were* used in the construction of the early pyramids, both stepped and true. Remains consisting of limestone chips, tafla clay and gypsum have been excavated at Saqqara near to Sekh-emkhet's unfinished pyramid, at Meidum, at Lisht, at Abydos, and also at Giza. Here especially the remains of two retaining walls, between 15 and 20 feet apart, have been unearthed to the south of the eastern mastaba field, and it is supposed that they would have enclosed a fill which formed a straight ramp up to the mastabas themselves to assist their construction. Furthermore, Zahi Hawass has stated: 'We have found that Khufu's [ramp] was on the south side of his pyramid, and so was that of Menkaure. Khafre's ramp seems to have been on the east, but we are still investigating it'.[159]

Furthermore, as will be seen later, the logistics of building the pyramids themselves – in terms of the numbers of men involved – are not as bad as the alternative camp would often have us believe, so availability of unskilled manpower for building ramps should not have been a major constraint. By the same token, the materials from which they were constructed were readily on hand, and in part derived from the waste products of the actual quarrying and construction. Such ramps would also have been relatively easy to dismantle, albeit that huge quantities of debris would have been created – which at Giza were often dumped back in the quarries. And, while there is no doubt that, for example, the debris from the ramps used at the Great Pyramid would have caused problems for the quarrymen and other builders working on the Second Pyramid, nevertheless a ready source of ramp material was therefore available to them.

Diodorus seems to confirm the ramp theory:[160]

> . . . the mounts [i.e. construction mounds] were made of salt and salt-petre, and that they were melted by the inundation of the river, and being so dissolved, every thing was washed away but

the building itself. But this is not the truth of the thing; but the great multitude of hands that raised the mounts, the same carried back the earth to the place whence they dug it.

For his part, Pliny seems to echo his predecessor, but then adds a new twist:[161]

The most difficult problem is, to know how the materials for construction could possibly be carried to so vast a height. According to some authorities, as the buildings gradually advanced, they heaped up against it vast mounds of nitre and salt; which piles mere melted after its completion, by introducing beneath them the waters of the river. Others, again, maintain, that bridges were constructed, of bricks of clay, and that, when the pyramid was completed, these bricks were distributed for erecting the houses of private individuals. For the level of the river, they say, being so much lower, water could never by any possibility have been brought there by medium of canals.

Whatever the details concerning the disposal of the ramps, a number of factors concerning their use can be postulated. First we know from the NOVA Experiment that a 2-tonne block on a lubricated sledge can be dragged fairly comfortably up a ramp with an inclined slope by as few as ten men. Second, although the length of the ramp – and the distance the blocks have to be hauled – increases as we get higher up the edifice, this is compensated for by the fact that both the number and the size of the blocks reduce. For example, Lepre suggests that in the Great Pyramid the blocks in the first five courses are considerably larger than the 2.5-tonne average, with heights of 58, 45, 44, 42 and 40 inches respectively; after this they gradually reduce in height from 36 inches in the middle to about 20 inches at the top.[162] Third, unless multiple ramps were used, there would be only one drop-off point to the course currently under construction at any one time, and this would severely reduce the speed and efficiency of the process. Fourth, there is general agreement that the feasible slope up which such blocks could be dragged is somewhere between 1 in 8 and 1 in 12; we have chosen the midpoint, 1 in 10, in any assumptions below, and this is the figure postulated as reasonable by Hopkins during the NOVA Experiment. Fifth, the ramps would need to be wide enough so that two teams could pass each other, one coming up and one coming back down. And, sixth, we can suppose that the hauliers would have been allowed to rest at predetermined intervals, and this would have been facilitated by chocking the sledge with wooden wedges.

There are two main types of ramp: the straight ramp, which is favoured by Edwards, and the spiral ramp, favoured by Lehner (although he suggests that a combination of the two may have been used even on one edifice). Each will now be considered in turn.

Straight ramps
The idea that a straight ramp would have been used alone is in our view unlikely, primarily for reasons of efficiency and space. Whether it ran perpendicular to one face, or alongside it, it would suffer from a number of significant defects. First, it would be extremely long – for example, assuming a maximum gradient of 1 in 10, to reach the summit of the 480-foot-high Great Pyramid it would have to extend for 4,800 feet, which is nearly a mile. Space alone would become a major problem. Second, because the ramp would be largely freestanding, and unsupported by the emerging edifice itself, it would have to be relatively wide with strong retaining walls. Third, each time a course was completed the ramp would not only have to be extended at its commencement, but also increased in height *along its whole length* to maintain a consistent gradient; this exercise would represent a severe disruption, which could be conducted only *between* the courses, not as a concurrent exercise. And fourth, although multiple ramps would probably be required, to allow more than one point of access, the headaches already described for a single ramp would be multiplied.

Lehner analyses the possibility that a straight ramp may have been used at the Great Pyramid.[163] He suggests that the quarry used – lying just south of the centre of what is now the causeway to the Second Pyramid – was much too close for a straight ramp to start anywhere near it and still be long enough to reach the top with the required slope. Furthermore, hieroglyphs and graffiti reveal that the contemporary mastaba cemeteries to the west and east of the edifice were already in progress early in Khufu's reign – in years 5 and 12 respectively[164] – therefore neither of these areas could have been used for a straight ramp. Finally, the northern edge not only drops off severely but any ramp at that side would be far away from the quarries. To support his view that spiral ramps were the predominant choice Lehner also indicates that the transport roadways from the quarries found to the southwest of the Red Pyramid come right up to the base of the edifice.

There is no doubt that spiral ramps would have been the overall better option for the construction of most of the early pyramids – although that is not to say that a relatively short straight ramp used in conjunction might not have its uses in specific circumstances, especially for the lower courses.

Spiral ramps

A ramp that spiralled round the pyramid would overcome all the objections to straight ramps mentioned above. First, in the case of the Great Pyramid it would not encroach on the surrounding structures or be compromised by the proximity of the quarry. Second, it would not need to be as wide – at least in its foundations – because it would be supported by the emerging edifice itself, and arguably would need only one external retaining wall of lesser strength. And, third, each time a course was completed it would need to be extended only at its end, and even this task could be all but completed concurrently, thus ensuring minimal delays between courses.

A multitude of configurations for spiral ramps have been proposed over the years, many of which are complex and quite baffling. The vast majority of these can only be checked with the assistance of 3–D scale models.

For this reason we will examine a relatively simple design, and the benefits and problems associated with it. The most straightforward method would be to construct a single ramp which, if applied to even the largest edifice – the Great Pyramid as shown *to scale* in Figure 16 – would allow the full height to be attained via a 1-in-10 slope, with only two sides (or possibly just three) needing 'double-tiers'. This means that the lower tier must be wide enough on these sides to support the second

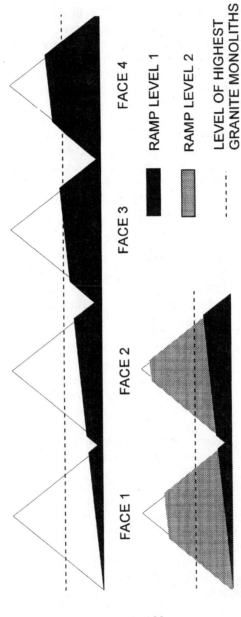

FACE 1   FACE 2   FACE 3   FACE 4

■ RAMP LEVEL 1

▨ RAMP LEVEL 2

- - - LEVEL OF HIGHEST
      GRANITE MONOLITHS

FIGURE 16: SCALE DIAGRAM OF SPIRAL RAMP ON THE GREAT PYRAMID WITH A SLOPE OF
1:10

tier *and* continue to allow room for two sledges to pass each other – effectively double the width of a second tier. In the scale diagram the width of the ramps is 20 feet for the lower tier and 10 feet for the upper tier. (Note also from the dotted line that even the unique monoliths forming the roofs of the King's and Relieving Chambers in the Great Pyramid could be set in place using the *full width* of the lower tier of the ramp *before* the upper tier was required; however, these huge blocks would present other difficulties, which will be discussed later.)

A single ramp such as that shown in Figure 16 would be wide enough to have a single 'up-track' and a single 'down-track', allowing multiple teams to be dragging sledges up and down in single file at any one time with room to pass each other. However, it would allow only one drop-off point at any one course – dictated by the point at which the slope of the ramp brings it level with that course. This would mean that the blocks would have to be dragged from that point across the flat surface to the point at which they were required. Because this would be a relatively slow and inefficient process, particularly on the larger lower courses, we realised that it would be possible to build *multiple* ramps in the early stages and still achieve the same final result. For 'Stage 1', a ramp such as is depicted on 'Face 1' in the diagram would be erected on *all four* sides – giving *four* drop-off points; then for 'Stage 2' these would be built up into the higher ramp seen on 'Face 2', but not only on 'Face 2' itself but *also* on 'Face 4' – giving *two* drop-off points. After this the plan would have to revert to the single ramp previously postulated, but a significant proportion of the masonry would now be in place – including in the Great Pyramid most of the complex blocks surrounding the chambers and passageways in the superstructure.

The other possible problem associated with this design is that the ramps would have to be wide enough at all levels to manoeuvre the blocks round the corners. Concentrating on the average 2.5-tonne core blocks, these are not huge (say of the order of $3\frac{1}{2}$ feet square on each side) and a width of something like 10 feet of ramp would probably suffice. However, there are two improvements that could be suggested.

First, Selim Hassan discovered two objects at Giza dating to the Old Kingdom, which he could only deduce were primitive pulleys.[165] These were made of hard red basalt, measured approximately 10 inches high by 7 inches wide, and were like segments cut down the centre of a mushroom, with three grooves for ropes at the top – each about 2 inches in width – and a hole in the base, which was probably used to attach them to a wooden frame. Although Hassan deduced that they may have been used as part of a block-and-tackle lifting system, they could equally well have been used to assist the hauling ropes in changing direction – especially when the sledges were being pulled round corners.

Second, it would not be unreasonable to suggest that the ramps could be widened – perhaps considerably – just after the corners; this would allow more room for the hauliers to carry on relatively straight until the block had reached the corner, and then swivel it.

If the unique problems of the huge monoliths in the super-structure of the Great Pyramid are ignored for the moment, then there are only two potential problems presented by the spiral-ramp theory. First, it has been suggested by opponents that, since this method would completely cloak the pyramid, it would prevent the 'backsighting' necessary to ensure that the orientation and alignment remained consistent as the edifice grew in height. However, as Lehner points out,[166] if the front faces of the casing blocks were left substantially undressed until the structure had been completed – which we may be fairly certain they were – then it is clear that, whatever ramps were used, the accurate sighting of already laid blocks was not the prime method used for controlling orientation. Second, we support Kerisel's theory that the cracks in the ceiling blocks in the King's and Relieving Chambers in the Great Pyramid were discovered *before* the edifice was completed. How could this be the case if the entire edifice was encased in a spiral ramp? After pondering this for a short time, we reached the conclusion that a properly stanchioned passage through the ramp would have been built into it at the point of the original entrance. This would allow continued access to the interior for completion of the various passages and chambers both above and even perhaps initially below ground, and during the later stages for inspection purposes, even while the upper reaches were still being completed.

As a balance of both evidence and logic, the spiral ramp was probably the *primary* mechanism used in the construction of the early pyramids – and certainly of the Great Pyramid when we consider the problems that leverage machines would have with the granite monoliths. That is not to say that, for example, a combination of straight ramps low down and leverage machines higher up could not have been used in one or several of the other edifices. Furthermore, whether the relatively simple design of the spiral ramp we have described above would be more or less appropriate than some of the more complex designs put forward is open to further discussion.

Cast blocks?

There is one relatively unique theory which should be considered, and which has received widespread exposure: that the pyramid builders did not have to raise the blocks into place because they cast them in molds *in situ*. This was first expounded by Professor Joseph Davidovits in *The Pyramids: An Enigma Solved*, published in 1988. Some pertinent comments have been made by Baldridge on the subject:[167]

> Polymer chemist Joseph Davidovits advanced an unconventional theory that the pyramid builders actually made the blocks by pouring a mixture of disaggregated limestone and a geopolymeric binder into wooden molds. This mixture then hardened and became almost indistinguishable from natural limestone. This would have allowed the workers to have simply passed potfuls of the mixture up the side of the GP, with no need for ramps and machines. Davidovits says that samples of pyramid casing stones reveal that they contained as much as 13 per cent of the binder; however Michael Tite says that his own analysis of pyramid stone did not produce the same features (Peterson 1984, p. 327). Geologist James Harrell, who has done extensive work on the provenance of pyramid stones, performed an analysis of the very sample that Davidovits used and concluded that it was natural limestone quarried in the Mokattam Formation (Harrell 1993).

The other main criticism of this theory – that the blocks

could not have been cast because they still contain the fossilised shells from which they derive their name – has been rejected by Davidovits's supporters. They suggest that the quarry material is loosely bound by clay, which releases in water so that the shells are also released, whereby they would then be reintroduced (often whole) into the aggregate. Be that as it may, there are three fundamental objections to this analysis. First, as far as we are aware, Davidovits is not suggesting that the granite blocks could have been cast, and consequently – at least as far as the Great Pyramid is concerned – he must be of the opinion that these blocks were pre-prepared and raised in the centre from the ground up as each course progressed, using either machines or small temporary ramps (if this were not the case he would have to revert to the full-ramp hypothesis, which would invalidate his whole argument). However, we will see later that we are not convinced that this would be logistically feasible. Second, the mere fact that the limestone blocks do not appear to have any uniform shape, especially in the core but also in the casing, would tend to argue against a casting theory – unless each block had its own wooden mould that was not built to any uniform pattern – which in our view would make no sense. Besides which there are too many anomalous shapes on the core blocks that would not be compatible with the use of moulds. And, third, why would some of the limestone core blocks have quarry marks on them if they were cast *in situ*? All in all this cannot be considered a serious threat to the spiral-ramps theory.

Completion

Positioning the core blocks
Much has been written about the core blocks of the pyramids, and as usual none have received more attention than those in the Great Pyramid itself. The alternative camp tend to play up the incredible and unique complexity of the blocks that surround the 'air' shafts; of those lining the upper part of the Descending Passage, whose joints are perpendicular to the slope of the passage, not to the horizontal; and of those that line the upper portion of the Ascending Passage and are similarly laid,

the arrangement of which is rendered even more complex by the presence of seven regularly spaced 'girdle-stones' – which revert to the true perpendicular and span the entire passage as one or at most two blocks. They have every right to trumpet the incredible and unparalleled complexity of these elements of the design, which would have significantly complicated the normal – and by comparison relatively simple – core laying process undertaken in all the other pyramids. However, do these factors in themselves prove anything other than the builders' dedication, excellence and organisation? We think not.

It is also clear that the quality of the core masonry varied from edifice to edifice, and even within the same one. Staying with the Great Pyramid, we have already seen that Vyse encountered wide, sand-filled spaces between the core blocks underneath the entrance to the Queen's Chamber. This would suggest they were quite irregularly laid. He records Perring on this issue as follows:[168]

> Mr. Perring observed, that the mortar used for the casing and lining of the passages was of lime only; that in the body of the pyramid it was composed of red brick, gravel, Nile earth, crushed granite, and calcareous stone, and of lime; and that for fillings in desert sand was employed in a grout of liquid mortar.

Yet Vyse also has this to say of the quality of core construction he encountered during his attempts to find an additional entrance in the southern face:[169]

> The stones were very large, and the half of each of them was keyed in under the upper layer, besides which, many of them were in slanting directions, although in horizontal courses; it became therefore necessary to break almost every block before it could be removed. The mortar was nearly as hard as the stone itself . . .

As for the Third Pyramid, we have already noted Latif's reports that during Youssef's attempts at dismantling it his huge workforce were able to remove only one or two stones each day. Furthermore, Latif asked an overseer who was superintending the removal of a block from this edifice, 'whether, if a thousand pieces of gold were offered to him, he would undertake to replace it in its original position; he answered, that if he were to be given many times that sum, he could not do so'.[170]

There is no doubt – from the pure fact that all the completed early pyramids are still standing substantially intact some 4,500 years after they were erected – that the quality of their core masonry was excellent in the places that mattered. So what can be said about the general procedures for laying this masonry? We can assume that the builders primarily worked on one course at a time – even if some of the internal structures of the Great Pyramid may have been erected several courses in advance, using temporary structures, to allow the master masons time to work on the more complex elements. The sledges would have been dragged off the ramps and across to as close to their intended position as space would allow. They would then most likely have been levered into their final position, assisted by the use of lubricating mortar. For blocks that required significant or highly accurate final positioning the levers could have operated in grooves cut for the purpose, although since these are not a universal feature of the core blocks, the alternative would have been to leave protruding bosses, which may or may not have been subsequently removed.

In a section in *The Complete Pyramids* entitled 'Trouble at the Top', Lehner admits that the NOVA team had great difficulty with the blocks on the upper reaches of their small-scale model, especially as space became limited. He therefore postulates that extra wooden ramps may have been erected around the edifice near its summit to assist its completion. However, it would be simpler just to make sure that the upper tier of the ramp was sufficiently wide – and as always extended horizontally somewhat – to allow all major manoeuvring to be completed. As far as we are aware the 10 feet we have proposed for the width of the upper tier is considerably more than the space in which his team were trying to operate.

Laying and dressing the casing stones[171]

If ramps were used the casing stones could be laid only at the same time as the core blocks on each course, rather than at the end from the top down. If machines were used, either would be feasible, but raising all these blocks at the end and then dragging them all round the edge into position in the limited space of narrow ledges would seem a less sensible option. If we assume they *were* laid course by course using ramps, there is much dispute about whether they would have been laid before or after the core blocks.

Based on his observation of small differences in the angles of the junctions of the casing blocks on the lowest course of the Great Pyramid, Petrie suggested that the casing blocks were laid first, with all their faces predressed, in order to ensure the overall accuracy of the course. Provided suitable gaps were left for the drop-off points from the ramps, this could make sense. However, it is now almost universally accepted that the front faces of the casing blocks were finally dressed *in situ* and top down, *after the completion of the structure*. This view is supported by the evidence of the Third Pyramid, where the granite casing on the lower courses remains undressed except at the centres of the four sides[172] – presumably because the edifice was completed in a hurry after Menkaure's death. This view is backed up by the completion of his temples using only mud brick.

If this example was pursued in all the edifices, there would be no point in laying the casing first, at least not for the sake of accuracy. Perhaps the Great Pyramid's accuracy was assisted by completing the lowest course from the outside in, with the facing of the casing blocks finished off at this point, although this procedure was not followed in subsequent courses. However, when we consider that the casing blocks also had to be manoeuvred into their final position using levers, albeit again with their mortar assisting with lubrication, questions of space arise irrespective of the order in which the blocks were laid. The positioning of the last blocks on each course would always represent the most difficult task.

It can be surmised that, for reasons of efficiency and time, the back, base and sides of the casing blocks would have been substantially dressed to fit the adjacent blocks before they were hauled up, leaving only final adjustments to these faces – and the complete dressing of the top and front – to be completed *in situ*. That all these tasks were performed with the utmost diligence is proved by the incredible accuracy of the fit of the casing blocks to their neighbours and to the accurately worked 'support' blocks behind them, especially when one considers that the side joints were not always perpendicular either to the horizontal or to the front face. As to the tools used for the final dressing of the casing, we know from part-completed blocks that this was performed with exquisite finesse by the simple use of small copper chisels whose blades were only about one-third of an inch wide, and which would have required repeated and regular sharpening to maintain their efficiency.

The idea that the *front* faces were finished only *after* the edifice was fully erected is supported by Masoudi, who relates that 'the Pyramid was constructed in steps, which were built up and completed from the top to the bottom, and effaced when the whole was finished'.[173] (Although this could of course be interpreted as suggesting that, as well as the finishing process, the entire casing blocks were left off until the end.) While this theory tends to be taken for granted, it does incorporate some severe logistical problems. If the casing blocks were all actually *laid* at the end from the top down – a possibility allowed for only by the use of leverage machines – then this additional procedure presents no problem; but we have seen that this would not be the most *efficient* solution even if this method were used. However, if they were laid course by course, as predicated by use of the ramp method, then there was no all-encompassing platform available to support the masons while they performed this final dressing. *If* we stick with the theory that ramps were used, *and* that the front faces were finished at the end, then we can conceive of only two possible methods of support: either some form of wooden scaffolding was erected on the ramps, although this would represent quite an undertaking; or alternatively multiple ropes were attached to the top of the edifice and let down the sides, with the masons working from some form of simple sling attached thereto. The latter would be the *only* option for finishing the facing at the end if leverage machines were used.

We will let you take your pick as to which of these various combinations of options you support. However, we would contend that all of them are entirely feasible, and they do allow us to explain how the construction of the majority of the early pyramids – and even the bulk of the Great Pyramid itself – was achieved.

Logistics

Classical historians present us with a variety of statistics about the number of men used and the time taken for the construction of the Giza Pyramids. For example, Herodotus reports that the Great Pyramid took 20 years and that the men 'worked in gangs of 100,000 for three months at a time'. Diodorus and Pliny agree about the time taken on the Pyramid, but both suggest that it required 360,000 men.[174] Meanwhile, Pliny also suggests, quite specifically, that all three were built in 78 years and 4 months – and in this connection it is of passing interest that the chronology we presented in Figure 10 gives a total for the reigns of Khufu, Djedefre, Khafre and Menkaure of 75 years, or 67 if Djedefre is omitted.

Regarding the time it took to build the Great Pyramid, these consistent Classical reports tally closely with the 23 years quoted earlier for Khufu's reign. That this amount of time is in the right ballpark is suggested by Lepre's report that one of the quarry marks in Campbell's Chamber suggests it was completed in 'year 17' of Khufu's reign.[175] And further by Lehner's report that quarry marks found on the back of two *casing* stones at the Red Pyramid, one from the base and one from about thirty courses up, show a difference of four years[176] (this could weaken the argument if the casing had all been put on at the end, but we have already suggested that this is unlikely). However, this is somewhat at odds with similar evidence presented by Edwards, who suggests that a block on the base of the same edifice dated to 'year 21' of Sneferu's reign, and one halfway up to 'year 22' – a difference of only one year for half the edifice.[177] The latter would suggest that the casing was all put on at the end. However, even Edwards suggests that there may be errors in this interpretation and, having been written in 1972, it is probably somewhat out of date.

If we use the largest and most complex edifice as our example, an extremely simplistic logistical analysis runs as follows: if the Great Pyramid contains approximately 2.3 million blocks, then at best it would require 274 blocks to be laid per day in a 23-year period (assuming that full years of 365 days were worked, with no holidays). With an average of 10 hours of daylight, this equates to 27 per hour, or approximately one block every 2 minutes! This does represent an incredible *average* rate, but the matter should not just be left there, saying, as many alternative researchers do, 'it cannot be done using conventional methods'. The different elements of the project need to be looked at, and the most likely areas of constraint in achieving this rate examined: or, in modern project-management speak, what are the tasks that are on the *critical path*?

Starting with the manpower, Lehner in particular has performed some detailed analysis which would suggest that the Classical reports are way above what would have been required to build the Great Pyramid.[178] He splits the critical tasks – those most likely to cause a constraint – into three:

- *Quarrying and initial dressing*: The total volume of the Great Pyramid is approximately 2.6 million cubic metres.[179] Assuming the full 23 years, this requires approximately 309 cubic metres of stone to be quarried and dressed per day. Based on figures from the NOVA Experiment, which used twelve men to produce 186 blocks with an average size of one cubic metre in 22 days (an average of 0.7 cubic metres per man per day), the Great Pyramid would require approximately only 450 men. However, Lehner is anxious to compensate for the fact that his men not only used iron tools, but also a mechanical winch to haul the stones out of the quarry. He therefore increases his estimate to 1,200 men, and possibly more (for the sake of argument, let us say 1,500 – a threefold increase).
- *Hauling*: Despite the fact that the NOVA team found that ten men could pull a 2-tonne block on runners up an inclined ramp reasonably easily, and despite the common view that at least on the flat an average man can pull one-third of a tonne by this method (which would reduce the figure to six), Lehner suggests that it should be assumed that the slightly larger 2.5-tonne-average blocks were

pulled by teams of 20 men (known to be one of the work-gang sizes commonly employed by the Ancient Egyptians). If it is then assumed that each team moved one block from the quarry into its position in the edifice every two hours, (a rate of five per day), 55 teams, or 1,100 men, would be needed. This analysis sounds about right. The ramps would need to be wide enough to allow the teams going up and coming down to pass each other, and for the sake of argument fifteen teams coming up, fifteen teams going down, both in single file, and 25 on their way to and from the quarry at any one time should not have made the area too congested. Clearly if too many men and teams were required to work concurrently, then congestion could be a logistical problem, but at the same time, the use of multiple ramps in the early stages would significantly reduce congestion. Lehner ends up with a final figure of 1,360, and we must accept that the numbers would have to be increased to allow for the far larger distance over which, for example, the casing stones had to be transported from Turah – but these extra teams would not increase the local congestion.

- *Setting and finishing*: This is the task that is really on the *critical path* of the logistics of this project. Could the setters and finishers have handled an average of 27 blocks per hour? Certainly this seems a reasonable rate on the lower courses where space was less restricted, even if we take into account that the casing and support blocks – which represent less than 5 per cent of the total volume – were far harder to position than the core blocks and required some dressing *in situ*, plus that the overall space available to work in would be reduced as the course progressed. However, it does tend to indicate that the bulk of the finishing work would have needed to be performed before the blocks were delivered. As for the unavoidable *in situ* finishing of the casing blocks and the more complex blocks lining the passages, chambers and shafts, it is not impossible that masons would have worked on these tasks at night using burning torches to speed up the process – and it is important to remember that the complex internal blocks represent a minute proportion of the total. As for the number of men required, Lehner suggests that a maximum of ten men could work on each block – split between masons and handlers – and would take an average of two hours to complete it. Since 55 blocks would be delivered every two hours, we can estimate that 550 setters would be involved at any one time. Would there be sufficient space for this number of men to process this number of blocks being delivered to the work-face? Probably yes, if one accepts the proposition that, compared with the average, the rate would be almost doubled in the early stages when the ramps were short and space was relatively unrestricted, and then progressively reduced until it was considerably less than the average at the top.

If we accept these broad logistics, the final tally for manpower is less than 4,000 men. A number of factors that we have so far omitted must now be added in: for example, all the men required to prepare food, mortar, make and maintain tools, build and extend ramps and roadways, excavate underground passages and chambers, and erect all the other edifices in the complex such as the enclosure walls, temples, subsidiary pyramids, mastabas, causeway (with its huge ramparts required to span the eastern cliff) and so on. However, none of these tasks is on the *critical path* in terms of requiring manpower which would not be available, or of holding up the main construction; the only possible exception is the underground passage and chamber, but work on this could still progress concurrently with the superstructure – and probably did until the point where the change in plan occurred.

Furthermore, we have not allowed for holidays or the fact that much of the unskilled labouring was performed seasonally by farmers during the three months of the Nile floods. It is clear that we could increase the overall figure five- or sixfold to 20,000–25,000 men and still be well within the potential constraints of the number of men available (estimates suggest that the population of Egypt at this time was of the order of 1.6 million). Of these, we might expect 5,000 or so to be skilled and permanently housed and working on the Plateau, and the remainder to be temporary agricultural workers.

What of the other pyramids? Only the most complex *individual* case has been taken so far. The only additional area for scrutiny is that of Sneferu's three pyramids, and in this case all the same logistics apply, except that the manpower may need to be increased to account for the larger overall volume in a similar timeframe. All the tasks on his *critical path* would have been the same or simpler by virtue of their being spread across three separate projects. Furthermore, it may be argued that, broadly speaking, differences such as the fact that his monuments are far less complex internally, and that his ancillary buildings were far smaller and simpler, cancel out against the fact that he did not have the vast resources of local limestone that were available at Giza.

None of the foregoing should tempt us to underestimate the magnitude of the task facing the pyramid builders, especially those who took on the significantly increased complexity of the Great Pyramid. The management of these projects would challenge most experts in the field today, even with new-fangled software to assist them. Everyone involved in all of the pyramid projects would have had to be superbly organised, punctual, efficient, motivated and conscientious. We can propose from this that even the nonskilled workers were more likely to be conscripts than slaves, proud to be part of such an important and far-reaching community project. However, notwithstanding all this, we contend that all the work was logistically feasible for the advanced civilisation that Egypt clearly represented in the pyramid-building era – and some of whose values we might do well to emulate today.

Monolithic Mysteries?

Some readers may have become somewhat exasperated by our previous omission of by far the most complex and intriguing aspect of pyramid building – the quarrying, transportation, finishing and raising of the huge granite monoliths that form the roofs of the King's and Relieving Chambers in the Great Pyramid. However, we did not want to unduly complicate the foregoing analysis, which extends to *all* the early pyramids. But clearly if the issues are to be covered properly we cannot duck this complexity – even though members of the orthodox camp often do just that. Nor can we ignore the even larger limestone monoliths incorporated into some of the temples on the Plateau, which will be looked at shortly. But first the granite beams will be considered. And, in so doing, let us take the highest estimates for the weight of these beams – which is a massive 70 tonnes (although we should note that this estimate derives from one huge block in the floor of Lady Arbuthnot's Chamber, which measures 27 feet by 7 feet by 5 feet; the others are smaller).

Quarrying

There is no dispute that the both the granite and basalt used on the Plateau were quarried at Aswan, about 580 miles to the south. Lehner suggests it was all quarried by hand, based on the multiple dolerite 'pounders' weighing between 9 and 15 pounds (or 4–7 kilograms) which have been found at the quarries. These were sometimes used for shaping the stone, but we are inclined to agree with Edwards that in terms of quarrying they may have been used merely to establish grooves *on all sides* into which, once again, wooden wedges would be hammered and then soaked, with the expansion causing the stone to fracture. Grooves cut in to unremoved blocks in the quarries show that this was the method used, and we see no major problem with this aspect.

Transportation

Clearly the distances involved are now considerable. It is normally suggested that even blocks as heavy as these were also loaded on to barges. This would be by far the most efficient method to travel the distance, since the laying of quality roadways for over 500 miles – while hardly impossible – would have been an extremely time-consuming operation. But could the ancient Egyptians have constructed such a vessel? Let us put this in perspective. If we said that as a very rough guide the average man weighs 100 kilogrammes, then 10 men would weigh a tonne, so 70 tonnes would represent 700 men. If this sounds high, ancient inscriptions appear to suggest that this was indeed the method used.

A relief on the causeway of the Fifth Dynasty king Unas at Saqqara shows a barge laden with two granite columns which match those found in his pyramid temples (see Figure 17). The accompanying inscription indicates that the columns are 20 cubits in length, although since this equates to about 28 feet – and from the scale of the man in the relief and the known size of the columns – it is probably referring to their combined length. We do not know how much they weighed, but if each was 14 feet long and, judging by the scale, approximately 3 feet in diameter, we can see that their combined volume would

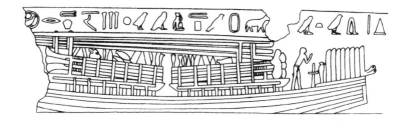

FIGURE 17: RELIEF OF GRANITE-LADEN BARGE FROM
UNAS'S CAUSEWAY[180]

not have been that much less than that of a typical block from
the Relieving Chambers – which would have been slightly longer
(to fully span the walls, which are already 17 feet apart) and
about 5 feet square.

When stones of this weight were being loaded on and off
the barges, clearly there was a significant danger of capsizing.
However, Lehner suggests that they would have either built
embankments around the barge at each end and then dug it
out, or used narrow canals and placed wooden support beams
across the banks and through the support trellises under the
columns (as shown in the relief), then weighted the barge down
or up to manoeuvre it in and out from underneath.

For transporting the blocks overground from quarry to barge,
and then from barge to pyramid, we can assume from the
statue-hauling relief depicted in Figure 13 that loads of this
weight were still transported using the lubricated-sledge-and-
roadway method, albeit that the quality of the roadway would
have to increase with the size of the load. As to the number of
men required, if using the previous assumption that one man
can pull one-third of a tonne *on the flat*, then a 70-tonne load
would require 210 men. This is pretty much in line with the
172 men, split into four ranks, hauling the 60-tonne statue
depicted in the relief.

It should be noted that the methods described above for the
quarrying and transportation of huge monoliths are not confined to elements of the Great Pyramid alone. For example,
when we explored the Red Pyramid – the chambers of which

are entirely lined with beautifully finished granite blocks – we noted that the lintel blocks immediately above the passages were substantially larger than the others, presumably in order to provide better support. We then established that they measured 9 feet 6 inches wide by 6 feet high by 4 feet deep. These dimensions, although considerably less than those of the largest blocks in the Great Pyramid, would still mean they weighed 20 tonnes or more. There is, however, one big difference: these blocks are only a few feet up from ground level.

Erection

The major problem area is how did the Ancient Egyptian builders lift 70-tonne blocks as high as 200 feet up into the superstructure of the Great Pyramid? The three 'orthodox' possibilities are as follows.

- *Simple levers*: Tompkins reports that the engineer Tons Brunes 'has demonstrated how a block as large as the beams of the King's Chamber could be comfortably raised by a single man with the dexterous use of balancing wedges'.[181] We have no more details on this assertion, but one thing is clear from our earlier discussion about the lack of space when using levers: the only way in which this could possibly work is for *all* the heavy blocks to be pre-prepared and placed in the centre of the foundation, and then lifted course by course as the edifice progressed. There are a number of factors that suggest that even this was not the method used. First, it would be extremely time-consuming for a prolonged period, when logistics demand high efficiency. Second, although we do not know what materials Brunes supposedly used, we doubt that simple wooden levers and wedges would easily bear the weight of these blocks. Third, this would have to mean that the replanning theory for the Subterranean Chamber was incorrect.
- *Leverage machines*: It is clear that Lepre's machine is designed to take only 2.5-tonne blocks, and it already appears too large to fit on the casing ledge alone. He admits that it would need a much larger machine with far bigger counterweights to lift the monoliths. Would there be space for this? And, even then, how would one lift the necessarily larger counterweights required by the machine in the first place? He offers the use of multiple smaller machines working in tandem as an alternative, but this is not an efficient solution either. These methods might work if all the larger blocks were

placed in the centre at the start to provide sufficient space, but there are strong arguments against this. Furthermore, the ropes and bosses required would have to be much stronger for blocks of this size – we certainly would not want to stand anywhere near the machine when it was lifting a 70-tonne block into midair! Baldridge suggests that it would have been easy enough to place the granite blocks at the centre at the start and then build small *temporary ramps* drag them up to the next course each time. His argument does appear logically sound, but given the logistics of the *critical path* – relating to the speed at which the blocks on each course had to be processed – this solution may be less efficient.

- *Ramps:* Turning to our favoured method of spiral ramps, we can conceive the following. Suppose our previous estimate of the number of men required to drag a 70-tonne block on the flat is increased from 210 to 280 to allow for the 1-in-10 slope. This may seem a relatively small increase to allow for the slope, but our original estimate was on the high side since we took on an average of one-third of a tonne per man, whereas it is equally often suggested that half a tonne per man is a valid average.[182] This revised figure is based on a quarter of a tonne per man. Let us further assume that they were arranged in four ranks of 70 men. Would these men be able to negotiate a 20-foot-wide ramp – which it would still be because the second tier would not yet be built? We think the answer is yes. However, what happens when at a corner? With the aid of multiple proto-pulleys as discussed previously, it is conceivable that after each 'haul' one row of men would move round the corner, but with a block of this length and size we can only guess that the ramp would have to be widened after the corner for some distance, perhaps to 40 feet or even more. This *seems* a feasible solution. The other alternative would be to build a straight ramp up to this point in the edifice: at about half the height – the floor of the King's Chamber lies at 139 feet, while the roof of Campbell's is at 208 feet – this would require a ramp of about half the length, or half a mile. There is no theoretical reason why this should not have been used in conjunction with a spiral ramp, but it does seem a massive extra effort to solve this one problem. And, if one attempts to fall back on a straight ramp or ramps alone, one is faced with all the difficulties previously discussed.

That these blocks were manoeuvred by conventional means is suggested by the existence of a number of 'construction bosses' which protrude from the blocks in the north walls of at least two of the Relieving Chambers.[183] Nevertheless, the alternative camp would probably have a field day picking holes in this analysis, and in truth we cannot be sure ourselves of the validity of our favoured solution – which, having discounted the use of leverage-machines or central-ramps on the basis of the tight logistics, remains the 'spiral-ramp-with-extended corners'. The only way to be certain would be to perform a large-scale experiment, which for obvious reasons is unlikely to happen. Accordingly we must examine the 'alternatives' shortly, to see if they provide a better answer.

Working with hard stone

As for the methods used to work the harder stone, most Egypto-logists now agree that the work required more than just pounders (see Plate 25). Lehner suggests that the Ancient Egyptians used copper saws to obtain straight edges, and tubular copper drills to hollow blocks out – for example the insides of the coffers.[184] Since he is aware that even tempered copper cannot work hard materials like granite on its own, he suggests that the drills and saws were used in conjunction with an 'abrasive slurry of water, gypsum and quartz sand'. Indeed he reports that he has found this mixture, tinted green by the copper, in the base of cuts on basalt blocks on the Plateau – and he is at pains to point out that it was the slurry that performed the cutting, while the copper tools themselves effec-tively acted only as a 'guide'; indeed the steel 'saws' used to cut granite nowadays have no teeth at all. For those unhappy with the concept of slurry, it has been suggested that diamond tips would be required to cut through the hard quartz layers in the granite, but these are not found naturally in Egypt. Petrie's perhaps better suggestion was tips of powdered corundum. Meanwhile, it is argued that the dressing of hard stone was performed using the pounders once again, with final polishing achieved by the use of an abrasive paste made of, for example, powdered pumice – which is still in use for this task in Egypt today.

Are these theories acceptable? They have been mercilessly hammered by the alternative camp, and in truth we have been inclined to agree with their criticisms. The 'alternatives' will be examined shortly, but it should be remembered that there are two questions that need to be answered: the first is whether copper was indeed the only metal from which tools were made; and the second is the nature of the power source for the saws and drills.

Limestone megaliths

A number of the temples on the Plateau – the two next to the Sphinx, and those to the east of the Second and Third Pyramids – contain even larger blocks, albeit of limestone. The largest of these megaliths is estimated to weigh as much as 200 tonnes, and the smallest as much as 50 tonnes! Very little has been said about them so far – and of course the orthodox camp ignore them completely and stick to *pyramid*-construction theories only – but they may be the 'straw that breaks the camel's back'. However, let us attempt to use an orthodox approach first and see where it leads. First, it should be remembered that these blocks would have been quarried locally on the Plateau, so there was no requirement to drag them long distances. Second, provided adequate roadways and sledges were used, it is *conceivable* (although by no means *conclusive* since other factors may come into play) to extrapolate the previous analysis and suggest that blocks of this size could be dragged along the flat, and that – although the largest would require a minimum of 600 superbly drilled men[185] – space would not be an issue.

But, when we consider that blocks of this size were sometimes placed *one on top of another*, the question must be raised as to how they were erected. A possible clue of sorts came from a perusal of Vyse's *Operations*. In excavating the deep shaft of Campbell's Tomb, Vyse found a huge coffer at the bottom which was resting on several feet of sand.[186] In assessing how it was lowered down, he postulated that the shaft had been filled with sand, the coffer placed on top, and then the sand gradually removed. This made us consider the possibility for the Sphinx and Valley Temples that, since they were effectively underneath the 'natural' sand level at the lower side of the Plateau, the blocks may have been placed in a similar way by a process of excavating the sand, piling it up, excavating it again and so on. However, we then come to the Second and Third Pyramid temples: these are much higher up on the Plateau, so the same theory does not work.

Two alternatives can be suggested for these. Perhaps a straight ramp was used, but we must remember that – unlike the vast flat surface presented by the course of a pyramid – the 'walls' in this case leave no room for the hauliers to continue to lift the block once they have reached the top of the ramp. Of course they may have been able to overcome this by dropping down on the other side and continuing their pull, but the angle would be less efficient and ultimately the opposite wall would surely get in the way of 600 men, even if they were in multiple ranks. So perhaps they would have been forced to build up sand embankments all over the emerging edifice at each course. This might work, but they would have to be highly reinforced to take this kind of weight without subsidence. It has even been suggested that the only ramps that could take this kind of load would have to be made of the same material themselves – stone.

All of this leaves us with a vague feeling of unease. It is as if, having come so close to apparently reasonable orthodox explanations for all the pyramid building, we are becoming desperate to think of one method after another, almost off the cuff, in an attempt to explain the construction of the temples. Although we clearly do not agree with the alternative camp's suggestion that these temples – which include the two so clearly attached to the Second and Third Pyramids – were constructed long before the pyramids using different technology, the feeling that this just will not do is reinforced by their highly pertinent question: *If the use of such large blocks is going to cause so many headaches, why bother? Why not just use smaller ones?* Of course we can argue that the use of the 70-tonne monoliths in the Great Pyramid was a structural necessity, but that argument cannot apply to these *megaliths*, which are repeatedly encountered in the various temples on the Plateau. It is perhaps for this reason, more than any other, that we must ask whether there is another more sensible, and indeed logical, explanation.

Appropriate Alternatives?

Recapping briefly, we have left three 'strands' open in all the foregoing analysis – three areas in which it might be suggested

200

that orthodox explanations are inadequate. These are, first, the manoeuvring of the granite monoliths in the heart of the Great Pyramid; second, the raising of the limestone megaliths in the temples; and, third, the tools used to fashion the hard stones. Since the first two go hand in hand, they will be dealt with first.

Confusing the issue

A number of alternative researchers, including Alford, Hancock and Bauval, make great play of interviewing modern crane engineers, establishing that there are only a handful of cranes in the world today that could lift weights in excess of 200 tonnes – and even then only in a 'static' environment (i.e. getting them to move around on tracks with such a weight would be harder still).[187]

This may be true, although we gather that the reality is that some are capable of static-lifting as much as 2,000 tonnes; but then our modern society would not dream of taking the time to construct something as low-tech as a huge ramp. That these observations are something of a red herring is proved by the fact that most of them do not go on to imply that the Ancient Egyptians did have even more advanced cranes or similar. For example, Hancock and Bauval, although deserving credit for asking the right questions, leave the issue entirely open:

> Either the people who designed these hulking edifices had knowledge of some technique that made it *easy* for them to quarry, manipulate and position enormous pieces of stone, or their way of thinking was utterly different from our own – in which case their motives and priorities are unlikely to be fathomable in terms of normal cross-cultural comparisons.

However, having applied these remarks specifically to the Sphinx and Valley Temples, we find that they are in fact attempting to use this line of argument to justify a much earlier date for the Sphinx – conveniently ignoring the existence of the other similar structures several hundred yards to their west, which are inextricably linked to the Second and Third Pyramids. This does not really help anyone's understanding.

A worldwide phenomenon

As for Alford, in his earlier work *Gods* – although the *conclusions* he draws come under the 'millennium madness' category – he does bring out some invaluable evidence that the ability to manipulate huge megaliths in ancient times was not confined to Egyptian civilisation alone, but appears to have been a worldwide phenomenon. His most telling evidence comes from the ancient foundations underlying the Roman 'Temple of Jupiter' at Baalbek in the Lebanon – a site that he brought back into public focus after it had been inaccessible for many years due to warfare.[188] Here, three granite megaliths known as 'the Trilothon', each weighing a staggering 800 tonnes, have been placed in a wall on the *sixth* level. They average 64 feet in length, 15 feet in height, and 12 feet in depth. Admittedly they were quarried at a site only one-third of a mile away, and there was no great incline between the two, but the ground is by no means flat. Alford's photograph of the perfectly squared block known as the 'stone of the south', which remains in the quarry and is estimated to weigh 1,000 tonnes, is truly impressive.[189]

Meanwhile on the other side of the world in South America, at the ancient site of Puma Punku near Tiwanaku in Bolivia, red sandstone blocks weighing in excess of 100 tonnes have been found in the 'shattered remains of a partially excavated structure'; and, at Sacsayhuaman near Cuzco in Peru, a similar block weighing 120 tonnes is found in the base of a wall. There are many other examples, including sites where the blocks may be somewhat smaller, but the route from the quarry requires the negotiation of steep mountains and valleys. All these sites are ancient – and some would argue that no one really knows exactly how ancient they are – and all the blocks described above have clearly been quarried, transported and shaped to fit their surrounds.

We know that many of these ancient civilisations had an entirely different mind-set, and indeed that their whole concept of time and effort would be complete anathema to the modern Western world. But, even if we accept this, can we seriously suggest that they were prepared to manoeuvre stones of this magnitude using simple ramps and levers – even if it were proved possible, which is not a foregone conclusion – when there is no obvious structural reason why they could not have used multiple smaller blocks?

Sonic levitation?

The possibility that some form of levitation may have been used, perhaps using vibration and harmonics, has been postulated by alternative researchers for some time. Following from the pertinent question they raise about the apparent lack of *need* to use such large blocks, they suggest that a civilisation that had mastered some form of levitation technology would deliberately choose to use larger blocks because this would be more efficient. Some even suggest that, although a civilisation as advanced as the Ancient Egyptians would have been *able* to devise the wheel, their ability to overcome the effects of gravity was the exact reason why they did not *need* it.

These are huge claims, and on the face of it would have to imply a far greater level of technological advancement than one can easily accept, but we do not resort to such possibilities lightly. Let us therefore examine what the alternative camp have to say about these issues.

Andrew Collins deserves credit for collating a number of historic references to the Ancients' apparent ability to move blocks by what we would regard as nonconventional methods.[190] First he examines a passage written by the Arab historian Masoudi, whom we have already encountered several times, concerning the erection of the Egyptian pyramids. This passage is reproduced by Vyse as follows:[191]

> In carrying on the work, leaves of papyrus, or paper, inscribed with certain characters, were placed under the stones prepared in the quarries; and upon being struck, the blocks were moved at each time the distance of a bowshot [about 150 cubits, or 210 feet], and so by degrees arrived at the Pyramids. Rods of iron were inserted into the centres of the stones, that formed the pavement, and, passing through the blocks placed upon them, were fixed by melted lead.

It has been suggested that the rods of iron were somehow instrumental in this process, but our reading of it is that apparently these were merely used for fixing the blocks in place on the pavement – and of course there is no evidence of this method being used. Also, the use of iron at this time is not accepted by Egyptologists. The idea that the blocks could move unaided for some 200 feet 'upon being struck' primarily because they had some 'magic spell' underneath them does seem somewhat far-fetched. But was Masoudi just inventing the whole thing because the Arabs understood even less about how the blocks might have been moved than we do now, or was he distorting an original truth?

Next Collins turns to the South American legends, which we would expect to exist given the structures examined above.[192] He reveals that the local Indian legends about the building of the temple complex at Tiahuanaco in Bolivia suggest that it was constructed at the 'beginning of time' by the legendary founder-god Viracocha or Thunupa. They claim he emerged from an island in the nearby saltwater Lake Titicaca – which itself appears intriguingly to have been thrust upward to 2 miles above sea level by a gigantic convulsion in relatively recent prehistory. This god is depicted on what was the centrepiece of the complex, a huge block known as the 'Gateway of the Sun', and is identified by scholars with the similar founder-gods of a variety of other South and Meso-American cultures, wherein he goes by the various names of Quetzalcoatl, Votan and Kul-kulkan.

The ruins contain a number of blocks weighing around 100 tonnes, and – most important for our current theme – the legends say that *the* Viracocha (the collective name for the god and his followers) caused the blocks to be 'carried through the air to the sound of a trumpet'. An alternative theme is that they created a 'heavenly fire' which 'was extinguished at their command, though the stones were consumed by fire in such wise [sic] that large blocks could be lifted by hand as if they were cork'. Is it just a coincidence, when one is considering the possible worldwide spread of a culture that could perform such apparent 'miracles', that Viracocha and his equivalent founder-gods are consistently described as fair-skinned, blue-eyed, fair-haired and tall in stature – the exact opposite of the indigenous locals?

Moving north to the Yucatan, Collins relates the Mayan legends concerning the construction of the temple complex at Uxmal – supposed to have been performed by an antediluvian race of dwarfs of whom it is said, 'Construction work was easy for them, all they had to do was whistle and heavy rocks would move into place' (although even these powers were apparently insufficient to allow them to escape 'the Deluge').[193]

If we move back to the Near East we find more legends, this time from early Greek historians who recorded that the walls of the ancient city of Thebes were built by Amphion, a son of Jupiter, 'to the music of his harp', while his 'songs drew even stones and beasts after him'. Another version claims that when he played 'loud and clear on his golden lyre, rock twice as large followed in his footsteps'.[194] And of course, on a more destructive but similar note, there is the biblical 'Fall of Jericho', in which Joshua is told how to bring the walls tumbling down by the 'captain of the host of the Lord':[195]

> And ye shall compass the city, all ye men of war, and go round about the city once. Thus shalt thou do six days. And seven priests shall bear before the ark [of the covenant] seven trumpets of rams' horns: and the seventh day ye shall compass the city seven times, and the priests shall blow with the trumpets. And it shall come to pass, that when they make a long blast with the ram's horn, and when ye hear the sound of the trumpet, all the people shall shout with a great shout; and the wall of the city shall fall down flat, and the people shall ascend up every man straight before him.

Are these all just distorted ancient legends, or could they contain some seed of truth? In attempting to answer this question, the best place to start is in the mysterious land of Tibet. A select band of European travellers who were able to visit remote monasteries in the 1930s have provided remarkably consistent eyewitness accounts of ancient sonic levitation techniques still practised at this time by the Tibetan monks. All reported that heavy stone blocks were moved without human intervention, other than the accompaniment of the process by the playing of a variety of horns and drums. We do not have the space here to go into great detail – indeed this subject deserves a whole book in its own right – but we refer readers to two works. First is the one first-hand account, that of a German traveller called Theodore Illion, who wrote up his experiences in a book called *In Secret Tibet*, which due to the resurgence of interest in these topics has fortunately now been reprinted. Second is Collins,[196] to whom all credit should be given for obtaining translations of the work of the Swedish engineer Henry Kjellson, who in his *Forsvunden Teknik* published in 1961 provides second-hand accounts of separate visits by a fellow Swede, a Dr Jarl, and an Austrian named Linauer. Both these works contain detailed diagrams of the amazing techniques observed by the visitors. We can only agree wholeheartedly with Collins when he bemoans the tragic loss of this Ancient Knowledge, which – as far as we in the West are aware – has been all but obliterated since the brutal occupation of Tibet in the 1950s by the Chinese.

Our only consolation is that a variety of Western researchers have been attempting to recreate these techniques for more than a century. The first was John Worrell Keely of Philadelphia, who over a period of 50 years in the second half of the nineteenth century developed and refined his 'sympathetic vibratory apparatus'. This was used to levitate metal balls and other heavier weights, to rotate large wheels, to power engines, and even to disintegrate granite by resonating in sympathy with the quartz therein.[197] From descriptions his apparatus relied on the use of spherical objects made from a combination of copper, gold, platinum and silver, and on the blowing of a sustained note on a simple trumpet, all of which shares many similarities with that reported by the visitors to Tibet many years later. Keely performed myriad demonstrations for interested observers in his laboratory – all of whom apparently came away suitably impressed – and he did attempt to put his apparatus into commercial production. Unfortunately this was hampered by the fact that it had to be tuned to the natural frequency of its surroundings, including that of any observers or operators. This and a major disagreement with his investors, after which he destroyed most of his research notes, meant that – despite his earlier efforts to share them – his secrets went to the grave with him.

By contrast the next major figure – an eccentric Latvian immigrant to the United States called Edward Leedskalnin – claimed that 'he knew the secret of how the pyramids were built' but was always determined to keep it to himself. Chris Dunn has investigated what he dubs the 'Coral Castle Mystery', whereby in the first half of the twentieth century Leedskalnin built himself a 'castle' constructed entirely from blocks of coral at Homestead, Florida.[198] There is every reason to suspect that he achieved this single-handed, despite being only 5 feet tall and weighing about 110 pounds, without the use of modern construction machinery – which becomes all the more intriguing when one establishes that a number of the blocks he used weighed between 20 and 30 tonnes. The average block weight was more than 2 tonnes, the total 1,100 tonnes, and his creation took some 28 years to complete. Despite visits from engineers, technologists and even the US government, he refused to divulge his secret right up to his death in 1952. However, from the remaining contents of his simple workshop – which is open to the public along with the rest of the site – Dunn suggests that Leedskalnin had discovered some means of locally reversing the effects of gravity; indeed he speculates that he generated a radio signal that caused the coral to vibrate at its resonant frequency, and then used an electromagnetic field to 'flip' the magnetic poles of the atoms so they were in opposition to the Earth's magnetic field rather than attracted to it. If Dunn's theory is right, this method is more akin to the experiments with antigravity devices that have been conducted for many decades.[199] However, one little twist to this story tends to indicate that, whatever Leedskalnin did, he did not require excessive equipment. He had in fact started his construction near Florida City, but had moved it all to Homestead after being attacked by thugs. A local truck driver who assisted him in transporting the blocks apparently reported that Leedskalnin asked to be alone for a moment while they were preparing to load a 20-tonne obelisk, and was amazed to hear a great crash only seconds later – and rushing back found the little man dusting off his hands, the obelisk being fully loaded and ready!

Moving right up to the present, and to confirm to the cynics among you that the foregoing is not just myth or trickery, an American acoustics engineer, Tom Danley, has worked for a number of years in research connected with this field. He and two colleagues from a company called Intersonics developed acoustic levitation and positioning devices that have also been tested by NASA – primarily, it appears, for their application to the suspension of solids and liquids without the need for containers.[200] The abstract from their US Patent No. 5036944, dated 6 August 1991, describes their research in the following broad terms:

An acoustic levitator includes a pair of opposed sound sources which have interfering sound waves producing acoustic energy wells in which an object may be levitated. The phase of one sound source may be changed relative to the other in order to move the object along an axis between the sound sources.

Although it would appear that Danley and his colleagues have been working with relatively small objects, it is clear that at least one set of basic principles is now scientifically in place.

In an interesting twist, Danley became involved with the examination of the Great Pyramid in 1996 via his friendship with the American documentary maker Boris Said. Danley himself has been almost completely silent on the nature of his acoustic experiments therein – because his work was conducted as part of an expedition led by the American millionaire Joseph Schor, under the terms of a nondisclosure agreement. These are all central characters to the politics of the last part of this work, and as such these issues will be examined in far greater detail later. In the meantime we do have some scant details from Said of Danley's work:[201]

In the Great Cheops Pyramid in the King's Chamber an F-sharp chord is resident, sometimes below the range of human hearing. Former NASA consultant Tom Danley feels the sound may be caused by wind blowing across the ends of the air shafts and causing a pop-bottle effect. These vibrations, some ranging as low as 9 hertz down to 0.5 hertz, are enhanced by the dimensions of the Pyramid, as well as the King's Chamber and the sarcophagus case inside. According to Danley, even the type of stone was selected to enhance these vibrations.

Furthermore, American mysteries researcher JJ Hurtak, director of the Academy for Future Science, has suggested that 'this chord [F-sharp] is the harmonic of planet Earth' to which native Americans still tune their instruments, and is 'in perfect harmony with the human body'.[202] Since these sounds are primarily infrasound (below the level of human hearing), and we cannot be certain whether or not the casing originally covered the shafts up, in our view it is unlikely that they were deliberately designed to produce this effect. Meanwhile Dunn, although not an acoustics expert, suggests that Danley may be mistaken about the source of the infrasonic vibrations, arguing that they come not from the shafts but from the Earth itself, magnified by the acoustic properties of the Great Pyramid. He also reveals that Danley's experiments suggested that the granite blocks forming the floor of the King's Chamber were sitting on 'corrugated' support blocks, which would cause minimal disruption to their ability to resonate. In 1995 Dunn conducted his own experiments, during which he found that when he struck the coffer it registered the note A with a frequency of 438 cycles per second (remember Greaves and others had always noted that it 'rang like a bell'), and further that the whole chamber was designed to amplify and resonate that frequency and octaves thereof. According to Dunn this has been confirmed by other researchers he has contacted.[203]

Several other British researchers of our acquaintance, including David Elkington and David Ritchie, are working along similar lines, although at the time of writing their work remains unpublished. One in particular, John Reid – a sound and acoustics engineer – prepared a brief paper for us which summarises his recent research. He states that, when he visited the Great Pyramid in late 1996, he was 'struck by the remarkable acoustic resonance of the King's Chamber and its sarcophagus', and that, when vocalising various tones while lying in the sarcophagus and then standing beside it, he was staggered by the intensity of the reflected energy: 'The effect of lying in the sarcophagus whilst toning its prime resonant frequency is almost like taking a bath. Waves of sonic energy wash over your body almost like water'. He then describes two subsequent research visits the following year, by which time he was armed with a battery of instrumentation:[204]

> The data obtained from my research visits in February and November 97 could easily persuade me that the King's Chamber and its sarcophagus were designed to acoustically couple, in order to enhance certain rituals which I believe were performed in the chamber. Three solid pieces of empirical data correlate very closely but of course this could still be coincidence and further research is needed to strengthen the case. When the results of my preliminary investigation are published, many people will be excited by what they read and they may believe I am being over cautious in my conclusions. However, if one wants to be taken seriously by the scientific and Egyptological communities one must observe caution, unless the evidence is overwhelming. I define my current results as merely 'intriguing'.

Reid has also revealed to us that he has obtained interesting results in the Red Pyramid, which makes us feel far more comfortable about his grasp of *context* than that of many of his fellow researchers. Indeed his agreeable understatement of his work contrasts favourably with the egotistic trumpet-blowing encountered so often, and we look forward to his publishing his results in the autumn of 1999. Although we clearly do not agree with, for example, Dunn's assertion that these acoustic properties were deliberately built into the Great Pyramid in order to create a resonant chamber that formed part of an energy plant, we do believe, along with Reid and others, that it is *possible* they were incorporated deliberately – perhaps into most of the early pyramids – as part of a ritual associated with the king's journey to the afterlife. But what has all this got to do with the *method* of construction of the pyramids?

The answer, and the reason we have briefly covered the topic of the pyramids' acoustic properties, is that, *if* we postulate that the pyramids were *deliberately* designed on the basis of acoustic knowledge, it can only enhance the possibility that the Ancient Egyptians *also* knew how to harness the clearly related principles of sonic levitation.

Advanced machining technology?

The other 'strand' that we previously left open is the issue of the tools used to work the harder stones like granite and basalt. We have seen that the orthodox camp accept that saws and tubular drills were used, and that although they assume copper to be the only metal available they point to a variety of 'slurries' or 'impregnations' being used on the cutting edges.

The first issue that we can sensibly question is the metals available. Only copper tools have been found so far in Old Kingdom remains. However, Petrie was quite convinced that bronze must have been used – he found green traces in cuts just as Lehner has, but of course these could derive from either metal. Despite the fact that all the bronze tools found so far date from the Middle Kingdom at the earliest, it should be remembered that, as far as we are aware, all the descriptions of the small hook found *sealed* inside one of the Queen's Chamber shafts suggest that it is made of bronze. However – even though the Ancient Egyptians could have devised a special means of tempering bronze to a harder finish – even this would have required crystalline tips or slurries to be effective on hard stone, so its use or otherwise makes no great difference in our view. What could make a significant difference is if iron was used – and we should recall the discovery of the 'iron plate', possibly plated with gold, found by Hill at the mouth of the southern King's Chamber shaft. Most of the orthodox community has attempted to play down this find, suggesting – in our view with no good reason given the detailed certification provided – that the plate was a later intrusion. Nevertheless, Petrie appears convinced of its provenance,[205] as for example is Lepre, although strangely both seem to derive only extremely narrow implications from the find. Both suggest that iron plates may have been used to protect the underside of limestone blocks to which levers were being applied, and Lepre suggests the levers themselves may have been made of iron. But surely if this material was available it would have been used to produce chisels, saws and drills, which would have been far superior to anything made of copper or bronze in terms of both effectiveness and durability.

Since we believe such iron tools may well have been used, we must answer the question as to why none have been found that date to the Old Kingdom. Our view is that, first, even relatively few copper tools have been recovered when one considers the huge numbers that must have been used at the time the early pyramids were being built. And, second, iron tools would clearly be subject to disintegration by rusting – especially given the high level of nitrates in Egyptian soil – which would make their chances of survival over such a prolonged interval virtually nil. Be that as it may, there are in fact much more important questions to examine regarding the nature of the power source for the drills and saws.

Many alternative researchers in recent years have picked up on some of the more controversial comments made by Petrie about ancient machining methods. For example, he fundamentally disagrees with suggestions that a slurry or powder was used on hard stone, asserting that the narrow grooves and clearly defined drill marks that he found could be created only by 'fixed jewel points'[206] (although modern experience tells us that either method will work). He also suggests that the more precious jewel-tipped tools would have been few and far between, and would have been carefully guarded and recycled – this explaining why we have not found any examples. However, he goes much further than this, arguing from the remnants of diorite and granite vases and bowls that they show all the hallmarks of having been produced on a *lathe*. For example, careful measurement of one fragment of open bowl revealed that it had been turned from two different centres of rotation – in other words, the piece had been removed and then aligned slightly differently in the lathe. A similar bowl revealed a similar but this time deliberate repositioning, which had been used to machine an internal lip on the rim – and the small but clear cusp between the two angles of cut had not been removed by polishing.[207]

But most controversially, although he makes no specific mention of high-speed, powered machine tools, he does make an observation about the speed of the tube drills:

The amount of pressure, shown by the rapidity with which the drills and saws pierced through the hard stones, is very surprising;

212

probably a load of at least a ton or two was placed on the 4-inch drills cutting in granite. On the granite core, No. 7, the spiral of the cut sinks .1 inch in the circumference of 6 inches, *or 1 in 60, a rate of ploughing out the quartz and feldspar which is astonishing.* Yet these grooves cannot be due to the mere scratching produced in withdrawing the drill, as has been suggested, since there would be about $\frac{1}{10}$ inch thick of dust between the drill and the core at that part; thus there could scarcely be any pressure applied sideways, and the point of contact of the drill and granite could not travel around the granite however the drill might be turned about. Hence these rapid spiral grooves cannot be ascribed to anything but the descent of the drill into the granite under enormous pressure; unless, indeed, we supposed a separate rhymering tool to have been employed alternately with the drill for enlarging the groove, for which there is no adequate evidence.

We were intrigued by the suggestions of tube drilling, and closely inspected a door-hinge hole in the Valley Temple which remains perfectly spherical although with a slight taper, and extremely smooth to the touch (see Plate 26). That it was formed by tubular drilling is further evinced by the rough stump of the core that was left unsmoothed at the base of the hole, the striations in the sides, and the complete absence of chisel marks – although intriguingly other hinge holes in the edifice clearly *have* been rough-chiselled. Furthermore, on a visit to the Petrie Museum in London we examined granite core 'No. 7' as described in the extract above, and exactly the same features can be seen in reverse (see Plate 27); indeed, since Petrie found this item in the Valley Temple, and its red colour and dimensions match the hole we inspected, there is even a possibility that the two may 'match'.[208] We wanted to know more . . .

The work of the alternative researchers who have brought Petrie's observations to light in recent years has in the main improved the quality of research in this area for two reasons. First, researchers like Graham Hancock – in his earlier work *Fingerprints of the Gods* – and the Canadian journalist Robert Mckenty have searched through the collections of the Cairo Museum and others, bringing us amazing reports of an incredible multitude of beautifully crafted bowls and vases fashioned from granite, diorite and basalt, many of which come from mastabas at Abydos and Saqqara and date to pre- and Early Dynastic times. Not only is the quality of these artefacts far superior to those of later eras – showing the sort of incredible quality and passion that is perhaps best exemplified by the statue of Khafre discussed previously – but their abundance seems to suggest that their creation was no great achievement. Above all, they clearly support Petrie's contention that lathes were used, especially to turn out the inside of thin-necked vases the bowls of which then widen considerably – and even more so when one finds that at least one example of such a vase was machined virtually to a point at the base, but so symmetrically inside and out that it still balances upright (see Plate 30).[209]

Second, a number of engineers have come forward and brought their analytical skills to the table – professionals whose practical experience in this instance is more relevant than the more academic knowledge of Egyptologists. Since these relative newcomers tend to be less vociferous in their condemnation of the orthodoxy, and rather suggest quite reasonably that the skills of the two disciplines should be brought together to attempt to solve the more complex enigmas of ancient Egyptian technology, we wholeheartedly endorse their approach. So what do they have to say?

The main professional proponent of the suggestion that we need to completely revise our view of ancient Egyptian technology is Dunn. For many years he has been developing a case that, in its relatively unique application of professional engineering expertise, appears at first sight extremely sound. His arguments regarding technology alone are many and varied, and must be distilled here to the bare essentials.

Dunn starts by comparing the levels of accuracy applied to the Great Pyramid's construction with those of modern building projects. He suggests that the facing and squaring of the casing stones – with a mean variation on the larger lower ones of a mere 0.01 of an inch over an area of 35 square feet, while the gaps between them averaged only 0.02 of an inch – is incredibly accurate even when compared with the tolerances used in most modern machine shops for large construction parts. And, when he reveals that a professional limestone quarryman in Indiana told him that on similar work he uses tolerances of about 0.25 of an inch, we tend to sit up and take notice.[210] Even more astounding, when Dunn measured the interior of the King's Chamber coffer he found it was accurate to within 0.002 of an inch – and he found similar accuracy in other coffers.[211] A civil engineer informed him that when levelling foundations they tend to work to a variance of 0.02 of an inch *per foot* – this would produce an acceptable variation of over 15 inches in the 756-foot sides of the Great Pyramid's base, and yet what we find is less than 1 inch.[212] As a further example, we have already seen that the Descending Passage was cut to an accuracy of 0.25 of an inch over its entire 350-foot length.

Dunn primarily suggests that this incredible engineering accuracy would be necessary only if the *purpose* of the edifice required it. But we feel that his argument falls down when we consider that, for example, the accuracy of the facing of the casing stones would not be critical to the functioning of the edifice as a power plant as he describes it. We have seen that a more valid explanation is that any inaccuracy in the first course – which is where the casing examined comes from – would have a significant knock-on effect further up, whereas we cannot be sure that the same level of accuracy would have been maintained all the way up the rest of the edifice. Furthermore, he admits that this same level of accuracy is repeated elsewhere, for example in the interior of the coffer in the Second Pyramid – and yet the interior design of *this* edifice clearly could not support his intricate power-plant theory.

Moving on to the *methods* employed, Dunn first looks closely at two errors originally noted by Petrie in the manufacture of the King's Chamber coffer:

> On the north end is a place, near the west side, where the saw was run too deep into the granite, and was backed out again by the masons; but this fresh start they made still too deep, and two inches lower they backed out a second time, having cut more than .10 inch deeper than they had intended . . . [Petrie also noted a similar saw-cut error in the underside of the coffer in the Second Pyramid.][213]

. . .

On the east inside is a portion of a tube-drill hole remaining, where they had tilted the drill over into the side by not working it vertically. They tried hard to polish away all that part, and took off about 1/10 inch thickness all around it; but they still had to leave the side of the hole 1/10 deep, 3 long, and 1.3 wide; the bottom of it is 8 or 9 below the original top of the coffer [all inches]. They made a similar error on the north inside, but of a much less extent. There are traces of horizontal grinding lines on the west inside.[214]

Dunn suggests that these errors would not have been committed if the saw and drill were being operated by hand, since the feed rate would be so slow that they would have been noticed and corrected long before they became so pronounced. He therefore suggests that all this must point to the coffer having been machined at high speed.[215]

In support of this argument Dunn turns his attention to the drill cores, and Petrie's observation about the 'astonishing' feed rate of 0.1 of an inch per revolution on the 6-inch circumference (a diameter of 1.9 inches) of the granite core 'No. 7' to which we previously referred.[216] He reports that two separate machinists have informed him that the fastest modern diamond drills, rotating at a maximum of only 900 r.p.m. because higher speeds cause overheating, cut through granite at the rate of 0.2 of an inch per minute – which equates to 0.0002 of an inch per revolution. Although he does not mention the diameter of the holes being bored when these rates are quoted, which we can only assume must make some difference, they are unlikely to be significantly larger – certainly not large enough to make up for a feed rate that is apparently 500 times faster! He and certain colleagues have therefore come to the conclusion that not only were the drills *not* powered by hand, but that there is only one technology of which we are currently aware – and with which we have only recently started to experiment – that *can* explain the extraordinary feed rate: the use of ultrasound. Furthermore, Dunn suggests that an analysis of the core also reveals that the 'spiral groove cut deeper through the quartz than through the softer feldspar' – to be clear, he means that the groove itself goes deeper towards the *centre* of the core in the quartz layers. Since we know that ultrasound causes quartz to vibrate to the point where it softens considerably, he argues that this confirms his suggested solution.

We remained impressed by Dunn's theories for a long time. However, when we came to study his work in detail a few alarm bells started to sound.[217] A close examination of his suggestion as to how the ultrasonic drill would have worked reveals the following problem. He clearly appreciates that an ultrasonic drill bit cuts via a high-speed vertical *pounding* action – not by rotation. In fact using ultrasound rotation is only optionally used at very slow speeds to advance the drill into the hole. Consequently he is forced to attempt to explain the concentric grooves, (clearly caused by relatively high-speed rotation), as the result of several possibilities: 'An uneven flow of energy may have caused the tool to oscillate more on one side than the other, the tool may have been improperly mounted, or a buildup of abrasive on one side of the tool may have cut the groove as the tool spiralled into the granite.' To be fair, he then concedes that a non-ultrasonic but conventionally rotating drill bit may have been used, and that the grooves would therefore be explained by the rapid *withdrawal* of the drill. That this logic is unfortunately muddled is revealed by the fact that it is from the spacing apart of these very grooves that he and Petrie deduced the incredibly high feed rate in the first place.

Where does this leave us? We would have been torn between attempting to amend Dunn's analysis, and accepting an apparently flawed orthodox stance, had it not been for the fortuitous intervention of John Reid – whom we have already mentioned in connection with his theories of pyramid acoustics. Reid has enlisted the help of Harry Brownlee – an expert stonemason and sculptor – and together they have studied the tubular drill cores that so amazed Petrie and Dunn. They make the critical distinction, not effectively made by Dunn, between the *horizontal* striations that are found on *all* cores – these being *separate* grooves, which are on close inspection randomly spaced – and *spiral* striations, which are genuinely connected spiral grooves. Petrie reports that he found these latter on only *one* piece, which he examined – our old friend drill core 'No. 7', whereon he describes four connected spiral turns. Reid and

Brownlee have examined and photographed this core in minute detail, and report that even on this they can detect only *horizontal* striations (see Plate 28); they can only conclude that there may be some confusion in the labelling of the artefact at the museum, and in order to cover all possibilities they provide explanations for both types of striation, which do not rely on highly advanced machining methods. Via Reid, Brownlee gave us the following statement:[218]

You will find similar tube drill cores lying in the waste heaps of any modern workshop where granite is drilled. The *horizontal* striations seen on the Petrie cores are a function of the amount of wobble on the drill bit due to eccentricity in the bit or wear in the bearings of the shaft. We can assume that the ancient Egyptian craftsmen would have faced even greater difficulty in producing and maintaining wobble-free bits with shafts made from wood. On modern cores, new drills in good machines produce very faint striations, but worn drills in worn machines give very similar effects to those seen on the Petrie cores. I believe that Petrie was correct in his assumption that the ancient Egyptians used bronze tubular drills in which diamonds or corundums were embedded, not only in the tip *but also in the wall*, as part of the casting process. The particles in the drill walls, coupled with pieces of quartz dislodged from the granite, are responsible – along with the wobble – for the omnipresent and actually random *horizontal* striations.

If Petrie did observe *spiral* striations, despite our inability to trace them on drill core No. 7, I believe they would have been caused by the withdrawal of the drill whilst it was still turning. Petrie mentions that this had been suggested but dismisses it because he assumes that a buffer of dust would build up between the drill and the core which would prevent such score marks. What he failed to consider was that the drill bit would have had a considerable wobble whilst it was turning, the side-thrust of which would allow any of the sizeable chips of diamond or corundum embedded in it to produce the spiral grooves as the slowly-turning drill was *extracted* at far greater speed than it drilled. My concept of the machinery they used would allow the drill to be raised and lowered with ease – despite the requirement for a superimposed weight of at least one tonne – while the animals which probably provided the motive force would not stop during this operation, so the shaft would continue to rotate. Indeed I suspect that the drill would need to have been regularly withdrawn in a simple and non-disruptive manner in order that the build-up of waste could be cleared.

As a result I disagree with Petrie's assumption that a feed rate of 1 in 60 was achieved for this particular core. Even modern, diamond-tipped, water-cooled drills cannot produce such a result, and as for any suggestion of ultrasound being employed – as has been recently suggested – not only is this unrealistic for obvious reasons, but from my experience ultrasound produces cores which are totally *free of striations*.

As further evidence of the existence of the play in the shaft, you only have to look at the triangular indent on the east wall of the King's Chamber sarcophagus to see that the tubular drill employed had a large amount of slap in its bearings, which caused it to wander off its perpendicular plane and penetrate past the vertical datum of the wall. However the deviation was sufficiently slight to be not immediately visible to the naked eye of the operators until it had progressed for several inches. They tried to polish out the indent made by the drill tip but couldn't remove it completely, and left the tell-tale evidence. As for the wandering saw marks, these are only about 1 mm deep and could easily have gone unnoticed up to this depth, especially since they would probably have used blocks of stone or wood attached to the granite block to act as guides – a method we still use in the field today – which would have masked the cut.

As for the suggestion that the quartz layers were cut deeper than the feldspar, when a diamond or corundum-tipped tubular drill meets a region of quartz which is imbedded in the softer feldspar, some of the quartz may be ripped out, depending upon the crystal's orientation and grain direction with respect to the tool angle. What sometimes remains is a shallow indent lying below the level of the adjacent feldspar, giving the appearance that the tool had cut deeper into the quartz than the feldspar.

This all starts to make some sense at last. And in order that they 'put their money where their mouth is', Reid and Brownlee plan to begin constructing a half-scale granite replica of the King's Chamber sarcophagus soon, which they hope will shed light on some of the mysteries surrounding the real thing. But what about Dunn's suggestion that the bowls and vases previously mentioned would have been impossible to create by hand?[219] Brownlee makes the following comments:[220]

> Even with the best modern tools and machines we would not find it easy to manufacture such artifacts, yet these near perfect bowls and vases are there for all to see and testimony to the great skill of the ancient craftsmen. Following our manufacture of the half-scale sarcophagus, John and I will try to emulate their results and produce some lathe-turned bowls and vases using hand made tools on a potters wheel-style lathe. In so doing, we hope to rediscover methods of manufacture which were forgotten thousands of years ago.

Conclusion

We have come a long way since the start of this chapter, and indeed there are still areas where we have only skimmed the surface. These issues have a far broader significance than just the determination of how the pyramids were built, since any evidence of advanced technology must be explained – how could it have been developed, and would it imply that advanced civilisations have existed on this planet for far longer than is traditionally accepted? So what have we actually concluded?

As far as the construction of the pyramids is concerned, we have gone to a great deal of effort to prove that the bulk of the orthodox explanation appears to hold water – even in terms of the raising of the granite roofing monoliths to a considerable height in the Great Pyramid. We did, however, become uneasy when we came to the considerably larger megaliths used in the temples on the Plateau, especially when we found evidence of similar blocks dotted around the Ancient World. Our investigation led us to believe that the supposed myths of sonic levitation may have some foundation in truth, especially when we considered the evidence suggesting that such techniques survived in Tibet until relatively recently. This suspicion was strengthened by evidence of their possible re-creation by a few Western pioneers in the last two centuries, by the ongoing work of modern scientists, and by suggestions of the acoustic knowledge incorporated into the designs of the early pyramids.

We have all seen simple phenomena, like an opera singer striking a note that can make a glass shatter, or a 'magician' levitating a person in midair – indeed many of us will have been involved in demonstrations whereby we ourselves are left supporting someone with just the tips of our fingers. Surely we do not have to understand the details of *how* such things work to believe that they *do* work. Since the orthodox explanation of the manoeuvring of huge megaliths feels increasingly contrived as the weights go up, is it not just as reasonable, if not more so, to suggest that sonic levitation may have been used – at least selectively? Or alternatively that our ancient forebears in some way harnessed their ability to exercise 'mind over matter'? After all, this is an ability we still retain – as witnessed by the occasional reports of, for example, a desperate mother lifting a car off her trapped child – albeit that most of us have forgotten how to deliberately harness these innate skills.

Of course to the extent that levitation of blocks may have been achieved by what we might term rather more 'spiritual' techniques, we are not necessarily required to search for 'lost civilisations'. And, as for the suggestion that advanced machining techniques which required an electrical or other power source were used, we have seen that the evidence is mixed. Here in particular we laymen can exercise logic as much as we like, but ultimately we are in the hands of the professionals whose expertise alone can provide the real answers. Furthermore, it is clear that further practical experiments of the type planned by Reid and Brownlee will reveal far more than acres of paper ever can. Accordingly, we await the results of their experiments with great anticipation. At the moment we can say that their interpretation appears to answer most of the difficult questions satisfactorily without the need for recourse to highly advanced technology – although to accept this explanation for the achievements of the Ancient Egyptians and others we must appreciate that their minds worked in very different ways from our own: they had a totally different concept of time and patience and dedication, which puts us to shame. For example, Dunn suggests that a beautifully worked schist 'goblet' in the shape of a trumpet may be far more than just a simple drinking artefact for use about the house or temple. He believes that it resembles a 'Helmholtz resonator', which would be used to amplify vibrational energy.[221] Although his contention is probably invalidated in that it has a flat and not a rounded base, to create such a beautiful artefact from such hard material to make even a goblet used for important rituals would require enormous dedication and skill.

Is that it? Well, not quite . . .

Not quite, because some of the objects that Dunn and others have identified still leave us baffled. For example, the function of a schist bowl with three lobes folded towards the centre is almost impossible to determine (see Plate 29). Like the 'goblet', it has been expertly crafted from extremely hard material and can be inspected in the Cairo Museum. And even Dr Zahi Hawass himself, after examining an early Egyptian skull, suggested the following in an interview:[222] 'One of the workmen had had a brain operation and this man lived another two years. Just think about it – a doctor 4,600 years ago could perform a successful brain operation!' These Egyptian relics form only a small selection of a multitude of anomalous ancient artefacts that have been found all over the world. Can we therefore be so hasty to reject the notion of advanced technology – and indeed of previous advanced civilisations – in antiquity? This is a huge subject, which must await another book.

In the meantime, on this subject at least, we feel the maintenance of an open mind emptied of ingrained preconceptions is the only appropriate stance.

CHAPTER

FIVE

LEGENDS OF THE HALL

At the end of the last chapter we considered the possibility that some sections of the Ancient Egyptian community, and indeed of other civilisations of the Ancient World, may have been more advanced than modern man, not only in certain aspects of 'technology', but also in their ability to harness the massive potential of the human brain. It was also suggested that if this were the case, then we would have to ask where such knowledge originated.

The orthodox camp would suggest that the archaeological record of the previous millennia does not support a theory of progressive advancement, while the alternative camp counter on two fronts. First, they suggest that some of the surviving edifices we have already considered, and other anomalous arte-facts from around the world, are not being analysed and interpreted with proper objectivity – or are being ignored completely. Second, they claim that we may have to look back many millennia for the real development stages, and that the archaeological record for this period was obliterated by the Deluge, which all religions of the world report, an event for which there is increasing geological evidence. They further argue that if this occurred around 12,000 years ago, all we see are 'pockets' of rebuilding around the world by survivors of the catastrophe who retained the 'Ancient Wisdom'.

This is necessarily an extremely brief summary of the general arguments in this area, and the whole subject will form the basis of a later work. But suffice to say that one of the critical pieces of evidence that advanced civilisations had inhabited this planet long ago would be the discovery of a cache or 'time-capsule' of records handed down by these ancient forebears. It is argued that such a cache would have represented a closely guarded secret, protected and preserved by an elite of 'shaman

223

priests', who were the real source of power in the Ancient World, and it is not beyond the bounds of possibility that such 'guardians' still exist.

In this chapter we will therefore start by reviewing the various 'legends' that indicate that such knowledge was indeed preserved – and we must bear in mind that Giza is not necessarily the only suggested location. The readings provided by the infamous American seer Edgar Cayce in the middle of the twentieth century will then be examined. Cayce's work has undoubtedly proved the prime motivation for the 'new seekers' of such records at Giza – especially in the build-up to the new millennium – since he supposedly predicted that this was the time for their discovery. These seekers have in fact dominated the more recent surveys and explorations of the Plateau, and are at the very heart of the political wranglings that will be considered in Part III. We will therefore examine the potential reliability of Cayce himself, and of his methods and readings, and we will look to establish whether his work is corroborated by other esoteric sources. Finally, we will look at the personalities involved in the organisation set up to preserve his work and continue research into these and other areas – the 'Association for Research and Enlightenment' or ARE – and also attempt to establish how likely it is that the 'time is nigh'.

Before we start, it should be remembered that certain of the topics covered in a previous chapter, such as the idea that the Great Pyramid contained a timeline of biblical prophecy, or that mathematical and geodesic knowledge may have been incorporated into its design, are considered by some to represent aspects of the 'knowledge repository'. However, in our view these issues are separate, and if anything they only prove that knowledge was being *applied*; they do not represent the *source*.

The Hall in Antiquity

It is a common misconception that Edgar Cayce was the first person to promote the concept of the 'Hall of Records'. While he certainly seems to have coined this popular term, there is no question that the idea was already firmly entrenched in historical legends. Indeed there are aspects of some ancient

Egyptian texts that have been used to provide support for this concept – and it is with these that we will begin our search . . .

Egyptian enigmas

In *On the Shores of Ancient Worlds*, published in 1974, Andrew Tomas suggested that there may be a link between the Hall of Records concept and one of the oldest ancient Egyptian legends – that of Isis and Osiris.[223] In condensed form this legend claims that Osiris came down from the heavens to civilise mankind, assisted by Thoth, the Egyptian god of Wisdom, whose Greek counterpart is Hermes. However, Osiris was killed by his brother Seth, and Isis was forced to retrieve his body from Byblos in the Lebanon. Determined to finish the job, Seth then cut the body into fourteen or sixteen parts, scattering them over Egypt – which Isis also then retrieved and reassembled. Tomas's contention is that the fragments of Osiris's body may have represented a 'ready-made cosmic culture including artefacts of sophisticated science which the priesthood were told by the donors to preserve in secrecy . . . in caches planted by the superior civilisers before they left'. He further contends that the places in which the 'body parts' were buried – including the delta towns of Athribis, Bubastis, Busiris, Sais and Balamun, then, moving south, Heliopolis, Memphis, Faiyum Lake, Cusae, Siut, Abydos, Dendera, Thebes and Elephantine – would subsequently have had permanent 'markers' erected over them, almost certainly in the form of pyramids and temples. This is an interesting suggestion, albeit that it is contained within a book whose main theme is that Earth was originally colonised by visitors from 'outer space'.

More recently three other researchers have suggested that a reinterpretation of certain ancient Egyptian texts may indicate the location of the Hall of Records at Giza. The most lucid proponent of this theory is Andrew Collins, whose *Gods of Eden* was published in 1998. His detailed analysis starts with an examination of the text known as the *Book am-tuat*, or the *Book of What is in the Duat*, translated by Sir EA Wallis Budge in his three-volume work, *The Egyptian Heaven and Hell*.[224] The *duat* is commonly understood to represent the Egyptian concept of the underworld, but all Egyptologists agree that this relatively late New Kingdom text – which would have been used primarily to assist the deceased on their journey to the afterlife – is an edited version of an older text which in the Old Kingdom would have had a different emphasis, primarily celebrating the journey of the sun 'underground' through the twelve hourly divisions of the night. Furthermore, Collins quotes the celebrated Egyptologist Selim Hassan, who suggested that the section dealing with the Fourth and Fifth Divisions of the *duat* – the journey through the kingdom of the god Seker, more usually referred to as the 'Land of Sokar' – may well represent an even older and originally separate text which was then combined with others. Crucially, Hassan suggests that 'the Fifth Division (as well as the Fourth Division) was originally a version of the *duat* and had its geographical counterpart in the Giza necropolis'.[225]

Collins elaborates from this as follows: Sokar was the god of the Memphite necropolis, which encompassed all the major pyramid sites including Giza; the 'descending passage' in certain depictions shows a sometimes 'ribbed' extension to the ceiling, which might be compared to the Grand Gallery in the Great Pyramid,[226] and the passage at this point is referred to as 'the way of Rostau', which is the Egyptian name for Giza.[227] In the Fifth Division the solar barque encounters a bell-shaped object surmounted by two hawks (see Figure 18), which Collins and others believe represents the infamous *benben* stone known to have been erected at Heliopolis, and also the *omphalos* found there and all over the Ancient World. They believe that these in turn represent the 'point of first creation' during what the Ancient Egyptians referred to as the 'first time' or *zep tepi*. Beneath the 'bell' is a representation of the 'primeval mound', and beneath this again an ellipse, containing the hawk-headed Sokar standing on a two-headed and winged serpent, and each side of this ellipse is guarded by a sphinx. Budge suggests that the ellipse represents 'an oval island in the river of the *duat* . . . and it is formed wholly of *sand*'.[228] Collins contends that all this points to a 'physical representation of the *duat* underworld [which] awaits discovery beneath the sands of Giza'. Intriguingly, although Collins does not choose to emphasise this

FIGURE 18: THE FIFTH DIVISION OF THE DUAT[229]

aspect, Budge's translation of part of the text relating to the journey through the Fourth Division reveals the following description of the gods encountered: 'Those who are in this picture, in their forms of their bodies, are the hidden [travellers]

227

upon the way of the *holy country whose secret things are hidden*'.[230]

On its own this may or may not be regarded as significant support for the concept of a Hall of Records at Giza. It should be noted that the *Book of Gates*, which also deals with the twelve divisions of the underworld, does not contain the same information – in fact the kingdom referred to in the Fourth and Fifth Divisions is not even the Land of Sokar. However, Collins goes on to discuss another set of texts commonly referred to as the *Edfu Building Texts*, which are inscribed on the walls and columns of the Temple of Horus at Edfu.[231] They tell the story of the 'first time', and how the world was brought into being by the *shebtiu* gods, whom Collins also refers to as 'Elder Gods', suggesting they were a race of bird-shamans who inhabited the 'Island of the Egg' in a lake at a place referred to as Wetjeset-Neter. Although the original temple on this island was subject to a terrible destruction – and the description of the island surrounded by water, and its destruction, perhaps echoes the legends of Atlantis, which will be discussed later – it was subsequently rebuilt by another race of *shebtiu*, also referred to as *netjeru* gods. Having protected the site from flooding by the use of relics stored within the island known as *iht*, these gods ultimately spawned the *shemsu-hor*, a race of semidivine beings also known as the 'followers of Horus', the predecessors of the human Horus-Kings who ruled pre-Dynastic Egypt.

Collins emphasises that the main link between these two texts is Osiris, since not only is he the god who ruled the *duat*, but also the island in the *Edfu Texts* is supposed to represent his first resting place. Collins uses this connection to link Osiris with Giza, supported by the reference in the Inventory Stela to the 'House of Osiris, Lord of Rostau'; and also quotes an extract from the Dream Stela, which refers to Giza as the 'splendid place of the first time'.

That such an island may have existed next to the Plateau is supported by several pieces of evidence reviewed in previous chapters. First, a natural or man-made lake, fed by the Nile, almost certainly came as far as the eastern sides of the Sphinx and Valley Temples. Second, the reports of, for example, Herodotus ('a conduit was built so that the Nile would encircle an island on which, they say, Cheops himself is buried'), and Hokm ('he commanded in the meantime to build the Pyramids, and that a vault or cistern should be made, into which the river Nile should enter'). Collins also indicates that even Dr EAE Reymond, whose translation of the *Edfu Texts* he uses, suggests that this island, and its temple and subterranean vaults, may well have been a genuine physical structure.

Collins then ponders the possible nature of the contents of such chambers, and their general layout. He argues that the 'egg' by which the island was named was also referred to as the 'embryo' or 'seed', and also the 'Sound Eye', which was the 'centre of the light which illumined the island' – and which had also contributed to the original destruction of the island. He then quotes a spell from the so-called *Coffin Texts* as follows: 'This is the sealed thing, which is in darkness, with fire about it, which contains the efflux of Osiris, and it is put in Rostau' (Spell 1080). Ultimately he suggests this may have been some form of crystal deposited in a central chamber underneath the island, flanked by twelve further chambers in a circle – each representing one of the divisions of the *duat* – which had to be negotiated in various rituals before the central chamber could be accessed. Collectively he refers to them as the 'chambers of creation', and suggests that they must be located to the east of the Plateau, buried somewhere underneath the modern village of Nazlet el-Samman. Although this interpretation clearly moves away from the conventional concept of a Hall of Records, it is interesting nonetheless.

The second researcher to have worked along similar lines is Joseph Jochmans, and in fact his work preceded that of Collins. However, since his *The Hall of Records* was self-published in 1985, and even we were unable to obtain a copy from Jochmans himself,[232] we have not used it as our main reference on the basis that any of you wishing to trace it would have great difficulty. Furthermore, it has to be said that Jochmans's style, his poor referencing and layout, and some of his more fanciful distortions regarding Giza, all make his work a poorer source. All the key points that are worthy of consideration are included in Collins's work as already described.

The third researcher with similar ideas is Nigel Appleby, who in fact repeats Collins's lines of argument almost word for word, except that he disagrees about the location for the buried chambers. Appleby argues they are some five miles northeast of Giza, as dictated by both 'sacred geometry', and by the position of the star Sirius in relation to the belt stars of Orion as represented by the pyramids. Since his book, *Hall of the Gods*, was removed from the shelves only weeks after its publication in 1998 under accusations of plagiarism, and because this episode is an important one in terms of recent political machinations, we will return to Appleby in Part III.

As to providing a brief insight into our views on these various interpretations of Ancient Egyptian texts, in no way do we support them completely. At the very least, Jochmans, Collins and Appleby all support a much earlier date for the edifices on the Plateau, and this is integral to much of their theorising. Furthermore, we know that undue reliance on the interpretation of any ancient texts is fraught with danger, let alone those of Ancient Egypt whose hieroglyphs may well contain all sorts of hidden meanings. However, some aspects of these interpretations are interesting, and it is not impossible that the texts do indicate something intriguing that has yet to be discovered at Giza. As to whether or not this might represent a Hall of Records, we must delay judgement until a great deal more evidence has been examined.

Another Ancient Egyptian text that may shed some light on the issue is the *Westcar Papyrus*.[233] One part of the text relates how Khufu consulted a 'magician' by the name of Djedi: the conversation goes something like this:

> Khufu: 'What of the report that you know the number of the *ipwt* of the *wnt* of Thoth?'
> Djedi: 'I know not the number thereof, but I know the place where it is [*or* they are] . . . in a box of flint in a room called "Revision" in Heliopolis.'

Apparently Khufu had been searching for this information for some time because he wanted to use it in building his 'horizon', which we may assume to mean his tomb or pyramid. But what was, or were, the *ipwt* of the *wnt*? These terms have caused endless speculation: Sir Alan Gardiner's tutor, Professor Adolf Erman, had originally translated them as something like 'the *keys* of the *sanctuary* of Thoth', and concluded that *they* were small enough to be hidden in a flint box. Although there appears to be no dispute over the translation of *wnt* as 'sanctuary', Gardiner disagreed with the association of the term *ipwt* with 'locks', on the basis that the determinative hieroglyph on which this interpretation was based appeared only once in the multiple renderings of the term. He preferred instead the translation 'the *secret chambers* of the sanctuary of Thoth'.

What does all this mean? Whichever of these translation is right, we might assume that Khufu wanted to be able to access Thoth's sanctuary. For what purpose? It has been argued that the knowledge therein could have assisted him merely to construct his pyramid, or perhaps he wanted to store such information in his edifice, or perhaps he wanted to build his edifice *near to* or *on top of* Thoth's chambers. However, all these interpretations ignore the presence of the foregoing phrase: Khufu wanted to know, and Djedi knew the whereabouts of, *the number* of the keys or chambers of Thoth's sanctuary. If we take Gardiner's translation of 'chambers', which is the only one that would have any great significance in this context (after all, it would not be a great help to Khufu to know how many keys Thoth had on his keyring!), then, as the *Hermetica* expert Adrian Gilbert has pointed out, this could mean one of two things: either Khufu simply wanted to replicate the number of Thoth's chambers in his pyramid; or, on a more profound level, he wanted to use Thoth's 'science of numbers' in the construction of his edifice; this could involve, for example, the *pi* and *phi* relationships discussed earlier.[234]

We can only conclude that it is a mistake to suggest that this text supports the idea that Thoth's 'Ancient Wisdom' was, or even still is, secreted somewhere at Giza. Nevertheless, it *could* still be seen to support the general argument that such knowledge did exist somewhere.

Classical confirmation?

None of the Classical historians we have previously encountered has anything useful to say that might shed light on the existence or location of a Hall of Records – except perhaps Herodotus, whose reports of an 'island' underneath the Great Pyramid on which Cheops (Khufu) was buried we have already noted. And of course Pliny's 'well' might be regarded as having some form of connection to such an underground island. It should also be noted that Herodotus is sometimes misquoted in relation to the 'labyrinth', which he inspected near to Lake Moeris. Although he reports that it 'outstrips even the pyramids' and that the Egyptian priests 'absolutely refused to show the underground rooms, on the grounds that there lie the tombs of the kings who originally built the labyrinth', he does *not* – at least in the translation we consulted – report that these underground rooms contained numerous statues and scrolls, as Tomas, for example, suggests.[235] (Since we are about to rely heavily on Tomas's work in the rest of this section, and we have not had the time to check back to the source for the remainder of his references, we must hope this is an isolated mistake. In any case, we do not rely unduly on these reports in reaching our eventual conclusions – they are included more to allow readers to evaluate all the possible evidence.)

Other Classical historians do, however, appear to offer us some interesting reports. According to Tomas the Roman historian Eusebius, writing in the third century AD, reports that in compiling his 'King List' Manetho 'copied from the inscriptions which were engraved in the sacred dialect and hieroglyphic characters upon the columns set up in the Siriatic land [now Lebanon] by Thoth, the first Hermes'. He further argues that this view is supported by Flavius Josephus, a Hebrew historian of the first century AD, who reports that the ancients, afraid that 'their science should at any time be lost to men', engraved their discoveries upon pillars in 'the land of Syria'.[236] A possible connection with Baalbek is established by Tomas. He suggests that the oral traditions of the Roman priests at Baalbek claimed that a labyrinth had been built underneath the massive platform shortly after the Deluge.[237]

A similar set of ideas is put forward in a note by Dr Sprenger on a translation of a Coptic manuscript in Vyse's *Operations*. Although the scribes to whom he refers are unfamiliar to us, he reports the following:[238]

Moses, of Chorene, seems to allude to this account when he mentions that Valarsaces sent to his brother Arsaces (the governor of Armenia), a learned man called Mariba to inquire into the ancient history of Armenia. This person is supposed to have found, amongst the archives of Nineveh, a book, translated from Chaldaic into Greek by order of Alexander the Great, which contained historical records of the most remote antiquity. Valarsaces ordered them to be inscribed upon a column; and the author derived from this monument a considerable part of his history. Cedrenus also says, upon the authority of an apocryphal work ascribed by the Egyptians to Hermes, that Enoch, foreseeing the destruction of the earth, had inscribed the science of astronomy upon two pillars ... Cedrenus was a monk, and lived about 1050.

Moving back to Egypt, Tomas quotes the Roman historian Ammianus Marcellinus of the fourth century AD, as follows: 'Inscriptions which the ancients asserted were engraved on the walls of certain underground galleries constructed in the interior of certain of the pyramids, were intended to preserve ancient wisdom from being lost in the Flood'. Furthermore, he says that Eusebius (again) reported that Agathadaemon had deposited scrolls in the sacred libraries of the temples of Egypt before 3000 BC, while c. 300 BC Crantor stated that there were certain pillars or towers in Egypt that contained a written record of prehistory.[239] Finally Tomas reports that in the fourth century BC Plato, in his *Timaeus* and *Critias* – the most famous source of Atlantis legends – states that as recently as 560 BC there were secret halls in the 'Temple of Neith' at Sais, which contained historical records that had been kept for more than 9,000 years.[240] Meanwhile, Bauval and Hancock note that the *Book of Sothis*, attributed by some to Manetho and commented on by the Byzantine historian Georgios Syncellus in the ninth century AD, suggests that important records were brought to Egypt after the Deluge.[241]

From this it is clear that the classical accounts tend to vary in the extent to which they suggest that ancient records were kept secret, and also in the locations of such records. Do we conclude from this that they are all wrong – or should we consider the possibility that accurate and highly revealing records

233

may have been available at least to a select few all over the Ancient World?

Arab accounts

In contrast to the 'legends' discussed so far in this chapter, the Arab accounts tend to concentrate on the Giza Pyramids alone. We saw in Chapter 1 that Mamun's interest in the Great Pyramid would have been roused by the Arab reports, which continued relatively unchanged for centuries, and at that point we reviewed Hokm's account of how the knowledge of 'profound sciences' and 'what is and what shall be' was placed in the Giza Pyramids by King Saurid so that it would be preserved during the Deluge.

We also mentioned that the accounts of Masoudi and Makrizi are pretty much the same. However, there are a few additional details in these, some of which may have some basis in truth while others are simply amusing. In providing the translation reproduced by Vyse, Dr Sprenger notes that Makrizi in particular emphasises that 'subterraneous passages', rather than the superstructures of the pyramids, were the depositories for the stored writings and artefacts.[242] Further, Makrizi supports Hokm's and Herodotus's contention that channels from the Nile fed these underground passages.[243] However, both Masoudi and Makrizi suggest that the passages lie 40 cubits (approximately 55 feet) underground – and, although Hokm says that the *gates* to them lie at this depth,[244] this does not even represent the depth the descending passages achieve. To add to the general confusion, Masoudi relates the tale of a man who visited the pyramid and was lowered down 'the well' by means of a rope which broke at a depth of 100 cubits (140 feet). The man apparently reappeared some hours later ranting 'he who meddles with and covets what does not belong to him is unjust'. He further relates that other explorers found a variety of amazing artefacts in the underground chambers, all of which seem highly fanciful – a view reinforced by the fact that the man whose rope broke supposedly carried on falling for a further three hours![245]

Edrisi's relatively 'sober' account suggests not only that on the roof of the Queen's Chamber were 'writings in the most ancient characters of the heathen priests' (see Chapter 1), but also that 'the two Great Pyramids have a subterraneous communication'.[246] Latif notes that 'the opening into the interior [of the Great Pyramid] leads to narrow passages, to deep wells, and to pits and precipices' (again see Chapter 1).

Despite the general unreliability of most of the Arab accounts, it could be argued that these excerpts provide some support for the concept of an underground complex at Giza.

Secret doctrines

The 'Hermetic' tradition forms the basis for many of the 'secret doctrines' still preserved by sects such as the Freemasons and Rosicrucians. It was developed openly in Europe during the Renaissance of the Middle Ages, but was based on various ancient Greek and Coptic texts which suggest that the information therein came from the secret writings of Hermes. Hermes is the Greek equivalent of Thoth, the Egyptian god of wisdom, and many scholars now believe that the origin of these texts is Egyptian. Adrian Gilbert has researched this subject in some detail, and was responsible for republishing Walter Scott's original 1924 translation of the *Hermetica* in 1992. He quotes the following extract, supposedly a statement by Thoth (Hermes) himself:[247]

> They [Isis and Osiris] will get knowledge of all my hidden writings, and discern their meaning; and some of these writings they will keep to themselves, but such of them as tend to the benefit of mortal men, they will inscribe on slabs and obelisks.

Not only does this support a number of the 'legends' we have already reviewed, but it also reaffirms the provenance of doctrines whose continued influence is simplistically demonstrated by the fact that we still use the term 'hermetically sealed'. We do not have the space to delve into the details of these doctrines in this work,[248] and in any case the real 'meat' arguably remains hidden from all but the highest initiates – or in some cases may even have become distorted or lost its original meaning. Nevertheless, there are a few aspects that can be revealed that may shed important light on the concept of the Hall of Records.

Taking Freemasonry first, Collins asserts that much of their modern doctrine is based on the *Book of Enoch*, in which Enoch, the patriarch, is clearly associated with Thoth-Hermes. This work has been pieced together over the centuries from a variety of manuscripts, and although it is not appropriate to go into detail here, it is clear from its contents why the compilers of the Old Testament omitted it – since it raises some intriguing and, for the dogmatic early Christian Church, embarrassing issues. Of particular interest to us is the suggestion therein that before the Deluge Enoch constructed 'nine hidden vaults' one on top of another, in the lowest of which he deposited a 'gold triangular tablet' (or a 'white oriental porphyry stone' in another tradition) bearing the 'Ineffable Name' of the Hebrew God, while a second tablet inscribed with information from the 'angels' was kept safe by his son Methuselah. Above the vaults Enoch also constructed two 'indestructible columns', on one of which were inscribed the 'seven sciences' of mankind, while on the other an inscription stated that 'a short distance away a priceless treasure would be found in a subterranean vault'. The book states that thereafter King Solomon discovered the vaults and incorporated the pillars, or copies thereof, into his temple. These two symbolic pillars form part of every Masonic 'temple' even today.[249]

Turning to the Rosicrucians, Tomas reports that their 'manifesto', the *Fama Fraternitatis*, which first emerged in 1614, describes the opening of the tomb of Master Christian Rosenkreuz:[250]

The sepulchre had seven walls with doors leading to storehouses of books and scrolls. A circular altar stood in the centre, covered with hieroglyphics. The vault was brilliantly illuminated by an artificial 'sun' in the ceiling.

More specifically in relation to Giza, in 1936 the then 'Grand Imperiator' of the Rosicrucian Order, H Spencer Lewis, wrote in *The Symbolic Prophecy of the Great Pyramid* that the Giza Plateau was riddled with underground chambers – an idea we have already encountered numerous times. However, he appears to suggest that this entire network *had already been discovered*.[251] It would appear that this was a somewhat confusing interpretation of the facts relating to the clearance of the Sphinx and its surrounds, and of the discovery of the 'Water Shaft' underneath the Second Pyramid's causeway and various other nearby structures, by Selim Hassan (see Chapter 1). In fact Lewis's diagrams of this network of supposed chambers and passages were almost identical to diagrams (see Figures 19 and 20) drawn up by HC Randall-Stevens – whose work will be considered later because it was supposedly *channelled* to him via the 'spirit voices' of ancient Egyptian initiates. Although it is suggested that the latter drew his versions sometime between 1925 and 1927, they were not published until long after Lewis's. Accordingly, it is unclear from whom they actually originated, but that one of those two men was a plagiarist is clear.

It would appear that the doctrines of both of these orders – and others such as the Knights Templar, who published Randall-Stevens's work – are intriguing, and may indeed have some origins in Ancient Wisdom that was passed down perhaps across many millennia. However, we cannot help but feel that they have become distorted over the ages. For example, Chris Knight and Robert Lomas, in their excellent 'insider' account of Freemasonry called *The Hiram Key*, published in 1997, reveal that as far as they could tell the modern initiates have little or no clue as to the real meaning, symbology and origins of their rituals and beliefs – and their book is the account of their attempt to rediscover this information. Meanwhile, the *details* of the modern Rosicrucians' accounts of secret chambers underneath and initiation rights carried out at the Sphinx and Great Pyramid appear to owe more to fantasy than fact.

Blavatsky bombshell!

Many of you will have heard of Madame Helena Petrovna Blavatsky. Born in Russia in 1831, she travelled extensively in India and the Far East before returning to England, where, in 1875, she founded the Theosophical Society. Essentially the Theosophists' doctrine is that all religions in the world can be traced to one extremely ancient source, and that mankind had evolved over many millennia through a series of 'root races'. When these ideas surfaced in her first book, *Isis Unveiled*, they so astounded the orthodox religious and scientific communities that she was mercilessly castigated for being unscholarly and lacking any real evidence or proof. In the introduction to her second book, *The Secret Doctrine*, first published in 1888, Blavatsky appears in retrospect to accept that the presentation of her first work may have been something of a misjudgement, and she consequently altered her approach considerably, as we will shortly see. Despite this, *all* of her work has been dismissed even by most alternative writers to this day as unscholarly, amid continued claims that either it was based solely on channelled communications with her 'grand masters' or, worse still, she made it all up. This attitude has been reinforced by both her own and her followers' insistence on using terms such as 'magic' and 'occultism' – which are even more stereotyped than 'Atlantis', and tend initially to put off even the most open-minded of researchers, ourselves included.

That the basis of her work is not entirely 'channelled messages' is intimated in her introduction, part of which explains the *Book of Dzyan*, on which much of *The Secret Doctrine* is based:[252]

> One of the greatest, and, withall, the most serious objection to the correctness and reliability of the whole work will be the preliminary STANZAS [of the *Book of Dzyan*]: 'How can the statements in them be verified?' True, if a great portion of the Sanskrit, Chinese and Mongolian works quoted in the present volumes are known to some Orientalists, the chief work – that from which the STANZAS are given – is not in the possession of European Libraries. *The Book of Dzyan* (or 'Dzan') is utterly unknown to our Philologists, or at any rate was never heard of by them under its present name. This is, of course, a great drawback to those who follow the methods of research prescribed by official Science; but to the students of Occultism, and to every genuine Occultist, this will be of little moment. The main body of the Doctrines given is found scattered throughout hundreds and thousands of Sanskrit manuscripts, some already translated – disfigured in their interpretations, as usual – others still awaiting their turn. Every scholar, therefore, has an opportunity of ver-

ifying the statements herein made, and of checking most of the quotations [Blavatsky's capitals].

As to the suggestion that she made it all up, it is not appropriate to go into her work in detail here. All we can suggest is that those readers who are interested might study the words quoted above, and perhaps read at least the introduction if not the whole 1,000 pages of the two volumes of *The Secret Doctrine*. From this one's own conclusions may be formed. For what it is worth we would suggest that Blavatsky's approach does *appear* reasonably scholarly – there is certainly a huge gulf between the thoroughly referenced nature of her work and the channelled material of, for example, Edgar Cayce, which will be examined shortly. A similar gulf exists between Blavatsky's *apparently* unselfish motives – the motto of the society being 'There is No Religion or Law Higher than Truth' – and those of, for example, Zecharia Sitchin, which were criticised earlier. However, it must be admitted that her detractors suggest that her work was not totally reliable.

The format of this two-volume work is that the first, *Cosmogenesis*, deals with the creation of the cosmos and of Earth, and the second, *Anthropogenesis*, with the various stages of mankind's development on Earth. Each begins with a selection of stanzas from the *Book of Dzyan*, followed by a lengthy commentary explaining and cross-referencing them to other works and ideas. Giza and the pyramids obtain only relatively brief mentions,[253] and the Hall of Records is not mentioned per se at all. But the potential explosiveness of Blavatsky's work, and perhaps the answer to the whole riddle of secreted Ancient Wisdom, lies in the following excerpt. Although she does not mention exactly where she was when she was studying the manuscript – for obvious reasons given the requirement that only a small part of the 'universal and perennial wisdom' should be released to mankind at large – she does provide clues:

> However it may be, and whatsoever is in store for the writer through malevolent criticism, one fact is quite certain. The members of several esoteric schools – the seat of which is beyond the Himalayas, and whose ramifications may be found in China,

Japan, India, Tibet, and even in Syria, besides South America – claim to have in their possession the *sum total* [Blavatsky's italics] of sacred and philosophical works in manuscripts and type: all the works, in fact, that have ever been written, in whatever language or characters, since the art of writing began; from the ideographic hieroglyphs down to the alphabet of Cadmus and Devanagari.

It has been claimed in all ages that ever since the destruction of the Alexandrian Library, every work of a character that might have led the profane to the ultimate discovery and comprehension of some of the mysteries of the Secret Science, was, owing to the combined efforts of members of the Brotherhoods, diligently searched for. It is added, moreover, by those who know, that once found, save three copies left and stored safely away, such works were all destroyed.[254]

. . .

Moreover, in all the large and wealthy lamasaries, there are sub-terranean crypts and cave-libraries, cut in the rock, whenever the *gonpa* and the *lhakhang* are situated in the mountains. Beyond the Western Tsaydam, in the solitary passes of *Kuen-lun* [Karakorum Mountains, Western Tibet] there are several such hiding places. Along the ridge of Altyn-Toga, whose soil no European foot has ever trodden so far, there exists a certain hamlet, lost in a deep gorge. It is a small cluster of houses, a hamlet rather than a monastery, with a poor-looking temple in it, with one old lama, a hermit, living near by to watch it. Pilgrims say that the subterranean galleries and halls under it contain a collection of books, the number of which, according to the accounts given, is too large to find room even in the British Museum.[255]

. . .

. . . some of the doctrines of the Secret Schools – though by no means all – were preserved in the Vatican, and have since become part and parcel of the mysteries, in the shape of disfigured additions made to the original Christian programme by the Latin Church. Such is the now materialised dogma of the Immaculate Conception. This accounts for the great persecutions set on foot by the Roman Catholic Church against Occultism, Masonry, and heterodox mysticism generally.[256]

She is also quite clear about the reason why such information has been hidden for so long – and will largely remain so unless and until the Western world undergoes a dramatic transformation. In the first place, she discusses how the Christian Church especially attempted to destroy all the evidence.[257]

> However superhuman the efforts of the early Christian fathers to obliterate the Secret Doctrine from the very memory of man, they all failed. Truth can never be killed; hence the failure to sweep away entirely from the face of the Earth every vestige of that Ancient Wisdom, and to shackle and gag every witness who testified to it. Let one only think of the thousands, and perhaps millions, of manuscripts burnt; of monuments, with their too indiscreet inscriptions and pictorial symbols, pulverised to dust; of the bands of early hermits and ascetics roaming about among the ruined cities of Upper and Lower Egypt, in desert and mountain, valleys and highlands, seeking for and eager to destroy every obelisk and pillar, scroll or parchment they could lay their hands on, if it only bore the symbol of the *tau*, or any other sign borrowed and appropriated by the new faith; and he will then see plainly how it is that so little has remained of the records of the Past. Verily, the fiendish spirits of fanaticism, of early and mediaeval Christianity and of Islam, have from the first loved to dwell in darkness and ignorance . . . Both creeds have won their proselytes at the point of the sword; both have built their churches on heaven-kissing hecatombs of human victims.

She then indicates why, as a result of such brutal suppression, mankind's descent into genuine profanity has led to the need for only a slow and gradual dissemination of the lost wisdom:[258]

> For it is not the fault of the initiates that these documents are now 'lost' to the profane; nor was their policy dictated by selfishness, or any desire to monopolise the life-giving sacred lore. There were portions of the Secret Science that for incalculable ages had to remain concealed from the profane gaze. But this was because to impart to the unprepared multitude secrets of such tremendous importance, was equivalent to giving a child a lighted candle in a powder magazine.

At the very least this is powerful stuff! As for the Great

241

Pyramid itself, Tomas reports that one of Blavatsky's students by the name of AP Sinnett wrote the following:[259]

> . . . one purpose of the Great Pyramid was the protection of some tangible objects of great importance having to do with the occult mysteries. These were buried in the rock, it is said, and the pyramid was reared over them . . .

He goes on to suggest that 'Khufu simply restored some portions of the pyramid, closing secret chambers and leaving his cartouches', which is of course an excellent forerunner of Alan Alford's 'adoption' hypothesis. Although we accept that the edifice *may* have been constructed by Khufu on a site which he knew was important, or even that he may have discovered some secret cache of import and buried it far beneath his edifice, we cannot accept Sinnett's muddled suggestion that the pyramid itself was constructed long before, that the 'cache' was secreted both deep underground *and* in the Relieving Chambers, and that Khufu then adopted it – including somehow breaking into and removing the 'upper' cache and then perfectly resealing the chambers. That Sinnett was perhaps a less than worthy student is suggested diplomatically by Blavatsky herself.[260]

Preliminary conclusion
From all the above, it would appear that the weight of evidence supports the idea that secret records of mankind's ancient past and knowledge do indeed exist in various locations in the world. However, the evidence linking them to Giza is far less substantial, so that the best we can say of the Plateau is that there are many varieties of rumours and legends suggesting it may have some sort of underground complex, which may lead to undiscovered chambers way *beneath* the Great Pyramid. For any further conclusions about a Hall of Records at Giza, we must now turn to the man who has been the primary motivator of the 'new seekers' on the Plateau . . .

The 'sleeping prophet'
In the first half of this century, the American seer Edgar Cayce forged a worldwide reputation as a psychic, healer and prophet.

While in a meditative trance he performed thousands of 'readings' for individuals, providing them with details of their past lives which often stretched into remote antiquity. Although he was unaware of the contents of his readings while in his trance-like state, they were invariably transcribed. Over a period of time these transcripts forced him to believe in a number of concepts including, for example, reincarnation, which he initially found deeply troubling given his devout and orthodox Christian beliefs. These readings are well documented and preserved, both in the ARE library and in the hundreds of books that have been written about him.

Much of this reputation was gained as a result of Cayce's ability to make 'holistic' medical diagnoses. These commenced in 1901 when, under hypnosis, he correctly diagnosed a throat condition of his own which caused him to lose his power of speech, and which had a psychological cause in stress. There is little doubt that his success in this field has been proven by the subsequent developments in holistic medicine that have shown it to be soundly based, and this evidence alone appears to validate him as a genuine psychic rather than a complete crank. Accordingly, in our view his work is deserving of scrutiny.

The Atlantean connection
To evaluate what he had to say about the Hall of Records, we should appreciate the wider 'Atlantean' context in which this topic was framed. Cayce's readings suggested that a significant number of his 'subjects' had enjoyed previous incarnations in Atlantis, the mythical world popularised by Plato and endlessly discussed and searched for ever since. Indeed they suggested that he himself was the reincarnation of a priest of that era by the name of Ra-Ta, and that the reincarnation of so many 'entities' from Atlantis, Lemuria and other prehistoric civilisations in the current time was deliberate, in order that they could bring about and oversee 'great earth changes'. Although the language used is often stilted and difficult to follow, from his many readings over a prolonged period we can attempt to piece together a history of Atlantis, and indeed of mankind's origins.

The prime sources for readings on this subject are *Edgar*

Cayce on Atlantis, prepared by his son Edgar Evans Cayce in 1968, and – somewhat unexpectedly – *The Egyptian Heritage* by Mark Lehner, published in 1974 before his conversion to the orthodox cause. Over a period of 22 years between 1923 and his death in 1945, Cayce gave somewhere in excess of 1,000 readings involving the subject of Atlantis. They form about 20 per cent of his total readings, while the vast bulk (60 per cent) relate to medical and healing issues.

In brief, the readings suggest that the Earth was first populated ten and a half million years ago by 'spiritual entities', which only gradually took physical form – and even then they were originally asexual, taking some time to separate into males and females. The Atlantean civilisation, which had emerged at least as far back as 50,000 years ago, was repeatedly destroyed – sometimes by natural catastrophe, finally at its own hand by abuse of its primarily crystal-based technology. Its history was forged by conflicts between the 'Sons of the Law of One', who attempted to remain true to the righteous path, and the 'Sons of Belial', who indulged themselves in sexuality, and abused power and technology. The latter gradually gained the upper hand until, aware of their imminent destruction, a number of the more enlightened made their escape to all parts of the globe. It was these 'refugees' who brought civilisation to, for example, Egypt in about 10,500 BC,[261] and set up a number of Halls of Records to preserve Ancient Wisdom and warn mankind of the fate that had befallen Atlantis.

Multiple records

According to the readings there were three main sites in which these records were buried:

> . . . in the sunken portion of Atlantis, or Poseida, where a portion of the temples may yet be discovered under the slime of ages of sea water – near what is known as Bimini, off the coast of Florida. And in the temple records that were in Egypt . . . Also the records that were carried to what is now Yucatan, in America, where these stones (which they know so little about) are now – during the last few months – being uncovered. In Yucatan there is the emblem of same [a crystal or 'firestone']. Let's clarify this, for it

may the more easily be found. For they will be brought to this America, these United States. A portion is to be carried, as we find, to the Pennsylvania State Museum. A portion is to be carried to the Washington preservations of such findings; or to Chicago.[262]

This reading was given on 20 December 1933, but as far as we can ascertain no one has yet traced these Yucatan temple stones with their 'emblem' to any of the locations suggested. One of the other readings says of the Yucatan records that 'the temple there is overshadowing same',[263] while others suggest that this is the 'Temple of Iltar' – the leader of the Atlantean evacuees to the Yucatan.[264]

The Hall of Records at Giza
The most specific reference given by Cayce for the location of the Hall at Giza is as follows:[265]

In position this lies – as the sun rises from the waters – as the line of the shadows (or light) falls between the paws of the Sphinx, that was set later as the sentinel or guard and which may not be entered from the connecting chambers from the Sphinx's right paw until the time has been fulfilled when the changes must be active in this sphere of man's experience. Then [it lies] between the Sphinx and the river.

Most researchers are aware of this last reading, and it has been the major source of the frenzied speculation regarding the 'entrance', which it suggests lies in the vicinity of the Sphinx's right paw. Partly because of its somewhat vague terminology, few have attempted to use it in suggesting a specific location for the Hall itself. However, Peter Lemesurier – who we have already seen is the modern standard-bearer of the pyramid 'timeline' hypothesis – has used it to suggest that the Hall should lie on a bearing between 23.5 and 27.75 degrees north of due east from the front of the Sphinx. He further says that this points to a 'low mound between the Sphinx and the Nile which is at present used as a midden by the inhabitants of ... Nazlet', and is 'just beyond the low wall diagonally across the road from the Sphinx, and directly opposite [i.e. to the north of] the

Son-et-Lumiere seating'. In fact while we were in Nazlet we did hear reports that this refuse tip had been explored, but were unable to confirm them or inspect it closely for ourselves.[266]

Finally, Cayce's readings seem to suggest that the buried Hall may be in the shape of a pyramid itself,[267] while the information therein is primarily *written* in a mixture of ancient Egyptian and Atlantean script.[268]

Practical corroboration?
We have already suggested that Cayce's medical diagnoses and healing powers have been pretty well confirmed. A scholarly and long-overdue critique of Cayce's readings and beliefs has been recently prepared by K Paul Johnson, whose *Edgar Cayce in Context* is the first serious work to be produced by someone largely independent of the ARE. Johnson suggests that 'it can be said with confidence that the general health guidelines found in the readings have been increasingly confirmed in the half-century since Cayce's death'.[269]

Turning to his many prophecies, particularly about significant 'earth changes', which were to include not only the 'Second Coming' of Christ but also massive geological upheaval in the Americas and elsewhere, these are analysed in detail by Johnson.[270] Most have not been fulfilled, especially since in the main the readings suggest that they were due to happen at the latest by 1998. However, one did suggest that the remains of part of Poseida or Atlantis would rise again in 1968 or 1969,[271] which has been linked to the reading quoted above in respect of Bimini – and in 1968 the so-called 'Bimini Road' was discovered by Dr Mason Valentine. This huge underwater causeway is 300 feet wide and 1,600 feet long, and consists of a series of slabs 8 to 10 feet square. Arguments about whether or not these are man-made, as well as further excavation and research, continue to this day. However, in *The Stargate Conspiracy*, Clive Prince and Lynn Picknett suggest that the 'road' had been known about for far longer, and indeed that its 'discoverers' were ARE members.

It is also interesting to note that he describes apparently advanced technologies being used in Atlantis, and some would argue that a few of these appear to have been invented only since the time of his readings. For example, he mentions 'ships that sailed both in the air and under the water'; 'death rays or super cosmic rays that will be found in the next 25 years'; 'universal forces not of the present'; 'transmission of thought through ether'; 'overcoming gravity'; and 'the terrible mighty crystal' or 'firestone' from which emanated invisible rays and powered various craft and other apparatus – among other things.[272]

But what of the accuracy of his readings in relation to Giza? They assert that the Great Pyramid was erected between 10,490 and 10,390 BC, and the Sphinx at a similar time; that the pyramid was not built primarily as a tomb – even though the others were; and they explicitly support the pyramid 'time-line' hypothesis.[273] All these suggestions go against our previous arguments. On the other hand, the readings do suggest that the pyramid was constructed 'by the use of those forces in nature as make for iron to swim – stone floats in the air in the same manner'.[274] This suggests the use of levitation techniques to which we previously gave some support.

Attempts at practical corroboration of his nonmedical readings and prophecies therefore produce somewhat mixed results.

Esoteric corroboration?
So how do Cayce's Atlantean readings stand up if we examine the possible sources of esoteric, rather than practical, corroboration? The manuscript-based accounts prepared by Blavatsky in *The Secret Doctrine* have a great many similarities with Cayce's readings, not least in their descriptions of the five 'root races' of mankind that have so far existed on this planet. However, not only does Johnson provide a thorough comparison of Cayce's 'Christian theosophy' with Blavatsky's 'Esoteric theosophy',[275] but he also reveals that these readings started only in 1923, when a prosperous printer by the name of Arthur Lammers came to him for a reading. Cayce's biographer, Thomas Sugrue, reveals the following:[276]

> He [Lammers] mentioned such things as the mystery religions of Egypt and Greece, the medieval alchemists, the mystics of Tibet,

yoga, Madame Blavatsky and theosophy, the Great White Brotherhood, the Etheric World. Edgar was dazed.

Not only this, but Cayce then stayed with Lammers for several weeks, although the association was apparently short-lived. The crucial issue here is that Lammers had read extensively on theosophical topics, and must surely have discussed them at length with Cayce during this period. Around this time Cayce also struck up a close friendship with a financier by the name of Morton Blumenthal, who, according to Johnson, was also an avid theosopher. This collaboration lasted seven years, and Blumenthal was closely involved in both the running and the financing of various Cayce projects at the time. Johnson even reveals that Cayce had given a lecture on medical matters to the Birmingham Theosophical Society in 1922, the year *before* he met Lammers.[277] If one also considers that his readings were 'prompted' by questions from his subject, we have the very real possibility that Cayce was merely regurgitating from his subconscious that which had already entered his conscious mind, with a few additions and distortions which would inevitably arise.

Nor should the fact that sometimes consistent details were repeated in readings many years apart be regarded as destroying this hypothesis, since we are of the view that the *subconscious* mind remembers and can reproduce everything that ever gets stored within it. This is not to suggest that Cayce was in any way 'faking' anything, merely that his readings may indeed have been influenced by knowledge imparted to him by acquaintances and subjects – a conclusion repeatedly drawn by Johnson in relation to the 'non-medical' readings. At the very least it lays bare the myth that he had no interest in or knowledge of theosophical doctrines.

More detailed accounts of Atlantis published by authors before and during the period of Cayce's readings also contain many similarities. These include, for example, W Scott-Elliot's *The Story of Atlantis* of 1896 – which was partially based on channelled material – and Lewis Spence's multiple nonchannelled books on the subject, for example, *History of Atlantis* of

1926. Had Cayce read or been told about their work? Who can say?

Moving more specifically to Egypt, Lehner notes that several of Cayce's readings contain references to the *Book of the Dead*.[278] How much did he know about Ancient Egypt from his theosophist acquaintances? In particular, was he aware of the contemporary work of Randall-Stevens? We have already noted that the latter received channelled material on Atlantis and the Hall of Records, which supposedly came from ancient Egyptian initiates called Osiraes and Oneferu.[279] Although his material came via a similar channel, Randall-Stevens was wide awake when he heard his 'voices' and knew their supposed identities, whereas Cayce was in a trance and never knew the apparent source of his information – although we may perhaps assume it was his own Ra-Ta 'entity'. Furthermore, Randall-Stevens had apparently led a fairly normal life and was a well-known singer, with no previous history of channelling and 'little interest in occult matters', when he received his first communication in 1925. Nor, on the face of it, did he attempt to draw any conclusions from his writings – which were all in the form of dictations from his voices – merely recording them conscientiously and making sure they were shared with the rest of the world. Moreover, a number of witnesses supposedly attested to the way in which his drawings – which included detailed pictures of the faces of his 'initiates', despite the fact that he had no apparent history of artistic ability – progressed quickly and sometimes upside down, in a similar way to a 'wireless picture machine' (the equivalent of the modern fax).

Randall-Stevens's voices produced detailed reports of Atlantis, and even a genealogical tree of mankind's earliest ancestors.[280] But what did they have to say about Giza? They concur with Cayce's readings that all the edifices on the Plateau were erected in great antiquity after the destruction of Atlantis, along with a 'Temple of Ptah' somewhere in the south. Both complexes were said to be 'Temples of Initiation' for 'schooling intended neophytes in the mysteries of the divine Cosmos' – and further they were closed down twice during times when 'unholy forces' took over Egypt. However, a ruler who brought the south and the north together called Mentos – surely identifiable with Menes – supposedly brought sufficient stability that the temples were reopened during the intervening period of his reign. Sometime later Khufu and his two successors appropriated the Giza pyramids as tombs without realising their true purpose, and the subsequent kings replicated the pyramid shapes for their sepulchres.[281]

His voices continue by describing the nature of the temples and passages of initiation at Giza. They suggest that subterranean passages connect all three pyramids and the Sphinx, and detailed plans of the underground network were transmitted as a series of drawings (see Figures 19 and 20). They go on to describe at some length the nature of the initiation process, which involves a number of stages at various times. Stage one included passing through the 'Temple of Purification' – the Sphinx Temple; lying in a sarcophagus in the small chapel in front of the Sphinx; entering the 'Halls of Mystery' beneath it; leaving the body in the 'Chamber of Transmigration' to journey on the astral plane in the 'Chambers of Darkness'; passing through the 'Temple of the Lotus'; overcoming the 'Halls of Ordeal' under the Third Pyramid, which subjected the initiate to appalling mind games called the 'Ordeal by Suggestion'; and finally entering the 'Halls of Light', or the 'House of Osiris' – also described as a 'House of Stone' surrounded by a lake of crystal water. Stage two involved mastering the 'branch of the divine tree of mysteries' known as 'concentration', or unlocking the 'latent powers of the mind which lie dormant within each individual'. The other stages or 'degrees of initiation' are not described in detail.[282] This description ends with a suggestion that mankind has evolved an even greater potential for destruction than that of Atlantis, specifically in terms of 'vast magnetic fields flowing out into space', which are upsetting the natural balance.[283]

Randall-Stevens emphasises that he did not travel to Egypt to see Giza for himself until 1927–8, *after* he recorded the initial information contained in *The Book of Truth: The Voice of Osiris* between 1925 and 1927 (this was later incorporated into Part I of his *Atlantis to the Latter Days*). However, the drawings we have reproduced in Figures 19 and 20, which were supposedly prepared at this time, show a flight of steps in front of the

Sphinx very similar to those described, for example, by Vyse in *Operations* – they date to the Graeco-Roman period and were built on top of the Sphinx Temple. Although the verbal transmissions repeatedly mention the latter as an integral part of the initiation ceremonies, it is clear from the diagrams that he is referring to the Valley Temple, while the Sphinx Temple per se is not discussed – in fact, it was exactly during this period that Baraize was unearthing and excavating the edifice. This discrepancy tends to ring alarm bells.

This account is more detailed than any other regarding the possible nature of the 'masonic centre' of Giza. While we have a degree of sympathy for the general principle of initiation procedures being carried out there, we cannot accept the suggestion that the edifices were built in great antiquity and appropriated in the Fourth Dynasty. Despite Randall-Stevens's apparent reliability, his books were published by the 'Knights Templars of Aquarius' of Jersey, and, since they contain a great deal of detail and names that do correlate far better than usual with known Egyptian deities and kings, we cannot help but feel that somewhere along the line elements of both conjecture and known information may have been mixed together in apocryphal form to support that body's doctrine. This is, however, pure guesswork, which we cannot substantiate other than by falling back on the archaeological evidence.

A great many similarities with Cayce's readings can also be found in an unusual source – the 'crystal skulls', of which a variety have now been found. Although scientific testing has proved that some of these are fakes manufactured in the last two hundred years, this is apparently not the case with all of them. In *The Mystery of the Crystal Skulls*, published in 1997, Chris Morton and Ceri Louise Thomas describe a wide array of legends surrounding the skulls, particularly those of Native Americans. In particular they traced the skull discovered in Lubaantun in Belize in 1924 by Frederick Mitchell-Hedges, now kept by his daughter Anna in Kitchener near Toronto. Not only has the scientific analysis of this skull apparently failed to undermine its authenticity as a possibly extremely ancient artefact, but the Canadian psychic Carol Wilson has attempted to reveal its secrets by channelling. In brief, the information

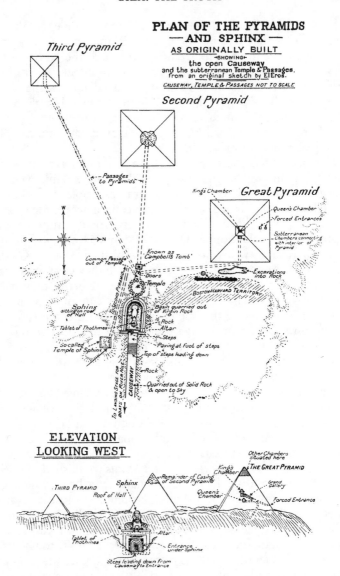

FIGURE 19: RANDALL-STEVENS'S GROUND PLAN OF THE
'MASONIC CENTRE' OF GIZA[284]

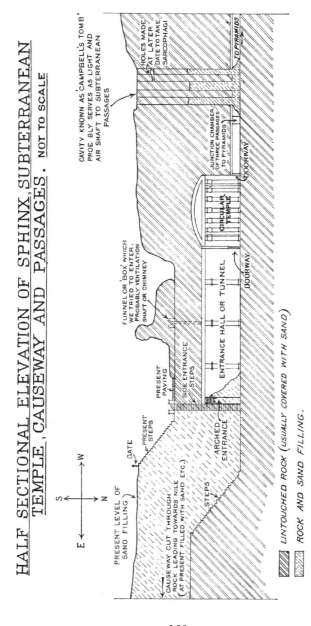

HALF SECTIONAL ELEVATION OF SPHINX, SUBTERRANEAN TEMPLE, CAUSEWAY AND PASSAGES. NOT TO SCALE

CAVITY KNOWN AS 'CAMPBELL'S TOMB' PROB.BLY SERVES AS LIGHT AND AIR SHAFT TO SUBTERRANEAN PASSAGES

HOLES MADE AT LATER DATE TO TAKE SARCOPHAGI

TO PYRAMIDS

JUNCTION CHAMBER OF THREE PASSAGES TO PYRAMIDS

DOORWAY

CIRCULAR TEMPLE

FUNNEL OR 'BOX' WHICH WE TRIED TO ENTER. PROBABLY VENTILATION SHAFT OR CHIMNEY

DOORWAY

ENTRANCE HALL OR TUNNEL

PRESENT PAVING

SIDE ENTRANCE STEPS

GATE

PRESENT STEPS

ARCHED ENTRANCE

STEPS

PRESENT LEVEL OF SAND FILLING

CAUSEWAY CUT THROUGH ROCK LEADING TOWARDS NILE (AT PRESENT FILLED WITH SAND ETC.)

S

E — W

N

UNTOUCHED ROCK (USUALLY COVERED WITH SAND)

ROCK AND SAND FILLING.

FIGURE 20: RANDALL-STEVENS'S DIAGRAM OF THE TEMPLES UNDER THE SPHINX[285]

forthcoming was that it had been made by 'thought form'; it had been on earth for 17,000 years; and it was designed as a telepathic link to other dimensions to inform us of our past and warn us of an impending catastrophe, involving a shift in the Earth's magnetic field, rising sea levels and disappearing land masses.[286] Inasmuch as it revealed that other similar skulls exist undiscovered beneath the ocean bed, while others still have not been 'given form' yet, there is little doubt that these artefacts fit the description of potential stores of 'records', which could be argued to corroborate the general principles of a source of ancient wisdom already elucidated.

The final piece of possible esoteric corroboration involves a book written in 1997 by an English medium, Ann Walker, called *The Stone of the Plough*. Although she describes herself as a 'simple housewife', for a number of years Ann Walker has been channelling messages from a spirit called 'White Arrow'. Her record of events that happened between 1993 and 1995, including two trips to Egypt, suggests that she received a number of communications from White Arrow and various 'aliens' in the form of diagrams and a mixture of Coptic and demotic Egyptian texts. These were interpreted by a scholar called Abdel Hakim Awayan, who lives in the village of Nazlet next to the Giza Plateau. She also received assistance in interpreting star maps from Adrian Gilbert.[287] The interpretations supposedly reveal the true nature of mankind's origination on another planet; the 'five stages' of mankind's evolution on Earth; and a number of 'keys' which would allow the Hall of Records to be found. One of these keys lies in the tomb of Imhotep at Ti in Saqqara, another at the base of a well near or under the Step Pyramid, and the third at Giza itself.

In particular the transmissions suggest that the Hall of Records is in fact the 'pyramid-shaped' spaceship that first brought our ancestors to Earth, lying buried underneath the Giza Plateau between the Great Pyramid and the Sphinx. It is reported to contain information about our past – including how our ancestors were four male and four female 'gods', whose original planet was destroyed by their own abuse despite White Arrow's attempts to warn them; and about our future – suggesting that the destruction of the rainforests is altering the tilt of the Earth's axis by 5 degrees, which will bring us into the path of a comet that will hit us in 2042 unless we rebuild the forests.

Intriguingly, Walker also reports that she provided a copy of her communications to an Egyptian government minister and, although he is not named, since his office is 'next to the pyramids' we can only conclude that he must be none other than Dr Zahi Hawass himself. Not only does she report that he signed an affidavit saying 'Ann Walker tells the truth of the Hall of Records', but also that he asked her to be interviewed in a television studio straightaway.[288]

Even to the open-minded there appear to be a number of inconsistencies and problems with this story. First, Walker reveals that White Arrow is none other than Jesus Christ himself, and suggests that an inscription in the Queen's Chamber – a cross (representing 'purity' or 'white') and the word 'Arrow' – is the great proof of his previous incarnation. However, this has not been noted by anyone else and, even if it were there, could have been drawn at any time in at least the last 1,200 years. Second, Walker claims the 'Plough' represents the constellation of the Great Bear, and yet the spaceship is identified by White Arrow as coming from the stars from which the pyramids at Giza take their alignment[289] – which could only mean either one of the pole stars or the constellation of Orion. To confuse the issue further, the interpreter Hakim suggests that the planet, named Molona, lay in our own solar system between Mars and Jupiter (shades of Sitchin's 'Twelfth Planet'?) and was destroyed about 17 million years ago;[290] in any case, there are severe cosmological objections to the 'exploded-planet' hypothesis. Third, White Arrow reports that a number of spaceships made it to Earth, which would tend to suggest it was widely colonised at the outset. Hakim seems to confirm this, and suggests that Giza was recolonised by Atlantean escapees in about 20,000 BC (partly using the *Edfu Texts*, which have already been discussed). Yet White Arrow also says quite clearly that the 'Atlantis' legends derive from the original destruction of our ancestors' planet, supposedly 17 million years ago. Fourth, the suggestion that the destruction of the rainforests could affect the Earth's tilt and 'weaken its fault-lines' sounds somewhat 'out of balance' itself.

Subsequently, Walker has apparently been led by White Arrow to turn her attention to a similar set of records buried in Mexico at 'Hill (or Cerro) Rabon'. We understand that publication of her work on this site will be forthcoming – as will that of another researcher by the name of Lynn Hermann, a member of the ARE.

It is of course extremely hard to judge whether these varied and numerous 'esoteric' sources of information may be regarded as corroborating or just copying each other. It could be argued that once a combination of the ancient Egyptian and other texts and Madame Blavatsky and her contemporaries got the ball rolling, everyone else simply copied from them with a few embellishments. But, despite the clear objections that we have voiced regarding certain elements of this 'evidence', such a line of thinking would perhaps represent an unfairly cynical and generalised rejection of a significant body of work.

The time is nigh

The discovery of the Hall at Giza was supposedly prophesied by Cayce to occur some time during the latter part of this decade, with the year of 1998 often mentioned by alternative researchers as if it were set in stone. That those commentators who were foolish enough to pin their hopes on this particular date have been left with egg on their faces is self-evident – unless of course they take refuge in the conspiracy theory that it has already been found but has been kept secret by the authorities. However, they would have done well to realise that this was not necessarily what Cayce's readings predicted. The following is the revealing and honest comment made to us by the ARE on this subject:[291]

> One interesting thing that seems worth noting is the consistent correlation between finding the Hall of Records and 'changes in the earth.' This seems more prevalent than a correlation with 1998, although the readings indicate 1998 as a pivotal year.

In fact the period 1958–98 appears to be the critical one for

Earth changes. This is amply demonstrated by the following reading (in which the grammar of the transcription is accurately copied but particularly poor):[292]

As to the changes physical again: The earth will be broken up in the western portion of America. The greater portion of Japan must go into the sea. The upper portion of Europe will be changed as in the twinkling of an eye. Land will appear off the east coast of America. There will be the upheavals in the Arctic and in the Antarctic that will make for the eruption of volcanoes in the Torrid areas, and there will be shifting then of the poles – so that where there has been those of a frigid or the semi-tropical will become the more tropical, and moss and fern will grow. And these will begin in those periods in '58 to '98 when these will be proclaimed as the periods when His light will be seen again in the clouds.

Although in other readings Cayce emphasises that the build-up to these changes would be gradual and not cataclysmic, clearly the predictions of geophysical upheavals described above have not come to fruition. As to whether the spiritual 'light' of the 'Second Coming' of Christ has returned to the Earth in this period, we leave it to you to make up your own mind – although for what it is worth we see Western society spiralling progressively downhill in a materialistic orgy of indulgence. Furthermore, it is not irrelevant to note that the concept of the return of Christ ought to represent a political 'hot potato' for those attempting to convince the Egyptian authorities of their right to explore the Giza Plateau based on Cayce's prophecies.

Meanwhile, *all* the readings relating to the discovery of the Hall of Records at Giza merely suggest this will happen at the time of these changes. For example:[293]

Yet, as time draws nigh when changes are to come about, there may be the opening of those three places where the records are one, to those that are the initiates in the knowledge of the One God: The temple by Iltar will then rise again. Also there will be the opening of the temple or hall of records in Egypt, and those records that were put into the heart of the Atlantean land may also be found there – that have been kept, for those that are of that group. The records are One.

No specific date is ever mentioned in these readings, so we can see that the assumptions about 1998 relied entirely on linking the two sets of information together. In fact to some extent it would be more appropriate to interpret Cayce's readings as indicating that 'windows of opportunity' exist for the opening of the Hall of Records, many of which have already passed us by. The reason for this appears to be that the human race cannot have this wisdom revealed until it is ready to appreciate it – and that time has not yet been right. We can only assume that many of those who now frantically seek the Hall have the arrogance to assume not only that mankind has reached this enlightened stage, but also that they personally have the requisite integrity and level of spiritual enlightenment to find it and comprehend its secrets. In the light of the behaviour we will later disclose on the parts of most of the major players in this drama, this seems unfounded to put it mildly.

Keeping the faith
The Association for Research and Enlightenment was formed in 1931; it is sometimes also referred to loosely as the Edgar Cayce Foundation, which, since the mid-1990s, has been a separate but related organisation.[294] Apart from sponsoring a variety of research into holistic medicine, which was one of its major objectives from the outset, it was also set up to ensure that preservation of and further research into Cayce's work could continue after his death. Membership, which numbered some 3,300 people in the mid-1960s, has steadily expanded with 'New Age' awareness so that it now stands at something like 30,000. Well-known modern supporters who visit the headquarters at Virginia Beach include the actress Shirley MacLaine and the author Dannion Brinkley.

Clearly our main area of interest is the ongoing involvement of the ARE and its members in research attempting to verify the predictions concerning the discovery of a Hall of Records at Giza. We have intimated that a key figure in this process was

Mark Lehner, from whose earliest work *The Egyptian Heritage* we have extensively quoted. Much has been made, especially by authors such as Hancock and Bauval,[295] of the apparent contradiction of this early involvement of someone who would later become such a bastion of orthodox Egyptology. But is this so very strange? Let us look more closely . . .

Lehner has never made any secret of his early affiliation. According to Johnson, 'Lehner had been mentored as a young man by Hugh Lynn and Charles Thomas Cayce [Edgar's son and grandson respectively], and an ARE couple, Arch and Ann Ogden of Florida, had funded his education in Cairo at the urging of the elder Cayce'.[296] However, even when he wrote *The Egyptian Heritage* Lehner was clearly having trouble reconciling Cayce's view of the age of the pyramids with the archaeological evidence. Commenting on the Relieving Chamber cartouches, he wrote:[297]

> If we take the Ra Ta period as historical fact, then we must entertain the idea – fantastic as it may seem – that these cartouches were placed in the Pyramid by the followers of Ra Ta as a 'red herring' for modern man until the time was right for the real meaning of this Pyramid to be brought to light. This, of course, would require considerable prophetic skill . . . [to know that] thousands of years later there would be a ruler named Khufu . . .

Is it so strange that, the more he learned in the field and from other Egyptologists, Lehner should have allowed these doubts to eventually overcome him? It is quite clear from our own general prevarication in this chapter that we too have gone through similar agonies, admittedly in a much shorter timeframe, in attempting to resolve the dilemma that possibly sound, general theosophy can be interwoven with interpretations of the age of the edifices on the Plateau, which are clearly at odds with the archaeological evidence. You will see how we resolve these contradictions in the conclusion shortly, but our thought processes may not have been so very different from Lehner's.[298] As for the ARE board's reaction to his progressive change in stance, they remained on good terms and were even brave enough to sponsor the first stage of his Pyramids Carbon-Dating Project in 1984 – knowing full well that the results might put paid to this important aspect of Cayce's readings, as they indeed did (see Chapter 2).

It has also been suggested that the ARE had a hand in Dr Zahi Hawass's education. Johnson reports, 'Later, Hugh Lynn was instrumental in furthering the graduate education of Zahi Hawass, now the Egyptian Government Official in charge of the Giza site, in Egyptology at the University of Pennsylvania'.[299] Unlike Lehner, Hawass has strenuously denied this link – and we will return to this subject in Part III.

Apart from the various characters already mentioned in connection with the ARE, there are two others who, as lifelong members, play a key role: they are Dr Joseph Schor of the Schor Foundation, a wealthy man who has sponsored and led most of the expeditions in search of the Hall of Records at Giza in the 1990s, and his colleague in many of these endeavours, Joe Jahoda. We will return to these pivotal figures later.

Conclusion

The overriding focus of this chapter has been the possibility that a Hall of Records exists at Giza. We have seen that, despite the considerable quantity of historical and other evidence that could be used to support such a contention, the main motivator for the 'new seekers' has been the readings of Edgar Cayce. We do not consider that he was in any sense attempting to delude the public, and that he has some degree of psychic ability is generally accepted based on his medical readings. Nevertheless, even his own umbrella organisation has been forced more and more to emphasise the usefulness of the latter, at the possible expense of any reliance on his 'Atlantean' readings and prophecies for the future, many of which have not been fulfilled. It is also clear that Cayce could have been influenced by a number of acquaintances who had a provable interest in theosophical doctrines.

As to the other 'major players' whose work appears to support Cayce in relation to Giza – from the Arab chroniclers to the channellers such as Randall-Stevens and others – all their accounts have defects of detail or contradictions that suggest that they should not be taken too literally. To regard many of them as apocryphal and as 'pointers to possibilities' is perhaps the kindest and safest approach.

Does this mean that we have concluded that Giza has no hidden cache of knowledge to offer up? Not necessarily. Whatever the objections, if one adopts the 'no-smoke-without-fire' philosophy, then it may well be that something of great import still awaits our discovery there. But *if* this were the case we would argue that it would be something buried long before the edifices were constructed, perhaps most likely a chamber far beneath the Great Pyramid. Meanwhile, ancient rumours of an *extensive* underground network beneath the Plateau are still peddled with great enthusiasm by local Egyptians, whose livelihoods to some extent depend on their continuation. Furthermore, a variety of researchers and writers who are either too credulous or too concerned with making money and reputations ensure that they are kept in the public eye. Many of these rumours we *know* from first-hand experience to be false, as will be seen later.

If such a chamber does exist at Giza – and it is a big *if* – there are nevertheless four further questions that should be examined. First, what would it contain? We have already seen that Cayce suggests *written* texts, but alternatives have been put forward. These include artefacts that would prove significant technological advancement in themselves; some kind of 'thought form', perhaps encoded in a crystal, which could be accessed only by someone with the appropriate integrity and enlightenment; an interdimensional gateway of some sort; and harmonic properties related to an initiation process which could release the spirit into the astral plane. And of course these possibilities are not mutually exclusive.

Second, has it been discovered already? For example, Khufu could have discovered it before he built the Great Pyramid. Meanwhile, it is not impossible that the Egyptian authorities have found something recently – maybe even in 1998, which would have fulfilled Cayce's prophecies – but have kept the incredible find from the world at large. We are open-minded about the former possibility, but the latter conspiracy theory – while it is attractive to any newcomer impressed by the work of Hancock, Bauval et al. – is one that appears less and less likely the more one learns about the subject.

Third, if we accept that it has not been discovered in modern times, when will it come to light? We have seen that Cayce's readings and other esoteric sources point to a time of spiritual change, not explicitly tied into the year 1998, so all is not lost. But is mankind at such a turning point? Despite our sympathy for new-age believers who within their various groups are buoyed with enthusiasm, and the fact that pessimism is not going to help mankind to move forward, we look around us with eyes wide open and see a different story – one of a world that is increasingly and massively dominated by materialism and power. Whether this apparently terminal decline can be reversed in the ordinary course of events, or would need a natural, technological, economic or political catastrophe to shake it free from its malaise, is anyone's guess.

Fourth, how deep is the cache buried? This issue is often overlooked in the fervour surrounding the 'search', but it is quite clear that the water table at the Plateau *does not lie very far beneath the Sphinx*. In fact a survey conducted by the National Research Institute of Astronomy and Geophysics in the early 1990s revealed that the water level was a mere 7 metres (23 feet) below the base of the monument. This was significantly *lower* than the water level of only 2 metres (6 feet) which they indicate had prevailed for the previous 50 years, the drop possibly caused by the then recent construction of a sewage system in the village of Nazlet.[300] If a cache of some sort was buried there at any depth, it would certainly have had to be 'hermetically sealed' to avoid destruction. Even if this were the case, how would it be opened without breaking the seal? The same is to some extent true of any chamber that might lie under the Great Pyramid, since, although it is on higher ground, the Subterranean Chamber and the vertical shaft that descends from it are already at a considerable depth.

All in all we do not find the evidence for the existence of a Hall of Records at Giza particularly persuasive, and future chapters will be found to reinforce this opinion. Nevertheless, we have gone into some detail in this chapter because there *is* considerable evidence of one sort or another that, in our view, suggests that such records may indeed exist in a variety of forms in *other* locations around the world. Since Blavatsky and others, who claim to have already inspected some of their contents, argue that they confirm an extensive and advanced prehistory for mankind on Earth, the implications, if they are telling the truth, are astounding. Indeed, these implications are far more significant than a parochial and limited concentration on Ancient Egypt and the Giza Plateau, as important as this topic is. We hope we have therefore done enough to excite interest in this fascinating subject without straying too far from the subject matter at hand. Meanwhile, further consideration of these broader issues must wait, as we have already hinted, for another work.

Part II
MODERN METHODS

CHAPTER

SIX

THE HUNT FOR SECRET CHAMBERS

Beginning in the mid-1960s, the hunt for hidden chambers on the Giza Plateau took on a new impetus with the use of modern electronic detection equipment. Long gone were the days when the likes of Belzoni, Caviglia and Vyse could tunnel and blast their way through the pyramids, and technologies such as gravimeters, resistivity surveys, acoustic sounding and ground-penetrating radar were brought into play.[301] The overall aim of most expeditions was to apply nondestructive methods in the service of archaeology, in order to discover what lay hidden beneath the sands – and in the monuments – without the need for an excavation. Any archaeological excavation or dig is by nature destructive, since layers of soil (or in this case sand) are methodically stripped away. However, these modern methods could offer a view of the subsurface without disturbance. Expedition leaders convinced the Egyptian Antiquities Organisation (EAO) of the potential discoveries these modern methods could make without damaging their monuments, which led to a period of cooperation between the EAO and various foreign institutions and individuals. This chapter will examine the period from the mid-1960s to the early 1990s, which was one of relative cooperation in which the EAO proved itself open to many new ideas and suggestions. As will be seen later, this is in stark contrast to the public rows and claims of cover-ups that erupted during the 1990s.

The Joint Pyramid Project

In 1965 a scientific proposal was submitted to a group of Egyptian physicists and archaeologists to search for undiscovered chambers in the Second Pyramid. The logic of the American team, led by Dr Luis Alvarez, was that since 'there were two chambers in the [superstructure of the] pyramid of Chephren's

267

father (Cheops) and the same number in the pyramid of his grandfather (Sneferu), the absence of any known chambers in the stonework of Chephren's Second Pyramid at Giza suggests that unknown chambers might exist in this apparently solid structure'.[302]

Alvarez proposed that a nondestructive approach to probing the Second Pyramid could be achieved by placing cosmic-ray detectors in the Upper Chamber. Cosmic rays emanating from space have the ability to penetrate dense materials such as rock but in doing so they lose some of their energy, so the amount of energy recorded in a 'spark chamber' indicates the density of the material. The data can then be recorded on magnetic tapes and analysed by computer.[303] In the case of the Second Pyramid the cosmic rays would pass through an average of 100 metres of limestone blocks before being recorded. Should a portion of those rays pass through a void in the structure of the pyramid the apparatus would then detect a slightly larger energy value that would indicate the possible presence of a concealed chamber within the core masonry. If such a hidden chamber was detected the investigators planned to drill a borehole through the limestone blocks and use optical equipment to see what lay within.

The proposal received a favourable response from the authorities and the 'Joint Pyramid Project' was established on 14 June 1966 as a collaboration between physicists from the Ain Shams University of Cairo, the University of California and archaeologists from the Egyptian Antiquities Organisation. The project was also supported by the US Atomic Energy Commission – who helped finance the design and construction of the detection apparatus – the Smithsonian Institution, the IBM corporation, Hewlett-Packard, the National Geographic Society and the Egyptian Surveying Department, who supplied critical measurements of the pyramid to the project scientists.

However, it was not until early 1967 that the detectors were set up in the Upper Chamber, the delay occasioned by the breakdown in diplomatic relations during the outbreak of the Six Day War. But by the spring of 1968, cosmic-ray data began to be recorded on magnetic tapes, and by September 1968 the team had recorded the path of over 2 million cosmic-ray particles. The data was sent to Ain Shams for analysis on the university's computer, while additional data was later analysed at the Berkeley Laboratories.

Mysterious developments?

In *Secrets of the Great Pyramid*, Peter Tompkins quotes a report in the London *Times* as follows:[304]

As Dr Lauren Yazolino, Alvarez's assistant, returned to the United States to analyze the tapes on the most up to date computer at Berkeley, a correspondent from the London *Times* visited Cairo to check on the results locally. At Ein [Ain] Shams University, John Tunstall found an up to date 1130 IBM computer surrounded by hundreds of tins of recordings.

'It defies all known laws of physics,' Tunstall quoted Dr. Amr Goneid, who had been left in charge of the pyramid project since the return to America of Dr. Yazolino.

According to Tunstall's report, each time Dr. Goneid ran the tapes through the computer a different pattern would appear and the salient points which should have been repeated on each tape were absent. 'This is scientifically impossible,' Tunstall quoted Goneid, explaining that the earlier recordings which had raised hopes of a great discovery were now found to be a jumbled mass of meaningless symbols with no guiding pattern whatever.

Tunstall asked Goneid: 'Has all this scientific know-how been rendered useless by some force beyond man's comprehension?' To which Goneid is reported to have answered: 'Either the geometry of the pyramid is in substantial error, which would affect our readings, or there is a mystery which is beyond explanation – call it what you will, occultism, the curse of the pharaohs, sorcery, or magic; there is some force that defies the laws of science at work in the pyramid.'

Meanwhile in his *Return of the Gods*, the infamous Erich von Däniken picks up on this 'mystery' but misleads the reader into believing the Egyptologists ignored this data:[305]

The very expensive experiment, in which several American institutes, IBM and Cairo's Ain Shams University were involved, ended without any clear results. The head of the archaeological research at the time, Dr. Amr Gohed [Goneid], told journalists that the findings were 'scientifically impossible': he added that either the 'structure of the pyramids is chaotic' or there is 'some mystery here that we have not explained'. The archaeologists generally ignored these baffling results.

However, in reality there was no mystery. As the team members revealed in an article in *Science* magazine, the computer program relied upon extremely accurate measurements of the pyramid's geometry, and similarly accurate positioning of the equipment in the chamber. But in fact the gap between the two spark chambers created an inactive area that was not allowed for in the original computer simulation, and this in turn gave a false signal suggesting the presence of a 'Grand Gallery' in the Second Pyramid in a similar position to that in the Great Pyramid. When the team subsequently adjusted the simulation by taking into account the gap, the image on the analysing equipment disappeared. Meanwhile, another false signal, initially indicating the possible presence of a chamber some 30 metres (nearly 100 feet) above their equipment, was found to be caused by the offset of the Upper Chamber from the exact centre of the pyramid:[306]

Because of the displacement of the Belzoni Chamber to the north and east of the center of the pyramid's base, the apparent chamber mapped itself onto the southern part of the western face of the pyramid. The relative increase in counting rate was about 10 percent, as expected. The angular size of the anomaly could be related to distance only by assuming a certain size for the floor area of the 'chamber'. If we assumed that the anomaly came from a room the size of Cheops' King's Chamber, it had to be about 30 meters away, and its plan position turned out to be almost exactly central.

Unfortunately, this large and persistent signal, together with a larger signal over a smaller angular range, disappeared as we learned more exactly all the dimensions of the apparatus and of the pyramid that were important in the simulation program. (We had not anticipated the need for such accurate data.)

By 1970 the Joint Pyramid Project had explored only 19 per cent of the total volume of the Second Pyramid. But having

Plate 1 (above): The original entrance to the Great Pyramid. Note the visitors, whose size puts the massive scale into perspective, in front of the forced entrance below and to the right.

Plate 2 (top right): Original casing stones at the base of the Great Pyramid. The huge size can be gauged by the 12-inch ruler against the base.

Plate 3 (middle right): The Sphinx with the Great Pyramid in the background. Note the various repairs at the lower levels.

Plate 4 (bottom right): The granite coffer in the Upper Chamber of the Second Pyramid. Note the lid is intact, not broken in two as often reported.

Plate 27 (above): Granite drill-core No. 7. (Copyright The Petrie Museum of Egyptian Archaeology, UCL, UC. 16036/John Reid)

Plate 28 (right): Close-up of drill-core No. 7. Note the irregularity of the grooves, which suggests ultrasonic machining was *not* used. (Copyright The Petrie Museum of Egyptian Archaeology, UCL, UC. 16036/ John Reid)

Plate 29 (above): Schist bowl with lobes. Its function remains unclear. (Courtesy The Cairo Museum)

Plate 30 (above): Taper-necked bowl with pointed base. How was it machined so accurately? (Courtesy The Cairo Museum)

Plate 22 (left): Corbelled roofing in Sneferu's Northern Pyramid at Dashur. This forms the prototype for the Great Pyramid's Grand Gallery. This shot also shows the modern wooden staircase which has been erected to allow easy access into the highest chamber.

Plate 23 (below): Huge lintel block in the Red Pyramid, measuring 9 feet 6 inches by 6 feet by 4 feet.

Plate 24 (left): The ground plan of the Giza Pyramids superimposed on a photograph of Orion's belt stars. Note that the offsets and sizes do not match up.

Plate 25 (below): Basalt paving stone from the Great Pyramid's mortuary temple. The underside of the straight edge admits no light, indicating the quality of workmanship employed.

Plate 26 (right): Granite door-hinge recess in the Valley Temple. It is perfectly spherical, and entirely smooth to the touch. Meanwhile, the sunken edges at the bottom of the hole are indicative of tube-drilling.

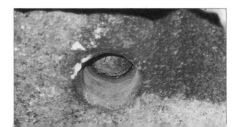

Plate 13 (above): The Valley Temple, looking west. Note the huge limestone blocks which form the core of the walls, and were quarried from the Sphinx enclosure. Some weigh as much as 200 tonnes!

Plate 14 (above): The right-hand entrance into the Valley Temple. The granite blocks which line the walls are exquisitely wrought, and still in fine condition thanks to being covered in desert sand for millennia.

Plate 15 (left): Granite wall blocks in the Valley Temple. Not only are these huge and finely wrought but they do not assume regular shapes, which makes the precision of their jointing all the more admirable.

Plate 16 (below): A granite casing block outside the Valley Temple. Our admiration for the exquisite carving of the concave face is increased by the fact that many such blocks lie scattered around the temple's base.

Plate 17 (above): The north wall of the Second Pyramid's mortuary temple. Again, some of these blocks weigh as much as 200 tonnes, while their extensive weathering appears to have been caused by wind and sand.

Plate 18 (left): Granite lining blocks in the Third Pyramid's mortuary temple. These blocks are exquisitely finished on the front, while the easier-worked limestone core blocks have been shaped to receive them at the back.

Plate 19 (right): The Step Pyramid of Djoser at Saqqara, looking north. Although not as massive as the Great Pyramid, this is still an enormous edifice, as can be gauged from the horses at the base. This is the first of the truly great pyramid structures, and the quality of the core masonry can be gauged by the fine state of preservation.

Plate 20 (left): The Bent Pyramid of Sneferu at Dashur, looking southeast. Another massive pre-Giza edifice, not only still in fine repair but uniquely with much of its limestone casing still intact. Again the car at the base gives an idea of scale.

Plate 21 (right): Casing stones on the north face of the Bent Pyramid. As well as demonstrating the quality and precision of their outer faces, this shot clearly shows how the casing blocks were matched up to the core blocks behind them.

Plate 9 (above): Square recess on the south wall of the Upper Chamber in the Second Pyramid. This is clearly not a shaft like those in the Great Pyramid.

Plate 10 (right): The Upper Chamber in the Third Pyramid, looking west. This chamber has been carved entirely from the bedrock. Note the small side-chamber in the west wall, and the passage leading down to the lower chambers.

Plate 11 (above): Round recesses on the south wall of the Upper Chamber in the Third Pyramid. Again these are clearly not shafts as in the Great Pyramid.

Plate 12 (right): The Lower Chamber in the Third Pyramid. Apart from the more celebrated King's Chamber, this is the only chamber in the three main Giza Pyramids to be granite-lined. It was here that Vyse discovered the empty but decorated basalt coffer which was later lost *en route* to England.

Plate 5 (left): Campbell's Chamber. The ceiling is covered in graffiti, effectively making the original quarry marks difficult to spot.

Plate 6 (right): Lady Arbuthnot's Chamber. Note the huge granite monoliths which form the low, flat ceilings – each thought to weigh as much as 80 tonnes!

Plate 7 (right): Nelson's Chamber.

Plate 8 (right): Wellington's Chamber.

Plate 31 (left): Weathering channels in the south wall of the Sphinx enclosure. These are the weathering patterns which have created all the controversy over the age of the Sphinx, and are judged by some to have been caused by running water. The same patterns can be seen in the west wall.

Plate 32 (right): Weathering on the Second Pyramid's north and west enclosure walls. These exhibit hard-edged fissures which are in stark contrast to the more rounded channels in the Sphinx enclosure.

Plate 33 (left): The western entrance to the Valley Temple. Note that the doorway is formed from granite lining blocks which lie underneath a massive limestone lintel. Yet some researchers argue that the granite lining was a later addition!

Plate 34 (below): The western doorway to the Valley Temple from the inside. Once again the granite lining underneath the massive limestone lintel is clearly displayed.

Plate 35 (above): The 'short' piece of wood before the bend in the northern Queen's Chamber shaft. Note the two holes which make it similar to drawings of the missing Dixon piece of cedar wood. (Courtesy Rudolf Gantenbrink)

Plate 36 (above): The 'hook' before the bend in the northern Queen's Chamber shaft. It is not dissimilar to the Dixon hook. The Dixons' metal clearing rod is on the right. (Courtesy Rudolf Gantenbrink)

Plate 37 (left): The metal and 'long' wooden rods before the bend in the northern Queen's Chamber shaft. It has been suggested that this piece of wood is an original artefact, but it appears to be another clearing rod which has snapped off. Since it lies *underneath* the metal rod at the corner, it was probably also introduced by the Dixons. (Courtesy Rudolf Gantenbrink)

Plate 38 (right): The metal and 'long' wooden rods after the bend in the northern Queen's Chamber shaft. Note how the wooden rod has whiplashed across to the left as it broke, pushing the floor chippings across with it. Also the square object at its end, which may have been some form of scraper used to retrieve artefacts. (Courtesy Rudolf Gantenbrink)

Plate 43 (above): The chamber at the second level of the Water Shaft. This shot shows the antechambers in the far (north) and right-hand (east) walls. The coffer in the middle antechamber of the west wall can just be seen on the left, while on the floor are piles of bone fragments. The wheel in the far right cell was clearly part of an old water pump, and it is lying against another coffer. The remaining antechambers are empty.

Plate 44 (right): One of the huge granite coffers in the second level of the Water Shaft. This is the one in the middle antechamber of the west wall. The lid has been slid to one side, while the interior was littered with debris including the tin cans of the excavation workers.

Plate 45 (left): The lid of the coffer in the entrance to the third level of the Water Shaft. This is as we saw it facing east towards the entrance, where it was originally found. Supported by timbers after the excavation of the chamber, it is clear that it was removed from the coffer by ancient tomb-robbers.

Plate 46 (left): The third level of the Water Shaft. Taken from the entrance looking west, the edges of the shaft leading down to this level can be seen at the top. In the centre is the water-filled recess containing the coffer. It is surrounded by a rectangular platform at the corners of which the possible remnants of columns can be seen. The water-filled 'moat' which surrounds this platform can just be seen on the left. Meanwhile, the two baskets on the far edge of the platform once again contained bone fragments.

Plate 39 (left): The start of Caviglia's Tunnel off Davison's Chamber. This shot was taken at the mouth of the tunnel, in the southeast corner of the chamber. After about 10 feet it curves round to the right to follow along behind the south wall.

Plate 40 (right): The end of Caviglia's Tunnel off Davison's Chamber. At the end is a small grotto in which one can just about stand, with short *original* excavations heading forwards, upwards, downwards and to the left (south). This is just one of the excavations, all of which reveal nothing but core masonry, and confirm that rumours of clandestine tunnelling are entirely false.

Plate 41 (left): Burlap bags containing chips of stone in Wellington's Chamber. These are almost certainly the product of recent clearing of the debris left by Vyse's blasting of the vertical access tunnel.

Plate 42 (right): The entrance to Baraize's Tunnel in the rump of the Sphinx. Once again this tunnel comes to a dead-end after a short distance. This shot also clearly shows the repairs carried out on the body, older at the top, newer at the base.

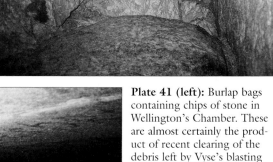

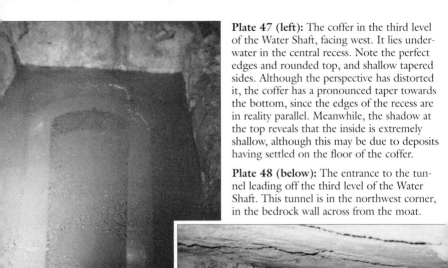

Plate 47 (left): The coffer in the third level of the Water Shaft, facing west. It lies underwater in the central recess. Note the perfect edges and rounded top, and shallow tapered sides. Although the perspective has distorted it, the coffer has a pronounced taper towards the bottom, since the edges of the recess are in reality parallel. Meanwhile, the shadow at the top reveals that the inside is extremely shallow, although this may be due to deposits having settled on the floor of the coffer.

Plate 48 (below): The entrance to the tunnel leading off the third level of the Water Shaft. This tunnel is in the northwest corner, in the bedrock wall across from the moat.

Plate 49 (above): Close-up of the tunnel leading off the third level of the Water Shaft. It is only possible to crawl in for a short distance before the tunnel narrows down rapidly, and this is as far up as one can place a camera. It is clearly revealed as a natural fissure in the bedrock, and not as a man-made tunnel as some have suggested.

Plate 50 (right): Celebrations! The authors after another daring night raid. Ian is on the left, Chris on the right.

scanned an area 35 degrees from the vertical the team were able to draw some definitive conclusions:[307]

> If the Second Pyramid architects had placed a Grand Gallery, King's Chamber, and a Queen's Chamber in the same location as they did in Cheops' Pyramid, the signals from each of these three cavities would have been enormous. We therefore conclude that no chambers of the size seen in the four large pyramids of the Fourth Dynasty are in our 'field of view' above the Belzoni Chamber.
>
> We can say with confidence that no chambers with volumes similar to the four known chambers in Cheops' and Sneferu's pyramids exist in the mass of limestone investigated by cosmic ray absorption.

The project eventually drew to a close in 1974, still with no chambers having been located in the Second Pyramid's super-structure. However, it was swiftly followed by another joint American–Egyptian project . . .

SRI International

Based in California, SRI International – previously known as the Stanford Research Institute – became involved in a variety of projects in Egypt during the 1970s. The scheme was a con-tinuation of a joint American–Egyptian project set up in 1974 to apply modern geophysical techniques to the field of Egypto-logy. The joint team was composed of scientists from SRI and once again Ain Shams, supported by archaeologists from the EAO. The team leaders were Lambert Dolphin, Senior Physicist with SRI, and Ali Helmi Moussa, Chairman of the Department of Physics at Ain Shams.

It is rarely reported that the 1977 survey was not confined to the Sphinx and the Giza Plateau. Additional surveys were conducted south of Giza at Saqqara and at the Valley of the Kings near Luxor. Dr Gamal Mokhtar from the EAO also expressed an interest in survey work being carried out at Alex-andria and the ancient city of Tanis in the Delta region. As these areas are outside the scope of this book, we intend to focus on the SRI's work at Giza and their subsequent findings, but it is important to emphasise the broader context and overall aims of the project, which are normally ignored.

Unforeseen problems

Ground-penetrating radar (GPR) employs high-frequency radio waves to penetrate below ground level producing an image of the subsurface features. Waves are transmitted downward by an antenna and reflect off the substrata, and the resulting signals are displayed as a profile. The method sounds relatively simple, but the depth to which the system can explore is constrained by a number of factors, including earth type. Certain soils and rocks, especially those with a high moisture content, affect the strength of the returning signal, resulting in a loss of radio frequency. At first glance one would think that the seemingly dry conditions at Giza would have been perfect for employing GPR, but conditions of high humidity prevail, while the natural water table – which is not far below the surface – adds to the moisture absorbed by the porous limestone that makes up the bedrock and monuments of the Plateau. The SRI team found the GPR equipment virtually useless when trials were carried out in 1974:[308]

> SRI hoped that radar probing of the pyramids in search of unknown passages or chambers would be feasible. However, it was found that the Giza area rock (and most of the limestone rock found in other archaeological sites in Egypt as well) exhibits very high in situ radio frequency losses so that radar probing is limited, for all practical purposes, to depths of a few meters even when a choice of operating frequency is optimal.
>
> These unexpectedly high radar losses are due to high porosity and poor quality of the rock (the limestone could also be classed as fine-grained sandstone), and the high ambient humidity (75% to 85%) of the Nile Valley, the latter due to prevailing winds blowing south from the Mediterranean Sea, and to the capillary action from the Nile plain.

The team therefore decided to apply acoustic sounding, resistivity and magnetometry surveys during their subsequent 1977 field season in Egypt. But they were to find that even this combination of methods is not a foolproof way of locating unknown man-made chambers . . .

Huge caves at Giza!
The rock of the Giza Plateau is formed from sea sediments laid down millions of years ago. It is mostly limestone rock of varying grades of competency interlaced here and there with layers of sand and gravel. Fault lines are especially noticeable around the area of the Second Pyramid. The subsurface of the Plateau is honeycombed by ancient underground water courses which have formed natural voids or 'solution cavities' in the soft limestone rock. Mark Lehner spoke of these cavities at a lecture in 1998 and added, 'There's huge caves at Giza, there's a cave you can get lost in. There is a cave at Giza in this limestone and nobody saw the end of it'.[309] Therefore it is easy to see how the researcher can be lulled into thinking that, in this rich archaeological area, they have located an undiscovered room or tunnel – when in reality what lies beneath their feet is a water-formed cavity or natural fault. It is vital to bear these problems in mind when reviewing the recent reports of various individuals claiming to have located secret chambers.

In 1977 the results of the SRI surveys were published in a paper entitled 'Applications of Modern Sensing Techniques to Egyptology'. The report is generally divided into research and results by method rather than locality, but we will examine it in relation to the two main areas of the Plateau that were tested: that is, the interior and exterior of the Second Pyramid, and the interior of the Great Pyramid. A few surveys were also conducted around the Third Pyramid but no anomalous areas were detected. Furthermore, they conducted a number of surveys around the Sphinx, but these will be considered in a separate section.

The Second Pyramid
The Second Pyramid was the main focus of the SRI's attention during the 1977 season at Giza. Around the perimeter they carried out a number of resistivity surveys searching for tunnels or chambers, followed up by acoustic sounding to verify the more interesting 'signatures'. In particular at the northwestern

end of the west face they identified anomalies as much as 6 metres (18 feet) deep. But in this heavily faulted region of the Plateau it was difficult for the team to place any significant interpretation on their findings. Switching their attention to the interior of the Second Pyramid, the SRI decided to follow up on the work of the Joint Pyramid Project, but, knowing their predecessors failed to locate any unknown chambers in its superstructure, they decided to probe the bedrock beneath it. Setting up their equipment in the upper (or 'Belzoni's') chamber, the team conducted acoustic soundings through the floor.

At a depth of about 21 metres (69 feet) and again at 33 metres (108 feet) the returning echoes indicated the presence of two large anomalies (see Figure 21). Do these represent additional rock-cut chambers similar to that in the Great Pyramid? The SRI suggested that a small-bore hole should be drilled down through the bedrock, so that by inserting a bore-scope camera they would be able to identify whether the anoma-

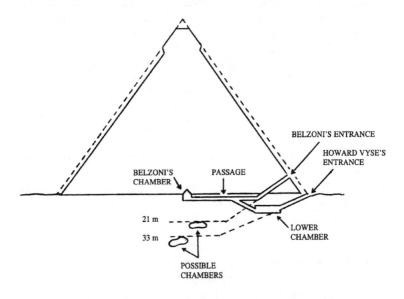

FIGURE 21: THE TWO ANOMALIES DETECTED BY SRI
BENEATH THE SECOND PYRAMID[310]

lies were natural voids or man-made chambers. Unfortunately, although the EAO gave permission to drill, no funds were available for the task and the nature of the cavities remains a mystery. Lambert Dolphin considers that they are the ones most worthy of attention, remarking, 'These anomalies under Belzoni's chamber are real and strong. This is all bedrock, and [they] could be faults or cracks, but they are big anomalies.'[311] Meanwhile, tests in the horizontal passageway leading to the upper chamber revealed the presence of another anomaly some 4 metres (13 feet) below the floor, which the team similarly thought 'could be a tunnel and should be checked by drilling and bore-scope observation'.[312]

It is possible that these two sets of anomalies are in some way connected, since an additional passageway would be required to reach any new chambers in the bedrock. Any future mission to investigate below the Second Pyramid could have a positive result by discovering a previously unknown chamber, although it would clearly have to be prepared for the disappointment of finding only natural cavities.

The Great Pyramid
The acoustic survey carried out in the Great Pyramid was limited to a single night's work with only two sets of data being taken – one in the King's Chamber and another in the antechamber leading to it. Problems arose when the individual stone blocks making up the pyramid's construction began reflecting multiple waves back to the receiving equipment, causing severe 'clutter'. However, results from measurements taken in the antechamber did reveal the presence of an anomalous echo 7.25 metres (24 feet) beneath the floor, approximately halfway between the King's and Queen's Chambers (see Figure 22). The SRI report suggests the echo is a possible cavity close to the point where the original pyramid 'plan' was supposedly altered. Therefore, it could be simply a small void left behind during the change in plan, or even a large crack. Of course we cannot entirely rule out the possibility that it represents an additional small chamber, but we must remember two important issues. First, a single night's work with only two sets of acoustic data encumbered by severe clutter

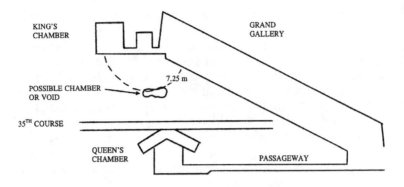

FIGURE 22: ANOMALY DETECTED BY SRI BETWEEN THE
KING'S AND QUEEN'S CHAMBERS[313]

problems is not a solid basis upon which to make a judgement.
Second, we should recall Vyse's comments about the large 'sand-filled' cavities between the core blocks, which he encountered
in the area of the Queen's Chamber entrance. The SRI results
could easily reflect such a cavity from which much of the sand
had drained over time.

At the time of the brief acoustic survey in the Great Pyramid
the SRI's plan was merely to determine the scattering effects
of the individual pyramid blocks, not to make a concerted effort
to locate hidden chambers (see Figure 23). From these results
they believed it would be possible in the future to detect both
known and unknown chambers or cavities within the core
masonry by adjusting the sound frequencies to eliminate the
clutter that confused the readings. They also suggested that with
improved equipment 'the acoustic sounder may have some use
even in the block and mortar parts of the pyramids' and recommended that 'more acoustic measurements within pyramids are
in order'.[314]

Of course the alternative camp have had a field day with this
'finding' of a 'secret chamber'. In *The Hall of Records*, Joseph
Jochmans completely misinterprets the SRI's findings and subsequent recommendations while throwing in an air of
conspiracy and obstruction for good measure:[315]

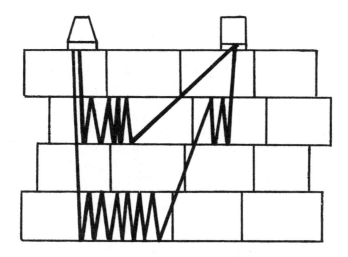

REVERBERATING SCATTER

FIGURE 23: ACOUSTIC 'SCATTERING' EFFECT OF
INDIVIDUAL PYRAMID BLOCKS[316]

So far to date, the Egyptian government has not seen fit to take action on these recommendations, even though they may have the potential of leading to a great discovery, perhaps even greater than that of Tutankhamun's tomb. One explanation given for the apparent reluctance to begin the search is that the Egyptians, sensitive to the fact that the Pyramid is their national treasure and number one tourist attraction, are fearful to let anyone damage the monument by drilling or extensive diggings. Adding to the general discouragement of further research is the Egyptian Department of Antiquities, whose members are notoriously conservative, and are therefore unwilling to admit to the possibility that other enigmas in the Pyramid have yet to be found. Their attitude is that, since we already know that the Pyramid was a tomb of a Pharaoh, there are no more mysteries to be had, and therefore it would be a waste of time to search for more. In truth they are worried that future discoveries would upset presently held theories, upon which many present reputations and authority is based. But one wonders if, perhaps behind this facade of official fears and conservatism, there might be certain individuals who are working to maintain the restraints on exploration, for very different reasons. These individuals, working on a higher level of awareness, know the secret chambers exist, but they also know that the time is not right for the world to learn of their contents. There must yet be a Transformation, both in the Earth and in mankind itself, before the day of opening arrives.

The simple fact of the matter is that further work was not conducted because the SRI's findings were not conclusive, and because problems with the equipment had to be resolved. When we contacted Dolphin for his explanation, his reply not only indicated that the anomaly was possibly just a large crack, but also flatly contradicted Jochmans's statement that the Egyptian Authorities would not allow further exploration to take place:[317]

> [The anomaly is] probably an empty void, but possibly only a large crack. The foundation of the King's Chamber goes all the way to the base of the pyramid and is separate from the foundation of the rest of the pyramid. It is possible these two sections have settled at different rates leaving a big crack.
>
> *We had permission to drill a hole from the Grand Gallery into this void, but we elected not to mar the pyramid on such scant evidence.*

And that, as the saying goes, is from the 'horse's mouth'! End of conspiracy.

Surveying the Sphinx

In recent times, interest in what lies beneath, within and around the Sphinx has captured the imagination of the public, researchers, writers, theorists, mystics and crazies alike, to such an extent that it is perhaps the only monument in Egypt that can compete with the Great Pyramid for the world's constant attention. According to some, as we have seen, the Hall of Records – or at least the entrance to it – lies hidden beneath it. In Chapter 1 we briefly mentioned Emile Baraize's work at the Sphinx, which started in 1925. As we will now be looking at the SRI surveys in the Sphinx enclosure it is necessary first to further elaborate on Baraize's excavations – and in particular on his rediscovery of three shafts in or under the monument.

The Sphinx shafts

Working on behalf of the Egyptian Antiquities Service as it then was, Baraize excavated the Sphinx enclosure and made repairs to the monument between 1925 and 1936. Finding the monument almost covered to its neck, he had the sand removed and built a retaining wall above the enclosure to halt further encroachment. He found the monument to be in poor condition with large cracks, and many of the pharaonic repair blocks had fallen away. During his restoration of the body, Baraize discovered two entrances at ground level that led to dead-end passageways underground. One is located on the rump just north of centre, the other on the left or northern side of the monument, approximately halfway between the front and rear paws. Baraize explored both entrances, and then resealed them with repair blocks and cement. His field notes and some 226 photographs, housed at the Centre Waldimir Golenischeff in Paris, were never widely published and the passageways were largely forgotten.

Over a ten-year period beginning in 1977, the EAO carried out a series of sporadic surveys and restoration projects on the Sphinx. During the early part of these projects the overseer of the workmen, Mohammed Abdelmawgud Fayed, reported the existence of the shaft in the rump to the EAO officials. As a small boy Mohammed had worked at the Sphinx with his father during Baraize's restorations, and was around seven years old when this shaft was originally discovered. In 1980, Zahi Hawass and Mark Lehner checked Mohammed's story by having one restoration stone removed, and re-examined the rump shaft. Although we will return to this shaft in Part III, suffice to say that they reported that it went a short distance both up and down, but led nowhere.

We met Mohammed during our research trip to Egypt in the autumn of 1998. Now an old man, he lives with one of his sons, Gouda, at their home opposite the Sphinx in Nazlet el-Samman. Another son, Ahmed, is a well-known lecturer and tour guide for the ARE. Mohammed confirmed the story of the rump passage to us, and remarked that nothing of any consequence was found during the restorations conducted either by Baraize or subsequently by Hawass and Lehner. He also remembered that the lowest part of the passage reached the water table. The entrance to this shaft can still be seen today from the western end of the Sphinx enclosure.

Although Mohammed did not remember seeing the second entrance – to the shaft on the northern flank – the Centre Waldimir Golenischeff did lend a series of Baraize's photographs to the EAO. From those photographs the northern shaft was rediscovered by Hawass and Lehner and found to be a dead-end passageway under the belly of the monument, which they then resealed.

The third shaft found by Baraize was the one on the top of the Sphinx's body behind the head, which had been bored to a depth of 27 feet by Vyse and Perring (see Chapter 1). This was reinvestigated by Hawass and Lehner, who found the broken-off boring rod left in from when the drill had stuck, and a fragment of the damaged back of the Sphinx's headdress.

These, then, are the three known shafts or tunnels associated with the Sphinx. However, since they still represent a source of great speculation for the alternative camp we will return to them in Part III, along with another rarely mentioned feature – a small chamber behind the Dream Stela.

The initial SRI survey

During 1977 the SRI team laid resistivity 'traverses' in front of the Sphinx's paws, along its flanks and diagonally across the left-hand rump (see Figure 24). As a result of these tests a number of small anomalies were found to exist. The traverse in the vicinity of the left-hand hind paw indicated the presence of a possible tunnel aligned on a northwest–southeast axis. On the southern flank, close to a Roman altar, two overlapping traverses indicated the presence of an anomaly which the SRI team identified as a possible vertical shaft.

If we consider the position of the two known shafts beneath the Sphinx in relation to these results, then perhaps both anomalies come as no great surprise. The anomaly on the southern flank is of course on the opposite side to the known northern shaft, but it is possible that the survey detected the end portion of that shaft. In any case it was described by

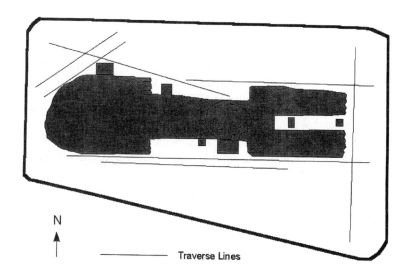

N

——————— Traverse Lines

FIGURE 24: THE SRI'S RESISTIVITY SURVEY AROUND THE
SPHINX[318]

Dolphin as being only a 'minor anomaly, nothing very big or
very long'.[319]

Turning to the results at the front of the monument, we must
remember that this is the area identified by Cayce as concealing
the entrance to a passage which leads to the Hall of Records –
and as such it has been one of the main focal areas of the
alternative camp. So what *did* the SRI find here? Their inability
to draw a definitive conclusion is demonstrated by this extract
from their report:[320]

> There are two anomalies in front of the front paws of the Sphinx.
> The bedrock in front of the Sphinx is covered with Roman-era
> paving stone – and poor electrical contact between the paving
> stones and bedrock gave somewhat noisy resistivity traverses.
> However one anomaly occurs on a large electrode spacing, sug-
> gesting a cavity or shaft as much as 10m [33 feet] deep. The
> cavity, if present, is probably filled with rubble.
>
> The resistivity anomalies we found around the Sphinx are
> not defined sufficiently to allow us any absolutely certain con-

clusions, and we feel that a more detailed survey should be conducted.

Again we asked Dolphin for his opinion concerning these anomalies. He emphasised that under the bedrock there are a number of cracks and small cavities and advised us not to put too much credibility on the results obtained around the Sphinx during 1977. He added that the Sphinx fieldwork that followed in 1978, funded by the ARE, was more thorough and included drilling to check any anomalies found. So let us now turn to this later project . . .

The Sphinx Exploration Project

In keeping with his desire to affirm his father's prediction about the Hall of Records, Hugh Lynn Cayce, the then president of the ARE, set about organising a mission to Egypt, and the Sphinx Exploration Project was born. Its purpose was to establish whether or not an underground chamber or chambers existed near the Sphinx. The project eventually became a joint cooperation between senior members of the ARE, SRI and the EAO. The ARE contingent was headed by Hugh Lynn Cayce, while Joe Jahoda – who, as we have already mentioned, had been a member of the ARE since his early teens – became the project's Technical Director. In a communication with us, Jahoda described how he was recruited into the project by Hugh Lynn:[321]

I will never forget going to ARE in '76 to buy a book at the bookstore and bumping into Hugh Lynn in the old white building at 67 Street and casually talking about the weather when, equally casually, he asked, since I was an engineer, if I could help organize the technical phase of the expedition. Then followed a series of discussions and written documents with SRI until we developed a protocol, specifications, and procedures for the entire program testing and data collection for probing under the Sphinx electronically to determine the presence of any type of anomaly or chamber or tunnel.

The SRI agreed to add the ARE–sponsored project to their 1978 field season at Giza and Saqqara. Working with the SRI that year was a drilling company owned by Kent Wakefield of Westec Metals. While working in New Mexico, Dolphin had met Wakefield and discussed the work that had been going on in Egypt. Wakefield, who appears to have been treasure hunting while in New Mexico, immediately became interested in assisting and formed a new company, Recovery Systems International (RSI), for the purpose of this venture. RSI brought with them to Egypt around $500,000 worth of drilling equipment, air compressors, optical instruments and supplies. This was a stroke of luck for Hugh Lynn, as any anomalies located around the Sphinx could be checked by drilling and inserting a bore-scope camera.

The EAO supervisors for the Sphinx Exploration Project were Zahi Hawass and Mark Lehner. This was four years after Lehner had written *The Egyptian Heritage*, and by this time he had already had considerable exposure to the 'bedrock realities' of Egyptian archaeology. Nevertheless, although not the avid Cayce-ite he may once have been, he still did not reject the predictions out of hand. In any case, it was a chance for him to repay his debt to Hugh Lynn for his assistance with his education.

Patti Burns and John Tanzi, technicians with the SRI, laid a series of resistivity and acoustic surveys around the Sphinx and in the Sphinx Temple. A number of anomalies were detected, so RSI was brought in to drill down and investigate them with bore-scope cameras. Five 4-inch holes were dry-drilled with air being used to blow the holes clean. Two of these were drilled in the floor of the Sphinx Temple: 'In one of the drillings the drill rod seemed to give way and they poured water down that hole, and it seemed to drain away. So they thought they really had a chamber there. They put the bore-scope camera down and it was just Swiss-cheese-like solution cavities.'[322] Meanwhile, the other three holes were drilled around the Sphinx. One of the largest anomalies was detected close to the Sphinx's right paw, but when they drilled on it all they found was a small crack in the bedrock and the water table below.

Contrary to the story put about by many alternative researchers, the SRI had permission to drill wherever they wished – but Wakefield's investors stopped putting money into the project and RSI ran out of funds. Both Dolphin and Jahoda indicated to us that Wakefield was under the impression he would make a large return for his investment, in antiquities, publicity or film rights. The drilling equipment was eventually donated to the EAO and 'put in a locked warehouse, but within a year or so it had been stripped and pillaged'.[323] Later, back in the USA, SRI and RSI ended up in court with SRI attempting to collect a balance of payments owed to them from RSI, but by this time RSI had become bankrupt.

So Hugh Lynn's project at the Sphinx had failed to find any sign of passageways leading to a Hall of Records as predicted by his father. Dolphin sums up his views on the project, and Hugh Lynn's reactions to the results, as follows:[324]

My overall impression is that the entire Sphinx area had no significant anomalies other than minor cracks here and there.

At the time this work did not seem any more important than any of the other tasks we had in front of us, and the Cayce funding allowed only a limited amount of time and effort. Hugh Lynn and I talked after the work for him was over and I remember he felt quite satisfied with our work, and of the opinion that his father's best work was in healing people and not in archaeological predictions. I had the distinct feeling Hugh Lynn was quite satisfied there was no Hall of Records anywhere under the Sphinx.

But overall, to this day, I would say the seismic anomalies under Belzoni's chamber are far more worthy of attention. I really think the question of possible chambers under the Sphinx is a dead issue. I just don't believe there are any there.

For his part, Hawass often refers to the SRI when countering claims of a chamber or Hall of Records beneath the Sphinx: 'People say that beneath the Sphinx there is a room and such things. It's all total nonsense. In 1977 [in fact 1978] the Stanford Research Institute did drilling everywhere around the Sphinx and they found nothing.'[325]

By contrast, Jahoda still believed the drillings did not go deep enough to locate a chamber. He continued to be optimistic of one day finding Cayce's mysterious chamber, and has since become involved in other expeditions to Giza, which will be examined later on.

The Queen's Chamber

Operation Khéops

Two Frenchmen, Gilles Dormion (a design technician) and Jean-Patrice Goidin (an architect), visited the Great Pyramid in March 1985 and made observations that led them to suspect the existence of a hidden system of passages and chambers. They hypothesised that the system visible today is a ploy to mislead tomb robbers, and that Khufu's real burial chamber is to the side of the Relieving Chambers. They also noted that some of the stone blocks in the walls of the horizontal passage leading to the Queen's Chamber were laid in a different way from all the others: 'The walls of the long, very low, passage leading to the chamber are lined with a crosswise [or cross-shaped] arrangement of stones, the perfect symmetry of which is illogical.'[326] What Dormion and Goidin noticed was that the blocks in the passageway were laid one above the other so that the joints formed a cross-shaped pattern, and this arrangement was totally unlike that in any other passage in the Great Pyramid. They theorised that this could indicate the presence of a concealed storeroom, possibly containing the pharaoh's belongings needed in the afterlife. In fact, another anomalous arrangement in this passage had excited the curiosity of JP Lepre when he examined the edifice back in 1978. He noted that two of the floor blocks had effectively been 'cut in half', while the six wall blocks on either side were double the size of the normal blocks. Nevertheless, this led him to similar conclusions.[327]

Back in France, Dormion and Goidin obtained significant support for a project to carry out work inside the pyramid from a number of French organisations: the Ministry of Foreign Relations, the Electricity Board, the Office of Geological and Mining Research, and the Geophysical Prospecting Company. The project became known as 'Operation Khéops'.

Returning to Egypt in early September 1986, they began microgravimeter surveys within the Great Pyramid. Tests in the Relieving Chambers did not produce clear results, although some kind of anomaly was detected. But other readings did seem to indicate the existence of a cavity behind the west wall

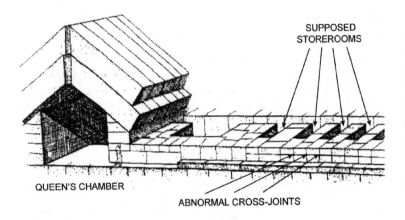

FIGURE 25: CAVITIES BEHIND THE WEST WALL OF THE
QUEEN'S CHAMBER PASSAGE[328]

of the Queen's Chamber passage (see Figure 25), just as they
had suspected.

The EAO gave permission for the drilling of three small holes
in the wall, which can still be seen at the base today, plugged
by metal caps. The first hole was bored at 35 degrees, and
showed only several blocks of stone separated by mortar. The
second hole was bored at 40 degrees, and revealed the same.
However, the final hole, drilled to a depth of 2.65 metres (nearly
9 feet), revealed a cavity containing sand of a very fine quality.
Dormion and Goidin pondered on how to probe deeper into
the cavity through the sand:[329]

> How can we find out what is behind the sand? How can we find
> out if there is not a door beyond, a door that this time opens
> onto the store-rooms? We must organise more, deeper, drillings,
> of at least 4m [13 feet]. This would not be easy to organise on
> account of the narrowness of the passage, and in the absence of
> a recess that can only be a handicap for the operators.

They decided they needed to perform more sophisticated
surveys and planned to return with GPR equipment. But in

February 1987 they heard that a Japanese team from Waseda University had beaten them to it . . .

Waseda University

Japanese archaeologists from the Egyptian Culture Centre at the Tokyo-based Waseda University conducted their 'Pyramid Investigation Mission' at Giza during 1987. During their first trip, between 22 January and 9 February, they followed up on the French team's findings with the use of GPR equipment, and also conducted surveys within the Sphinx enclosure. Meanwhile, their second trip, from 12 to 23 September, essentially repeated the same surveys but with improved equipment and techniques.[330] It is inappropriate to present a detailed account of all their work here, but their follow-up on the French team's work – and in particular their analysis of the sand from the cavity – is worthy of further investigation.

Using GPR they surveyed the floors and walls of the Queen's Chamber. Results from the north wall indicated the presence of a cavity about 3 metres (10 feet) behind it. This cavity was judged to be some 1.5 metres (5 feet) by 1 metre (3 feet), i.e., also to the west of the horizontal passage. Moving their equipment into the passage itself they surveyed the entire length of the west wall. Reflections from the GPR waves indicated that the cavity was perhaps a concealed passageway running parallel to the horizontal passage:[331]

> This newly discovered passage starts from a point only one block's width away from the northern wall of [the] Queen's Chamber. The reflection ends at a point approximately 30m [98 feet] north of [the] Queen's Chamber. Therefore the passage is thought to come to an end here or turn west at a right angle.

The Waseda researchers also detected the presence of what appeared to be a cavity beneath the floor of the horizontal passage some 1.5 metres (5 feet) below its surface. They believed this cavity might be as much as 3 metres (10 feet) deep and that sand was present inside it.

Are these just cavities similar to those detected by Vyse? Or are they sand-filled 'chambers', and if so are they connected?

Two modern British researchers believe the latter is the case, and we will examine their theory in Part III. But let us now turn our attention to the sand from the cavity behind the passage wall, about which some members of the alternative camp have made some extraordinary claims . . .

Special sand?
The sand discovered inside the pyramid by Dormion and Goidin was analysed by the Japanese team using microscopic observation and X-ray photography. It was then compared with samples of sand from the Giza and Saqqara areas. Contrary to rumours that still seem to circulate even today, the Japanese did not report any evidence that the sand from the cavity was 'radioactive'. However, they did find that it was composed of more than 99 per cent quartz grains between 100 and 400 microns in size, whereas the samples taken outside the pyramid and from Saqqara were composed of calcite, quartz and plagioclase, with the grain size much smaller at between 10 and 100 microns. Further investigation revealed that this type of sand is termed 'weeping', 'whispering' or 'musical' sand, because of the sound it makes when walked on or blown by the wind. So from where had it come?

The Waseda researchers were informed by a local Egyptian about an area where a deposit of sand was known to make similar sounds. This area turned out to be near El Tur, in southern Sinai, a few hundred miles southeast of Giza across the Red Sea. However, although the report does not make it entirely clear whether or not they tested this sand to see if it matched, Waseda team members also noted that the formation and deposition of the quartz sand in the region of El Tur was probably caused by the weathering of granite deposits originating at Mount Sinai or its immediate area.[332]

The observations made by the Japanese researchers raise several important questions. Why did the Ancient Egyptian architects choose to transport a potentially large quantity of quartz sand to Giza, and place it in a cavity behind the Queen's Chamber passage? And since granite deposits are also found at Aswan in southern Egypt – which we have already seen was the main source of this material for the pyramid builders – do similar weathered sand deposits exist there too? Only further study of the sand found in the Great Pyramid will reveal its origin, although not its purpose. This can be understood only by further investigation of the cavity or cavities behind the horizontal passage. Meanwhile, we should note that it has been suggested that the sand was placed in the Great Pyramid to act as a 'shock-absorber' against earthquakes – although why local sand could not have been used is not readily apparent.

More Secret Chambers?

In 1992 another team used nondestructive methods, this time to survey the area around the Subterranean Chamber in the Great Pyramid.[333] The project was instigated by Jean Kerisel, whose theories regarding the pyramid we considered in Chapter 3. Motivated by Herodotus's 'canal' accounts, and the archaeological evidence for the existence of such a canal outside on the Plateau, Kerisel started by considering the level to which the water under the Great Pyramid would come. He did this by using a combination of Vyse and Perring's calculations when they had the vertical shaft off the Chamber dug to a depth of 38 feet, and his own calculations. He considered that the depth achieved by Vyse's shaft was sufficient to reach the probable level of a canal, but that it must have been in the *wrong place*.

His team therefore commenced by using GPR in October 1992, with the following results:

> By this method, we detected, under the floor of the horizontal corridor [leading to the Subterranean Chamber] (to the right of the niche) an interface that could be the roof of a corridor oriented SSE NNW. This roof was found to be at the depth that the descending corridor would reach if it were to be extended. The corridor, if it is empty, would be about 1.60m [5 feet] in height and rises slightly, opening into the pit that we will come to later.

Then in December they switched to using microgravimetry, with the following results:

> At the spot where the radar had detected a kind of passage, the micro-gravimeter detected nothing, which indicates that the

passageway has been filled in. On the other hand, in the horizontal passageway it detected a very clear local anomaly of a mass defect in the west side, at 6m [20 feet] before the entrance to the chamber. According to our calculations, it corresponds to a vertical pit of at least 5m [16 feet] in depth, square in section with sides of about 1.40m [4 feet], in immediate proximity to the west wall.

From this Kerisel concluded:

The passageway detected by the GPR could simply be a marl [fine-grained sedimentary rock] zone of the type of strata that one sees on the head of the Sphinx: but it would be rather exceptional that it should be so thick. As for the micro-gravimeter, it could have detected a sizeable volume of dissolution of the limestone by underground water, that is to say a sort of deep grotto: such a geological accident could exist.

He suggests that he wanted to perform drilling to investigate the anomalies further, and that he was preparing an appropriate request to the authorities. However, at the time of writing we are not aware of such work having been performed.

Finally, Lepre – although not working with modern technology, and relying instead on good-quality observation alone – notes some further anomalies which might be indicative of additional chambers. The main one is the relatively loose jointing around the bottom-left block in the west wall of the King's Chamber, which is revealed if a layer of nonoriginal plaster is scraped away. This is in stark contrast to the extremely fine joints in the rest of the chamber, and he argues that this is exactly the sort of place where an additional passage to another chamber would be located.[334] He also singles out for further investigation the huge deep shaft located between the Great Pyramid's east face and its mortuary temple; and a large 4-feet-by-10-feet stone paving block with high-precision joints lying at an acute angle across what would have been the line of the casing stones on the north face of the edifice, 70 feet from the northeast corner.[335]

Conclusion

In this chapter we have attempted to provide a background to the history of exploration at Giza from the mid-1960s up to the 1990s. It is by no means a complete history, as other surveys and excavations were being carried out during this period, mostly by more orthodox archaeological institutions.[336] Those academic bodies have published their findings widely in journals, reports and books. On the other hand, the expeditions that we have reviewed above are more often than not omitted even from popular books dealing with orthodox Egyptology. To some extent the same could be said for the writings of the alternative camp, and furthermore, even when they do get a mention, they are selectively quoted or just badly researched in order to support a variety of often conspiratorial theories. We trust that we have done enough to prove that, during this period leading up to the 1990s at least, conspiracy was not the order of the day.

What is our summation of the findings themselves? There are multiple problems with the technology which need to be ironed out, all of which takes a great deal of time and money. We have also seen that in the interior of the edifices there are many 'natural' explanations for cavities, even if the readings are correct – including sand infill and foundation slippage. The same is true of the bedrock under and around them, which is peppered with natural caves and cavities.

However, there is no doubt that further exploration in certain areas is warranted, and in some cases this has indeed happened. But we must wait for Part III to review the results.

THE AGE OF THE SPHINX

The question of the age of the Sphinx has puzzled scholars for many centuries. Almost as many rumours abounded regarding this enigmatic monument in antiquity as did about the pyramids themselves, albeit that for much of the time it was buried up to its neck in sand. Not long after Caviglia cleared the front and discovered the Dream Stela of Thutmose IV in 1818, scholars were able to translate it and found a possible reference to Khafre thereon. Quoted in Vyse's *Operations*, Samuel Birch had the following comment to make:[337]

> In the thirteenth line part of a cartouche occurs, which is apparently the prenomen of the king Ra shaa f, or Shafre, supposed to be Chefren (Khafre); but the fracture in the inscription makes it impossible to determine in what manner the name is mentioned.

Despite the lack of context for this partial inscription, Gaston Maspero, for example, claimed that it meant that Khafre *refurbished* the Sphinx. By contrast most Egyptologists used it to set them on the route to the modern orthodox view that he was responsible for the *building* of the monument. This view became increasingly confirmed as the surrounding monuments were unearthed over subsequent decades, including the Sphinx and Valley Temples, and the Second Pyramid's causeway and mortuary temple – and as it became clear that a standard pattern was applied to all the complexes. But in the late 1970s an unorthodox researcher entered the fray and argued that weathering patterns on the Sphinx indicated that it was much older than the orthodoxy presumed. Since that time a plethora of often ill-informed books and articles have represented this as incontrovertible scientific support for the existence of advanced civilisations in antiquity. The researcher was the author and Egypt tour guide John Anthony West . . .

The Lion Man

West elucidated his theories in a book entitled *Serpent in the Sky*, first published in 1979. Subsequently he managed to persuade a geologist, Dr Robert Schoch from Boston University, to assist his research, and the pair made a preliminary 'unofficial' trip to Giza in June 1990. This was followed by an official EAO-sanctioned research trip in April of the following year, which received some financial assistance from the ARE, and included a geophysicist, Dr Thomas Dobecki from McBride Ratcliff & Associates of Houston, and a documentary producer, Boris Said. These trips were highly successful for West in that Schoch especially became convinced that the basic premise was correct; indeed he has gone on to become a champion of the cause in his own right, albeit that – as we will see – his redating is not necessarily as radical as West's.

The findings were publicised widely, partly as a result of West's subsequent tie-up with Hancock and Bauval. However, West effectively became *persona non grata* with the Egyptian authorities, and was refused permission to undertake further research at the site amid accusations that he was 'searching for Atlantis'. Although we will return to these important political issues in Part III, suffice to say for now that although West's eloquent but vitriolic attacks on orthodox Egyptology cannot have helped his cause, this turn of events was unfortunate – because for once it appeared that a member of the alternative camp was attempting to use experts in the appropriate field to examine a hypothesis that would undoubtedly have dramatic implications were it proven to be correct.

Nevertheless, in the fullness of time West and Schoch's theories have had ample time for full development and elucidation. It is, however, less well known that other scientific experts have had equal time to study the evidence and develop a strong opposing case. So in this chapter we will examine the merits of both sets of arguments, and also the variety of ancillary evidence presented by West and his supporters to back up his claims for the great antiquity of the Sphinx.

But first, let us see what set West on his path. *Serpent in the Sky* was primarily a study of the high state of culture of early Egyptian civilisation. Referencing the work of freethinking philosophers such as Rene Schwaller de Lubicz and George Gurdjieff, West could not accept that such high culture could develop 'overnight'. And, when he came to a passing reference by Schwaller that the 'severe erosion of the body of the Great Sphinx of Giza is due to the action of water, not of wind and sand', he considered the supposedly arid climate of northern Egypt in the last 4,500 years and formed the startling conclusion that this must point to its being far older than convention suggested. His euphoria at answering the 'sudden civilisation' dilemma, and at the implications of this seeming proof, were expressed in his own words as follows:[338]

> If the single fact of the water erosion of the Sphinx could be confirmed, it would in itself overthrow all accepted chronologies of the history of civilisation; it would force a drastic re-evaluation of the assumption of 'progress' – the assumption upon which the whole of modern education is based. It would be difficult to find a single, simple question with graver implications. The water erosion of the Sphinx is to history what the convertibility of matter into energy is to physics.

Of course these assertions are perfectly correct – but with one fatal flaw: the question, as with all ones of such extreme consequence, is *not* a *simple* one!

Preliminaries

We have already seen in earlier chapters that the Sphinx is carved out of the solid limestone bedrock on the eastern edge of the Plateau, and that only its head is above the natural level of the ground, while its body has been carved out by excavating an 'enclosure' around it. Although those unfamiliar with the Plateau can become confused because of the extensive brick repairs that have been undertaken for millennia to shore up the deteriorating monument, especially at the base of its body, it is important to emphasise that it is primarily made of solid bedrock, not of constructed blocks (see Plate 3).

Because the Plateau naturally slopes down towards the eastern edge, the enclosure walls are relatively high at the back of the monument, but decrease in height as they near the front. Meanwhile, the falling off of the ground immediately to the north means that the northern enclosure wall is not as high as its southern counterpart, while at the front the ground has been completely levelled to erect the Sphinx Temple. Despite these variations the enclosure still forms a pit into which sand is naturally blown off the higher reaches of the Plateau, while at the same time any running rainwater tends to drain off into it – especially on its western and southern sides. Even the casual observer can see that the enclosure walls on these two sides contain deep, wide, rounded and vertical fissures (see Plate 31) which on the face of it appear to have resulted from water cascading over them, searching out and wearing away any natural indentations or areas of softer rock, assisted by the gravel and sand that would be carried along with it. That these fissures become less pronounced on the southern wall as one moves down the slope to the east appears to add weight to this observation.

There are two major arguments that cause West and Schoch to suggest that this must indicate an earlier date for the Sphinx. The first is that for the bulk of its 'orthodox' life it has been buried up to its neck in sand, thus reducing the ability of rainwater to flow over the enclosure walls. The second is that the climate in northern Egypt has been arid for the majority of this time. So let us first examine the reliability of these two claims.

Up to his neck

In *Serpent*, West estimates that the Sphinx has been buried for something like 3,300 years of its 4,700-year orthodox life.[339] Since he is using a different chronology which places Khafre's reign some 200 years earlier than the dates we have used, and since some of his data was prepared before the recent Sphinx surveys that have shed more light on the issue, let us take a moment to re-estimate. In *The Complete Pyramids*, Lehner clearly describes the various repair stages that form the basis of our analysis, presented below in table form to show the 'state' of the enclosure at various times.[340]

PERIOD	YRS	STATE	DESCRIPTION
2500–2100 BC	400	Clear	From time of construction to 'disorder' of 1st Intermediate Period
2100–1400 BC	700	Blocked	No reports of restoration or worship
1400–1200 BC	200	Clear	'Phase I' restorations by Thutmose IV (c. 1400 BC) and then by Ramesses II (c. 1200 BC)
1200–600 BC	600	Blocked	No reports of restoration or worship
600–500 BC	100	Clear	'Phase II' restorations during Saite Period
500–300 BC	200	Blocked	Herodotus (c. 400 BC) doesn't even mention Sphinx's head
300 BC–300 AD	600	Clear	'Phase III' restorations during Graeco-Roman Period
300–1900	1600	Blocked	Known to be buried until Baraize cleared it properly in 1920's (Caviglia and others only cleared a small proportion for a short time)
1900–2000	100	Clear	Remained clear since

These revised estimates indicate that West's original figures remain more or less valid – a reasonable estimate is that it has been buried for something like 3,100 years of its orthodox 4,500-year existence, or roughly two-thirds.

The Egyptian climate

When West first elucidated his hypothesis in *Serpent*, he assumed that the weathering he had observed – particularly on the Sphinx itself rather than the enclosure walls – had been caused by the extensive flooding of the Plateau at the end of the last Ice Age and during the periodic 'great' Nile floods which followed *c*. 15,000–10,000 BC.[341] Schoch corrected him on this, pointing out that the weathering of the walls was the more revealing piece of evidence, and indicating that in his opinion this would have been caused by heavy precipitation or rainfall rather than flooding. In an article written in 1992 for the Egyptology periodical *KMT*, Schoch describes the climate of northern Egypt from ancient times.[342] He suggests that heavy rainfall occurred during the so-called 'Nabtian Pluvial', which started *c*. 10,000–8000 BC and lasted right through to *c*. 3000–2000 BC. It would appear that there were variations during this period, with particularly heavy rainfall *c*. 9200–6000, 5000, and 4000–3000 BC; and the experts he quotes seem to be unanimous that the arid climate that has persisted in the modern era commenced in approximately 2350 BC. This is only 150 years after the conventional date for the carving of the Sphinx.

Meanwhile, geologist James Harrell from the University of Toledo, one of the opponents of the West–Schoch hypothesis, writing in the same journal in 1994, describes how even during the time of this arid climate there are infrequent but heavy, intense and sudden rainstorms in the area, during which rainwater infiltrates the sand and limestone before it can evaporate. He further suggests that this intensity can result in groundwater flows and even surface run-off.[343] This analysis is corroborated by a number of accounts from explorers visiting the Plateau in relatively recent times. For example, Vyse makes the following observation in his diaries:[344]

An Englishman (Goodman), whom I had sent to Alexandria with the packet for Mr. Hamilton, returned with a letter from Colonel Campbell, and entered my services. He informed me that the weather had been unusually stormy at Alexandria. We had also experienced at the pyramids heavy showers and strong gusts of wind chiefly about sunset. The ground at Gizeh, and also that of Thebes, is in many places broken up by ravines or channels, which are supposed to have been caused by heavy rains. Mr. Wilkinson and also Mr. Hamilton mention periodical showers; and pits have been formed near the entrances of some of the tombs at Thebes, apparently to secure them from damp. Yet although heavy showers do occasionally occur, continued rain is exceedingly rare, and it can hardly be supposed to have fallen in sufficient quantities to have made these deep channels, which are probably, therefore, the repeated effects of violent winds.

Ignoring Vyse's amateur geology, we can see that he found heavy rainfall was not an unknown occurrence even in the single year he spent at the Plateau. And some two centuries before this Greaves had noted what appeared to be relatively constant rain during his brief visit:[345]

... for two months, namely December and January, I have not known it rain, so constantly, and with so much violence, at London, as I found it to do at Alexandria ... And not only there, but also at Grand Cairo, my very noble and trustworthy friend Sir William Paston, at the same time observed, that there fell much rain.

Meanwhile, it is also well known that repeated flash floods plagued the Valley of the Kings at Luxor, 500 miles to the south of Giza, to such an extent that the tomb of the sons of Ramesses II (known as 'KV5'), unearthed only relatively recently by the archaeologist Kent Weekes, was full to the brim with debris washed into it over the last three millennia which had taken on a 'cement-like' consistency – making its excavation extremely difficult.

Finally, the comments of the Egyptologist Alexander Moret are also highly revealing:[346]

Rain-storms are sometimes mentioned in the Egyptian texts. It should be noted that the temples of all periods have channels, on the roofs (with spouts) and underground, to carry off rainwater.

From this it is clear that, although the heaviest and most persistent rainfall in the area occurred prior to 2350 BC, such weather was not an uncommon feature for many centuries thereafter, almost up to the present day. This situation is somewhat different from that normally described by members of the alternative camp when discussing the Sphinx's age – that no rainfall of any consequence has fallen since the date when Egyptologists say the Sphinx was built.

Weathering

The arguments put forward by West and Schoch on the one hand, and Lehner and Harrell on the other, and elucidated in a number of articles in *KMT* between 1992 and 1996, tend to become somewhat belligerent at times – perhaps to be expected given the high stakes involved. They also pay at least as much attention, if not more, to ancillary issues such as weathering on other edifices away from the Sphinx, and other contextual issues. Not that these are irrelevant, but when one reviews the various articles one tends to become lost in a sea of attack and counterattack, with each author also concentrating on his perceived 'strongest ground', which ends up obscuring the basic issues at stake. Nevertheless, we will attempt to pull out and summarise these key issues – aided by the work of the geologist Lal Gauri from the University of Louisville, who has worked extensively with Lehner at the Sphinx in the last two decades, and who is fortunately very focused and clear in his explanations.

Types of weathering

From the variety of sources we have consulted, the different types of potential weathering appear to be divisible into three main categories, although the different geologists place varying emphases and interpretations thereon:

- *Precipitation weathering*: According to Schoch, this tends to produce a 'rolling and undulating vertical profile' with a 'smooth and polished' surface, and is caused by rainwater coursing over the rock.
- *Wind-sand weathering*: According to Schoch this tends to attack the 'less competent' layers of rock, producing sometimes heavily

undercut and random shapes, while any fissures affected tend to remain narrow, jagged and rough.

- *Chemical weathering*: According to Gauri, this is caused by water seeping into the pores in the rock, which then evaporates from the heat of the sun and crystallises the chemical 'salts' present (such as halite and gypsum), which in turn then expand and pressurise the pores. However, according to Schoch this mechanism produces only surface flaking and deterioration.

By our own reckoning, chemical weathering can be subdivided into three further categories, depending on the source of the water:

- *Capillary weathering*: This applies when a structure, such as the Sphinx and its enclosure, is sufficiently close to the subsurface water table that water can be sucked up into the pores of the rock via the process known as capillary action.
- *Wet-sand weathering*: This applies where the rock is encased in wet sand, which transfers its moisture into the rock. Of course the sand is originally moistened either by precipitation – which can also produce this chemical effect without the sand – or by capillary action. This type of weathering can clearly act on the Sphinx and its enclosure even when it is encased in sand.
- *Atmospheric weathering*: This derives from the humidity of the atmosphere, which is high at the Giza Plateau, and which causes condensation to form on the rock and be sucked into the pores via capillary action at night when it is cool, evaporating again when it heats up. It can of course primarily apply only to rock that is exposed to the atmosphere.

There is one overriding issue which we should bear in mind when considering the question of weathering at the Sphinx – it would appear that weathering patterns do *not* provide foolproof evidence for dating purposes. This is for several reasons, and we will examine each in turn . . .

Indistinguishable weathering
The first reason is that different types of weathering, however 'obvious' their cause might look to the casual observer, are not easily distinguishable. This issue was raised by West himself right at the start of the debate, although perhaps not given the

prominence it deserved. He reports in *Serpent* that when he consulted geologists they were initially cautious about making any positive judgements about the causes of weathering at the Sphinx since 'in many cases, erosion by wind and sand could be strikingly similar to erosion by water'.[347] Despite his and Schoch's continued assertions that the vast bulk of the geological community has always been behind them – for example, they supposedly received unanimous support when they presented their case to the Geological Society of America's annual convention in San Diego in October 1992 – it seems to us that the geological evidence is by no means as clear as they and their supporters would have us believe.

Overlaid weathering

The second reason is that different weathering agents operating in different eras can overlay each other, effectively wiping out the previous 'evidence'. Schoch himself admits that any wind-sand or chemical weathering tends to overlay previous precipitation weathering, thereby obscuring it, but he refuses to accept that this is a major detraction from his argument.

Rapid weathering

This 'overlay' problem is brought even more into focus by the observations made by Gauri et al. in a paper written for *Geoarchaeology* magazine in April 1995 – and it is a great shame that this was not reproduced in *KMT* to add substance to the main debate. Gauri is an undoubted supporter of *atmospheric* chemical weathering as the main cause. Although we will see shortly that this view may need some adaption when related to the history of the often buried Sphinx enclosure, he presents clear evidence that long periods of time are *not* required for such weathering to take place:[348]

> A large amount of debris due to weathering at the base of the walls around the Sphinx has accumulated where, at the end of Baraize's restoration about 1926, a clean surface had been produced. This is despite frequent cleaning in recent times. Further, Figure 8 shows a limestone block lying at the ditch of the Sphinx intended to be used in a recent restoration. Within one season

considerable exfoliation had occurred, the edges had worn away, and a rounded weathered surface had formed. Thus, it is clear that long periods of time are not necessary for the deep weathering of certain rocks to occur.

This view is supported by comparative photographs presented by Lehner and taken in 1909 and 1994, showing the significant weathering of the front wall of the Valley Temple in only 85 years.[349] Furthermore, he reports that during his extensive work at the Sphinx in recent decades he has observed large sections of limestone as much as one foot across and half an inch in thickness regularly falling off the body of the monument in front of his own eyes.[350]

To be fair, although the issue does not appear to be mentioned in the papers we have consulted, we should also note that acid rain and a general increase in pollution resulting from modern industrialisation in the vicinity of the Plateau may well have played their part in speeding up the rate of deterioration of the monument in recent decades. Schoch hints at this, suggesting that chemical erosion has taken place only in the last few hundred years, but there is no hard scientific data with which to test this hypothesis.

The nature of the rock

Gauri further indicates that the *extent* of weathering depends on the nature of the rock. The softest layers are those that contain only small pores, since when water seeps in and then evaporates, the 'mobilised salts' that crystallise exert a much greater pressure on smaller-diameter bores; the intrinsic salt content of the rock also plays a part. Therefore, for example, whereas the rock mentioned by Gauri in the above quotation was clearly of poor quality, he notes that the rocks used for the first repairs to the monument in pharaonic times were much more durable. Consequently he argues that 'the degree of weathering of the limestones at the Sphinx cannot be related quantitatively with the extent of the time passed since exposure to the environment'.

But perhaps Gauri's most critical argument is that it is the *rate* of change of the pore size (or 'lithology') in the rock that determines the weathering patterns produced:[351]

> The angularity or smoothness of a profile can be understood by the degree at which one lithology grades into another . . . A gentle gradation will produce a rounded profile and the profile will be angular if the lithology changes abruptly.
>
> . . . Figure 7, which shows an outcrop in the necropolis [to the south and west of the Sphinx], reveals a somewhat deeply notched thin softer [vertical] layer embedded in a thick harder layer. It is perhaps this type of profile that Schoch calls angular, but notice that the upper layers are distinctly rounded. *Thus, both an angular and a rounded vertical profile can be seen in one outcrop which is not possible under Schoch's thesis. Above all, the recent weathering of these strata is so intense that any relict profile will be modified in a short time, let aside the thousands of years that have elapsed since wet conditions prevailed in the area.*

We can deduce from these observations that rates of chemical weathering are sufficiently rapid, and their effects on different types of rock *even in the same location* sufficiently varied, that no valid observations about the age of a structure can be derived from weathering evidence alone.

We should also note in passing that the Sphinx's head is comparatively unweathered. This is because it comes from the highest and relatively hard stratum known as 'Member III', and consequently no valid comparison can be made with this in order to support or disprove any of the weathering theories relating to the body and the enclosure walls.

Does all the foregoing invalidate the West–Schoch hypothesis entirely? They argue that this analysis is at least partly flawed for a number of reasons, to which we will now turn . . .

Atmosphere alone?

First, they suggest that because the Sphinx enclosure has been filled with sand for a significant part of its orthodox life it cannot have been atmospherically weathered, as Gauri suggests, for much of this time. But it is at this point that we can bring the wet-sand and capillary mechanisms of chemical weathering into play. The former is particularly supported by Harrell,

303

although he tends to suggest that this would only occur at the base of the sand-filled enclosure via capillary action from the water table, whereas the deepest vertical weathering is at the top. However, if we accept that the 'arid' climate in Egypt has continued to produce sporadic but intense rainfall, then we can surely argue that this mechanism would have been at work from the top down as well.

This theory is particularly validated by an observation made by Gauri, who, when mapping the geological strata of the enclosure, went to shift some sand that had built up against the wall and found that, although dry on the surface, it was soaked a few inches underneath – as was the underlying bedrock.[352]

Sloping walls

Second, Schoch has emphasised that the enclosure walls are generally more eroded at the top than at the bottom, which appears at odds with the fact that the upper layers tend to be harder. However, Lehner argues that even the relatively uneroded eastern end of the south wall shows that it was deliberately cut with a slope in the original excavation of the enclosure.

The vertical fissures

Finally, West and Schoch have increasingly fallen back on the evidence of the deep, rounded, vertical hollows in the west and south walls of the Sphinx enclosure, insisting that these are *too* obviously weathered by precipitation for the other arguments about weathering to matter. We have some sympathy for this view, but again Gauri appears to have an answer.[353] He suggests that they represent faults in the rock originating from the time when the structural deformation of the whole Plateau caused the rock strata to tilt, perhaps millions of years ago, and that they were widened into cavities or channels by the 'hydraulic circulation of the underground water'. They were then exposed when the bedrock was excavated from the Sphinx enclosure.

One such fault line, the 'major fissure', runs diagonally across and right down through the Sphinx's body just in front of the rump. There are also two more – one in the middle of the body, the other behind the head – which are less well known. All three are clearly visible on old photographs, although they have now been substantially repaired.[354] In common with the *recesses* of the vertical fissures in the enclosure walls, these are *narrow* and *jagged*. The same type of fault lines can be found in many of the deep shafts on the Plateau, and even crossing the bedrock element of the Descending Passage under the Great Pyramid, all of which have been shored up with masonry.

Most important of all, Gauri maintains that not only has chemical weathering acted on these faults to produce a rounded profile on the outer edges both vertically and in places horizontally, but also the significant recent weathering debris on the floor and in the recesses shows that the process continues apace even today. West and Schoch contend that the chemical erosion process can produce only jagged profiles, and yet it is proved to have been operating with a vengeance on their *still-rounded* fissures in the Sphinx enclosure. So surely we must conclude that this weathering is capable of producing a rounded profile.

This important 'fault-line theory' was not particularly well explained by Lehner in his *KMT* contribution,[355] which allowed West to come back at him with some force[356] – although in fact he explains it far better in an article he wrote with Hawass for *Archaeology* magazine at about the same time.[357] However, in our view this explanation may well prove substantially correct, especially when we come to consider the context issues.

All this is not to say that rain erosion may not have played a significant part. As Gauri himself admits, 'rainfall, even in the modern desert environment, is a potent agent of erosion and may have contributed to the widening of the pre-existing channels'. In our view, even if we adopt the unrealistic scenario that the effects of chemical erosion have played a major part only in the last 50 to 100 years, our earlier climate review suggests that there may well have been sufficient rainfall during the 1,400 or so years that the Sphinx and its enclosure have been exposed to cause the weathering seen thereon – without having to go back further into prehistory. Of course this is all conjecture because there exists no hard scientific data for weathering rates that can be used to test any of the hypotheses. But, once again, we must conclude that the central West–Schoch hypothesis is clearly flawed, perhaps fatally so.

Making comparisons

We have already mentioned that the four main participants writing in *KMT* have gone to great lengths to analyse and compare the weathering on other structures on the Plateau and elsewhere. The following is our brief analysis of these parts of the debate:

- They discuss the various megalithic temples, including the Sphinx and Valley Temples and the mortuary temples of the Second and Third Pyramids. West and Schoch assert that the underlying precipitation weathering of the limestone core blocks of these edifices – which they suggest were built in the same early epoch as the Sphinx – can still be seen, especially if one stands back from afar. We do not find this convincing, and were certainly unable to detect any significant rounded *vertical* fissures in these blocks when we visited the Plateau, although they are heavily weathered in what appears to be a typical random pattern (see Plate 17). We should also remember that all these temples have, like the Sphinx, been buried under sand for most of their lives; while water run-off towards the two low-lying temples in front of the Sphinx could well mean that their sand covering was often wet.
- They discuss certain Old Kingdom tombs in the vicinity of the Sphinx (particularly that of Debehen, which is to the southwest), which according to West and Schoch do not exhibit typical water-weathering patterns. Much time is spent arguing about the various different strata of rock that exist in the Sphinx enclosure, and the way in which they correlate with the relevant other parts of the Plateau – an issue complicated by the fact that the strata do not lie horizontally. However, they seem to miss the point that these other structures are much higher up on the Plateau, and in any case do not lie in a hollowed-out enclosure, so even in this simple sense they cannot be sensibly compared with the Sphinx. Furthermore, Lehner indicates that these tombs have been covered by the mass of quarrying and ramp debris that litters the Plateau, especially in this area, and with probably relatively dry sand on top of that, for most of their existence.
- They discuss the First Dynasty mud-brick mastabas at Saqqara, which according to West and Schoch are not heavily weathered despite being made of inferior material. However, not only are these in a completely different location, but in fact most of them had collapsed even by the Third Dynasty and been subsequently built over.

- They discuss the 'Oseirion' at Abydos, which is normally associated with the New Kingdom ruler Seti I (Nineteenth Dynasty). West delights in comparing this edifice to the Valley Temple because of its similar freestanding granite pillars. However, not only do both he and Schoch accept that at the Valley Temple these undoubtedly date to the Fourth Dynasty anyway, but the resemblance is in any case only superficial in that the Oseirion does not incorporate the Old Kingdom style of granite-cased limestone-cored walls. In fact it is effectively constructed in an excavated enclosure in the ground, and – while this is certainly a unique arrangement – we cannot, for contextual reasons if nothing else, support West's contention that it was built in a much earlier epoch when it would have been above ground.

Although the issue is not discussed in the *KMT* debate, both West and Andrew Collins have also noticed vertical weathering profiles on the foundation walls of Saladin's medieval citadel, which is perched atop a cliff face between Giza and Cairo. However, since no one is clear as to whether this face is natural or was carved out when the castle was built, there is little valid comparison to be made.

Perhaps more interesting appeared to be our own observation that the structures most comparable with the Sphinx enclosure on the Plateau are the bedrock walls which have been excavated to the north and west of the Second Pyramid in order to provide a levelled foundation (see Plate 32). These do display vertical fissures but they are of the 'narrow, jagged and rough' variety which Schoch would put down to wind-sand weathering. But, whereas we had thought that these might lend credence to the West–Schoch hypothesis – since the enclosure is high up on the Plateau and would not naturally collect water – we can now see that these are probably yet more examples of originally subterranean faults which have been chemically weathered and perhaps to an extent have suffered wind-sand weathering. The lack of rounded features thereon would therefore be explained by differences in the rock – which is presumably harder and from a higher stratum – and by the relative lack of wetness of any sand and debris that would have covered them, given their raised position.

In summary, given our previous conclusions regarding the

inherent difficulties in comparing weathering patterns, let alone using them to draw conclusions about age, all these comparison attempts in our view represent something of a side issue.

Making a date

In his *KMT* paper, Schoch describes the results of seismic surveys undertaken by Thomas Dobecki on the floor of the Sphinx enclosure.[358] Survey lines were recorded along the two sides of the Sphinx (referred to as lines S1 and S2), along the rump (S3) and along the front (S4) (see Figure 26). Their interpretation of these surveys was that the bedrock underneath the enclosure floor was between 50 and 100 per cent more weathered at the front (to a depth of some 6 to 8 feet) than at the rear (only 4 feet). From this, Schoch concludes that the rear of the monument must have been excavated long after the front, and it is from this information as much as anything else that he derives his estimate of the date of the original carving. His logic is as follows. On the basis of the Inventory Stela and other contextual evidence, he assumes that Khafre did make some repairs to the Sphinx, and therefore suggests that it was he who carved out the rump. If this occurred some 4,500 years ago, then on the basis that the rump is between 50 and 100 per cent newer than the rest of the monument, the original carving of the front and sides must date back a further 2,500 or so years minimum and 4,500 years maximum, giving a range of 7000 to 5000 BC. However, he concedes that the date may be earlier still, given the nonlinearity of weathering rates.

Unfortunately this line of argument is – like the Sphinx enclosure itself – deeply flawed, for the following reasons:

- First, Schoch clearly makes the assumption that the subsurface weathering has been caused by rainfall seeping down through the bedrock floor of the enclosure – and not by any wet sand or capillary action from the water table. If the Sphinx enclosure has been cleared of sand for only 1,400 years of its orthodox life (see previous estimates) then the extra 50 to 100 per cent weathering at the front and sides should have taken only an extra 700 to 1,400 years – provided the enclosure had been previously kept free from sand (although who knows what assumptions could be made in this

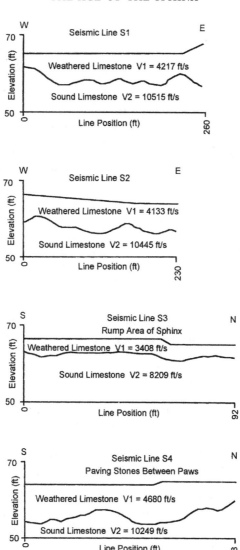

FIGURE 26: DOBECKI'S SEISMIC SURVEY RESULTS IN THE
SPHINX ENCLOSURE[359]

respect?). This would push the date back to between approximately 4000 and 3000 BC only.

- Second, the lines S3 and S4 show that the general level of the enclosure at the rear is of the order of 2 feet higher than at the front, so that any surface water in a cleared enclosure would tend to run to the front anyway, before it seeped through.

- Third, even the original interpretation of the data appears somewhat suspect: the lines S1 and S2 taken along the flanks show extremely nonuniform rates of subsurface weathering along the length of the enclosure, which would suggest that to base the analysis primarily on the two lines at the front and back only is completely invalid.

- Fourth, the entire analysis is a 'red herring', since it is almost certain that the subsurface erosion has been caused far more by hydraulic and capillary action over the many millennia since the bed was laid down than by relatively recent rainfall and exposure. Harrell even suggests that the seismic readings were merely picking up the break between the 'shoal reef' limestone of the 'Member I' strata and the underlying nummulite bank of the Mokkatam formation, but this analysis in itself seems flawed because according to Gauri the break between these beds slants across the Sphinx enclosure such that the upper layer is present on only one side.

- Fifth, Schoch himself accepts the existence of New Kingdom repair blocks on the *rump* of the monument, indicating that extensive weathering had taken place at the back, by his own admission since the *orthodox* carving date. So why could this rate of weathering not have applied all over?

- Sixth, and perhaps worst of all, it is clear that the west wall behind the rump – which according to Schoch's theory must have been carved out only *c.* 2500 BC – *shows exactly the same vertical and rounded weathering profiles as the south wall*. If they could be created on this wall after this date, then why not on the other – and why bother to attempt to redate the monument at all?

All in all, therefore, this is not one of Schoch's better performances. Nevertheless we should also record that Schoch attempts to place his 7000–5000 BC dating into the context of the advanced settlements known to have existed, for example, at Jericho and at Catal Huyuk in Anatolia, both of which have been dated to this epoch.

For his part West does not tie himself down to this 'conservative view' (his own description!), and instead argues that we must look even further back, perhaps as far as 10,500 BC or even earlier, for reasons we will review shortly. He further suggests that all other evidence of an earlier advanced civilisation in this area was destroyed by the cataclysmic flooding that occurred at the end of the last Ice Age, and is now either buried at the bottom of the subsequently formed Mediterranean, or under the desert sand that now occupies the ancient more westerly course of the Nile.[360] In this context it is interesting to note that, in a documentary made for the BBC's *Timewatch* programme entitled the 'Age of the Sphinx', independent advice was sought from the University of Sheffield's Drylands Research Unit. Dr Sarah O'Hara thereof pointed out that between 10,000 and 20,000 years ago the climate in this area was *completely dry*. This seems somewhat at odds with the concept of post-Ice Age floods, but if it is correct it has significant implications for West's 'nonconservative' early date for the Sphinx.

Meanwhile, both West and Schoch have suggested that isotopic analysis (the testing of radioactive isotopes to determine how long rock has been exposed to the elements) should be performed on the limestone of the Sphinx to test its date – although Gauri argues that this will not work, precisely because continued erosion has removed the relevant surface material. Perhaps performing such tests on the always-exposed and harder-materialed head could, in part, overcome this objection. But as far as we are aware, at the time of writing no such tests have been performed.

Finally, we should note that Dobecki's seismic surveys also recorded the possibility of a rectangular man-made chamber beneath the paws of the Sphinx, which West has suggested would correlate with Edgar Cayce's predictions.[361] However, we will leave this issue for a later chapter.

Context Revisited

Let us now turn to the contextual issues raised by West and Schoch. West in particular makes great play of the fact that the attribution of the Sphinx to Khafre relies entirely on circumstantial evidence, although he is somewhat disingenuous when he quotes Selim Hassan in support of this view, since the latter

311

makes it quite clear in *The Sphinx: Its History in the Light of Recent Excavations* that he nevertheless supports the conventional dating.

Restoration

We have already seen that in *The Complete Pyramids* Lehner provides a detailed analysis of the various phases of repairs carried out on the Sphinx. His attribution of the earliest phase to the time of Thutmose IV is based partly on the Dream Stela, which describes how the Sphinx asked the king to rescue it from its sand covering. However, West and Schoch use the Inventory Stela to suggest that Khafre merely repaired the monument, since it says that the 'House of Isis' was discovered by Khufu beside the 'House of Harmakhis' (i.e. the Sphinx), indicating that it already existed even in Khufu's time. We saw in Chapter 2 that in our view the content of this stela cannot be taken literally. West insists that it can because the information would not be essentially altered any more than a twentieth-century copy of the Bible. However, given the extent to which it is clear that when it was first drawn up, the Old Testament especially was hopelessly distorted from the older texts on which it was based, we take this suggestion with a hefty pinch of salt. Furthermore, if we appear arbitrarily to be prepared in one paragraph to accept the evidence of one stela and not another, it should be made clear that – apart from our reservations about the Inventory Stela cited previously – this is additionally because, first, the Dream Stela is a contemporary original and not a much later copy; and, second, there is a great deal of circumstantial evidence to support the Dream Stela, such as the numerous mud bricks found inscribed with Thutmose's name by Hassan in the enclosure, originating from an inner wall which he erected therein;[362] the same cannot be said for the Inventory Stela.

In any case, it is more important that West and Schoch go on to argue that the oldest repair blocks on the Sphinx's body themselves date to the Old Kingdom. It is true that the style of the earliest repair blocks does date them to this period. However, Lehner points out that Thutmose and his successors had no qualms about stripping Old Kingdom structures to provide themselves with materials – and that they even admit to this in the Dream Stela. He asserts that the pivot sockets on the back of the granite slab from which the stela itself is constructed exactly match those in one of the doorways in the Second Pyramid's mortuary temple, suggesting it was a lintel therefrom; and, more important, that the blocks used to repair the Sphinx's body at this time almost certainly came from the walls of the Second Pyramid's causeway.[363] Although Lehner initially had doubts about this issue, he is now firmly convinced that the first repairs were New Kingdom, and in our view this is a reasonable suggestion.

For his part, Zahi Hawass appears to be less sure and suggests that the 'Member II' limestone of which the body is primarily composed was in such poor condition when the body was *first excavated* that it was impossible to sculpt with any accuracy, forcing the original sculptors to case almost the *entire* body with higher-quality blocks that could be worked.[364] However, West and Schoch have pointed out that, if the blocks removed from this member were of sufficient quality to construct the Valley and Sphinx Temples, it was good enough for carving the Sphinx, and we tend to agree with them. Nevertheless, it is certainly conceivable that *certain parts* of the newly exposed bedrock in Member II were sufficiently flawed – such as the 'major fissure' in front of the rump – that Old Kingdom masonry was immediately applied.

West and Schoch have also suggested that the core had eroded by as much as 3 feet before the Phase I repairs were carried out, which they say must have taken place in only 300 years at the most.[365] But if these were New Kingdom repairs, and wet-sand and capillary weathering while the enclosure was filled are taken into account, then we have a far longer, 1,100-year period in which this could have occurred.

The restoration evidence, therefore, does not on balance support an earlier dating for the Sphinx.

The Temples

In the mid-1980s, the geologist Thomas Aigner conducted a detailed survey which attempted to map the strata seen in the Sphinx enclosure into the huge limestone core blocks that make up the Sphinx and Valley Temples. His work proved conclusively that the blocks in the Sphinx Temple come from the middle and lower layers and often display a distinguishing yellow band of softer material. Whilst the origin of the blocks used in the Valley Temple proved less easy to determine, the suggestion that they were quarried first from the upper layers of the Sphinx enclosure is still that favoured by Lehner and others.[366]

We have already seen that West and Schoch, in accepting this evidence, propose that these temples also date back much earlier than Khafre's reign – and in fact, since their similarity with the mortuary temples of the Second and Third Pyramids is unavoidable, when pressed they suggest that these too should be redated. However, it is clear to us from previous analysis that all these structures, with the possible exception of the Sphinx Temple, fit perfectly into the *context* of Old Kingdom pyramid complexes; as a result, they are all contemporary with each other, and, more important, with the Sphinx. Furthermore, Lehner points out that emplacements exist for multiple statues of Khafre in all of these temples (bar that associated with Menkaure), and that, as well as the life-size statue found in a pit by Mariette, several fragments of these have been unearthed that also bear Khafre's name.[367] Meanwhile, Hassan was the first to indicate that a trench cut parallel to the Second Pyramid's causeway on its north side, which would have been used to mark the boundary between the complexes of the two large pyramids, carries right down into the Sphinx enclosure and had to be blocked with masonry to prevent water draining into it (suggesting there was plenty of rainfall at the time). He therefore argues that the enclosure must have been excavated after the main complex had been laid out.[368]

As for the possible anomaly of the Sphinx Temple, it sits on the same terrace as the Valley Temple, which is inextricably linked by the causeway to the Second Pyramid. The fronts and backs of the two temples are in virtual alignment, while both share the same style of limestone-core walls faced with granite inside and out – albeit that the exterior facing of the Sphinx Temple appears not to have been completed, suggesting that it was the last edifice built in Khafre's reign (a theory born out by the fact that its core blocks come from the lower levels of the enclosure). Furthermore, Herbert Ricke, who carried out a detailed study of the Sphinx Temple between 1967 and 1970, concluded that its open court was nearly an exact copy of the one in the Second Pyramid's mortuary temple.

Turning a blind eye to this mountain of contextual evidence, but nevertheless accepting that the granite facing of the Valley and Sphinx Temples is Old Kingdom style, West and Schoch suggest that this must have been a later addition to the much earlier limestone cores. They attempt to back this up by suggesting that the backs of the granite facing blocks have been cut in 'irregular, undulating patterns' to fit *already weathered* limestone core blocks.[369] However, in our view this suggestion is totally insupportable. First, they also suggest that the worst-weathered limestone blocks were also cut back to provide a smoother surface – this tempts us to ask why they would bother to shape both surfaces, and to ask how they can tell the limestone blocks were weathered in any case if they had been smoothed out. Second, it is clearly easier to shape the softer limestone cores to fit the irregular backs of the much harder granite facings than vice versa. That this was the method used is evident in the Third Pyramid's unfinished mortuary temple, in which the builders were in the process of fitting the lowest tier of facing to the limestone core blocks in the south wall of the north corridor when the work was abandoned: the overhang of the limestone blocks above indicates clearly that they were cut back *in situ* to fit the shape of the back of the facing (See Plate 18).[370] And, third, Lehner maintains that close examination of the granite blocks that do remain *in situ* on the Valley Temple shows that the core limestone behind them is *not* weathered.

However, the most damaging evidence against the 'two-stage construction' argument lies in the layout and design of the Valley Temple itself, elements of which are so clearly contrary to the theory even to the casual observer that we are amazed that the issue is not raised in any of the papers we have consulted. During our research trip we noticed that in the western entrance, which leads on to the Second Pyramid causeway, a huge granite lintel forms the top of the doorway but is intricately worked into the surrounding limestone blocks, and especially is surmounted by a limestone block so massive that it must be one of the largest in the edifice (see Plates 33 and 34). Furthermore, there is a set of recessed chambers off each side of the passage on the north side leading to this doorway, each of which displays an integral granite lining. Therefore, apart from the fact that a granite lining on a limestone core is typical of Old Kingdom temple style, we find it impossible on a practical level to conceive that these granite elements could have been added as part of a second-stage construction.

Symbolism

As we will see in a later chapter, the authors Graham Hancock and Robert Bauval have teamed up with West to use his revisionist theories to support their claim that the layout of the Giza Pyramids was *designed c.* 10,500 BC to reflect the three belt stars of Orion. They argue that this assumption is strengthened by the Sphinx's leonine form, which reflects the fact that it was carved during the precessional age of Leo, which spans this date.

Without going into too much detail at this stage, there are a number of objections to this hypothesis. For example, the astronomer Dr Ed Krupp, Director of the Griffith Observatory in Los Angeles, suggests:[371]

> There is no logical reason or evidence to associate the Sphinx with ... Leo the Lion ... Why is the one constellation we know the Egyptians recognized as a lion nowhere near Leo but in the north circumpolar zone? Leo [is] a constellation not recognized by Egyptians before the Ptolemaic era.

Furthermore, it is surely no coincidence that Djedefre, Khufu's short-lived successor, was the first Fourth Dynasty pharaoh to incorporate the name of the sun god Re or Ra into his name – a tradition that continued with Khaf-re and Menkau-re. On this basis it is surely sensible to suggest that the Sphinx was erected facing due east, towards the sun as it rises at the equinoxes, in this very epoch when the sun cult came to prominence. This view is backed up by Ricke, who argues that symbolically the Sphinx Temple was the first solar temple associated with an Old Kingdom pyramid complex.[372]

Again, therefore, we do not believe that the symbolic evidence supports a redating of the Sphinx.

As a slight aside, in many of the depictions of sphinxes, including on the Dream Stela, and in the Fifth Division of the *Book am-tuat* which we discussed in chapter 5, they are found in pairs acting as protectors. This has led the Egyptian researcher Bassam El Shammaa to conclude that the remains of a second Sphinx, which was destroyed in great antiquity, lie buried behind the Valley Temple. However, his theory appears to be primarily based on the Inventory Stela which is not in itself a reliable source, and in any case we are not entirely convinced that his interpretation that it mentions two Sphinxes is actually correct.

The face

Much has been made of the extent of the likeness of the human face of the Sphinx to that of Khafre, best known from his life-size statue in the Cairo Museum. In *Serpent*, West accepted that the resemblance is 'too close to ignore, but not close enough to prove Chephren [Khafre] was the builder'.[373] However, when Lehner attempted a computer simulation, which effectively mapped Khafre's face on to that of the Sphinx,[374] West was outraged, declaring it a 'technological tautology'. He therefore sought the opinion of Frank Domingo, a senior forensic artist with the NYPD, who after a detailed study concluded:[375]

> The proportions in the frontal view and especially the angles and facial protrusion in the lateral views convinced me that the Sphinx is not Chephren. If the ancient Egyptians were skilled technicians and capable of duplicating images then these two works cannot represent the same individual . . .

It is true that the Old Kingdom sculptors certainly did seem to pay great attention to reproducing the faces of their kings with a high degree of accuracy. However, at a 'nonforensic' level, Domingo's reconstructions and Khafre's face from the statue do, from the front view at least, look strikingly similar in our opinion – except that the Sphinx's jaw is rather more squared.[376] Turning to the lateral view, once the nose is reconstructed, the Sphinx's face is nowhere near as negroid-looking as it usually appears, and indeed if it is tilted forward somewhat it once again appears very similar in our view. Certainly the profile of the eyes, nose and lips is remarkably consistent, even if their relative positions do not match exactly.

West and Schoch's attitude to this issue is somewhat confusing. At various times they have emphasised the negroid features of the Sphinx's face, while at other times accepting that the *nemes* headdress and plaited beard thereon are clearly of Dynastic style. They have also argued that it must have been *recarved*, perhaps even by Khafre himself – which confuses the argument even more, especially in respect of Domingo's analysis.

Nevertheless, this latter view has often been expressed even by Egyptologists, on the basis that the head does appear to be rather out of proportion – that is, too small – for the rest of the body. Lehner has attempted to counter this argument by suggesting that the body is too long, a situation forced on the sculptors when they discovered the 'major fault'. A shorter body would undoubtedly bring the proportions more into balance, but the head would probably still be on the small side. Although *by definition* all sphinxes have human heads, Hassan points out that they were not really known in pre-Dynastic times, and that the only known predecessor is a small female sphinx statue found in the ruins of Djedefre's pyramid complex at Abu Roash.[377] If the Great Sphinx of Giza was not only the best known and largest, but also near enough the first, then we cannot use precedent to discount the possibility that the face was at some point recarved.

Some have suggested the face would have been originally that of a lion, while the researcher Robert Temple believes it to have been that of a dog. However he also accepts the orthodox age for the Sphinx, but – based on Herodotus's accounts – suggests that the weathering has been caused by the enclosure being filled with water by a race of alien visitors who were amphibians.[378] Since the water would drain away without constant refilling, we do not regard this as very likely.

All things considered, we believe the contextual evidence swings the balance in favour of the suggestion that the Sphinx's face is indeed that of Khafre, and that it was never recarved.

Conclusion

There is one piece of attribution evidence related to the Sphinx that we have not previously mentioned. In 1979, while clearing a mound of debris in the northeast corner of the Sphinx enclosure as part of the original Sphinx Restoration Project, Zahi Hawass's team found three limestone core blocks intended for the Sphinx Temple, which had been left behind when the work was abandoned. In the debris *underneath* them they found numerous pieces of Old Kingdom pottery. Similar pottery was found in the hard-baked and previously undisturbed construction debris in the quarrying channels on the western 'ledge', which is raised up from the floor of the enclosure behind the rump and almost certainly results from its being abandoned before it was completely levelled (Lehner compares its unfinished state to that of the floor of the Subterranean Chamber in the Great Pyramid). Meanwhile, when the holes drilled by the SRI in 1978 in the floor of the Sphinx Temple were examined, the sticky clay therein was found once again to contain Old Kingdom pottery, and also a number of dolerite pounding stones which as we have seen are typical period tools.[379]

When we consider this comparatively *hard* evidence, the contextual evidence, and the fact that even the geological argument for the redating of the Sphinx is itself flawed at best, then we must surely draw the conclusion that the Sphinx and its associated temples were indeed built during the Fourth Dynasty, almost certainly by Khafre – and not many millennia before, as West, Schoch and now many other members of the alternative camp would have us believe.

We must emphasise that this does not mean that we wish to denigrate the often significant contribution made by West. For example, we have already seen that we do not necessarily disagree with his contention that highly advanced civilisations existed on this planet in great antiquity, but we do not agree that the Sphinx is prime evidence of them. We feel we need to look further afield, including outside Egypt, to test this hypothesis – a suggestion with which West does not disagree. Furthermore, his main contribution in *Serpent* was to examine the issues of symbology and esoteric wisdom in Ancient Egypt, which are of crucial importance in their own right. Finally, even if his Sphinx redating theories are incorrect, his vociferous advocacy thereof has played a part in forcing the Egyptological community to come out of their trenches and become more visible to members of the public, and especially those with alternative leanings. Partly in order to refute the West–Schoch hypothesis, Lehner and Hawass especially have given a number of lectures and taken part in debates and documentaries that might not otherwise have caught the public's attention. In the final analysis, this can only improve information flow and the quality of the various ongoing debates.

CHAPTER

EIGHT

The Enigma of the Shafts

We saw in an earlier chapter that – in terms of the general context of the purpose of the pyramids – there is really only one significant enigma that remains almost impossible to resolve: the purpose of the 'air' shafts in the King's and Queen's Chambers. So let us now revisit these aspects of the Great Pyramid's design . . .

Ventilation Revisited

It would appear that the shafts in the King's Chamber were always designed to run right through the edifice unhindered. They are certainly open at the chamber end, and it is possible that Latif's account of 'openings which admit air and light' indicates that they were always open on the outside, even when the casing was still intact as he reported – although the function of the 'Iron Plate' discovered by Hill at the mouth of the southern shaft remains unclear.

One of the most convincing explanations that these shafts were indeed devised to ventilate the chamber is provided by JP Lepre, who makes several important points.[380] First, the chamber is high up in the superstructure, and since warm air rises it is consistently 10 to 20 degrees hotter than the under- or near-ground chambers in both the Great and all other pyramids. Second, although clearly the dead king himself did not need fresh air, the assortment of high-ranking priests and dignitaries involved in the burial ritual would expect comfortable conditions. Third, although we have already recorded the oft-touted claim that the temperature therein remains at a constant 68 degrees irrespective of the season, Lepre found from a series of measurements taken at different times that it can fluctuate between 70 and 80 degrees – but suggests this is because the northern shaft is 'punctured' by Caviglia's tunnel running along-side it, which has reduced its efficiency.

However, as we have already noted, this theory takes a severe knock when we come to the Queen's Chamber shafts. These were originally blanked off by 5 inches of nonremovable masonry on their inside ends – in other words, the blocks in which they commence had been deliberately hollowed out for several feet from their back faces, but in both cases the channel stops short from being carried right through to the front. Piazzi Smyth's record of the Dixon brothers' own testimony was quite specific about this:[381]

> ... Dr. Grant and Mr. Dixon have successfully proved that there was no jointing, and that the thin plate was a 'left', and a very skillfully and symmetrically left, part of the grand block com-posing that portion of the wall on either side.

Clearly this was no simple blanking mechanism. A number of Egyptologists have attempted to explain these features of the Queen's Chamber shafts as a corollary of the replan theory, whereby they were left unfinished as part of the process of abandonment in favour of the King's Chamber. Again, Lepre's explanation is by far the most detailed and lucid.[382] Not only does he add weight to the replan theory by pointing out that the red ochre lines used to align the blocks in the Queen's Chamber passage remain faintly visible, whereas they would have been polished away were it completed, but he also suggests that the shafts come to exactly the level of the pointed roof of Campbell's Chamber – and that the reason for this is that the architects had to keep the Queen's Chamber in reserve for a burial in the event of Khufu's sudden death *until the King's Chamber and its necessary Relieving Chambers had been com-pleted* (by contrast, others speculate that the fact that they go past the height of the King's Chamber *floor* is sufficient to quash the replan theory). On this basis he suggests the 'lasts' could have been knocked out should the chamber have been required in a hurry.

However, there are a number of objections even to Lepre's analysis. First, he suggests that the Queen's Chamber shafts both travel to within about 20 feet of the outside of the edifice, but unusually for him he does not reveal how he arrives at this conclusion. We will see shortly that more recent exploration has revealed that the southern shaft stops more like 50 feet from the outside, while the full extent of the northern shaft remains a complete mystery – so we can only assume his distances were based on mere speculation. Second, and more significant, is the fact that, although the shafts take more or less the shortest route to the outside of the edifice, it would have been far easier in construction terms for them to have been routed *horizontally* through one course of masonry. More than anything else, this piece of reasoning tends to demolish the ventilation theory.

As previously noted, the complexity of the compound angles required in the blocks that encase the shafts in order that they can run obliquely is quite stunning, and does indeed suggest massive dedication to an important cause.[383] It has been suggested that they form part of some kind of ritual associated with the king's journey to the afterlife, and we have already indicated that we have some sympathy with this view. In this connection Robert Bauval has suggested that they line up with important stars, and we will examine this assertion in the next chapter. But first some important additional information needs to be established.

A New Perspective

Much has been made of the direction of travel of the shafts from a side or vertical perspective. However, the *lateral* course of the shafts, revealed by looking *down* through the edifice, is less well appreciated. So let us examine this in more detail.

When they first cleared the King's Chamber shafts, Vyse and Perring carefully mapped them and established that the southern one is 174 feet long and inclined at 45 degrees, while – because the King's Chamber lies south of the centre line but they both exit at the same height – the northern one is longer at 233 feet and less inclined at 31 degrees. However, they also angle obliquely in a *lateral* direction in order to exit in the centre of the north and south faces of the edifice, and the reason for this is that they commence well to the east of the centre line of the pyramid. But as can be seen from Figure 27, the inner ends of the King's Chamber shafts could have been placed more or less in line with the east side of the coffer on the central north–south axis, entirely avoiding the need for lateral deviation. To add to the intrigue, close investigation using Caviglia's tunnel, which runs alongside the northern shaft, reveals that it veers sharply northwest after a few feet, and returns to a northerly direction only after some 25 feet. It is clear from the scale diagram that it does not need to do this in order to avoid the antechamber or the southern tip of the Grand Gallery, because it already starts well to the west of them. Why these even greater degrees of complexity?

By contrast, because the chamber itself is smaller, the Queen's Chamber shafts could never have commenced sufficiently far west to run directly along the centre line. In fact they lie more or less in the centre of the chamber, the result being that the two sets of shafts are more or less in perpendicular alignment with each other at the start. Again it is intriguing that, like its King's Chamber counterpart, the northern Queen's Chamber shaft kinks significantly to the west, although after a considerably greater 40 or so feet, and – although this occurs at about the level of the base of the Grand Gallery – again there is no obvious need for this change of direction because the shaft is already well to the west of the potential obstacle. Other than that we know it then travels in this northwesterly direction for some distance, but we do not know what happens thereafter.

Unfortunately, none of this analysis helps us to understand why the shafts were built, and if anything it only adds to the enigma. Are the deviations in the two northern shafts required to circumvent as yet undiscovered chambers or passages? That is anyone's guess, although such considerations may be useful inputs if further nonintrusive surveys were performed. Nevertheless, it is important to appreciate these attributes at least in order to be able to evaluate all theories put forward, as will be seen later. In the meantime, yet more information can be revealed . . .

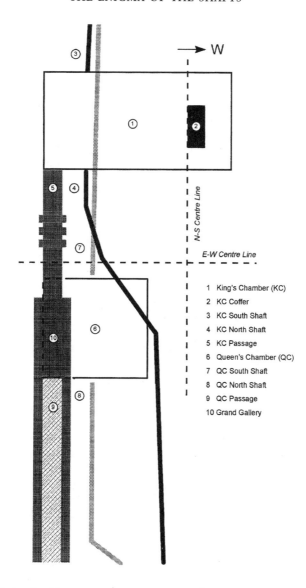

FIGURE 27: THE KING'S AND QUEEN'S CHAMBER SHAFTS
VIEWED FROM ABOVE[384]

Opener of the Ways

Rudolf Gantenbrink is a Munich-based robotics engineer who has spent much of his life designing and building high-technology equipment to allow cameras to film inaccessible places – for example on oil rigs. Over the years he became intrigued by the Great Pyramid, and in particular by the enigmatic 'air' shafts. As a result, in 1990 he presented a proposal to the German Archaeological Institute in Cairo (GAIC), directed by Rainer Stadelmann, to investigate the shafts using robotic technology. By coincidence, at about the same time the GAIC received a commission from the EAO to install ventilation systems in the Great Pyramid. This was the first stage in a plan put forward by Zahi Hawass, who ultimately hopes to install such systems in all the pyramids to reduce the moisture from the thousands of visitors' breath, which over the long term is having a similarly detrimental effect on the interior of the edifices as atmospheric weathering is on the outside.

The two pieces of work were effectively combined, allowing Gantenbrink to explore the shafts under a permit from the EAO on the basis that he also find time to install the ventilation systems. During the first phase in 1992, he started by clearing the King's Chamber shafts of reaccumulated debris – which he achieved using the high technology of lowering an old car axle down on a length of rope! He then explored them using a small and relatively simple robot with a miniature camera attached to relay pictures, which he pulled up and down the open-ended shafts using cables. Although little new was revealed about the shafts themselves, much was learnt about the requisite technology during this exploratory operation. Having cleaned and explored the shafts, Gantenbrink installed two fans, one at the end of Caviglia's tunnel, which runs alongside the northern shaft, and one in the mouth of the southern shaft, which succeeded in reducing the humidity in the King's Chamber, and to a lesser extent the pyramid as a whole.

Fired with enthusiasm, and knowing that for the following year he would switch his attention to the Queen's Chamber shafts, Gantenbrink returned to Germany to improve his design, and over the next few months he and his team developed a truly marvellous piece of robotic technology. In order to be able

326

to cope with the slope of the shafts without the use of cables to pull it through, he incorporated a remote-control system coupled with the ingenious use of hydraulically controlled upper and lower tracks. Fitted with powerful lamps and an improved camera with better vertical and horizontal range, his robot was ready – and poised to make probably the most celebrated discovery of the twentieth century in the Great Pyramid. He called it Upuaut – after the Egyptian god whose name means the 'opener of the ways'.

More artefacts?

So much attention has been paid to Gantenbrink's discoveries in the southern Queen's Chamber shaft, to which we will turn shortly, that it is often overlooked that he first explored the northern shaft, with some interesting results. In both *The Orion Mystery* and *Keeper of Genesis*, Robert Bauval does draw attention to this exploration, indicating that Upuaut's camera picked up two 'distinct objects – a metallic hook, and an apparent baton of wood'.[385] He goes on to assert that these are similar to the objects found by the Dixons, and to this day continues to make great play of the fact that they have not been retrieved – emphasising that the wood would be carbon-datable, ostensibly an important piece of research since the original 5-inch baton has, as we have already seen, been missing for many years.

Let us therefore examine these claims. Gantenbrink was kind enough to provide us with rarely seen video footage shot when Upuaut was exploring the shafts in 1993, which has allowed us to examine it in detail.[386] It is quite clear that as Upuaut ascends the northern shaft, in which the walls and ceiling are in the main extremely roughly finished in contrast to the relatively smooth floor, the camera picks up a tubular iron rod abandoned by the Dixons, which lies along the right-hand wall before crossing the floor to bend round the left-hand kink at about 40 feet along; the rod is about two-thirds of an inch in diameter. As Upuaut gets to the kink and peers round, we see that the rod is jammed hard up against the right-hand wall, clearly as a result of the Dixons ramming it in thinking that they had met an obstruction that they could clear – after all, they probably assumed the shaft ran straight. But also as we approach the kink there is indeed a length of wood, which is square in section and broken off at the near end, lying right across the shaft and disappearing round the kink. As we round the corner, we see that it is tucked up along the left-hand wall (see Plates 37 and 38). Is this an original artefact left in the shaft when it was constructed and similar to the missing piece of cedar wood, as Bauval claims? In our view it is highly likely that the answer to this question is an emphatic 'no'!

There are a number of reasons for reaching this conclusion. First, let us compare the 'new' length of wood with the 'old' Dixon piece. The new one has accurately machined and squared sides, free of any marks or cuts, and is clearly considerably longer – perhaps as long as 4 or 5 feet, although it is difficult to tell exactly due to the lack of perspective. By contrast, the old one was reported to be just under 5 inches long, and had *notches* cut in it. The only attributes they really share are a similar cross-section of about one-third of an inch, and the fact that they are both broken off at one end. Second, it is clear from studying the position of the wood that it is highly likely to be just another length of rod that has been used in an attempt to clear or explore the shaft. It too has become stuck around the kink, but instead of jamming tight as the metal rod did, it has snapped under the pressure applied and the broken end has whiplashed across the floor of the shaft, scraping some large chips of stone along the ground with it as it went; the whole ensemble lies piled up against the left-hand wall after the bend, but jutting out before it.

It is also interesting to note that at the far end of the wooden rod there appears to be a square-shaped object which, although the image is not particularly clear, may represent some form of scraper attached to the end of it – which was perhaps designed to drag out and retrieve objects in the shaft. As to who might have used this wooden rod, it would appear that it travels *underneath* the iron rod at the kink and, although the analysis is not foolproof, this could indicate that it was used by the Dixons themselves before they had the jointed iron rod made up. Since Bauval is at pains to point out how he studied the video with Gantenbrink at great length in his Munich home just after it was taken, and since he also includes a still frame of the 'new' wood as it lies before the kink in *Keeper of Genesis*,[387] we cannot help but feel that this analysis would also have been readily available to him.

However, the story of the 'new wood' does not end here. A much shorter video produced by Gantenbrink shows what is possibly *another* piece of wood, this time indeed much shorter and looking as if it has two holes in it, which would correlate with the fittings on the 'Dixon hook' (see Plate 35). It appears to lie a few feet back down the shaft from the kink, pushed up quite close to the right-hand wall by the Dixons' iron rod. *This discovery has not been previously disclosed.*

As far as the 'new' hook is concerned, Bauval is perhaps on stronger ground. We were at first confused because we were unable to locate it in either of Gantenbrink's videos, but a still shot helpfully provided for us by him from Upuaut's camera does show an object lying on the floor further back down the shaft, this time on the left of the Dixons' metal rod, which at this point is hard up against the right-hand wall (see Plate 36). Life-size, it is almost impossible to tell what this small object is, but an enlargement of the shot reveals what do appear to be two rounded 'hooks' just like those on the Dixon artefact, albeit that the left-hand one is bent round considerably more. And from the few spots of reflection it does appear that it may be metallic – although Bauval's assertion that it is made of gold appears to be an exaggerated assumption. At something like half an inch across the prongs, the new artefact is of similar size to the old one – judging from a photograph of the latter reproduced by Lehner, which we assume is life size.[388]

What do we glean from all this? If efforts should be made to recover anything from this shaft, in our view it is the previously undisclosed *shorter* piece of wood – if that is indeed what it is – that is *possibly* an original artefact, and should therefore be carbon-dated; quite why Bauval concentrates on the longer piece is a mystery to us. As for the hook, even if it is an original artefact, it will be only a copy of the one we already have.

But perhaps more important still, Gantenbrink was unable to manoeuvre Upuaut around the kink, not least for fear of its becoming jammed. This leaves us with the still-unanswered question: *What lies at the end of this northern shaft?*

Gantenbrink's 'door'

Let us now review the video footage from the southern shaft. Over a much longer distance than that travelled up the northern shaft, Upuaut's progress repeatedly threatens to be interrupted by irregularities in the walls and floor at 39, 59, 98, 154 and 177 feet along. These consist of 'steps' of between half and one and a half inches at the joints between either the floor or wall blocks, probably caused by subsidence. It is clear that the shafts have been created by placing blocks hollowed out into an inverted 'U' shape on to predominantly flat floor blocks, although in at least one place the floor block itself is clearly relieved to a depth of about an inch; furthermore the joints in the floor and 'wall' blocks do not normally coincide. It is also interesting to note the presence of red ochre 'cutting and alignment' marks on the wall blocks where they jut out.

Having managed to negotiate these obstacles, Upuaut carries on until at just over 200 feet all four sides of the shaft smooth out noticeably with the use of the same higher-quality Turah limestone as is used on the external casing – and there ahead, about 213 feet along, its camera picks out what has ever since been referred to as a 'door'. This description derives from the fact that the limestone slab that blocks the shaft has what appear to be two copper handles attached, each about 2 inches long but only a quarter of an inch wide; in fact the left-hand one is much shorter, but what appears to be its broken-off portion lies on the floor of the shaft a few feet back down. Meanwhile, Upuaut's red laser spot disappears under a slight gap all along the bottom edge of the 'door', and especially a triangulated section broken off at the bottom right-hand corner. Since it is still some 50 feet from the outside of the edifice, there is plenty of room for a secret chamber to lie behind it, although Gantenbrink himself has always taken great pains to emphasise that he makes no predictions about such issues.

What Next?

The discovery of 'Gantenbrink's door' was trumpeted in the worldwide press, and the situation was not assisted by, for example, Professor Edwards's light-hearted remark at the time – that it might conceal a statue of Khufu gazing in the direction of Orion – being widely misrepresented as the considered opinion of an expert. To this day dedicated 'Egypt followers' in the West remain up in arms at the authorities' apparent indifference to and failure to 'open' it, and there are a number of political and conspiracy aspects to this delay which will be considered later. However, without wishing to pour too much cold water on the fires, we should at this point remember two factors that put the discovery into better perspective. First, the shaft and 'door' itself measure only about 8 inches square; is it therefore likely that a chamber of any size would lie behind it? And, second, close scrutiny of the magnified shots of the edges of the 'door' in the video – with prodigious use of the PAUSE button – in our view reveals that the right-hand wall, ceiling and floor all carry on back behind the edges of the block as before. However, while the lower half of the left-hand edge is so closely jointed that no crack at all is discernible, the upper half is the only section where it is impossible to tell whether the wall carries on or not. It is therefore *possible* that it represents a sliding 'portcullis', which emerged from a recess in the left-hand wall (and not from above as many have suggested). But in our view it is just as likely that it is a small individual block, which may even have been cemented in place.

However, such an analysis still leaves us with an enigma: if the 'door' is only an immovable block of limestone, why are it and the surrounding blocks made of Turah limestone, and why use a small sealing block rather than the face of the next large core block to finish off the shaft if it was just abandoned? Perhaps even more perplexing, what do the 'handles' represent? There is one suggestion that springs to mind, as trite as it might seem in relation to such an awe-inspiring edifice: that is that the 'handles' in particular are nothing more than a practical joke, played not by the designers and architects but more likely by one of the workmen responsible for finishing the shaft. If he were of a humorous nature, one can imagine his relishing the thought of the false excitement they would cause when discovered millennia later. Far-fetched? Perhaps, perhaps not.

So what should be done next? Attempting to move the 'door' itself seems fruitless: if it is a portcullis, sliding it sideways would almost certainly fail for lack of capability to exert the appropriate force by remote control; and if not, pushing it further back up the shaft, even if possible, would surely risk damage behind it. Gantenbrink himself, anxious only to ensure that his discovery is properly scientifically investigated, has sensibly suggested a number of largely noninvasive options: these include passing a current across the 'handles' to see if there is a connection at what, if there was, he would consider to be the 'front' side (although the back as we look at it); the use of either ultrasonics or the release of gas to determine whether a chamber exists, and if so its volume; and the insertion of a fibre-optic camera into the crack at the bottom – or if this were unsuccessful through a small-bore drill hole. Of course it is anyone's guess as to how deep such a hole would have to be to 'strike it rich', if indeed it ever did; and the authorities would look pretty foolish if they trumpeted such an 'unveiling' operation without first carrying it out to ensure there was something to unveil. Yet, as we will see later, this is actually what appears to be happening in the run-up to the millennium.

Perhaps the most constructive suggestion in our view, and one that arguably requires considerably less technology, is to explore the rest of the *northern* shaft first. Indeed this suggestion has been put to Hawass by Gantenbrink, but it is not easy to establish the former's priorities. We have seen that Gantenbrink was afraid that Upuaut would become stuck if he tried to manoeuvre it around the kink; this was quite understandable, since he was short on time and had some $250,000 of his own and his sponsors' money tied up in the robot. But surely, with proper backing and planning, it is not beyond our ability to insert a small fibre-optic camera into a flexible but strong rod which could be juggled around the kink – after all, it is only some 40 feet up the shaft. Or if for some reason this approach failed, to remove the various rods and debris from the shaft and then use perhaps a slightly shorter version of Upuaut to manoeuvre around it. By establishing how far this shaft goes, in what direction, and what lies at the end of it, we may find considerable clues as to the nature of 'Gantenbrink's door' – and whether or not it is worth investigating further.

As we have already indicated, this is not the last we will hear of the 'door' and the shafts, but the political and more recent developments must wait for Part III. And we will now turn our attention to Bauval's star-alignment theories . . .

CHAPTER

NINE

TWINKLE, LITTLE STAR

In 1994, Robert Bauval and Adrian Gilbert published *The Orion Mystery*, the first of a number of popular bestsellers dealing with Giza. The theories underlying this work were primarily Bauval's handiwork,[389] and he used computer simulation to suggest that the 'air' shafts of the Great Pyramid aligned with four major stars with religious significance *c.* 2500 BC, and – more controversially – that the three Giza Pyramids were *laid out* to correlate with the belt stars of the constellation of Orion *c.* 10,500 BC. Along with the theories surrounding the redating of the Sphinx and the discovery of 'Gantenbrink's door' – both of which Bauval has been keen to associate himself with – these have become probably the most widely publicised 'pyramid revelations' of the 1990s. So let us now examine how well they stand up to close scrutiny . . .

Shaft Alignments

Early pioneers
Taking the supposed alignments of the shafts in the Great Pyramid first, we should be quite clear that Bauval was not the first person to postulate such a function. In broad terms we have already seen that most Egyptologists down the ages who have not found the 'ventilation' theory convincing have suggested that the shafts may have a ritual function related to the passing of the king into the 'realms of the heavens', and this theory is still widely supported today.

However, as Bauval properly pointed out in *The Orion Mystery*, the first researchers to suggest that specific astronomical alignments existed had done so back in 1964. The Egyptologist Alexander Badawy first postulated the idea, and asked an astronomy professor, Virginia Trimble, to confirm his hypothesis.[390] Concentrating on the King's Chamber alone, they first pointed out that the angle of the northern shaft is approximately 31 degrees, while the latitude at Giza is approximately 30 degrees. Using the same logic that we used in Chapter 3 when discussing the siting of polar stars up the Descending Passage of the Great Pyramid, this means that in principle it is quite safe to argue that this shaft was built to point to a circumpolar star – which, due to the effects of precession, was probably Thuban (alpha Draconis) at the time the pyramid was erected. This contention is strengthened by the fact that the Ancient Egyptians were highly conscious of these stars, which they referred to as the 'indestructible ones' or the 'imperishables' on the basis that they were always visible to them.

Meanwhile, they also looked at where the southern King's Chamber shaft pointed. In order to understand their analysis, it is first important to appreciate that star coordinates are measured in angles of declination from the celestial equator, which at Giza, with its latitude of approximately 30 degrees, is 60 (90 minus 30) degrees above the southern horizon (see Figure 28). Badawy postulated that it might point to the belt stars of the Orion constellation, one of the few constellations that all scholars accept were known by the Ancient Egyptians – and this had important significance as the celestial representation of their god Osiris. Indeed, the *Pyramid Texts* found in the Fifth and Sixth Dynasty pyramids of Unas and Pepi II at Saqqara suggest that the king ascended into the 'southern skies' in the region of the constellation of *sah(u)*, which undoubtedly represents Orion. However, he needed Trimble to establish the true position of the belt stars in the epoch when the pyramid was built – which our earlier chronology dates between 2551 and 2528 BC – after taking into account the effects of precession which have caused them to rise higher in the sky on the meridian, the celestial north–south line, since that time.

Remembering that it is possible, based on other chronologies and carbon-dating evidence, that the dates we have quoted may be several hundred years too recent, we can select Trimble's main figures as follows:[391] Between 2800 and 2500 BC, she found that, at their culminations (or highest points) on the meridian, Al Nitak (zeta Orionis) moved from −16° 33′ to −15°

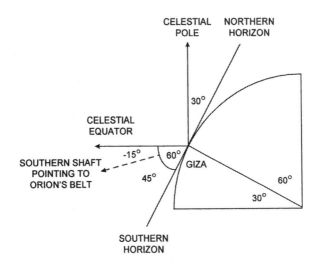

FIGURE 28: THE DECLINATION OF ORION AND THE
DIRECTION OF THE SOUTHERN SHAFT

04', Al Nilam (epsilon Orionis) moved from −16° 17' to −14°
46', and Mintaka (delta Orionis) moved from −15° 49' to
−14° 17'. With its steeper angle of approximately 45 degrees,
in broad terms it seemed clear that the southern shaft did effectively point at these stars, whose declination was of the order
of the requisite −15° in the appropriate epoch (see Figure 28).

But was this *deliberate*? After all, it may be pure chance, or
it may be that, of the multitude of bright stars in the sky at this
declination, any number of others could have passed over the
shaft during a 24-hour rotation of the sky. Trimble at least was
aware of this latter possibility, but when she examined the
charts she found that no other stars of comparable magnitude
had declinations between −16 and −13 degrees during this
period. Combined with the circumpolar direction of the
northern shaft, this evidence looks persuasive (this may even
provide a rationale for why the King's Chamber was offset from
the centre line). Mark Lehner certainly seems convinced,[392] as
does Paul Jordan, who also adds a few extra thoughts:[393]

Since Orion, as Osiris, is a known constellation of the Ancient Egyptians and Osiris was the god of the underworld and of resurrection, it was informed speculation to conjecture that the southern shaft of the King's Chamber played some part in the beliefs of Khufu's time about the fate of the dead king in the afterlife. (Orion's annual reappearance in the night sky, after seventy days of invisibility, at about the time of the summer solstice, may have contributed to the resurrection myth of Osiris, along with the more or less simultaneous inundation of the Nile.)

It is also interesting that according to most traditions, the process of cleansing, embalming and mummifying the pharaoh's body lasted 70 days before he could be buried.

Bauval's extensions

Bauval wondered why no one had ever extended this analysis to the Queen's Chamber shafts and, convinced that the more recent explorations indicated they had not been abandoned, he set about establishing what stars they may have pointed to in the pyramid-building epoch. Taking the southern shaft first, he initially used its angle of approximately 39 degrees provided by Petrie to establish that, according to his precessional calculations, it would have pointed to Sirius – which lies just beneath Orion and represents the Egyptian goddess Isis, Osiris's consort.[394]

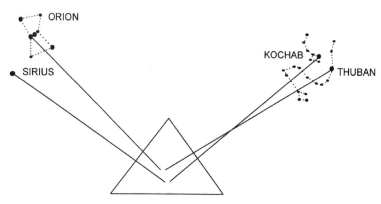

FIGURE 29: BAUVAL'S SHAFT ALIGNMENTS[395]

This suggestion has gained considerable support, and not just in alternative circles. For example, the Griffith Observatory director, Ed Krupp, whose relatively orthodox views we encountered previously, remarks,[396] 'Bauval's suggestion that we have at least a Sirius alignment from the Queen's Chamber is reasonable.'

However, Bauval seems to be on less stable ground when he turns to the northern shaft. Having settled on a date of 2450 BC for the alignments of the other three shafts (we will examine the reasoning behind this shortly), and using the same approximate figure for its slope of 39 degrees, he concludes that it too lined up with a star – this time Kochab (beta Ursa Minor), one of the four stars forming the head of the Ursa Minor Constellation. He supports this by suggesting that this was known as the 'celestial adze of Horus' or the 'adze of Upuaut' – the adze being used in conjunction with the *pesh-en-kef* tool in the 'opening of the mouth' ceremony. That he is perhaps a little desperate to prove a significant alignment for this last shaft is reinforced by his suggestion that the inexplicable kinks in both northern shafts are *deliberate* so that they too are shaped in the form of the 'sacred' adze.[397]

Objections

We have provided only a brief analysis of Bauval's arguments above for good reason. Much of his work on the shaft-alignment theory is taken up with an obsession for refining shaft angles in order that exact precessional dates can be calculated for the alignments, and thereby the Great Pyramid's construction be supposedly dated. At one point he is forced to agonise over whether a 140-year gap in his calculations for the two southern shafts is acceptable, given the more likely construction period of 20 years.[398] Rudolf Gantenbrink was performing his exploration of the shafts at exactly the time *The Orion Mystery* was being written, and preliminary figures for the angles of the shafts provided by him were used by Bauval to update his calculations, which had previously been based on Petrie's figures.[399] As a result he claimed that the correct date was between 2475 and 2400 BC, settling on an average of *c.* 2450 BC.[400]

Of course, even if these calculations were reliable, his claims that 'this was news' might be regarded as something of an overstatement given its proximity to the established date. However, the truth is that they are open to all sorts of objections.

- First, Bauval appears to have made no attempt to question the possibility that other stars may have occupied the same area of sky as his chosen targets for the two Queen's Chamber shafts at other times of the day or night. By contrast, this is exactly what made Trimble's original analysis so persuasive.
- Second, Gantenbrink revealed in an interview with us in January 1999 that there are considerable deviations in the angles from the horizontal measured by Upuaut along the entire explored lengths of the Queen's Chamber shafts; these are as much as 7 degrees[401] in the 40 or so feet of the northern shaft, and 0.2 of a degree in the 200 feet of the southern one. Unlike their King's Chamber counterparts, where such deviations can perhaps be ignored because the exact exit point is known, these cannot. Gantenbrink apparently discussed these issues with Bauval at the time, and was unimpressed by the 'unscientific' bias which their omission from *The Orion Mystery* indicated.
- Third, Bauval's entire analysis is predicated on the assumption that the shafts effectively travel due north–south in the vertical plane. However, his own analysis of the adze shape of the two northern shafts reveals that he is quite aware that this is not true. Meanwhile, we saw long ago that even Vyse realised that both King's Chamber shafts must run obliquely in the vertical plane in order to exit in the centre of the edifice. Gantenbrink has also revealed that the southern Queen's Chamber shaft does the same, and not even he or anyone else has the faintest idea what direction its northern counterpart might eventually take, except that it was last seen by Upuaut heading northwest after the kink! (Refer back to Figure 27.) All these factors render any attempt at unduly accurate or prescriptive analysis completely invalid.
- Fourth, the angles quoted by Bauval appear in any case to be questionable.[402] Gantenbrink admitted to us that he was not prepared to disclose the exact data to Bauval at the time because it had not yet been published through the appropriate scholarly channels. Apparently the conversation in relation to the relatively unexplored northern Queen's Chamber shaft went something like 'Is it less than 40 degrees?', then 'Is it more than 39 degrees?', etc., etc. This would

explain why, when compared with the exactness of his other figures, Bauval describes this angle in no more accurate terms than 'he [Gantenbrink] thought it might be closer to 39 degrees', which even in itself is relatively meaningless given the 7 degree variation we mentioned earlier. Meanwhile, for the southern Queen's Chamber shaft Bauval quotes Gantenbrink with a figure of 39 degrees 30′, which is close enough to the true figure confirmed to us of 39 degrees 36′ 28″[403]. For completeness, the angles of the King's Chamber shafts measured accurately by Gantenbrink were 45° 0′ 0″ exactly for the southern one and 32° 28′ 0″ for the northern one; but these refinements do not substantially affect Trimble's original analysis – she had used 44° 30′ and 31° respectively – since it was not so prescriptive anyway.

As far as the issue of using the alignments to attempt to date the pyramid is concerned, Krupp has this to say:[404]

> I certainly don't take seriously these precessional discrepancies of a few centuries in the agreement of star alignments with the shaft orientations. There are many reasonable sources of error here – date of construction, date of design, Egyptian astronomical calculation, construction accuracy, intended alignment targets, and so forth, to accommodate the 'errors' cited. I actually get the feeling that no one in this business, except Badawy (deceased) and Trimble, know the first thing about error analysis.

Furthermore, apart from anything else, precession produces very slow changes in the context of a few centuries, and is far too forgiving a mechanism for accurate dates to be derived.

But does the general principle of 'star alignments' still hold true? Gantenbrink himself has more recently attempted to perform a study of the Great Pyramid's design from an architect's perspective, reaching some intriguing conclusions.[405] He suggests that the pyramid was clearly designed just as we would today by defining 'primary' construction points, which can be retrospectively established because they will always have whole-number values (of course this analysis relies on determining the units of measure, and Gantenbrink uses the 'ell', which is 0.5236 of a metre and gives a base of 440 × 440 ells). However, he also looks for whole-number ratios and distances between points, and finds that the angles of the two King's Chamber shafts are based on complementary ratios of 11:7 and 7:11. He therefore concludes that their angles derive from these simple construction ratios, and that the additional fact that they both exit at the same height conclusively proves that they were not designed based on stellar alignments. Of course this line of argument tends to go against the replanning theory, which we previously supported at least in part, but it is nevertheless another highly useful contribution which may well strengthen the case against the shaft-alignment theory.[406]

Conclusion

What are we to conclude from all this? Again, we are forced to remain open-minded at present. Clearly, astral connections and symbolism did play a part in the Fourth Dynasty, and certainly during Khufu's reign, despite the fact that the solar cult was fast gaining ground (we will examine these symbolic issues in more detail shortly). Badawy and Trimble's original work, replete with error analysis and only broadly prescriptive, remains reasonably compelling when viewed in the light of the *Pyramid Texts*. And, despite our disagreement with Bauval's attempts to be overly prescriptive about the angles of the shafts and the precessional dates the alignments might imply, his basic addition of Sirius into the equation may be a useful insight – albeit that it tends to tie 'Gantenbrink's door' into Isis rather than Osiris, a symbolic issue which does not appear to have been properly explored.

However, the practical objections are numerous: in the first instance, the fact that *all* the shafts travel horizontally for at least the first 6 feet, that both the Queen's Chamber shafts were originally blanked off at their inner and outer ends, that we do not know whether or not the casing stones ever covered the exits of the two King's Chamber shafts, and that the original function of Hill's 'iron plate' remains obscure, makes it pretty clear that they were not intended for any sort of direct observation. Meanwhile, we are faced with the significant deviations in the two northern shafts, and we do not know what lies behind 'Gantenbrink's door' or where the northern Queen's Chamber shaft ends up. The problem with this is that it takes only *one* shaft to have no real stellar alignment for it to cast doubt on the entire theory – unless perhaps the Queen's-Chamber-abandonment theory is evoked. In summary, therefore, we feel that we must await further exploration of the Queen's Chamber shafts in the hope that this will shed new light on the enigma.

The Orion Correlation

Let us now turn our attention to what was definitely an entirely new and original piece of analysis on Bauval's part – his view that the three Giza Pyramids were *laid out* to reflect the three belt stars of Orion. Before we look at this basic premise, and any objections thereto, we should be aware that he and Gilbert postulated wider correlations with other stars in the constellations of Orion and Taurus – and most of the published attacks on the correlation theories have concentrated on these latter because in truth they are an easy target. However, in our view this tends to obscure the more significant basic premise, and the two should therefore be examined separately.

The basic premise

One night in 1983, while they were stargazing in the dunes of Saudi Arabia, an acquaintance pointed out to Bauval that one of the stars of Orion's belt is slightly offset and smaller. His immediate inspiration was that the three Giza Pyramids might have been built to represent them. He researched the matter, and read about the Ancient Egyptian religious principle of 'as above, so below' – meaning that the *duat* of heaven supposedly had a counterpart on Earth whose centre point was Rostau, which, as we have already seen, is quite reasonably linked with the Giza Plateau. He also established that the Milky Way was considered by the Ancient Egyptians to represent the River Nile, and realised that, if one stood at the north end of the Plateau and looked south, at the meridian there were the three belt stars of Orion represented by the three pyramids – the smallest offset slightly at the top – with the Milky Way or Nile to the left as it should be (see Figure 30).[407]

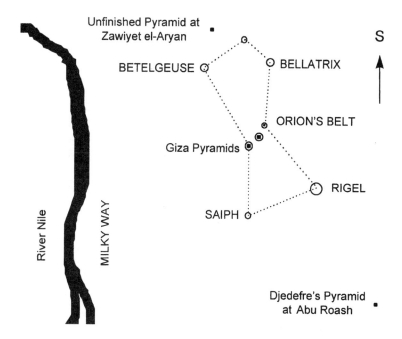

FIGURE 30: THE 'BROAD' ORION CORRELATION[408]

Back in the 1980s, Bauval gained some immediate support for this basic premise from unlikely quarters: for example, Professor Edwards wrote:[409]

> ... I am very much in agreement with your contention that the stars in Orion's belt were an important element in the orientation of the Great Pyramid. I think you have made out a very convincing case that the other two pyramids at Giza were also influenced by it.

And Dr Jaromir Malek of the Ashmolean Museum followed this up with:[410]

> ... I would be prepared to consider seriously the observation that the Giza pyramids were positioned or sited in a manner as to represent the three stars of Orion.

343

Correlation issues

Let us make our own examination of the physical correlation. Starting with the detailed mapping, in Plate 24 we have superimposed the outline of the three Giza Pyramids on to a magnified photograph of the belt stars, scaling it so that the centre points of the two larger pyramids line up on the centres of the two stars they are supposed to represent. We can immediately see that both sets of three objects are relatively equidistant, so the general scale of this localised mapping does not present a problem. We can also see that the offset of the Third Pyramid, although not completely accurate, is in the right direction and is no further off than one would expect given the fact that the Ancient Egyptians did not – at least we assume – have magnification telescopes. Furthermore, this offset is clearly visible with the naked eye.

However, there *is* a problem when we come to the relative sizes. Mintaka, the uppermost star, which is supposed to represent the smaller Third Pyramid, is not *noticeably* smaller than its two counterparts when viewed with the naked eye, nor even in the magnified photograph we have used in Plate 24.[411] Just to check this point we consulted the star catalogues and established the 'visual magnitude' or brightness of the three stars – which is the key issue here, since it correlates with observation with the naked eye and ignores the stars' distance from Earth.[412] Remembering that the *lower* the magnitude index the *brighter* the star, we can see from the data in Figure 31 that it is actually Al Nilam, the Second Pyramid equivalent, that is the brightest of the three, and is more or less the same amount brighter than Al Nitak, the Great Pyramid equivalent, as the latter is than

FIGURE 31: THE VISUAL MAGNITUDE OF THE BELT STARS
OF ORION[413]

Pyramid	Star	Visual Magnitude
Great Pyramid	Al Nitak or zeta Orionis	2.05
Second Pyramid	Al Nilam or epsilon Orionis	1.70
Third Pyramid	Mintaka or delta Orionis	2.23

Mintaka. These figures are not easy to compare in percentage terms because a jump of one unit of magnitude produces a change in brightness of 2.5 times. However, to the extent that these variations are visible, they do not reveal Mintaka as substantially smaller than the other two – and certainly not 80 per cent smaller, as the Third Pyramid's base area is compared with its two larger counterparts.

The only other direct criticism of the basic correlation theory is one regularly voiced by Krupp, as follows:[414]

> Once you accept the shaft alignment premise, however, the Orion's Belt ground plan falls to pieces. You have to turn Egypt upside down to make it work, and the shafts tell us the Fourth Dynasty Egyptians meant north when they said north and south when they said south.

However, we have already seen that Bauval's analysis is based upon looking *south* across the Plateau, and lining the pyramids up with Orion as it would be seen above the *southern* horizon. This also ensures the Nile is in the correct position, on the left, to correspond to the Milky Way. Since Orion clearly does occupy the southern and not the northern skies, and this was as much a symbolic mapping as a 'scientific' one, we find this criticism of the basic theory unconvincing.

Practical and contextual issues

It has been suggested that the reason the three pyramids are offset from each other on a diagonal is that the surveyors needed a clear view north to the pole stars in order to cardinally align their descending passages; but perhaps, once this had been achieved at the Great Pyramid with such accuracy, its cardinal lines could have been used without further stellar observation being necessary.

In *The Complete Pyramids*, Lehner suggests that the three pyramids at Giza were built with their southwest corners aligned to follow the edge of the Mokattam formation before it drops off into the valley. This diagonal runs approximately northeast to southwest, and he argues that such a siting kept them all at roughly the same height.[415] However, Bauval argues against this, questioning why Khufu should have sited his pyramid directly over a large mound of bedrock, which as we have already seen would have caused significant problems with surveying, and arguing that it would have been more logical to have built it on the flatter and higher ground to the west.[416] In support, Jean Kerisel supports the contention that the topographical features of the plateau are not sufficient to explain their layout.[417] And in a slight about-face, Lehner also observes that not only do the southwest corners all line up, but also that the west sides of the Great and Second Pyramids align with the fronts or east sides of the Second and Third Pyramids' mortuary temples respectively, while the south side of the Second Pyramid aligns with the south side of the Sphinx enclosure and bisects the Sphinx and Valley Temples. He therefore concedes that perhaps the layout was inspired by 'some religious or cosmic impulse beyond the purely practical', and although he briefly dismisses the *broader* correlation theory there is nothing intrinsically in this analysis that, in our view, is at odds with the *basic* correlation.

A possible contextual objection is that, as we have already noted, there was at least one interruption to the flow of building at Giza, and possibly two. Khufu's successor, Djedefre, built his pyramid north at Abu Roash, and Lehner suggests that the Unfinished Pyramid at Zawiyet el-Aryan may be the work of a king called Nebka, who may have reigned briefly between Khafre and Menkaure. Even if only the first of these is correct, why would Djedefre depart from a ground plan of such significance? Bauval suggests that his pyramid does in fact align to one of the other stars in the Orion constellation, as will be seen later, but because we believe this broader correlation is fundamentally flawed we do not accept this explanation. However, it has been suggested that Djedefre was somehow an outsider. For example, Selim Hassan argues that he was Khufu's son by a Libyan wife, and this caused succession problems.[418] Alford maintains he was a usurper who came to the throne by murdering the heir apparent and marrying his widow – and was then himself assassinated by Khafre after an eight-year reign.[419] Although neither of these assertions is backed up by references as to where the information comes from, it is fair to say that they could explain Djedefre's departure from the plan. As for Nebka and the Unfinished Pyramid, it is still unclear whether or not they really do interrupt the chronology of the plan.

However, undoubtedly the most damning practical objection is the evidence of the *replanning* of the Second and Third Pyramids. We have already seen in Chapter 2 that the Second Pyramid was either shifted a long way to the south or, more likely, trebled in size from a consistent northern edge, while the Third Pyramid was doubled in size around a consistent centre point. If representing the relative size and position of Orion's belt stars was so important from the *outset*, then surely such replanning would be unthinkable.

Symbolic issues
The foregoing discussion about Djedefre brings us on to another point: it is clear that he was the first Fourth Dynasty king to place significant emphasis on the emerging sun cult by adopting the title of 'son of Ra' via incorporating 're' into his name. This would perhaps serve as an additional explanation for his departure from the basic correlation plan were it not for the fact that Khafre and Menkaure, as is clear by the 're' element of their names, continued with the sun cult enthusiastically *but still returned to the supposed plan.*

From a broader perspective Bauval often accuses Egyptologists of historically ignoring stellar alignments because of their preoccupation with the emergence of the solar cult in the Fourth Dynasty, but in our view this is a gross oversimplification. In truth many Egyptologists accept now, and have in the past, that the two concepts may well have existed quite happily side by side. In fact, sun worship appears to have made a tentative start as far back as the Second Dynasty, as indicated by its second king's name of Ra-neb or Neb-re – albeit that the cult was not to emerge into true prominence until the Fourth Dynasty. Furthermore, Jordan observes:[420]

Since the time of the Meidum pyramid, the provision of temples on the east–west axis of the pyramids points to the solar component in beliefs about the royal dead, even though the pyramid interiors remained (mostly) on a north–south axis that probably goes back to the stellar orientation of the Dyn. III step pyramids. Where religion was concerned, the Egyptians were never absolutist and would not abandon a good old idea because a good new idea had come along: they were even able to sustain simultaneously several formally quite contradictory ideas, like many religious people. So a dead king might spend eternity sailing from horizon to horizon with Re in his sun boat at the same time as dwelling with the circumpolar stars, that never set with the passing nights and seasons.

Meanwhile, Bauval and Gilbert point out that the name of the pyramid at Abu Roash is 'Djedefre is a *sehetu* star', and suggest that *sehetu* or *sahu* is linked with Orion.[421] This tends to indicate that he respected the solar and stellar cults at the same time. Accordingly, Egyptologists in the main do not reject the possibility that the stellar cult continued to have influence after the solar cult emerged.

On the other hand, if the sun cult was *excessively* dominant in the Fourth Dynasty then perhaps we do have reason to question some of Bauval's theories. Hassan has this to say:[422]

> Coming to the question of the true pyramid form, we know that the early object of adoration in the solar temple of Heliopolis was a triangular, or pyramidal stone, called the *Ben-ben*, on which the Sun-god in the form of a phoenix, was wont to perch. It is this *Ben-ben* mounted on the top of a high pillar, which is the obelisk, a famous cult object for the Sun-worshippers. Therefore, we may see in the Pyramid nothing but a gigantic *Ben-ben*, and imagine that the king chose this form of tomb in the belief that, buried in the heart of the most sacred solar-symbol, his mortal body would be safe for all eternity.

Others have suggested that the pyramid shape is a representation of the rays of the sun, especially when they are emerging from clouds – although Gilbert has scoffed at this on the basis that there rarely are clouds at Giza. Whether or not the latter is true, *if* the 'true' pyramid form is symbolically the *ben-ben* then this may cast doubt on both the shaft alignment and the Orion correlation theories – although we would then be required to accept that the sun cult really took off some time before with Sneferu.

Moving on to another symbolic area, we should perhaps examine whether or not the linking of Orion with Osiris in the Fourth Dynasty is as much of a foregone conclusion as is normally suggested. If the link had not been established then, this would significantly weaken Bauval's arguments. Writing in the 1930s GA Wainright, the then chief inspector of the EAO, suggests that Osiris appears in the *Pyramid Texts* only at the *end* of the Fifth Dynasty, and that 'he did not reach the position of national god of the dead until the 12th Dynasty.' By the same token he argues that the widespread worship of Isis as his consort is also a relatively late development.[423] However, Jane Sellars, who studied Egyptology at the University of Chicago's Oriental Institute and has earned widespread respect since her *The Death of Gods in Ancient Egypt* was published in 1992, suggests that these two were always ranked alongside the earliest gods of pre- and Early Dynastic times, Horus and Seth. Accordingly, and being poorly qualified to judge such weighty issues, we feel compelled to reserve judgement.

Dating issues

Perhaps the most widely publicised aspect of the Orion correlation theory, and certainly the most controversial, is Bauval's suggestion that although the pyramids were *built c.* 2500 BC, their *layout* reflects Orion's belt *c.* 10,500 BC. In fact, this issue is given very little prominence in *The Orion Mystery*, occupying only a couple of pages, and appears to be almost a throwaway suggestion; nor is it mentioned in the British documentary hosted by Emma Freud, *The Great Pyramid: Gateway to the Stars*, which accompanied the book and was first aired in 1994. Certainly the discussion is so vague and nonspecific that the underlying rationale is not immediately clear.[424] We are provided with a brief description of how precession affects the height of the Orion constellation above the southern horizon as it crosses the meridian – specifically that Al Nitak starts the 26,000-year precessional cycle at its lowest declination of approximately 11 degrees above the horizon *c.* 10,500 BC, and halfway through, or 13,000 years later in *c.* 2500 AD, it is at its highest point of approximately 58 degrees above the horizon. We are then told swiftly:

> But what now emerges from the visual picture of the southern sky at the epoch *c.* 10,400 BC is this: The pattern of Orion's Belt seen on the 'west' of the Milky Way matches, with uncanny precision, the pattern and alignments of the three Giza pyramids!

And that's it . . . You have to examine the accompanying diagram to appreciate the nature of the 'match', and even then it takes a while before the rationale becomes clear. It is suggested that whereas in 2500 BC the Milky Way lies at an oblique angle to the meridian, in this earlier epoch it is more 'vertical' so that it better mirrors the course of the Nile. However, this mirroring is hardly a fleeting occurrence or a factor that can sensibly be used to pinpoint a specific date. So, although the issue is not elucidated, it becomes apparent that the key element is that the belt stars have to adopt the same 45-degree angle to the meridian at their culmination as the diagonal of the two larger pyramids does to the north–south axis on the ground. However, the only thing the accompanying small-scale diagram does is to show that the angle of the constellation as a whole does vary *between* the two ends of the precessional half-cycle.[425] We are given no hard data whatsoever about this angle in the different epochs.

We have now taken the trouble to check this data. The angles formed in different epochs by the line joining the centre points of the two main stars of Orion's belt, Al Nitak and Al Nilam, when the former is at its culmination on the meridian on the southern horizon, are shown in Figure 32. There are a number of highly interesting observations that can be made. First, the angle is only 45 degrees *c.* 12,000 BC, *not* 1500 years later as Bauval and Gilbert suggest – at this later time the angle is only 35 degrees, which is not even close. Second, the 45-degree angle does not return until *c.* 4500 AD, and because of the compound angles involved, the data does not move in step with the precessional cycle – which reaches its 'outer limits' *c.* 10,500 BC and 2500 AD. And, third, the rotational motion of Orion around the sky ensures that the required angle is regularly achieved at

FIGURE 32: THE ANGLE OF THE TWO LARGER STARS OF
ORION'S BELT ACROSS THE EPOCHS[426]

EPOCH c.	ANGLE (°)	EPOCH c.	ANGLE (°)	EPOCH c.	ANGLE (°)
14,500 BC	60	7500 BC	14	500 BC	20
13,500 BC	56	6500 BC	12	500	24
12,500 BC	51	5500 BC	11	1500	33
11,500 BC	43	4500 BC	11	2500	38
10,500 BC	35	3500 BC	12	3500	42
9500 BC	25	2500 BC	14	4500	46
8500 BC	19	1500 BC	17	5500	51

other times of the day when it is not on the meridian. We can therefore see that not only do Bauval and Gilbert pinpoint the wrong epoch for their own analysis, but the analysis itself is extremely unsound. After all, why should the angle *have* to form a match only on the southern horizon at the zenith? This is surely being unduly selective.

The conclusion drawn from the scant analysis in *The Orion Mystery* is that the pyramids were operating as a 'Great Star Clock of the Epochs', pointing to the 'first time' or *zep tepi*. Quite why they supposedly do this remains unclear. Initially one gets the impression it is just to demonstrate the Ancient Egyptians' knowledge of precession – although if they had been making observations for only a few hundred years, as is at one point suggested, then while the change in declination may have been obvious the change in *angle* of orientation at the zenith would have been so minute as to be undetectable. And in any case we have proved that the angle that is supposedly critical to the mapping of Orion on to the ground plan does not vary in step with precession anyway.

However, Atlantis and the Cayce readings then creep in briefly, and the stage is set for Bauval's follow-up work with Hancock, *Keeper of Genesis*. In this, the whole prehistoric layout and dating issue is given much more significance, and we will examine the additional conclusions drawn therein shortly.

351

Conclusion

A great deal of ground has been covered in discussing the basic Orion correlation theory. We have seen that the mapping of the two sets of three objects on to each other appears quite reasonable, as does the fact that it is based on looking *south* rather than north. We have also seen that Djedefre's departure from the supposed plan can perhaps be explained, while the possible symbolic objections about the pre-eminence of the sun cult in the Fourth Dynasty, and of Osiris's late rise to prominence, are not sufficiently certain as to undermine the basic theory.

However, we have also seen that there remain two objections that are far less easily dismissed. First, to the naked eye the belt star Mintaka is not significantly smaller than its two counterparts, and certainly not enough to account for the significant reduction in size of the Third Pyramid. Second, the virtually conclusive evidence regarding the large-scale replanning of both the Second and Third Pyramids seems to us to put the final nail in the coffin. As for the suggestion that the plan was devised *c.* 10,500 BC, this is arguably the weakest element of the entire theory. And without it we are forced to question whether the supposed 'Orion correlation' ever really deserved the significant publicity and attention it has been accorded.

The Broader Correlations

Let us now turn our attention to the 'broader correlation' theory, which originally stemmed from Bauval's belief that *all* the Fourth Dynasty pyramids must be accounted for if the theory was to 'hold water.'[427] This he explains partly on the basis that, while these pyramids used architectural elements to assist the pharaoh on his journey to the afterlife, their poorer quality successors used the copious *Pyramid Texts* inscribed on their chamber walls to achieve the same result – a new approach that might be summed up as 'to write is as good as to do'. The broader theory is split into two parts.

First, staying with the constellation of Orion, Bauval suggests that Djedefre's pyramid at Abu Roash corresponds with the 'bottom left' star, Saiph, and the Unfinished Pyramid at Zawiyet el-Aryan with the 'top right' star, Bellatrix. If you refer back to Figure 30 you can see that, on the properly scaled map with the belt stars carefully lined up with the three Giza Pyramids, this assertion is a gross distortion. However, the sleight of hand does not end here. Although most commentators have drawn the equivalent map, they fail to point out that it is not the same as Bauval's for a very good reason. He has departed from his *south*-oriented approach, and presents a schematic of Orion at a far shallower angle by switching to how it looks on the *eastern* horizon at its heliacal rising just before the sun comes up. This point is not made clear by Bauval, at least not in such a way that the inconsistency is highlighted, but it is clear that he cannot have it both ways. The mapping works either on the southern horizon, as he has suggested for the Giza Pyramids, or on the eastern horizon – but to argue that it does both for different purposes is having one's cake and eating it. Even if such a trick could be justified, which it cannot, it is still clear that the scale he has used remains hopelessly distorted.[428] Whatever angle he slants Orion at, on a properly scaled map in which the Giza alignments are strictly adhered to, the outlying stars are too far out to match up.

Turning to the second element of the broader theory, Bauval attempts to find a match for the remaining Fourth Dynasty pyramids, those of Sneferu at Dashur. Seemingly unaware that there is good cause to believe that Sneferu also built the pyramid at Meidum, but at the same time conscious of the fact that even he cannot distort the scale of his maps sufficiently to map these into the Orion constellation, Bauval looks elsewhere. The Hyades, the 'head' element of the Taurus constellation, appear to fit the bill, partly because of references in the work of Jane Sellars, which link them to Seth, and partly because they are in roughly the right place. Accordingly, Bauval maps the Bent and Red Pyramids on to Ain (epsilon Tauri) and Aldebaran (alpha Tauri) respectively. However, this time his scaling is even more outrageously distorted – so much so that we have not provided a reproduction, since a true-scale map would not even allow the Giza Pyramids to be separately identifiable.[429]

Much has been made by commentators who oppose the Orion correlation theory of the number of stars for which no equivalent pyramid exists. For this, it has to be said that Bauval and Gilbert's protestations that these were either never built or have not yet been discovered are pretty weak – especially since the uncorrelated stars Rigel and Betelgeuse are by some margin the brightest in the constellation (with visual magnitudes of 0.12 and 0.5 respectively). Nevertheless, we are amazed that the major assaults on the theory have concentrated on this clearly weak aspect, without any real attempt to analyse and constructively criticise the *basic* hypothesis. For example, the supposed 'official rebuttal' of the theory, written by Robert Chadwick, a history professor from Quebec, and published in *KMT* in 1996, does exactly this.[430] If this is the best rebuttal against the general theory that has yet been produced, it is perhaps little wonder that it has managed such a long but hardly deserved shelf life.

In an article in *Quest for Knowledge* magazine in 1998, Adrian Gilbert makes some attempts to defend the theory, but his arguments – in particular in relation to the omission of Rigel and Betelgeuse, and to the inaccurate scale mapping of the broader plan – are frankly unconvincing.[431]

In the final analysis, it is interesting to note that Bauval himself has issued a 'positioning statement' on the broader theory:[432]

All this, and the positional discrepancy first pointed out by Dr. Jaromir Malek in 1994 of these two pyramids [at Abu Roash and Zawiyet el-Aryan] in relation to the Giza/Orion's belt datum compels me now to discard them as part of the overall star correlation plan instigated at Giza or assume, at best, the possibility that the 'unfinished' state of these pyramids reflects their 'inaccurate' astronomical positioning relative to Giza. As for the two Dashur pyramids, these are known with a reasonable degree of certainty to have belonged to the pharaoh Snefru, father of Cheops. I maintain my view that these two pyramids strongly appear to represent the two principal stars of the Taurus-Hyades constellation, although not necessarily tied to the datum or node of Giza.

This may not be the full retraction that is arguably merited, but is a start. Meanwhile, perhaps the most telling comment on the broader theory is that, given their clear level of advancement, if the Ancient Egyptians had *wanted* to match the sky with multiple edifices on the ground they would have done a much better job!

Keeper of Genesis

Following the huge success of *The Orion Mystery*, Bauval teamed up with the already well-established author Graham Hancock to write a new bestseller, *Keeper of Genesis*, and Gilbert became somewhat excluded from the party. Published in 1996, for the most part this was only an update of its predecessor, although it had a fundamentally different and conspiratorial tone – an issue to which we will return in Part III. However, it did bring in a few new issues and placed greater emphasis on some of the old ones.

The most obvious addition was a tie-up with John Anthony West, since Bauval and Hancock clearly felt that his increasingly celebrated attempts to redate the Sphinx tied in nicely with their own search for the 'first time.' In effect this was a mutual-admiration society, since West's own theory supposedly benefited from reciprocal support – indeed it can be no coincidence that from the early 1990s he started to converge on a 10,500 BC date for the age of the Sphinx, especially since the Cayce readings suggested a similar epoch. To cement their emerging relationship, the 'three musketeers' appeared in front of the cameras for the *Mystery of the Sphinx* documentary, produced by Boris Said and hosted by Charlton Heston, which first aired as an NBC TV special in 1993. As a result, whereas in *The Orion Mystery* absolutely no mention of the Sphinx is made, the whole of the first two chapters of *Keeper of Genesis* are devoted to the monument, and much of them to West's theories.

Ignoring the political and conspiratorial elements, plus the in-depth study of Egyptian texts used as supporting evidence, the 'new improved' theory runs as follows:

• First, greater emphasis is placed on the way in which the 'spot-on' alignments of the Great Pyramid's 'star shafts', acting as 'precise time-markers', date the edifice to *c.* 2500 BC.[433] However, we have already seen that, in fact, precession is very forgiving where dating is concerned, producing relatively slow changes, and that the shafts themselves are full of deviations, so that at the very least *less* emphasis should be placed on such rigid dating interpretations, not more.

- Second, it is interesting to note that the 'broader correlation' theory is entirely omitted from this revised work.

- Third, the importance of the angles of Orion's belt stars in justifying the 10,500 BC 'layout' is properly emphasised this time, although needless to say the hard data is still not forthcoming.[434] However, the suggestion that 'it is not until 10,500 BC however . . . that the perfect correlation is finally achieved with the Nile mirroring the Milky Way and with the three pyramids and the belt stars identically disposed in relation to the meridian' is somewhat at odds with the hard data we produced previously. Meanwhile, it is made clearer that the reason this date is important is that it *also* marks the beginning of the precessional half-cycle of Orion at its lowest culmination on the meridian, which is equated with the 'first time' of Osiris. Since this latter observation is astronomically correct, one is tempted to conclude that it has been used to 'fudge' the clearly incorrect basic Orion 'correlation' date.

- Fourth, it is asserted that the Sphinx is an 'equinoctial marker' because it faces due east to the rising of the sun at the equinoxes – although it is made clear that this is true across all epochs. In conjunction with the supposed geological evidence, and backed up by textual references to the Sphinx as 'Horus in the Horizon', it is suggested that the Sphinx must be associated with the ruling constellation at the time of its construction – that is, Leo, whose precessional age supposedly lasted from *c.* 10,960 to 8800 BC.[435] However, we have seen in a previous chapter that there are severe doubts that the constellation of Leo was recognised by the Ancient Egyptians prior to Ptolemaic times.

- Fifth, it is suggested that the astronomical model on the ground works like the 'cog-wheels of a clock' to date the 'first time' and the beginning of Egyptian civilisation, by using the combined 'thought-tools' of the Sphinx's gaze at the eastern horizon marking the general precessional age of Leo, while the fine tuning is achieved by the sliding scale of Orion's belt angle moving progressively antic-lockwise as it culminates lower and lower on the meridian until the requisite 45-degree angle is achieved, supposedly, in 10,500 BC.[436] However, even if this theory were correct, we have seen that the angle is achieved much earlier at *c.* 12,500 BC, *which takes us out of Leo and into the previous precessional age of Virgo anyway*. And furthermore, as Krupp has consistently pointed out, once Leo is brought into play simultaneously with Orion, the Milky Way lies *between* them in the sky in *any* epoch, clearly putting the Sphinx on the wrong side of the Nile.

• Sixth, three further attempts to justify the 10,500 BC date are made, as follows. It is claimed that at this time Al Nitak's setting point is 27 degrees west of south, the same angle as that from the centre of the Second Pyramid to the edge of the Third Pyramid's easternmost satellite. Further, that at its lowest point in the precessional cycle Sirius was exactly on the horizon only at this latitude (because of the additional 'proper motion' caused by its proximity to the Earth), although it is admitted that this only indicates a date of somewhere between 11,500 and 10,500 BC. Lastly, that the angles of the Great and Second Pyramids' causeways of 14 degrees north and south of east respectively correlate with the 'cross-quarter' points of the rising sun between the equinoxes and the solstices – and that, although this is true at all epochs, only at the halfway point between the winter solstice and the vernal equinox in 10,500 BC does Leo have just its head and shoulders above the horizon, simulating how it appears when 'buried' in its enclosure.[437] These additional pieces of 'corroboration' are frankly so selective and contrived that we will not be considering them further.

So none of these additions strengthens the previous theories, and in some ways they arguably weaken them. Finally, Bauval and Hancock turn their attention to the issue from which the title of the book is derived: they postulate that the 'star clock' is in fact a 'treasure map', completed by mapping the position of the sun beneath the horizon when Leo is just fully risen in the pre-dawn of the vernal equinox. Translated on to the ground this supposedly marks a spot about 100 feet beneath the Sphinx's hind paws, wherein lies something of 'momentous importance' – even 'genesis' itself; and, although the Hall of Records is not mentioned by name, the implication seems clear.[438] However, in our view, irrespective of all the foregoing criticisms, not only does attaching such importance to a some-what arbitrary position of the constellation of Leo seem unwarranted, but furthermore, the astronomical arguments at this point become extremely confused – Bauval and Hancock seem to switch seamlessly from discussing the 'vernal point' of the sun's rising on the horizon for which the constellation of Leo forms a backdrop, to a 'vernal point' underneath the horizon based on the arbitrary position of the constellation just above it.

It is perhaps indicative of the massive attention attracted by the various conspiracy theories in *Keeper of Genesis* that this latter – the one really new piece of analysis – has been virtually overlooked ever since. At least it does attempt to provide a reasonable answer as to what this 'star clock' is for, which was conspicuously lacking in the previous work. As to the 8,000-year gap between the supposed date of the layout of the pyramids and their construction, Bauval and Hancock suggest that either the ground plan was physically established in the earlier epoch – 'perhaps in the form of low platforms' – or that the knowledge required to establish it was preserved and handed down by the 'followers of Horus', who had probably inhabited the Giza area throughout the intervening period.[439] However, given that the logic underpinning this new piece of analysis is of a consistently poor quality, the lack of publicity it has attracted is probably fortunate.

Judgement Day

We have seen that in reality *The Orion Mystery*, apart from highlighting the previously sound research of Badawy and Trimble and perhaps bringing ancient Egyptian texts into more public focus, adds precious little to our understanding of the Giza Plateau. It sold well arguably because it was the first published work to feed off the discovery of 'Gantenbrink's door', which it did mercilessly even though there is still no proven connection between the two sets of analysis – and in fact Gantenbrink's detailed mapping of the Queen's Chamber shafts arguably detracts from the unduly prescriptive nature of Bauval's 'star-alignment' theory. Meanwhile, his 'Orion correlation' theory, even in updated form, ultimately falls down in every aspect. *Keeper of Genesis*, in attempting to rehash and expand upon the same hypotheses, similarly adds little – but is in turn bolstered by West's proposed redating of the Sphinx, and a large helping of conspiracy and Atlantean theory. We do not enjoy criticising the work of fellow writers and researchers. However, we have devoted no little space to these theories in this chapter because they have gained an enormous following, and we do not believe the arguments against them have been properly established and presented before now.

In the final analysis, once again we must reiterate our view that the Ancient Egyptian astronomers probably *were* far more accomplished than was once believed, and that a select band of 'survivors' from a previously destroyed high civilisation in remote antiquity *may* indeed have educated them – either directly or by leaving some form of records. But we also believe that, unlike West, with whom we have some sympathy, the authors of these two works – despite presenting some occasionally useful insights – are guilty of selectively using the evidence to support their theories, rather than arriving at those theories as a result of an even-handed analysis of the evidence as they attempt to establish proof of such knowledge and civilisations. And that arguably, they damage the credibility of more scholarly searches for the truth in so doing.

Part III
POLITICS ON THE PLATEAU

TEN

FOOL'S GOLD

The Giza Plateau represents many things to many people: a place for theorists to let their imaginations run wild; a holiday destination for the tourist; a playground for the wealthy researcher; a place of pilgrimage for the 'new age' fraternity. But behind this apparently peaceful scene lies a battleground of politics, egos, public squabbling and alleged cover-ups. Nor are the battle lines always clearly drawn between the alternative and orthodox camps – of late the conflict has often taken place entirely within the former, leading to a most uncivil war between what one person described as 'EGOgyptologists'. But ego is perhaps only a part of the story: power, money and fame also have roles to play in this unfolding drama.

In this chapter we will examine some of the most destructive politics to invade the Plateau in the last decade, involving a few central characters. We will begin with John Anthony West's Sphinx Project of the early 1990s, before turning our attention to the multiple Schor Foundation Expeditions of the mid-to-late 1990s, and finally the ongoing saga of Gantenbrink's 'door'.

The Sphinx Project
We have already seen that John Anthony West's 'official' field trip in April 1991 was recorded by the film producer Boris Said. However, their collaboration was to end in tears, and, since they have both played an important part in the Plateau politics of the 1990s, it is instructive to appreciate how this split arose.

Early days
Although West and Said had known each other since childhood, they had pursued entirely different careers. Before he became a documentary-film producer, Said's competitive nature took him into the world of motor racing and the US Bobsled Team, where

he took part in three Olympics as the team's driver. West on the other hand became a novelist and dramatist. Moving from New York to Europe in 1957, he lived in Britain and pre-hippie Ibiza, writing short stories and plays. While researching for his book *The Case for Astrology* (co-authored with Jan Gerhard Toonder) in the late 1960s, West commenced a study of Eastern and Western philosophy, religion and mysticism – and, as we have already seen, was particularly taken by the work of the French scholar Rene Schwaller de Lubicz. The latter's interpretation of the sacred geometry and symbolism of Ancient Egypt differed from the orthodox Egyptological view in almost every aspect, and made a lasting impression on West, who even travelled to France to stay with Schwaller's stepdaughter, Lucie Lamy. Lucie herself was no stranger to her stepfather's work, having accompanied his research team to Luxor and written her own book, *Egyptian Mysteries: New Light on Ancient Knowledge*. His influence on West's work was nowhere better manifested than in *Serpent in the Sky*, and, as we have already seen, it was his observation regarding the apparent water-weathering of the Sphinx that prompted West to question the orthodox dating of the monument.

Raising funds
In order to place the investigation on a formal footing in advance of the 'official' research trip, West and Said became partners in a company they called 'The Sphinx Project'. They agreed that West would focus on the research while Said would film and document the expedition, and set about attracting funds. The bulk of the $175,000 raised came mainly from friends and contacts West had developed through his tours to Egypt.[440] Meanwhile the ARE, with an obvious interest in the age of the Sphinx and its relationship to the Cayce readings, agreed to invest $10,000 – on the basis that two of their members could travel with the expedition. The two chosen were senior members Joe Jahoda and Dr Joe Schor.

The ARE connection
As we have already seen, both of these men have been members of the ARE since their teens, starting in 1951 when they took

part in a study known as Project X, initiated by Hugh Lynn Cayce. They were part of a delegation of seven college students invited to the headquarters at Virginia Beach to study his father's readings and apply them to everyday life – and by the end of the three-week period the two young men had become so fascinated by the readings relating to Egypt, the Sphinx and the Hall of Records that they decided they would one day travel to Giza to locate it.[441] But a lot of water was to pass under the bridge before they had an opportunity to put their pledge into action.

Schor began a long professional career in the pharmaceutical industry after receiving his PhD in biochemistry at Florida State University (FSU) in 1957. Having joined Forest Laboratories in 1977, he researched 'sustained-release' technology and cardio-vascular medicines and established himself as the inventor and co-inventor of patents in these fields. He eventually became the company's Vice President of Scientific Affairs, with technical responsibility for research, development and governmental affairs.[442] Given his lifelong career in medicine, it is perhaps the case that Schor's interest in the Cayce readings is far broader than just the Hall of Records, and encompasses the medical diagnoses as well. Meanwhile, we have already seen in Chapter 6 that Jahoda did get a brief but somewhat abortive opportunity to explore the Sphinx in 1978 with the SRI's 'Sphinx Exploration Project', but the following year business commitments came to the forefront when he started a company called Astron Corporation. Originally, Astron was in the business of researching and developing esoteric technology for the US government, but it soon expanded into the telecommunications industry, producing a wide range of antennae for UHF satellite systems, direction-finding equipment and cellular phones.

Accordingly, when they joined West and Said's trip in 1991, albeit only as observers, Jahoda and Schor at last had an opportunity to go to Egypt together to pursue their boyhood dreams – some 40 years after Project X had sparked their curiosity.

West versus Hawass
Said's documentary of West, Schoch and Dobecki's work, *The Mystery of the Sphinx*, was first aired as an NBC TV special in

1993. Hosted by Charlton Heston, it attracted huge audiences and was even nominated for two awards. But the programme went far beyond the mere presentation of the geological and seismic work. Strong elements of Cayce's predictions and of the legendary continent of Atlantis were introduced, suggesting that Egypt's heritage perhaps owed its beginnings to some lost civilisation. Dobecki's tentative seismological finding of a 'man-made chamber' underneath the Sphinx's paws, which we reported briefly in Chapter 7, was presented as a fact that corroborated Cayce's prediction of an entrance to the Hall of Records at this spot.

The Egyptian authorities' reaction to this programme was both understandable and predictable – they went absolutely ballistic! Dr Zahi Hawass, the Director of the Giza Plateau, had already expressed his displeasure at the team's 'unscientific' methods. However, after the documentary had been aired he famously described its linking of Atlantis to the Giza monuments as 'American hallucinations' – as it effectively suggested that Egypt owed its ancient history, technology and impetus to the legacy of a lost civilisation as perceived by an American psychic. In Europe or America we might take these claims with a pinch of salt, but for the Egyptians it was akin to suggesting to the French that the British had built the Eiffel Tower, or to the Americans that the Russians had erected the Statue of Liberty.

A vitriolic slanging match between West and Hawass ensued, and West was effectively locked out of any further research at Giza. Under ongoing fire from West's supporters, in an interview conducted by *KMT* in 1997 Hawass explained that his exclusion was in no sense a personal decision, and that all permits for exploration on the Plateau had to be authorised by the 22 members of the Permanent Committee of the Supreme Council for Antiquities (or SCA, as the EAO had been renamed in 1994); and, further, that any research mission had to be properly backed by an academic or other recognised institution. When pressed as to why West had ever been allowed a permit in the first place without being connected to an appropriate body, Hawass replied that 'The Permanent Committee decided it was a mistake in West's case, and it has become much stricter about permissions'.[443] Meanwhile, at this same relatively late date, West was still expressing his displeasure at what he called 'smear campaigns from a variety of academic sources, led mainly by Seth himself, in his most recent incarnation as Zahi Hawass'.[444]

West versus Said

Meanwhile, all was not well within the the Sphinx Project itself, and West and Said's business relationship ended amid recriminations, with West alleging that Said had improperly used expedition funds for his own purposes.

In the meantime, Said wrote and produced a compilation video in 1997 called *Behind the Scenes: Legends of the Sphinx – A Search for the Hall of Records in Egypt*,[445] in which he discusses the continuing saga of the Sphinx before turning to a variety of other issues. It begins with his review of the making of *The Mystery of the Sphinx*, including clips therefrom, and he recounts that his film 'followed the adventures of John Anthony West', but makes no mention of their business partnership. He further suggests that he and West spent two years trying to get permission from the Egyptian authorities to excavate the 'chamber' beneath the paws of the Sphinx detected by Dobecki – although quite how this would have been achieved when their company was already in debt is not revealed. He also suggests that Robert Schoch submitted an independent application to the SCA for permission to continue his research at Giza, but the application was rejected.

Conclusion

West has become a slightly acerbic character and, although this is perhaps not surprising, he cannot consider himself blameless for his exclusion from the ongoing explorations on the Plateau. However, we do not question his integrity. He has done what he genuinely believes to be right, and perhaps his only failing is to be a little too arrogant in his beliefs, and too vitriolic (albeit often with terrific dry humour) and insensitive in his attacks on those who disagree with him on issues which, as we have seen, are by no means as black and white as he suggests. As for Said, he does not come out of this episode smelling of roses – and the odour increases as new episodes unfold, as we will shortly discover.

The Schor Foundation Expeditions

Following their somewhat muted role as observers of West's Sphinx Project expedition, Schor and Jahoda were even more determined to follow up with one of their own. At the end of 1994 Schor retired from Forest Laboratories, thus allowing himself the time to organise such a venture, and submitted a proposal to the SCA for the Schor Foundation to conduct acoustic and radar surveys on the Giza Plateau under the direction of his old college, the FSU. An annually renewable five-year licence was granted.

The Sphinx revisited

In April 1996 the joint Schor Foundation–FSU team arrived at Giza. Representing the FSU were three professors of geology – Dr Alan Zindler, Dr Leroy Odom and Dr James Tull – and a professor of archaeology, Dr Daniel Pullen. The Schor Foundation's team was headed by Schor himself, and included Jahoda – who was by now Technical Director of the Foundation – and both Dobecki and Said, who were brought in from West's old team. Said conducted the filming while Dobecki carried out GPR surveys in the Sphinx enclosure, and it was subsequently claimed that his tests in front of the monument reconfirmed the existence of the possibly man-made 'chamber' beneath the paws, which he had postulated during the 1991 Sphinx Project. This anomaly was described as measuring approximately 30 by 40 feet (9 by 12 metres) and lying approximately 16 feet (5 metres) below the paws. Meanwhile, at the other end of the enclosure between the rump and the western wall, Dobecki identified another anomaly some 15 feet (4.5 metres) below the surface, and it was suggested that this represented a tunnel emerging from the rump of the Sphinx and heading west in the direction of the Second Pyramid.

The sound man cometh

The Schor expedition returned to Egypt in November 1996 with the addition of Tom Danley, the acoustics engineer we introduced in Chapter 4. Through his acquaintance with Said his research into acoustic levitation had been featured in the documentary *The Mystery of the Sphinx* and the latter suggested he should accompany the team to Egypt. Accordingly he was hired to take sound and vibration measurements inside the Great Pyramid, his experiments involving the placement of accelerometers (vibration detectors) in the King's and all five Relieving Chambers.

We have already commented briefly on the findings of this research in Chapter 4, but of more importance now is the fact that, while placing his equipment in the Relieving Chambers, Danley noticed what he believed to be evidence of a clandestine tunnelling operation. Once again this 'evidence' provided even more explosive fuel for attacks by the 'conspiracy camp', although we will leave the close scrutiny of his claims for a later chapter.

Little else of note seems to have occurred on this expedition, and the team returned to the US with their data and film footage of Danley's experiments.

More shafts and tunnels

Returning in February 1997, the Schor Expedition team set about exploring the 'Water Shaft' under the Second Pyramid's causeway, which as we saw in Chapter 1 Selim Hassan had initially investigated in the 1930s. In his time the lowest or 'Third Level' had been completely under water, but the Schor team found it only partially flooded, and while attempting to obtain a level platform for their cameras they scraped away some debris on the floor and discovered the top of a sarcophagus lid. Again we will examine this discovery in far more detail in a later chapter, for – like Danley's 'clandestine tunnel' in the Great Pyramid – this shaft has become the focus of much speculation and rumour.

During this expedition the team also conducted GPR surveys between the Great Pyramid and the three small satellites on its east flank, revealing an anomaly that the team claimed represented a tunnel between the two. As a 'test case' the Schor Foundation team were allowed to investigate this anomaly during a more recent mission in September 1998, by drilling a hole and inserting a bore-scope camera. The importance of this case was emphasised at the ARE's annual convention in August 1998, when Hawass announced that if the radar showed 'evidence up there, for sure we'll look what's under the paw of the Sphinx'. In other words, if they discovered a man-made tunnel at this point, thereby proving the effectiveness of radar to Hawass's satisfaction, they would be granted permission to investigate the 'big one' – the anomaly under the Sphinx's paws. The stakes were set high, but unfortunately disappointment was the only result – the camera revealed nothing more than a natural cavity, and Hawass's scepticism was reinforced: 'They found absolutely nothing'.[446] This was a major setback for the Schor Foundation, although we will return to what appears to be an 'about turn' on this issue in the last chapter.

Men from Mars

At this point it is worth introducing two new figures who, despite being somewhat on the fringes of the current discussion, are well-known names who will reappear later on. JJ (Jim) Hurtak, a disciple of the 'mysteries school', accompanied the Schor team on the February 1997 mission, and had originally been a staunch supporter of the 'structures on Mars' hypothesis. This fuelled further conspiracy rumours of the 'NASA involvement' type, primarily because of his connection with Lambert Dolphin and Richard Hoagland – the two founder members of the 'Independent Mars Project', which they set up in 1983. Hoagland is a former NASA consultant, and in particular has been one of the prime campaigners for the 'Face on Mars' theory with which many readers will be familiar.

Briefly, two NASA space probes, Viking II in 1976 and Mars Global Surveyor in 1998, have photographed an area of Mars called Cydonia, and at one point in the scans an image of a giant face appears, which is claimed by some to be man-made rather than a natural feature. Of course if this were correct it would have the astounding implication that some form of intelligent civilisation existed on Mars millions of years ago, when it was possibly habitable. Hoagland goes further than this, and in the *The Mystery of the Sphinx* a sizeable piece of time is devoted to a film of a lecture given by him in which he draws parallels with the Great Sphinx. Most visually startling is his demonstration that if the two halves of the image are separated and mirrored to produce two symmetric images, one gives the clear impression of being a humanoid face while the other is unquestionably leonine. However, we do not accept the implication in the documentary that this is evidence that the Sphinx was carved by the survivors from Mars escaping a comet impact on that planet a mere 12,000 years ago, and furthermore the most recent photographs have tended to reinforce the view that the phenomenon is a natural geological feature only.

Conclusion

In truth, we have come to the conclusion that both Schor and Jahoda are men of integrity who have behaved admirably while their motives have come under repeated and heavy fire from jealous rival camps, as we will see shortly. We also believe they have had relatively unselfish motives in searching for a Hall of Records near the Sphinx. However, we cannot help but come to the conclusion that their search is either fruitless or has been misdirected.

We have already seen that confidence in GPR readings and seismic surveys is by no means absolute, especially on a Plateau honeycombed with natural underground cavities and fissures, and consisting of variable-quality limestone bedrock whose strata do not lie flat. There have, however, been suggestions that the quality of the equipment and interpretation of its data have improved substantially since the time when the SRI, for example, were performing ground-breaking work in the late 1970s. We thought we would check out an expert's opinion on this, and who better to ask than Lambert Dolphin, who had led those original expeditions and remains an expert on the subject?[447]

> Our 1974 radar work was very careful. We measured radar losses by every means we could think of – all the way down to 30 MHz and up to about 150 MHz. (Most commercial cart radars are about 150 MHz or higher – losses in rock climb steeply with increasing frequency.)
> I am not convinced anyone has meaningful radar data in Egypt.

In physics we used to say 'there is no such thing as 200 Db in a radar system' (twenty orders of magnitude between radar power and minimum detectable received signal wattage). In Ground-Penetrating Radar 100 Db is a practical total dynamic range. A few feet of even good grade Egyptian limestone easily eats up 100 Db.

A radar placed on the ground or within a tomb in Egypt will show a profusion of echoes. These however all prove to be 'clutter' – echoes from near-surface scattering which takes place right near the surface of the ground between transmitting and receiving antennas. Unless the radar operator knows what he is doing he will misread these clutter echoes as echoes from subsurface cavities which they are not. We proved this because we could not get radio waves more than a few feet ONE WAY from the surface into a shallow tomb.

Someone is going to have to let me see their actual records before I am prepared to change my mind about the uselessness of GPR in Egypt. Good radar results there would mean the rock properties have changed enormously in 20 years – not likely.

Furthermore, although we cannot be sure about the exact locations of the SRI's 1978 drillings when compared to Dobecki's 'chamber', Dolphin made it clear to us as we saw in Chapter 6 that one of the largest anomalies they detected was close to the Sphinx's right paw, and that when they drilled on it all they found was 'a small crack in the bedrock'. In the almost hysterical climate that has built up in the run-up to Cayce's 'prediction year' of 1998, and now the new millennium, any further drilling in this area without extremely persuasive new evidence would indeed only invite further unfounded speculation. It is therefore little wonder that the authorities should adopt this cautious approach – our only concern being that they seem to have been inconsistent and far less cautious in their approach to the exploration of 'Gantenbrink's door', as we will see later.

Trouble in the Alternative Camp
In addition to their failure to locate a Hall of Records, unfortunately the Schor Expeditions were also continually dogged by political in-fighting – becoming a target not only for rivals in

the alternative camp but also for disgruntled parties within their own ranks . . .

Schor versus West

Almost as soon as the Schor Foundation expeditions began they ran into problems with other alternative researchers. In December 1995, prior to the first expedition, West had written to Schor suggesting that they should work together, but the latter replied that a proposal had already been submitted to the SCA for approval, and that he wished to keep the team as defined therein.[448] West appears to have presumed that his and Schoch's exclusion represented a 'Schor takeover bid' of his earlier work at the Sphinx.[449] But it seems more likely that the antagonism between West and Hawass would have severely compromised the mission should West have been included – indeed we have already seen that the Egyptian authorities were at this time refusing both him and Schoch permission to conduct further field research.

West's close friends Robert Bauval and Graham Hancock then took up the cudgels on his behalf. In fact they had initially been invited to participate in the expedition by Schor, but in an admirable display of unity they seem to have taken exception to West's exclusion, as well as objecting to signing a nondisclosure agreement.[450] Predictably this led to repeated and very public accusations from West, Bauval and Hancock that Schor was operating in secret, which caused massive problems for his various expeditions – but we will leave further examination of these issues for the next chapter.

Schor versus Said

However, Schor was not immune from trouble *within* his own team as well, the main 'problem' being Said. Continuing his version of events in the *Behind the Scenes* video, Said recounts how, while on holiday in Egypt in 1995, he met with Zahi Hawass and discussed the making of another documentary. Back in New York he set about raising some capital – although he does not disclose from whom – and returned to Egypt in October of the same year with a small film crew. Said alleges that, during this new round of filming, Hawass asked him what it would take to create another network special: he replied that it would need something extraordinary, like the discovery of a new tomb or the opening of a secret tunnel. He further alleges that Hawass then suggested that the film crew should follow him to the Sphinx, where he was filmed inside the tunnel in the rump proclaiming the following:[451]

> Even Indiana Jones will never dream to be here. Can you believe it? We are now inside the Sphinx in this tunnel. This tunnel has never been opened before. No one really knows what's inside this tunnel. But we are going to open it for the first time.

This now infamous footage was incorporated into a short promotional video called *The Secret Chamber*, which Said claims he then took to Joe Schor – two months later signing a joint-venture agreement with the Schor Foundation that he would document the exploration to locate a secret chamber beneath the paws of the Sphinx.

This is not quite the version of events put forward by Schor and Jahoda, the latter informing us that it was they who first contacted Said – and the promotional video was actually filmed when he was already working under their auspices and funding. Meanwhile, referring to the nondisclosure rules to which all team members had signed up, Jahoda continues as follows: 'Boris started out breaking these rules by releasing to Bauval and others a copy of an experimental six-minute pilot film [*The Secret Chamber*] in which we were all playing around. Zahi pretended to be Indiana Jones and in dramatic fashion announced the finding of a tunnel . . . etc.'[452]

Although it was not publicly shown at the time, the release of this video into the hands of the rival camp significantly added to the Schor group's problems, since Hawass's statements were used to back up the accusations of secrecy and cover-up. Everyone – ourselves included – was unable to work out why Hawass should make such a statement on video when all his other pronouncements have been so 'anti-alternative'. Was there really a conspiracy going on? Perhaps Jahoda has at last provided us all with the answer – it was *fun and games*!

In a further twist, the FSU team members were incensed that

their names were being linked with Dobecki's seismic surveys and a 'secret chamber' at the Sphinx. Odom in particular was scathing in his attack on Hawass for failing to make the appropriate distinction.[453] At about the same time, Pullen was objecting to the use of their names in the credits for the *Secret Chamber* promo.[454]

Unsurprisingly the February 1997 expedition ended with Schor and Said parting company. Said went on to claim that Schor's licence had been revoked at the end of 1996, and that they had been operating in Egypt under *his* commercial film licence during 1997. But Jahoda informs us, 'Joe Schor nor myself have ever received a formal letter from anyone in Egypt cancelling our 5-year permit to perform radar analysis at the entire plateau . . . Zahi has stated on many occasions, including to Boris, that our permit was never, never cancelled'.[455]

Since they were allowed to return in September 1998, as we saw previously, this would appear to be the correct version of events. The situation rapidly deteriorated after Said revealed important information about the expeditions' discoveries on various radio talk shows,[456] and Schor's reaction was to file a lawsuit against him for alleged breach of confidentiality. The legal rights to the film footage shot by Said during the various expeditions became a complex bone of contention – as Schor had financed the expeditions he retained *legal* title thereto, while Said held the *marketing* rights. The case eventually went to court.

Whether or not the film footage of the Schor expeditions will be publicly aired remains to be seen. Danley feels particularly frustrated with this issue as he would like to present a technical paper on his tests in the Great Pyramid, but is unable to do so till one year has elapsed from the time the footage is first shown in public.[457]

Conclusion

In our view none of these machinations reflect well on those characters involved in attacking the Schor Expeditions. Once again they seem to have been motivated by poor research, mistrust, jealousy and ego, rather than any genuine desire to ensure that integrity was applied to the investigation of the precious monuments of the Plateau. The one area where any attacks may have some validity is that, several years on, the official reports presented by the Schor team to the Egyptian authorities remain unpublished.[458] However, this would appear to represent a holdup with the authorities themselves rather than any attempt by Schor to hide information, and it is an issue to which we will return in the next chapter.

Open That Door!

Let us now turn our attention to the ongoing saga of the 'opening of Gantenbrink's door'. For reasons we will cover in the next chapter, and circumstances that were in our view primarily beyond his control, Rudolf Gantenbrink became *persona non grata* with the Egyptian authorities when his discovery was sensationalised by the press in 1993. As a result he was denied the right to bring his work to its logical conclusion by further exploration, and the robot Upuaut languishes in the British Museum, to which it was donated. Apparently Dr Nur El-Din, the then chairman of the SCA, even declined Gantenbrink's offer to train an Egyptian team to use it themselves.[459] However, worldwide media and public pressure continued to be brought to bear on the authorities to discover what lay beyond the 'door' – and they needed at least to be *seen* to be doing something about finding someone to fund and construct a new robot.

El-Baz to the rescue

In November 1995 the California Chapter of the American Research Center in Egypt (ARCE) organised a conference entitled 'The Origins of the Egyptian State and the Preservation of Its Legacies', held at the UCLA. Among the speakers was Zahi Hawass, who under continuing public pressure announced that the Egyptian authorities would be taking up the issue of Gantenbrink's 'door' and attempting to see what lay beyond it sometime in May of 1996.[460] Four months after the conference, and only two months before the project was due to begin, the *Egyptian Gazette* of 31 March contained an article indicating that the project would now be delayed until September 1996, and conducted by an international team led by the Egyptian scientist Dr Farouk El-Baz – along with a 'Canadian contingent'.

Dr El-Baz is a founding director of the Department of Remote Sensing at Boston University, and has a long and distinguished career. In 1964 he gained a PhD in geology from the University of Missouri-Rolla and held teaching posts at Assiut University in Egypt and the University of Heidelberg in Germany. Between 1967 and 1972 he participated in the Apollo space programme as secretary of the Site Selection Committee for the lunar landings, as well as being chairman of the Astronaut Training Group and principal investigator for Visual Observations and Photography.

El-Baz is also respected for his pioneering work in the application of space photography and space-borne imaging radar to locate sources of ground water in arid and desert terrain; and his current research involves the broader application of remote sensing systems to the fields of geology, geography and archaeology. If Gantenbrink was not going to be allowed to do the job himself, the choice of El-Baz seemed an excellent one – he had all the necessary qualifications and connections to meet the SCA's now stringent requirements, while his Egyptian–American background could bridge the gap between any cultural differences and head off potential misunderstandings. What could possibly go wrong?

The Zuuring Affair

At the 'Quest for Knowledge' conference held at the Business Design Centre in London in May 1996, Robert Bauval and Graham Hancock revealed that a Canadian by the name of Peter Zuuring would be heading a new attempt to probe Gantenbrink's 'door'. They showed a photograph of him sitting at a table with Joe Schor and Joe Jahoda at the 1995 ARE annual convention – although they did not reveal whether the two were joint investors in the new project or merely having breakfast together. Then, in an update to *Keeper of Genesis*, published in the paperback edition in 1997, they revealed more information. Referring to the 'Canadian contingent' mentioned in the *Egyptian Gazette* article, they suggested the following:[461]

The Canadian element, 'Amtex', is headed by Peter Zuuring, a wealthy Dutch-Canadian businessman, who told us that he had shown the Egyptians how the door could be opened 'relatively inexpensively . . . We're working with Spar Aerospace to design a miniature arm with tools that could first tap the door, knock it and try to lever things a little bit to see if there's anything loose. But I think ultimately we'll go straight through'. In two conversations, Zuuring told us that he thought it unlikely that the project could start as early as September 1996: the following year, he said, 1997, was far more likely. The objective, which might take some time, was to raise the huge sum of US $10 million to promote a staged 'live opening' of the door on international television networks. 'I'm working with a private guy who is a personal friend of Hawass and we are absolutely going to drum this thing to death. Whatever the event we are going to stage, it will be televised live'.

The year 1996 came and went, and so did the early part of 1997, and yet no exploration took place and no official statement was released. An Internet rumour suggested that El-Baz and two assistants had penetrated beyond the 'door' with a fibre-optic camera lens, and that behind it lay a 7-by-5-foot (2-by-1.5-metre) chamber containing a statue of a black male holding a sacred *ankh* symbol. Although this rumour was intriguing, it did not originate from a reliable source, so we decided to investigate matters ourselves. We contacted El-Baz in September 1997 and asked if there had been, to the best of his knowledge, any further explorations of the Queen's Chamber southern shaft, and whether he had personally been involved – even in an advisory capacity. He replied that he had not, and that 'I was informed over one year ago that a Canadian team may propose a special imaging system to go beyond where the German team had explored, but I have not heard anything since'.[462] As is so often the case, the Internet rumour turned out to be just that – a rumour. But what in any case was the situation with Zuuring's proposed project?

In January 1998 we contacted the manager of public affairs at Spar Aerospace in Toronto, Lynne Vanin, who told us, 'I am not aware of any such project at Spar.' Further enquires two months later received the same reply: 'I'm sorry but I cannot find any information on this project.'[463] Adopting a different tack, although it proved impossible to track down Zuuring himself, we were able to piece together what had taken place thanks to a resident of Zuuring's home town of Belleville, Ontario – although this is one of the few occasions in which we have been asked to keep our source anonymous to protect their privacy.

According to our source, it appears that Amtex Software Incorporated produced CD-ROM games. In the spring of 1997 an environmental audit was carried out on the building housing its offices, and the auditor found them 'to have been rapidly vacated with much software and personal items strewn about'.[464] The reliability of our source appeared to be confirmed when we contacted the local Chamber of Commerce in July 1998, who informed us that Amtex had gone bankrupt and Zuuring had disappeared.[465] We also learnt from our source that Peter Zuuring's brother Hans had shed considerable light on the situation: 'Peter called him [Hans] and explained that he wanted to travel to Egypt to visit the pyramids to research information for an interactive CD-ROM game. He asked Hans to travel with him. Hans agreed and proceeded to arrange for time off work (a university professor) and replacement teaching staff as well as purchasing desert clothing, etc. A day or two before their departure, Peter called him and said he was out of money, and the trip was off.'[466]

So once again an enigma played up by the alternative camp is perhaps explained. It would seem that Peter Zuuring foxed Hawass and the Egyptian authorities into believing he wanted to carry out a serious scientific mission to open Gantenbrink's 'door', when in all likelihood he saw an opportunity to travel to the Giza Plateau and, with the blessings of the SCA, conduct research for an *interactive computer game*! Nevertheless, it is arguably quite reasonable to question the judgement of the authorities in allowing a man with little apparent track record to derail a project that, despite our reservations about what the 'door' might truly represent, is still of no little importance – especially when they had supposedly taken the trouble to secure the services of someone of the calibre of El-Baz.

Schor steps in . . . and out

Unsurprisingly the saga of Gantenbrink's 'door' continues. In January 1998 Zahi Hawass was interviewed on US radio's *Art Bell Show*, during which he stated that he hoped to get beyond the 'door' by May of 1998. As usual the month of May came and went without any announcements or apparent further developments, although Hawass did find the time to participate in a debate with Graham Hancock, John Anthony West, Ed Krupp and others – on a cruise in Alaska of all places. But in July 1998 we received information that indicated that Joe Schor was backing the construction of a sophisticated robot.[467] This of course would take considerable financing, and we were subsequently able to establish that on 9 February 1998 Schor sold 45,445 common shares in Forest Industries valued at \$2,729,879.[468] Here was perhaps an indication that things were moving forward – although of course the two issues could be unrelated. But who, we wondered, would be entrusted with the task of constructing such a sophisticated robot?

Then in September 1998 we received the following communication from the researcher and author Ralph Ellis:[469]

> I had a chat with Robert Bauval on the 21 July at his home in Buckinghamshire. He mentioned in passing that the new robot that would penetrate the Khufu pyramid shafts was designed and operated by NASA personnel. This investigation was planned to go ahead this winter/spring . . .

At the same time two British researchers, Peter Renton and Paul Ellson, told us that Hawass had apparently informed Schor that another group had put in a bid for the project.[470] And Jahoda subsequently confirmed their remarks: 'Yes, Joe looked into helping to get a robot to help Zahi get the project going, but since then Zahi has found another approach and apparently [it] will be put into operation at the end of this year [1999]'.[471]

Exactly who this group is remains a mystery at the time of writing, since nothing further has appeared publicly from Robert Bauval regarding NASA involvement, while Gantenbrink denies any knowledge of an expedition. Hawass has been reported as saying that the 'door' will be opened during the millennium celebrations at the Plateau as 'Egypt's gift to the world'.[472] In April 1999 we did contact him to ask about these plans, but he replied that this information will all be revealed in a book he is due to publish with Mark Lehner called *Giza and the Pyramids*,[473] so for the moment we can reveal nothing else. However, we have already expressed our view that the investigation would in reality have to occur long before this time, and that if nothing is found the authorities will be left with much egg on their faces if they continue to trumpet the 'live millennium opening'. Although it remains to be seen if this is merely another in a long line of false promises, a Trojan horse to attract tourism, or a commitment to a serious scientific project to resolve the enigma of Gantenbrink's 'door' – some seven years after it was first discovered – we at least are not holding our breath.

ELEVEN

FALSE PROPHETS?

Let us now turn our attention to the highly pervasive but often confusing role played by Robert Bauval and Graham Hancock in the 'plateau politics' of the 1990s.

Genesis of Conspiracy

We have already made numerous references to the work of these two mavericks in previous chapters, and indicated that their most successful book collaboration remains *Keeper of Genesis* (published in the US under the title *The Message of the Sphinx*). We have also seen that, apart from the dubious nature of the theories expounded therein, which appear to be largely a rehash of those in Bauval's earlier *Orion Mystery*, the whole tone of the later book is massively conspiratorial – effectively any consistency of theory and argument is relinquished to make way for the primary goal, which is to attack the Egyptian authorities and other researchers involved with them at every turn.

A casual perusal of the book leaves one confused about where they stand on a number of important issues, and indeed confusion and innuendo appear to be the two major weapons used in creating this 'bestseller'. To recap:

- In Chapter 1 we saw how Bauval's tie-up with Hancock produced a fundamentally different slant on the issue of the Dixon relics, in which Dr Edwards is made out to have been involved in a conspiracy to hide the carbon-datable 'cedar wood' artefact found in one of the Queen's Chamber shafts. However, the label on the cigar box in which they were kept, as inspected by Bauval himself, made it clear that this piece went missing long before the British Museum ever got involved. In his enthusiasm for the main conspiracy theme, he has allowed himself to arrive at a perverse interpretation of the available evidence, and in doing so has shown scant regard for the reputation of Edwards, who, by the time that Bauval's accusations were made, was old and frail.

- In Chapter 2 we saw that they accuse Egyptologists of 'intellectual chicanery' over their acceptance of the authenticity of the Khufu cartouches in the Relieving Chambers but dismissal of Hill's 'iron plate'. In essence they are themselves guilty of double standards in reversing the situation, especially since in reality they do not actually disagree with the orthodox dating of the pyramids. Again, this is based on a perverse interpretation of the evidence and arguments to bolster conspiracy theories, while leaving their own arguments shot full of logical inconsistencies. Their confusion about dating is exacerbated by their continued attacks on the Egyptian authorities for supposedly ignoring the evidence of carbon dating surveys. However, not only has Mark Lehner, for example, continued to perform such studies with great dedication, but in any case they appear to ignore the potential unreliability of such tests.

- In Chapter 4 we revealed that they cast severe doubt on the ability of the Ancient Egyptians to construct the pyramids with orthodox methods, which – although their analysis contains no great depth and ignores much of the evidence – has some validity. However, they offer no real alternative solution, and are in fact only using this to bolster the case for an earlier date for the Sphinx. Again, the logic is confused, and the primary aim seems to be to attack the orthodox community.

- We saw in Chapter 5 that they make a major issue out of Lehner's apparent U-turn away from the Cayce prophecies and towards the orthodox position. They admit that they revised the first draft after correspondence with Lehner, and undoubtedly toned down their attacks, and they are good enough to reproduce a lengthy explanation provided by Lehner in an appendix, but the reader is still left with a sense that something is afoot.

- We saw in Chapter 8 that they attack the authorities for their failure to retrieve the remaining piece of wood from the northern Queen's Chamber shaft revealed by Upuaut, when in fact this is almost certainly another clearing rod used by the Dixons. Bauval was still hammering this point as recently as the end of 1998 in a South African M-Net TV documentary made by *Carte Blanche*, in which he states, 'It is an unquestionable fact that it [the wood] is contemporary with the monument. We are absolutely sure about this.' We also saw that it is another much smaller piece of wood revealed by Upuaut that is the likely original artefact, one Bauval misses completely. And, once again, if they accept the orthodox dating, this is really not a major issue. They also attack the authorities for their failure to explore behind Gantenbrink's 'door', an attack that has some validity but in no way presents a balanced view of the possibility that there may be nothing behind it at all.

- In Chapter 10 we saw that they backed their colleague (some use the word 'mentor') John Anthony West in accusing Joe Schor of being in collusion with the authorities in covering up explorations at the Plateau – an important issue to which we will shortly return. We also saw that they were the first to go public with Zahi Hawass's infamous 'Indiana Jones' quip culled from Boris Said's *Secret Chamber* promo, and the first to suggest the involvement of Peter Zuuring and even NASA in the opening of Gantenbrink's 'door', all of which have a more rational explanation than conspiracy and cover-up.

All of this leaves a slightly unpleasant taste in the mouth. However, the fun was only just beginning . . .

The 'Real' Gantenbrink Story

We have hinted in previous chapters that there was more to the story of how Rudolf Gantenbrink's discovery of the 'door' in the southern Queen's Chamber shaft came to be leaked to the press – resulting in his 'exclusion' from further work – than meets the eye. The 'official' version from Hawass ran as follows:[474]

Gattenberg [sic] was a full member of the team and did some very important work, but he finally abused our trust. He leapt to his own conclusions about some things and, without consulting Dr. Stadelmann or myself, he went to the press and made a lot of money selling a video of what his robot saw, and stated things that had not been proven at all. He said his robot had discovered a secret door. What door? All that can be said is that a block of some sort . . . has been found . . . In the first place, this news should have been announced in Egypt, with the permission of the Supreme Council for Antiquities; and secondly, the factual information should have been presented rather than sheer speculation. By making a media circus, Gattenberg [sic] not only violated the terms of his contract with the German Institute, but he also broke faith with the rest of the investigating team.

In August 1998 Robert Bauval himself took somewhat belated responsibility for the discovery being leaked to the worldwide press in the following statement on our *EgyptNews* mailing list: 'If anyone must be blamed, then let it be me. For it was I who brought Rudolf's discovery of the "door" to the press's attention in April 1993.'[475] Of course it was clear from both of Bauval's books that he had been heavily involved, but he had always made out that he had acted altruistically and with Gantenbrink's full support.[476] Then in January 1999 the normally reticent Gantenbrink finally decided to speak out on the affair, and again chose *EgyptNews* as the prime vehicle to make a statement. Commenting first on Bauval's use of his name in a list of speakers at a forthcoming conference which he had no intention of attending, and having apparently asked Bauval to remove his name no fewer than 33 times, he continues as follows:[477]

Although, I have had a lot of experience seeing my name misused for profit reasons – and especially so related to the name Robert Bauval – but this is a new direct attempt of an ongoing violation of my person. Like breaches of copyright, promotions for conferences, incorrect quotes, edited statements, etc. Even by knowing that I am definitively not at all sharing their views about the Egyptian history they are repeatedly trying to make people believe that I back up their theories.

I DO NOT BACK UP THEIR THEORIES AND VIRTUAL DISCOVERIES!

I would like to point out here that the ongoing misuse of my name through different 'new age' parties for their marketing strategies, has led – and will further lead – to the strange situation of the Pyramid's air shaft exploration. Relating this true scientific project permanently to virtual discoveries, halls of records and lost civilization theories, makes it untouchable for serious scientists. This is the true reason why the important and most necessary investigation of the Northern shaft of the Queen's Chamber is blocked from scientific research for six years.

This posting predictably generated a flurry of defensive responses on *EgyptNews* from both West (who attacked Gantenbrink's scientific credentials, apparently because he does not support the Sphinx weathering theory) and Hancock (who accused Gantenbrink of acting like a 'spoilt child'). Meanwhile, Adrian Gilbert, Bauval's co-author on *The Orion Mystery*, had this to add about a lawsuit that followed the initial discovery, relating to the legal rights to Upuaut's video footage:[478]

These rights were obviously crucial as Rudolf had invested a lot of his own time and money in this project, it was only right that he should have a return on this investment. It was not us who denied him this but rather others. We in fact set him up with a contract from the BBC. They were supposed to show his documentary alongside ours in a Pyramid evening. Instead they included the cream of his footage in our programme [*The Great Pyramid: Gateway to the Stars*] and went back on any agreement they had with him to show his Upuaut Documentary in full. I am not privy to the terms of their agreement but this later became the subject of a court case. The basis of the BBC's defence was on who really owned the copyrights over Gantenbrink's footage of the discovery: he or the German Institute under whose umbrella he was working.

None of this had anything to do with 'The Orion Mystery', which was by then a bestseller. Much to my annoyance Robert felt he had to get himself involved in the court case, on the side of the BBC. This for a time poisoned relations between him and Rudolf, which till then had been very cordial. The unfortunate side-effect of all these proceedings was that the German Institute became 'embarrassed' and Rudolf was banned from doing any further work in the Great Pyramid.

Subsequent to the publishing of 'The Orion Mystery', for various reasons, the partnership between Robert Bauval and I broke up and instead he teamed up with Graham Hancock as his writing partner. Together they wrote 'Keeper of Genesis', which put a most unwelcome light on current investigations around the Giza area, implying various conspiracy theories. They now, I think, recognise that this was a mistake and that the book would have been better had it stuck to facts and theories concerning astronomy and the dating of the sphinx. Further appearances of Robert on television discussing theories concerning pyramids on Mars and their hypothetical connection with the pyramids of Giza served only to discredit him in the eyes of Egyptology and the scientific community. This, unfortunately, tarnished the very good work contained in 'The Orion Mystery',

which five years after publication remains unrefuted in all its
major aspects.

Despite the fact that we do not agree with Gilbert's contention
about the Orion correlation, his public statements do tend to
be a breath of fresh air in the stale and usually odorous political
climate that has developed. Following these various postings,
Gantenbrink responded with additional information as
follows:[479]

1. The first broadcast of filmed material from the shafts was done
by a production called 'The Great Pyramid – Gateway to the
Stars' which first presented the Bauval / Gilbert star correlation
theory world-wide in public, shortly before their book came out.

2. This material was stolen from a home video sample tape.

3. The material was altered by stitching out the time code that
had been copied on to the images for security reasons.

4. The material was released against a documented interdiction
from myself and the German Archaeological Institute in violation
of my copyright.

5. The material was released without any clearance of the
Supreme Council of Egyptian Antiquities.

6. The material was illegally rebroadcast after an injunction
issued by the High Court in London.

7. This world-wide 'first time' broadcast of shaft material, clearly
linked our find to a highly controversial theory.

8. The broadcast led to a legal case at the High Court in London,
and to heavy protests from the German Archaeological Institute,
the British Museum, and the Egyptian Supreme Council of
Antiquities.

We were able to further clarify this situation with Gantenbrink when he came to London to meet us shortly after this
furor erupted.[480] He told us that Rainer Stadelmann, the director
of the German Archaeological Institute in Cairo (GAIC), had
been responsible for cancelling a press conference that had been
scheduled to announce the discovery of the 'door'. It would

appear that Hawass's suspension two days before the discovery (an issue to which we will return in a later chapter) did not help matters because he had been extremely supportive and helpful in an unofficial as well as an official capacity, while in Gantenbrink's own words 'what we found was a question mark' – in other words, this was a discovery that could only lead to mostly unscientific speculation (as it of course did), and the Institute perhaps got cold feet.

Gantenbrink was annoyed by this turn of events, not for himself, but for his eighteen sponsors, who deserved some return on their investment. To placate them he edited his video footage and made a copy for each of them, also passing a copy to Stadelmann and the Egyptian Ministry of Culture. While in his view the facts of his discovery should have been officially announced, he was quite aware of the protocol that no scientific details should be released until proper reports had been pre-pared and scrutinised by the relevant authorities, in this case the GAIC and the SCA. With this in mind, he clearly marked all the videos 'for demonstration only, not for broadcast', and, when Bauval kept requesting more information just as *The Orion Mystery* was nearing completion, he gave him a copy to placate him, on the apparent understanding that he was not to use any still shots or to falsely use Gantenbrink's name in connection with his shaft alignment and other theories. Accord-ingly Gantenbrink professes that he was 'amazed' when *The Orion Mystery* and the various newspaper articles and television documentaries appeared, all linking his discovery inextricably with Bauval's theories.

In particular he says this was all the ammunition Stadelmann needed to disown the project completely – although, to correct the popular misconception that he was 'dismissed' from Giza, he states categorically that as a result of all this it was he who wrote to Stadelmann to dissociate himself from the GAIC. His decision was reinforced by the fact that he never had a contract with the GAIC, that he was confirmed as the project leader but never paid, and that the institute gave him virtually no support during his exploration of the shafts – Uli Kapp, a surveyor, not an archaeologist, was provided but was removed on other business during the last critical week, while the SCA provided various inspectors from the Plateau, but again no archaeologist, as was officially required.

We do not suggest that Bauval deliberately set out to jeopardise Gantenbrink's position, and it is true that he has remained vociferous in lobbying for his being allowed to return to complete his investigations of the shafts. However, it is quite clear that he must have known he was breaking his unofficial word to Gantenbrink in playing to the press as he did, and in relentlessly linking the discovery of the 'door' to his theories – even if he was too naïve at the time to understand the official protocol, or too disrespectful and impetuous to realise the damage his unsanctioned breaking of the rules would cause. To take all this on his shoulders when he had nothing whatsoever to do with the official exploration was an unwarranted intrusion to say the least, and it cannot be a coincidence that he must have realised the discovery would assist his own book sales. Any subsequent attempt to repair the damage is, in our view, too little too late – especially since it is clear that at least as late as the middle of 1997 Hawass was still labouring under the impression that the leaking of the story was all Gantenbrink's fault.

To compound the matter, Bauval clearly did not learn from his mistake – committing exactly the same error in conjunction with Boris Said to disrupt the Schor Foundation expeditions, as we will see shortly. One mistake may be just that, but two seems to be something of a habit.

On the Offensive

Following the publication of *Keeper of Genesis*, Bauval and Hancock engaged in a frenzy of activity to promote their book and the conspiracy theories therein. They appeared on countless radio shows and documentaries, and wrote numerous articles and letters for the press, many of which appeared on the then rapidly emerging Internet – the latter especially acting as a magnet for conspiracy theorists who picked up the base material and spread it far and wide, introducing their own distortions and innuendo along the way to devastating effect. They also spoke at a number of conferences. Their September 1996 appearance at a conference entitled 'Return to the Source:

Rediscovering Lost Knowledge and Ancient Wisdom', held at the University of Delaware and sponsored by the Society for Scientific Exploration, was pretty much typical, as video footage reveals. Having appeared on *The Art Bell Show* the night before, they are in fine fighting form, and it is true that they do make a formidable pairing when speaking. The audience is clearly the typical American 'new-age' set who have been primed to accept just about anything their saviours come up with – and any 'narrow-minded' and 'job-protecting' scientists or Egyptologists in the audience would have been quite reasonably intimidated into silence in such an atmosphere.

The question-and-answer session at the end builds to a suitably sycophantic climax, with Hancock self-righteously proclaiming 'we are absolutely opposed to any secrecy and exclusivity of knowledge', and accusing Schor and the authorities of operating behind a 'veil of secrecy, confusion, disinformation and dishonesty'. Powerful stuff. But then out of the audience comes a quiet, slightly nervous voice: it is Joe Jahoda, who, as technical director of the Schor Team, tries to actually *inform* the audience what is really going on. A less political or abrasive character you could not meet, and when the 'dynamic duo' invite him up on to the stage to take questions from the audience you know that the poor man, who arrives on stage with a carrier bag which presumably acts as his briefcase, is going to be like a lamb to the slaughter. He bravely attempts to explain the protocol regarding the issuing of reports to and then by the authorities, but is constantly interrupted and in the end stands forlornly to one side, able only to repeat 'I am just a simple scientist' before he is drowned out by the wave of accusations once again. Anyone watching this hapless encounter can be left in no doubt – these guys are bullies, and are perfectly capable of making mincemeat of an easy target.

Jahoda's reception is in stark contrast to that of the 'guru' himself, West, who is invited on stage along with Robert Schoch to a hero's welcome and even more rapturous adulation than that reserved for the duo themselves. Always ready with his acerbic wit, which makes him more likable, he joins in the 'fun'. Hancock goes on to inform the audience that, on *The Art Bell Show* the night before, 'We called for an International Public

Enquiry into what has been happening at Giza in the last couple of years. We feel, lame dog though it is, that UNESCO is the International body [for the job]', and that 'there is a seething can of worms there which is greatly to the disadvantage of the entire human race'. Turning to Gantenbrink's 'door' he states proudly, 'I believe these are sacred monuments. They should not be subjected to this kind of obnoxious behaviour.' It is perhaps reasonable to suggest that the truly obnoxious behaviour is being played out right in front of the audience's eyes.

Baiting the authorities

We have already referred to the *Carte Blanche* documentary, which was in fact filmed in two parts, the first in 1996 when the conflict was at its height. When interviewed at this time Hawass, who is clearly seething about the attacks, says of Bauval, 'The man is an amateur. He should not write about the pyramids. That type of person looks for two things: to become famous and make money!' This early part of the film captures the deep animosities perfectly.

Subsequently the battle spilt over into the pages of *KMT*, initiated by an interview with Hawass in the summer 1997 edition, in which among other things he attempts to put the record straight about West's exclusion from the Plateau:[481]

> The Committee [of the SCA] does not play favourites, it looks for scholars with worthy projects. It also does not believe that the monuments of Egypt should be used to make money; they are not for sale to the highest bidder. If scholars give lectures about their work in Egypt, and make some money from these, this is generally to finance their next season of work, and there is no problem with that. But it is those persons who want to exploit the monuments for profit that cause the problems; and they make problems even for legitimate scholars, because of the way they abuse the monuments to make money.

In West's case, this is perhaps a little harsh. Predictably he, Schoch, Bauval and Hancock responded with a joint letter to the winter 1997 edition, in which, among other things, they question Hawass's 'extraordinary hostility' to their claims of an earlier Sphinx and his 'public contempt' for Edgar Cayce and his readings. In support of this they bring in the issue of Hugh Lynn Cayce's claims about assisting Hawass's education at the University of Pennsylvania, and suggest that 'we can think of no reason why he should have invented such a claim', before noting the ARE's support for various expeditions and Hawass's involvement in Said's *Secret Chamber* promo.[482]

In the following edition, Hawass responded to various general points before turning to the issue of his supposed educational assistance by asserting 'the Hugh Lynn Cayce I knew would exaggerate things', and further that Robert Smith, who as we have already seen was the author of Hugh Lynn's biography, wrote to Hawass subsequently to apologise for not having checked his facts with him first.[483] In the same edition Lehner goes further, quoting Smith himself in saying that 'Hugh Lynn was essentially a story-teller'. He continues that it was he, Lehner, who introduced Hugh Lynn to Hawass and also to Frank Blanning, who had been the dean of students at the American University in Cairo. When the latter became the head of the Cairo office of the Fulbright Council for Educational and Cultural Exchange, he was responsible for awarding Hawass his scholarship in the same way as all the other recipients – and it was only this casual acquaintance that presumably allowed Hugh Lynn in 'story-telling' mode to claim that he had obtained Hawass's scholarship for him.[484]

Another piece of the 'innuendo jigsaw' had been set aside.

Baiting Schor

Even before *Keeper of Genesis* was published, although we cannot be sure of the full extent of the communication between the parties, it would appear that Schor had enough advance warning of its contents to be on his guard. When he found out that a planned newspaper serialisation was going to imply that he was inextricably linked to the ARE and would be searching for the Hall of Records, and that a new licence had been granted to his team even though West and Schoch had been refused permission to conduct further work, he threatened Hancock and Bauval with a libel action – perhaps to distance himself from adverse publicity that could harm his relationship with the authorities.[485] Although both he and Hawass were publicly proclaiming that the Schor projects were primarily preservation- and safety-related, this was in truth somewhat disingenuous, and the serialisation went ahead in the *Daily Mail* of 2 May 1996 without the threat being carried through.

Meanwhile, we have already seen in Chapter 10 that Bauval and Hancock had originally been invited to join the Schor expeditions, but refused on the basis of West's exclusion and the requirement that they should sign nondisclosure agreements. These were the two major bones of contention that they exploited to the full in their public utterances – for example, as we have already seen, at the 'Return to the Source' conference. Not only were they intent on halting Schor's missions, but they also wanted to ensure that any of his team's findings were brought to the attention of the public as soon as possible. In this they were aided by Said, who released a copy of the *Secret Chamber* promo to Bauval – who in turn milked Hawass's 'Indiana Jones' quip for all it was worth. By the time he made his *Behind the Scenes* video compilation, Said was getting fully stuck into Schor over secrecy and cover-ups as well:[486]

> Finally I've become convinced that Dr. Schor never wanted to go public with this information at all. I believe it was always his intention to keep news of the secret chamber and its contents from the public.

Bauval, Hancock and West must have felt they were making some real progress in their 'war' against Schor when during a conference in November 1996 West met with Dr Ali Hassan, who had just been appointed as the new head of the SCA, and who according to them professed himself 'totally unfam- iliar and unaware of the involvement of the Edgar Cayce Foundation and its members at Giza since the 1970's', and promised that 'no license to undertake digging under the Sphinx, or of opening the door in the Pyramid would be implemented before he verified the situation left to him by his predecessor, Dr. Nur El Din'.[487] And shortly afterwards, in conjunction with Said, they were claiming that the war had been won – and that the Schor team's licence had been revoked. This is how their own 'fanzine' *Hieroglyph* described their victory in May 1998:[488]

One of the major aims of *Hieroglyph* at its inception was to provide updated information on the strange goings-on at Giza as outlined in *Keeper of Genesis*. In early 1997, the situation seemed critical as work on the opening of the door at the end of the Queen's Chamber air-shaft, discovered by Rudolf Gantenbrink, and the exploration of hidden chambers under the Sphinx had been 'officially' halted and were feared to be on the verge of being carried out in secret. *Hieroglyph* is glad to report that the tide seems to have turned. Graham Hancock told *Hieroglyph* in an exclusive interview, 'There's been a curious series of developments over the last year. Robert Bauval and I had found ourselves, together with John Anthony West, in a position of antagonism and opposition to the way that archaeological projects were being managed on the Giza plateau, and we felt that the Schor Foundation/Florida State University project had many aspects about it that were unsatisfactory. We fought a public campaign on this issue during 1996 and 1997 to draw public attention to what we thought was wrong. The result of this attention was the Egyptian authorities, particularly the Chief Inspector of Antiquities Dr. Zahi Hawass, receiving literally thousands of letters from all around the world protesting the way that project had been administered, and indeed authorised. And it's fairly clear that the decision to cancel that project on the part of the Egyptian authorities was in part a response to all of the public interest in this matter. It's clear that the Egyptian authorities are interested and do listen to what the public has to say.'

For his part, West had this to say:[489]

This guerrilla campaign against formidable odds evidently had its intended effect. The Schor takeover bid, after several expeditions to Egypt . . . seems to be at a standstill . . . Recently, perhaps out of frustration, Hawass in Egypt has stepped up the campaign of vilification and abuse in what he describes as a 'public relations counter-attack'.

So were the 'dynamic duo' really protecting the world's most famous archaeological site from unscrupulous predators anxious to recover ancient wisdom for themselves and for commercial exploitation? Or were they 'false prophets', engaged in their own cynical agenda of self-promotion? Let us examine the facts.

We have already seen that West's exclusion from the Plateau owed far more to his, Bauval's and Hancock's incautious desire to trumpet the 'incontrovertible evidence' for an earlier date for the Sphinx – in the process linking it with Atlantis (however much West may profess now that he never made such a link[490]) – rather than to any conspiracy by the authorities. As for the issue of signing nondisclosure agreements, about which Bauval and Hancock were so indignant, Schor himself has informed us that, as he was financing the mission, he wanted an opportunity to recoup his investment by having the first opportunity of releasing the findings.[491]

Undoubtedly he was also aware of the problems that Gantenbrink had encountered when his discovery of the 'door' in the southern Queen's Chamber shaft had been almost immediately leaked in sensationalised reports to the press – by the same Robert Bauval who was now objecting to a nondisclosure agreement – causing him to be ostracised by the authorities. So it would seem that Schor was not only protecting his own investment, but also meeting the criteria laid down by the SCA forbidding unauthorised publicity. 'Joe felt one had to follow the letter of the law in every respect,' reports Ray Grasse, who was an observer during the second Schor expedition.[492]

Above all, we have seen quite clearly, both from Jahoda's comments that their licence was never revoked and from the fact that they were back at the Plateau in September 1998, that Bauval and Hancock did not 'win the war'. Their triumphant and smug claims to have stopped the Schor expeditions were completely false. Nevertheless, what impact did they have? Here is Jahoda again:

> I never understood why Bauval and Hancock tried so hard to delay and hurt our mission. We were all working on the same program I thought ... to get to the truth. They had requested that everyone write a letter and get the project stopped and

opened up etc. They apparently received 23,000 letters all negative, etc. My estimate is that it cost us 2 years of delays . . .
minimum.[493]

I do not wish to reopen graves, however each of the individuals
involved, who mounted massive verbal campaigns in the press,
at lectures, and in books will have to answer, perhaps in their
minds, perhaps in the future, perhaps now, for the problems they
have caused in delaying the work for about 2 years. Some of the
reasons were outright poor follow-up and investigations of
the facts. Some were based on bias, some because they felt they
deserved to be there, and some . . . to sell papers, books, and
lectures . . . to earn a living following years of experience and
automatic reflex actions. Do I feel badly towards them and their
actions? Intellectually yes. Inwardly no . . . We are all behaving
in a manner which is less than perfect. All performing our roles
and going through the motions which in our model of the universe
is correct. Forgiveness is our only possible response . . . one to
the other, as I hope they will forgive me for any of my less than
perfect actions. Looking back, the attacks hurled at us were
terrible. I witnessed that period first hand. We, as well as Zahi,
were accused of everything from stealing, hiding, rejecting
people's help who were entitled to be there by virtue of their
previous work, etc., etc. If they only knew the honesty that existed
within the expedition, the honesty of Joe Schor and Zahi etc.
they would never have made those unsubstantiated accusations.
I could never believe the junk they were throwing around . . . for
their own reasons . . .

Through it all, Zahi came out a champion, a knight in shining
armour. He was vilified, his job was threatened by the many
attacks and 23000 letters and e-mails etc., but he remained firm
always protecting the monuments and the plateau. Joe Schor
likewise, remained firm through attacks you would not believe.
He never returned attack for attack, instead in quiet dignity he
did not answer his critics. A gentleman and a man throughout. I
admire these men for their behavior.[494]

And we admire you, Joe, for your dignity and forgiveness,
and for helping us to set the record straight.

Conclusion

It is clear that, although Bauval, Hancock and to a lesser extent West did not ultimately prevent the Schor expeditions from continuing, they did manage to massively disrupt them. By doing so, the progress of externally funded expeditions on the Plateau in general was also disrupted. It is no exaggeration to say that their own obnoxious behaviour in opposing the Schor expeditions may have even played a part in the delays to the further exploration of the Queen's Chamber shafts, which they proclaimed themselves so anxious to have investigated.

Meanwhile, although we accept that the authorities' approval of projects that were supported by conspicuously ARE affiliates even if not by the ARE itself was not handled as well as it might have been, and that they certainly lost the PR battle with Bauval and Hancock over this issue, we can see on sober reflection that the accusations of conspiracy and cover-up were based on a tangled web of intrigue which was more often than not a misrepresentation of the *motives* of the people and organisations involved, and in some cases even of the *facts* themselves. At the end of the day, the reason the Schor Expeditions were allowed to continue while West's and Gantenbrink's were not was that the Schor team knew what the rules were, and managed to stay close enough to Hawass that the massive problems caused by the leaks of Said and indirectly Bauval and Hancock were managed one way or another, so that it remained clear that they themselves were trying to abide by the rules.

Nevertheless, it is also fair to say that the substantial delays in releasing the results of expeditions frustrate researchers anxious to know more about, for example, Danley's acoustic tests – and as we have already seen it frustrates the team members themselves even more. The disruptive consequences for ongoing relations of releasing information early through unofficial channels are such that we can only condemn such action. However, we would suggest that the authorities themselves should perhaps be a little more sensitive to the desire of researchers and the public to be kept properly informed, and that they might consider making revisions to or improving the efficiency of their lengthy protocol, which requires that all 22 members of the Supreme Council have to approve any report before it can be released.

About Turn!
Despite the prolonged ferocity and intensity of Bauval and Hancock's attacks on the Egyptological establishment, there were signs by late 1997 that they were softening their approach. If you thought events were difficult to follow up to now, hang on to your hats . . .

The entente cordiale
It would appear that Robert Bauval had somewhat more constructive discussions with Zahi Hawass and Joe Schor as well, at the ARE's annual convention in August 1997. Then in December 1997 Graham Hancock apparently spent some time in the company of Hawass being shown round all the 'secret' places on the Plateau, including for example the Relieving Chambers and the various tunnels in the Sphinx.

Then in May 1998 a conference entitled 'The Pyramids, the Sphinx, the Mystery' was held during a cruise in Alaska on the MS *Statendam*. Organised by Visions Travel and moderated by Art Bell, the speakers included West, Hancock, Hawass, Ed Krupp and Danion Brinkley (a well-known author on 'alternative' topics). Although the opposing sides continued to disagree about the theories, it *appeared* that a new air of dialogue and mutual respect was taking shape. This was trumpeted in a variety of statements released after the event. The first was issued by West and Hancock shortly after the cruise, responding to accusations (which we will consider in a later chapter) that Hawass had been suspended:[495]

> As is widely known we ourselves have had serious differences with Dr. Hawass over many years. However over the past six months we have been engaged in a civil and increasingly amiable dialogue with Dr. Hawass. This dialogue has convinced us that our differences with him, however acrimoniously expressed, were largely due to mutual misperceptions . . . We would like to state, for the record, that while our disagreements with Dr. Hawass over matters Egyptological still continue, we are in the process

of exploring them with him in depth with the kind of civil and courteous debate that are appropriate for science and scholarship. We are now absolutely convinced that the precious monuments of the Giza plateau could not be in better hands than those of Dr. Hawass. We have seen him at work. We have seen his passion and genuine love for the pyramids and the Sphinx. And we have seen that above all else he is determined to ensure the preservation of these monuments for the future. There are no conspiracies. There are no hidden finds. There is no skullduggery.

Then Bauval and Hancock issued a similar public statement about Mark Lehner in July, which contained almost identical phraseology.[496] And Bauval took our breath away after the ARE annual convention of August 1998: ' . . . we will not allow this to degenerate again in a morass of political confusion and media hype. The stakes are too high for egos to get in the way of the search for the truth'.[497]

What *incredible* arrogance! After being the prime motivators of a massive public campaign to ensure that innuendo and doubt pervaded every aspect of exploration on the Plateau, which was arguably fuelled more by their *own* egos than by any desire to protect the monuments or obtain the truth, and having exploited the media with great expertise themselves, here they were acting as if butter wouldn't melt in their mouths! As for the suggestion that they were engaging in 'the kind of civil and courteous debate that are appropriate for science and schol-arship', one wonders why they had not noticed that this might have been appropriate from the outset.

This about-turn caused a variety of reactions. Some of their followers remained somewhat blind to the faults of their heroes so that they did not question their actions at all, merely lauding them all the more for their belated appearance at the 'nego-tiating table'. Meanwhile, in other quarters the seeds of mistrust that they had so successfully sown turned back on them with a vengeance in a poetic form of karmic rebalance. Alan Alford, a diehard of the anti-orthodox school if ever there was one, accused them of 'sleeping with the enemy', while others went further and suggested openly that they had sold out and joined the conspiracy – and were now acting as the very agents of disinformation that they themselves had previously fought so hard to expose.[498] Such innuendo directed at *them* for a change was in our view poetic justice, even if, as always, false.

We might be able to accept that their about-turn is the responsible and positive action they make it out to be if they showed a bit more humility about the whole issue, and actually *apologised* for all the vexation and disruption they have caused for so many people who had far more constructive ways to spend their time than fending off their unwarranted accusations. However, all they have ever (at least publicly) done is suggest the whole thing was a misunderstanding on *both* sides. Wrong. The misunderstanding was all theirs. If Hawass is being apparently cordial to them now, it is only because they have generated such a following that from a public-relations point of view he could no longer afford to ignore them. But we suspect that his understanding of their motives and theories remains the same as it ever was – that they appear to be self-publicists whose science and scholarship are arguably no better now that they were when they started.

Hancock's uncompromising attitude to criticism was aptly demonstrated in his response to Adrian Gilbert's posting on *EgyptNews* when the 'Gantenbrink Affair' blew up in January 1999, as we discussed earlier: 'Gilbert is wrong to suggest that Bauval and I now "recognise" that certain chapters of "Keeper of Genesis" were "a mistake". We're content with what we wrote, and regret nothing.'[499] Meanwhile, Bauval's arrogance also remains undented, and if anything is strengthened; we will see just how absolutely this is the case in the ensuing chapters.

Hall? What Hall?

One other aspect of this whole sorry saga that is, for once, comic in its transparency is the efforts of the 'three musketeers' to distance themselves as far as possible from the Hall of Records as the end of 1998 approached, as was demonstrated in their appearances in the *Carte Blanche* documentary.

In the first part, shot in 1996, we are for once shown the diagrams from *Keeper of Genesis* that pinpoint the location of the Hall under the rear paws of the Sphinx (which we referred to in Chapter 9). However, in the second part, shot in 1998, we are first treated to Hancock solemnly informing us that 'a very unseemly feeding frenzy around the Hall of Records has erupted in the last two or three years'; that 'it could just be all Scotch mist'; and that it is 'mostly modern speculation' which is not backed up by mythology. He even refers to it as the '*damned* Hall of Records'. A bit ungrateful, we think, given that it is this very concept to which their best-selling book owed some measure of its success. Nevertheless, in true Hancock style, the pronouncement is made straight-faced, without any trace of irony. Perhaps he and Bauval would come across better if they displayed a bit of humour and self-deprecation, and didn't take themselves so *very* seriously.

Meanwhile, Bauval limits himself to 'I am beginning to think that the chamber itself is not important'. For his part West confidently informs us that 'the notion of the Hall of Records comes from one source and one source only . . . and that is Edgar Cayce' (a statement that is in any case not necessarily true, as we saw in Chapter 5), and that while his health diagnoses were fairly reliable, his predictions about world events were 'pretty flawed'. Meanwhile, *with* a trace of irony, West does at least admit that 'in a way we are largely responsible for getting the world so excited about it'.

Divergent Paths?

Following their successful collaboration on *Keeper of Genesis*, Bauval and Hancock turned 'extraterrestrial' in a risky venture along with the researcher John Grigsby. Their *Mars Mystery*, published in 1998, picked up on the work of Richard Hoagland and others to postulate from the face and other structures in Cydonia that Mars had once been inhabited, and that the population was wiped out by a huge cometary impact less than 20,000 years ago. Although they do not appear to emphasise the parallels with the Sphinx or any direct link between the two civilisations, they do suggest that the same fate could befall Earth, and that the structures may be a warning. Although its release coincided with a Hollywood blockbuster dealing with the threat of cometary impact, and the book is described once again as a 'number one bestseller', it in fact received a less than rapturous reception on both sides of the Atlantic. A glance

401

through the customer reviews on the Amazon Internet book-shop reveals that the majority of the feedback was negative, with comments like 'utter disappointment', 'disjointed' and 'fragmented' the order of the day.[500] Had the 'dynamic duo' for once misjudged the feelings of the people? After all, one did not have to be too bright to realise that such a threat is with us millennia after millennia, and that it is just another factor in the huge game of cosmic chance. Meanwhile, new pictures from Mars Global Surveyor made the 'face' look less and less like an artificial structure.

But perhaps there is a more subtle reason why this book was so far from the roaring success these authors would normally expect. We have it on good authority that their original follow-up book proposal under the working title *The Philadelphia Connection* was even more explosive in its accusations of conspiracy and cover-up at the Plateau, including large helpings of NASA involvement over the last 30 years and full parallels being drawn between the monuments of Giza and Cydonia. However, it would appear that further research led to the 'about-turn' that put paid to this line of enquiry.

In any case, as the 'Author's Note' in the US edition makes clear, *The Mars Mystery* was primarily Hancock and Grigsby's work, and in the US it was released under Hancock's name only. Then in September 1998 he published a new book called *Heaven's Mirror* with his wife, the photographer Santha Faiia, in conjunction with a series of three 50-minute documentaries called *Quest for the Lost Civilisation* on Channel 4. These looked at the archaeo-astronomy of various sites around the world, including Stonehenge, Angkor in Cambodia, Nan Mador in Micronesia, and Easter Island, among others. As with Giza, his proposition is that, although many of these sites are relatively recent constructions, they all supposedly demonstrate a knowledge of precession that ties them into his favourite date . . . you guessed it, 10,500 BC. Without having yet studied this new work in any depth ourselves, there are signs that this analysis is even more flawed than his and Bauval's Giza–Orion correlation. Alan Alford has provided a preliminary rebuttal of the Angkor–Draco correlation on his web site, which once again centres around stars that do not have matching temples and vice-versa,[501] while Ed Krupp suggests, 'He matches monuments around Angkor Wat with northern Mesopotamian and Mediterranean constellations in a way that has more internal contradictions than his Giza stuff'.[502]

Hancock is now reported to be working on a long-term project to dive on many underwater sites off the coastline around the world, especially in the Pacific, and at the same time to examine local mythology in an attempt to locate definitive proof of a 'lost civilisation' from antiquity – his line of reasoning being that these sites would have been *above* water before the last Ice Age.[503] Provided he leaves his obsession with archaeoastronomy and the date of 10,500 BC to one side, we think that this is an eminently sensible project. Since he has now become a recognised television personality, if he plays to his strengths we believe he has the chance to make a highly valuable contribution to public awareness of the *possibility* that the distant origins of mankind are not necessarily those we have always been led to believe.

All this has kept Hancock so busy that he and Bauval have not been working as closely together of late, although their public pronouncements are still extremely supportive of each other. Meanwhile, in the intervening period Bauval's focus has remained firmly fixed on Giza, as we will see in the following chapters.

TWELVE

In 1995 three young men – Nigel Appleby, a design engineer and military artist, Adam Child, a British Telecom development manager, and Bill Shirley, a captain of the Royal Signals unit of the British Army – came together to form an expedition team called 'Operation Hermes'. Based on Appleby's research, which clearly owed something to Edgar Cayce's predictions, the team's broad aim was to mount a series of expeditions to locate various Halls of Records around the globe – in Egypt, South America, Tibet and Antarctica. Appleby and Shirley drew upon their military experience and connections to recruit members of both the Territorial and regular army units into their organisation,[504] which soon swelled to 18 members – including several geologists from Bradford University. They also secured the services of GSB Prospection, a geophysical exploration company specialising in noninvasive surveys, which gave them access to high technology equipment.

Hermes Rising

Deciding to focus on Egypt in the first instance, they contacted the Egyptian authorities and tendered an initial proposal, which received a favourable response. Zahi Hawass faxed Appleby in March 1996 with the following:[505]

Further to earlier conversation. Provisional approval is no problem and given hereby. Final approval subject to committee of 22 of which I am one. I see no problem if all details scientifically prepared and the team has Ph.D. qualified members in Archaeological Surveying. Supreme Council of Antiquities insist on Ph.D. qualification and association with Institute or association. You have supplied details and at this stage meet requirements. Please send in full application as soon as possible to process fully.

Things were looking good for the team, but to turn the dream into reality they needed significant funds – and what better way to raise them than to go public and look for sponsorship. From working in virtual obscurity, Operation Hermes was projected on to the world stage on 10 August 1997 when the *Sunday Times* boldly published an article by the journalist Cherry Norton headlined 'RAIDERS OF THE LOST ARCHIVES FIND PHARAOHS' RECORDS'. The article announced that Appleby and Child would not be looking for the fabled 'Hall' under the Sphinx, but at a site some 9 kilometres (5 miles) north-northeast of Giza. It went on to explain briefly that Appleby had spent years gathering data, deciphering ancient codes and observing stellar alignments relative to the pyramids, before being able to pinpoint the site. What lay hidden beneath the sands was graphically portrayed in an accompanying illustration – the 'Hall' being described as constructed of 'granite and sheathed in gold', and enclosed in a small pyramid now buried under 30 feet (9 metres) of sand. For a respected and somewhat conservative newspaper this was indeed an exceptional article, and one more usually found on the pages of the tabloids. Perhaps most surprisingly of all, Appleby and Child were already claiming that they had been 'given permission by the Egyptian authorities' to survey the site. The story led to a worldwide media scramble, with Appleby's phone ringing virtually nonstop.

Seeing the potential of a bestseller, the literary agent Simon Trewin made contact with Appleby and suggested that he should publish his research in a book. After lengthy discussions Trewin and Appleby agreed a deal with the publishers Random House. But, although the *Sunday Times* article had brought Operation Hermes much-needed publicity and Appleby a lucrative book deal, it was something of a double-edged sword. The sensationalised nature of the article itself was in any case not something the SCA would look upon in a favourable light, but to publicly claim they had been granted permission when they had only been given 'provisional approval' was a serious mistake. The then head of the SCA, Dr Ali Hassan, and Zahi

Hawass published several articles in the Egyptian press rejecting Appleby's claims. An opportunity to repair this rift presented itself when, in mid-October 1997, five members of Operation Hermes (although not Appleby himself) travelled to Egypt to carry out a preliminary survey of the projected site, which to their immense relief they found to be on private *undeveloped* land. But they failed to take full advantage of their visit by arranging a meeting with the relevant Egyptian officials to placate them.

Nevertheless, the team received another publicity boost when Appleby appeared on the South African TV documentary show *Carte Blanche* in November 1997.[506] During this programme he revealed more of what lay behind his theory regarding the location of the 'Hall', suggesting that, if the three pyramids at Giza mirrored the stars in Orion's belt, then Sirius should also have an earthly counterpart. Whereas Robert Bauval had merely used Sirius as an alignment for the southern Queen's Chamber shaft, Appleby conjectured that when Sirius's position in relation to Orion was marked on the ground there should be an important monument at that location – perhaps the Hall of Records itself.[507] To confirm that his projection was correct, Appleby first turned to the Fibonacci Spiral,[508] suggesting that if the Sphinx is used as the starting point and the spiral is extended out for 144,000 feet, then the point at which it ends concurs with his projection for the star Sirius. He also applied a number of other rules of 'sacred geometry' – which his research had revealed were consistently applied in ancient monuments all over the world – all of which apparently confirmed his theory.

Operation Hermes' rise to fame was indeed swift, and by keeping the public informed through a dedicated web site they tapped into the huge Internet audience.[509] The *Hermes Web Station* evolved into a highly professional presentation of all the aspects of the organisation, including objectives, equipment, planning, preparation and news updates, while an online discussion list added an interactive element for the public at large to ask questions or post messages. A sister organisation, Hermes Foundation International, was also established with its own web site. Unlike the military style of its big brother, the latter was pitched towards a 'new-age' audience from whom it hoped to attract much-needed funds, with suggested packages of private or corporate sponsorship ranging from £1,000 to £10,000. With training weekends a regular feature of their preparations, a complete infrastructure in place and a date set for their main expedition to Egypt in July 1998, the team were confident of success. Meanwhile, leaving the finer details to his colleagues, Appleby went into self-imposed isolation to complete his book within a 12-week deadline.

Hermes Falling

In early June 1998 Appleby's book *Hall of the Gods* was published – but within a week it was withdrawn from sale amid a legal threat of plagiarism brought primarily by the British author Ralph Ellis. Some weeks later the main expedition to Egypt was cancelled. The decline and fall of Nigel Appleby and Operation Hermes was as swift as its rise. But what are the events that led to such a dramatic U-turn? The answer is by no means simple . . .

Let us first investigate the complications behind the cancellation of the Hermes expedition. Shortly after the publication of the article in the *Sunday Times*, a number of interested parties made contact with Appleby and his team. One such person was Gerald O'Farrell. It would appear that shortly after Appleby met O'Farrell, he became convinced not only of his academic standing – referring to him as 'Dr' O'Farrell[510] – but also that he could be of great value to the Hermes organisation. Seemingly a close friend of Dr Ali Hassan, he might help smooth the way for their expedition to Egypt. Of course this must have seemed like a godsend for Appleby, as the team had not yet received formal written approval for their mission to proceed, and Operation Hermes would now have their very own academic Egyptologist who could champion their cause. This is made quite clear in a report drawn up for Robert Bauval and Graham Hancock by the researcher Simon Cox, who interviewed Appleby in September 1997; the report consists primarily of 41 numbered points, at least three of which demonstrate not only Appleby's belief in O'Farrell's claims but also his key role in negotiating with the Egyptian authorities:[511]

9. Dr. Gerald O'Farrell is the name cited most often in connection with academic credibility, with the added point that he is an emeritus professor, (info yet to be corroborated) based at a British university . . .

10. It was stated that Dr. O'Farrell was a close friend of Ali Hassan, the Egyptian antiquities member, and that as of this weekend (Sept 7/8) he was in Cairo meeting Mr. Hassan . . .

38. Appleby remained adamant that Ali Hassan would indeed grant them a licence, with Dr. O'Farrell playing a pivotal role in this.

It would seem then that the team believed that any problems they had previously created with the authorities could be smoothed over by O'Farrell. But what Appleby and his team did not realise was that O'Farrell was not quite the man of influence they believed him to be, and in reality could do little to help their cause. For he was neither an academic Egyptologist nor the holder of a doctorate. This was obviously in complete contrast to what Appleby had reported to Cox. So had Appleby misunderstood what O'Farrell was telling him in their many conversations?

Exactly when Appleby must have realised that he was not going to get his permit is hard to define. Certainly in May 1998 he still appeared to believe the mission would go ahead as planned when the *Daily Telegraph* gave a full-page spread to an interview with him in which it was stated:[512]

In three weeks time Appleby will fly out to Egypt with his team of 23 geophysicists, archaeologists and support staff to start probing an area of farmland on the rapidly expanding fringes of Cairo.

Appleby has managed to persuade the Egyptian Antiquities Organisation – the official body which oversees Egyptian Heritage – of his case. The organisation has given permission for his expedition on two conditions: that he is not allowed to do any digging and that he takes with him Ph.D.-qualified geophysicists.

Whether these words can be attributed to bravado or a committed belief that everything would turn out all right is unclear;

but Appleby was certainly not doing himself any favours by again publicly claiming he had permission when in truth he had not. This article also contained a highly damning statement that Appleby later claimed he did not make: referring to a lost advanced civilisation, he is reported as saying: 'The Egyptians were barbarians by comparison, who merely inherited knowledge of this glorious past in the form of myths and legends.' The Egyptian authorities' reaction to Appleby's apparent statement was poignantly expressed in an unusually reserved statement by Zahi Hawass on 7 June:[513]

> We would like to state that Hermes Operation Ltd. has not been granted official permission by the Supreme Council of Antiquities to do any kind of archaeological work or survey at or near the Giza Pyramids. Also we reject the statement made by Mr. Appleby in the London *Daily Telegraph* 'that the Egyptians were barbarians', who did not build the pyramids at Giza.
>
> We have to say that the ancient Egyptians were intelligent and made contributions to the ancient world not only in building the pyramids but also in science, art, astronomy and technology.

This was shortly followed on 15 June by articles in three Egyptian newspapers stating that Appleby and his team did not have permission and would not be allowed to bring their expedition to Egypt.[514] In addition the *Daily Mail* on the same day quoted Hawass as saying, 'No permission has been given to anyone to look for the Hall of Records.' To the highly determined adventurer the message finally came through loud and clear: don't call us – we'll call you! Even the British Embassy in Cairo advised Operation Hermes not go ahead with their trip, and suggested that Appleby should arrange a meeting with Dr Hawass to sort out their differences.

At this point the sensible approach would have been to retire from the affray, let the heat die down and make another attempt at a much later date. But Appleby – ever the soldier – was in 'refuse-to-lose' mode. He first attempted to go through 'senior officials in Cairo' to put pressure on the authorities; and when this tactic failed he then argued that, as his projected site for the Hall of Records was on private land, his team would not need a permit. But this was all a fruitless exercise, for even *with* a permit, clearance from Egypt's security services was still required. And without that Operation Hermes would not even have been allowed to *step* on Egypt's soil, let alone *survey* some of it.

This whole saga was creating problems not only for the authorities in Egypt, but also within the alternative research field as well. During a meeting which Chris attended with Robert Bauval and Ralph Ellis at the time, Bauval expressed his displeasure at the waves being created within Egyptian circles by Appleby's actions. This seemed somewhat hypocritical, as Bauval himself was no stranger to creating similar waves in the not too distant past – but perhaps he felt that his new *entente cordiale* with the authorities was being threatened. He also seemed concerned by Appleby's claim that they did not need a permit to survey private land – concerned enough, in fact, to telephone Hawass, who proceeded to calm his fears by stating that Appleby could not do anything without a permit, private land or not.[515] Meanwhile, Graham Hancock was at the same time claiming that Operation Hermes was a 'scam' to dupe the public.[516] What on earth did all this have to do with them? you might ask. What indeed? More will be revealed shortly.

Despite Appleby's dogged persistence, his group have never made it back to Egypt to explore the chunk of arable land under which they believe the Hall of Records lies. Moreover, it is unlikely that this claim will ever be proved or disproved, because the ever-increasing suburbs of modern Cairo are expanding into the undeveloped Egyptian countryside at a rapid rate – making it almost inevitable that the site will be buried underneath a concrete tower block. Despite our own view that Appleby's theory of the location is flawed – since it relies at least in part on the Orion Correlation theory about which we have already expressed considerable doubts – Operation Hermes was at least during its inception well organised, and the team highly motivated. In 'going public' they effectively excluded themselves from any serious consideration by the Egyptian authorities, but without the publicity they could not attract the funds they required. It was a 'Catch 22' situation, and they took a gamble – a gamble they were destined to lose.

Meanwhile, amidst all this confusion the situation was further complicated when Appleby's book was withdrawn from sale amidst allegations of plagiarism – a subject to which we will now turn.

Fall of the Gods
On 2 June 1998 Appleby's book *Hall of the Gods* was published by William Heinemann, an imprint of Random House, but, as we previously indicated, within the space of a few days it was withdrawn from sale. A number of authors including Robert Bauval, Graham Hancock, Christopher Knight and Robert Lomas had written to the publishers alleging plagiarism – but little did they realise that their letters were not the reason for the swift withdrawal of the book. Rather this was down to the efforts of one author, Ralph Ellis, who was tenaciously battling to save his work from being abused. The following is the inside story on the events leading up to this drastic action.

In the beginning . . .
In the spring of 1997 Ellis had completed his manuscript for a book that was eventually published under the title of *Thoth, Architect of the Universe*. Sending it off to literary agents, publishers and other authors, he received little encouragement for his hard work other than suggestions that he should make it less complicated and more readable. Finally Ellis received a response which he describes in the revised second edition of his book as follows:[517]

> A kindly old gentleman said he could be of assistance and could I meet him as soon as possible! Without a second thought, I was in a meeting, which went extremely well. The gentleman was suitably impressed with my ideas and the world, it seemed, would soon be flicking through the next best seller on the news-stands. The old adage was as true as ever: if it seems too good to be true, it is probably just that.

Although Ellis does not name this 'old gentleman', he was in fact none other than Gerald O'Farrell – the same person who had contacted Appleby in August 1997. Subsequently Ellis was introduced to Appleby by O'Farrell, who had been flitting between the two researchers. Ellis and O'Farrell had had many discussions during June and July concerning their shared interests, and on at least one occasion explored the Wiltshire countryside together, since the former had made certain observations concerning some of the prehistoric monuments found there which he had incorporated into his manuscript. Then in late August a disagreement developed between the two when O'Farrell proved unable to deliver on his promises:

> The confident talk at the meeting was one thing, but the reality of the situation was quite another. The editing of my manuscript never happened, publication was suddenly not as straightforward as had been promised, the finance for further investigations fell through. The whole escapade was turning into a charade.

Eventually they went their separate ways. But then Ellis got wind of another author who had submitted a book proposal that seemingly incorporated ideas and concepts from his own manuscript – and the author turned out to be Appleby. It was too much of a coincidence that they could have been working on exactly the same concepts independently, so Ellis decided to protect his work by the only method he believed was available to him – he published his book himself. After he had waded through all the machinations of printing, publishing and distribution, *Thoth* was eventually published in November 1997 and his copyright secured. Appleby then purchased a copy of the book and wrote to Ellis requesting permission to use diagrams, pictures and lengthy quotes, and the two eventually came to an agreement about what could and could not be used. Knowing that Appleby had already incorporated 'similar' concepts into his own book proposal, Ellis was perhaps taking a risk in allowing him to use any of his material – but, hoping for some additional exposure for his own work and believing his copyright to be secure, Ellis thought there was little to be concerned about. How wrong he was . . .

The Giza debate

At the end of March 1998, Chris co-organised a two-day conference in London which focused on the Giza Plateau. The format was a series of lectures presenting both the orthodox and alternative points of view, followed by a debate with questions from the audience. Speakers included Dr Ali Hassan, John Anthony West, Adrian Gilbert, Bassam El Shammaa, Andrew Collins, Robert McKenty and Nigel Appleby. Other members of Operation Hermes were also in attendance, manning an information display on the Hermes Foundation and their forthcoming expedition, while Ralph Ellis took the opportunity of promoting his book at the event with a small stand located in the same room as the Hermes team.

Day one passed with Appleby and Ellis conversing in an amicable manner, with no indication that the latter was in for a major shock during the following day's presentations. Taking the stand, Appleby delivered a lecture on his forthcoming book to a captivated audience. Within the first few slides he had used one of Ellis's diagrams, and he proceeded to incorporate Ellis's work throughout his lecture – justifying himself by claiming they had both been independently following the same line of reasoning:[518]

> A guy who has now become a good friend of mine, Ralph Ellis, is probably hiding at the back of the room somewhere. He's done an awful lot of research on the same sort of stuff I have done.

Moving ever deeper into the realms of Ellis's work, Appleby proceeded as follows:

> Ralph, he's come to the same conclusions. No insult to him, he has gone around the houses in a very, very nice long way, and backed it up with even more scientific fact than I could possibly do. I just came to the conclusions dom, dom, dom, and it all seemed to fall into place. So poor Ralph seems to have worked a lot harder than I had to. But he certainly validates what I was saying and vice versa.

413

Meanwhile, referring to Ellis's theories about Stonehenge, Appleby had this to say:

> Again poor Ralph Ellis, he had to do the work the hard way, using complex mathematics within it to come to the same conclusions. I, being the way I am, I sneaked down to Stonehenge, I scaled the fences, I climbed inside and just got a tape measure out.

What audacity! Here we had in the same room the author whose work Appleby was presenting as parallel research, while using his images and concepts. And, to top it all, the evidence that this was Ellis's work was on sale in the adjacent room! Appleby was indeed a cool customer. This is how Ellis himself describes his reaction:[519]

> I sat at the back of the Hall with my eyes opening widely, not believing my ears or eyes. Here were large sections of my book, *Thoth*, being delivered by another author.
>
> I could understand that someone may have had the same ideas as me, even though it was a coincidence that these ideas should surface at the same time. However to stand there and use my diagrams, my pictures, my words and the measurements that I had made with my own two hands on the pyramids of Egypt, was beyond belief. Here, too, were the diagrams that we had agreed would not be used; they had been lifted directly from the book without a please or a thank you. The lecture went on with numerous selections from my book.

Let battle commence

To Ellis's credit he did not bring Appleby back to reality there and then, but returned home to recheck their original agreement. He sent two letters of complaint to Appleby, to which no reply was forthcoming, so to force the situation he then wrote to Appleby's publishers forbidding the use of 'any quotation, diagram or picture' from *Thoth*. This had the desired effect, and a series of communications between the two authors ensued. However, Appleby maintained his stance that they had been conducting parallel research while claiming that Ellis's theories originated with Gerald O'Farrell:[520]

Please remember it was Gerald O'Farrell who recommended that I contact you as you and I were following identical paths of research. This excited me as I had assumed I was alone in my findings. It gave me a tremendous boost to find out that we were in agreement on so many aspects. Also as Gerald informed me at the time, it was he that introduced you to the Avebury and Stonehenge concepts only last year.

It seems highly likely that in fact O'Farrell had not introduced *Ellis* to these concepts, but rather *Appleby*. This was all too much for Ellis, and in a blanket ban he refused all permission for any of his work to be used in *Hall of the Gods*. Appleby's editor, Maria Rejt, then faxed Ellis a letter on 16 April 1998 acknowledging his refusal, to which he replied by sending a copy of his book to her highlighting the material to be removed from Appleby's manuscript. The following day he received a fax from Appleby stating that he would remove all references to him and his theories, and all relevant diagrams and photographs. But his relief was short-lived . . .

Six weeks later on publication of *Hall of the Gods* Ellis found to his horror that it still contained large sections lifted from his own work. Writing an angry letter to Random House, he sent them a copy of *Thoth*, again highlighting the relevant plagiarised sections. On 5 June Ellis received the following response from Rejt: 'I am writing to confirm we have ceased distribution of HALL OF THE GODS and are now in the process of withdrawing the book from sale', while on 19 June Random House made a statement in the trade journal the *Bookseller*, admitting 'clear evidence of plagiarism'.

Meanwhile a total of eleven other authors had also complained to Random House about the book. But Appleby was defiant, and denied any plagiarism – admitting only to 'errors in writing procedures'. Fighting back, he sent scathing communications to these authors presenting himself as the victim of professional jealousy. It was not until after 20 June that the other authors came to learn of Ellis and his fight to protect his copyright, and they banded together effectively as a 'pressure group' – coordinated by, you've guessed it . . . Robert Bauval. They attempted to get Appleby to back down from his dogged persistence to have his book put back on the shelves, with Bauval himself particularly adamant about putting a stop to Appleby's shenanigans and totally against any compromise.[521] On 1 August Bauval sent a 22-page information and fact sheet for posting over our *EgyptNews* mailing list to keep the Internet community informed, although reaction thereto was minimal as no serious conclusions could be drawn from its content.

Meanwhile, out of the public eye a war of words was being waged between Appleby and this group of authors, and between lawyers representing both parties. On 31 July the solicitors representing Ellis and Bauval posted a letter setting out the authors' grievances against Appleby's use of their work, and included in the communication were two sets of proposed agreements which they suggested could resolve the dispute and avoid any legal action.[522] One was between the aggrieved authors and Appleby himself, proposing that he must admit his plagiarism and breaches of copyright, apologise therefor, and not attempt to have his book republished in any form whatsoever. The other agreement was between them and Random House, proposing that the latter must admit and undertake the same.

In response Appleby's solicitors sent a letter which still denied plagiarism and argued that any extracts were covered under the standard 'fair usage' provisions.[523] Bauval was having none of this, and suggested the authors could prove otherwise in a court of law.[524] In addition to the letter of denial, Appleby's solicitors proposed a single and more simplified agreement which would effectively let both Appleby and his publishers off the hook without either of them having to admit to plagiarism. Again, Bauval's response was that he and the other authors wished to stick to the original draft agreements.

A strange turn of events

According to Ellis, things started to go really awry during the first weeks of September 1998. He reports that Bauval had been having a series of lengthy discussions with representatives of Random House and Appleby during which the latter had 'revealed all', the result being that he received a fax early on the Saturday morning of 12 September which proposed a single watered-down version of the original agreements, to be signed by each of the authors whose copyright was infringed, as follows:

THE PARTIES AGREE AS FOLLOWS

1. Mr. Appleby acknowledges that he has incorporated unlicensed elements of the author's original creative work in the book and apologises for this.

2. Mr. Appleby undertakes that he will not republish the book in its originally published form. However, should the book be republished in a different form, then Mr. Appleby undertakes not to use the title 'Hall Of The Gods' and to abide to items 4 and 5 here below.

3. Mr. Appleby undertakes to destroy any copies of the book that may come into his possession in excess of his complimentary copies already received from the publishers.

4. If Mr. Appleby wishes to use any material from the author's published works at any future time he undertakes that there will be no plagiarism, breach of copyrights or misrepresentation.

5. If Mr. Appleby wishes to use any material from the author's published works at any future time he undertakes that he will approach the author in writing and will not use such material until he receives approval in writing.

6. In consideration for Mr. Appleby's undertaking, the author agrees that he will not bring any legal action or take any other action whatsoever against Mr. Appleby in relation to the contents and publication of the book.

As an airline pilot by profession he was blurry-eyed after a long-haul flight and, needing time to think, he merely sent a fax to Appleby acknowledging that Bauval and Appleby had come to an agreement, adding that he *might* be in a position to sign a similar agreement the following week. Ellis relates that, within minutes of sending his fax to Appleby, Bauval was on the phone demanding to know why he had not signed the revised agreement. Pointing out that he had the chance of a publishing deal with Random House himself, Bauval recommended that if Ellis wished to pursue a similar opportunity he should sign the agreement immediately. Ellis sensibly replied

that he wished to confirm this deal with Random House personally and see what was actually on offer. After all, the very same
publishing house had had to withdraw Appleby's book from
sale because of his own persistence in the face of adversity.
According to Ellis, Bauval responded by indicating that:

> If I did not sign immediately he would withdraw all support and
> I would return to anonymity, I would never hear from him again
> – at that point I said 'goodbye Robert' and put the phone down.

The following Monday when office hours had once more
been resumed, Ellis rang Random House to check on the validity
of the supposed publishing contract, but he reports that nobody
there would speak with him. He followed up by dispatching a
letter to them but did not receive a reply. So Ellis had no way
of verifying that an alleged publishing contract was in the offing,
and was also confused as to why a one-time supporter and
champion of his cause was now seemingly pressurising him into
signing a watered-down version of the original agreement that
was far from watertight. And what was the significance of the
dropping of the other agreement forcing Random House to
admit their own liability in this affair? Despite being offered a
few carrots, Ellis did not consider himself a donkey, and
realising that the new agreement contained too many loop-holes
he refused to sign. Eventually he went on to instigate criminal
proceedings against Appleby.[525]

Conclusion
Whatever we may think of his theories, in our view Ralph Ellis
comes out of this whole affair as one of the few involved whose
integrity remains intact. In the face of much adversity and
pressure he stood his ground, and won through in a world with
which he was not overly familiar – a literary world filled
with political and personal aspirations that rarely bares its face
to the public.

Meanwhile, Nigel Appleby's rapid rise and fall perhaps leaves
him with memories he would rather forget. He had claimed
much but delivered little. And, despite the fact that he was given
only three months to complete his manuscript, it is quite clear

that his work did significantly plagiarise the work of at least two authors – Ellis and Andrew Collins in particular – both of whom have produced comparisons with their respective works, which leave no room for doubt on this issue.[526] Despite the fact that his book did contain several original ideas, he claimed that it was the culmination of over twelve years of personal research – whereas in varying degrees it appeared to be in large part the culmination of twelve other authors' research.

As for Robert Bauval, Appleby claims, 'I had made the Orion–Giza connection in 1983 while at college due to a connection of ancient sites in Colchester that married up to the Orion constellation.'[527] However, in comparison with the two authors mentioned above, Bauval's own case for plagiarism seemed less sound. And, in any case, once Ellis had ensured that the book was pulled from the shelves, the massive publicity surrounding this rare plagiarism case made it highly unlikely that any publisher would touch Appleby ever again – even though the 'amended' agreement appeared to suggest that he could rewrite the book under a new title. So why was Bauval so anxious to press the point home? And was he not once again acting as the ringleader in a saga that was not primarily his concern? As usual, there was more to this than met the eye, and there was more confusion to come. He and the other authors had issued a public statement in August 1998 which stated in no uncertain terms:[528]

We, the Authors, namely Graham Hancock, Robert G. Bauval, Colin Wilson, Christopher Knight, Robert Lomas, Andrew Collins, Simon Cox and Alan Alford hereby confirm that we have absolutely no affiliation or business involvement – *nor intend to have in the future* – with the Hermes Foundation International, Hermes Operation Ltd. and/or its associates, partners, directors or sponsors.

Nevertheless, only a month later Bauval issued a statement via Collins's web site inviting Appleby and 'a few key members of his Operation Team' to join him on a trip to Egypt![529] Yet again Bauval was indulging himself with another massive U-turn, and if his swift resumption of relations with his former foe was difficult to understand, it may have had something to do with the release of his latest book ... because *Secret Chamber: The Quest for the Hall of Records* was published in November 1999 – by Random House!

THIRTEEN

THE HUNTER

Larry Dean Hunter is one of the brightest minds of these last few decades. Born on May 11th, 1950 – a scientist, researcher, inventor and independent Egyptologist . . . In the village of Nazlet el-Samman, he has celebrity-like status. Walk with Larry down the streets and alleys of the village and you may hear that mantra 'Laaary . . . Laaary . . . Laaary' filling the air from the voices of people you pass by, including old women and young children. He receives this attention from his keen and compassionate ability to touch the lives of each and every person he meets.[530]

This is how Larry Hunter was described by a former colleague, Amargi Hillier, when he agreed in early 1998 to help him to publish his conspiracy and secret-chamber theories on the Internet. By August of the same year, Hillier was telling a very different story. So who is Larry Hunter, and what has he been up to at the Plateau in the last few decades? Is he an almost messianic figure, or yet another misguided self-publicist? Let us enter into his world of undercover investigations, politics and cover-ups to find out . . .

Revelations!

Hunter reports that he was formerly in the US Navy and was also involved in naval intelligence. He was trained in navigation techniques both ancient and modern, and one of his areas of interest in Egypt has been to re-evaluate Robert Bauval's 'broader' Orion Correlation theory, supposedly conducting a more accurate mapping using Global Positioning System (GPS) satellite technology to locate ancient underground sites at all of the correlation points – including the villages of Birak al-Khiyam, Ahmerah and Nazlet el-Batron.[531] As a preliminary to his conspiracy theories, he reveals that when he located these sites the locals would usually inform him that they had been visited by a 'Dr' somebody-or-other many years before. Although Bauval and Graham Hancock were apparently due to travel to Egypt with him sometime around 1995 to investigate his new theories and sites, he suggests with some disgust that they pulled out.

Another of his major theories, which is similar to those we dismissed in Part I, is that the Great Pyramid is a giant solar-powered energy generator, and he has even gone as far as to secure a patent for this technology.[532] As part of this research he has also supposedly studied the work of the 'pyramidiots' we reviewed earlier, in particular pyramid geometry and its relationship to the orbital characteristics of the Earth in the solar system. He even goes as far as to argue that a network of similar structures may have existed all over the ancient world – despite the fact that the true pyramid form appears to be almost exclusive to Egypt – and that they may have been used not only for energy generation but also to assist interplanetary and interstellar travel. In conjunction with this he suggests that the pyramid structures photographed near to the 'face' in the Cydonia region of Mars are probably equivalents, and that in investigating them NASA is covering up the fact that it has already confirmed these theories. Hmm . . .

This is useful background information for the two main topics we want to cover in this chapter. First, Hunter claims to have discovered a secret chamber in the Great Pyramid which has been covered up by the Egyptian authorities for many years. And second, and not entirely unrelated, he has investigated the cover-ups and corruption, and points the finger most vehemently at Zahi Hawass – even claiming that he is part of an 'antiquities mafia' that has been operating in Egypt for several decades, and that he was suspended at one point for antiquities fraud.

In the middle of all of this, Hunter became involved with Richard Hoagland in supporting Tom Danley's claim (which we mentioned briefly in Chapter 10) that 'clandestine tunnelling' was taking place in the Great Pyramid in attempts to get behind Gantenbrink's 'door'. However, this is a whole separate 'can of worms' which will be left for a later chapter.

The Hall of Osiris

Hunter's most sensational claim is that there exists in the Great Pyramid a secret chamber which, among other things, contains the body of Osiris – hence the 'Hall of Osiris'. He claims that he first became aware of this back in June 1979, when he was exploring the Subterranean Chamber and crawled to the end of the small tunnel that leads off it to the south. With no torch, as he crawled along in the darkness he made 'owl noises' in an attempt to bounce sound off the end of the tunnel so that he would not bump into it. But to his great surprise he found he was getting strange echoes, which he subsequently investigated by having an assistant bang the coffer in the King's Chamber. In his own words:[533]

> The sound does indeed come from the King's Chamber through unknown passageways and into an undiscovered and unopened chamber and through the roof at the end of the dead-end passage off the Subterranean Chamber . . .

Having apparently pieced together 'hundreds of testimonies from people who have entered in and worked in this secret chamber', Hunter provides the following details about the Hall of Osiris. He starts by revealing its history, suggesting that the authorities knew about it at the latest in the early 1970s, when Ahmed Kudry, the then director of the Giza Plateau, bored a horizontal tunnel about 12 feet (4 metres) up from the bottom of the Well Shaft, which heads to the south[534] for about 35 feet (11 metres). At the end it supposedly opens into the massive 250-foot (76 metres)-high secret chamber on its northern wall. As to how Kudry knew where to direct the tunnel, Hunter reveals that the chamber had in fact already been discovered even long before this:

> Kinneman and Petrie were known to have found a secret entrance to the Great Pyramid in the area near the cemetery in the village of Nazlet el-Samman. There are holes near the cemetery in this spot. In the southern-most hole, if you go down about 50 metres [165 feet], there are two doors. One door will lead all the way to the Great Pyramid and the other under the Sphinx . . . Then

in 1973 the antiquity people started to dig down from near the toilet of the pyramid director's office. From these rooms under the office, are passageways that lead under and into the Great Pyramid . . . The director then, Ahmed Kudry, later wanted to make an entrance to this room from inside the pyramid itself.

He also reveals that Hawass knew about the chamber at this time, since he was asked by Kudry to install a spiral staircase from the new tunnel down to the floor. Moving on to the details of the chamber itself, Hunter tells us that it is more or less square, so that its base diameter is about the same as its height, and that it lies between the King's Chamber above and the Subterranean Chamber with its small south passage below. In case you think this is amazing stuff, you ain't heard nothing yet! He continues that a huge shaft through the centre line of the edifice continues up through a gap in the ceiling of the chamber right through to the top of the pyramid and also down for *thousands* of feet from a gap in the floor.

For those of you who have not switched off already, we should perhaps point out a few purely practical problems with this scenario just to make sure you are on the ball. First, it would be a close call as to whether the Queen's Chamber would be somewhat in the way of this secret chamber; and, second, the possibility of such a huge chamber being able to support the weight of masonry above it is virtually nonexistent. Meanwhile, it is a little unclear exactly where the vertical shaft is supposed to emerge at the top of the pyramid.

But let us not allow such trivialities to distract us from this fascinating adventure. Hunter continues that there are massive columns stretching from floor to ceiling in each corner of the chamber, while in the south wall nine doors lead to tunnels which travel underground to connect the edifice with all the other ground counterparts of the Orion constellation. Furthermore the chamber and the rooms at the base of the vertical shaft contained 'ancient capacitors' which are linked to crystal technology, while at floor level on the east wall the biblical 'Ark of the Covenant', no less, lay secure at least until 1979; behind the Ark were written the names of those who 'were and are to control it' in hieroglyphs and Arabic, but apparently Hawass has either removed these names or covered them up. And we are not finished yet: 'Near the Ark was a body, however it was reported to be shrivelled up or not well preserved . . . The south wall has been described as "glowing", "coloured" or illuminated of its own accord . . . It was reported that robes were also found . . . containing glass disks sewn into them . . . [which] could only be made with fusion power. They were reported to have healing properties . . .' Meanwhile, the underground roadways that branch off from the chamber and the base of the vertical shaft are sometimes as much as 30 feet (9 metres) in diameter, and one travels a full 120 kilometres to the Fayum and is 'lined with 144,000 statues standing in a line supported with gold canes'! These roadways also house many doors and further chambers containing, presumably, more artefacts of various kinds.

Finally Hunter tells us that high up on the west wall of the chamber is a walkway, with five doors leading off to rooms on its south side, while the north side runs along behind the south wall of the King's Chamber (let us once again ignore the fact that, based on his own dimensions of 250 feet wide, this west wall itself may lie far to the west of the King's Chamber – depending on where on the north wall the access tunnel emerges, something we are not told). The middle door takes you down a corridor for 35 feet (11 metres) to a large room in which – unless it has been removed by irreverent fiends – a body lies 'sleeping' or 'getting stronger' on a central dais, surrounded by a 'light field' of some sort, and wearing a 'pinkish-coloured' robe bearing . . . the cartouche of Osiris! According to Hunter, this is what Danley's 'clandestine tunnel' is aiming for – and behind Gantenbrink's 'door' is a small chamber containing a small black basalt statue of Osiris holding a sacred *ankh* and staring through a small hole in the far wall, which in turn looks on to this larger chamber.

Hunter versus Hawass

In November 1988, while on one of his many trips to Egypt, Hunter attempted to inform the authorities of his 'discovery' and to obtain permission for official testing of his preliminary findings. Hawass appears to have been relatively offhand with him, and in a likely attempt to get rid of someone who was making a nuisance of himself he told Hunter to write a report for the authorities. This Hunter did, delivering a copy to Hawass, Farouk Hosney, the Minister of Culture, and to the Tourist Police. The eight-page report included details of acoustic tests supposedly performed in the presence of two Plateau inspectors who worked for Hawass, but was also relatively scathing about the latter's apparent indifference – which cannot have endeared Hunter to the people he was trying to win over, albeit that none of his later conspiracy theories were aired therein.[535]

Despite various confrontations with Hawass and others on the Plateau and in Hosney's office at this time, in which Hunter was supposedly verbally abused and threatened with arrest and deportation, Hawass subsequently agreed to go into the pyramid with him to investigate his claims. He tends to make a big deal of the fact that Hawass admitted that he had visited the Subterranean Chamber only once before, but given the exhausting crawl down the lengthy Descending Passage we do not find this particularly surprising. When he asked Hawass to crawl further down the 'south tunnel' with him, Hawass refused since he was not wearing rough clothes, and again Hunter makes a big deal of the fact that if he had read the report he would have known he needed to go down this tunnel – but again we find all this behaviour perfectly in keeping for a relatively senior and busy official. Meanwhile, Hunter returned to the pyramid shortly afterwards without official permission, and recorded the echoes from the King's Chamber at the end of the tunnel on tape and video.

Returning to Egypt a year later, Hunter – apparently blissfully unaware that the authorities have to put up with this sort of nonsense from cranks all the time – describes his rather self-important indignation when he discovered that no action had been taken about his report. He decided that something was amiss and to take revenge, since he was by now pretty certain that Hawass was up to no good and was covering things up.

His major piece of 'evidence' was the testimony of Ahmed Shire, a guard in the Sphinx enclosure, who apparently told him that on the afternoon of 7 February 1988 he saw several people from the Antiquities Department standing on the Sphinx's right shoulder just after a 700-pound (320-kilogram) chunk had fallen from that very part of the monument, while a crowbar lay ominously on the ground. Buoyed by apparently supporting rumours from the villagers of Nazlet – and despite the fact that this well-known event almost certainly occurred as a result of the continuing deterioration of the monument, as well as that any act of sabotage would hardly be conducted in the middle of the day – Hunter went to the Egyptian press, who gave the story front-page coverage. The implication was that Hawass had orchestrated the event to get Kudry fired, so that he could take over as director of the Plateau.

The antiquities mafia

Hunter's story then skips forward to early 1993, by which time he was convinced that the secret chamber had been known about by the authorities for some time. At this time the then head of the SCA, Dr Mohammed Bakr, was himself alleging that an 'antiquities mafia' had been in control for the last 20 years – and according to Hunter, threatening 21 possible felony charges against Hawass for stealing artefacts, including supposedly one statue that sold for $10 million and three other items which netted a total of $22 million. Hunter says that as a result Hawass 'fled' to the US, returning only once Bakr had been removed and replaced by Dr Nur El-Din several months later. The reality appears to be that Bakr *did* make these allegations about a 'mafia', but that in respect of Hawass a statue was stolen by persons unknown, and that as the man in charge he was forced to take the blame and was suspended, only to be subsequently reinstated by El-Din.

Meanwhile, Hunter links all of this in a rather confusing way to the problems over Gantenbrink's 'door', with allegations that Hawass and Bauval were colluding with Gantenbrink in secret and that the latter had no permit for his work. Since at this time Bauval was already starting to give the authorities a pretty hard time, the extent of double-dealing required to make this last aspect of Hunter's story hang together taxes even the sharpest brain. And in any case we also know from Gantenbrink himself that Hawass was suspended two days *before* his discovery of the 'door'.

We also find Hunter suggesting that the contents of the secret chamber were being smuggled out via the underground tunnel that passed underneath Hawass's toilet to an underground warehouse somewhere to the north of the Plateau. We are confidently informed that the Queen of England has one of the capacitors – although quite what she would do with it is unclear – and the Jet Propulsion Laboratories have several others!

Then we turn to the events of July 1997, when the police apparently raided many homes in the village of Nazlet in the middle of the night, while at around this time at least one house in the nearby village of El Koom Late, which was supposedly on top of one of the underground tunnels, was demolished. Unfortunately none of this is coherent enough for one to establish the argument Hunter is trying to derive from these events. However, we have had independent confirmation that ten officials from the Antiquities Service *were* suspended on the insistence of the Mayor of Giza after the house in El Koom Late – which was a protected building – was pulled down. It would appear that these officials uncovered some sort of antiquities recovery operation taking place at the house, and took immediate action; however, it is not clear that Hunter's allegation that they were themselves involved in the antiquities fraud stands up. Meanwhile, an *eleventh* official, supposedly Hawass, was apparently spared by intervention from a senior figure – although again the reason for this is unclear.

Although Hunter's previous accusations had mainly been confined to the local Egyptian arena, a press release issued by himself and Hillier in mid-1998, which was reproduced in a variety of places on the Internet, really opened up the debate. It suggested that at a meeting in March 1998 with an anonymous Egyptian government official they were informed of a document signed by a 'high' official which yet again suspended Hawass from his post as director of the Plateau, and ordered him to be transferred to a temporary position with the 'Sound and Light' show. The added implication was that Hawass was blatantly ignoring this edict.

In the new spirit of détente that they had by now fostered

with Hawass after the Alaska Cruise, and perhaps with Hunter's attacks on Bauval's Orion correlation and his role in the Gantenbrink affair in the back of their minds, John Anthony West and Graham Hancock were quick off the mark to counter this one. Their public statement, again posted to various places on the Internet on 17 May 1998, suggested that such rumours of the suspension of their new 'buddy' were complete rubbish, and that Hunter's postings were the 'Egyptological equivalent of [Internet] child pornography'. Although Hillier correctly thought their turn of phrase rather distasteful, it does convey the extreme contempt in which they held Hunter's allegations against Hawass – and as a refutation of the supposed suspension, it was probably correct.

Within this story we find the usual accusations that the cover-up is intended to prevent the truth about the real origins of man from coming out, that NASA are involved, and the hopeful lament that perhaps the secret chamber will be opened only by those with a true heart – this despite the accompanying allegations that the chamber had been known about by the 'dark side', who had been systematically pilfering and selling off its contents, for many years. Even Mark Lehner is not spared from Hunter's wrath, since as well as the usual innuendo regarding his about-turn away from Cayce's prophecies, we are informed:

> Before they [Hawass and Lehner] even went to Virginia Beach they had done work north of the Sphinx, a little to the east, where they had taken out several statues but officially reported only finding one. We know the man, a 13-year old boy at the time, in the village of Nazlet el-Samman that was lowered by a rope who saw these three statues and vase. Hawass told the boy not to mention the two other statues and the boy was instructed the same by Mark Lehner.

We have not met Lehner personally, but we find these allegations about a man whose only apparent 'crime' has been to change his mind about something as he learnt more and more about it particularly distasteful.

Seeing Sense

Although he was responsible for publishing most of the information we have presented above in a lengthy article under the title 'The Hall of Osiris' on his well-known *Amargiland* Internet web site, Amargi Hillier began to have doubts about Hunter very shortly after they teamed up together. As we indicated at the outset, by August 1998 when he issued a statement about the removal of this article from his site, he was indicating that he no longer wanted to work with Hunter: 'I do not support his work, his methods of investigation, his tactics, his morals or his motives.' He then went further in September in a public statement which we posted to our *EgyptNews* mailing list. We reproduce a lengthy extract from this below, because not only does it shed light on Hunter and his beliefs and methods, but is also, we believe, a brave attempt by a man we have met and spent time with to be honourable in the face of adversity, and to admit his mistakes; would that there were more like him:[536]

As many of you know, approximately 6 months ago I began to publish on the internet a series of news flashes which suggested that there was some sort of black-market mafia established within the Egyptian Antiquity department and the Egyptian government. Posted online were reports that suggested a suspension of Dr. Zahi Hawass, the current Undersecretary of State for the Giza Monuments. Soon following, was a rather long article entitled the 'Hall of Osiris', which I personally wrote, that attempted to detail this so-called corruption; labeled under the guise of an 'investigation'. However, the term 'investigation' was very misleading since, as an online journalist, I did not fully investigate the information that was published on my web site. Let me clarify the situation that took place.

I only acted as a writer for a person who claimed to have 'investigated' this so-called corruption for over 15 years. This person was Larry Hunter. Hunter had approached me to take a look at his 'facts' and asked if I would be interested in putting together the information and writing the data that would be released to the public. He approached me for three reasons: 1) My web site is widely popular with an extensive amount of worldwide viewers. 2) I was currently living in Cairo, Egypt. 3) Hunter felt I could handle the level of information he was suggesting. Being admittedly new to the scene, I was compelled with

Hunter's information . . . which was reinforced by the fact that Hunter has known many people in the village of Nazlet-el-Samman for almost 2 decades. In other words, I thought he had a case, so-to-speak; even I was hearing some of these stories from the mouths of villagers. So, in haste, I agreed to help him and we began to publish the information which you all remember appeared on the internet in the spring of 1998.

Publishing in haste was, without a doubt, a reflection of my inexperience in the matters concerning the Giza monuments and antiquities here in Egypt. Suggesting that this was an investigation was very misleading, as it was NOT investigated on my part. It was only the words and thoughts of Larry Hunter. Surprisingly early into this work, I began to see many red flags with the personality of Hunter. These began to plant seeds in my mind that perhaps his information was not credible. Larry Hunter began to tell me that he was the reincarnate of a very ancient Egyptian god; describing to me a time when he was in the Great Pyramid during a 'stellar alignment' when a 'force' passed through his body and spoke to him giving him a new name. That name was 'Osiris' . . .

It came to a point that I was feeling just too uncomfortable with the situation and really began to question the information he was putting forth about Dr. Zahi Hawass. People from all over the world were sending letters to my personal e-mail saying things like . . . 'if Hunter has been at this for almost 2 decades, where is the evidence?' It wasn't long after that I came to the same conclusion . . . there was and still is no evidence for what Hunter is suggesting.

In my heart, I ached with pain. Not for the dismissal of Hunter and his so-called investigation. On the contrary, cutting ties with Hunter was quite relieving. The support I received in Egypt and around the world was overwhelming after this decision. But the pain I felt was that I had unfairly accused a man, with serious allegations against him. That man was Dr. Zahi Hawass. It can be too easy to jump on the bandwagon of 'secret doings going on in the great pyramid', but it is much more difficult to use your mind to analyze data efficiently, separating truth from fallacy. How could I accuse a man of serious crimes without even investigating on my own?

As stated in one of my news flashes, Hawass had openly invited me to come and meet with him to discuss these issues. This was weeks before the release of the 'Hall of Osiris' article. Hawass, through a man named Ferganni Al-Komaty, invited me to come and sit with Dr. Zahi Hawass and enjoy a game of back-gammon and conversation, as well as full access to the closed Great Pyramid to search around for any and all signs of secret diggings or hidden rooms. Did I take Dr. Zahi Hawass up on his offer? No! I declined, and weeks later I released the article that suggested Dr. Zahi Hawass was a thief. Poor journalism I would say . . .

After a thorough and personal investigation into the claims made by Larry Hunter, I can now state without any doubt that Hunter's facts are wrong regarding Dr. Zahi Hawass and the Antiquity organization in Egypt. Hunter has absolutely no evidence for what he is suggesting and, from what I gather, is going to be suggesting on his new upcoming web site . . .

I witnessed him [Hunter] boast many times to several people about the vast riches he was going to make after he put together his video. He expected to sell it by appearing on the Art Bell radio show in America. He even told people here the details by calculating the dollar figures to them: Art Bell's total viewers with one percent purchase of a video at X dollars would make him such and such millions of dollars. This he stated many times to people who often live and raise a family on under a meager $100 dollars a month. This boasting does not reflect experience in this country.

Hunter was never afraid to say to me that he wanted Dr. Zahi Hawass dead so he could take charge of the pyramids . . . Art Bell finally asked Hunter to be on the show to discuss the serious allegations Hunter made against Dr. Zahi Hawass. Hunter declined as he told me he didn't have his video ready yet.

My more recent statement released in August, as well as per-sonal follow-up statements issued on various internet forums, reminded people that I wanted to have nothing to do with Larry Hunter and his 'investigation'. Now I can further add to that statement by saying I feel Hunter's sources are not credible, his facts are not factual and his investigation is unprofessional. Basically, what he is saying about Dr. Zahi Hawass is not true. I feel that Hunter is acting in retaliation to Dr. Zahi Hawass' refusal to let him to do research in the Great Pyramid, over ten years ago . . .

Dr. Hawass' feelings towards Larry Hunter is quite simple. Dr. Hawass is not bothered in the least by what Hunter is suggesting since the stories that Hunter hears from the villagers are just not factual. This reveals to me, a man that is working on more important things than to worry about an American man who thinks he is the reincarnated Osiris or the messiah who wants to take control of the pyramids. Larry Hunter has said to me many times in the past . . . 'The pyramids are mine, Amargi' . . .

With an inspector assisting, I personally climbed up the treacherous grotto in the currently closed Great Pyramid. Now I fully understood why this shaft is off limits to the public. It is a very dangerous climb and descent, and I myself even became extremely nervous as I got high into it . . . with my back and elbows harshly rubbing against the walls of this very narrow almost vertical shaft, my hands and feet grasping sweatily to the crumbling stone foot holdings, all the way up. After 5 meters [16 feet], it was very obvious there would be no way that anybody could secure enough footing or space to dig through solid rock. As my heart pounded wildly, I had already passed the area that Hunter suggested there was a gate to enter the secret passageway. Much to the inspector's concern for my safety, I continued on up for the sake of informing the worldwide public that there was absolutely no entrance to any secret room. This is exactly what I found inside the entire length of the grotto shaft: nothing. Nor did I expect to find anything. I will publish photographs of this area soon.

Larry Hunter has also suggested that a living body was found inside the Great Pyramid that was secretly removed within the last couple of years . . . What wasn't reported to you is that Hunter told me many times, that he had been told that the body looked like him . . . Larry Hunter has also openly told people in America and in Egypt that his name is inscribed upon the wall of the 'secret room' above the Ark of the Covenant, which he claims was found and removed. His name, according to Hunter, appears at the top of the list of 1,000 names of those who would be in charge of this Ark . . .

I respect the work of Dr. Zahi Hawass and what he is trying to do here. Perhaps, as a service to him, I can help tell the world exactly what is going on here so we can start to finally end these crazy rumors of 'secret diggings' and such.

Of course this 'treachery' did not go down well with Hunter and his supporters. Hunter suggests that Hillier has merely gone over to the 'dark side', especially since he has now been able to build some bridges with Zahi Hawass. But one consolation we can also take from all this is that, whatever else he may be, Hawass does in reality appear to be a very forgiving man.

Meanwhile, Hunter started his own Internet web site in late 1998, albeit that it is clearly still under development at the time of writing, and contains little of the detail of Hillier's original article as yet. However, the signs are that he has not changed his mind at all, and that in time all the same material will be regurgitated, although we do find him adding a new string to his bow in discussing the Hall of Records itself:[537]

> During my June [1998] trip, he [Ahmed Fayed] was well enough to accompany me to the piece of property he used to own and granted me permission to do an interview on video with him revealing the location of a temple that he and his father had unearthed in 1956; over 42 years ago . . . The 'Hall of Records' is covered by six feet of dirt west and north of the Sphinx, bearing 062 degrees from the right paw of the Sphinx.

Also reproduced on his site is an aerial photograph pinpointing the location of this 'temple', and it appears to be near the last building on the right in the parade of houses and shops to the northeast of the Sphinx, about 600 feet (180 metres) from the front of the monument. He further suggests that this Hall of Records is a 'library' to help us understand the technology of the pyramid, among other things. His ghostwriter on the site continues:

> Since the powers to be have kept the truth from humanity, Larry took it upon himself to exercise his own learning abilities and re-discovered many secrets of this ancient culture. By utilizing reverse engineering he has been able to see things no one else could see. The things written in the 'Hall of Records'. The knowledge is out. They can't stop it now. The word.

So it looks as if someone else has been taken in by 'the Hunter'. And, just to prove that some people never learn, another supporter has entered the fray. On his web site,[538] John Carlo reveals that in August 1998 he and his wife travelled to Giza where the villagers told him about everything going on with Hawass, corruption and so on. So he contacted Hunter and is now trying to organise a petition via the Internet to present to Hawass on his return to Egypt in June 1999 – as well as, for good measure, to the Egyptian Ambassador in Washington, the United Nations and the major media networks. Again we are treated to the usual Cayce and Hall of Records stuff, as well as – despite the obligatory protestations that 'love and truth must prevail' – the similarly routine vitriol against the authorities.

We are sure that he means well, but Carlo would do well to consider the views of a man like Hillier, who has spent more than just a few weeks in the village, and also to look behind the scenes before he jumps to the conclusion, as have so many before him, that it is up to him to save the world. We have heard all this talk from the villagers ourselves, and it is clear that many of them truly dislike Hawass. However, one must consider that some of them, as desperate as they are for tourist dollars, resent his rumoured plans to buy out their homes in order to build a traffic ring road around the Giza Plateau; and further that they are perfectly capable of using whatever tactics they see fit to exploit the gullibility of foreigners, as well as sometimes each other, in their efforts to get rid of him.

Unfortunately this saga shows no signs of abating. At the beginning of April 1999, a series of postings by Hunter, Hillier and various others to the *Giza* Internet mailing list, which is hosted by Carlo, revealed that the animosity between the two sides is as strong as ever, and arguably getting stronger.[539]

Conclusion

We have seen that at least some of the rumours of corruption in the Egyptian authorities put about by Hunter do appear to have some foundation in reality. However, his insistence on linking his corruption charges to rumours of secret chambers in the Great Pyramid and supposed clandestine tunnelling, all of which we know to be false, leaves us with little faith in his more detailed interpretation of events.

As a final example of his train of thought, Hunter has suggested that Jim Hurtak was able to 'raise' the Dream Stela between the paws of the Sphinx by chanting the '72 names of

God', and that he supposedly went rapid rafting under the Plateau:[540]

> I have heard that J.J. Hurtak went rapid rafting under the Giza Plateau. He reportedly showed a video of it to a group of people that attended a seminar of his in Australia.

Hurtak's response to this suggestion was highly revealing:[541]

> I think that Larry Hunter wants to put HIS OWN FACE on the face of The Sphinx! Personally, I cannot believe that Hunter has A SINGLE SHRED of credibility left with ANYONE!

And on that note, we will move on . . .

FOURTEEN

THE WATER SHAFT

We have already referred to the fact that, in recent years, the Water Shaft, which lies underneath the Second Pyramid's causeway, has received increasing attention from a variety of sources. So let us now devote ourselves to this saga, which shows little sign of abating (refer to Figure 33 for clarification of the layout of the shaft).

Early Days
When Zahi Hawass first started to speak publicly about the shaft in 1998, he often gave the impression that it represented a new discovery. However, as we will now see, this is far from the truth.

Hassan thwarted
We have already seen in Chapter 1 that the shaft was excavated in part by Selim Hassan in the 1930s. Frustratingly, despite the meticulous way in which Hassan documented his work in the multiple volumes of his *Excavations at Giza*, this work is hardly mentioned. Volume 5 does contain the following under the heading of 'Shafts Of The Saitic Period':[542]

> The most striking example of this type of shaft is that which was cut in the causeway of the Second Pyramid and discovered by me in our sixth season's work. Upon the surface of the causeway, they first built a platform in the shape of a mastaba, using stones taken from the ruins of the covered corridor of the causeway. In the centre of this superstructure they sank a shaft which passed through the roof and floor of the subway running under the causeway to a depth of about 9.00m [30 feet]. At the bottom of this shaft is a rectangular chamber, in the floor of the eastern [he in fact means *northern*] side of which is another shaft. This

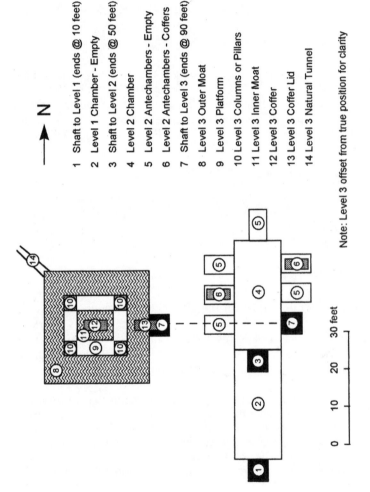

N

1 Shaft to Level 1 (ends @ 10 feet)
2 Level 1 Chamber - Empty
3 Shaft to Level 2 (ends @ 50 feet)
4 Level 2 Chamber
5 Level 2 Antechambers - Empty
6 Level 2 Antechambers - Coffers
7 Shaft to Level 3 (ends @ 90 feet)
8 Level 3 Outer Moat
9 Level 3 Platform
10 Level 3 Columns or Pillars
11 Level 3 Inner Moat
12 Level 3 Coffer
13 Level 3 Coffer Lid
14 Level 3 Natural Tunnel

Note: Level 3 offset from true position for clarity

0   10   20   30 feet

FIGURE 33: A SCHEMATIC DIAGRAM OF THE WATER SHAFT

descends about 14.00m [45 feet] and terminates in a spacious hall surrounded by seven burial chambers in each of which is a sarcophagus. Two of these sarcophagi, which are of basalt and are monolithic, are so enormous that at first we wondered if they contained the bodies of sacred bulls. In the eastern side of this hall is yet another shaft, about 10.00m [33 feet] deep, but unfortunately it is flooded. *Through the clear water we can see that it ends in a colonnaded hall, also having side chambers containing sarcophagi.* We tried in vain to pump out the water, but it seems that a spring must have broken through the rock, for continual daily pumping over a period of four years was unable to reduce the water level . . .

However, Nigel Skinner-Simpson, a fellow researcher to whom we are indebted for scouring Hassan's voluminous work to locate this description, unfortunately found that the volume that should have contained the details – that relating to his excavations during the 1934–5 season – made no mention of the shaft at all. Meanwhile, we ourselves were able to establish that an article headed 'SUBWAY FOUND BELOW THE PYRAMIDS', which appeared in the *Daily Telegraph* of 4 March 1935, also dealt with its discovery:

A subway connecting Khephren's Pyramid City to Cheops' Pyramid City has been discovered in the course of recent excavations. This had been cut through the living rock. More remarkable still, a shaft, 11 yards [33 feet] long, was found to lead from the subway to the heart of the rock. When examined, it was found to end in a chamber some 6 yards by 11 yards [18 by 33 feet]. From one side of it there was a second shaft leading 16 yards [48 feet] farther down into the rock and ending in a hall somewhat larger than the upper chamber, with seven smaller chambers leading from it. In two of these, basalt sarcophagi were found. From one of these side-chambers a third shaft runs down another 14 yards [42 feet] into the rock, *ending in a colonnaded hall, in which three more basalt sarcophagi were found.* So far, the bottom-most chamber, which is some 65 yards [195 feet – this is clearly a mistake] below the surface of the causeway, has not been investigated, as it is partly under water . . . The chambers are, according to Prof. Selim Hassan, the Egyptian excavator, of the Saitic period (about 600 B.C.).

At the time we were uncovering this information, these two descriptions seemed to fit pretty much what we were hearing from other sources – except for one detail: the *multiple* sarcophagi in the lowest-level chamber. The importance of this will become apparent later, but we were all desperate for more information. Skinner-Simpson had also revealed to us one other source, the one that fired his interest in the Water Shaft in the first place. This was H Spencer Lewis's *The Symbolic Prophecy of the Great Pyramid*, which, as we have already seen in Chapter 5, is unfortunately not the most reliable of sources. Nevertheless, in the appendix Lewis indicates that his information is based on an article by Hamilton M Wright, which appeared in the January 1935 edition of a 'magazine edited in Egypt and more or less privately published in London'.

Skinner-Simpson has exerted a great deal of energy in attempting to trace this unnamed publication – primarily because Lewis also suggests that the article includes original photographs taken by Wright with Hassan's permission – but unfortunately so far without success.[543] Meanwhile, we have in Lewis's work a quote from a Mr Mahmoud Derwish, who was in charge of part of the excavations, suggesting that the lowest-level chamber 'apparently contains a sarcophagus'; that is, only *one*.[544] Having appeared reasonably reliable up to this point, however, Lewis's account then appears to drift into a description of what he would *like* to have been discovered, rather than what actually *was* discovered:[545]

A description of the chambers and rooms beneath the sands connected by these secret passageways reveals that there were inner courts and outer courts and a Chapel of Offering cut into one of the huge rocks with three pillars in its centre. The three pillars representing a triangle are highly significant points in the study and analysis of the purpose of these underground chambers.

Another chamber, much like a burial chamber but undoubtedly a room of initiation and reception, was found at the end of a sloping passage, cut deep into the rock in the west side of the Chapel of Offering. In the centre of this chamber was another large sarcophagus of white Turah limestone, and there were examples of excellent alabaster vessels found in the chamber.

The walls are beautifully painted and sculpted with scenes and inscriptions and the Lotus flower is an important emblem in the pictures. Other chambers were discovered with pillars in the centre and in some of these were carved figures of a young woman in a beautiful gown, plainly indicating a ceremonial robe.

There are many magnificently carved figures in these various underground rooms and chapels, temples, and hallways, also many beautifully coloured friezes. In examining the *photographs* of some of these we are deeply impressed with the improved form of the art, showing the distinctive characteristics of the period that followed Amenhotep's mystical reawakening of Egypt.

The foregoing facts are just a few of the many contained in Dr. Hassan's latest report. They verify in part at least the things indicated on the two diagrams shown in this book [those taken from Randall-Stevens] . . .

Since he mentions photographs and Hassan's report, we can only assume that this account is not entirely made up. One possible explanation, hinted at by the term 'inner courts and outer courts', is that excavation work was taking place on the Sphinx Temple and perhaps also the Second Pyramid's mortuary temple at this time. Since Lewis repeatedly refers to the Second Pyramid's causeway as being 'subterranean' – which it was only to the extent that it had only recently been freed from the sand that covered it – this perhaps allowed him to justify to himself the use of considerable poetic licence in implying that all these temple chambers and passages are 'underground' and 'secret', thus bolstering his interpretation and reproduction of Randall-Stevens's diagrams of the initiation chambers beneath the Sphinx. All in all these latter elements are, in our view, best ignored – and certainly cannot relate to discoveries in the Water Shaft itself, the lowest level of which, as all the reports make quite clear, was underwater and could not properly be explored.

Lehner swims
Hassan was not the only person to enter the shaft prior to the mid-1990s. Joe Jahoda has been reported as saying that he saw the lowest level while he was at the Plateau with the Sphinx Exploration Project back in 1979, accompanied by Mark Lehner, and that the water level was higher than it is now.

Meanwhile, Hawass did report in his unpublished lecture to the ARE's annual convention in August 1998 that Lehner used to swim regularly in the lowest level of the shaft.

Furthermore, in the *Mysteries of the Pyramids* video produced in 1988 and hosted by Omar Sharif, Lehner is filmed at the lowest level alongside a 'shallow pool surrounding two deteriorating columns of stone, and remnants of a human skeleton half-buried in the rock. Lehner then pitches a pebble into the water and states that the point of impact marks the place where two shafts under the water go further still'.[546] Intriguingly, this clip was cut from a revised version of the video produced in 1994 – perhaps because by this time he had realised that speculation about additional shafts, whatever its original source, was unwise and unhelpful.

Hyping It Up!

Said speculates

In Chapter 10 we briefly referred to the fact that the Schor Foundation team entered and filmed the Water Shaft in February 1997. In his *Behind the Scenes* video, Boris Said recounts that he first entered it with a guide back in 1992,[547] and then again in November 1996 during the 'Danley' visit. He proceeds to recount the story of how two little boys were playing in the bottom of a well in 1946 when it caved in, and they fell into a 'room-like cavern' and on to a 'polished black granite sarcophagus lid'; apparently they looked around, and 'there was a tunnel also filled with sarcophagi'; he then suggests that, although scared out of their wits, the boys still took the time to cover over the lid and the tunnel with stones to hide them, while much later the chamber became flooded after the building of the Aswan Dam. Implying that it was the lowest level of the shaft into which they had tumbled, Said shows some footage taken at this time and emphasises a 'pile of rocks' on one side, but, although the footage is unclear and brief, he actually appears to be discussing what we now know to be the remnants of one of the 'columns' referred to by Hassan. In any case, this attempt to link what they found in the shaft to the 'boys' story' – the purpose of which is to sustain the possibility of additional tunnels, as we will see shortly – is doomed to failure, not least because Hassan makes it quite clear the lowest level was completely flooded only some twelve years before their supposed adventure.

The sequence of film and narration in this compilation of Said's is confusing because he then shows more footage, which purports to be from the same trip, in which the sarcophagus lid is found – but we are convinced that this did not occur until the following Schor Expedition in February 1997. It is also confusing in that the first clip commences with a mock-up in which the real location of the shaft under the Second Pyramid's causeway is clearly arrowed, while the second – in an apparent attempt to throw explorers off the scent and keep the location of the shaft a mystery – shows initial footage of the team entering what looks like Campbell's Tomb lower down the Plateau, before switching to the genuine interior.

Nevertheless, the second and longer clip, actually from February 1997, shows that the water level has dropped somewhat – revealing a square chamber cut from the bedrock, the central floor of which is covered in earth, boulders and general debris, while around the outside a 'moat' of water remains on all sides. It then homes in on the team scraping away the dirt on the floor in the entrance to this lowest level in an attempt to gain a level platform for their fixed TV camera, and uncovering the top of a dark granite sarcophagus lid in the process. There is one very important feature of this clip – it shows quite clearly that the lid is *in the entrance* and not in the centre of the chamber *when it is first discovered* hidden in the debris. This point was later confirmed to us by Jim Hurtak, who told us,[548] 'I have in my possession a picture taken by my wife of the sarcophagus lid as it was being uncovered. It is clearly not positioned over/on the sarcophagus . . .' The significance of this will become clear later.

Finally Said shows a third clip, again from this later visit, which has Thomas Dobecki performing a seismic survey on top of the sarcophagus lid.[549] Said reports that 9 feet (3 metres) underneath an 'anomalous cavity', perhaps as much as 8 feet (2.5 metres) wide and with a 'domed ceiling', descends at an angle of 25 degrees towards the Sphinx in the east; and further, somewhat inexplicably, that in their opinion it must be a 'man-made' feature because it is 'deeply dipping'. He also implies that it ties into the anomaly located 15 feet (4.5 metres) underground detected by Dobecki's seismic survey in April 1996 at the back end of the Sphinx enclosure, which we discussed in Chapter 10. Since much continues to be made of this apparent 'discovery', we will return to it later.

Referring back to his trip into the lowest level of the shaft with Said in November 1996, Danley makes the following observations:[550]

> ... at the far wall it [the water] was about 8 feet deep and while clear, had an Alkaline crust that irritates the skin. To the right is a large pile of stone that rises up out of the water to meet the ceiling. This (behind the pile of stones) was where the cave leading to the Sphinx was believed to be ... There are the remains of two pillars which probably held up the ceiling and there was a good deal of debris around, including human bones and shards of pottery. I also saw cracks leading from the floor/wall joint going out and sloped downward which suggested to me that the 'floor' was continuing to sink (like maybe there was another void below this room). Later, when the GPR was brought down, the actual tunnel was found under an 18 inch thick, black stone slab, under about a foot of dirt ... in fact if you were in the bottom you stood over it when you got off the ladder. It was WHEN the slab/void below it was discovered that the expedition 'fell apart' and Boris and Dr. Schor parted company and everyone was told not to talk about it. Boris then went on as many radio shows as possible to talk about the discovery and raise funds to go back (now that Dr. Schor was out of the picture).

We can see from this that Danley describes the remnants of the pillars or columns mentioned by Hassan as well as human bones, which supports Lehner's earlier observation, and also confirms the positioning of the sarcophagus lid in the entrance. And he ends by introducing the political angles which follow on from our observations in Chapter 10 about Said suggesting that Joe Schor's licence was revoked at around this time. The implication made by Said, Danley and others is that when Zahi Hawass found out about the discovery of the lid and the possible tunnel underneath it, he wanted to take over the whole show for himself. We have already seen that in fact Schor's licence was not revoked, and it would appear more likely that he was simply not that interested in the Water Shaft, preferring far more to concentrate on the supposed chamber under the front of the Sphinx. However, Hawass's subsequent actions do leave something to be desired, as we will see shortly.

Meanwhile, as Danley suggests and we discussed previously, Said did do his best to cause a furore – especially about the seismic-survey results and the supposed conspiracy of silence. He repeatedly broke the terms of his nondisclosure agreement by appearing on radio shows,[551] and publishing still photos captured from his film footage on his *Magical Eye* Internet web site – which incidentally closed down in late 1998, apparently because Said both lost his webmaster and was 'rapidly losing interest in Egypt'.[552] He has now turned his attention to ancient underwater structures in Okinawa and the Pacific Rim.

Hawass confuses

Since mid-1998 confused accounts of the Water Shaft have been emanating from Hawass. He gave it a brief mention in May 1998 at the 'Alaska Cruise' debate, suggesting that a sarcophagus, giant cavern and tunnels had been found underwater and that divers had to be used to conduct the preliminary investigation. Then at the ARE's annual convention in August 1998 he went into more detail. Although he studiously avoids any mention of Hassan's work, he does reveal that the shaft has been known about for some time, for example by Lehner, and describes the real location – that is with the entrance in the tunnel under the causeway. He goes on to discuss the second level, comparing the two huge sarcophagi, each estimated to weigh some 25 tonnes, to those in the Serapeum at Saqqara, and indicating that they found this chamber full of stones and debris, which included fragments of pottery and bone.

He then moves on to the enigmatic third or lowest level, and explains that having been told about the seismic survey under the lid he decided to hire contractors to pump out the water for fifteen days and then excavate the chamber properly. What was revealed was a water-filled 'depression' in the centre, containing a sarcophagus, which he does not describe in great detail, and surrounded by a rectangular platform on which stood the remains of *four* pillars, which would have once reached up to the ceiling, one in each corner. So far so good.

However, he then confuses the issue by making two apparently conflicting suggestions. First, he says that his first impression when he saw this level was 'this is what Herodotus saw' – he is of course referring to the latter's description of Khufu being buried on an island surrounded by water (see extracts in Chapter 2). But later on he suggests that the central rectangle is in the shape of the hieroglyph for *brw*, meaning 'place' or 'land', and that both during and after the New Kingdom the Plateau was called *brw Osiris neb Rostau* – in other words, the 'Land of Osiris, Lord of the Underground Tunnels'.

From this somewhat contrived logic, and a similarly contrived comparison with the Oseirion at Abydos, he deduces that the third level must represent the 'tomb of Osiris' (although, without mentioning it, he is probably also aware of the Greek inscriptions on the paws of the Sphinx, which suggest it is 'the guardian of the tomb of Osiris', as we saw in Chapter 1). Of course this cannot be both Khufu's burial place and symbolically that of Osiris, and in any case Hawass's own dating of the lowest level of the shaft to the New Kingdom or even the later Saite Period clearly precludes it from being associated in any direct way with Khufu – so we are forced to deduce that his emphasis on Herodotus was only his *first impression*. Nevertheless, these ongoing musings confused everyone enormously for some time: what on earth was Hawass going on about? However, at the end of his ARE speech he drops a clue:

> We are planning to take it up [the sarcophagus lid], take it out, and see what's inside that, what it could contain – a body, a symbolic object of the god Osiris?

Although this was clearly at odds with the evidence that the lid had been removed from the coffer long ago, Hawass went on to suggest that this operation would take place the following October. He further increased speculation levels by suggesting on his own Internet web site, *The Plateau*,[553] that he would present two lectures to the National Geographic Institute in early December 1998 at which more would be revealed – but, when the lectures were given, the shaft received not even a cursory mention.

Meanwhile, at the ARE convention he also describes a small-diameter 'tunnel' in one corner of the third-level chamber, which he says they tried to investigate by sending a small boy crawling into it. However, it narrowed to such an extent that even the boy could progress for only about 9 feet [3 metres]. This is the tunnel referred to by Danley above as 'the cave leading to the Sphinx', and Hawass further muses that it may have been dug by 'treasure hunters' in ancient times. We will see shortly how ridiculous both of these suggestions are.

Hunter attacks again

Of course, all this confusion was too much for Larry Hunter. Having apparently seen at least some of Said's film footage of the shaft, and desperate to attack Hawass on any issue he possibly could, he used the latter's apparent failure to mention previous excavations to suggest that he is a plagiarist – even christening him 'Zaki', although quite what this is supposed to mean escapes us.[554] And, just to make sure that, as usual, he confused the matter still further, Hunter opened his attack with the following:

> I have heard that J.J. Hurtak went rapid rafting under the Giza Plateau. He reportedly showed a video of it to a group of people that attended a seminar of his in Australia.

We have of course already seen Hurtak's response to this suggestion in the previous chapter, and to preserve everyone's sanity we will move swiftly on.

Time for Truth!

Of course all this speculation and excitement meant that the Water Shaft was a must for us on our research trip in the autumn of 1998 . . .

We go down!

As with our exploration of the Relieving Chambers, where we were lucky that the ladder at the top of the Grand Gallery was in place, we found that, although the entrance in the tunnel under the causeway was barred with an iron gate and railings, the bars at the top had been bent down just enough to squeeze over. We are not embarrassed to report this, nor do we consider it irresponsible, especially when we point out that of all the risks we took on the Plateau to bring out the truth this was by far the greatest. The gap at the top is some 8 or 9 feet off the ground, but only about 18 inches deep, with a steep drop down into the first shaft on the other side. Laden with cameras and flashlights as we were, this was not an easy or pleasant manoeuvre for six-foot-tall men, and we do not recommend it.

All was as we expected to find it on the first two levels, except we were somewhat disappointed to discover that the two huge sarcophagi on the second level, whose lids were slid to one side, appeared to have been used as rubbish bins by the workers – with baked-bean tins and other detritus scattered therein – while piles of charred human bones lay around on the floor (see Plates 43 and 44). The charring confused us somewhat, although we have been told that the grave robbers would sometimes burn any bodies they found in order that the spirits of the deceased could not attack them as they worked. Meanwhile, the first antechamber on the left was empty but contained two narrower depressions in the floor for smaller sarcophagi, while we were intrigued to find simple crosses which reached from floor to ceiling and wall to wall 'painted' on the back wall of each antechamber, using what appeared to be some form of red ochre.

Still, anxious to see the much-vaunted third level for ourselves, we climbed carefully down the ladder with only our flashlights to guide us, and at the bottom turned round to survey the scene. Danley and others have remarked on the amazing feeling engendered by this chamber, and we have to say that, with the light from the torches shimmering off the water around the edges on to the walls, our initial reaction was 'wow, this place is *really special*'. As we advanced towards the centre of the chamber, our breath was taken away by what we saw next.

The pictures that had been put into circulation by Said and others had shown the chamber before it had been excavated, but now we were confronted by something hardly anyone had seen before . . .

The water in the depression in the central platform did have a deposit of some sort floating on the top, which in our initial euphoria appeared like small flower petals but was clearly the 'alkaline crust' mentioned by Danley. But to our great surprise, given the excavation and clearing work that had taken place relatively recently, when this layer was moved to one side the water was absolutely crystal-clear underneath – as it was in the 'moat' around the edge. And there in the centre lay a light-coloured sarcophagus, perfect in every respect, with a rounded top end and slightly tapered sides (see Plate 47). It was let into the 'floor' to an unknown depth, and appeared extremely shallow inside – too shallow even for a human body, unless the lid was hollowed out. On reflection we realised that the light colour, which did not match the lid, may have been caused by a thin film of the alkaline deposit attaching itself to the granite, while there may also have been a layer of 'silt' on the inside – albeit that through the water the inner 'floor' of the sarcophagus looked pretty flat.

Finally prising ourselves away from this magnetic sight, we surveyed the rest of the chamber (see Plate 46). There were the remains of the four pillars, one at each corner of the platform, with matching protuberances from the ceiling, at least for the far pair – suggesting that these would have been carved from the bedrock as the chamber was created, but had been eroded to mere stumps over the years by the water. The lid remained partially buried in the entrance, although now supported at the front by wooden joists since the recent excavation had removed the stone and debris from underneath where it jutted out from the entrance into the chamber (see Plate 45). At the far side of the platform lay a basket containing bone fragments, although there was no sign of the skeleton mentioned by Lehner in the *Mysteries of the Pyramids* video – we must assume that this was taken away for analysis. And then we noticed the tunnel in the far right-hand corner, which both Hawass and Danley had mentioned.

A narrow plank of wood ran across the 'moat' from the central platform to the tunnel's entrance and, unstable as it was, one at a time we climbed across (see Plate 48). Although the entrance was about 3 feet in diameter, after only a few feet the tunnel became so narrow that we could go no further. Stretching in as far as we could with one arm, we took photographs which subsequently revealed a narrow and winding tunnel which can only be a *natural cavity* in the bedrock, carved out over time by water (see Plate 49). So much for Hawass's suggestion that it was carved by robbers – just how tiny does he think these ancient marauders were? Furthermore, Danley's suggestion that it headed in the direction of the Sphinx was revealed to be entirely false – it heads off from the far right-hand corner of the chamber, that is in a *northwesterly* direction, almost directly opposite to the orientation of the Sphinx, which lies due *east*. We also investigated several additional small cavities in especially the left-hand or south wall, but they were all revealed to be natural imperfections in the rock, which went back for no real distance.

How significant is it?

The most important issue we must resolve in attempting to gauge the real importance of the Water Shaft is its age. We have already seen that Hassan regards it as Saite Period, or 26th Dynasty, *c.* 600–550 BC, while Hawass presents conflicting reports about whether he agrees and regards one or both levels as Saite Period, or instead earlier New Kingdom creations of the Eighteenth Dynasty *c.* 1550 BC. For a while we were intrigued by the unusual shape of the coffer in the third level, which as we have indicated is clearly rounded at the end and tapered towards the bottom – a style with which we were not familiar, and which is certainly completely different from the huge parallel-sided sarcophagi in the second level. However, again Nigel Skinner-Simpson has researched the point thoroughly, and reported to us: 'I drew a picture of it for someone in the Dept. of Egyptian Antiquities, British Museum. He immediately identified the shape as dating from the 26th Dynasty'.[555] Such a late date does not fit well with tales of underground passage systems built for initiation rituals at the same time as the Sphinx.

Were there ever multiple sarcophagi in the third level, as suggested by Hassan and in the *Telegraph* report? It seems to us unlikely given the layout of the chamber, with its central depression allowing room for only one, and no antechambers. It is of course possible that Hassan, looking underwater, somehow saw the lid in the entrance as well as the coffer in the centre, and thereby concluded that there were at least two – although we would be surprised if all the debris that covered both items by the time of modern excavations was not present in his day too. As to when the lid was removed, clearly the shaft had been robbed in antiquity just like most of the others on the Plateau.

Turning to Dobecki's seismic survey and suggested passage heading in the direction of the Sphinx, there are several points to be made. First, we have seen that the late date of the shaft does not make such a connection very likely. Second, we have seen how unreliable such technology is on the Plateau anyway. Third, for the passage to head in the direction of the Sphinx to the east it would have to pass out of the chamber back in the direction of the entrance – in other words, we must ask how the survey was able to detect an anomaly that after only a few feet headed out under the bedrock wall. Or alternatively, have the team got their directions mixed up, as for example Danley had with the natural cavity in the corner of the chamber? Fourth, the Sphinx is some 825 feet (250 metres) away down the Plateau – a long way for an underground tunnel to travel. And, fifth, we must question whether in this particular instance the switch between the granite material of the lid and the more normally tested bedrock limestone underneath has not rendered the data unreliable. For example, the team mention a 'domed' shape: since we have seen that the coffer itself is quite shallow, and therefore that the lid is probably hollow, are they perhaps just picking up the change in material (albeit that this would make their estimate of the 'anomaly' being 9 feet down way too high)? All in all we think this 'discovery', like so many others using similar technology on the Plateau, is highly suspect.

Finally, let us turn to the water in the shaft. As we have

already seen, it is this above all that makes the third-level chamber have such an impact on observers, and also has invited comparisons with the Oseirion at Abydos. But we must ask ourselves whether these two edifices were originally constructed to have water-filled surrounds. The answer must surely be no. At the very least in the case of the Water Shaft we know that the level of the water has changed enormously only in the last half-century. Hassan found the third level full to the ceiling, while Said reported that in 1992 it was within 2 metres thereof, and in 1996 within 7 metres. Meanwhile, when the shaft was robbed probably not long after its construction, we can surmise that it must have been virtually or completely empty of water. Consequently we can assume that the 'symbolic' level we now see, whereby the coffer is just covered in the centre while the outer trenches form a 'moat', is pure chance – and in fact the result of Hawass's pumping operations.

All of this is somewhat at odds with the general consensus that the building of the Aswan Dam has raised the level of the underlying water table at the Plateau by some 8 metres, but presumably other factors – such as new irrigation and drainage systems near the Plateau – also have an effect.[556] It is also unclear just why Hassan's attempt to pump out the water failed while Hawass's succeeded, since the level has remained consistent since this operation – unless we put this down to more modern technology. We should also ask ourselves why the water remains crystal-clear. When we went in, the whole third-level chamber had been disrupted – rock and other debris had been disturbed as part of the excavation only a few months before, and we found that the remains of the columns, for example, were in very poor condition, crumbling away like a loose clay – and yet the water was perfectly clear. Despite the fact that the water was clearly not flowing, it was not stagnant either. When we also take into account that if the water had been artificially introduced it would just evaporate or leak through the bedrock floor over time, and that the level has altered up and down over time independent of pumping operations, we can only conclude that it must derive from the water table. This in turn strengthens our argument that, as boring as it is to dismiss such a wonderful visual effect, the water in the lowest level-chamber is not part of an original symbolic design.

This having been said, it is of course possible that the water in the 'moat' around the outside may hide additional tunnels lower down, although almost certainly not where Dobecki's survey suggested. Although when we went down the water was clear, it was not possible in the limited time available for us to examine all four sides in detail, and in any case there is still rubble and debris underwater, which could mask other features. When Skinner-Simpson visited the shaft with an inspector at about the same time, he was told that the authorities intended to make a further exploration of the 'moat', especially on the far or west side where it appears quite deep. However, once again, we are not holding our breath in anticipation that they will find something.

Above all we should remember that the whole Plateau is littered with similar shaft tombs dating to various dynastic eras, and, while some of these have yet to be properly explored, there is only one real conclusion to draw from the considerable weight of evidence: just like the pyramids themselves, they are all tombs.

Pulling in the Punters

Despite having satisfied ourselves that this shaft was not quite the amazing discovery everyone was suggesting, we were still intrigued by what Hawass might be up to. We were soon to find out . . .

Early in 1999 rumours started to circulate that Fox TV were going to stage some live openings of tombs on the Plateau, and that the Water Shaft may play a part. We then received intelligence from a fellow researcher who had been down the shaft since our visit that the authorities were preparing to put the lid *back on to* the sarcophagus in the third-level chamber. Had Hawass been using his Herodotus and 'tomb-of-Osiris' suggestions to hype up the punters for a major and totally artificial unveiling?

Eagerly we awaited the programme, which was due to be shown in the US on 2 March. We had a contact in the States ready with video recorder to rush us a copy as soon as it aired.

But come the day we found that Hawass had somewhat 'pulled his punch'. Initial reports indicated that the view inside the coffer was pretty poor, and nothing of any real interest was discussed. When we obtained our video copy, we went to work and found that these reports were true.

The programme, entitled *Opening the Lost Tombs – Live* and hosted by the US broadcaster Maury Povich, is long and involved. It opens with a raft of references to all the 'alternative favourites' – lost civilisations, alien visitors, Edgar Cayce, the Hall of Records, the Face on Mars, the 'helicopters' inscribed in the tomb of Seti I at Abydos, the Orion Correlation,[557] the Age of the Sphinx, Gantenbrink's 'door', and the 'pyramids-not-tombs' theory. It then spends about an hour and a half switching between West, Bauval, Hancock and Hoagland ruminating on their pet subjects. Interspersed in these interviews are two 'live openings': the first at the 'tomb of the unknown', although this is soon revealed to be that of Kai, one of Khufu's officials; and the second at one of the Third Pyramid's satellites. These turn out to be pretty damp squibs, with a few skeletons and one mummy coming to light in tunnels and chambers that have clearly been excavated and opened before the event by hard-working Egyptian labourers.

Finally we are taken down the Water Shaft. We are first treated to a graphic reconstruction of the various levels, which is in itself badly researched and wrong in that it shows the first-level chamber on an east–west instead of north–south axis, with the result that all the remaining chambers are rotated clockwise through 90 degrees. At the entrance, Hawass regales us once again with tales of Herodotus and Osiris – although the date 500 BC does slip out quietly – and insists that this is his 'greatest adventure ever'. We gloss over the second level, and then at the top of the last shaft he breathlessly announces that this will be 'one of the most amazing things you will ever see!' Finally we descend to the lowest level, where a team of workmen appear to have just lifted the lid off the sarcophagus using ropes, chains and pulleys suspended from the ceiling. Hawass gets the female presenter to measure its length – about 9 feet (3 metres) – and rambles on about its combined weight of some 11 to 12 tonnes, and how it would have been lowered down by filling the shaft with sand and then removing it. But we are given only the briefest of glimpses into the water underneath, and the coffer itself is hardly even visible! Meanwhile, although throughout the programme we have been treated to speculation about finding previously undisturbed mummies, the *contents of the sarcophagus are not mentioned at all*! It is as if they were irrelevant! *We* know it was empty, but what were the viewers supposed to think?

As he has several times previously in the programme, Hawass pauses at this point to counter the Cayce theories – although his brief refutations are hopelessly outweighed by the exposure given throughout the programme to the 'alternative team' drafted in for the occasion. However, he then turns to the 'tunnel' in the far right corner and says enigmatically, 'But to be fair, I did not excavate this tunnel yet, and really I don't know where it leads . . . but I always say that you never know what the sands and the tunnels of Egypt may hide . . .' Given what we said earlier about the clearly natural origin of this cavity, we feel that he should perhaps have confined his show-manship to his excellent impersonation of Charlie Chaplin when he got the television cables wrapped round his legs in Men-kaure's Queen's Pyramid, and nearly became one of his own mummies in the empty sarcophagus! The programme ends shortly afterwards with Povich ruminating once more about the Hall of Records and the chamber under the Sphinx's paws.

Why does Hawass cooperate with such nonsense? you might ask. When agreeing to work with Fox, he clearly had in mind Said's advice to him of several years previously: if you want to create another commercial success like the *Mystery of the Sphinx*, you need something extraordinary, like the discovery of a new tomb or the opening of a secret tunnel. So the answer is really very simple: Hawass is a considerable self-publicist, and believes that – for all his vehement opposition to the alter-native camp – such programmes increase tourist revenue. We might also ask why he made such a huge fuss over the *Mystery of the Sphinx* and then several years later happily cooperated with this similar production? Perhaps again the answer is simple: this time round it was his show, and it would be the Plateau's coffers that received the money from it.

However, it is clear to us that Hawass's 'duality' of serious Egyptologist and one-man PR machine, while perhaps essential to his role as director of the Plateau, undoubtedly leads to confusion, which he does little to minimise – and continues to foster unhelpful conspiracy theories instead of damping them down.

FIFTEEN

TUNNEL TALK

Let us now turn our attention to three of the most publicised rumours of 'clandestine tunnelling', all which have also been used by members of the alternative camp to further accusations of conspiracy and cover-up against the authorities on the Plateau.

Danley's Tunnel

We saw in Chapter 10 that when Tom Danley was performing his acoustic experiments in the King's and Relieving Chambers, as part of the Schor Expedition in November 1996, he supposedly came across evidence of a clandestine tunnelling operation.

Hoagland and Hunter reveal all

This issue was first brought to the attention of the public by Richard Hoagland, who posted a report on his *Enterprise Mission* Internet web site in June 1997, which contained the following extracts:[558]

> . . . a member of the Schor Expedition approached the Enterprise Mission a few weeks ago, and offered to publicly reveal several crucial details of what has been occurring 'behind the scenes' on the Plateau. This individual had become convinced, over the increasingly interminable 'delays' and 'excuses' issuing from key authorities in Egypt, that it was the intent of some members of the Egyptian government NOT to reveal these exciting new archaeological discoveries, brought to light by Schor's investigation – ever – but to 'sit on them' . . . indefinitely. By offering to make certain details public – including actual video and instrumental readings substantiating these heretofore hidden new discoveries – this individual hoped to inform *other* members of the government of Egypt of the apparent 'agendas' of some . . . to

create sufficient *public political pressure* to bring this intolerable situation 'to a head' . . .

. . . revealed in our conversations was the unmistakable possibility of a 'hidden excavation' proceeding for the last several months *inside* the Great Pyramid itself!

The time line for this activity – 'none' in April, 1996; the initial beginnings of a 'clandestine tunnel,' above the King's Chamber itself, actually videoed by Schor's party, in November, 1996; and the introduction of a (literally!) 'hot' new power cable to these upper chambers, extending upward from the famed 'Grand Gallery,' in February, 1997 – left little doubt that someone was secretly driving a new tunnel deep into the Pyramid. There also seemed only one objective for such elaborate and obviously clandestine tunneling activity: The so-called 'Isis Chamber' (so-termed by us) – hidden behind the now-infamous 'Gantenbrink Door' . . .

. . . according to our careful analysis of Schor's on-site witness – 'someone' was apparently physically attempting – by digging a clandestine tunnel toward the hidden chamber from above the King's Chamber to do just that – *without* the rest of the world finding out about it!

The report continues by saying that Hoagland asked Larry Hunter to investigate further – describing him as 'a colleague, and independent researcher with almost 20 years of detailed, on-the-ground experience in Egypt'. Hunter was due to travel to Giza shortly after the story first broke, and he came back with a series of supposedly 'dramatic, highly revealing' photographs which showed evidence of: 'fresh snow drifts of highly powdered limestone, covering almost all available surfaces within the Pyramid'; 'the presence of the new power cable'; 'burlap bags of *freshly-tunneled limestone rocks* – just sitting on the Great Step'; and 'a *fraying rope* – dangling provocatively over the edge of the Davison tunnel far above'. In addition, the report indicates that:

Before leaving Cairo . . . Mr. Hunter deposited copies of this evidence with the appropriate military and civil authorities in Cairo, officially charged with overseeing the archaeological well-being of the Giza Plateau, and its crucial monuments. In particular, Larry left copies of all the photographs displayed with this article with Mr. Mohammed Sherdy – Assistant Managing

Editor of 'El Wafd' ('The People'), a leading Cairo daily news-paper. Mr. Sherdy, in turn, promised a 'full investigation' of this compelling evidence of 'clandestine tunneling' inside the Great Pyramid . . .

These claims were given significant publicity when Hoagland and Hunter appeared together on *The Art Bell Show* in the same month, with Bell himself supporting them vociferously.[559]

Danley fills in the gaps

Along with many others we decided that this was strong stuff, and managed to establish that the anonymous Schor team member was indeed Danley, who apart from anything else was intensely frustrated at not being able to reveal the findings of his acoustic research to the world at large. In August 1997 we contacted him for more details, and he replied as follows (note that his account is slightly confusing in that he numbers the chambers with the King's as *one*, Davison's as *two*, and so on):[560]

Perhaps I can shed a little light on the tunneling, at least based on what I saw when I was there . . . While placing the [acoustic] sensor in the second level [Davison's Chamber], I noticed the entrance to a tunnel into the wall to the left of the entrance which if I recall correctly was identified . . . as one of several old 'robbers tunnels'.

While waiting for the film crew to setup, I turned on my head lamp and crawled into it. It was small, just big enough to crawl into on your hands and knees, it immediately turned right and followed along the granite wall . . . After about 8–10 feet, I reached the point where the original work stopped, and after crossing a very small 'room' it continued and looked like new work. This went for perhaps another 25–30 feet in the same direction (parallel to and just outside of the granite wall of the second chamber). The digging was being done by hand, using the typical pointed chisel hammers that are commonly used there to work limestone. The conditions the people, whoever they were, worked in were terrible, just crawling on one's hands and knees once, raises a major cloud of dust and made my miner's cap light seem like a laser beam in the darkness.

In the third chamber [Wellington's], there were many burlap

bags of stone chips (from the work on the second chamber), all heaped against the wall just around the corner of the entrance. Also a large number of plastic water bottles were in the pile of trash next to the bags of stone. There was no sign of any recent work being done on any of the other chambers although I thought I saw a 'room' through a large crack in the wall of the fifth chamber [presumably Lady Arbuthnot's if he is being consistent] but when the film crew sent the fiber optic camera in, it was just a long row (more than 40 feet, the length of the fiber optic) of big stones with the lower corners broken off.

Regarding the digging, I mentioned the tunnel and bags of tailings to our 'escort', an inspector at Giza and he asked for a map, which I drew for him. The next day he went up to see for himself and then reported it to his boss (which he had said he was a little reluctant to do) . . .

While we did have to run several cables into the upper chambers, none were 'power' and none were permanent. There is a . . . handhold rope that is anchored to the floor about 1.5 feet inside the tunnel in the wall . . . you grab this rope to help climb over the end of the ladder and into the tunnel . . . I wish I could tell more about what I saw and did and discovered in the Pyramid, but right now I can't due to a non disclosure agreement.

So what Danley was suggesting was that Caviglia's original tunnel off Davison's Chamber, which we described in Chapter 1, was being extended. Hoagland and Hunter's 'careful analysis' had then interpreted this as heading to the 'Isis' chamber, which they postulated lay behind Gantenbrink's 'door'.

Even without the benefit of our own exciting, risky and 'clandestine' first-hand exploration of this tunnel in the autumn of 1998, which we describe in the Introduction, it is clear that this analysis should have raised alarm bells. For example, anyone who takes the trouble to examine proper reports or diagrams of Caviglia's original tunnel would realise what Danley himself indicated to us – that after the right-hand turn the tunnel runs along behind and parallel to the south wall of Davison's Chamber. Since Danley also makes it clear that the supposed 'extension' continues in the 'same direction', it is clearly heading *west* – not to the *south*, where it would need to head if it were going to meet up with the end of the southern Queen's Chamber shaft. In fact Hoagland and Hunter are clearly aware of this while they are speaking on *The Art Bell Show*, but the observation is passed off with 'it would be easy to branch off to the south'. Meanwhile, the logic of quite why the 'tunnellers' would spend so much time taking the tunnel a total of *60 feet* – as they suggest in this interview – in the *wrong* direction, when they still had of the order of 100 feet to travel south, is quite beyond us.

We go in!
Notwithstanding this, we still felt the issue needed to be resolved once and for all. We wanted to see this extension with our own eyes. What we found revealed that these reports, put about with such self-importance by Hoagland and Hunter and the many others who followed their lead, were not just a trifle misleading. Two and two had been put together to make considerably in excess of four, but so certain were they of their 'careful analysis' that the vitriol directed at the authorities, and Zahi Hawass in particular, was enough to make even those who think that he is not exactly perfect wince and feel sorry for him. So what is the real truth?

First, we compared the tunnelling we saw with diagrams of Caviglia's original tunnel made by Vyse's assistant, John Perring, in his own study called *The Pyramids of Gizeh* (see Figure 34). It is quite clear to us that they are one and the same. Danley suggests that after the right-hand turn in the tunnel, which takes it round behind the granite blocks of the south wall, he crawled for something like 10 feet (3 metres) before reaching what he describes as a 'very small room'. This is more or less correct, except the 'room' is an area where the tunnel, which is only about 3 feet 6 inches (1 metre) in diameter, has been suddenly extended downward and upward, so it is possible to stand up. It has also been extended for several feet to the left, i.e. the south, and again in front, i.e. to the west. In fact this front extension is in two parts – a lower section and an upper section. But what it *does not do* is extend forward for anything more than a few feet (see Plates 39 and 40).

Quite how Danley thought that it had been *recently* extended for another 25 to 30 feet (8 to 9 metres) is quite beyond us. All

461

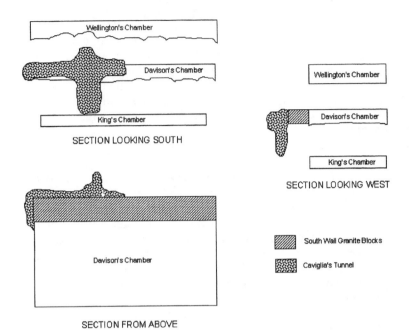

FIGURE 34: PERRING'S MAPS OF CAVIGLIA'S TUNNEL[561]

we can suggest is that it is extremely hot and claustrophobic in the tunnel, making a prolonged stay unpleasant. We ourselves were limited for time anyway, but spent ten to fifteen minutes each taking photographs and making notes which we could then compare – there was far too little room for both of us to be in there at the same time, even if we had not both been overweight! In any case it was uncomfortable work, which would leave the fittest person sweating profusely, let alone us.

Furthermore, if at that time there was a great deal of dust in the passage as Danley describes, which when disturbed made his miner's light 'like a laser beam in the darkness', this cannot have helped his view. When we were in there there was no dust (we will reveal why shortly), and our powerful torches allowed a detailed close-up examination of the walls at the end of the passage – which not only revealed that they did not extend any

462

further than a few feet, but also that the chiselled surfaces did not look fresh, and had no 'inconsistencies' that could have concealed a new extension. As for the extra 20 to 25 feet (6 to 8 metres) added by Hoagland and Hunter – well, clearly they felt in need of a bit of extra length.

Second, the burlap bags seen by Danley in Wellington's Chamber were still there when we examined it (see Plate 41). We think it is highly likely that both these, and those observed by Hunter on the Great Step, contained debris from Vyse's original blasting of the tunnel to access the upper Relieving Chambers, which the authorities had presumably at last decided to clear up. That in Wellington's Chamber would have been accumulated from therein and the chambers above it, the rest cleared out completely. It is also appropriate to ask why on earth the 'tunnellers' would take the trouble to carry bags of chippings *up* to the next chamber, when it would be easier to leave them in Davison's or take them right outside. Meanwhile, since both Danley and Hunter report extensive dust everywhere, we can only assume that this clearing-up operation was being carried out in 1996–7, and that by the time of our exploration in late 1998 it had all been swept away or settled.

Third, the 'power' cables mentioned were almost certainly used to light the Relieving Chambers; this would have been required both for the debris-clearing operation just described, and also for the detailed photographic study of the 'quarry marks' carried out by Hawass, which we have tied down to a date of November or December 1996. In any case, we are tempted to ask why power cables would be required for anything other than lighting if, as Danley suggests, the 'tunnellers' were using only chisel-hammers.

Fourth, although rather irrelevant, it is amusing that Hoagland and Hunter describe the 'dangling rope' hanging into the Grand Gallery as the method by which the bags were lowered, yet Danley clearly indicates that the purpose of this short and frayed rope was to assist the awkward process of entering the access tunnel to Davison's Chamber. It had 'frayed' away completely by the time we entered the passage, which made our attempts to negotiate the step off the unstable ladder and into the narrow passage rather scary at 30 feet above the unforgiving blocks of the Grand Gallery floor – although at the same time comical, each of us suggesting that the other looked like a 'beached whale' trying to wriggle back into the water!

We also went into the three remaining Relieving Chambers above Wellington's, aided by a series of rickety iron or wood ladders which certainly help rather than hinder. They were all free of debris, and nothing untoward was to be seen. It is also worth noting that everywhere in the main chambers and passages of the Great Pyramid was evidence that genuine restoration work was in progress, including the remortaring of joints, filling in of cracks and treatment of the limestone blocks. All this pointed to the fact that the edifice had been closed to the public for over a year for exactly the reason Hawass claimed – for much needed repairs, and to give it a rest from the relentless onslaught of tourists.

Cox's Tunnel

At the end of March 1998 Simon Cox, a British freelance researcher who studied Egyptology at University College in London, was giving a tour of the Giza Plateau to the authors Clive Prince and Lynn Picknett, who were on their first visit to Egypt. The day before the Great Pyramid was due to close for a long period of restoration, they took the opportunity to explore its interior. Making their way from the Grand Gallery to the King's Chamber, Cox suddenly saw something unusual that he had not noticed in his prior visits – a locked metal grille that protected the entrance to a winding tunnel heading off roughly in a northwesterly direction.

A few weeks later on 18 April the *Daily Mail* published an article headed 'EGYPT IS HIDING MAJOR FIND AT THE GREAT PYRAMID, SAY BRITISH EXPERTS: WILL THIS TUNNEL LEAD US TO THE TREASURE OF THE PHARAOH?' The article begins:

> British researchers claim the 'discovery of the century' has been made at the Great Pyramid of Giza. The team believes the Egyptian authorities are carrying out secret excavations on a tunnel which may lead to three previously unknown chambers. They say they have taken video footage inside the pyramid which backs up their claim. The day after they did their filming, the authorities

closed the pyramid for an eight-month 'renovation project'. The team claims this is simply a cover for the excavation. 'It is the discovery of the century' Simon Cox, one of the researchers said yesterday. 'This find could solve the greatest mystery of all time. The scale of it is just amazing.'

The article then suggests these chambers might represent 'treasure troves full of gold coins or just empty rooms', and a graphical illustration shows them high up in the body of the Pyramid. It continues:

He [Cox] came across a metal grille in a wall inside the antechamber leading to the King's Chamber. 'I'd never seen it before,' explained Mr. Cox 'The grille was rusty but the mortar holding it to the wall was new' . . . Electric cables ran along the ceiling, indicating that lighting or machinery was being used. Because filming is forbidden the team used a hidden video camera to record their find. Sources have since told them workers found the tunnel using sonar equipment then discovered the three new chambers . . .

'It is no coincidence the pyramid has closed down now,' said Mr. Cox. 'It gives them an opportunity to explore these new areas without anyone knowing.'

On his return from Egypt Cox gave private viewings of his video evidence to friends and colleagues – including to Chris and another researcher, Jeff Brown, during a meeting in the South of England. Let us allow Chris to describe what took place in his own words:

In early April 1998 Simon, Jeff and myself met up for a meeting at Jeff's home to discuss a trip to Egypt. Simon had just returned from his latest visit and claimed to have video footage backing up his belief that a new tunnel had been excavated in the Great Pyramid from somewhere near the King's Chamber. Jeff put the tape in the video player and we sat back to watch. The lighting in the Great Pyramid wasn't very good, but you could see Simon at a grille which was apparently on the right side of the passage leading to the King's Antechamber. There was a distinct humming noise which sounded like a fan, a bit like the one in the King's Chamber itself, but quieter. In the video the Egyptian guide turns to Simon and says 'ventilation', while his reply sounds something like 'ventilation my ass' – I think we can safely assume he did not agree with the guide. That was it really – nothing spectacular. Simon mentioned that he had been in the pyramid many times and had not noticed this grille earlier. I was certainly no expert having only visited the pyramid briefly twice before. But I could not see how an excavator could move tonnes of rubbish past such a publicly accessible area without anyone noticing it. The video showed very little and I did not think much more about it, until a few days later when the *Mail* article was published. To say the least I was quite surprised Simon's story had made it into a top daily newspaper!

Following the *Mail*'s lead we posted the story over our *EgyptNews* mailing list, and almost immediately received the following reply from the researcher Chris Dunn:

> In February, 1995, while participating in a documentary with Graham Hancock and Robert Bauval, I noticed that there was no padlock on this gate, that is located in the west wall of the passage leading from the Grand Gallery to the Antechamber. And I was able to crawl along the passage with my flashlight/torch. I found that the passage led to the northern shaft and then veered to the right and followed the shaft for about ten feet where it terminated with the same kind of fan that is installed in the mouth of the southern shaft in the King's Chamber. (These fans, as I understand it, were installed by Rudolf Gantenbrink.) The cable running along the ceiling of the passage was there simply to power the fan.

Checking the story further, we received confirmation from Rudolf Gantenbrink that this is exactly where he placed the second of his fans, as we discussed in an earlier chapter. As well as sending us a photograph of the tunnel ending in a wall with the fan inset, he explained that this tunnel was another dug by Caviglia in the 1820s during his attempt to trace the course of the northern King's Chamber shaft – which we described in Chapter 1. So in fact there was no clandestine tunnel, and no cover-up. Not only had Cox clearly failed to gain access to the tunnel proper in order to substantiate such publicly aired claims, but he also failed to research the issue with any 'real' authority who would have known about Gantenbrink's work – and even then the sound of the fan, being the same as that in the King's Chamber, should have provided a clue.

Cox was quick to realise his mistake, and on the day following the appearance of the article asked us to publish his 'retraction' over *EgyptNews*. It suggested that he had been misquoted – especially on the issue of the 'treasure' – but as the following extract indicates it was perhaps not as full and complete a retraction as it should have been:

> The whole point of the report was obviously not to highlight some previously known tunnel, it was to highlight the fact that possible workings are going on within the fabric of the Great Pyramid. *I myself can confirm that within Davison's Chamber the old workings of Caviglia seem to have been re-opened on the south granite wall* and also that as of last month, there seem to be fresh activity in the subterranean chamber. I intended to highlight these facts and also to ask the question as to why this 'tunnel' near the King's Chamber, seems to appear intermittently by this I mean that the metal grille is sometimes there and is sometimes not.

Caught up in the rumour mill, and with Richard Hoagland and Larry Hunter's reports of Caviglia's other tunnel still unrebutted, Cox clearly still supported the general suggestion of clandestine tunneling and could not let the conspiracy accusation drop. Yet again this saga demonstrates how, like a computer virus, the fever of conspiracy spreads to amateur and professional researcher alike – burrowing its way into the brain and bypassing intellect and reason, only to emerge reinforced not only on the Internet but even on the pages of a national daily newspaper. In truth, we ourselves had not dismissed *all* of these claims at that time either. However, we did know that a lot of badly researched rubbish was being given a great deal of publicity, and resolved to try to rectify the problem by investigating the origins of the rumours first-hand. The rest, as they say, is history.

The Sphinx's Rump

In the general atmosphere of mistrust that has dominated the mid-to-late 1990s, the other clandestine tunnel that everyone has been discussing is the one in the Sphinx's rump (see Plate 42). Given Zahi Hawass's supposedly joking announcement in Boris Said's *Secret Chamber* promo that 'nobody really knows what is inside this tunnel', which we discussed in Chapter 10, and all the talk of chambers under the Sphinx and underground passages connecting them to the Water Shaft, this is perhaps hardly surprising.

We have already seen in Chapter 6 that Baraize had entered the 'rump tunnel' in the 1920s and found nothing, and similarly that Hawass and Mark Lehner had reopened and explored it in the early 1980s. This is how the former described what they found:[562]

> One part of the passage winds down under the Sphinx before it comes to a dead end about 4.5 meters [15 feet] below floor level. The other part would be an open trench in the upward curve of the rump except that it is covered by the layers of ancient restoration stones. In 1980–81, we found that the lower part did indeed come to the water table, and just above this point the debris contained modern items – glass, cement, tin foil – evidence that Baraize had cleared and refilled the bottom of the passage before he sealed the opening by his restoration of the outer layer of masonry 'skin'. The passage is crudely cut, its sides are not straight, but there are cup-shaped footholds along the sides. It looks like an exploratory shaft.

However, the confusion over this issue was not helped by the *Mysteries of the Pyramids* video produced in 1988, in which Lehner is seen crawling inside the entrance to the tunnel and once inside climbing down, then up, then down again, etc. The editing allows one to believe that in fact this could be quite a substantial passage, perhaps winding deep into or under the body of the Sphinx.

We decided to check it out with an independent source, someone we knew had been able to gain access to this tunnel in recent years. Although this person has understandably asked to remain anonymous, since the authorities are rightly extremely protective of the Sphinx and its enclosure, more so than any other part of the Plateau, we showed them the footage and asked them to comment on how it compared to what Hawass had described and they had seen. Their response was unwavering: *all three were consistent.* The Lehner footage merely swaps repeatedly between the downward and upward sections of the tunnel. The only differences that our source could detect were, first, that the water table has receded in recent years, or at least was not present at the base of the shaft at the time they went in – which leaves no room for lingering doubts that something else might have been under the water; and, second, that the 'roof' of the upper section had been concreted over, and was rather poorly supported by wooden beams when they surveyed it.

It remains unclear whether this shaft was excavated as a tomb in Dynastic times, or is a later exploration. But, whichever is the case, there is almost certainly no secret tunnel that connects with other passages or chambers. It is, literally and figuratively, another dead end.

In an interesting aside, our source also revealed that they had been inside a small chamber behind Thutmose IV's Dream Stela, which lies between the paws of the monument. Apparently this is very small, no more than 4 or 5 feet (1 to 1.5 metres) in diameter, and is accessed by dropping down through a small hole in the ceiling, which is normally covered by an iron trapdoor. Not only is it empty, but it leads nowhere. Above all our source was able to inspect the back of the base of the Dream Stela from within this chamber, and revealed – in case there was ever any doubt – that Larry Hunter's suggestion that Jim Hurtak had somehow been able to 'raise' it was absolute nonsense. It is firmly embedded at its base, and clearly has been ever since it was erected.

Conclusion

These are just three of the more celebrated rumours of clandestine tunneling which we have been able to investigate closely, and can reveal to be completely unfounded. This is in addition to the information we have already reviewed suggesting it is unlikely that there is any man-made chamber under the Sphinx's paws, any extra tunnels leading off the Water Shaft, or even, arguably, anything of any interest behind Gantenbrink's 'door'. There are many, many more rumours and stories we could relate, usually originating from locals who like a good story, and subsequently propagated with almost religious fervour by gullible or self-promoting so-called 'researchers', but frankly they would not be worth the paper they were written on.

During our most recent research trip, on our first night in Nazlet we sat with a charming local man who had trailed us all round the Plateau into 'secret tombs' which no one was allowed to visit, while we attempted to quiz him about access to the Water Shaft. Hot and thirsty, we were delighted to be taken to his humble home to drink beer, and feast on chicken and bread cooked expertly by his wife, and eaten off a tray on the floor while his pet pigeons pecked courageously away with us. The discussion in broken English was most convivial, and ended with excited drawings on scraps of paper of a 'secret chamber' buried deep beneath the Great Pyramid. The meal was well salted, but the story needed to be taken with more than just a pinch!

In our view all of these rumours have a rational explanation which has little to do with conspiracies and cover-ups, and a great deal to do with poor-quality research, misinterpretation, suspicion and self-promotion. It is time this nonsense came to an end, and energies were focused on more serious and pressing issues – unless of course one takes the view that it is all rather amusing and part of life's rich tapestry. Which, on balance, we do not.

CHAPTER

SIXTEEN

Epilogue

Since this work was originally published, there have been various developments worthy of mention which, broadly speaking, can be split into two categories. First, we have engaged in a number of discussions regarding the various theories analysed in Parts I and II. Second, the 'show' goes on, and a number of important political and explorational aspects have unfolded further. We will deal with each of these in turn.

Moving the Debate Forwards

Our original research for this work led us to conclude that most of the alternative theories about the age, purpose and construction of the Pyramids, about the age of the Sphinx, about the Orion correlation, about Gantenbrink's 'door', and about secret chambers and tunnels in and under the various edifices of the Plateau, were deeply flawed. Broadly speaking this is still our position. However, a number of constructive ongoing discussions with fellow researchers have led us to modify the details of some of our analysis. (These extensive discussions can be followed in full by visiting our *Giza: The Truth Discussion Site.*[563]) Since this is exactly what constructive debate and ongoing research should achieve, we are happy to present these developments.

A Reader Writes . . .

By far the most revealing new piece of research to come to our attention is that of British geological engineer, Colin Reader, on the age of the Sphinx. He sent us his paper *Khufu Knew the Sphinx* shortly after this work was originally published, and it was immediately apparent to us that he had some new ideas which deserve serious consideration.[564] Unlike John Anthony West and Robert Schoch, whose theories we examined in

Chapter 7, he does not attempt to push the age back by more than a few hundred years – in fact only to the early dynastic period *c.* 2800BC – and he also makes a considerable effort to fit his revised chronology into the proper archaeological context of Giza as a whole.

Two primary pieces of evidence exist that Reader suggests force us to consider a pre-Fourth Dynasty date for the monument, neither of which, as far as we are aware, have been properly elucidated elsewhere. The first forms the basis for his refutation of Lal Gauri's chemical-weathering hypothesis which we previously supported. He draws our attention to the *distribution* of weathering patterns between the western Sphinx enclosure wall and the rump of the monument itself, indicating that, whereas there is significant widening and rounding of the *vertical* joints in the enclosure wall, there is little evidence of this in the rump. We questioned whether these joints – which were originally sub-surface geological fault lines – really do continue into the body of the monument at all, but Reader provided us with evidence from one of Gauri's own papers that they do.[565] Since the strata to which we are referring are the same in both locations, and there is only approximately twenty metres distance between the wall and the rump, and because chemical weathering primarily depends on air temperature and humidity, he contends that some other weathering agent *must* be responsible for the differentiated patterns observed on the enclosure wall – and that that agent is surface water run-off.

Reader's second observation concerns the quarry used by Khufu's builders as the main source of limestone for the Great Pyramid. It is clear from Figure 35 that this quarry eventually occupied almost all the space between the Second Pyramid and the Sphinx enclosure, albeit that there is a suggestion that it was extended to the west during Khafre's reign. It is also clear that, once used, this quarry would have been back-filled with limestone chips and other debris from the construction process. Reader suggests that, as soon as this quarry was excavated and even once it had been back-filled, it would have all but eradicated the ability of rain water to run-off from the previously extensive catchment area to the west of the Sphinx enclosure. This is because, for surface run-off to occur, the rate of rainfall

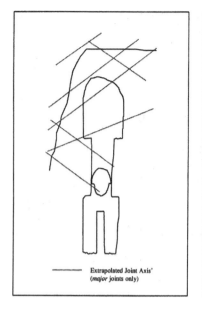 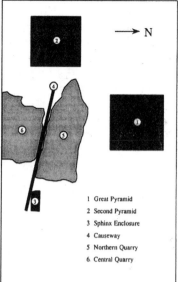

1 Great Pyramid
2 Second Pyramid
3 Sphinx Enclosure
4 Causeway
5 Northern Quarry
6 Central Quarry

Extrapolated Joint Axis'
(*major* joints only)

FIGURE 35: THE JOINTS IN THE SPHINX ENCLOSURE, AND
THE KHUFU AND KHAFRE QUARRIES[566]

must exceed the rate at which the surface and immediate sub-surface can absorbe it, and sporadic but heavy rainfall *prior* to the quarrying would have quickly exceeded the ability of the original limestone bedrock to absorbe it. By contrast, the rainfall would have to be far more intense to achieve run-off over the significantly more permeable in-fill of chippings and wind-blown sand *after* quarrying and back-fill had taken place. Even then, run-off would only occur if the various fills reached the original level of the limestone across all parts of the quarry – otherwise the run-off would be halted by the eastern quarry wall, or at least by some form of ascent out of the dip created by the only partial back-filling of the quarry. He suggests that just such a dip does form part of the post-quarry topography.[567]

Reader goes on to argue that his case is strengthened by a close analysis of the north enclosure wall. He points out that there is a significant and clear break between the weathered

473

surface of the bulk of this wall and the vertical and non-weath-ered portion that lies at its eastern end – in fact, that portion which has been quarried immediately adjacent to the north wall of the Sphinx Temple. He further points out that, whilst there is no doubt that the bulk of this temple is contemporary with the carving of the Sphinx, because the blocks can be matched with the appropriate strata in the Sphinx enclosure, there is room for doubt about the source of the blocks for the Valley Temple (with which assertion we now agree, and have amended the wording in Chapter 7 accordingly). Whilst we have pre-viously argued strongly against any attempt to suggest a two-stage construction for the Valley Temple, and continue to so do, Reader's suggestion of a two-stage construction for the Sphinx Temple should not be dismissed lightly. He argues that a smaller version was constructed at the time the Sphinx was carved, which was then extended to the north and south during the Fourth Dynasty – hence the relatively unweathered 'new' enclosure wall to the north.

To complete his analysis, he suggests that a portion of the Second Pyramid's mortuary temple may also have been orig-inally constructed along with the Sphinx and Sphinx Temple, only to be extended later, and that the two 'proto-temples' formed the eastern and western elements of a complex clearly designed in early or even pre-dynastic times as part of a solar cult. This would explain why it was Khaf-*re*, not Khufu, who extended these existing structures and incorporated them into his pyramid complex – as part of the re-emergence of the solar cult. He backs up his assertions by listing a number of pieces of archaeological evidence for activity at Giza from as early as the late pre-dynastic period.

Although we await further research by Reader, we find his arguments reasonably persuasive. Accordingly the age of the Sphinx remains, in our view, an open question. But while we now accept that there may be reason to question Gauri's chemical-weathering hypothesis, his redating is significantly less than that proposed by Schoch, let alone that of West, and involves pushing the age back by no more than *c.* 300 years. This is primarily based on respect for the archaeological context and, as a result, requires assumptions about the ability of the heavier rainfall pre-2350BC, and especially pre-Khufu, to effect sufficient weathering. In our view this is a more reasonable approach than Schoch's use of seismic surveys to suggest a much older date, while West's attempts to push the date back even further have no contextual or logical grounding other than the readings of Edgar Cayce and Bauval's astronomical 'lock' on 10,500BC (see below).[568]

Our original support for the orthodox position on the age of the Sphinx, as still described in Chapter 7, received heavy criticism from West himself, much of it unfortunately of a personal rather than theoretical nature. However, we have had considerable constructive debate with a number of the key researchers in this area, which has resulted in a number of new papers by ourselves, Schoch, Reader, geologist James Harrell and David Billington being made available through our web site. In our view, this has all helped to move the debate forwards.

The Sphinx Enclosure

Our view of the extent to which the age of the Sphinx remains an open question has been reinforced by more recent research that we have conducted regarding the periods for which it has been buried in sand. In Chapter 7 we saw that the consensus view is that it has been in this state for approximately two-thirds of its orthodox 4500-year existence. We also saw that, based on the evidence of the Dream Stele between the paws, Thutmose IV's supposed clearance of the enclosure *c.* 1400BC is thought to represent the first time this had taken place since its construction. Yet in fact there is little within the text of the stele to justify this assumption, because the relevant line simply states: 'The sands of the Sanctuary, [Setepet] upon which I am, have reached me.' This is by no means a clear indication of the volume of sand within the enclosure, and one could equally argue that there was only a relatively small buildup around the base. Moreover, further careful study of other New Kingdom iconography and texts strongly suggests to us that the Sphinx was free of sand long before Thutmose's restoration. Indeed, it may even be that the monument only became truly buried during Egypt's Christian or early-Islamic period in the middle of the first millennium.[569] This fresh analysis could significantly extend the time period available for weathering to occur – both from water run-off resulting from the flash floods that, as we have seen, still occur in the modern 'arid' period, and from further chemical action on the originally water-weathered channels.

To close this subject, a number of the key researchers into the age of the Sphinx are now in constructive communication, and we can only hope that at some point a cross-disciplinary team will be allowed to submit a proposal to conduct further much-needed research on site. Such a proposal would receive our whole-hearted support.

Orion Recorrelated?

Another area in which we have engaged in extensive post-publication debate via our web site is in respect of the Orion correlation theory (see Chapter 9), and there are two major areas of discussion. The first involves criticisms that Robert Bauval has made concerning our comments on the 10,500BC dating. We used SkyGlobe to derive the angles of the belt stars in the different epochs, as presented in Figure 32 (in fact we have updated these figures slightly having re-checked our measurements), since this was the software used by Bauval himself when he wrote *The Orion Mystery*. However, he points out that this software fails to take into account such complex astronomical factors as proper motion, nutation, aberration and refraction, merely accounting for precession. To establish these figures properly, he asked Professor Mary Bruck, a former lecturer in astronomy at Edinburgh University, to calculate them. Her results indicate that the angle formed by the line running through Al Nitak and Al Nilam at culmination in 10,500BC was between 40 and 43 degrees from the horizontal, the variation being dependent on whether or not nutation was allowed for in the calculations. Bauval's assertion that this is pretty close to the required 45-degree angle is a fair one.

One is entitled to ask how he thought the angle was 45 degrees using SkyGlobe when he originally presented his theory. The answer is that the 'lock' on the 10,500BC date was always much less the precise angle of the belt stars, and much more the facts that, at this date, firstly the constellation of Orion was at its lowest point in the precessional cycle (which we cannot dispute), and secondly that, at the *exact* point of the sunrise on the vernal equinox of that epoch, not only did the constellation of Leo provide the backdrop in the east but Orion was also exactly at its point of culmination in the southern sky. (The emphasis on these latter points is somewhat underplayed in Bauval's previous work, which is where the confusion arose for us, and we are sure for a great many other people.[570]) However, even *if* this latter assertion is true, and we have not had the time to obtain the appropriate software to check it, it is clearly an astronomical 'coincidence'. Although we accept that the Ancients read much into such events, this one is undoubtedly rendered less symbolic if the Sphinx was not there at this time – which we do not believe it was.

However, there are far more fundamental issues at stake than the supposed date correlation. The other significant area of discussion on the site has focussed on our two *main* criticisms that we believe completely undermine the basic Orion Correlation theory. These are included in Chapter 9, but in outline they are: first, the massive differential between the size of the Third Pyramid and that of Mintaka relative to their earthly and celestial counterparts; second, the significant evidence for major replanning of the Second and Third Pyramids, in terms of size and possibly also location.[571] Both of these detract from the fundamental hypothesis of a correlation in the ground plan to such an extent that the dating issues become irrelevant.

Further constructive discussions with a number of other key researchers regarding this theory, including Egyptologist Kate Spence, astronomers Ed Krupp and Tony Fairall, and John Legon, can be found on our web site.[572]

Dunn's Determination

We have also engaged in a spirited discussion with Chris Dunn about 'advanced machining' (see Chapter 4).[573] Having read our report of John Reid and Harry Brownlee's inspection of Drill Core No. 7, which suggested that it did not exhibit *spiral* striations, Dunn flew to London to inspect the core for himself. His report came up with two important new findings.[574] First, although on initial inspection he thought that Reid and

Brownlee must be right, he still decided to check for spirals by wrapping a length of thread around the apparently random and unconnected striations. He found that the groove varied in depth as it circled the core, and at some points there was just a faint scratch, difficult to see with the naked eye. Nevertheless, he suggests that he *did* find spiral striations – although not a single spiral with a pitch of .100 inches as described by Petrie, but two intertwined spirals of similar pitch.

We had already suggested that, even *if* spiral striations were found, they could easily be the result of the drill bit being *withdrawn* from the workpiece, thus telling us nothing about the feed rate of the drill. Prior to his report, Dunn had also accepted this possibility. However, during his visit, he measured the depth of the grooves at up to .005 inches, and now suggests that there would be insufficient lateral force to create such deep grooves when the bit was merely being withdrawn.

At the time of writing we have been unable to substantiate whether or not these new elements of Dunn's analysis are sound. However, he had previously maintained that the primary aspect which made him consider ultrasound was the fact that the quartz was cut deeper than the surrounding feldspar, but in correspondence it is clear that he accepts Brownlee's suggestion that this may have been caused by ripping. Since his report adds nothing definitive on this subject, it remains unclear exactly what conclusions he draws from his new analysis, and indeed whether or not he believes it reinforces his suggestion that ultrasound was employed.

Meanwhile our attention has also been drawn to two other important sources which argue that conventional drilling methods were employed by the ancient Egyptians. The first is a book originally published in 1930, by Somers Clarke and R. Englebach, entitled *Ancient Egyptian Construction and Architecture*. Although we have not yet been able to obtain a copy, we are informed that it contains an Egyptian illustration of a weighted drill being used, and mentions evidence of tubular bits. The second is a series of highly enlightening experiments performed by Denys Stocks of Manchester University, in which he uses wet sand as a grinding slurry, that have produced granite drill cores with striations appearing highly similar to those on No. 7.[575]

Above all, the practical experimentation already performed by Stocks, and planned by Reid and Brownlee, is more likely to resolve the issues than any amount of theoretical speculation. Nevertheless, this is probably a debate which is set to run and run . . .

Acoustic Anomalies
Another update on the theory front concerns ongoing research into acoustics, which we briefly mentioned in Chapter 4. David Elkington, Paul Ellson and John Reid have now published their detailed findings in *In the Name of the Gods* (Green Man Press, 2001) and although we cannot go into details here they are well worth examining.[576]

Sonic Levitation?
The final theory update concerns our previous suggestion in Chapter 4 that we could not provide a logical explanation as to how the 200-tonne megaliths were raised up into the walls of various of the temples. Reader once again has an important contribution to make, and in a paper specially prepared for our web site he demonstrates, using detailed calculations of thrust and stability, that a sand ramp *would* be able to support such huge blocks during construction. Moreover, another correspondent, George Forrest, has suggested that the logic behind using such huge blocks was their stability in the earthquake conditions that we know affected the Plateau to some extent in the past. So perhaps this is another enigma that has now been solved.

The Show Must Go On

Gantenbrink's Door
Original plans to 'open Gantenbrink's door' during the millennial celebrations were shifted to January 2000 long before the event itself. Then, in early 1999, Zahi Hawass announced that the project would not proceed before May 2000, and would be a co-operative venture with the National Geographic Society.

In mid-1999 he again confirmed that the expedition would take place sometime during the spring of 2000, but it is no great surprise that it has never come to fruition. Nor have the prospects improved over time, because in April 2001 Hawass was interviewed about any new proposals, to which he replied: 'We hope soon that some people will come . . . I'm not in a hurry'.[577] Clearly the saga of the opening of the 'door' and the further exploration of the northern shaft goes on and on, and we can only hope that sooner or later the authorities will prove us wrong by waking up to the importance of exploring them both.[578]

Schor to Return?

We saw, in Chapter 10, that the Schor Foundation failed to prove the reliability of ground-penetrating radar and bore-scope camera technology in locating possible man-made cavities beneath the Plateau during their Autumn 1998 expedition. Everyone thought that this was their last chance, but Hawass announced, in August 1999, that he would give them one 'last' chance to prove Cayce's claims of a Hall of Records hidden beneath the Plateau. This expedition was due to take place during November or December 1999, but some 18 months later it too has failed to materialise. We finally had the pleasure of meeting up with Joe Schor personally in London in February 2001, and he confirmed that he is still persevering with his plans and now has access to some state-of-the-art three-dimensional radar equipment. Unfortunately, seemingly as a result of the Egyptian authorities' continued caution over the possible political repercussions of such expeditions, his team has still not been given the full green light to leave for Giza.

Even if they do finally make it, will they ever find anything? Given all the evidence we have presented already about natural cavities and the unreliability of the technology, let alone the limited likelihood that a physical Hall of Records exists at Giza, we very much doubt it. But, once again, we would be delighted to be proved wrong.

More Secret Chambers

In Chapter 6 we mentioned Gilles Dormion's 1986 'Operation Kheops'. In 2000 he and a joint French and Egyptian team discovered previously unknown tunnels and chambers in the pyramid at Meidum, and he has now proposed a new project to drill in the Great Pyramid and use fibre-optic technology in an attempt to locate similar hidden chambers. However, he still uses GPR to pinpoint his target, which as we have seen can be misleading.[579]

However, more recent suggestions by British researcher Mark Foster, details of which can be found on our web site, could perhaps provide him with the most appropriate target for his drilling. We have not previously mentioned that there are a set of passages about 90 metres to the east of the Great Pyramid, just north of its original causeway, and that Flinders Petrie was the first to draw attention to the fact that they appear to represent a copy of the Descending and Ascending Passages. As Foster points out, it would hardly serve any purpose to dig these 'trial passages' out of the bedrock as a learning exercise for the real ones that are positioned largely in the superstructure – so what are they for? He emphasises that they include another *vertical* passage rising from the intersection of the two main ones, and arguably this is a clue as to where Dormion should concentrate his efforts.

A Final Word

Although we have been somewhat scathing about a number of people in this book, because we believe they merit some degree of criticism, it should be clear that we have only done this when we question their motives. Those with whom we disagree purely on an intellectual level we hope have received somewhat kinder treatment. Nor have we allowed our views to be biased by personal acquaintance, for there are some who have been criticised even though, for example, they may have helped us with our research. It gave us no pleasure to do this, and we realise that we leave ourselves open, in a few cases, to accusations of being disingenuous, but in our view this is the price one must pay for being entirely honest and open-handed in one's treatment of the facts.

Above all, it is in no sense *our* right to act as judge and jury on people's actions. Instead you, the readers, will make up your own minds about the ins and outs, whys and wherefors, and rights and wrongs of the tangled web of politics and intrigue which we have laid before you in this book. So should, indeed *must*, it be.

Since the book was originally published, we have been accused repeatedly of uncritically accepting the orthodox standpoint. In fact, the truth is that, like so many others, we were in danger of uncritically accepting the *alternative* standpoint before we conducted the detailed research on which this work is based. We hope that we have redressed the balance somewhat so that readers have the chance to consider *both* sides of the arguments, and make up their own minds accordingly. Although we feel we have been able to rationalise many of the 'enigmas' of the Plateau within an orthodox context, in no sense do we feel that all of the magic and excitement of Giza and its incredible monuments is removed as a result. Almost certainly the ancient Egyptians did have an advanced understanding of acoustics which was coupled with an esoteric world view of breathtaking wisdom and complexity. As long as we devote our attention to those issues that remain genuinely unexplained, there is *plenty* of truth still waiting to be discovered . . .

Were the Giza Pyramids Covered in
Hieroglyphs?

We made a brief mention of this possibility in Chapter 1, based on the descriptions of the Great and Second Pyramids' casing provided by Latif early in the thirteenth century.

Initially Latif's observations seemed exciting. We wondered whether anyone had tried to find any of the original casing blocks from the Great Pyramid, for example in the Grand Mosque of Sultan Hasan, which was built in 1356, supposedly almost entirely using these blocks.[580] Could these reveal anything about the true mysteries of the edifices and their builders? However, on sober reflection, we began to accept the conventional wisdom that no other report from antiquity suggests that the exterior of the Great Pyramid, or any of the others, was inscribed. We then concluded that Latif observed and exaggerated the type of graffiti that has been left by tourists on attractions throughout the ages – and there is no doubt that, despite the lack of cheap air travel, Giza was as essential an element of the well-travelled tourist's agenda in antiquity as it is now, especially in Roman times.

Nevertheless we remained puzzled as to quite why such graffiti would have been 'unintelligible' to him. We then uncovered the comments on this matter made by a scholar called De Sacy, who appears to have been a contemporary of Vyse. While commenting on Latif's account, he makes the following observations:[581]

> The weight of his testimony is also increased by the words of Abd Allatif in some lines further on, wherein, speaking of the traditions which existed relative to the destination and origin of the pyramids, he says, 'I have written at length upon the subject in my great work, and I have related what others have said of these buildings: I refer those of my readers to that work, therefore, who are desirous of further details. I confine myself here to give an account of what I myself have seen.'

I have said that many other Arabian writers before Abd Allatif agreed with him respecting hieroglyphical inscriptions on the Pyramids, I will now quote some of them. Masoudi, an author who flourished in the beginning of the fourth century of the Hegra [*c.* ninth century], and who wrote in Egypt, says, 'The Pyramids are buildings of immense height, and of wonderful construction; the surfaces are covered with inscriptions, written in the characters of ancient nations and kingdoms which no longer exist. What this writing is, and what it signifies, are not known.'

Ebn-Khordadbeh, a traveller, and author of *A Geographical Description of the Mahometan Countries*, written in the third century of the Hegra [*c.* eighth century], in a passage quoted by Makrizi, thus expresses himself, 'All the mysteries of magic, and all the recipes of the medical art, are written upon these Pyramids in Musnad characters.'

Makrizi also quotes from another writer: 'We have seen the surfaces of the two Great Pyramids covered with writings from the top to the bottom. The lines were close, and well inscribed opposite each other. They were written in the characters that were in use among those, who constructed the buildings, the letters are now unknown, and the sense cannot be discovered.'

Ebn Haukal, a traveller and writer of the fourth century of the Hegra [*c.* ninth century], states also, that the exterior faces of the Great Pyramids were covered with writing, in characters, which he calls Greek-Syriac (if there is no mistake in the manuscript of his work, belonging to the Library at Leghorn, and which I have now before me). But, according to the passage quoted by Makrizi from Ebn Haukal, the characters were Greek.

William de Baldensel, who travelled in the Holy Land and in Egypt in the beginning of the fourteenth century, asserts, that he saw, upon the two Great Pyramids, inscriptions in various characters . . .

It must be at the same time confessed, that, according to the accounts of various travellers the highest part of the revetment of the Second Pyramid, which is still to be seen, is without any hieroglyphical writings. This, however, only proves that the whole of the entire surfaces were not covered with them. It is also said, that no remains of hieroglyphics whatever are to be found, either upon the numerous fragments which are scattered about the base of the Pyramids, or upon any of the pieces of granite or marble which formerly made part of their revetment, and which are to this day to be found at Gizeh and elsewhere, where they serve for lintels, thresholds, and door-posts; but it may be doubted whether this fact has ever been satisfactorily ascertained, which after all affords only a negative argument.

So Latif's account was clearly not uncorroborated! Meanwhile, the argument regarding the lack of inscriptions on the remaining casing at the top of the Second Pyramid does not seem sound to us, since it might be reasonable to expect such inscriptions to occupy the lower courses of the edifice. As for the relatively small number of other *known* fragments that survive from both edifices, and are still in place, in the Cairo Museum, or elsewhere, we agree with De Sacy's observation that the lack of inscriptions thereon does not merit throwing out the possibility altogether. Furthermore, we do know that, apart from Herodotus's descriptions of the inscription of the rations required by the builders on the Great Pryamid, Diodorus records that Menkaure's name was inscribed on the north face of the Third – although such inscriptions would hardly represent the revelation of deep mysteries.

However, if we are to stand by our comments about *context*, the fact that the significant quantity of casing that remains intact on the Bent Pyramid bears no inscriptions must count against the general possibility of their existing on other edifices. Furthermore, we have seen that Greaves, whom we regard as a highly scholarly and observant man, surveyed the Giza Pyramids closely and – while he appears to indicate that the casing on the Second and Third Pyramids was still substantially intact – does not make any mention of inscriptions. One possible explanation for this is that during the intervening centuries they may have become progressively worn away by continued weathering from wind and sand – and this suggestion is perhaps supported by the dates of the various accounts, in that we have a number from the eighth and ninth centuries, but only Latif from the early thirteenth and de Baldensel from the early fourteenth. Or perhaps they were eradicated by locals in a fit of religious fervour. In either case, it would appear that if they did exist they were more likely to have been painted on than inscribed with chisels, which probably increases the likelihood of their not being original inscriptions. All in all, then, another enigma that remains unresolved.

As an aside, Edwards discusses the possibility that the pyramids were originally red-painted, like the Sphinx.[582] Chemical analysis performed by A Pachan on casing fragments from the Great and Second Pyramids apparently revealed non-natural chemical elements, which he deduced were the remnants of such a covering, but others have argued that this is only a natural ageing effect, which is also responsible for their patina. Perhaps conclusively, the hieroglyph consistently employed to represent a pyramid in inscriptions from Old Kingdom mastabas consists of a predominantly *white* structure, with a thin red base (hence the red granite at the base of the Second and Third Pyramids), and a blue or yellow capstone (signifying grey granite or a gold overlay respectively).

Appendix II

More on the Pyramids-as-Tombs Debate

We indicated in Chapter 3 that there are a number of arguments which the alternative camp uses to counter the pyramids-as-tombs theory. Let us now examine each in turn.

Looting Evidence?

How much physical evidence of looting remains? The answer is vast – so vast that with the exception of the special factors surrounding the Great Pyramid (which we have considered separately), it cannot be seriously disputed. It starts with the pre- and Early-Dynastic mastaba tombs, and one of these even now has the ancient robbers' wooden mallet wedged under the lid of its coffer. Arguably it was precisely because Djoser was aware of the widespread looting of his predecessors' tombs that he had Imhotep come up with a larger-scale and more ingenious solution – and this same factor was the motivation for the rapid advance in the sophistication of pyramid building that ensued.

As for the early pyramids themselves, we have already noted that Vyse and Perring comment extensively on the amalgam of rubbish and debris from broken sealing blocks and portcullises which the latter encountered when he entered the pre-Giza pyramids. In particular, Perring found late-style hieroglyphs near the entrances to the Bent Pyramid, which suggested that it had been robbed at least while such writing was still in use,[583] while we have also seen that he encountered massive vandalism in the interior of the Red Pyramid.

Turning now to Giza, to the Second Pyramid, we will examine in more detail the evidence of how and when it was looted. We can only speculate, but the following is our best guess at what might have happened. The presence of the intrusive tunnel indicates that the Arabs, whose graffiti Belzoni found in both chambers, had probably forced this entry either because by their time the original entrances were obscured by sand and debris which had piled up around the base, or because the casing stones concealing at least the upper entrance had been replaced, after earlier intrusions, by

487

restorers.[584] This latter explanation would certainly be consistent with the idea that Mamun or a contemporary forced the entrance into the Great Pyramid for the same reason. Meanwhile, Belzoni found that the portcullis in the lower passage was completely broken up, while that in the upper passage was intact but had been raised a few inches off the ground. This is somewhat confusing, because from his descriptions it would appear that the sealing blocks in the upper passage had been broken up, while those in the lower passage were subsequently found intact by Vyse. We can only conclude that the upper passage had been used to enter the edifice in far earlier times, by robbers who knew where the entrances were, and that they had raised the upper portcullis without breaking it. This must have slipped back down again subsequently, perhaps because its temporary supports were disturbed. Meanwhile, it is anyone's guess as to who broke up the lower portcullis, although clearly the operation must have been conducted from the inside. As far as actual looting is concerned, we know that Belzoni found that the floor blocks of the upper chamber had been dug up and lay strewn around, and that he found that the coffer lid had been pushed to one side. The coffer itself contained assorted rubbish.

Turning to the Third Pyramid, although we have seen that it was assaulted by Saladin's son in a highly unsuccessful attempt to dismantle it, it has no intrusive entrance like its two counterparts on the Plateau. Vyse himself tunnelled into the centre, but without breaking into any of the passages. Nevertheless, it is clear from his description that it had been entered before. The sealing blocks that had plugged the main descending passage had been clumsily removed, as had some of those that plugged the antechamber. The portcullises had been broken up, and fragments remained strewn around. The floor blocks of the upper chamber had been removed to reveal the passage to the lower chambers, as had the blocks that sealed off the western antechamber. And finally even the blocks that sealed the obsolete upper passage had been broken up, and various tunnels had been dug as extensions to the top of the passage in the search for other chambers in the superstructure. Since the upper chamber contained Arabic graffiti similar to those in the Second Pyramid, it is clear that it had been breached in Arab times at the latest. However, we also know that the remains found in the upper chamber date to the Saite Period, so it had been entered long before. The only possible puzzle is why in this case the Arabs did know about the original entrance, and we must conclude that it was not covered in debris, and further that either it was not (at least by then) concealed by casing stones, or the stones were easier to locate. Of course the latter explanation is rendered more plausible on this edifice by the way in which the casing stones are smoothed flat around the entrance.

So, aside from special considerations of the Great Pyramid, which we considered in Chapter 3, it is clear that the looting evidence is persuasive. But the alternative camp make a series of additional claims to which we should now turn.

Missing Mummies?

We have already seen that the alternative camp's most common and ostensibly valid argument is that no original kings' mummies have ever been found in any of the pyramids. In fact some of them, Alford for example, have more recently qualified this by restricting their assertion to the pre-Sixth Dynasty pyramids only. This is sensible, not least because in 1971 a French archaeological team led by the Brugsch brothers found the complete mummy of a young man in the coffer of the pyramid of the Sixth Dynasty king Merenre at Saqqara. There have been suggestions that this is a later intrusive burial from the Eighteenth Dynasty, but the mummy, which was removed to the Cairo Museum, has still not been scientifically tested to determine its true age.[585]

What of the early pyramids? Is this suggestion correct? Let us take a look at the evidence. A number of mummies have been found in the satellite pyramids on the Plateau, especially those attached to the Third Pyramid. Although as far as we are aware these have not been conclusively dated, and although there are those who would argue that this proves nothing about the main pyramid structures themselves, we view it as important circumstantial evidence. More intriguing are the fragmented and definitely human remains found among the debris in the chambers of the Red Pyramid in 1950, which still had dried skin attached and appeared to indicate mummification. According to George Johnson, writing recently in the Egyptologists' journal *KMT*, these were examined by Dr Ahmed Mahmud el Batrawi and he concluded – admittedly on hardly scientific evidence – that they were fragments of Sneferu's mummy.[586] Clearly it would assist the debate if they were re-examined using modern carbon-dating techniques. There are of course the Arab rumours, for example that of Hokm, which we have already reproduced, that Mamun found a richly decorated body inside the coffer in the King's Chamber – but these tend to be from the less reliable sources and must therefore be discounted.

These elements aside, all the other remains found *inside* the Third and Fourth Dynasty pyramids are clearly from later *intrusive* burials. We have already seen that Vyse found human remains and fragments of a wooden coffer in the Third Pyramid, which dated to the Saite Period, and that this period was one in which such practices may have been commonplace. Similarly that Belzoni discovered the bones of a bull in the coffer in the Second Pyramid. Meanwhile, Petrie reported that he found ox bones in the second chamber of the Red Pyramid, which may of course mean that the human bones previously mentioned date to the same burial – and further that at Meidum he found ' . . . pieces from a wooden sarcophagus . . . which had been very violently wrenched open and destroyed', although this discovery is called into question since in his later biography he recalls ' . . . finding pieces of wooden canopics, but nothing else'.[587]

So, while there is ample evidence of *intrusive* burials, the evidence for *original* mummies in the earliest pyramids is poor. However, the alternative camp are forced to apply an additional clause in attempting to make this argument stick – that the robbers would not have gone so far as to steal the mummies themselves. This seems a strange line of argument. If the 'contemporary-robbery' theory is correct, it clearly demonstrates that not all Ancient Egyptians were entirely devoted to matters spiritual. If they were prepared to defile the tombs by entering and robbing them of their treasure, indeed of all the accoutrements that were supposed to allow the king to continue in the afterlife, they would hardly be squeamish about removing perhaps the best souvenir of all – the king's mummified body.

There is another possibility that must be admitted at this stage: that for one reason or another the kings were not actually buried inside their monuments, but elsewhere. This is a possibility, which we examined in Chapter 3 and, as we have seen, in the *context* of this debate, even this theory does not automatically imply that the pyramids themselves must have been constructed for more mysterious purposes.

Stolen Sarcophagi?

Although they are in evidence in all the other early pyramids, the alternative camp go on to point out that none of Sneferu's three pyramids has been found to contain any trace of a sarcophagus. At first sight this does appear incongruous, even when one considers the double-edged sword that he could only have been buried in one place – an issue to which we will return. However, again, the alternative camp have to argue that these *could not* or *would not* have been removed to make their argument stick. We would contend that, even if the coffers were in some cases too large to be removed, especially if there remained much rubble cluttering the passages, even fragments of them would surely represent a significant trophy for the robbers to place in their living room – or sell. In fact we have excellent evidence that the ancient robbers did indeed break the coffers up, which comes from the pyramid of the Sixth Dynasty king Pepi I at Saqqara. In its main chamber Petrie found a black basalt coffer with particularly thick sides which had been '*broken up by cutting rows of grooves in it, and banging it to pieces*'.[588]

As a corollary, Alford makes great play of the fact that in the Red Pyramid the concealed passage that leads from the second into the third chamber has been enlarged by hacking at the granite floor blocks. Since he does not accept the pyramids-as-tombs theory, he argues that something other than a coffer must have been removed from here – albeit that the remaining passages are still of the same original diameter, so that he asks, 'Was an artefact broken up to facilitate its removal?'[589] This would tend to indicate that even he must at least accept the *principle* of breaking artefacts up to remove them. However we tend to concur with the view that the passage was enlarged for a different reason – to remove the large granite blocks, which as we have seen had been taken up from the floor of the third chamber, to get them out of the way. Since the excavation of the floor continues to a depth of some 14 feet they would certainly have been a hindrance.

Lidless Sarcophagi?

It is sometimes suggested that the fact that the coffer in the King's Chamber of the Great Pyramid is lidless, and that no traces of this lid have been recorded, means that it never had one and cannot be regarded as a sarcophagus. There are three arguments against this. First, all the other coffers that have been found have had lids – including that in the Second Pyramid, whose lid remains *in situ* in the upper chamber, and that which Vyse discovered in the Third Pyramid's lower chamber, whose lid had been removed and lay fragmented in the upper chamber. Second, as we have seen, we believe it is entirely possible that the lid was broken up and removed even *before* Mamun entered the chamber, again because even fragments of it would have made excellent souvenirs. Third, and most conclusive of all, a rarely publicised piece of analysis of the coffer by JP Lepre in *The Egyptian Pyramids*, published in 1990, indicates that it bears all the hallmarks of *having been designed to take a lid*:[590]

> The lid, which is now missing, is calculated to have weighed over two tons. Traces of angled grooves and three pinion holes used, along with a resinous glue, for the fastening of the lid are still barely discernible at the top edges of the sarcophagus.

As a diversion on the matter of the design of the coffers, Lepre's reconstruction drawings indicate that a dovetail joint would have prevented this coffer's lid from being lifted, and that it would have to be slid off from the far side (nearest the west wall of the chamber). This was prevented by the granite fastening pins, which would have been pressed right through the lid once it was in position. That these must have been camouflaged in some way is suggested by the fact that the original robbers broke off a large segment of the corner of the coffer in attempting to prise the lid upward – this damage being still readily observable. This design is similar to that used on the Second Pyramid's coffer, which Petrie describes as having a projection on the base of the lid which fitted into undercut grooves in the top of the coffer. He suggests *bronze* pins in the lid located in corresponding holes in the west side of the coffer, the holes being filled with heated resin – traces of which he found, along with traces of cement on the top of the coffer, which suggested it had been sealed all round.[591]

Oversize Sarcophagi?

Detailed surveys of dimensions have revealed that the coffers in the Great and Second Pyramids are too large by a small margin to fit down the passages leading to the chambers. Consequently, these at least must have been placed *in situ* during the construction. The alternative camp make great play of this, suggesting that it eliminates the possibility of funeral processions. However, this seems quite absurd: we would suggest that the chances of ever conducting some semblance of a funeral procession while attempting to manoeuvre a stone coffer – which at between 3 and 4 tonnes could never be lifted by hand in the confined spaces – are absolutely nil. Since they could not form part of the procession, it would make sense whenever possible to place them *in situ* during construction. The procession would then be confined to the much easier task of carrying a wooden internal coffer.

In any case, the fact that both Sekhemkhet's and Nebka's sarcophagi were found inside the burial chambers of their clearly *unfinished* pyramids at Saqqara and Zawiyet el-Aryan respectively indicates that this practice was quite normal.

Sealed Sarcophagi?

Perhaps the most intriguing find in this whole field was made in the early 1950s by Zakaria Goneim. While excavating the pyramid of Sekhemkhet at Saqqara, he found in the main burial chamber an alabaster sarcophagus which was unique in having a sliding door at one end. Furthermore, to get to the underground chamber he had had to remove sealing blocks at the entrance, about halfway along the passage, and at the doorway to the chamber – all of which appeared intact. In the sand which filled the top of a vertical shaft that dropped down through the superstructure to join the descending passage, he found some bones and multiple papyri written in demotic Egyptian (dating them to the 25th Dynasty or later), but in the passage beneath the shaft he found a hoard of gold jewellery, which he dated to the Third Dynasty. Since there was no trace of any other robbers' tunnel, all these factors pointed to this being a genuine undisturbed burial. Goneim's excitement mounted when he came to examine the coffer itself, because the grooves for the sliding panel were sealed with a layer of plaster. However, when he lifted it up, lo and behold! Nothing. No mummy, nothing. The coffer was completely empty.[592]

We cannot blame the alternative camp for the importance they attach to this discovery, for it does cause Egyptologists some problems. Some report the find and then move on rapidly. Some suggest that it means that this was a 'dummy' burial intended to fool robbers, and this may indeed be the case despite the fact that some jewellery was found – after all, the place was hardly littered with funerary artefacts. Some suggest that Sekhemkhet was buried in the mastaba on the south side of his pyramid, but the wooden coffer found therein was small and contained the bones of a child, and although its style was Third Dynasty, Sekhemkhet was known from reliefs to have lived into adulthood. Others still suggest that the mummy must have been stolen immediately after the internment, before the coffer and edifice were sealed. Since the sealing was effected entirely by the use of blocks, which would have taken time to put in place unlike the lowering of portcullises, this is not impossible, but is it likely?

What can we make of this? The first point is that the edifice was clearly unfinished. Although a large amount of work was put into excavating a series of 132 subterranean 'cells' off a U-shaped corridor outside the base of the edifice, which became a common design for stepped pyramids, the superstructure never attained its full height, and the main burial chamber remained roughly hewn from the rock. This is consistent with the fact that Sekhemkhet, who was Djoser's son, reigned for only six years. Since it would have been impossible to complete the work above and below ground in a reasonable timeframe, perhaps he was buried in a less impressive but complete structure elsewhere. Since the sarcophagus had already been placed in the chamber, it may have been regarded as more effort to retrieve it than to build a new one. And, since it was there, perhaps it was sealed so that it did act as a dummy burial. We have also already considered the theory that kings were not necessarily buried in their pyramids, but elsewhere, which may account for this apparent anomaly.

Alternatively, we should perhaps question the validity of the claim that the edifice had not been entered before. Certainly Lehner hints that all is not as clear-cut as it may seem when he says there is 'some dispute whether the tomb was unviolated',[593] and it would be interesting to examine Goneim's original account to see if it overstates the case. It certainly seems unusual that *every* other mastaba and pyramid from this era bears the signs of forced entry in antiquity except for, apparently, this one. It is even more suspect when one considers that the mastaba on the south side clearly had been looted. Why would robbers bother with this and not the pyramid itself? And we know that the pyramid attracted attention, given the papyri Goneim found and the fact that its stones were quarried just like all the others.

However, this is pure speculation, which we normally try to avoid. The simple fact of the matter is that, even if the edifice was intact and the coffer was always empty, this is an *isolated incident* which again cannot be taken out of the general context. After all, the object in question is still a coffer with a form of lid, and, given the rest of the evidence we present, what else is it supposed to be? What does its being empty prove? That none of the early pyramids was ever used as a tomb? One swallow cannot a summer make.

Many alternative theorists quote the physicist Dr Kurt Mendelssohn, who in his *Riddle of the Pyramids*, published in 1975, suggests that this is *not* an isolated incident:[594]

> *The fact that the sarcophagi in the Khufu and Khafre pyramids were found empty is easily explained as the work of intruders*, but the empty sarcophagi of Sekhemkhet, Queen Hetepheres, and a third one in a shaft under the Step Pyramid, pose a more difficult problem. They were all left undisturbed since early antiquity. As these were burials without a corpse, we are almost driven to the conclusion that something other than a human body may have been ritually entombed.

We need to address various issues raised by this statement: First, his interpretation of the circumstances of Queen Hetepheres' burial is entirely at odds with that of Egyptologists. Her lavish burial accoutrements were discovered by the Harvard-Boston Expedition team led by Reisner in 1925, at the base of an 85-foot-deep vertical shaft, which may have formed part of the original design of the northernmost of the Great Pyramid's satellites. It was clear from the infill, which came right to the top of the shaft, and the completeness of the collection of artefacts, that this tomb had not been robbed. However, the various items of furniture and pottery were smashed and jammed into a space that was too small, with little attention to detail; this led Reisner to conclude that this was a *reburial* after her original tomb – possibly at Dashur – had been ransacked and the mummy stolen.[595] Furthermore, the canopic vase that contained the queen's internal organs was also found in the chamber, with the sealing intact; in fact it would be highly revealing for such remains to be carbon-dated, if they still exist. (Lehner amends Reisner's theory somewhat and suggests that her mummy was deliberately removed to the main chamber of this pyramid as part of a replan, with a different set of accoutrements. However, in our view this is less likely, especially given that the canopic vase remained.) To suggest this was an undisturbed original chamber with an intact but empty sarcophagus is disingenuous at best.

The same is true of what Mendelssohn says about the shaft under the Step Pyramid. It is unclear exactly what shaft he is talking about, and he may even be confusing the issue by referring to the deep 'southern shaft', which lies to the south of the entire complex. In any case, we can find no reference to an undisturbed chamber that was found with an intact but empty sarcophagus in this complex – while we are aware of plenty of evidence that it was extensively looted in antiquity, and that there were multiple burials in the many ancillary chambers of the underground complex.

Above all, it is clear from our emphasis in italics in the quotation above that Mendelssohn does accept that the coffers in the Giza pyramids may well have been emptied of their contents by robbers. Furthermore, he also observes that:[596]

> ... while the *funerary function of the pyramids cannot be doubted,* it is rather more difficult to prove that the pharaohs were ever buried inside them ... there are too many empty sarcophagi and, what is worse, rather too many empty tomb chambers, to make the idea of actual burials unchallengeable.

Given he accepts that the coffers of most of the early pyramids were not originally empty, *and* that the edifices had a funerary function, and yet still suggests that 'something other than a human body may have been ritually entombed' (even in empty sarcophagi!), this suggests at the very best an apparent desire to overcomplicate the problem. The ingenuity is compounded when Alford, for example, uses this very same quotation from Mendelssohn to support his supposed 'burial' of the pyramids-as-tombs theory.[597]

Multiple Sarcophagi?

If we are to be ruthlessly nonselective in our appraisal of the evidence, we must now turn to an issue that we have not seen raised by any of the alternative theorists, but which might at first appear to support their case. This is the possibility of multiple sarcophagi in one pyramid. While this factor quite reasonably goes unremarked in respect of, for example, the Stepped Pyramid, since the multiple subterranean chambers were clearly designed to house more than just Djoser himself, it is rarely reported that there may have been more than one coffer in both the Great and Third Pyramids. In Part I we have already reproduced the extract from Edrisi's account of the interior of the Great Pyramid, which suggested that an 'empty vessel' similar to that in the King's Chamber was housed in the Queen's Chamber. If this account is correct, it raises some interesting issues. First, it could support the idea of an original multiple burial inside the edifice – indeed we are tempted to ask whether it could be this, and not the shape of the roof, that caused the Arabs to christen it the 'Queen's Chamber'. Alternatively it might be argued that it remains consistent with the replanning theory, since – if this additional coffer were larger than the passages and placed *in situ* during construction, like its counterpart in the King's Chamber – it would have remained in place but empty. (Lepre considers the possibility that the Queen's Chamber originally contained a coffer, but is clearly not aware of this possible supporting evidence.)[598] Whichever is the case, we must also wonder who might have broken it up and removed it in the four hundred or so years between the time Edrisi saw it and when, for example, Greaves explored the edifice.

This is not the only enigma that Edrisi's accounts present, because he also reports the existence of an additional coffer in the *Third* Pyramid:[599]

A few years ago, the red Pyramid, which is the Third, or smaller one, was opened on its lower skirt on the north side; but it is not known who opened it. An alley was found leading down about twenty draas, or more; and on its extremity a narrow place that affords room for one person only [the partially blocked ante-chamber]. After which, a road is entered, of difficult and fatiguing passage, where one creeps along upon the stomach for above twenty draas more, until an oblong square room is reached [the upper chamber], in which several pits are seen, that were dug by those who went in quest of treasures. From thence another room [the chamber with cells] is entered, the four walls of which are formed by six or seven chambers with arched doors, as are the doors over the small private chambers in the baths. *In the middle of the space on the side, and round which these chambers extend, is a long blue vessel quite empty.* The Shereef Abou Al Hosseyn, of the family of Mymoon Ibn Hambe, has told me that he was present when the opening into this Pyramid was effected by people who were in search after treasures. They worked at it with axes for six months, and they were in great numbers. *They found in this vessel, after they had broken the covering of it, the decayed, rotten remains of a man, but no treasures on his side, except some golden tablets inscribed with characters of a language nobody could understand.* Each man's share of these tablets amounted to one hundred dinars.

Again, if this account is accurate it raises a number of issues. First, Vyse found no trace of this vessel, and also commented that no coffer could have been removed from the Third Pyramid by the time he entered it because the antechamber still retained most of its original sealing blocks. However, he was referring to the removal of a coffer *intact*, while we have already seen that they were often broken up to effect their removal. However, since Edrisi also appears to have seen this coffer *in situ* and first-hand, again we do not know who might have effected such a removal, or when – although in this case they would have had several hundred years more until the time Vyse entered the edifice.

Second, it is unlikely that the body found in this other coffer represented an intrusive burial, since it was apparently accompanied by gold tablets; and furthermore the replanning theory does not fit this find, since both lower chambers would have been constructed simultaneously. So we must conclude that, in this case, the existence of two coffers would represent a deliberate multiple burial – which is arguably out of character for the Giza Pyramids.

Third, the fact that neither of the coffers or the gold tablets had been removed before would suggest that the edifice had not been looted previously, or at least only on a few occasions when the robbers already had more than they could carry.

Fourth, why does Edrisi not mention the main lower chamber? We can only assume that it remained blocked off at this time.

Who can judge the extent to which these accounts are accurate? Both appear to be first-hand reports (albeit that the *contents* of the blue coffer are reported second-hand), and appear to be detailed and accurate in all other respects. It is impossible and arguably worthless to speculate further on these finds and their multiple and often conflicting implications. However, the evidence, such as it is, is at the very least intriguing, and should not be omitted from a detailed study such as this.

Multiple Chambers?

For completeness, and since it is another of the arguments raised by the alternative camp, we should remind ourselves of the possible reasons why multiple chambers are encountered in many of the early pyramids. As we have already seen, there are four. First, they may represent replanning exercises. Second, they may represent multiple burials. Third, they may represent deliberate decoys to fool robbers. And, fourth, they may represent a deliberate element of the rituals associated with the king's journey to the afterlife, whereby an additional chamber or chambers were required to house the *ka* statue representing his spiritual double.

It is also clear that we need not be unduly insistent on selecting just *one* of these theories and applying it to *all* the pyramids. There is no reason why each should not be applied to different edifices, and even to different parts of one edifice. And in our view all of these are satisfactory explanations which do not require us to re-evaluate the basic pyramids-as-tombs hypothesis.

Multiple Pyramids?

We have already noted the final general objection made by the alternative camp – that Sneferu built *three* pyramids, despite the fact that he could be buried only once. We should commence our investigation of this issue by examining the orthodox camp's rebuttal, which suggests that design faults encountered in two of the edifices twice required him to erect a new tomb. The argument commences with the premise that the outer layers of his pyramid at Meidum collapsed *during his reign* because they were not properly keyed into the central stepped core. This is backed up by the fact that the sole chamber in this structure was undoubtedly left unfinished, as demonstrated by the rough state of its corbelled roof. Supposedly his run of bad luck continued when the Bent Pyramid showed signs of deterioration and cracking during construction, partly because the ground on which it was erected was unstable. This is supported by the fact that the upper chamber – which is in the superstructure – still contains the original wooden beams at floor level which were arguably introduced to prevent its inward collapse due to the huge pressure of the surrounding masonry.

They further suggest that this is why the angle was reduced, to lower the weight of the masonry above the chambers – although in the final analysis this still did not do enough to convince the king that the edifice was safe. Finally, they say, Sneferu turned to the Red Pyramid, which was deliberately built with a shallow angle to assist the speed of construction for the now ageing king. This is all tied up with what one might term the 'evolutionary-design' theory, which suggests that Sneferu's architects and builders were experimenting with designs for the first 'genuine' (that is, not stepped) pyramids, while at the same time attempting to place chambers in the superstructure rather than below ground. This theory is undoubtedly supported by the fact that the chambers in the Red Pyramid do show few signs of cracks, except in the huge lintels above the passages, and these cracks probably formed when the blocks plugging the passages were removed.

Unfortunately for Egyptologists, and for us as supporters of the pyramids-as-tombs theory, this somewhat outdated analysis has been revealed to be flawed in two areas. First, it is now almost universally accepted – even by the orthodox community – that the Meidum 'collapse' occurred well after Sneferu's death. Alford points out that New Kingdom graffiti have now been found under the mounds of debris.[600] Meanwhile, George Johnson suggests that the similarity of the debris found at Meidum with that at the Red Pyramid indicates that the Meidum pyramid did not collapse at all, but was merely quarried for stone long after its construction, as were the casings of most of the others.[601] Second, and worse still for the 'evolutionary-design' theory, the quarry marks on a number of casing stones from both the Meidum and Red Pyramids indicate that construction on both ran *concurrently*. First we have Johnson's version of this:[602]

> Significantly the mason's graffiti dating the building phases of the Sneferu monuments verify work was under way at more than one pyramid at the same time. Graffiti found on limestone blocks during the clearance of the northwest corner of the Meidum Pyramid in 1984 date to the thirteenth, sixteenth and eighteenth occasions of

the 'cattle count' of Sneferu and are from the same period the Red Pyramid was under construction. At the latter site Stadelmann found the earliest graffiti dating to the year of the thirteenth 'occasion' of Sneferu, and the latest to the twenty-fourth cattle count.

Writing at a time when the attribution of these pyramids to Sneferu was less certain than it now is, and with what may now be superseded information, Edwards also refers to this issue but the 'overlap' appears somewhat shorter:[603]

[The relationship of the outer Meidum pyramid] to the Northern Stone [Red] Pyramid may be indicated by some casing blocks which are dated in the twenty-first and twenty-third years of the reign of an unnamed king, while similar blocks dated in the twenty-first and twenty-second years of Sneferu have been found at the Northern Stone Pyramid.

Edwards goes on to suggest that the marks on the Meidum blocks came from the upper courses, while those at the Red Pyramid were from the lower courses. Meanwhile, Lehner suggests that the Bent Pyramid was commenced in the fifteenth year of Sneferu's reign, and the 'return to Meidum' occurred 'probably in the 28th or 29th year of his reign'. He also mentions quarry marks on the Red Pyramid, with one from low down dating to the 30th year, while one 30 courses higher is dated four years later (this is all despite the fact that the chronology he uses gives Sneferu only a 24-year reign).[604]

Whatever the finer details, Egyptologists have responded to this evidence with the following revised analysis. The inner stepped core of the Meidum Pyramid is laid in the old-fashioned style with the blocks inclined in towards the centre, while the outer layer uses the later style of horizontal courses also found in the upper section of the Bent Pyramid and the entirety of the Red Pyramid. The revised chronology therefore suggests that Sneferu first built the stepped Meidum Pyramid, then abandoned it in favour of the more ambitious Bent Pyramid. When the latter was deemed unstable, he had the Red Pyramid erected to a different design again, but *at the same time* had the Meidum Pyramid completed also in the new style. According to the German Egyptologist Rainer Stadelmann, the Meidum Pyramid – and possibly the Bent Pyramid also – was completed as a cenotaph rather than a tomb.[605] This makes some sense, especially since we have seen that the interior of the Meidum Pyramid was never completed.

What does all this mean for the pyramids-as-tombs theory? If the Meidum Pyramid ended up as a cenotaph, and the Bent Pyramid was either the same or was abandoned due to poor positioning and a flawed design, then the Red Pyramid remains Sneferu's one and only true funerary edifice. This view is supported by the fact that the only real remains of a mortuary temple of any size found next to one of these pyramids – modest though it is in comparison with those at Giza – are on the east side of the Red Pyramid. The Meidum Pyramid has only a small chapel on the east side and no valley temple, while the Bent Pyramid has the same small chapel and a very small valley temple. It also appears that the Red Pyramid's mortuary temple was completed in a hurry using mud bricks, while there is no causeway to speak of and the remains of a rudimentary valley temple have never been properly excavated. This all suggests that the temple and pyramid were required urgently when the king died.

Conclusion

We have seen that all of these arguments against the pyramids-as-tombs theory can be effectively countered.

Appendix III

The Great Pyramid's Security Features

We indicated in Chapter 3 that in order for us to be able to evaluate how and when the Great Pyramid may have been breached, we needed to review the orthodox theories as to the security arrangements for its unique interior. This might also help us to evaluate the purpose of some of the more detailed features, which might otherwise be regarded as unexplained enigmas – such as the regularly cut recesses in the Grand Gallery walls.

The Entrance

Starting at the outside, we have Strabo's supposed report of a hinged door block. The original existence of this is normally taken for granted, but – although this is a point rarely picked up by the alternative camp – it begs the question as to why it would be necessary if the pyramid was to be used only once, as a tomb, before it was sealed up. The standard response is that it was required to allow the priests to enter the building to perform maintenance and inspections. However, this argument runs directly contrary to the evidence that we have already reviewed, for example in relation to the Second and Third Pyramids, that *the descending passages were sealed with blocks*. Although we have no concrete evidence that this was also true of the Great Pyramid's Descending Passage, we should ask ourselves why, if context is king, the Great Pyramid should have been any different from its counterparts. Clearly the Ascending Passage was sealed with blocks, so why not the Descending Passage also?

Is there physical evidence for a hinged-block system? The casing stones around the original entrance have now been stripped, as have many of the core blocks behind them, so it is impossible to judge. However, the huge double gables over the 'inner' entrance, albeit that they were built for support rather than decoration, somehow do not appear to us consistent with the idea of a small hinged door. Meanwhile, Egyptologists such as Petrie and more recently Lepre have conducted detailed analyses of the way the 'doors' might have worked, based primarily on the fact that the Bent Pyramid's western entrance apparently shows signs of just such a system.[606] The blocks on either side of the entrance are reported to contain distinct sockets in which the hinges would have swivelled, while the floor – although now filled in – originally contained a deep recess which would have been necessary for the block to swivel inward (this is Lepre's reappraisal of Petrie's theory, which suggested, apparently incorrectly and based on Strabo's original description, that it would have swivelled outward). Lepre also suggests that the Meidum Pyramid contains similar sockets. We can only say that we have been unable to inspect these entrances for ourselves. But even if Lepre's analysis is correct, at least in relation to the western entrance of the Bent Pyramid – which is unique in itself anyway – we are inclined to think that it does not carry over to the monuments on the Giza Plateau.

Let us now examine Strabo's account in more detail. It is by far the shortest and least detailed of those prepared in Classical times. What is more, the translation of his work that is normally reproduced is as follows: 'A stone that may be taken out, which *being raised up*, there is a sloping passage'.[607] However, an original translation of Strabo's *Geographica* dating to 1857, which we consulted and have already reproduced, merely says, ' . . . a stone, which may be taken out; when that is *removed*' – not 'raised up'. The translation of the original Greek is clearly important.

Edwards and Lehner both admit that, if a hinged door had existed in Strabo's time, it could have been put in place only long after the edifice had first been violated.[608] We were prepared to write this off as an unlikely theory which relies too heavily on Strabo's account until we considered the following. Whoever dug the intrusive entrance tunnel – and in our view it is highly likely that this was Mamun – was clearly unable to locate the original entrance. Furthermore, unlike the situation at the Second Pyramid, in this case the forced entry is *below* the real entry, so accumulated sand and debris cannot be the solution as to why the explorers could not locate it. For this reason, at whatever time this tunnel was created, the original entrance must have been cleverly concealed. This view is supported by the fact that reports of Mamun's exploration do not mention his fighting his way through insects, bats and their excreta in the various passages – a common feature of future explorers' accounts – which suggests that his entrance was the first to open the edifice up to vast numbers of such creatures. Since, as we have already seen, there is every reason to believe the edifice had been entered long before this, the original entrance used by all previous explorers cannot have been left open.

Therefore we can only surmise that someone – possibly Saite Period restorers – had either fitted a hinged block, or had accurately refitted the missing casing stones. The case for the former is enhanced by the fact that it is likely that the interiors of all the edifices were repeatedly entered at least in pre-Classical times, and in accepting this inevitability the development of such an entry mechanism may have proved less of an effort than continually refitting the casing blocks. It may even be argued that the priests at this time would have allowed restricted entry to the edifice for the important, initiated or wealthy – in just the same way as is now being proposed for the edifice to prevent it from rapid decline due to the incursion of thousands of tourists every year.

A Dummy Chamber?

The next point we should consider about security is that some Egyptologists have suggested that the Subterranean Chamber was deliberately built as a decoy, to prevent robbers from searching for the real chambers up in the superstructure. Given the emphasis that was placed on security, this is at first sight a plausible theory. However, we have already seen that there is persuasive evidence that this chamber has such an unfinished appearance because it was abandoned in favour of the higher chambers as part of a replanning exercise. Furthermore, if it were built as a decoy they would surely have finished it so it looked like a proper chamber. These two theories are mutually exclusive, and we are minded to stick with the latter.

The Plugging Blocks

We have already agreed with Vyse's suggestion that the Descending Passage was originally plugged with limestone sealing blocks, perhaps as far as its junction with the Ascending Passage. Moving on, we have the granite plugs that block the bottom of this latter passage. We know that these would have been concealed by an angled limestone block in the roof of the Descending Passage, which would have been indistinguishable from the rest of the ceiling. Three of these blocks are still in position, and they are the ones that are by-passed by the additional intrusive tunnel.

There are two questions that arise concerning these blocks. The first is: Were they slid into place or built *in situ*? And the second: How many of them were there originally? Furthermore, these two questions are interrelated.

The most convenient theory is that they *were* slid into place, because this would explain the existence of the regular slots cut into the side ramps of the Grand Gallery – which Borchardt surmised were used to house wooden beams which held the plugs in place while they were being stored therein. Alternatively, it has been suggested that these blocks are such a tight fit in the Ascending Passage itself that there is no way they could have been slid down without snagging, and that consequently they must have been built *in situ*. However, this is not as valid an argument as it at first appears, for a number of reasons:

- First, Lepre produces some highly important and rarely publicised measurements which show that the Ascending Passage is uniquely *tapered*, unlike all the other original passages in the pyramids, which are always built with great precision to consistent dimensions.[609] Where it emerges into the Grand Gallery it measures 53 inches high by 42 inches wide; halfway down it measures 48 by 41½ inches; and at the bottom (where the three plugs are now) it measures 47¼ by 38½ inches. In the few places where the passage is not worn away by visitors, it is clear that it too was originally finished with great precision, so we must conclude that this taper of 5¾ inches in height and 3½ inches in width over the 124 feet of its length is deliberate. The clearance remains sufficiently small that the blocks would still have been in grave danger of snagging as they neared the bottom, but a number of researchers have suggested that the process was assisted by a lubricating mortar – of which traces have been found.
- Second, the distance between the ramps on either side of the Grand Gallery is exactly the same as the width of the top of the Ascending Passage, suggesting it was deliberately designed to hold the plugging blocks.
- Third, Noel F Wheeler, the Field Director of Reisner's Harvard-Boston Expedition, wrote a paper published in the periodical *Antiquity* in 1935, which again provides rarely publicised evidence:[610] He noted that there are five pairs of holes in the walls at the base of the Grand Gallery, in the 'gap' between the end of the Ascending Passage and the continuation of the sloping floor of the Gallery – this gap occasioned by the branching off of the horizontal passage that leads to the Queen's Chamber. He argues that these were used to locate wooden beams that supported a 'bridge slab', which would have provided a continuation of the sloping

floor. It would have been at least 17 feet long, thick enough to support the plugs as they slid down, and would also have effectively sealed off the passage to the Queen's Chamber – which shows no signs of having been itself sealed with plugs. Although no traces of this slab have ever been found – in our view because it was probably destroyed by robbers in early antiquity, after which the debris would have been cleared out by restorers – this would be a necessity for the 'sliding plugs' theory to work. In support of this theory, there are 5-inch 'lips' on both sides of the gap upon which the slab would have rested.

- Fourth, Borchardt's replanning evidence regarding the change in orientation of the blocks from which the Ascending Passage is formed precludes the possibility that the plugging blocks were placed *in situ*. Since he theorised that the lower section of the passage was originally solid masonry, which was subsequently carved out, the plugs would still have had to be slid down it, albeit for a shorter distance.
- Fifth, Lehner notes that in the Bent Pyramid's small satellite there is a short ascending passage which may represent an admittedly far smaller-scale prototype for that in the Great Pyramid.[611] At the point where it increases in height from the normal few feet, there is a notch in the wall which he believes may have been used to locate a wooden chock which, when pulled away by rope, would have released the plugging block or blocks it was supporting.

There is one additional feature of the Grand Gallery that we must examine. On each side a groove – about 7 inches high and 1 inch deep – has been cut into the third layer of corbelling along its entire length. Lepre suggests that this was used to locate a wooden platform, presumably accessed by a ladder at each end, which at this height would still be 6 feet wide, along which the funeral cortège would have progressed – thereby avoiding the plugging blocks housed below.[612] (Some Egyptologists have suggested that the blocks themselves were housed up on this platform, with the cortège passing below, but we find this an unlikely scenario which would require far greater complexity in getting the plugs down again. Also, the wooden boards would have had difficulty in supporting the weight of the blocks.) In addition, at the top of the grooves there are rough chisel marks running along their entire lengths, from which Lepre argues that whatever was housed in the grooves was valuable to robbers and well worth the effort of removing. He therefore surmises that the platform may have comprised cedar panels inlaid with gold. Although this platform would have been somewhat higher than appears necessary, and although we are not entirely convinced by Lepre's explanation of the chisel marks, this theory appears the most plausible so far put forward.

Even though they accept that a funeral procession would involve only an inner wooden coffer while the granite one remained *in situ*, some alternative researchers have still argued against this theory by suggesting that this supposedly sombre and formal occasion could hardly be expected to be conducted while effectively negotiating an obstacle course. However, we regard this argument as fatuous, since the processions that had to negotiate the cramped space and steep incline of the descending passages in all the other pyramids would have faced equally awkward conditions.

All of this seems to us to point towards the 'sliding-plugs' theory being the correct one. Furthermore, it appears to offer a reasonable explanation for the otherwise enigmatic features of the Grand Gallery. Although in no way would we wish to denigrate the exquisite design and execution of this remarkable feature of the edifice, we are forced to conclude that it had a primarily functional rather than symbolic purpose.

We must now turn to the equally vexing question of how many blocks were actually used to seal the Ascending Passage. Given our preference for the 'sliding-plugs' theory, we know that there would have been provision to house about 25 of them in the Grand Gallery. We also know that the grooves for locating the chocks, and indeed for the overhead walkway, run along the entire length. But does this mean that this many were actually used? We know that the intrusive tunnel at the bottom of the Ascending Passage by-passes only the three that remain *in situ*. We can see no reason for previous intruders to have broken up a full 22 massive granite blocks *from the top down*. After all, what would be their motivation to perform such a mammoth task in the first place if they had already entered the upper chambers? And in any case why would they leave the last three in place? It is possible that additional *limestone* plugs were used, so that whoever performed the tunnelling got past the granite blocks and then continued on through these softer plugs themselves. However, we find it more likely that only three blocks were ever used.

Given that the Gallery was clearly designed to house so many more, we must then ask why the change of plan came about, and indeed when. After all, the decision would have to have been reached at the latest before the roof of the Gallery was completed in order that the chosen number of plugs could be lowered into it, and yet after the first three corbels of the Gallery's walls had been completed with their various niches and grooves. As unsatisfactory as it is to indulge in mere speculation, we can only suggest that it was decided at this point that, in combination with the other security features discussed in this section, three plugs would be enough. This would certainly have saved significant time and effort, notwithstanding that short cuts are not a regular feature of this edifice. (There is another alternative, which is that Khufu decided at this point that he wanted to be buried elsewhere; a possibility we have already discussed.) Meanwhile, we should note that the *chisel marks* indicate that it must have been decided that the possibly gold-inlaid walkway should still run the entire length of the Gallery.

The Portcullis System

We have already noted that the granite-lined King's Antechamber contains four sets of slots in the side walls for portcullises to be lowered into position. We have also noted that this is a feature present in many of the other pyramids, although this particular arrangement is more complex than most. Each of the three main sets of slots is 3 feet deep and 21½ inches wide, while the northernmost slots reach down only to the level of the passage roof. Two granite slabs are still *in situ* in the latter, but a significant space remains above them. Since the west, south and east walls of the Antechamber itself, and the passage, are also lined with granite, we can assume that this was the material from which the portcullises would have been made. The whole of this section of the interior was clearly intended to be extremely hard to break through.

Once again we must turn to the invaluable scholarship of Lepre to assist our understanding of this mechanism.[613] He indicates that there are three channels cut into the south wall of the antechamber, each about 3½ inches wide, which would have been required in order that the ropes used to lower the portcullises into place would not snag between the slab and the wall. Although he points out that there is some doubt over the oft-touted possibility that wooden rollers may have been housed above the slots, around which the ropes would have operated, he suggests that the slabs in the northernmost slots would have acted as counterweights – thereby rejecting the other oft-touted suggestion that the uppermost of them is missing. He also indicates that from the rear or northern side of the upper counterweight protrudes a semicircular boss – although again he points out that it does not seem to be properly designed to act as a boss around which a rope could have been secured, and is forced to leave its true function as a matter for further study.

It is often suggested that no fragment of the three missing portcullises has ever been found, and from this many alternative researchers – and even some Egyptologists – deduce that they were never even fitted. In the first instance, the continued presence of the counterweights – which are above the level of the passage and therefore would not obstruct the progress of an intruder – suggests to us that the portcullises were originally in place but were broken up by the early robbers. Again we would suggest that, as with the 'bridge slab', the debris from this operation would have been cleaned up by restorers. However, in addition to this evidence, Lepre produces a real *coup de grâce* on the matter: *he has matched the four blocks of fractured granite found in and around the edifice to the dimensions of the portcullises.*[614]

In brief, each of the main slabs would have been a minimum of 4 feet high by 4 feet wide – probably more depending on the degree of overlap into the slots – and most significantly about 21 inches thick (to allow a tolerance of $\frac{1}{2}$ inch in the slots). He examined the four blocks – one lies near the pit in the Subterranean Chamber, another in the niche in the west wall just before the entrance to this chamber, another in the grotto in the Well Shaft, and another outside the original entrance – and established that, while they were all less than 4 feet in height and width, they were all 21 inches thick! (Note that there is a loose block of granite in the King's Chamber, but this is known to come from the floor and was therefore omitted from the analysis.) As if this were not sufficient evidence, he found that three of the four blocks have $3\frac{1}{2}$-inch holes drilled in them – in fact the one in the pit has two, and the one near the entrance three. Furthermore, the holes in the latter are spaced $6\frac{1}{2}$ inches apart. So he established that not only do the holes have the same diameter as the channels for the ropes in the south wall of the Antechamber, but they are also spaced the same distance apart. Although Lepre is unable to provide a foolproof explanation as to how these four fragments ended up in their present locations – he suggests a variety of high jinks by early visitors to the monument – nevertheless this strikes us as pretty convincing evidence that these are indeed fragments of the original portcullises.

The Well Shaft

It is appropriate now to turn to the question of who dug the enigmatic Well Shaft, and why. It has been suggested that it was dug by the earliest robbers, who needed a mechanism to get into the upper reaches of the edifice, and who knew the internal layout sufficiently to dig upward from the bottom and still find the base of the Grand Gallery. However, there are a number of factors that suggest that this analysis is incorrect. First, it is clear that the top end of the shaft was originally sealed by a block which fitted into the ramp in the west wall of the Grand Gallery, and clearly mere robbers would not have concealed their tunnel in this way. Second, it would be infinitely harder to excavate this tunnel upward rather than downward – it would require platforms, and the fragments of rock would continually fall into the workers' faces. Third, at the bottom the shaft continues a little below the level of the Descending Passage, which it would not do if it had been dug from there in the first place. Fourth, the top third of the shaft runs through the superstructure (the remainder through the bedrock), and the uppermost section of this was not tunnelled through the masonry but deliberately built into it *during construction*[615] (this would also support the replanning theory, in that the lower part of this top third would have been tunnelled through the masonry after it was decided to abandon the Subterranean Chamber). And, fifth, any intruder who had discovered the upper reaches of the edifice by by-passing the granite plugs would have had no reason to then dig this additional shaft.

It is therefore almost certain that the Well Shaft was dug at the time the edifice was constructed. It is likely that its purpose was to provide the workers responsible for sliding the granite plugs into place at the foot of the Ascending Passage with a means of escape; after all, the distance involved and the weight of the plugs (even if there were only three) meant they would not have been able to release the chocks from beneath the passage 'remotely' by rope. We can surmise that, once the plugs had been released, they would have let themselves down into the shaft; and that once they were all out they would probably have hidden the bottom of the shaft with an appropriate block so that it would not be discovered.

It is perhaps enigmatic that the tunnel was designed to travel for such a long distance – several hundred feet – in a vertical and then southerly direction, when it could have been made far shorter either by travelling vertically down, or even better by sloping in a northerly direction at a respectable distance underneath the Ascending Passage. However, Maragioglio and Rinaldi suggest that it was dug to provide additional ventilation for the Descending Passage and the Subterranean Chamber during their construction, and as an ancillary motive this might explain the lengthy course.

Of course this analysis must be considered in conjunction with the considerable complications regarding whether the Well Shaft was dug with official sanction or in secret, and also who rediscovered it and when, which we considered in Chapter 3.

Appendix IV

Features of the Major Third and Fourth Dynasty Pyramids

This table provides a summary of the features of the major Third and Fourth Dynasty pyramids, and should be used both as a general reference and as a guide to the progression of pyramid building in this period. It

Name	Location	N/S	Casing	Steps/Ext. Angle	Entrances/Passages/Angles	Chambers
Djoser (Step Pyramid)	Saqqara	No	Limestone	6 uneq	Sloping trench/ramp from outside; deep vertical shaft in cntre	Central plus mult int passages, galleries, & chambers
Sekhemkhet	Saqqara	Yes	? (quarried so much that only small inner core left)	7 but in cmplt	Sloping trench/ramp from outside; vertical shaft from 2nd tier	Central plus mult int/ext passages, galleries, & chambers
Khaba (?) (Layer Pyramid)	Zawiyet el Aryan	Yes	? (quarried so much that only small inner core left)	6/7 but in cmplt	Ext steps/passage to T junct psge; ext vert shaft to junction	Central plus mult ext passages & chambers
Sneferu	Meidum	Yes	Limestone (coating & 'pyramid' core gone)	7/8 @ 75 then 51.8	1 1 28	1 in s/s (at ground level)
Sneferu (Bent Pyramid)	Dashur	Yes	Limestone (angled down)	54.5 then 43.3	2: in N/W faces to lower/upper chambers; 25 (N) 30 then 24 (S)	1 subter. with antechamber; rough passage link to 1 in s/s (at grnd level)
Sneferu (Northern Stone or Red Pyramid)	Dashur	Yes	Limestone	43.5	1 1 27	3 in s/s (2 at ground level, main slightly raised)
Khufu (Great Pyramid)	Giza	Yes	Limestone	51.8	1 Many 26	1 subter.; 2 in s/s plus ante/relieving chambers & GG
Djedefre	Abu Roash	Yes	Granite	48–52	Sloping trench/ramp from outside; deep vertical shaft in cntre	1 central

also demonstrates the consistency of some of the key features of these pyramids. The primary source of the data is Edwards' *The Pyramids of Egypt*, with additional data added from a variety of sources.

Pcullis Doors	Coffers	Mummies/ Bones	Other	Re-wrks	Surrounding Buildings	Ownership/ Markings
No	Not in Central; 2 alabaster in smaller	Bones in central plus of child in one coffer	None (although clearly repeatedly plundered)	4	Mortuary temple (to N not E) with courtyds; serdab; mastaba; many others; high decorated walls	Reliefs, inscriptions and statues of Djoser
3 intact slabs (suggest never robbed)	Alabaster with lid and *sealed* sliding panel	None	3rd Dyn gold jewellery in passage; wreath on coffer	?	Walled enclosure with mastaba and prob mortuary temple; (poss unfinished due to King's early death)	King's name on clay jar stoppers
No	None	None	None (appears unfinished and never occupied/ used)	?	None (unfinished)	King's name on stone vessels in mastabas to north
No	Fragments of wooden coffin	None	None (although clearly plundered)	3 (orig step)	Sat. pyramid; mastaba; small mortuary temple; encl walls; walled causeway; valley temple	Old name of locn translates as 'Sneferu endures', plus textual refs
2 side (only 1 shut but decoratd *inside*)	None	None	Baskets; 5 bats in box in floor cavity; (probably plundered)	1(?)	Sat. pyramid; small mortuary temple; encl walls; walled c'way; decorated valley (?) temple	Sneferu red quarry marks on core blocks plus on stelae and columns
No	None	Fragments of human remains in main chamber	None	0	Small mortuary temple; encl walls; no real causeway; small valley temple	Sneferu red quarry mark on casing block; textual refs
Slots for 3 vert but no traces	Granite, no lid	None (plundering depends on well shaft)	Sticks/Balls/ Hooks in shafts	2(?)	Sat. pyramids; mortuary temple; encl walls; walled causeway; valley temple	Khufu red/black quarry marks in relieving chmbrs & core blocks; textual refs
No	No	None	None	?	Sat. pyramid; mortuary temple; encl walls; long causeway; valley temple?	Votive Pottery

Name	Location	N/S	Casing	Steps/ Ext. Angle	Entrances/Passages/ Angles	Chambers
Khafre (Second Pyramid)	Giza	Yes	Limestone/ Granite	52.3	2 (one on ground outside); 2 (plus conn); 26 (upper) 22 (lower)	2 subter
Menkaure (Third Pyramid)	Giza	Yes	Limestone/ Granite	51.3	1; 2 (upper terminates in body); 26	3 subter plus antechamber & 6 cells

APPENDIX IV

Pcullis Doors	Coffers	Mummies/ Bones	Other	Re-wrks	Surrounding Buildings	Ownership/ Markings
Yes	Granite, let into floor, with intact lid	Bull's bones	None (clearly plundered)	1(?)	Sat. pyramid; mortuary temple; encl walls; walled causeway; valley temple	Statue in pit in Valley Temple; textual refs
Yes	Decorated basalt (lost by HV) plus sep wood lid	Saite period fake 'bones' in upper chamber	None (clearly plundered)	1	Sat. pyramids; mortuary temple; encl walls; walled c'way; valley temple	Restored name on wooden coffer; textual refs

517

Appendix V

Chronological Summary

The following are approximate summaries of events mentioned in this book.

Exploration Chronology

Date (c.)	Event
2500 BC	Giza Pyramids and Sphinx built. Probably looted substantially over next few centuries.
1400 BC	Restoration of Sphinx by Thutmose IV.
1200 BC	Restoration of Sphinx by Ramesses II.
600 BC	Various Saite Period restorations and resurrection of Fourth Dynasty cults.
440 BC	Herodotus writes about the pyramids.
330 BC	Alexander 'the Great' destroys the library at Heliopolis.
20	Strabo writes about the pyramids.
77	Pliny writes about the pyramids.
820	Mamun explores the Great Pyramid.
9th century	Hokm writes about the pyramids.
950	Masoudi writes about the pyramids.
1220	Latif writes about the pyramids.
1245	Edrisi writes about the pyramids.
15th century	Makrizi writes about the pyramids.
1638	Greaves explores the Great Pyramid.
1765	Davison explores the Great Pyramid.
1798	Napoleon's *savants* including Jomard explore and map the Plateau.
1818	Belzoni explores the Second Pyramid. Caviglia explores the Great Pyramid and clears the front of the Sphinx.
1820	Champollion deciphers the Rosetta Stone.
1837–42	Vyse and Perring explore all three pyramids and the Sphinx.
1855	Mariette excavates the Valley Temple.
1872	The Dixon brothers explore the Great Pyramid.

1880	Petrie surveys and explores the Plateau.
1881	Maspero unearths the *Pyramid Texts* at Saqqara.
1906	Reisner excavates Third Pyramid's mortuary and valley temples.
1910	Holscher excavates the Second Pyramid's mortuary temple.
1925	Cole and Borchardt survey the Plateau.
1925–36	Baraize excavates the Sphinx.
1935–6	Hassan excavates the Sphinx and Sphinx Temple, and the Water Shaft.
1946	Lauer excavates the Great Pyramid's mortuary temple.
1963	Maragioglio and Rinaldi survey the Great Pyramid.
1967–70	'Joint Pyramid Project' examines Second Pyramid for hidden chambers.
1974–7	SRI examine Great and Second Pyramids and Sphinx for hidden chambers.
1978	The SRI/ARE 'Sphinx Exploration project' examines the Sphinx for hidden chambers.
1984	Phase 1 of 'Pyramids Carbon-Dating Project'.
1986	Dormion and Goidin examine Great Pyramid for hidden chambers.
1987	Waseda University examine Great Pyramid and Sphinx for hidden chambers.
1988–98	'Sphinx Restoration Project' led by Hawass.
1989	Hawass examines remains of Great Pyramid's valley temple.
1991	Lehner directs the 'NOVA Pyramid-Building Experiment'.
	West, Schoch and Dobecki conduct on-site investigation into age of Sphinx.
1992	Kerisel examines Great Pyramid for hidden chambers.
1993	Gantenbrink explores Queen's Chamber shafts and discovers artefacts and 'door'.
1995	Phase 2 of 'Pyramids Carbon-Dating Project'.
1996–8	Various Schor Foundation expeditions to Plateau to locate hidden chambers near Sphinx and elsewhere.
1999	Hawass reports that he plans to open Gantenbrink's 'door' just after millennium.

Theory Chronology

Date (c.)	Event
1859	Taylor publishes *The Great Pyramid: Why Was It Built and Who Built It?*
1865	Smyth surveys the Great Pyramid and postulates the 'pyramid inch'.
1888	Blavatsky publishes *The Secret Doctrine*.
1923–45	Cayce provides prophecies regarding Atlantis and the Hall of Records.
1926	Randall-Stevens receives channelled diagrams of initiation chambers under the Sphinx.
1931	Formation of the Association for Research and Enlightenment.
1971	Tompkins promotes mathematical properties in *Secrets of the Great Pyramid*.
1976	Sitchin suggests Great Pyramid is beacon for ancient spacecraft in *The Twelfth Planet*.
1979	West proposes earlier date for Sphinx in *Serpent in the Sky*.
1980	Sitchin suggests Vyse forged the quarry marks in *Stairway to Heaven*.
1985	Jochmans publishes *The Hall of Records*.
1994	Bauval and Gilbert postulate the 'Extended Shaft Alignment' and 'Orion Correlation' theories in *The Orion Mystery*.
1996	Alford suggests Great Pyramid is energy generator in *Gods of the New Millennium*, and supports Sitchin's argument re. Vyse forgeries.
1998	Collins examines evidence for sonic levitation in *Gods of Eden*. Renton promotes 'Wand of Isis' theory. Dunn promotes advanced machining technology and suggests Great Pyramid is energy generator in *The Giza Power Plant*.
1999	Reid and Brownlee experiment with non-advanced machining technology.

Politics Chronology

Date (c.)	Event
1993 onwards	The Said/West 'Mystery of the Sphinx' documentary puts forward alternative theories to worldwide audience. A huge row ensues with the authorities; subsequently West is excluded from further on-site investigations; West and Said part company.
1996–7	Bauval and Hancock spawn multiple conspiracy theories in *Keeper of Genesis*, followed up by public arguments with authorities and Schor.
	Danley reports clandestine tunnelling in Great Pyramid. Hoagland and Hunter pick it up and spread more conspiracy rumours.
1997	After falling-out with Schor, Said produces 'Behind the Scenes' documentary, which adds fuel to Schor cover-up theories. Schor files law suit against him.
1998	In major about-turn, Bauval, Hancock and West enter into entente cordiale with authorities and Schor.
	Appleby's Hermes expedition is refused permission to go to Egypt. His book is withdrawn from sale for alleged plagiarism from a number of authors. Ellis leads the effort, and eventually commences criminal proceedings against him. However, Bauval co-ordinates the other authors, then in another about-turn invites Appleby to join lecture tour in Egypt.
	Hunter and Hillier get together to promote former's theories about 'Hall of Osiris' hidden in Great Pyramid. They allege conspiracy and cover-up by the authorities, and another public argument ensues. Then Hillier denounces Hunter, and apologises to the authorities.
	Rumours about the Water Shaft and clandestine tunnels in the Great Pyramid increase. We enter both areas and obtain photographic evidence that nothing of great interest is going on.
1999	Bauval firms up his plans for 'Project Equinox 2000' and the 'Magic Twelve', although they change regularly.

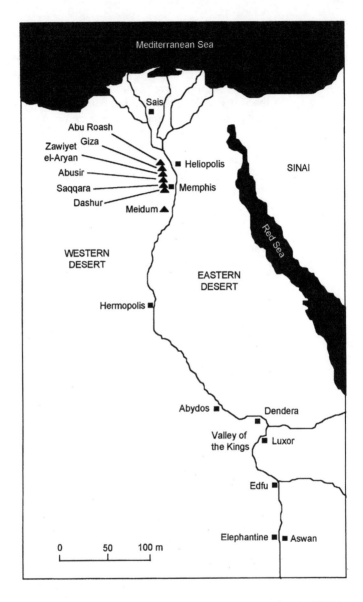

Mediterranean Sea

Sais

Abu Roash
Giza
Zawiyet el-Aryan
Abusir
Saqqara
Dashur
Meidum

Heliopolis

Memphis

SINAI

Red Sea

WESTERN DESERT

EASTERN DESERT

Hermopolis

Abydos

Dendera

Valley of the Kings

Luxor

Edfu

Elephantine   Aswan

0   50   100 m

APPENDIX VI: MAP OF THE MAJOR PYRAMID SITES

NOTES

Chapter 1: Early Explorations

[1] Vyse, *Operations*, Vol. II, Appendix, pp. 109–24.

[2] This translation is taken from Greaves, *Pyramidographia*, pp. 81–3. John Greaves explored the Great Pyramid in 1638, and wrote about his work and its history. We will introduce him properly later.

[3] Vyse, *Operations*, Vol. II, Appendix, pp. 321–30. This summary of Masoudi's account was apparently prepared by Dr Sprenger from a collection of Arab manuscripts which reproduce Masoudi's work (including those of Makrizi, whom we will mention shortly), and compared where possible with the highly damaged original manuscript of Masoudi himself.

[4] Greaves, *Pyramidographia*, pp. 83–4.

[5] Makrizi's account can be found in Vyse, *Operations*, Vol. II, Appendix, pp. 352–7. His work appears to be primarily a repetition of that of his predecessors.

[6] Both the following extracts are taken from Greaves, *Pyramidographia*, p. 84.

[7] This is taken from a translation of Edrisi's *History of the Pyramids* by JL Burkhardt, reproduced in Vyse, *Operations*, Vol. II, Appendix, p. 335.

[8] Vyse, *Operations*, Vol. II, Appendix, pp. 340–1.

[9] Lehner, *The Complete Pyramids*, Chapter II, p. 41.

[10] Pliny, *Natural History*, Book 36, Chapter 17, p. 336.

[11] Vyse, *Operations*, Vol. II, Appendix, p. 342.

[12] Greaves, *Pyramidographia*, p. 94, Footnote.

[13] Ibid., p. 62.

[14] Ibid., p. 93.

[15] Pliny, *Natural History*, Book 36, Chapter 17, p. 338.

[16] Greaves, *Pyramidographia*, p. 87.

[17] Belzoni, *Narrative . . .*, p. 422; the translation is by a Mr Salame. Note that in *Operations*, Vol. II, Appendix, p. 116, Vyse reproduces this and an alternative translation by Professor Lee of Queen's College,

Cambridge, as follows: 'The master Mohammed, son of Ahmed, the stone-cutter, first opened them; and upon this occasion were present El Melec Othman, and the master, Othman, and Mohammed Lugleik.'

[18] Edwards, 'The Air Channels of Chephren's Pyramid', *Studies in Honour of Dows Durham*, Boston, 1981, pp. 55–7.

[19] The Egyptologist JP Lepre, in *The Egyptian Pyramids*, Chapter V, p. 114, suggests that the shaft was an original feature which was dug to a depth of 60 feet, but he does not mention his source. However, we will see later that Vyse is quite specific that it was mainly dug through virgin bedrock by his own men.

[20] These are reproduced in Vyse, *Operations*, Vol. II, Appendix, p. 290.

[21] Ibid., Vol. II, Appendix, p. 291.

[22] Ibid, Vol. I, pp. 12–13.

[23] The details of this excavation come from ibid., Vol. III, Appendix, pp. 107–17. It consists of an account of Caviglia's work taken from Salt's papers.

[24] Ibid., Vol. III, Appendix, p. 111, Note 4.

[25] From an interpretation of the smaller Ramesses II stela by Birch included in ibid., Vol. III, Appendix, p. 117, Note 9.

[26] In fact, we have been informed that as of March 1999 these blocks have now been replaced as part of the ongoing restoration of the edifice by the authorities, so that the floor is once again complete.

[27] Vyse, *Operations*, Vol. I, pp. 223–4.

[28] Note that Vyse did not extend Caviglia's tunnel alongside the northern shaft at all.

[29] Ibid., Vol. I, pp. 205–7.

[30] Birch's description and interpretation of the hieroglyphs is contained in ibid., Vol. I, pp. 279–84.

[31] The upper cartouche has been copied from a drawing of the marks in Campbell's Chamber in ibid., Vol. II, after p. 158; the lower one from a drawing of the marks in Lady Arbuthnot's Chamber in ibid., Vol. II, after p. 14. Those in Nelson's Chamber can be found in ibid., Vol. II, after p. 158.

[32] Ibid., Vol. I, pp. 166 and 287.

[33] Perring's calculations in ibid., Vol. II, Appendix, p. 113, are as follows: estimated original volume of masonry: 89 million cubic feet; estimated space occupied by original chambers and passages: 56 thousand cubic feet. The proportion is therefore only 0.06 per cent.

[34] Ibid., Vol. I, p. 159.

[35] Hancock and Bauval, *Keeper of Genesis*, Chapter 6, pp. 110–5.

[36] Vyse, *Operations*, Vol. I, p. 276. Perring and Mash also produced certificates, which are reproduced by Vyse.

[37] Hancock and Bauval, *Keeper of Genesis*, Chapter 6, pp. 111–12; the tests were carried out by Dr MP Jones, Senior Tutor in the Mineral Resources Engineering Department at Imperial College, London, and his colleague Dr Sayed El Gayer, who gained a PhD in Extraction Metallurgy from Aston University in Birmingham.

[38] Vyse, *Operations*, Vol. I, p. 286.

[39] Ibid., Vol. I, p. 185.

[40] The entire account of Vyse's opening of the Third Pyramid is provided in *Operations*, Vol. II, pp. 70–100.

[41] Ibid., Vol. II, pp. 85–6.

[42] Taken from Lehner, *The Complete Pyramids*, Chapter III, p. 135.

[43] Taken from Vyse, *Operations*, Vol. II, Plate 19.

[44] Smyth, *Our Inheritance in the Great Pyramid*, Chapter XIX, pp. 428–9.

[45] Bauval and Gilbert, *The Orion Mystery*, Epilogue, pp. 241–50.

[46] Hancock and Bauval, *Keeper of Genesis*, Chapter 6, pp. 116–22.

[47] Lehner, *The Complete Pyramids*, Chapter III, p. 112. He states: 'A few objects were reportedly found in the northern air shaft in the late nineteenth century, now on display in the British Museum'; and references a small picture of the ball and hook. In fact it is not clear from Smyth's account in which shaft they were found.

[48] Ibid., Chapter II, p. 61.

[49] Ibid., Chapter IV, p. 232. See also reconstruction pictures pp. 204–5 and 230–1.

Chapter 2: When Were the Pyramids Built?

[50] For a thorough treatment of the sources of the orthodox framework, and the chronology applied to it, see Jordan, *Riddles of the Sphinx*, Chapter 3.

[51] Ibid., Chapter 3, pp. 37–9.

[52] Data derived from information in Lehner, *The Complete Pyramids*, Introduction, pp. 8–9 and 17.

[53] Data derived from information in ibid., Introduction, pp. 8–9 and 17.

[54] Adapted from ibid., Introduction, pp. 16–17.

[55] Herodotus's entire account is contained in *The Histories*, Book 2, pp. 144–9.

[56] For example see ibid., pp. 147–8, paras. 131 and 134.

[57] Diodorus Siculus, *Histories*, Book 1, Chapter 5, pp. 65–7.

[58] Vyse, *Operations*, Vol. I, p. 226.

[59] Zahi Hawass, Interview in *KMT*, Vol. 8, No. 2, Summer 1997, pp. 19–20.

[60] Hassan, *The Sphinx . . .*, p. 95.

[61] Lehner, *The Complete Pyramids*, Chapter II, p. 38.

[62] In a lecture given by Hawass to the ARE annual convention in August 1998 at Virginia Beach.

[63] Sitchin, *The Stairway to Heaven*, Chapter XIII, pp. 253–82.

[64] This is clearly demonstrated by Mark Lehner in the *Mysteries of the Pyramids* documentary, produced in 1988.

[65] The Internet address of Stower's web site is: <http://www.dcs.shef.ac.uk/~martins/Pyramid>.

[66] A detailed photograph is available for inspection at Stower's web site.

[67] Vyse, *Operations*, Vol. I, pp. 226 and 237–8.

[68] Ibid., Vol. III, Appendix. The marks found at the various sites are described in the following pages: Abusir, pp. 22–37; Saqqara, pp. 53–5; Dashur, pp. 72–6; and the Turah quarries, pp. 93–103.

[69] Sitchin, *The Wars of Gods and Men*, Chapter 7, p. 136.

[70] This is taken directly from Stower's web site (see above), but came originally from an article entitled 'More on Forging the Pharaoh's Name', which appeared in the journal of the Ancient Astronaut Society, *Ancient Skies*, July–August 1983. Its author was the editor, Gene M Phillips, and his source, although not named, must have been Sitchin or Mr Allen (the 'reader') himself. The other articles, written by Sitchin, are 'Forgery in the Great Pyramid', included in the Association for Research and Enlightenment's in-house magazine, *Venture Inward*, November–December 1986, pp. 33–7; and 'The Great Pyramid Forgery', in *FATE*, July 1993, pp. 47–58. See Stower's web site for further details.

[71] Hancock and Bauval, *Keeper of Genesis*, Chapter 6, pp. 108–9. In fact they quote an additional source: Joseph Jochmans, *The Hall of Records*, Part One, Chapter II, pp. 194–6 (this book was self-published in 1985). However, Jochmans himself only copies from Sitchin, and adds nothing new.

[72] The full statement can be reviewed on Stower's Internet web site (see note 65 for address).

[73] Wilson, *From Atlantis to the Sphinx*, Chapter 3, pp. 66–72.

[74] Collins, *From the Ashes of Angels*, Chapter 22, p. 323. The detail in Note 5 reveals that his source was also Jochmans.

[75] Alford, *Gods of the New Millennium*, Chapter 4, pp. 85–8.

[76] Ibid., Chapter 3, pp. 77–83.

[77] Jordan, *Riddles of the Sphinx*, Chapter 7, pp. 94–6.

[78] Sitchin, *The Stairway to Heaven*, Chapter XIII, pp. 256–9.

[79] Lehner, *The Complete Pyramids*, Chapter II, p. 38.

[80] Alford, *The Phoenix Solution*, Chapter 4, pp. 94–5.

[81] Lehner, *The Complete Pyramids*, Chapter III, p. 79.

[82] Edwards, *The Pyramids of Egypt*, Chapter 4, p. 94.

[83] Vyse, *Operations*, Vol. II, Appendix, pp. 115 and 119–20.

[84] Lehner, *The Complete Pyramids*, Chapter II, p. 45.

[85] Ibid., Chapter III, p. 111.

[86] Alford, *The Phoenix Solution*, Chapters 3 and 4.

[87] Ibid., Chapter 2, p. 53.

[88] Lehner, *The Complete Pyramids*, Chapter II, pp. 66–7.

[89] *Venture Inward*, May–June 1986, p. 13.

[90] See Herbert Haas, James Devine, Robert Wenke, Mark Lehner, Willy Wolfli and Georg Bonani, 'Radiocarbon Chronology and the Historical Calendar in Egypt', *Chronologies in the Near East*, BAR International Series 379 (ii), pp. 585–606.

[91] Lepre uses the chronology developed by Sir Arthur Weighall in his *History of the Pharaohs* (1925).

[92] Hancock and Bauval, *Keeper of Genesis*, Appendix 5, pp. 323–6.

[93] Alford, *The Phoenix Solution*, Appendix A, pp. 419–22. Some interesting further observations about the technique can be found in Dunn, *The Giza Power Plant*, Chapter 15, pp. 246–9.

[94] Ibid., Chapter 1, pp. 7–10.

[95] Lehner, *The Complete Pyramids*, Chapter II, p. 67.

[96] In a lecture given by Lehner to the ARE's annual convention in August 1998 at Virginia Beach.

Chapter 3: Why Were the Pyramids Built?

[97] Tompkins, *Secrets of the Great Pyramid*, Introduction, p. xiv.

[98] Lemesurier, *The Great Pyramid Decoded*, Chapter 1, p. 7.

[99] West, *Serpent in the Sky*, p. 13.

[100] Sitchin, *The Stairway to Heaven*, Chapter XII, p. 251.

[101] Alford, *Gods of the New Millennium*, Chapter 4, pp. 88 and 90.

[102] Alford, *The Phoenix Solution*, Chapter 3, p. 75.

[103] Dunn, *The Giza Power Plant*, Chapter 1, p. 11.

[104] Vyse, *Operations*, Vol. II, Appendix, p. 345.

[105] Belzoni, *Narrative . . .*, p. 430.

[106] Vyse, *Operations*, Vol. I, p. 287.

[107] Ibid., Vol. III, Appendix, p. 69.

[108] Ibid., Vol. I, pp. 224–5.

NOTES

[109] Vercoutter, *The Search for Ancient Egypt*, pp. 55–9 and 180–1.

[110] This is taken from a translation of a paper entitled 'The Pyramid of Cheops: Latest Research' written by Kerisel for the French *Revue d'Egyptologie*, No. 44, 1993, Section II. The section is entitled 'The Origin of the Breaches in the Superimposed Roofs of the King's Chamber'.

[111] Strabo, *Geographica*, Vol. III, Book 17, Chapter 1, p. 249.

[112] Diodorus Siculus, *Histories*, Book 1, Chapter 5, p. 66.

[113] Noel F Wheeler, 'The Pyramids and Their Purpose II: The Pyramid of Khufu', *Antiquity*, IX, 1935, pp. 179–80. This view has been supported more recently by Maragioglio and Rinaldi.

[114] See for example Lehner, *The Complete Pyramids*, Chapter II, p. 41.

[115] Vyse, *Operations*, Vol. II, Appendix, p. 345.

[116] Ibid., Vol. II, Appendix, p. 117, Note 2. The French reads: 'Nous avons regardé par une ouverture, qui etait faite dans *l'un de ces edifices*, et qui est profonde de cinquante coudées . . .'

[117] A long discourse on this issue is presented by Vyse in ibid., Vol. II, Appendix, pp. 340–1, Note 8. It is written by M De Sacy, and quotes a great many references which others might like to follow up. However, surprisingly, it appears to make exactly the same mistake in assuming Denys was referring to the Great Pyramid.

[118] Lehner, *The Complete Pyramids*, Chapter II, p. 41.

[119] Noel F Wheeler, 'The Pyramids and Their Purpose II: The Pyramid of Khufu', *Antiquity*, IX, 1935, pp. 181–2.

[120] Ibid., pp. 180–1.

[121] Diodorus Siculus, *Histories*, Book 1, Chapter 5, p. 66.

[122] Lepre, *The Egyptian Pyramids*, Chapter X, pp. 265–72.

[123] Collins, *From the Ashes of Angels*, Chapter 22, p. 323.

[124] Lehner, *The Complete Pyramids*, Chapter III, p. 114.

[125] Hancock and Bauval, *Keeper of Genesis*, Conclusion, p. 284.

[126] For example in ibid., Alford's *Phoenix*, and Lehner's *The Complete Pyramids* (Chapter I). The following translations are also readily available for those who would like to learn more: EA Wallis-Budge, *The Egyptian Heaven and Hell* (for the *Books of the Duat* and *Gates*); and Dr Raymond Faulkner, *The Ancient Egyptian Book of the Dead*, *The Ancient Egyptian Pyramid Texts* and *The Ancient Egyptian Coffin Texts*.

[127] A number of authors are quoted on these issues in Tompkins, *Secrets of the Great Pyramid*, Chapter XX, pp. 256–9. These include Helena Blavatsky, William Kingsland, Manley P Hall, Giorgio de Santillana and Henri Furville, among others.

[128] Tompkins, *Secrets of the Great Pyramid*, Chapter XXII, p. 284.

[129] For more details on these daily rituals see Lehner, *The Complete Pyramids*, Chapter IV, pp. 233–5.

[130] For a full discussion on this, and the reasons why it may also be incorrect, see Edwards, *The Pyramids of Egypt*, Chapter 7, p. 222.

[131] For a fuller discussion of the *phi* relationship and the importance of the Golden Mean see Tompkins, *Secrets of the Great Pyramid*, Chapter XV. Note that Tompkins argues that the incorporation of this proportion means that one side of the Great Pyramid is a geometrically accurate representation of the mapping of a quadrant of the globe on to a flat surface. While this is mathematically true, to us it seems to be something of a red herring.

[132] See para. 124 of the Herodotus extracts quoted in Chapter 2.

[133] In fact, the exact angles required for the two relationships are slightly different: the *pi* relationship requires an angle of 51 degrees 51′ 14″ (51.85404 in decimals), whereas the *phi* relationship requires only 51 degrees 49′ 38″ (51.82735 in decimals), to produce results accurate to 6 decimal places.

[134] Lehner, *The Complete Pyramids*, Introduction, p. 17.

[135] Alford, *The Phoenix Solution*, Chapter 2, pp. 40–1.

[136] Tompkins, *Secrets of the Great Pyramid*, Chapter XVI.

[137] Ibid., Chapter VII, p. 94.

[138] Ibid., Chapter IX, pp. 114–6.

[139] Vyse, *Operations*, Vol. II, Appendix, pp. 107–9.

[140] A fuller discussion of these issues can be found in Tompkins, *Secrets of the Great Pyramid*, Chapter XIII, and in de Santillana and von Dechend, *Hamlet's Mill* (1969), and Schwaller de Lubicz, *Sacred Science* (1988).

[141] Tompkins, *Secrets of the Great Pyramid*, Chapter XII.

[142] Ibid., Chapter XII, p. 148.

[143] Sitchin, *The Stairway to Heaven*, Chapter XII, pp. 232–4 and 251.

[144] Sitchin, *The Wars of Gods and Men*, Chapter 8, pp. 167–72. A further section about the construction of the pyramid is contained in Chapter 10, pp. 202–15.

[145] Alford, *Gods of the New Millennium*, Chapter 9.

Chapter 4: How Were the Pyramids Built?

[146] It will be difficult to provide accurate footnotes for each of the arguments used by each of these Egyptologists throughout, since each of us takes a significantly different approach in terms of the order in which we deal with the various issues. Suffice to say that the following

are the general references to their work: Lehner, *The Complete Pyramids*, Chapter IV, pp. 202–23; Edwards, *The Pyramids of Egypt*, Chapter 7; and Lepre, *The Egyptian Pyramids*, Chapter IX.

[147] For pictures of examples of these tools, which are now housed in the Cairo Museum, see Lehner, *The Complete Pyramids*, Chapter IV, p. 210.

[148] Taken from Edwards, *Pyramids of Egypt*, Ch. 7, p. 202.

[149] Ibid., Chapter IV, p. 203.

[150] Lepre, *The Egyptian Pyramids*, Chapter IX, p. 244.

[151] Taken from an article entitled 'Assembling Pyramid Proof' in *Ground Engineering*, January 1999, pp. 24–6. A full report by Dr Parry entitled 'On the Construction of the Great Pyramid at Giza' is available from the Department of Engineering at Cambridge University on request. We should also note that the Japanese team were impressively able to pull a similarly clad 2.5-tonne block using 18 men up a 1-in-4 slope with 'considerable ease'; we will see shortly that this is more than twice as steep as the gradients we assume to have been used for the sledge method later on, and would considerably shorten the length of ramp required. Nevertheless, we feel that the limitations of this method that we point out preclude it from further serious consideration. It would also appear that the ancient quadrant or cradle that they examined was a mere 9.2 inches long – which hardly suggests it was used for the purpose proposed.

[152] Lehner goes into considerable depth in describing the techniques that would have been used for initial surveying, alignment and levelling in *The Complete Pyramids*, Chapter IV, pp. 212–14.

[153] The experiment is described in ibid., Chapter IV, pp. 208–9.

[154] Lehner initially says '20 men or fewer', but subsequently refines this to 10 to 12 men on p. 224.

[155] Herodotus, *The Histories*, Book 2, pp. 144–5.

[156] Lepre, *The Egyptian Pyramids*, Chapter IX, pp. 254–62. In particular the diagrams of his machine can be found on pp. 258–9.

[157] Baldridge is a graduate of Edinburgh University's Centre for Cognitive Science. His theories are contained in an undergraduate paper written in 1995–6 entitled 'Moving and Lifting the Construction Blocks of the Great Pyramid', and reproduced on his web site at the following Internet address: <http://www.ling.upenn.edu/~jason2/papers/pyramid.htm>

[158] Taken from ibid., and reproduced with the kind permission of Jason Baldridge.

[159] Hawass, Interview in *KMT*, Vol. 8, No. 2, Summer 1997, p. 21.

[160] Diodorus Siculus, *Histories*, Book 1, Chapter 5, p. 66.

[161] Pliny, *Natural History*, Book 36, Chapter 17, pp. 337–8.

[162] Lepre, *The Egyptian Pyramids*, Chapter IX, p. 254.

[163] Lehner, *The Complete Pyramids*, Chapter IV, p. 217. Note also his depiction of the layout of the Plateau during the construction of the Great Pyramid on pp. 204–5.

[164] Alford makes great play of these discoveries to support his contention that the Great Pyramid was built in an earlier epoch, arguing that Khufu would not have diverted any resources away from the challenging new technology represented by his pyramid until it was completed. However, we are of the view that the logistics are not as bad as he suggests, that there would have been men to spare, and that the relatively simple mastaba structures would have added little to the overall effort of a team who were superbly organised in the first place. To us this also indicates that the layout of the entire complex was well understood early on.

[165] Hassan, *Excavations at Giza*, Vol. 10, 1938–9, Appendix, pp. 49–51. See also ibid., Plate XVII, or Lehner, *The Complete Pyramids*, Chapter IV, p. 211, for pictures.

[166] Lehner, *The Complete Pyramids*, Chapter IV, p. 216. Furthermore, during the Giza Mapping Project, Lehner found holes in the corner blocks of the Great Pyramid's southernmost satellite at various levels. Vertical poles set into these and rising through the ramps could have allowed backsiting to be performed.

[167] Baldridge, op. cit. The two references he quotes are, in full: Peterson, I, 'Ancient Technology: Pouring a Pyramid', *Science News*, 26 May 1984, Vol. 125, p. 327; and Harrell, James A, and Penrod, Bret E, 'The Great Pyramid Debate – Evidence from the Lauer Sample', *Journal of Geological Education*, 1993, Vol. 41, pp. 358–63.

[168] Vyse, *Operations*, Vol. I, p. 166, Note 7.

[169] Ibid., Vol. I, p. 166.

[170] Ibid., Vol. II, Appendix, pp. 344–5.

[171] Lehner goes into considerable depth in describing the techniques that would have been used for surveying and alignment as the pyramids rose course by course in *The Complete Pyramids*, Chapter IV, pp. 218–21.

[172] Protruding bosses are also readily visible on these unfinished casing stones, which would have assisted their handling using ropes given that they were not a standard cube shape.

[173] Vyse, *Operations*, Vol. II, Appendix, p. 329.

[174] Diodorus Siculus, *Histories*, Book 1, Chapter 5, p. 66; and Pliny, *Natural History* Book 36, Chapter 17, p. 337.

[175] Lepre, *The Egyptian Pyramids*, Chapter V, p. 109.

[176] Lehner, *The Complete Pyramids*, Chapter III, p. 104.

[177] Edwards, *The Pyramids of Egypt*, Chapter 7, p. 217.

[178] Lehner, *The Complete Pyramids*, Chapter IV, pp. 206–7 and 224–5.

[179] Calculated from the following formula: volume = area of base × height ÷ 3.

[180] Taken from Lehner, *The Complete Pyramids*, Chapter IV, p. 202.

[181] Tompkins, *Secrets of the Great Pyramid*, Chapter XVIII, p. 234.

[182] This higher figure is, for example, supported by Petrie. However, we should note that an entirely different analysis was supposedly provided to Hancock and Bauval (see *Keeper of Genesis*, Note 9 to Chapter 3, p. 342) by Kerisel, in the form of an unpublished manuscript of a book entitled *La Grande Pyramide et ses Derniers Secrets*, which was due to be published in 1996. Herein he suggests that any pressure exceeding 1.5 tonnes per square metre would cause the lubricant to seep away, and that, because of this and other factors, the friction coefficient would reduce the average to less than 0.1 tonne per man; therefore the figure quoted in the note for a 70-tonne block is 807 men – although in the main text this is magically reduced to 600 for no obvious reason (p. 32). We have been unable to ascertain whether this book was in fact published, but in any case – despite our possible agreement with Kerisel regarding the structural issues of the Great Pyramid – we feel that: (a) his analysis *may* be entirely theoretical and not practical, unlike the NOVA Experiment; (b) it takes no account of the evidence of, for example, the Djehutihotep relief; and (c) greater numbers of men would still not invalidate our basic analysis, since the granite blocks are relatively few in number, and there would be plenty of space available for more men.

[183] Lepre, *The Egyptian Pyramids*, Chapter V, pp. 108–9.

[184] Lehner, *The Complete Pyramids*, Chapter IV, p. 210.

[185] Based on Kerisel's figures as discussed above, Hancock and Bauval (see *Keeper of Genesis*, Chapter 3, p. 32) suggest this would require of the order of 1,800 men. We have suggested these figures are probably gross inflations anyway, but since in principle we agree with their arguments, even if only 600 men were involved, the issue requires no further comment.

[186] Vyse, *Operations*, Vol. I, pp. 220–1.

[187] For example, see Hancock and Bauval, *Keeper of Genesis*, Chapter 3, pp. 28–30; and Alford, *Gods of the New Millennium*, Chapter 3, p. 53.

[188] Alford, *Gods of the New Millennium*, Chapter 3, pp. 51–2.

[189] Ibid., Plate 3.

[190] Collins, *Gods of Eden*, Chapter 3, pp. 35–7.

[191] Vyse, *Operations*, Vol. II, Appendix, p. 325. The translation is once again by Dr Sprenger (see note 3).

[192] Collins, *Gods of Eden*, Chapter 5, pp. 58–60. Collins's primary source is Osborne, *South American Mythology* (1968).

[193] Ibid., Chapter 5, p. 61.

[194] Ibid., Chapter 5, pp. 62–5.

[195] Ibid., Chapter 8, pp. 98–104; the biblical extract comes from *Joshua* 6: 3–5 (Authorised King James Version).

[196] Ibid., Chapter 5, pp. 66–74.

[197] Ibid., Chapter 7, pp. 88–97. Collins's primary source is Pond, *Universal Laws Never Before Revealed: Keely's Secrets* (1990). See also Blavatsky, *The Secret Doctrine* (1888), Book I, Part III, Chapter X, pp. 554–60.

[198] Dunn, *The Giza Power Plant*, Chapter 6, pp. 109–19. He indicates that more information, including some of Leedskalnin's papers on electricity and magnetism, can be obtained from Coral Castle, 28655 S. Dixie Highway, Homestead, FL 33030, USA (tel. 305–248–6344).

[199] For example, the work of Nikola Tesla and others is covered in a number of books on antigravity by David Hatcher Childress, including *The Anti-Gravity Handbook*, *Anti-Gravity and the Unified Field* and *Anti-Gravity and The World Grid*.

[200] Readers wishing to learn more about this topic can visit the NASA Technical Report web site at the following Internet address: <http:// techreports.larc.nasa.gov/cgi-bin/NTRS>.

[201] Taken from an interview with Said conducted by *FATE* magazine in April 1998.

[202] Quoted from his appearance in the *Behind the Scenes* compilation video produced by Said in 1997, of which there will be more in Part III.

[203] Dunn, *The Giza Power Plant*, Chapter 8, pp. 139–43, and Chapter 9, pp. 158–61. The whole of Chapter 8 has some interesting further observations about resonance and harmonics, including a description of Tesla's near destruction of a large building in which he was experimenting.

[204] From a paper kindly prepared specifically for us by Reid in February 1999, which summarises his current research, although without details of the specific results, which should be published in the autumn of 1999. See also *Quest for Knowledge*, Vol. 1, Issue 9, pp. 16–17.

[205] Dunn, *The Giza Power Plant*, Appendix B, p. 264.

[206] Petrie, *The Pyramids and Temples of Gizeh*, pp. 74–8. This chapter, entitled 'The Mechanical Methods of the Pyramid Builders', is reproduced in full by Dunn in op. cit., Appendix A, pp. 257–62.

[207] In addition to Petrie's observations in the appendix, Dunn has prepared diagrams illustrating these principles operating on the artefacts in op. cit., Chapter 4, p. 82, Figure 19.

[208] A reproduction of Petrie's drawings of the specific artefacts that he felt showed signs of machining technology can be found in Dunn op. cit., Chapter 4, p. 73. Meanwhile, the hinge hole in the Valley Temple is in the upper lintel of the doorway to the chambers that lie in the southwest corner of the 'T-piece' of the main hall. Furthermore the Petrie Museum can be found at Malet Place, London WC1, and the items in question are mainly housed in 'Case J'.

[209] Ibid., Chapter 9, pp. 168–72. This includes another photo of the 'balanced' bowl.

[210] Ibid., Chapter 3, pp. 50–1 and 56.

[211] Ibid., Chapter 5, pp. 94–9.

[212] Ibid., Chapter 3, pp. 56–7.

[213] Ibid., Chapter 4, p. 76. Reproduced from Petrie, *The Pyramids and Temples of Gizeh*, p. 29.

[214] Ibid., Chapter 4, pp. 80–1. Reproduced from Petrie, *The Pyramids and Temples of Gizeh*, p. 29.

[215] Ibid., Chapter 4, pp. 77–81.

[216] Ibid., Chapter 4, pp. 83–6.

[217] Ibid., Chapter 4, pp. 87–91.

[218] From Reid's paper prepared for us in February 1999.

[219] For Dunn's explanation as to how the 'balanced' vase must have been machined see *The Giza Power Plant*, Ch. 9, pp. 170–1.

[220] From Reid's paper prepared for us in February 1999.

[221] Dunn, *The Giza Power Plant*, Chapter 9, pp. 169 and 172.

[222] From an interview with Dr Hawass conducted by 'Carte Blanche' in 1998. The details can be found at the following Internet address: <http://www.mnet.co.za/carteblanche/week/981206_egypt.html>.

Chapter 5: Legends of the Hall

[223] Tomas, *On the Shores of Endless Worlds*, Chapter 15, pp. 137–53.

[224] Budge primarily uses a version of the text found in the tomb of King Seti I of the Nineteenth Dynasty. Note that the other main text in *The Egyptian Heaven and Hell* is the *Book of Gates*, translated from a version found on the sarcophagus of the same king, which also deals with the Twelve Divisions of the *duat*. Meanwhile the other three main sets of ancient Egyptian texts, the *Book of the Dead*, and the *Pyramid* and *Coffin Texts*, are in 'spell' form.

[225] Collins, *Gods of Eden*, Chapter 12, p. 166. His discussion of the *Book of the Duat* can be found in this chapter. Meanwhile, we should also note that Mark Lehner had already to some extent paved the way for this analysis in his *The Egyptian Heritage*, Part 2, Chapter 2, p. 117–20. This was published back in 1974, and Lehner also references CJ Bleeker's *Egyptian Festivals*.

[226] An illustration can be found in ibid., Chapter 12, p. 165; this should be compared with various illustrations in Budge, *The Egyptian Heaven and Hell*, pp. 63, 71 and 87.

[227] This linking of Giza and Rostau (or Rosetjau) seems to be universally accepted – see for example Bauval and Gilbert, *The Orion Mystery*, Chapter 6, pp. 120–3.

[228] Budge, *The Egyptian Heaven and Hell*, p. 93.

[229] Taken from ibid., p. 103.

[230] Ibid., p. 70.

[231] Collins, *Gods of Eden*, Chapter 13, pp. 174–80. His source of translation is Dr EAE Reymond's *The Mythical Origin of the Egyptian Temple*. The remainder of his discussion of these issues can be found in chapters 13 to 15.

[232] We finally obtained a copy from Collins himself, who took the trouble to photocopy and bind all 155 pages of Chapter II for us. We have also noted previously that Lehner had to some extent paved the way for Jochmans's analysis – at least of the Fourth and Fifth Divisions of the *duat* – back in 1974.

[233] A commentary on this text was produced by the Egyptologist Alan Gardiner in the *Journal of Egyptian Archaeology* in 1925. This has been reproduced by Bauval and Gilbert in *The Orion Mystery*, Appendix 3, pp. 264–9.

[234] Gilbert summarised his position in a posting to our *EgyptNews* Internet mailing list on 15 August 1998. By the end of the posting, however, and in an apparent departure from his previously sound logic, he effectively reverts to Gardiner's scenario.

[235] Herodotus, *The Histories*, Book 2, p. 155.

[236] Tomas, *On the Shores of Ancient Worlds*, Chapter 15, p. 149.

[237] Ibid., Chapter 15, pp. 150–1.

[238] Vyse, *Operations*, Vol. II, Appendix, p. 330, Note 7.

[239] Tomas, *On the Shores of Ancient Worlds*, Chapter 15, p. 145. The Marcellinus report appears to be more or less confirmed by Collins in *Gods of Eden*, Chapter 12, p. 170.

[240] Ibid., Chapter 15, p. 142. The original source may be found in Plato, *Timaeus*, pp. 22–3 (Stephanus Edition) or pp. 34–6 (Penguin Edition).

[241] Hancock and Bauval, *Keeper of Genesis*, Note 1 to Chapter 5, p. 345.

[242] Vyse, *Operations*, Vol. II, Appendix, p. 324, Note 3.

[243] Ibid., Vol. II, Appendix, p. 325 and Note 4.

[244] Ibid., Vol. II, Appendix, p. 325, Note 5; and Greaves, *Pyramidographia*, p. 82.

[245] Ibid., Vol. II, Appendix, pp. 328–9.

[246] Ibid., Vol. II, Appendix, pp. 335–6.

[247] Excerpt from Gilbert's posting to our *EgyptNews* Internet mailing list on 15 August 1998. The source is Scott's translation of one of the books of the *Hermetica*, the *Kore Kosmu*, Section 66.

[248] Anyone wishing to further explore the various doctrines should consult Manley P Hall's *An Encyclopedic Outline of Masonic, Hermetic, Qabbalistic and Rosicrucian Symbolic Philosophy* (1901).

[249] Collins, *From the Ashes of Angels*, Chapter 2, p. 13; his source is Richard Laurence's *The Book of Enoch the Prophet* (1838).

[250] Tomas, *On the Shores of Ancient Worlds*, Chapter 15, pp. 151–2.

[251] Lewis, *The Symbolic Prophecy of the Great Pyramid*, pp. 123–31 and 184–90. Further information on the Rosicrucian concept of the initiation ceremonies carried out in the Great Pyramid is contained in an article entitled 'The Thought of the Month: Within the King's Chamber', *Rosicrucian Digest*, March 1954, p. 84.

[252] Blavatsky, *The Secret Doctrine*, Introduction, pp. xxii–xxiii.

[253] During a dissertation on sacred numerology, Blavatsky discusses Smyth's views about the incorporation of the *pi* relationship into the Great Pyramid and, pleasingly, remains unmoved by Petrie's apparent refutation of the theory based on his then relatively new measurements; that is to say she has a refreshingly objective view of the edifice, and her doctrine remains independent of such theories. She does, however, briefly discuss initiation ceremonies conducted in the King's Chamber in a footnote (see ibid., Book I, Part II, Chapter II, pp. 313–18). She further elucidates the nature of these ceremonies in ibid., Book II, Part II, Chapter XVII, p. 462. No other significant mention of the Great Pyramid or its counterparts is made, nor does she necessarily appear to attribute any great age to the pyramids or the Sphinx.

[254] Ibid., Introduction, p. xxiii.

[255] Ibid., Introduction, p. xxiv.

[256] Ibid., Introduction, p. xliv.

[257] Ibid., Introduction, pp. xl–xli.

[258] Ibid., Introduction, pp. xxxiv–xxxv.

[259] Tomas, *On the Shores of Ancient Worlds*, Chapter 15, pp. 147–8.

[260] Blavatsky, *The Secret Doctrine*, Introduction, pp. xvii–xix.

[261] A number of readings consistently mention this date; see *Edgar Cayce on Atlantis*, Chapter 5, p. 142.

[262] Reading 440–5; see ibid., Chapter 4, pp. 90–1.

[263] Reading 2012–1; see ibid., Chapter 5, p. 146.

[264] Reading 5750–1; see ibid., Chapter 5, pp. 114 and 118.

[265] Reading 378–16; see ibid., Chapter 5, p. 148.

[266] Lemesurier, *The Great Pyramid Decoded*, Chapter 8, p. 237, and Chapter 9, p. 300.

[267] Reading 2329–3; see Lehner, *The Egyptian Heritage*, Part 1, Chapter 7, p. 97.

[268] Reading 2537–1; see ibid., Part 1, Chapter 7, p. 99.

[269] Johnson, *Edgar Cayce in Context*, Chapter 1, p. 35.

[270] Ibid., Chapter 3, pp. 81–95.

[271] Reading 958–3; see ibid., Chapter 3, p. 83.

[272] Readings 2157–1, 262–39, 2913–1, 187–1, 519–1, and 440–5; see *Edgar Cayce on Atlantis*, Chapter 3, pp. 78–80, and Chapter 4 pp. 84–93.

[273] Readings 5748–6, 5748–5 and 2823–1; see Lehner, *The Egyptian Heritage*, Part 1, Chapter 7, pp. 87–8 and 91–3.

[274] Reading 5748–6; see ibid., Part 1, Chapter 7, p. 88.

[275] Johnson, *Edgar Cayce in Context*, Chapter 2, pp. 43–8.

[276] Ibid., Introduction, p. 6. The quote comes from Sugrue, *There is a River*, Chapter 15, p. 200.

[277] Ibid., Introduction, pp. 7–8.

[278] Readings 5748–2 and 706–1; see Lehner, *The Egyptian Heritage*, Part 2, Chapter 2, pp. 115–17.

[279] Background information from Randall-Stevens himself comes from *Atlantis to the Latter Days*, Foreword, and Part I, Chapters I–III.

[280] Ibid., Part II, between pp. 108 and 109.

[281] Ibid., Part I, Chapter VI, pp. 51–4. Footnote 2 on p. 54 also suggests: 'A stela in the form of a large stone scarab was found during excavations near the Great Pyramid in June 1954. The writing on it stated that he [Khufu] was buried near the south face of the Pyramid.' However, we can trace no reference for this supposed find.

[282] Ibid., Part I, Chapter VII, pp. 55–64.

[283] This at least is surely an accurate prediction of the type of technology being developed in, for example, the 'High-Frequency Active Auroral Research Program' (HAARP) run jointly by the University of Alaska and the US Military. For those of you unfamiliar with this project, it is a particularly perplexing one which is experimenting with the focusing of radio-frequency radiation on to specific parts of the ionosphere. That it could have dire consequences is explained in detail

by Nick Begich and Jeane Manning in *Angels Don't Play This HAARP* (1995).

284 Taken from Randall-Stevens, *Atlantis to the Latter Days*, Part I, Plate VI, between pp. 64 and 65.

285 Taken from ibid., Part I, Plate VII, between pp. 64 and 65.

286 Morton and Thomas, *The Mystery of the Crystal Skulls*, Chapter 7, pp. 68–79. Further information on the skulls can be found in an article by Charles Pelton entitled 'The Crystal Skull Enigma', *Atlantis Rising*, Issue 10, Winter 1997.

287 Walker, *The Stone of the Plough*, Appendix 1, pp. 317–20.

288 Ibid., Chapter 35, pp. 308–9. During a meeting with Walker on 21 March 1998, Chris asked to see the 'affidavit' but was told it was 'private correspondence'.

289 Ibid., Chapter 35, p. 311.

290 Ibid., Chapter 35, p. 312.

291 In an e-mail dated 19 August 1998 from their Member Services Department. The relevant readings quoted in this communication are as follows: 378–16, p. 2, para. 5; 1602–3, p. 6, para. 21; 3976–15, p. 2, para. 8; 294–151, p. 3, para. 9; 378–14, p. 3, paras. 6–7; 1602–3, p. 2, para. 8; 5748–5, p. 2; 5750–1, p. 4; 378–16, p. 3; 294–15, p. 3; and 5748–5, p. 1, para. 4. Meanwhile, Johnson notes that the ARE leadership's attitude towards '1998' had become increasingly ambivalent in the run-up; see *Edgar Cayce in Context*, Chapter 3, pp. 91 and 95.

292 Reading 3796–15; see *Edgar Cayce on Atlantis*, Chapter 6, pp. 158–9.

293 Reading 5750–1; see ibid., Chapter 5, p. 118.

294 For a description of its formation in Cayce's own words see A Robert Smith, *The Lost Memoirs of Edgar Cayce*, Chapter 22, pp. 202–7.

295 Hancock and Bauval, *Keeper of Genesis*, Chapter 5, pp. 93–104.

296 Johnson, *Edgar Cayce in Context*, Chapter 3, p. 68. The source reference is to the biography of Hugh Lynn Cayce written by A Robert Smith.

297 Lehner, *The Egyptian Heritage*, Part 2, Chapter 4, p. 132.

298 For more on this see the series of three articles written by Lehner for *Venture Inward*, January–February, March–April and May–June 1986.

299 Johnson, *Edgar Cayce in Context*, Chapter 3, p. 68. The source reference is to the biography of Hugh Lynn Cayce written by A Robert Smith.

300 From an article by Dr Hawass entitled 'History of the Conservation

of the Sphinx' reproduced at the following Internet site: <http://guardians.net/hawass/sphinx2.htm>.

Chapter 6: The Hunt for Secret Chambers

[301] These systems basically apply different methods to probe beneath the subsurface of the object being surveyed.

[302] Luis W Alvarez et al., 'Search for Hidden Chambers in the Pyramids', *Science*, Vol. 167, 6 February 1970, p. 839.

[303] The basic method had been established some ten years earlier, when in 1955 cosmic-ray detectors had been successfully utilised to establish the thickness of rock covering a 'powerhouse' in the Snowy Mountains of Australia.

[304] Tompkins, *Secrets of the Great Pyramid*, Chapter XXI, pp. 273–4.

[305] Von Däniken, *Return of the Gods*, pp. 152–3; his source is an article in a 1969 edition of the German newspaper *Der Spiegel*.

[306] *Science*, Vol. 167, 6 February 1970, p. 838.

[307] Ibid., p. 839.

[308] 'Applications of Modern Sensing Techniques to Egyptology: A Report of the 1977 Field Experiments by a Joint Team: Ain Shams University, SRI International & Organization of Antiquities', published by SRI International, Menlo Park, California, September 1977, p. 1.

[309] In a lecture given by Lehner to the ARE's annual convention in August 1998 at Virginia Beach.

[310] After SRI, 'Applications of Modern Sensing Techniques to Egyptology', Figure 95, p. 126. Reproduced by kind permission of Lambert Dolphin.

[311] E-mail communication with Dolphin, 7 February 1999.

[312] SRI, 'Applications of Modern Sensing Techniques to Egyptology', p. 64.

[313] After ibid., Figure 109, p. 141. Reproduced by kind permission of Lambert Dolphin.

[314] Ibid., p. 137.

[315] Jochmans, *The Hall of Records*, Part One, Chapter II, p. 185.

[316] After ibid., Figure 107, p. 139. Reproduced by kind permission of Lambert Dolphin.

[317] E-mail communication with Dolphin, 1 February 1999.

[318] After SRI, 'Applications of Modern Sensing Techniques to Egyptology', Figure 47, p. 66. Reproduced by kind permission of Lambert Dolphin.

[319] E-mail communication with Dolphin, 7 February 1999.

[320] Ibid., p. 67.

[321] E-mail communication with Jahoda, 9 November 1998.

[322] From a lecture given by Lehner to the ARE's annual convention in August 1998 at Virginia Beach.

[323] E-mail communication with Dolphin, 8 February 1999.

[324] E-mail communication with Dolphin, 10 February 1999.

[325] 'Pyramid Selling', *Sunday Times*, 20 September 1998.

[326] Dormion and Goidin, *Les Nouveaux Mystères de la Grande Pyramide*, p. 92.

[327] Lepre, *The Egyptian Pyramids*, Chapter V, p. 105. Lepre also noted that by diligent observation Smyth had noticed discrepancies in the orientation of the wall blocks of the Descending Passage about 35 feet in, accompanied by inscribed lines on the walls, leading him to believe that they pointed to a concealed entrance to an additional *Ascending* Passage. He was led to this conclusion by the fact that further down the passage he noticed a similar unorthodox joint in the floor underneath the entrance to the Ascending Passage proper. See ibid., Chapter V, pp. 73–4.

[328] After Dormion and Goidin, *Les Nouveaux Mystères de la Grande Pyramide*, p. 198, in acknowledgements of Albin Michel.

[329] Ibid., p. 199.

[330] Both seasons' work was published in two volumes by the Waseda University: 'Studies in Egyptian Culture No. 6' covers the 1987 season and 'Studies in Egyptian Culture No. 8' the 1988 season. The second volume is a far better publication than the first, which is mostly composed of GPR printouts and photographs of limestone and sand under laboratory conditions with accompanying text. Perhaps an interesting scientific paper, but archaeologically disappointing.

[331] Waseda University, 'Studies in Egyptian Culture No. 8', p. 50.

[332] For a brief analysis of the sand and the location of its possible source, see Shoji Tonouchi in ibid., pp. 86–7.

[333] See Kerisel, 'The Pyramid of Cheops: Latest Research', *Revue d'Egyptologie*, No. 44, 1993, Section III, pp. 4–8. This section is entitled 'Peculiarities in the Pyramid's Subterranean Domaine'.

[334] Lepre, *The Egyptian Pyramids*, Chapter V, pp. 103–4.

[335] Ibid., Chapter X, pp. 275–8.

[336] For a comprehensive list of excavations carried out at Giza and elsewhere see Lehner, *The Complete Pyramids*, Chapter II, pp. 68–9.

Chapter 7: The Age of the Sphinx

[337] Vyse, *Operations*, Vol. III, Appendix, p. 115. It has been suggested by West and others that the phrase 'Khaf' appears in many Egyptian words, but the decisive issue would appear to be Birch's statement that it appears in a cartouche, indicating it is part of a king's name. The situation is complicated by the fact that the original inscription on this line flaked off long ago due to exposure to the elements.

[338] West, *Serpent in the Sky*, p. 186.

[339] Ibid., pp. 190–5.

[340] Lehner, *The Complete Pyramids*, Chapter III, pp. 128–9. For references to Sphinx worship in ancient and classical times see also Selim Hassan, *The Sphinx . . .*, pp. 6–9.

[341] The entirety of West's original argument dating to 1979 can be found in *Serpent in the Sky*, pp. 184–220; meanwhile, in a later edition published in 1993 he updates his theories in Appendices I and II (pp. 221–32).

[342] Schoch, 'Redating the Great Sphinx of Giza', *KMT*, Vol. 3, No. 2, Summer 1992, p. 69, Note 10; he refers to the separate works of WC Hayes and KW Butzer.

[343] Harrell, 'The Sphinx Controversy: Another Look at the Evidence', *KMT*, Vol. 5, No. 2, Autumn 1994, pp. 72–3.

[344] Vyse, *Operations*, Vol. II, p. 2. See also Vol. I, pp. 145 ('At night there was a heavy storm of wind and rain') and 182 ('It rained early in the morning').

[345] Greaves, *Pyramidographia*, pp. 74–5.

[346] Moret, *The Nile and Egyptian Civilisation*, p. 35, Footnote 3.

[347] West, *Serpent in the Sky*, p. 189.

[348] KL Gauri, JJ Sinai, and JK Bandyopadhyay, 'Geologic Weathering and Its Implications on the Age of the Sphinx', *Geoarchaeology*, Vol. 10, No. 2, 1995, p. 130.

[349] Lehner, 'Notes and Photographs on the West–Schoch Sphinx Hypothesis', *KMT*, Vol. 5, No. 3, Autumn 1994, pp. 43–4.

[350] In a lecture given by Lehner to the ARE's annual convention in August 1998 at Virginia Beach.

[351] Lehner, op. cit., *KMT*, Autumn 1994, p. 127.

[352] Gauri is quoted in Schoch, op. cit., *KMT*, Summer 1992, p. 67, Note 7.

[353] Gauri et al., op. cit., *Geoarchaeology*, 1995, pp. 123 and 125.

[354] See photograph from the beginning of the twentieth century in Jordan, *Riddles of the Sphinx*, p. 6.

[355] Lehner, op. cit., *KMT*, Autumn 1994, p. 48, Note 10.

[356] West, open letter to *KMT*, Vol. 7, No. 1, Spring 1996, pp. 3–6.

[357] Lehner and Hawass, 'Remnant of a Lost Civilisation?', *Archaeology*, September–October 1994, pp. 45–6.

[358] Schoch, op. cit., *KMT*, Summer 1992, pp. 56–8.

[359] After West, *Serpent in the Sky*, Appendix II, p. 228.

[360] Ibid., Appendix II, p. 229.

[361] Ibid., Appendix II, p. 228.

[362] Lehner and Hawass, 'The Sphinx: Who Built it, and Why?', *Archaeology*, September–October 1994, p. 40. We had thought that this wall, reckoned to be as high as 24 feet, butted up against the enclosure walls, which could have had an impact on the weathering analysis. However, it is described as 'encircling the Sphinx like a giant cartouche', presumably in an ill-thought-out attempt to keep the sand at bay, and as such would presumably have been freestanding.

[363] Lehner, *The Complete Pyramids*, Chapter III, p. 132.

[364] From the lectures given by Lehner and Hawass at the ARE's annual convention in August 1998 at Virginia Beach. Hawass also emphasised that when they first started the Sphinx Restoration Project in the late 1970s they were both relatively young and eager, and, more important, *open-minded* about what they would find.

[365] West and Schoch's suggestions were put forward in the documentary *Mystery of the Sphinx*, produced by Boris Said and Bill Cote, and hosted by Charlton Heston. This was aired as a one-hour NBC TV special in 1993, and a longer 90-minute video is available.

[366] Lehner, *The Complete Pyramids*, Chapter III, p. 127. For more details on Aigner's study, see Lehner, 'A Contextual Approach to the Giza Pyramids', *Archiv für Orientforschung*, 32 (1985), pp. 136–58.

[367] Lehner and Hawass, op. cit., *Archaeology*, September–October 1994, p. 32.

[368] Hassan, *The Sphinx . . .*, pp. 88–92.

[369] Schoch, op. cit., *KMT*, Summer 1992, p. 55.

[370] Lehner, op. cit., *KMT*, Autumn 1994, pp. 42–4.

[371] In a posting to our *EgyptNews* Internet mailing list on 9 February 1999.

[372] Lehner, *The Complete Pyramids*, Chapter III, pp. 128–30.

[373] West, *Serpent in the Sky*, p. 207.

[374] Lehner, *The Complete Pyramids*, Chapter III, pp. 130–1.

[375] West, *Serpent in the Sky*, Appendix II, p. 232.

[376] Domingo's reproductions can be found in ibid., Appendix II, pp. 230–1.

[377] Hassan, *The Sphinx . . .*, pp. 63–70.

[378] Temple, *The Sirius Mystery*, p. 31.

[379] Lehner and Hawass, op. cit., *Archaeology*, September–October 1994, p. 37. The SRI drillings were discussed by Lehner in a lecture given to the ARE's annual convention in August 1998.

Chapter 8: The Enigma of the Shafts

[380] Lepre's lengthy discourse on the King's Chamber shafts can be found in *The Egyptian Pyramids*, Chapter V, pp. 94–101.

[381] Smyth, *Our Inheritance in the Great Pyramid*, Chapter XIX, p. 430.

[382] Lepre's similar discourse on the Queen's Chamber shafts can be found in *The Egyptian Pyramids*, Chapter V, pp. 111–14.

[383] This complexity is discussed in some depth in Hancock and Bauval, *Keeper of Genesis*, Chapter 3, pp. 57–60.

[384] Prepared with assistance from Rudolf Gantenbrink.

[385] Hancock and Bauval, *Keeper of Genesis*, Chapter 6, p. 122. See also ibid., Appendix 5, p. 326, and Bauval and Gilbert, *The Orion Mystery*, Epilogue, pp. 248–9.

[386] At the time of writing, Gantenbrink is constructing a web site on which he will place still photos taken from Upuaut's video camera, and other information on his surveys of the shafts.

[387] Hancock and Bauval, *Keeper of Genesis*, Plate 16.

[388] Lehner, *The Complete Pyramids*, Chapter III, p. 112.

Chapter 9: Twinkle, Little Star

[389] *The Orion Mystery* is written almost exclusively in the first person, which is perhaps a little surprising for a joint work. In any case, it is clear that that person is Bauval rather than Gilbert, and if the latter is somewhat excluded from our analysis no slight is intended.

[390] Trimble, 'Astronomical Investigation Concerning the So-Called Air-Shafts of Cheops' Pyramid', and Badawy, 'The Stellar Destiny of Pharaoh and the So-Called Air-Shafts of Cheops' Pyramid', both in *Mitteilungen des Instituts für Orientforschung der Deutschen Akademie der Wissenschaften zu Berlin*, Band X, 1964, pp. 183–7 and 198–206.

[391] Extracted from Trimble, op. cit., reproduced in Bauval and Gilbert, *The Orion Mystery*, Appendix 1, p. 255.

[392] Lehner, *The Complete Pyramids*, Chapter III, pp. 112–13; the

diagram captions describe the southern and northern shafts as oriented to Orion and polar stars respectively.

[393] Jordan, *Riddles of the Sphinx*, Chapter 9, p. 139.

[394] Bauval and Gilbert, *The Orion Mystery*, Chapter 7, p. 137.

[395] After ibid., Chapter 9, p. 182, Figure 15.

[396] Extract from e-mail from Ed Krupp to Michael Brass dated 30 April 1998, forwarded to us by the latter.

[397] Bauval and Gilbert, *The Orion Mystery*, Chapter 11, pp. 216 and 218, and Appendix 5, p. 286.

[398] Ibid., Chapter 7, p. 138.

[399] In fact, before Gantenbrink updated them the most accurate figures available had been produced in Maragioglio and Rinaldi's survey. However, he found that even this contained some inaccuracies and confusion.

[400] Bauval and Gilbert, *The Orion Mystery*, Chapter 9, p. 180.

[401] The angle of the northern shaft varies between 33.1 and 40.1 degrees.

[402] Bauval and Gilbert, *The Orion Mystery*, Chapter 9, pp. 179–80.

[403] In *The Phoenix Solution*, p. 426, Note 37, Alan Alford suggests that Gantenbrink gave him an angle of 32 degrees 36′ 28″, some 7 *degrees* less. However, we can only assume this was a typographical error.

[404] Extract from e-mail from Ed Krupp to Michael Brass dated 19 June 1998, forwarded to us by the latter.

[405] Gantenbrink, 'On the Great Pyramid', *Quest for Knowledge*, Vol. 1, Issue 10, 1998, pp. 26–9.

[406] It is only fair to note that Bauval is clearly aware of this architectural-design issue, and writes about it in *The Orion Mystery*, Appendix 5, pp. 281–7. However, there is insufficient detailed analysis herein to provide a serious refutation of Gantenbrink's hypothesis about the shafts.

[407] Ibid., Chapter 6, pp. 118–29.

[408] Figure drawn up to scale by superimposing a map of the major stars of the Orion constellation on to a detailed ground map, and lining up the belt stars with the three Giza Pyramids.

[409] Bauval and Gilbert, *The Orion Mystery*, Chapter 7, p. 133. However, it is fair to say that in the *The Great Pyramid: Gateway to the Stars* documentary, he seems considerably more circumspect when interviewed about Bauval and Gilbert's theories.

[410] Ibid., Chapter 7, p. 134.

[411] Nor is it in the photograph reproduced in ibid., Plate 8. Meanwhile, although we are not experts, the highly magnified shot reproduced in

Plate 7 appears to be distorting the relative magnitudes due to some sort of reflective 'halo' effect.

[412] By contrast, the 'absolute magnitude' attempts to take this into account, so a larger star which was further away might have the same visual but a larger absolute magnitude. Meanwhile the 'photographic magnitude' can differ again because the eye deals with the colours of the spectrum differently from a lens, and stars have different colours dependent on their temperature. However, this potential distortion of photographic images as against human vision can in this case be discounted because the three belt stars have a very similar colour index – varying between minus 0.19 and minus 0.22. We should also note that in the Orion constellation only Betelgeuse has a magnitude that varies significantly over time; and further that the two outer stars are 'doubles'.

[413] Data taken from the *Bright Star Catalogue*.

[414] Extract from e-mail from Ed Krupp to Michael Brass dated 30 April 1998, forwarded to us by the latter.

[415] Lehner, *The Complete Pyramids*, Chapter III, pp. 106–7.

[416] Bauval and Gilbert, *The Orion Mystery*, Appendix 9, pp. 301–2.

[417] In the *The Great Pyramid: Gateway to the Stars* documentary.

[418] Hassan, *The Sphinx . . .*, p. 91, Note 1.

[419] Alford, *The Phoenix Experiment*, Chapter 3, p. 69.

[420] Jordan, *Riddles of the Sphinx*, Chapter 9, p. 133.

[421] Bauval and Gilbert, *The Orion Mystery*, Chapter 6, p. 128.

[422] Hassan, *Excavations at Giza*, 1938–9, p. 10.

[423] Wainright, *The Sky Religion in Ancient Egypt*, Appendix, pp. 93–100.

[424] Bauval and Gilbert, *The Orion Mystery*, Chapter 10, pp. 198–202.

[425] See ibid., Chapter 10, p. 201, Figure 17, and p. 203, Figure 18.

[426] Data derived from SkyGlobe, version 4. This is an updated version of the software package used by Bauval and Gilbert, and the data therein has not changed. The angle was approximated by measurement with a protractor on screen in zoom mode. Although they point out that the data pre-10,000 BC has a higher margin of error, this is not sufficient to alter our broad findings. As one would expect, the zenith occurs at different times in each day in a given year, and in different times in each millennium even on the same day. For consistency we measured all figures on 21 June, adjusting for the time of the zenith as we went. However, the relevant angles are the same all year round, and change only slowly across the years.

[427] Bauval and Gilbert, *The Orion Mystery*, Chapter 6, p. 128, and Chapter 8, pp. 144–50.

⁴²⁸ See ibid., p. 298, Figure 27. It is interesting that in our edition, the paperback, this diagram has been placed completely out of context among the appendices, to which it clearly does not relate. In the main chapter where these issues are discussed, no equivalent diagram is produced.

⁴²⁹ Anyone who doubts this assertion should consult a map for themselves – for example, that in Lehner, *The Complete Pyramids*, pp. 10–11.

⁴³⁰ Chadwick, 'The So-Called "Orion Mystery": A Rebuttal to New-Age Notions About Ancient Egyptian Astronomy and Funerary Architecture', *KMT*, Vol. 7, No. 3, Autumn 1996, pp. 74–83. Apart from the obvious scale issue, he discusses the missing stars in the complete Taurus constellation, the fact that the latter was not recognised by the Ancient Egyptians, the Fifth Dynasty pyramids, which from Abusir are possibly included but from Saqqara are not, and the lack of stellar counterparts for the other structures on the Plateau, such as the temples and the Sphinx. All of these are arguably relatively trivial issues, especially if the main ones relating to the basic theory are being ignored.

⁴³¹ *Quest for Knowledge*, Vol. 1, Issue 10, July 1998, p. 19.

⁴³² Bauval, 'Position Statement Regarding the So-Called "Wider Plan" of the Star-Pyramids Correlation Theory', published on 24 July 1998 at the following Internet site: <http://www.m-m.org/jz/sphinxb98.html>.

⁴³³ Bauval and Hancock, *Keeper of Genesis*, Chapter 4, pp. 68–9.

⁴³⁴ Ibid., Chapter 4, pp. 70–6.

⁴³⁵ Ibid., Chapter 4, pp. 77–8.

⁴³⁶ Ibid., Chapter 4 pp. 78–81, Chapter 16, pp. 259–61, and Chapter 17, p. 264. See especially Figure 30, p. 81, and also Figure 56, p. 232.

⁴³⁷ Ibid., Chapter 17, pp. 265–78.

⁴³⁸ Ibid., Chapter 17, pp. 278–82. See especially Figures 68–9, pp. 280–1.

⁴³⁹ Ibid., Chapter 17, p. 263.

Chapter 10: Fool's Gold

⁴⁴⁰ This figure was provided in a telephone conversation with West on 8 November 1998.

⁴⁴¹ This information is based on e-mail communications with Jahoda between 14 and 16 January 1999.

⁴⁴² As reported in the *Florida State University Department of*

Chemistry Alumni Newsletter, Autumn 1996; see the following Internet web site: <http://www.chem.fsu.edu/news.htm>.

443 Hawass Interview, *KMT*, Vol. 8, No. 2, Summer 1997, pp. 18–9.

444 From *Egypt Update*, 19 July 1997, p. 2, sent out with West's Egypt trip brochure.

445 This video was promoted through Said's *Magical Eye* web site, which has since closed.

446 Quoted in 'Pyramid Selling', *The Sunday Times*, 20 September 1998.

447 In an e-mail from Dolphin dated 22 March 1999.

448 This letter was made public during a *Carte Blanche* documentary, *The Search for the Hall of Records*, partly filmed in Egypt during November 1998 and aired on South African M-Net TV the following month. A synopsis thereof can be found at <http://www.mnet.co.za/carteblanche/week/981206_egypt.html>.

449 From *Egypt Update*, 19 July 1997, p. 4, sent out with West's Egypt trip brochure.

450 William P. Eigles, 'West, Hancock & Bauval cut out of New Sphinx Research', *Atlantis Rising*, Issue 8, Summer 1996.

451 Taken from the short promotional video entitled *The Secret Chamber*, which is included in Said's 1997 *Behind the Scenes* video compilation.

452 In an e-mail from Jahoda dated 16 March 1999. See also Eigles, op. cit., *Atlantis Rising*, Issue 8, Summer 1996. Further to this, in the second part of the South African *Carte Blanche* documentary made in 1998, Hawass takes the host Derek Watts into the Sphinx's rump tunnel and once again, with a grin on his face, repeats the famous words: 'even Indiana Jones would not believe to be here'. Although he is playing with fire for an audience who might not understand the background, this reinforces our interpretations.

453 In a posting made by Odom to the *Nova* web site in February 1997.

454 In a posting made by Pullen to the *Sci.Archaeology* Internet news-group (according to the *Sphinx Group* web site).

455 In an e-mail from Jahoda dated 16 March 1999.

456 Said appeared with Danley on the *Laura Lee Show* on the 25 September 1997, and again on *The Art Bell Show* on 11 November 1997.

457 In a posting made by Danley to the *Ancient Wisdom* Internet discussion list on 4 March 1999.

458 The fact that these were prepared and presented was confirmed to us by Jahoda in an e-mail dated 30 March 1999.

[459] Bauval and Hancock, *Keeper of Genesis*, Appendix 6, p. 328.

[460] In a posting on the *Sphinx Group* web site in 1995 at the following Internet address: <http://www.m-m.org/<jz/sphinxb95.html>.

[461] Robert Bauval and Graham Hancock, *Keeper of Genesis*, Appendix 6, p. 328.

[462] In an e-mail from El-Baz dated 15 September 1997.

[463] In e-mails from Vanin dated 26 January and 10 March 1998.

[464] In an e-mail from our source dated 26 June 1998.

[465] In an e-mail from Ryan Weese, Tourism Coordinator for the Belleville Chamber of Commerce, dated 7 July 1998.

[466] In an e-mail from our source dated 26 June 1998.

[467] In a faxed copy of an e-mail passed to us anonymously and dated 22 June 1998.

[468] This data was sourced from the 'Index of Companies and Funds' supplied by the *Yahoo Finance* Internet search facilities at <http://biz.yahoo.com/I>, and also *EDGAR Online* at <http://people.edgar-online.com>.

[469] In an e-mail from Ellis dated 25 September 1998.

[470] In a telephone conversation with Renton and Ellson on 26 September 1998.

[471] In an e-mail from Jahoda dated 8 March 1999.

[472] In the Egyptian newspaper *Al Ahram* dated 5 November 1998.

[473] In an e-mail from Hawass dated 4 April 1999.

Chapter 11: False Prophets?

[474] Hawass, Interview in *KMT*, Vol. 8, No. 2, Summer 1997, pp. 20–1.

[475] In a posting to our *EgyptNews* Internet mailing list dated 13 August 1998.

[476] See Bauval and Gilbert, *The Orion Mystery*, Chapter 9, pp. 174–84; and Bauval and Hancock, *Keeper of Genesis*, Chapter 7, pp. 131–5.

[477] In a posting to our *EgyptNews* Internet mailing list dated 16 January 1999.

[478] In a posting to our *EgyptNews* Internet mailing list dated 19 January 1999.

[479] In a posting to our *EgyptNews* Internet mailing list dated 20 January 1999.

[480] The meeting took place on 25 January 1999.

[481] Hawass, Interview in *KMT*, Vol. 8, No. 2, Summer 1997, p. 19.

[482] *KMT*, Vol. 8, No. 4, Winter 1997, pp. 3–4.

[483] *KMT*, Vol. 9. No. 1, Spring 1998, pp. 5–6.

[484] Ibid., p. 6.

[485] See Bauval and Hancock newsletter, *Hieroglyph*, No. 1, January 1997, p. 2.

[486] Quoted from Said in his *Behind the Scenes* video compilation.

[487] See Bauval and Hancock newsletter, *Hieroglyph*, No. 1, January 1997, p. 3.

[488] Ibid., No. 2, May 1998, pp. 2–3.

[489] From *Egypt Update*, 19 July 1997, p. 4, sent out with West's Egypt trip brochure.

[490] For example, the last chapter of *Serpent in the Sky*, which deals with the Sphinx weathering, is provocatively titled 'Egypt: Heir to Atlantis'.

[491] In a telephone conversation with Schor on 9 March 1999.

[492] In an e-mail from Grasse dated 8 March 1999.

[493] In an e-mail from Jahoda dated 14 January 1999.

[494] In an e-mail from Jahoda dated 16 March 1999.

[495] In a public statement released in various places on the Internet dated 17 May 1998.

[496] In a public statement posted to the *Sphinx Group* Internet list dated 19 July 1998.

[497] In a posting to our *EgyptNews* Internet mailing list dated 13 August 1998.

[498] As was, for example, aptly demonstrated by the conspiracy researcher John Carlo in his 'Statement to Graham Hancock, Robert Bauval, John Anthony West and Amargi Hillier' on his web site at the following Internet address: <http.//www.angelfire.com/ak/DESERT-LION/hancock.html>.

[499] In a posting to our *EgyptNews* Internet mailing list dated 20 January 1999.

[500] At <http://www.amazon.com>.

[501] At <http://www2.eridu.co.uk/eridu/news.html#hancock>.

[502] Extract from e-mail from Ed Krupp to Michael Brass dated 19 June 1998, forwarded to us by the latter.

[503] See Bauval and Hancock newsletter, *Hieroglyph*, No. 3, September 1998, p. 3.

Chapter 12: The Appleby Affair

[504] Appleby served with the Territorial Army while Shirley was an officer with the Royal Corps of Signals.

[505] Appleby and Child supplied Chris with a copy of this fax at a

meeting on 16 June 1998. Although this copy does not bear a date, a press release posted on the *Operation Hermes* web site at <http://www.In-ter.com/Hermes/intro.htm> claimed Appleby received the fax on 11 March 1996. It should also be noted that we have not seen the original proposal, and are therefore unaware what claims the group made, and what exactly it was that Hawass was responding to.

[506] Note that this was an entirely separate *Carte Blanche* documentary from that mentioned several times in the previous chapter, and concentrated on Operation Hermes alone.

[507] Appleby's projections for the location of the Hall of Records can be found at <http://www.in-ter.com/Hermes/maps.htm>.

[508] The 'Fibonacci Spiral' is an extension of the 'Fibonacci Series', which we examined in Chapter 3.

[509] See address above. The site was still accessible at the time of writing.

[510] In his book, *Hall of the Gods*, Appleby mentions 'Dr' O'Farrell in the acknowledgements and again in an endnote reference (to Chapter 19, p. 392).

[511] Cox, 'Report on the Hermes Foundation for Robert Bauval and Graham Hancock', September 1997. Bauval published 95 per cent of this report and other documents on the Internet through our *EgyptNews* mailing list in a posting dated 1 August 1998.

[512] From the *Daily Telegraph*, 30 May 1998.

[513] Taken from the posting to our *EgyptNews* Internet mailing list made by Bauval on 1 August 1998, as mentioned above.

[514] The newspapers were *Akhbar Al Yom*, *Al Ahram* and *Al Goumhoria*.

[515] This meeting took place at Bauval's home in Beaconsfield on the 21 July 1998. The conversation with Hawass was replayed from a tape recording.

[516] Confirmed in an e-mail from John Anthony West dated 10 June 1998 in which he states, 'Yes, Graham tells me the Hermes thing is a scam, but that's all I know. I have a call in to him to give me details, but he is off promoting the new book.'

[517] Ralph Ellis, *Thoth*, Chapter VI, p. 133.

[518] The following quotes are taken from Appleby's lecture, which was captured on video.

[519] Ralph Ellis, *Thoth*, Chapter VI, p. 135.

[520] Extract from a fax from Appleby to Ellis dated 15 April 1998.

[521] This view was more than adequately expressed to Chris at the lengthy meeting he had with Bauval and Ellis on 21 July 1998.

[522] Copies were kindly supplied to us by Ellis.

[523] Dated 13 August 1998.

[524] In a fax received by Ellis dated 25 August 1998.

[525] See the *Mail on Sunday* of 11 October 1998. As at the time of writing the case has not yet been heard in the courts.

[526] These were posted to our *EgyptNews* Internet mailing list on 17 June and 3 July 1998 respectively.

[527] See Appleby, 'Operation Hermes: The Quest to Discover the Hall of Records', *Quest for Knowledge*, Vol. 1, Issue 12.

[528] In a statement posted to our *EgyptNews* Internet mailing list on 1 August 1998.

[529] In a statement posted to Andrew Collins's *EDEN* web site dated 18 September 1998, which was removed shortly after the trip was cancelled – seemingly due to a lack of interest from potential travellers.

Chapter 13: The Hunter

[530] This quote, and the rest of the information about Hunter in this chapter unless otherwise stated, is taken from an article headed 'The Hall of Osiris', which was published on the Internet at <http://www.amargiland.com/hall-of-osiris>. Although the article was removed from this web site by Amargi Hillier, its author, in August 1998, it is still the main historic source of information on Hunter's activities and investigations. We have used Hunter's name even when quoting from this document because, as will become clear, the theories and investigations therein are clearly his original work and not Hillier's.

[531] See Hunter's own Internet web site for more details at <http://larryhunter.com/Default.htm>.

[532] US Patent Number 04 509 501; see Hunter's web site for more details. He also appears to have formed some type of company, judging by his paper, which is headed 'Pyramid Sun Power'.

[533] Taken from Hunter's web site.

[534] In fact the 'Hall of Osiris' article says *west*, but this is clearly even more nonsensical and we have established that it is a mistake with Hillier.

[535] The report is reproduced on Hunter's web site.

[536] The *EgyptNews* posting was dated 23 September 1998.

[537] From a report on Hunter's web site.

[538] At <http://www.angelfire.com/ak/DESERTLION/john.html>.

[539] The list is maintained under the Internet address <Giza@onelist.com>.

[540] In a posting by Hunter to the *Sphinx Discussion Group* on the

Internet in September 1998. The idea of the 'hinging' stela may have derived from Spencer Lewis, who discusses it in *The Symbolic Prophecy of the Great Pyramid*, pp. 125–30.

[541] In an e-mail passed on to us by Boris Said and dated 6 November 1998.

Chapter 14: The Water Shaft

[542] Hassan, *Excavations At Giza*, Vol. 5, 1933–4, p. 193; taken from Nigel Skinner-Simpson's web site at the following Internet address: <http://wkweb5.cableinet.co.uk/nigelss/pages/shafted.htm>.

[543] The fascinating story of Skinner-Simpson's detective work on this issue can be found on his Internet web site.

[544] Lewis, *The Symbolic Prophecy of the Great Pyramid*, Appendix, pp. 187–8.

[545] Ibid., Appendix, pp. 189–90.

[546] William P Eigles, 'The Search for the Giza Hall of Records', *Atlantis Rising*, Issue 15, p. 56.

[547] According to Skinner-Simpson's web site, in his appearance on a radio show in September 1998 Said suggested that when he first went down the shaft in 1992 he did not notice the second level, the implication being that it was then somehow blocked off and had been opened up since. This appears ridiculous on two counts: first, it is impossible to access the third level without entering the second level proper; and, second, it was clearly not blocked off even when Hassan found it in the 1930s.

[548] In an e-mail from Hurtak dated 30 March 1999.

[549] Again from Said's radio appearance reported by Skinner-Simpson, he suggests that ancient texts indicate that sarcophagus lids were often used to cover the entrance to secret chambers or tunnels. This is supposedly why the survey was performed on the lid.

[550] In a posting by Danley to the *Sphinx Discussion Group* on the Internet in September 1998.

[551] For example, as we saw in a previous note, Said appeared on *The Laura Lee Show* with Danley to discuss these issues and others on 25 September 1997. He was on again as recently as 6 March 1999, this time with Jim Hurtak.

[552] In an e-mail from Said dated 27 October 1998.

[553] At <http://guardians.net/hawass/index.htm>.

[554] In a posting by Hunter to the *Sphinx Discussion Group* on the Internet in September 1998.

[555] In an e-mail from Skinner-Simpson dated 12 March 1999.

[556] It is interesting to note that Perring conducted a detailed examination of the water level in similar shafts at the high and low Nile points of the year in the 1840s, and found that, while the level of the river itself varied by about 20 feet, the water in the shafts varied by only about a foot; see Vyse, *Operations*, Vol. II, Appendix, p. 148.

[557] We are even treated to a reconstruction of Edgar Cayce in a trance suggesting that 'the Giza Plateau was laid out according to the stars'. We may be mistaken, but we are not aware of his ever suggesting this in his readings.

Chapter 15: Tunnel Talk

[558] The report can still be viewed in its entirety on Hoagland's *Enterprise Mission* web site at the following Internet address: <http://www.planetarymysteries.com/enterprisemission/pyramid.html>.

[559] The 'clandestine tunneling' accusations are primarily aired in the last quarter of the show. It can be replayed by visiting the following Internet site:
<http://ww2.broadcast.com/artbell/abell/9706/ab0626.ram>.

[560] In an e-mail from Danley dated 12 August 1997.

[561] After Perring, *The Pyramids of Gizeh*, Figures 1 to 3.

[562] Hawass, 'Responses to Your Questions', *PBS/NOVA* Internet web site, dated 10 February 1997; see <http://www.pbs.org>.

Chapter 16: Epilogue

[563] The site can be found at the following internet address:
<http://www.ianlawton.com/gttindex.htm>.

[564] Reader's full paper remains only self-published at the time of writing, but is reproduced on our web site. However, a shortened version entitled 'A Geomorphological Study of the Giza Necropolis, with Implications for the Development of the Site' appeared in *Archaeometry*, Vol. 43, Part 1, February 2001.

[565] His reference in a letter to us dated 14 December 1999 is to Gauri, *Geologic Study of the Sphinx*, NARCE 127.

[566] After Reader, *Khufu Knew the Sphinx*, Figures 2 and 3.

[567] However, more recent research has led us to question this aspect of Reader's argument, particularly in view of the fact that a number of shaft tombs in the region of the supposed quarry, including Campbell's, appear to cut through virgin bedrock right to the top.

[568] In fact West has more recently suggested that, in view of the inhospitable climate that would have accompanied the end of the last Ice Age *c*. 10,500BC, the date should be pushed right back to the *previous* precessional age of Leo *c*. 36,000BC – see the various papers on his web site at <http://members.aol.com/jawsphinx/index.html>. We have yet to hear any official comment on this from Robert Bauval and Graham Hancock, especially in terms of what this means for their theory about *zep tepi*, or the 'first time', and the layout of the Giza Plateau to reflect Orion's belt *c*. 10,500BC.

[569] For more details see the paper published on our web site entitled *A Reappraisal of the History of Clearance of the Sphinx Enclosure*.

[570] Although the explanation provided in his more recent book, *Secret Chamber*, Appendix 2, pp. 374-7, is far more lucid.

[571] We have fleshed out the replanning argument in particular in a paper published on our web site entitled *The Fundamental Flaws in the Orion-Giza Correlation Theory*.

[572] Two papers of particular importance to this debate can also be accessed. The first is a rarely-discussed paper by Egyptologist Jaromir Malek that first appeared in *Discussions in Egyptology*, No. 30, 1994. The second is Kate Spence's 'Egyptian Chronology and the Astronomical Orientation of Pyramids', *Nature*, No. 408, 2000, in which her theory casts some doubt on the ancient Egyptians' knowledge of precession.

[573] We have also had discussions with Dunn regarding his 'Giza Power Plant' theory that we mentioned briefly in Chapter 3, and he seems to have little defense against our suggestions that it completely ignores the religious context of pyramids in general, of their surrounding complexes, and of the texts found inscribed in the walls of their chambers from the Fifth Dynasty onwards. For more details see our web site.

[574] Dunn's full report of his visit to the Petrie Museum in November 1999 can be found on his web site at <http://www.gizapower.com/>.

[575] Stocks' most recent experiments were carried out in conjunction with the NOVA team, and a report of their achievements, including impressive photographs, can be found at <http://www.pbs.org/wgbh/nova/lostempires/obelisk/cutting.html>. Meanwhile, the results of his previous experiments were published in *Popular Archaeology*, April 1986, and in his article 'Stone Sarcophagus Manufacture in Ancient Egypt' in *Antiquity*, Vol. 73, No. 282, December 1999.

[576] For Reid's work on the Great Pyramid in particular see Chapter 12, pp. 394-8, and for the results of his cymatic experiments on the King's Chamber sarcophagus see the Plates section.

[577] See Hawass' web site at <http://guardians.net/spotlite/spotlite-hawass-2001.htm>.

[578] We might note that in *Secret Chamber* Robert Bauval gives his version of the events surrounding the discovery of Gantenbrink's 'door' (Chapter Eleven, pp. 239–85). We are also given to understand that Rudolf Gantenbrink is working on his own book, the publication date of which has yet to be announced.

[579] The current head of the SCA, Dr. Ali Gaballah, presented a paper on their findings to the Eighth International Congress of Egyptologists in Cairo. For more information see <http://www.iol.co.za/frame__decider.php?click__id=588&art__id=qw988132021939B221&set__id=1>.

Appendix I: Were the Giza Pyramids Covered in Hieroglyphs?

[580] Tompkins, *Secrets of the Great Pyramid*, Chapter II, p. 18.
[581] Vyse, *Operations*, Vol. II, Appendix, pp. 342–4, Note 9.
[582] Edwards, *The Pyramids of Egypt*, Chapter 7, p. 212.

Appendix II: More on the Pyramids-as-Tombs Debate

[583] Vyse, *Operations*, Vol. III, Appendix, p. 69.
[584] As to when the Arab incursion may have taken place, the evidence is mixed. The most obvious lead is the Arabic inscription, which Belzoni suggests dated to about a millennium before his time, i.e. the ninth century. However, Lehner suggests the thirteenth century, and neither indicates the basis for his assertion. We have already seen in a previous note that there are several apparent translations of the inscriptions anyway. Meanwhile, an extract from *Freemasonry from the Great Pyramid of Ancient Times*, self-published by Thomas Holland in 1885, suggests: ' . . . the enterprising Belzoni found its [the Second Pyramid's] entrance in the north front in 1818, and discovered at the same time that it had been previously forced open by the Arabian Caliph, Ali Mehemet, A.D. 782, more than a thousand years before' (p. 13). However, ultimately it is more important that we appreciate that the edifice had been breached long before the Arabs even entered Egypt.
[585] Lehner, *The Complete Pyramids*, Chapter III, p. 160.
[586] George B Johnson, 'The Red Pyramid of Sneferu Inside and Out', *KMT*, Vol. 8, No. 3, Autumn 1997, p. 25.

587 Ibid., p. 24.
588 Petrie, *The Pyramids and Temples of Gizeh*, Chapter V, p. 55.
589 Alford, *The Phoenix Solution*, Chapter 2, p. 35.
590 Lepre, *The Egyptian Pyramids*, Chapter V, pp. 92–3. Drawings of how the lid would have fitted are on p. 96.
591 Petrie, *The Pyramids and Temples of Gizeh*, Chapter III, p. 36.
592 Edwards, *The Pyramids of Egypt*, Chapter 2, pp. 56–60.
593 Lehner, *The Complete Pyramids*, Chapter III, p. 94.
594 Mendelssohn, *The Riddle of the Pyramids*, p. 75.
595 Lehner, *The Complete Pyramids*, Chapter III, p. 117.
596 Mendelssohn, *The Riddle of the Pyramids*, p. 74.
597 Alford, *The Phoenix Solution*, Chapter 3, p. 73.
598 Lepre, *The Egyptian Pyramids*, Chapter V, pp. 113–4.
599 Again taken from the translation of Edrisi's *History of the Pyramids* by JL Burkhardt, reproduced in Vyse, *Operations*, Vol. II, Appendix, p. 336.
600 Alford, *The Phoenix Solution*, Chapter 2, pp. 37–54.
601 George B Johnson, 'The Red Pyramid of Sneferu Inside and Out', *KMT*, Vol. 8, No. 3, Autumn 1997, p. 27, Note 8.
602 Ibid., p. 26.
603 Edwards, *The Pyramids of Egypt*, Chapter 3, p. 78.
604 Lehner, *The Complete Pyramids*, Chapter III, pp. 97, 99 and 104.
605 Ibid., Chapter III, p. 103.

Appendix III: The Great Pyramid's Security Features

606 Lepre, *The Egyptian Pyramids*, Chapter V, p. 72; his and Petrie's reconstructions are in Appendix B, pp. 293–5.
607 For example, this is the version used by Petrie and reproduced by Lehner in *The Complete Pyramids*, Chapter II, p. 39.
608 See Lehner, ibid., Chapter II, p. 39, and Edwards, *The Pyramids of Egypt*, Chapter 4, pp. 93–4.
609 Lepre, *The Egyptian Pyramids*, Chapter V, p. 77.
610 Noel F Wheeler, 'The Pyramids and Their Purpose II: The Pyramid of Khufu', *Antiquity*, IX, 1935, p. 166.
611 Lehner, *The Complete Pyramids*, Chapter III, p. 104.
612 Lepre, *The Egyptian Pyramids*, Chapter V, pp. 82–3.
613 Ibid., Chapter V, pp. 86–89.
614 Ibid., Chapter V, pp. 89–92.
615 Ibid., Chapter V, p. 117.

BIBLIOGRAPHY

Where later publications or editions have been used, the date of the first publication or edition is given in those instances where an understanding of chronology is considered important.

Alford, A., *Gods of the New Millennium*, Hodder & Stoughton, 1997

Alford, A., *The Phoenix Solution*, Hodder & Stoughton, 1998

Appleby, Nigel, *Hall of the Gods*, Heinemann, 1998

Baines, John and Malek, Jaromir, *Atlas of Ancient Egypt*, Oxford, 1980

Bauval, Robert and Gilbert, Adrian, *The Orion Mystery*, Mandarin, 1995

Bauval, Robert and Hancock, Graham, *Keeper of Genesis*, Mandarin, 1997 (distributed in the USA as *The Message of the Sphinx*)

Bauval, Robert, *Secret Chamber*, Century, 1999

Belzoni, Giovanni Battista, *Narrative of the Operations and Recent Discoveries Within the Pyramids, Temples, Tombs and Excavations in Egypt and Nubia*, John Murray, London, 1822

Blavatsky, Helena, *Isis Unveiled*, Theosophical Publishing House, 1972 (First edition, 1877)

Blavatsky, Helena, *The Secret Doctrine*, Theosophical University Press, 1988 (First edition, 1888)

Brunes, Tons, *The Secrets of Ancient Geometry*, Chronos, Copenhagen, 1967

Cayce, Edgar Evans, *Edgar Cayce on Atlantis*, Howard Baker, 1969

Clarke, Somers and Englebach, R., *Ancient Egyptian Construction and Architecture*, Dover, 1990 (First edition, OUP, 1930)

Collins, Andrew, *From the Ashes of Angels*, Signet, 1997

Collins, Andrew, *Gods of Eden*, Headline, 1998

Davidovits, Joseph, *The Pyramids: An Enigma Solved*, Hippocrene, 1988

Diodorus Siculus, *Histories*, J. Davis, London, 1814

Dormion, Gilles and Goidin, Jean Patrice, *Les Nouveaux Mystères de la Grande Pyramide*, Albin Michel, 1987

Dunn, Christopher, *The Giza Power Plant*, Bear & Co, 1998

Edwards, I.E.S., *The Pyramids of Egypt*, Ebury Press, 1972 (First edition, Penguin, 1947)

Ellis, Ralph, *Thoth, Architect of the Universe*, Edfu Books, 1998

Faulkner, Raymond, *The Ancient Egyptian Pyramid Texts*, OUP, 1969

Faulkner, Raymond, *The Ancient Egyptian Book of the Dead*, British Museum Press, 1996 (First edition, Limited Editions Club, 1972)

Faulkner, Raymond, *The Ancient Egyptian Coffin Texts*, Aris and Phillips, 1978

Furlong, David, *The Keys to the Temple*, Judy Piatkus, 1997

Greaves, John, *Pyramidographia*, George Badger, London, 1646

Hall, Manley P., *An Encyclopedic Outline of Masonic, Hermetic, Qabbalistic & Rosicrucian Symbolic Philosophy*, Philosophical Research Society, 1977 (First edition, 1901)

Hancock, Graham, *Fingerprints of the Gods*, Heinemann, 1995

Hassan, Selim, *Excavations at Giza*, Cairo Government Press, 1946

Hassan, Selim, *The Sphinx: Its History in the Light of Recent Excavations*, Cairo Government Press, 1949

Hawass, Zahi, *Secrets of the Sphinx*, American University in Cairo Press, 1999

Herodotus, *The Histories*, Oxford World Classics, 1998

Hodges, Peter, *How the Pyramids Were Built*, Aris & Phillips, 1993

Illion, Theodore, *In Secret Tibet*, Adventures Unlimited Press, 1991 (First edition, Rider, 1937)

Jochmans, Joseph, *The Hall of Records*, Self published, 1985

Johnson, K. Paul, *Edgar Cayce in Context*, State University Press, NY, 1998

Jordan, Paul, *Riddles of the Sphinx*, Sutton, 1998

Kingsland, William, *The Great Pyramid in Fact and in Theory*, Rider, 1932

Knight, Christopher and Lomas, Robert, *The Hiram Key*, Arrow, 1997

Laurence, Richard, *The Book of Enoch the Prophet*, John Parker, Oxford, 1838

Lehner, Mark, *The Egyptian Heritage*, Edgar Cayce Foundation, 1974

Lehner, Mark, *The Complete Pyramids*, Thames and Hudson, 1997

Lemesurier, Peter, *The Great Pyramid Decoded*, Element, 1997 (First edition, 1977)

Lepre, J.P., *The Egyptian Pyramids*, Mcfarland, 1990

Lewis, H. Spencer, *The Symbolic Prophecy of the Great Pyramid*, Rosicrucian Press, 1936

Lockyer, Norman, *The Dawn of Astronomy*, Macmillan, 1894

Maragioglio, Vito and Rinaldi, Celeste, *L'Architettura delle Piramidi Menfite*, Turin and Rapallo, 1963–77

Mendelssohn, Kurt, *The Riddle of the Pyramids*, Thames and Hudson Ltd, 1975

Moret, Alexander, *The Nile and Egyptian Civilization*, Kegan Paul, 1927 (trans. by M. R. Dobie)

Morton, Chris and Thomas, Ceri Louise, *The Mystery of the Crystal Skulls*, Thorsons, 1998

Osborne, Harold, *South American Mythology*, Hamlyn, 1968

Perring, John Shae, *The Pyramids of Gizeh*, London, 1839–42

Petrie, William Flinders, *The Pyramids and Temples of Gizeh*, Field & Tuer, London, 1883

Plato, *Timaeus and Criteas*, Penguin, 1977

Pliny, *Natural History*, Bohn's Classical Library, London, 1857

Pond, Dale, *Universal Laws Never Before Revealed: Keely's Secrets*, Message Co., 1990

Proctor, Richard, *The Great Pyramid, Observatory, Tomb, and Temple*, Chatto & Windus, 1883

Randall Stevens, H.C., *From Atlantis to the Latter Days*, Knights Templars, 1981 (First edition, 1954)

Reymond, E.A.E., *The Mythical Origin of the Egyptian Temple*, Manchester University Press, 1969

de Santillana, Giorgio and von Dechend, Hertha, *Hamlet's Mill*, Boston, 1969

Schwaller de Lubicz, Rene, *Sacred Science*, Inner Traditions, 1988

Scott, Walter, *Hermetica*, Solos, 1992 (First edition, 1924)

Scott Elliot, W., *The Story of Atlantis*, Theosophical Publishing House, 1984 (First edition, 1896)

Sellars, Jane, *The Death of Gods in Ancient Egypt*, Penguin, 1992

Sitchin, Zecharia, *The Twelfth Planet*, Bear & Co, 1991 (First edition, Stein & Day, 1976)

Sitchin, Zecharia, *The Stairway to Heaven*, Avon, 1980

Sitchin, Zecharia, *The Wars of Gods and Men*, Avon, 1985

Smith, A. Robert, *The Lost Memoirs of Edgar Cayce*, ARE Press, 1997

Smyth, Charles Piazzi, *The Great Pyramid: Its Secrets and Mysteries Revealed*, Bell, 1990 (reprint of *Our Inheritance in the Great Pyramid*, W.M. Isbister, 1880; First edition, A. Straham & Co., London, 1864)

Spence, Lewis, *History of Atlantis*, Senate, 1995 (First edition, 1926)

Strabo, *Geographica*, Bohn's Classical Library, London, 1857

Sugrue, Thomas, *There is a River: The Story of Edgar Cayce*, ARE Press, 1997 (First edition, 1942)

Taylor, John, *The Great Pyramid: Why Was It Built and Who Built It?* Longman, 1864

Temple, Robert, *The Sirius Mystery*, Arrow, 1999 (First edition, 1976)

Tomas, Andrew, *On the Shores of Ancient Worlds*, Souvenir, 1974

Tompkins, Peter, *Secrets of the Great Pyramid*, Galahad, 1997 (First edition, 1971)

Vercoutter, Jean, *The Search for Ancient Egypt*, Thames and Hudson, 1992

Vyse, Richard Howard, *Operations Carried Out on the Pyramids of Gizeh*, James Frazer, London, 1840–2

Wainright, G.A., *The Sky Religion in Ancient Egypt*, Cambridge, 1938

Walker, Ann, *Little One – Message from Planet Heaven*, Element, 1994

Walker, Ann, *The Stone of the Plough*, Element, 1997

Wallis Budge, E.A., *The Egyptian Heaven and Hell*, Dover, 1996

West, John Anthony, *The Case for Astrology*, Pelican, 1973

West, John Anthony, *Serpent in the Sky*, Quest, 1993 (First edition, Harper & Row, 1979)

INDEX

(Page numbers given in italic type refer to diagrams)

Giza: The Truth Web Site

For a complete and up-to-the-minute perspective on ongoing Giza research, visit the regularly updated 'Giza: The Truth Discussion Site' at www.ianlawton.com/gttindex.htm. Subjects covered include The Hall of Records, The Great Pyramid's 'Star Shafts', Pyramid Acoustics, the Age of the Great Pyramid, Pyramid and Plateau Geometry, The Purpose of the Great Pyramid, Pyramid and Temple Construction, Secret Tunneling, The Age of the Sphinx, The Orion Correlation, The Giza Power Plant, Advanced Machining, and Sonic Levitation.